In Sickness and In Wealth

IN SICKNESS AND IN WEALTH

American Hospitals in the Twentieth Century

ROSEMARY STEVENS

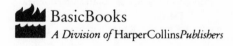

BasicBooks
A Division of HarperCollins*Publishers*

Library of Congress Cataloging-in-Publication Data

Stevens, Rosemary.
   In sickness and in wealth.

   Includes index.
   1. Hospitals—United States—History—
20th century. I. Title. [DNLM: 1. Hospitals—
History—United States. WX 11 AA1 S8i]
RA981.A2S74 1989   362.1'1'0973 88–47903
ISBN 0–465–03223–0 (cloth)
ISBN 0–465–03224–9 (paper)

Copyright © 1989 by Basic Books, Inc.
Printed in the United States of America
Designed by Vincent Torre
90 91 92 93 CC/RRD 9 8 7 6 5 4 3 2 1

Q. You can not put doctors and ministers who are engaged in the distribution of sweet charity in the line of men who are managing Standard Oil and the Sugar Trust.

A. I think human nature is the same.

Hearings in the Pennsylvania legislature
on state (tax) aid
to nongovernmental hospitals, 1910

After all, the chief business of the American people is business. . . . We make no concealment of the fact that we want wealth, but there are many other things that we want very much more. We want peace and honor, and that charity which is so strong an element of all civilization. The chief ideal of the American people is idealism.

Calvin Coolidge, speech to the American Society
of Newspaper Editors, 1925

The modern hospital, whether operated by a city, a church, or a group of private investors, is essentially a business.

Parker v. *City of Highland Park, Michigan,*
on hospital tort liability, 1978

CONTENTS

ACKNOWLEDGMENTS

No BOOK of this scope can be written without the support, advice, and criticism of colleagues and friends. For research funding I am grateful to the Commonwealth Fund, the National Library of Medicine (under research grant ROI-LM 03849), the Rockefeller Foundation (for a Rockefeller Humanities Fellowship in 1983–84 and for the opportunity to be a visiting scholar at the foundation's center in Bellagio, Italy), and the John Simon Guggenheim Foundation (for a Guggenheim Fellowship in 1984–85). Between 1983 and 1985 I was also a resident scholar at the Francis C. Wood Institute for the History of Medicine at the College of Physicians of Philadelphia.

I am especially grateful to my old colleagues and friends John D. Thompson and Brian Abel-Smith, both of whom have written major books on hospital history, for good advice and encouragement over almost three decades. I also fully realize how much this book has benefited from the willingness of colleagues to read and criticize all or part of the manuscript and to provide helpful comments at various stages. I should like to thank, in particular, Mark Adams, George Bugbee, David Drake, Robert Ebert, Gail Farr, John Whelen Farr, Jr., Vanessa Northington Gamble, Janet Golden, Frances Stuart Hanckel, Jack Hershey, Christopher Lawrence, Diana Long, Irvine Loudon, Edward Morman, Patricia Patrizi, Jack Pressman, Charles Rosenberg, and Robert Sigmond. The late Isidore S. Falk commented in detail on the early drafts of the first half of the book. Martin Kessler, my editor at Basic Books, read the evolving manuscript at critical stages and provided invaluable suggestions and needed encouragement.

David Babbitt worked as a superb research assistant, initially for one year and then in short additional periods throughout the project, as his own graduate work at the University of Chicago allowed. Students at the University of Pennsylvania also participated at different stages. I thank, in particular, James Capshew, Michael Keenan, Alejandra Laszlo, Deborah B. Leiderman, Lynn Nyhart, Jack Pressman, and Virginia Smith, each of whom worked for short periods on background research while they were graduate students. Jon Abramzyk, Jeffrey Closter, Lori Klein, Rosanne Miller, Michael Rahmin, Lois Schwadron, and Greg Weinstein worked on the project while they were undergraduates, as did Ellen Berkowitz of Bryn Mawr College. Jennifer Sabin suggested the book's title. Lori Cole, Greta Ilott, Patricia Johnson, Kathy Lin, Gael Mathews, Sandra Pascale, Linda Pascale, and Debra Seave Robinson provided excellent word-processing services over the seven-year period of writing, from very rough drafts to finished product.

One of the pleasures of doing research with a broad sweep of subject matter is the opportunity to find, to collect, and to think about materials across diverse fields and areas of interest. I owe a large debt to the helpfulness and interest of staff at major national associations: the American Hospital Association, the American College of Surgeons, the Joint Commission on Accreditation of Health Care Organizations, the American Medical Association, and the Blue Cross/Blue Shield Association. My thanks go, too, to the staff at the other collections I have used, particularly the National Archives, the Rockefeller Archives, the Library of Congress, the National Library of Medicine, the College of Physicians of Philadelphia—and, not least, the libraries and archives at the University of Pennsylvania. Many other research specialists, physicians, administrators, hospital board members, and university colleagues took time to talk to me about their own experiences and work. I hope you all know how much your help has been appreciated and will be kind in pointing out the remaining errors and omissions.

Last, but not least, thank you, Carey and Richard Stevens, for your tolerance, understanding, and support.

In Sickness and In Wealth

1

Introduction

MY FIRST EXPERIENCE with hospitals was as a child, seriously ill from scarlet fever in a hospital in Britain in 1945 before penicillin was generally available for civilians. Years later I became a hospital administrator and then a policy analyst and historian, first in Britain and then in the United States. The underlying questions of this book have run as a background refrain through other studies I have done of British and American medicine and through major changes in the American hospital system, from Medicare in 1965 to the economic turmoils of the present. Why do we have the hospital system we have? Where has it come from? What are its characteristics? How does it work—and why doesn't it work better? Institutions, like individuals, carry the burdens of their past experience. Hence this history.

American hospitals are regarded, variously, as the best in the world, as myopically biased toward high-technology medicine, as riven with problems of cost and accessibility, and as mirroring the social divisions of contemporary America. There is serious concern about a "two-class" or multitiered system of medicine. One out of every eight Americans has no hospital insurance. Investor-owned hospitals have established a strong, if minor, presence; and the idea that hospitals are charities, or even elements of a welfare state, has diminished almost to extinction. The appropriate roles for government, commercial enterprises, and voluntary nonprofit organizations in the provision of hospital service are all being questioned simultaneously. It is a good time to elucidate the fundamental attributes of the U.S. hospital system—in their organizational, professional, political, and economic contexts. This is a story of medicine, money, and power—of change and the continuity of conflicting ideals. I shall trace the hospitals from their expansion into a visible national movement at the beginning of the twentieth century to the massive corporate complex we have today.

American Dilemma: Technological versus Social-Welfare Goals

Collectively, hospitals have become one of the largest enterprises in the United States, spending $180 billion in 1987, employing 3.7 million people, and providing 34 million inpatient treatments and 311 million outpatient visits. Yet it is a troubled, conflicted "industry." I concentrate here on the institutions we normally think of first as "hospitals": short-term, acute general hospitals that include both medicine and surgery and account for 85 percent of all hospital expenses.[1] The essential historical dilemma for U.S. hospitals, I shall argue, is that they are both public and private institutions: both necessary social organizations *and* icons of American science, wealth, and technological achievement.

After decades of growth, hospital admissions and occupancy rates declined in the early 1980s; they are now shifting upward to cope with new challenges, from chronic disease to AIDS. Hospital administrators and boards have countered a tightening market by being aggressively competitive and profit-oriented, by forming alliances among hospitals and with physicians, and by extending the hospital's "products" through diversifying into such activities as nursing homes, rehabilitation centers, medical equipment firms, and management-consulting companies. The acquisition and management of capital has become as central to hospital policy-making as it is to corporations in other fields. In turn, local governments, hungry for tax revenues, are claiming that hospitals are "businesses" and should therefore be denied the traditional privilege of tax exemption.

Such activities seem to stamp the American hospital system as a multifirm business itself, pure and simple. But the picture is much more complex, for side by side with the philosophy of the marketplace, hospitals have represented charitable intent and public purpose. The power of the federal government over hospitals has rapidly increased in the past two decades. Indeed, federal government policy has been instrumental in driving hospitals toward a more competitive, market-oriented position. Federal regulation has also become vastly more detailed, managerial, and interventionist than ever before as hospitals have sought to maximize their services and income from Medicare and Medicaid and government has moved to thwart them—and to protect the social assumptions built into these huge programs for the elderly, the impoverished, and the disabled, in the face of rising costs.

The picture is further complicated by the fact that most general hospitals in the United States are voluntary not-for-profit organizations, neither government-owned nor designed to make profits for owners or shareholders. Today's voluntary not-for-profit hospitals provide 70 percent of the nonfederal short-term hospital beds in the United States; state and local governments provide 19 percent, and for-profit hospitals, 11 percent.[2] Historically, voluntary hospitals have occupied the middle ground between government and commerce, while serving (and being sustained by) both. The voluntary not-for-profit hospital, with its associated ideology of voluntarism and community, has contained and encompassed the central dilemma of U.S. national health policy: how to distribute the wealth of medical science and diffuse its technology across the population without establishing a massive welfare state.

When I arrived in the United States in the 1960s, I was struck by the incongruities of the American hospital and health-care system compared with that of my native country, Britain. There most hospitals are owned and operated as government institutions within an organized national health service, and services are available to all irrespective of income and are generally free of fees. In Britain, too, there is far less overt emphasis on medical technology and a willingness to wait for services that would not be tolerated by Americans. In the United States, in contrast, general hospitals are run under a variety of auspices. Seen through British eyes, they are luxuriously, even extravagantly, built and equipped. Much of hospital administration appears to revolve around patient-billing procedures and business offices. However, oddly enough, hospital volunteers are much more in evidence in the United States than in Britain.

Particularly mystifying are phrases which incorporate the vague words "voluntary" and "community," as in "voluntary hospitals" and "community hospitals," as if everyone knows what these terms mean. Are American ideas about voluntarism (whatever they are) archaic holdovers from an earlier period, or potent aspects of the continuing system? Are hospitals in transition from one form of organization to the next, whatever this might be? Were there once well-endowed voluntary hospitals providing virtually all of their services free (as current myth seems to suggest),

or have the hospitals long been multipurpose organizations, partly charities, partly businesses?

A major theme of this book is that American voluntary hospitals have
been expansionary, income-maximizing organizations throughout the century; that is, in many respects they have behaved as businesses. But a
second theme is that the hospitals have simultaneously carried symbolic
and social significance as embodiments of American hopes and ideals: not
only of science, technology, and expertise, but of altruism, social solidarity,
and community spirit. The ideal of "charity" has been at least as important
as the "business of business."

The role of voluntarism and of voluntary institutions as alternatives
to government in general and socialism in particular is a further major
theme. Voluntary hospitals have long served as the preferred alternative
to a government hospital or health-care system in the United States, a
country which has made no serious commitment to egalitarian goals as a
basis for providing social services. But this theme tells only part of the
story, because voluntarism in the United States is not merely an alternative
to government but an entrenched aspect of American corporate capitalism.
The voluntary hospitals are not fall-back organizations, existing only because government has not acted. They are instruments of America's version of the capitalist state—social structures established to maintain, interpret, and extend it, as essential in their way as business corporations. The
two forms of "privatization"—business and voluntary—are complementary and mutually supportive, with an overlapping cast of characters.
Government's role has been, in large part, to support both for-profit and
not-for-profit private enterprise—at least up to the present.[3]

In the United States the essential tension in the hospital system is not
a simple question of what is to be regarded as "public" (governmental) and
what "private" (nongovernmental). Indeed, I shall show that a great
strength of the voluntary nonprofit form of organization has been its mix
of public and private roles throughout this century. Tension lies, rather,
in conflicting models of hospital service which overlap both the public and
the private domains. On one side is a model of hospitals as a supply-
driven, technological system, analogous to an electrification system or a
system for producing military aircraft. Hospitals produce surgery, procedures, X rays, expertise, even babies. On the other is a model of hospitals
as community services, with lingering religious, humanitarian, and
egalitarian goals, more analogous to a system of schools.

The technological model assumes that hospitals exist primarily to
produce and to diffuse medical technology, the more advanced the better.
Corporate research and development in industry generates new technol-

ogy; medical schools and hospitals support and incorporate the technology and foster its diffusion. The costs are passed on to customers (patients), usually through their health insurers. The highest-status hospitals are those which have the latest appliances and techniques; thus the cycle of innovation continues. Corporations, technical experts, financiers, and managers are mutually dependent participants in this system, pursuing competitive advantage, efficiency, effectiveness, and profitability.[4] Any serious attempt to limit the expanding costs of the system or to cover a greater number of individuals at the same cost is countered by charges of "rationing" which appear intuitively countertechnological in intent, that is, as threatening the central tenets of excellence on which the technological system is based. Hence negative U.S. critiques of the British National Health Service tend to focus on its relative lack of hardware, procedures, and facilities.[5]

However, despite the appeal of a technological (or business) model for hospitals, the American ideology of community service also continues to be strong. Thousands of Americans serve without pay on hospital boards or give their time in charity as hospital volunteers. And generosity flows in an outpouring of funds in special appeals—for example, for a well-publicized child who needs a liver transplant. Hospitals are both an expression of American business enterprise *and* of American community ideals.

The ramifications of a hospital system which is neither strictly a technological system nor a community-service system—it is a hybrid—interweave through American hospital history. Indeed, there is considerable "play" in interpreting the system, for different purposes and at different periods. American hospitals can be seen as both efficient and greedy (or even antisocial) when they maximize their income and profitability. When they try to limit their admissions to patients who can pay, are they rational and responsible organizations which act to safeguard their very existence or are they failing in moral duty? And who is to decide? These questions form a continuing motif from past to present.

Hospitals are, of course, professional institutions, that is, places where physicians, nurses, therapists, and technicians work. But here is a further confounding set of factors. Doctors in the United States are still, for the most part, organized independently of the hospital, with the "privilege" of working there. There has long been an inbuilt conflict between the concept of the hospital as a doctors' workshop, subject to medical control, and the hospital as an independent corporate bureaucracy. None of these tensions is new. Their negotiation and partial resolution in different periods form a continuing refrain, from the early years of the century to the present. It is a refrain that we ignore at our peril.

Characteristics of the American Hospital System

The organizational, political, and economic identity of American hospitals as a unique *system* is a twentieth-century phenomenon. The earlier history of hospitals is well served by the masterful book by my colleague Charles E. Rosenberg, *The Care of Strangers: The Rise of America's Hospital System.* Rosenberg focuses first on the emergence of the American hospital between 1800 and 1850, and then on the major transformations that took place in this traditional institution between 1850 and 1920, in the context of the broader changes in American culture accompanying industrialization, urbanization, and immigration. There were in fact overlapping transformations: in conceptions of disease and of science, in the professions of medicine and nursing, in the balance of authority within the hospital, in the hospital's clientele (as paying patients were eagerly sought and proved willing to pay for the new hospital medicine), in hospital architecture and engineering, and, of course, in life on the ward. The historical narrative of *In Sickness and In Wealth* begins in 1900 (chapter 2), during the period in which these various transformations were being completed.

Emerging out of the history of American hospitals in the twentieth century is a set of culture-specific characteristics that mark hospitals as idiosyncratically "American" institutions. Together they form the evolving, collective personality of the hospitals themselves, the actors in the larger system. These characteristics form a subset of themes through this book. Six are of particular importance for understanding the system, past and present.

The first is the segmentation and diversity of hospital ownership in the United States. As major expressions of charitable, social, and economic interests, American hospitals affirmed the pluralism of American society and its division into diverse and competing ethnic, racial, and religious groups in the late nineteenth and early twentieth centuries. By 1900 the United States was dotted with hospitals run by hundreds of different private groups, including Roman Catholics, Lutherans, Methodists, Episcopalians, Southern Baptists, Jews, blacks, Swedes, and Germans, depending on the power structures of local populations. The patterns have also varied geographically, both within states and between regions. Voluntary hospitals have a particularly strong tradition in the Northeast, for example, while profit-making hospitals have long been most firmly established in the South and West.

A related aspect of pluralism is the large number of hospitals in the

United States and the fact that many are still quite small. Today, for example, despite wide publicity about hospital closures, particularly of small urban hospitals in low-income areas, one out of five U.S. hospitals has fewer than 50 beds.[6] Paradoxically, the scattering of hospitals in small local units has enhanced their receptivity to national goals and standards that establish rules of operation—standards initially set by the medical profession, more recently by the federal government. Hospitals became "standardized" between the two world wars through voluntary acceptance of physician-established accreditation requirements (chapter 3). Standardization not only defined the institution as a "hospital," but set a precedent for external definition of what hospitals do. In some ways U.S. hospitals are more highly (and centrally) regulated than those in Britain, even though the latter has a government-run National Health Service.

The linked ideas of voluntarism and community became, in parallel, a unifying and defining rhetoric. In the 1920s, for example, the hospital journals presented hospitals as consumer-oriented and community-sponsored institutions (chapter 5); in the 1930s, voluntarism became politicized, with the major hospital associations acting as effective national political lobbies (chapter 6); in the 1950s, community independence and institutional autonomy were stressed (chapter 9); in the 1960s there was a shift toward "grass-roots" representation, in rhetoric at least, and in the 1970s a turn toward entrepreneurialism and managerialism (chapters 10 and 11). Today hospital representatives are searching again for their "community role" and "voluntary mission." I will suggest that the vagueness and emotive cultural associations of words like "voluntarism" and "community" have served hospitals well throughout their history. The linked processes of national standard-setting and national rhetoric make it possible to write about American hospitals as a genre, despite the continuing heterogeneity of ownership and function across the United States.

If pluralism is one major characteristic of the American hospital system, a second is social stratification. American hospitals have long served as vehicles for defining social class and race, and for interpreting American attitudes to indigence; in the United States, poverty means failure. Hospitals such as Philadelphia General, Bellevue and Kings County in New York, Cook County in Chicago, and San Francisco General, imbued with the old almshouse tradition, were established as, and remained, institutions primarily for the very poor, and were associated with second-class social status and moral stigma. Even as these hospitals, like other hospitals, were "medicalized" in accordance with Progressive, scientific ideas in the late nineteenth and early twentieth centuries—and indeed, many became major teaching centers—they continued to attract a relatively large proportion of the poorest Americans and a relatively large proportion of racial and ethnic minorities. The poor, in turn, became the medical schools' "teaching material." These patterns continue today in the large proportion of Medicaid (welfare) patients treated in academic medical centers.

Until well after World War II, major differences in the kinds of diseases treated by governmental and not-for-profit hospitals in the largest cities added to the sense of social distinction. Yet outside the older industrial cities, local government hospitals have been not only the sole hospitals in many areas, but they have also played a role as community hospitals—that is, a role virtually indistinguishable from that of voluntary hospitals in a similar position—and have been as socially inclusive as local public schools.

Distinction between hospitals has been buttressed by the stratification of patients within hospitals according to ability to pay. U.S. voluntary hospitals have accepted private patients throughout the century. At the beginning of this century these patients were typically housed in separate buildings, in well-furnished private rooms rather than wards, with better food, cooked in separate kitchens, and with less restricted visiting hours. In the large cities there has been an exquisite social patterning of patients across the hospital system and within individual hospitals. American urban hospitals have never, as a group, served as egalitarian forces in the culture as a whole.

The money standard of success, infusing all aspects of hospital operation, is the third major characteristic of the American hospital system. The pay nexus extends from the selection and distribution of patients to decisions about services, and on to the values incorporated into the institutions themselves. Most U.S. hospitals were established without large endowments—indeed, on a shoestring. From the late nineteenth century on, U.S. voluntary hospitals have relied, to a great extent, on fees from paying patients. (Even in the mid-1930s well over two-thirds of the income of American hospitals came from patient fees.) I will argue that American hospitals have been successful in attracting paying patients largely *because* of the pay ethos. The hospitals presented themselves as having something valuable to sell: surgery, glamour, expertise, healthy babies.

Demonstration or show, even conspicuous waste, has been a lasting feature of American hospitals. Indeed, hospitals have been among the most luxurious and costly of American institutions—unnecessarily so, according to critics throughout the century. Part of the reason is undoubtedly the urge to appeal to upper-class patients. But the U.S. hospital is also a multipurpose social institution which embodies cultural ideas about moral worth. The twentieth-century hospital has symbolized the wealth and power structures of new and expanding American cities, the order and glamour of science, and the happy conjunction between humanitarianism and expertise in a society rife with money-making. An observer writing about the New York Hospital for *Harper's Monthly Magazine* in 1878 encapsulated the intertwining allure of technology, money, and religion. The hospital's elevator was described as larger than that of a fashionable hotel and as so smooth in motion that it was like a "mechanical means of getting to heaven."[7]

The pay nexus has been a useful vehicle for defining social class in the United States, sorting patients into different hospitals and different types of accommodation and providing a sense of social "place." In turn, the pay system led the hospitals to provide an array of facilities at different prices. The commitment to providing relatively luxurious care to the upper class and charitable care for the deserving poor at the beginning of the century left an embarrassing gap of services to the growing middle-class population. It was to fill this gap that American hospital trustees and administrators invented the "semiprivate" room. This curiously revealing term implies the provision of care in a room with more than one bed (and thus not strictly a private room), yet definitely not "public" accommodation—that is, a room distinct from the social stigma of care in a ward, with its negative connotations of indigence and failure. Today's hospital business offices are enmeshed in a plethora of arrangements for billing, third-party reimbursement, special discounts to certain buyers, and complicated auditing arrangements. Total coverage through the pay system continues to be elusive.

The pay nexus has also encouraged hospitals, for decades, to concentrate their resources in areas of maximum income (that is, profit centers), to limit the number of areas which run at a loss, and to be extremely sensitive to financial incentives. In these areas, as I shall show, hospitals have long been effective businesses. Since World War II, American hospitals have been driven by reimbursement incentives built into private insurance and, increasingly, into government schemes. Federal policy since the Medicare legislation (1965) has further emphasized the role of the hospital as an institution with something to sell for a price—that is, as a private contractor in the marketplace.

A fourth characteristic of American hospitals is their focus on acute care and technology, and surgery in particular. Hospitals have prospered because of their central place in medical technology, professionalism, and expertise. The American hospital has been—and is—a projection of a medical profession whose archetypes are science, daring, and entrepreneurship. Surgery is still the mainstay of the U.S. short-stay hospital, despite the advent of outpatient surgical facilities and the sophistication of nonsurgical procedures.[8]

The modern doctor, associated with the new hospitals, was—and is—a master engineer, a hero in the American mode, fighting disease with twentieth-century tools. But the early emphasis on surgery has focused hospitals, in turn, around technical spaces such as operating rooms. Generation after generation has characterized the twentieth-century hospital in industrial terms as a factory or workshop. The success and visibility of the hospital in providing acute, specialized care has also obscured its relatively limited role in the overall picture of health and disease. How much hospitals should expand their identity as community health centers forms a further interweaving theme in their history, from past to present.

The hospital's emerging technological role has been fostered by the medical and nursing professions in different ways. Doctors in an upwardly mobile profession claimed hospitals as their own domain; nurses were captured by the hospital and institutionally subsumed. The first professional nursing schools in the United States, based on the Florence Nightingale model, appeared in the 1870s. But nurses, like the hospital social workers who followed in the early twentieth century, were handicapped by appearing to be all-purpose female service workers, without a defined monopoly of scientific skills. Nursing also continued to embrace the model of the hospital as a "charity," with its associated notions of self-sacrifice and religious duty, long after doctors embraced the strong cultural associations between technology, expertise, business, and income.[9] The hospitals' two major professions have continued, in some ways, to express the ambivalence in the social values attributed to the healing role itself.

A fifth, related characteristic of American hospitals is the built-in tension between hospitals and the medical profession. To the American physician the hospital has been an extension of his or her private practice of medicine—and still is, to some extent. Doctors have pressed, successfully for the most part, to have access to hospitals as a matter of course. The average American hospital is an "open-staff" institution; that is, it expects to provide all qualified practitioners with hospital privileges, subject to the rules and regulations of the institution. A large hospital may have several hundred doctors associated with it, few of whom are there on a full-time basis. This open-staff system has made the hospital a technological center, but not necessarily an organizational center, for American medicine. Indeed, for much of the century organized medicine has effectively resisted a strong hospital role in the organization of health services as a whole.

But in turn, doctors, while powerful, have not been closely identified with the internal power structure of hospitals. They have existed as an amorphous mass of "others" essential to, but not fully part of, the organization. Throughout the twentieth century different groups have looked upon the hospital through different eyes, with different technological, organizational, and service agendas, and with different expectations. Administrators, medical staffs, and hospital boards operate in continual tension.

A sixth and final characteristic of American hospitals is the strong yet largely informal role of medical schools as an influence in the hospital system. Only a minority of hospitals had, and still have, primary affiliations with medical schools. Nevertheless, the most powerful hospitals continue to be teaching institutions, in terms of the prestige structures of medicine and of hospital administration. Medical-school faculties dominated the upgrading of surgery through the American College of Surgeons before and after 1920, and thus, in turn, the standardization of hospitals (chapter 5). The growing research focus of major medical schools in the 1930s and 1940s supported the production of knowledge rather than organizational affiliations as the main guide for hospital planning in the postwar years. The combination of medical schools and associated hospitals on one site into a "medical center" was also to provide a model for further development after World War II (chapter 8). Indeed, the American academic health center has become so large and unwieldy that there is now considerable concern about the relationship of the medical school to the academic health-center complex overall and about the school's relationship to its sheltering university, and further concern about the governance of the academic health center itself.[10]

The Process of Change

These six characteristics—segmentation, stratification, the money standard, technological identification, the division between doctors and hospitals, and an authoritative role for university medicine—act and react upon each other, forming different patterns through the decades. The result is a constantly negotiated hospital system, although obviously built on certain "givens." As multipurpose human repair shops, at any time the hospital's functions represent the skills and fashions of contemporary medicine, attitudes to diseases among populations, and the money available for hospital care. In short, hospitals are characterized by change. They are affirming and defining mirrors of the culture in which we live, beaming back to us, through the scope and style of the buildings, the organizational "personality" of the institution and the underlying meaning of the whole enterprise, the values we impute to medicine, technology, wealth, class, and social welfare.

This central observation about—or model of—organizational change should be stressed. As Rosenberg and others have emphasized, the hospital is not an inevitable institution. It is forged by individuals and it is sensitive to economic incentives and to other cultural rewards and disincentives— the messages, that is, in its immediate environment. There is no set design for the hospital's organizational role or for the structure or performance of the hospital system. Nor, I would argue, is there a predictable trajectory of change. If there were, hospitals in all countries would be the same. U.S. hospitals are adaptive, pragmatic organizations, with a long history of rapid adjustment to shifting environments and with a usefully vague, wide-ranging rhetoric, able to be used selectively as times change. As hospitals move within and affect their intertwining environments—social, cultural, professional, political, technological, and economic—the hospital system is constantly reinvented.

It is difficult to see how it could be otherwise, given the variety of social purposes hospitals serve and the diffusion of hospital decision-making among communities of interest—ranging, *inter alia,* from the major health professions, through local elites, to national lobbies, group purchasers, and government agencies. Nevertheless, I emphasize this point because recognition of U.S. hospitals as analogous to factories and/or businesses has made it tempting to critics throughout this century to assume that hospitals are embarked upon some predictable, evolutionary process of change similar to that already experienced by other industries.

One organizational theory has been to assume that technological systems follow certain rules of evolution. In the 1920s and 1930s, for example, a deterministic theory of "cultural lag" assumed that new technologies forced social organizations to adapt in certain ways (chapter 7). Since, according to this theory, there was a time lag before organizations caught up to their technological requirements, it followed, by no means incidentally, that shrewd organizational tactics and social strategies should be designed to hurry the process along, so that cultural adaptation might be eased. Doctors feared corporate domination by hospitals in the 1930s in part because they thought it was inevitable. Leading health-care reformers saw hospital-based medical practice and regional hospital planning as necessary responses to technical change. What we decide to do depends on where we think change is heading—and this may depend in turn on our interpretation of history. All of which is to say that ideas may carry political baggage with them.

Today, as in the past, how we interpret recent hospital history may affect our actions in the present. Paul Starr, for example, writing in the early 1980s, described a historical process wherein a long period of "medical domination" of health-care institutions had been recently overtaken by the "coming of the corporation."[11] It is easy to take such an observation— as many hospital observers now do—as a theory of inevitable (and future) change, and to draw the analogy between hospitals and industrial consolidation. If this analogy is extended, hospitals can be viewed as firms which will (indeed, *should*) move toward consolidation, while the small-scale local hospital can be seen as a vanishing breed, doomed to be replaced by larger, more complex, corporate organizations. Hospitals, then, would consolidate much as the manufacturing industries consolidated at the beginning of the twentieth century, following in turn the consolidation of the railroads. Indeed, if one believes hospitals to be inevitably heading toward large, corporate chains, why not speed up the process?

In such ways historical interpretations and policy intertwine. But such analogies beg the question of whether hospitals are legitimately businesses and, if so, what this means, or how far hospital service can usefully be compared to manufacturing industries, and indeed, whether any service industry can be appropriately compared to manufacturing.

Analogies are seductive and often useful. Yet the facts I shall present here do not bear out a smooth-flowing direction for hospital evolution. However tidily we like to reason, there is no inevitable historical process at work whereby hospitals move from small-scale, autonomous institutions to organizational cogs within massive systems. History shows, rather, that hospitals have embraced a variety of organizational objectives and political postures in different decades as they interact with shifting environmental incentives and restrictions. As political, cultural, and economic conditions have changed, so have the scope, priorities, and structures of hospitals.

Hospitals are powerful actors in social networks. As parts of the social system change—through war, for example, or governmental policy—hospitals modify their roles and scope. Their actions, in turn, play back into (and mold) the wider system. It is this continuous, dynamic process of change that I describe in this book. This idea, too, carries political implications. Its corollary is that future patterns of change are much more open than is apparent in the received wisdom about hospital policy today.

Whether hospital service moves (or is moved by public policy) toward increased definition as a "charity" or public service in the future (that is, as a gift from richer to poorer members of the population, or as a service made available to everyone under government auspices), whether hospital care is seen purely as a business transaction, designed to optimize medical technology, or whether it is some concocted mix of these approaches depends in large part on how we assess contemporary events in the framework of history. This book is offered, with humility, as an attempt to understand the assumptions underlying U.S. hospitals and the hospital system in the twentieth century; the values Americans ascribe to medical care, to hospitals as valuable social institutions, and to the provision of services to the whole population; and the evolving power structures of the system itself.

2

Charities and Businesses: Hospitals in the Early Twentieth Century

Between 1870 and 1917 the American hospital was transformed from an asylum for the indigent into a modern scientific institution. Hundreds of new hospitals sprang up under the aegis of religious orders, clerics, industrialists, women's groups, ethnic associations, and committees of established and aspiring elites in communities across the United States: in small towns across New England, in trade and industrial centers in the West, in cities like Milwaukee and St. Louis that were expanding rapidly under an influx of immigration, in market centers for farmers in Georgia and Illinois and for lumber workers in Wisconsin and Washington, and in the railroad depots of great companies like the Santa Fe—joining the older, usually larger hospitals in the more settled, established cities. Even small hospitals boasted well-equipped, marble-walled operating rooms, disciplined nursing schools providing willing workers to staff the wards, and a cadre of private attending physicians. The American hospital movement, wrote a journalist in the early 1890s, "is a striking instance of our advancing civilization."[1] The hospital, like the hotel, the factory, the club, and the symphony, was a manifestation of modern America.

So strong was the sense of hospitals as a national movement that the

U.S. Census Bureau included a special investigation of hospitals as part of its wider survey of "benevolent institutions" in 1904. A second survey in 1910 estimated the combined value of benevolent hospitals to be at least $306 million. More and more, wrote the census analysts, the hospital for the sick was a "public undertaking."[2] It is here that our story begins.

As a medical-treatment and nursing center the twentieth-century hospital was virtually a new institution—technological and interventionist. The best hospitals were models of cleanliness, efficiency, and expertise. Where only twenty or thirty years before there had been noise, dirt, and disarray, there was now control and organization: the rustle of the nurse's uniform, the bell of the telegraph, the rattle of the hydraulic elevator, the hiss of steam, the murmured ritual of the operating room. Digitalis, quinine, and mercury gave promise of relief to patients, while morphine, opium, cocaine, and sulfonal reduced the noisy manifestations of pain. The old "unruly" patient was rarely seen, and the fetid smell of festering wounds had been banished with antiseptics and unrelenting cleanliness. Control of disease and its symptoms was echoed in organizational control on the wards, where patients rested quietly under knife-edged sheets in an atmosphere of time-clock discipline and fresh air. The mood of medicine was optimistic. Henry James, returning from Europe in 1905, described Presbyterian Hospital in New York and Johns Hopkins Hospital in Baltimore as symbols of stillness, whiteness, poetry, manners, and tone— necessary values, he considered, amidst the violence, vulgar materialism, and hurly-burly of America.[3]

By 1900 American surgeons were operating, *inter alia,* to repair gunshot wounds and drain abscesses in the brain, to remove fluid accumulated in the chest during pleurisy, to relieve the "running from the ear" which often accompanied scarlet fever and other infections, to excise enlarged and infected tonsils and adenoids, and to remove benign and cancerous tumors in all parts of the body. The abdomen and pelvis were the particular "playground of the surgeon."[4] Appendectomies and gynecological operations were done in profusion and with enthusiasm. Nurses managed the hospital environment to ensure, as far as possible, safety from infection. (There was no penicillin until World War II.) Much of the nurse's work, too, was technological and interventionist in the first decade of the twentieth century: taking the patient's pulse, temperature, and blood pressure; regulating the body temperature through hot and cold packs; sterilizing instruments; preparing dressings; and acting as a laboratory technician. In some hospitals nurse-anesthetists were entirely responsible for administering anesthetics in 1910, particularly in the Midwest; in others nursing pupils were trained to give electrical, X-ray, and Finsen light treatments under general medical supervision.[5] Doctors and nurses combined to make the hospital a "hygienic machine" in which the patient's body could be restored, recalibrated, and repaired.

Between 1900 and 1917, patterns of influence, financial and political incentives, and expectations about the hospital's function were created that we still see today, both at the local and national levels. The medical profession was gaining a new identity and prestige through the successes and brilliance of surgery, through claims of expertise based on science, and through the strength of professional organizations. The American Medical Association became, for the first time, a powerful national force, after it reorganized in 1901 as the federated representative of state and local associations. Inside the hospitals authority was gradually being reshaped around the growing involvement of doctors in hospital routine, from patient admissions through authority over nursing procedures, to decisions about autopsies. In turn, the relative balance of power shifted from hospital trustees to medical decision-makers.[6]

However, the shifts were not all in one direction, that is, toward an institution dominated exclusively by a professional agenda. Set against these changes were continuing assumptions about the practices and benefits of charity that were to stamp the twentieth-century hospital as part of the fabric of American life at the local level. Charitable and medical interests worked together to establish domains of control and areas of consensus. Two other rivals for position—managers and nurses—were outgunned by the authority inherent in powerful local networks: of doctors and of charity-givers.

The principles of "scientific charity," articulated in the charity organization movement after the Civil War, left as their legacy belief in self-help rather than handouts, private efforts over those of government, and paternalism rather than egalitarianism. The American hospital expressed the preferences of both board members and physicians for a style of medicine that encouraged economic self-reliance by assuming that patients should pay wherever possible, that signaled the success of professional expertise, and that avoided, where possible, the worst diseases of indigence and failure.

Americans, like the British, believed that the theory of private charity, voluntarily given, "separates it entirely from socialism, as that word is commonly used."[7] But there were two basic differences in the application of hospital charity in the United States and Britain, giving American charitable hospitals special and unique characteristics by 1900. The first was the long acceptance of paying patients in U.S. hospitals, in a tradition that went back to the establishment of the Pennsylvania Hospital in 1751—the first voluntary hospital in the American colonies. The second was the equally long tradition of government aid to private charitable endeavors.[8] The American hospital was already a hybrid.

Establishing the Power Base: Patterns of Allegiance

There was no standard definition of a "hospital" in 1900. American hospitals were a heterogenous group of institutions in terms of both function and size. They fell roughly into four categories of ownership: proprietary, private charitable, religious, and governmental. The most prestigious hospitals were organized as charities, by individuals who were usually not medical practitioners—and who had agendas of their own.

Proprietary hospitals—that is, hospitals operated by proprietors or owners—were nearest to the day-to-day routine of many private practitioners, scattered across the country, who set up a few beds for the convenience of paying patients, sometimes in their own homes. Proprietary hospitals flourished in particular where other types of hospitals were unavailable, notably in the South and West. In North Carolina fifty-four of the sixty-five hospitals existing in 1916 were "stock hospitals," virtually all of them new hospitals opened by surgeons.[9]

There may have been as many as 1,500 to 2,000 proprietary hospitals in 1910 out of a total of over 4,000 hospitals of all kinds.[10] Eminent surgeons established their own small hospitals for private patients who preferred not to go to large institutions. Small-town doctors set up small units where no other hospital existed, and profit-oriented city specialists designed their own exclusive treatment centers, chiefly for women's surgery as this became a fashionable and lucrative field. Some of the profit-making medical schools also owned hospitals as a sideline. In Louisville, Kentucky, for example, medical-school professors ran a hospital as a profit-making venture. Such hospitals were essentially small businesses in character, intents, and methods.

Proprietary hospitals were important to the emerging structure of the American hospital system because the business model was an alternative form of organization to that of charity and governmental hospitals, a form to which doctors might possibly turn in earnest if their demands for hospital beds and clinical authority were not met. Proprietary hospitals were also a model for the wider hospitalization of upper-class patients. Paul Starr argues that the potential threat of competition from the proprietaries forced charitable and religious hospitals to modify their own practices by opening their staffs to additional doctors and allowing their medical staffs to charge fees.[11] But whatever the relative importance and influence of proprietary hospitals in different places, the form itself was important because it suggested a potential way of organizing hospitals in the future as privately held homes or clinics, that is, as businesses.

For physicians, however, it was both professionally and economically preferable to admit their private patients to hospitals run (and financed) by others, including religious groups, charitable associations, and local governments—always assuming that these hospitals allowed doctors to bill private patients for medical attention. Doctors who had access to private practice in independent hospitals were provided with a major social subsidy, for the separation of the cost of hospital operations from physician practice relieved doctors of the burden of capital costs, fund-raising, and any hospital operating losses, as well as from the headaches of hospital administration.

The traditional expectation that doctors would provide their services free to all hospital patients, irrespective of income, had gone by the board by 1910, even in the oldest, most conservative hospitals, although doctors were still generally expected to provide free care to low-income patients whom the hospital treated without charge in the wards. The practice of medical billing for hospital patients was particularly widespread outside the older eastern cities. In 1903, for example, hospitals like Presbyterian Hospital in Chicago and Lakeside Hospital in Cleveland allowed doctors to bill patients admitted to the wards, as well as to private rooms.[12] Private practitioners who held hospital appointments were natural supporters of charitable hospitals. In contrast, practitioners without such appointments saw hospitals (and their associated doctors) as potentially dangerous competitors. As the medical profession sought unity, locally and nationally, its members also sought access to hospitals as a matter of course—and as a matter of economics for the average practitioner.

The epitome of twentieth-century financial relationships between doctors in private practice and independent charitable hospitals—a new

American archetype—was in Rochester, Minnesota, where Drs. William and Charles Mayo dazzled visitors with their surgical technique and clinical success, drawing paying patients from far and wide. In 1904 alone the Mayos performed over three thousand surgical operations, with great success. Their patients were operated on and cared for in an associated but independent charitable hospital, St. Mary's, run by the Roman Catholic Sisters of St. Francis. The hospital ran on an even financial keel, but the doctors made substantial incomes, largely from their hospital work. The Mayo Clinic, incorporating a multispecialist group practice, was formally established in 1914, and the Mayos endowed the new Mayo Foundation with an initial gift of $1 million.[13] Although the Mayos' enormous success was virtually unique, the pattern of fee-for-service medical practitioners associated with charitable institutions (where much of the work was done, incidentally, by ill-paid or unpaid women) was repeated in town after town across the country. The doctors' quid pro quo for hospital access was donating services to the hospital where needed. A doctor thus received a double benefit: fees from paying patients and a reputation for charity. In addition, there was prestige, for hospitals were associated with social prominence and professional expertise.

From the perspective of the average practitioner, there were two general caveats to the system of relations between private doctors and charitable hospitals. First, it was obviously necessary to have a hospital appointment if one was to admit private patients. In the first two decades of the century, local groups of doctors pressed hospitals throughout the country to open their staffs to all practitioners. Second, doctors had no wish to be more restricted in their clinical work, professional behavior, and ability to charge fees in charitable, religious, or governmental hospitals than they would be in hospitals under their own direct control. They wanted, in short, professional autonomy. Two lasting themes of American hospital history were thus laid down well before World War I: the strong stance taken by organized medicine in favor of "open-staff" hospitals, and professional control of the hospital's clinical work.

Pressures for the open-staff system were particularly plausible on democratic grounds when the only local hospital was run by local government, that is, by a county, city, or town. Professional autonomy, on the other hand, was most compatible with the ideals of hospitals run by charitable groups, because board members, practicing charity, were less likely than elected officials to value the hospital as a vehicle for patronage and control—at least not for base political reasons. Government hospitals like Cook County in Chicago or Charity Hospital in New Orleans were regarded as political plums (and were notoriously corrupt) in terms of appointments, supplies, and contracts. Voluntary boards were, in contrast, more likely to view the hospital as a valuable instrument of professional expertise—in somewhat the same way that child welfare was being addressed through the expertise of caseworkers, or symphony orchestras were formed by upper-class committees as social vehicles for musical expression. These views harmonized nicely with the aspirations of private practitioners. The role of the board was to supply support to experts rather than to oversee their work.

The private charitable hospital, organized under nonsectarian auspices and run by a voluntary board of trustees, was the most prominent type of hospital in the early twentieth century. The third type, related to the second, was the religious hospital, owned or operated by a church, religious order, or a board representing religious interests. The 1904 hospital census reported 831 nonsectarian benevolent hospitals and 442 "ecclesiastical" hospitals in the United States, compared with 220 under federal, state, and local-government control. The single largest religious affiliation was Roman Catholic. Most of these hospitals were of recent origin. Frances Hanckel has calculated that over 80 percent of the private and sectarian charitable hospitals existing in 1910 were established after 1880, and 32 percent in the decade beginning in 1900.[14] Eager citizens, anxious to provide a place to take accident victims and sick transients, other than to a hotel or police station, clubbed together to establish a hospital, or alternatively invited a religious order or pressed local government to do it for them, depending on their trust in these various institutions.

Not only were private charitable and religious hospitals socially useful as instruments of charitable impulse, they were valued for their role as modern, "progressive" institutions. It was in society's interest to promote medicine, including medical education and laboratory research, wrote a major exponent of the practice of charity, Edward T. Devine, in 1904, in order to improve general levels of efficiency and skill in the population.[15] Hospitals also made economic sense in a technological, consumer-oriented culture. As "charities," they seemed to have everything in their favor. Income from paying patients, a major drive and rationale for widespread institutional expansion, represented almost half of the budgets of nonsectarian private charities in 1904 and almost three-fourths that of the "ecclesiastical" institutions (table 2.1).

Besides establishing the hospital itself, hospital boards and associated women's committees commonly established their own nursing schools as

TABLE 2.1

Nonproprietary Hospitals by Control and Source of Financing, United States, 1904

	Government	Private	Ecclesiastical	Total
Number of hospitals	220	831	442	1493
Number of patients, January 1, 1904 (thousands)	21	25	25	71
Number of admissions, 1904 (thousands)	263	480	322	1,065
Operating costs ($ millions)	6.6	13.9	7.7	28.2
Income from paying patients as percent of costs	7	45	71	43
Tax subsidies to private institutions as percent of costs	NA.	12	7	8
Other income as percent of costs	93	43	22	49
Average length of stay (days)	31	19	28	25
Cost per admission, 1903–4	$25	$29	$24	$26
Average number of patients per hospital, January 1, 1904	94	31	57	48

SOURCE: Calculated from U.S. Department of Commerce and Labor, Bureau of the Census, *Benevolent Institutions 1904* (Washington, D.C.: Government Printing Office, 1905), pp. 16, 23, 32.

well, whose pupils provided basic staff for the hospital. Upon graduating, the nurses went on to nurse patients in their homes or to work in public health. By 1912 there were more than 1,100 nursing schools, virtually all set up and run by hospitals, with 30,000 students. Even the smallest hospitals, those with under twenty-five beds, had training schools. Indeed, the school *was* the nursing staff; it existed in symbiotic—or parasitic—relationship to the hospital, like a proprietary school in the hospital's midst. Nursing schools were particularly important attributes of hospitals in the Northeast, somewhat less common in the Far West.[16]

Religious, ethnic, and linguistic diversity in the United States made schools and hospitals visible affirmations of the importance of immigrants and religious groups. Chicago, for example, the archetypal melting pot, had a very mixed array of fifty-nine hospitals in 1910, including fifty with nursing schools—and these figures exclude an unknown number of hospitals run by doctors on a proprietary basis. (In comparison, there were fifty-six community hospitals, including for-profit hospitals, in Chicago in 1980.) These hospitals ranged in size from fifteen beds, in small private units that were not much different from private houses, to 1,350 beds in the great Cook County Hospital for the indigent, which was also a major teaching hospital. Some hospitals attested to strong religious origins—like the 400-bed Michael Reese Hospital, run by the Associated Jewish Charities, the 300-bed Presbyterian Hospital, supervised by the Presbyterian Church, the 200-bed St. Bernard Hospital, conducted by the Hospital Sisters of St. Joseph, or the 200-bed St. Elizabeth's Hospital, run by another Roman Catholic order, the Poor Handmaids of Jesus Christ. Others reflected national origins, such as the 60-bed German American Hospital, the 50-bed Norwegian Tabitha Hospital, and the 40-bed Swedish Covenant Hospital; and some were expressions of the activities of nonsectarian private groups. Each had its own, individual sense of "mission."

Clubwomen, clergymen, bankers, and business leaders came together to establish hospitals as part of their commitment to ideals of Judeo-Christian obligation, to class and group solidarity, and to civic duty, that is, as a positive act of charity. They aimed to do good through exercising a disciplined sense of service to others. This usually meant service to the poor and unfortunate, but there was no necessary or concomitant commitment to giving away services predominantly (or even minimally) to the very poor. This is an important point to remember in today's debates about hospitals as "charities": the essence of the act was *giving* per se rather than giving to a particular population. An organization that provided useful services, for a fee, to self-reliant individuals could still be recognized as a public charity.

As the proportion of paying patients rapidly increased, so did acceptance of payment in principle; by 1900 payment was the "true scientific plan" for hospital charity.[17] America, proclaimed British hospital expert Henry C. Burdett, was the "home of the pay system."[18] Patients who could afford to pay more were often charged at rates above cost to help subsidize the poor, while additional funds were sought through private donations and government subsidy. Hence the patterns shown in table 2.1.

Assumptions about paying for care were folded into the prevailing language and expectations of the practice of charity, with its strong focus on the work ethic. The relatively well-endowed Presbyterian Hospital in Chicago is a good example. This hospital, designed for both paying and nonpaying patients from its beginnings in the 1880s, labeled those patients "productive" and "unproductive" respectively. Nevertheless, hospital spokesmen had no difficulty in describing Presbyterian as a "monument of charitable purpose and action" because it represented an "immense investment of capital and good will."[19] It was in the vein of charity as the act of giving, rather than the act of receipt, that medical planning expert Dr. John Shaw Billings, addressing the relations of hospitals to public health at a major conference in 1893, remarked: "I myself am of the opinion that hospitals supported by voluntary contributions confer quite as much benefit upon those who contribute the funds as upon those who are treated in them."[20] Service as a trustee was a statement of decency, a symbolic announcement that "We care." (It still is, to a large extent.) The amount of services actually given away depended, quite pragmatically, on what funds the hospital expected to have. Arthur Ryerson, the president of St. Luke's, Chicago, described the process in the 1890s: "I figure out my final income, and then earn enough money from my pay patients to come out square at the end of the year."[21]

The importance attached to private benevolence—the voluntary act of giving—had three structural and behavioral effects on hospital organization as a whole. First, it created strong local allegiances to particular hospitals, through a self-defined network of charity-givers. These allegiances lasted even as religious and ethnic affiliations weakened, as local populations became assimilated and/or moved to different areas; hence the survival of names such as Presbyterian, Methodist, Baptist, or Mount Sinai for hospitals which today are indistinguishable from nonsectarian institutions. Surgery made hospitals particularly thrilling as a basis for voluntary activity. Hospital sponsors and friends organized charity balls, oyster suppers, fairs, and other fund-raisers, while local women made jams and jellies, rolled bandages, provided linens and flowers, and visited and cheered the patients. These activities had the double value of raising money and fostering group solidarity. Participation in hospital work, like membership on the boards of other social and cultural institutions, defined and ratified social structures in the community through creating a visible, beneficent upper class (or often a set of competing elites) with its own continuing institutions.

Second, giving to a particular hospital created an array of hospitals with a strong sense of institutional identity but relatively little interest in serving the whole population for all their health needs. Different hospitals had little or no incentive to combine forces; heterogeneity in hospital control existed everywhere. In Kansas City, for example, at least twenty-two different hospitals were established between 1870 and 1915, but although some closed, none of them merged.[22] From the beginning of the century to the present, hospital boards and administrators have come together only where mutual gain was perceived and where, as far as possible, institutional autonomy could be maintained. Charles Rosenberg has caught the organizational process vividly in his phrase "inward vision and outward glance."[23] The hospital's community of interest looked inward to the needs and priorities of the medical profession, to the administrative and financing needs of the individual hospital, and to the patient as a bodily mechanism. Trustees, as well as doctors, showed little interest in the patient as a social being or family member. Nor was there much pressure to define the hospital as a center for public education, community health, or social reform.

Critics of the relatively narrow function of the hospital, "limited to the bare treatment of disease," stood out in stark relief—individuals like Sidney E. Goldstein at Mount Sinai Hospital in New York. The hospital, wrote Goldstein in the social reform journal *Charities and the Commons* in 1907, "does not feel itself an intimate part of the social order; it stands forbiddingly isolated and aloof."[24] His and others' pleas to consider the patient as a "social unit," the hospital as a center for education, and charity as a matter of changing health conditions through social reform fell on deaf ears. Hospital boards of trustees, borne along on the successful wave of scientific medicine, with its focus on the patient as a medical rather than a social subject, were happy to leave things as they were. At the same time, the commitment to the hospital as a center for modern medicine by trustees, associated doctors, and affiliates gave the voluntary form a strength and a stability that would ensure its survival through the years.

A third attribute of the tradition of private benevolence, following in a path that went back to the Elizabethan Poor Law, was the assumption by trustees and associates of the charitable hospital that local governments, rather than themselves, were the appropriate and essential residual caregivers. Governments, not hospitals, were to be charged with services to the "unworthy" and unwanted, that is, to social failures, including the down-and-out, the incurable, and the chronically sick. The charitable hospital was a household, run with goodwill for those deemed appropriate for admission through its portals; these individuals were expected to conform to household rules and to get well. It was taken for granted that local-government hospitals in major cities should support the role of the charitable (and incidentally the proprietary) hospitals by taking patients these hospitals were not prepared to admit. Implicit in the model of medical care of the poor were thus two very different kinds of institutions and two philosophies. Charitable and religious institutions provided services to the socially worthy (both paying and impoverished) and were oriented to diagnosis and cure. Government hospitals provided shelter and basic services as a backup system, on grounds of necessity and public order.

Since government hospitals provided a necessary support structure for the success of private charity in major cities, the number of local-government hospitals did not diminish when other hospitals opened, as one might intuitively expect. Instead, in tandem, government's role became even more important in the early twentieth century than it had been in the nineteenth. The two sets of institutions were interdependent. They still are, to some extent, although "patient dumping" from voluntary hospitals to governmental hospitals is now regarded as unacceptable. There were seventy-eight city and county general hospitals in 1910, some in the alms-house tradition, some attracting patients across a broader social spectrum. Over half had been established in the previous twenty years.[25]

Local government control did not, however, inevitably mean restriction to the poor. Here the theme of heterogeneity must be stressed. In isolated rural towns hospitals set up under local government auspices served much the same functions as religious and private charitable hospitals in other areas, drawing a substantial proportion of paying patients; and they have continued to do so throughout the century. But the hospitals which grew out of the old city poorhouses (almshouses) were vital twins of charitable institutions in major cities: huge hospitals like Bellevue in New York, Charity in New Orleans, and Cook County in Chicago. These often grim, barrackslike institutions carried the social stigma of poverty in American culture, were generally poorly funded, and were regarded by potential patients as socially second-rate. Such perceptions were indeed inevitable as long as admissions to local government hospitals were weighted toward the indigent while the charitable hospitals courted those who could pay. The perceptions were structured into the system, providing powerful indices of social class and race.

A few large city-owned hospitals did charge all patients who could pay, as a matter of policy, in the first decade of the century. Boston City Hospital was a case in point. However, it was also regarded as the only municipal hospital where standards of work equaled or excelled those in privately endowed institutions.[26] Even in Boston there were class differences between the clientele in the different types of hospitals, charitable and governmental. The largest almshouse hospitals, with their locked wards and punishment cells—sometimes present well into the twentieth century—their syphilis, alcoholic, and tuberculosis wards, their unmarried pregnant mothers and mentally disturbed old people, and their repressive rules and regulations were multipurpose medical and welfare institutions. Sometimes they even had their own special smell. Bellevue Hospital's first woman house physician (in 1902) remembered it as a "never-to-be-forgotten mixture of carbolic, soapsuds, dust, and musty wood."[27]

In the early 1900s, medical schools were courting city and county hospitals as laboratories for teaching and research. Staff at the Philadelphia General Hospital, for example, began their own publication of clinical studies at the hospital in 1890, and from 1904 listed in the annual report the names of studies where hospital "materials" (that is, patients) had been used.[28] The result, for these hospitals, was a partial, one-sided transformation: they became major clinical factories for scientific medicine while remaining centers for society's rejects.

Outside the major cities there were marked variations in local government care of the poor, even within a single state. In Illinois, for example, Cook County provided the most complete medical treatment to its indigent of all counties, with physicians on the premises of the hospital. At the other end of the scale, sixty-four of ninety-eight Illinois counties reported no institutional provision for the sick poor in 1903. In some counties medical care was given in general almshouses which were characterized by filth, flies, no shades or screens, no medical attendants or nurses, with the insane kept in iron-barred cages—conditions that would exist in some rural areas throughout the United States well into the 1920s, and probably well beyond.[29]

Proprietary, religious, private charitable, and local-government hospitals have provided the great bulk of hospital care in the United States throughout this century. Other hospitals were run, *inter alia,* by the federal government for sailors in the merchant marine, for those working on army posts, and for blacks freed from slavery after the Civil War; Freedmen's Hospital in Washington, D.C., is now Howard University Hospital, a major teaching hospital. A few states organized general hospitals, including the state miners' hospitals in Pennsylvania and West Virginia, representing state support of industry; and some business corporations, including railroads, and a handful of employee associations established hospitals as well. Patterns of hospital control and allegiance have varied from place to place, depending on industrial conditions and wealth, local power structures, the degree of unity and/or upward mobility in the social hierarchy, the effectiveness of municipal and county government, state enabling legislation, intergroup rivalries, and the specific interests of bishops, industrialists, doctors, and society women.

Illinois reported the largest cluster of Roman Catholic hospitals of any state in 1903 (43 out of a total of 118 hospitals). New York City had (and has continued to have) an unusually strong local government commitment, with over $11 million invested in its city hospital system in 1909, a far greater amount than any other city, and a strong system of subsidizing charitable hospitals as well.[30] The city of Cincinnati was unusual in taking special pride in its magnificent hospital building, the teaching hospital for its municipal university—and an architectural showplace for the region.

The value of this hospital's property in 1909 was almost 50 percent more than the entire Cook County Hospital in Chicago.[31]

Nevertheless, despite the heterogeneity, the most striking feature of the hospital movement was its simultaneous development across the country, as a wide variety of individuals, including practicing doctors and medical-school professors, perceived—independently—the manifold advantages of hospital provision. By 1910 there were as many hospitals in the United States per 1,000 population as there are today. Probably one out of every five doctors already had access to a hospital.[32] Both the charity-givers and the doctors had strong interests in establishing and expanding hospitals in their own communities. Each needed the other to realize these interests.

Charities as Businesses: The Pay System

As charities, hospitals were in a class by themselves by 1900. Relative to the other benevolent institutions, like homes for adults, for children, or for the blind and deaf, with which they were compared by the U.S. Census Bureau, hospitals were small, short-stay institutions. The average length of a hospital stay was twenty-five days in 1904, only nineteen days in nonsectarian charitable institutions (table 2.1). Hospitals were complex, expensive, and particularly attractive to paying patients. All charities charged where they could, as a matter of course. However, the rise of surgery created a new market of services to relatively well-off individuals who were not otherwise disabled or socially dependent. "Today," enthused a writer in *Popular Science Monthly* in 1913, "the patient approaches [the hospital] with confidence instead of apprehension, with alacrity instead of reluctance, and with the hope of life rather than the fear of death."[33]

Income from paying patients was particularly strong in the western states. Hospitals in thirteen U.S. states and territories drew 70 percent or more of their operating income from patients in 1903. In Utah and Oregon, government and private charitable hospitals together earned more from paying patients than they actually spent on hospital operations (table 2.2). Hospitals under a variety of ownerships benefited from paying patients.

TABLE 2.2

States Reporting the Highest Percentage of Income from Paying Patients to Nonproprietary Hospitals, 1903

	Income from Pay Patients, 1903 ($)	Percent of Cost of Maintenance, 1903	Number of Patients per 100,000 Population on December 31, 1904
Utah	89,004	116.2	56
Oregon	79,015	109.7	80
North Dakota	46,462	96.5	31
Indian Territory	13,590	93.4	8
Nebraska	156,400	89.3	40
Oklahoma	3,403	82.9	NA
South Dakota	43,417	79.9	23
Wyoming	21,419	79.2	62
Wisconsin	304,278	77.6	55
Washington	226,767	75.7	169
Minnesota	472,922	74.7	76
Iowa	253,598	73.7	37
Michigan	457,854	73.3	50
All states*	12,181,484	43.2	87

NOTE: Table includes all states where 70% or more of the income of governmental, ecclesiastical, and other private benevolent hospitals was derived from paying patients in 1903.
*Including states not listed in the table.
SOURCE: *Benevolent Institutions 1904*, p. 32.

In San Francisco, for example, the six charitable hospitals which took in more money from paying patients than their entire operating expenses in 1903 included the Lane Hospital (the teaching hospital for Cooper Medical College), Pacific Hospital (a private charitable corporation), St. Thomas Hospital (a private charitable corporation), the Protestant St. Luke's Hospital, and the Roman Catholic St. Joseph's and St. Mary's. The University of California even did quite well on outpatient service, receiving income from patients equivalent to two-thirds of its operating expenses. Although hospitals in the eastern states lagged behind, income from paying patients was increasingly important here, too, for paying patients were on the increase across the country. At the Union Protestant Infirmary in Baltimore, for example, 67 percent of the hospital's income came from paying patients in 1905, 79 percent in 1910, and 88 percent in 1915.[34] At Touro Infirmary in New Orleans, 49 percent of the receipts were from patients in 1900, 79 percent in 1914.[35]

How far the shift from charity to purchase had gone by the time of America's entry into World War I can be seen at a glance in table 2.3, which shows the distribution of beds and pay status in nongovernmental general hospitals in Illinois in 1917. Only 15 percent of the patients in these hospitals were true charity cases, treated for free; 77 percent paid full rates, and 9 percent paid for part of their care. Outside the cities virtually all care in Illinois was given either in county hospitals or on a paying basis. At the same time, another stratification had appeared in the hospital in the form of rooms of different sizes. Well over one-third of the service in nongovernmental hospitals in Illinois was given to patients in single rooms; less than one-third of the patients were in wards with five beds or more. Again, outside the cities, treatment in large wards was rare. These structures had

TABLE 2.3

Distribution of Beds in Privately Conducted General Hospitals, Illinois, 1917

| | | | Percentage of Beds in | | | | |
	No. of Hospitals Reporting	Total Beds	Wards of 5 Beds or More	3–4 Bed Wards	2 Bed Wards	Single Rooms	Total
Chicago	34	4,068	39	16	12	33	100
Other cities of 10,000 or more population	27	1,914	26	16	15	42	100
Other towns	29	827	9	15	10	66	100
Total	90	6,809	32	16	13	39	100

Pay, Part-Pay, and Free Service in Privately Conducted General Hospitals, Illinois, 1917

| | | Total Patients Seen in Previous Year | Percentage of Patients Who Were | | | |
	No. of Hospitals Reporting		Pay Patients	Part-Pay Patients	Free Patients	Total
Chicago	35	105,898	70	11	20	100
Other cities of 10,000 or more population	35	57,812	86	6	8	100
Other towns	36	13,532	91	6	3	100
Total	106	177,242	77	9	15	100

NOTE: Percentages may not add up exactly, due to rounding.
SOURCE: *Report of the Health Insurance Commission of the State of Illinois* (Springfield, Ill.: State of Illinois, 1919), pp. 85, 87.

nothing to do with medical treatment per se. They derived jointly from the goals of social stratification and of optimizing hospital income. Together, boards of trustees, superintendents, and associated physicians ratified the idea of hospital service as something to be paid for and to be available at different rates and prices, from the implied social success of the single private room to the social failure of the indigent wards.

The pay system made voluntary hospitals peculiar hybrids economically. They were "charities" in terms of the sources from which they drew money for buildings and other capital investments. Capital came almost entirely from private gifts, endowments, and donations until after World War II, and predominantly from these sources until the 1970s. In terms of day-to-day operations, however, the early-twentieth-century hospital was more like a business. The more attractive the hospital was to paying patients, the greater its income; the greater its income, the greater the level of medical facilities and amenities that it could offer, and in turn, the greater its attraction to paying patients, who might otherwise be treated at home. Hospitals had a clear incentive to build the demand for hospital service; that is, to behave as successful, competitive enterprises in which the goal was expansion of units sold, including surgical operations and filled private beds.

Opinions varied as to how much the hospital should actually be used. A committee of inquiry in New York in 1910 found that between 89 and 92 percent of all sickness in different districts of New York City was being cared for in private homes. The editor of the *New York Medical Journal,* which reported these findings, described them as a "shock," because they suggested underutilization of hospitals.[36] A careful study in Dutchess County, New York, in 1912–13, concluded that 15 percent of all seriously ill patients needed hospitalization for an array of noncontagious diseases, another 4 percent for contagious diseases, and 9 percent because the patients had unsatisfactory homes, due to crowding, sanitation, low-grade mentality, ignorance, shiftlessness, or poverty.[37] Most patients, particularly those not needing surgery, such as patients with pneumonia or a fever, could be taken care of just as well (if not better) at home where they could be cared for by a trained nurse, family members, or servants, rather than by inexperienced hospital pupil nurses; and where they would have comfort and privacy and avoid the risks of being treated in a bed adjacent to someone with, say, typhoid fever, insomnia, or delirium tremens.[38]

Hospitals countered unfavorable comparisons with home care by providing facilities that were both private and luxurious. Jefferson Medical College Hospital in Philadelphia, for example, quadrupled its budget between 1899 and 1916, from $64,000 to $277,000, largely by opening a new hospital with a luxurious private service. Private patients were given a room with bath, electrotherapeutic and hydrotherapeutic treatments, and had the use of private reception rooms, a roof garden, a sun parlor, and a separate diet kitchen. Surgery was performed in operating rooms separate from those used for other patients, and there was private nursing care of maternity patients.[39] Meanwhile, hospitalization was urged by a hospital's attending physicians on grounds of scientific necessity and quality of treatment. Professor of Surgery W. W. Keen at Jefferson, for example, stressed the hidden and massive dangers of the millions of bacteria that had become an almost palpable element of surgical thinking, following general acceptance of the germ theory. Seeking a striking illustration for a general audience, he wrote that "even the spotless hands of the bride, in the eyes of the surgeon, are dirty."[40] The assumption of professional control over these dangerous, unseen beings enhanced the authority and the mystique of the doctor and encouraged the image of the hospital as a necessary, scientific base for treatment.

The steam sterilizer was an important symbol of the new hospital-based technique. In the hospital, sterilization was done by steam at 240 degrees Fahrenheit, compared with the 212-degree boiling point at home; and all materials used for operations were sterilized to an extent not possible at home, as Professor Keen and others pointed out. The visual impact of the operating room and its antechambers, lavishly supplied with marble, suggested the perfect application of modern science. Eminent surgeon J. M. T. Finney remarked: "It would appear to the uninitiated impossible, in such a hygienic sanctuary, to commit a surgical sin" (although he criticized common lapses in surgical technique).[41]

Operations continued to be performed at home well into the twentieth century. Efficiency expert Frank Gilbreth, for example, brought a surgeon into his home laboratory in order to demonstrate surgical operating techniques during the wholesale removal of the family's tonsils.[42] Portable surgical kits continued to be marketed, including folding operating tables. Most surgeons were, however, readily able to convince patients to enter hospitals by World War I. It was difficult, if not impossible, for the modern man to object to removal of his appendix by an expert when others were entering into surgery with fortitude, or for the modern woman to say that she did not need an operation for, say, endometritis or for laceration of the cervix or an ovarian cyst, and it was impossible to insist on having it done at home over the objections of the surgeon.

The scientific justification for hospital admission was extended to diagnosis, even though in many, if not most, of the small hospitals, routine pathological services were not available before World War I. In the (ideal) hospital, wrote the superintendent of Johns Hopkins Hospital, "every body fluid is made the object of examination, the blood, the urine, the stomach contents, and the excreta, by the most clinical or chemical methods. The microscope is called upon to aid the investigation of tumors and new growths, and all the armamentarium of scientific research is called into requisition."[43] Joel Howell has recently argued, from studying the records of the Pennsylvania Hospital, that the new X-ray machines and pathological services were not central to actual clinical diagnosis in the hospital before World War I.[44] Nevertheless, hospital trustees and associated physicians believed strongly in the value of science and technology. Jefferson Hospital, for example, bought an X-ray machine soon after the discovery of the X ray by Röntgen in 1895, to "meet the call for the latest appliances." The hospital board's view was that it proved its value by "wonderful results."[45] Hospital administrators and boards fostered the images of science, engineering, and technology by choosing pictures of operating rooms, laboratories, and equipment to illustrate their annual reports. There was nothing inconsistent in board members seeing the hospital as both charity and engineering center. The more effective the institution in terms of treatment, the greater the social value of its charity—in terms of the value of the hospital itself and of the time and money that the members contributed.

Hospitalizing paying patients seems to have been more difficult, initially, in the country than in the city, perhaps because the cottage hospital of ten or twenty beds was not much different from the private home. But even in the country, hospital service was well accepted by World War I. Brattleboro Memorial Hospital, Vermont (established in 1904), is a good example. By 1911, this hospital usually had about fifteen patients in residence, with an annual total of over four hundred patients treated; the average length of stay was sixteen days. Three-fourths of the patients were operated upon—mostly abdominal and gynecological surgery, tonsillectomies, and adenoidectomies—and only a handful of patients were treated free. The hospital charged ward patients $10 a week, and private-room patients from $15 to $25. Like other hospitals it also added fees for technical procedures, including operating fees and anesthesia, fees for X-ray and electrical treatments, and additional fees for the X rays themselves. The charge for an 11-by-14-inch radiograph ranged from $3 to $10.[46]

In the cities, individuals used to shopping in huge, specialized department stores, like Wanamaker's or Filene's, to attending spas in the country for their health, and to dining in fashionable restaurants and hotels were attuned to seeing luxurious institutions as a preferred alternative to staying at home—symbols of all that was modern in America. Luxurious accommodations, like the scientific and technological image, provided a compelling attraction for patients. The two characteristics worked together, as they did in contemporary advertisements for upscale stores and automobiles. On the one hand, hospitalization was presented as less expensive (for equivalent service) than home treatment. On the other, quality seemed synonymous with expenditure.

U.S. visitors to Britain looked on the London voluntary hospitals as quaint and eccentric, marked with a sign, perhaps, over the hospital door—"Supported by Voluntary Contributions Only"—even though a number of patients might well have funds enough to pay.[47] London voluntary hospitals drew almost 90 percent of their income from voluntary gifts and investments in 1911. Although the newer, provincial hospitals outside London were building up a private clientele, largely by encouraging the growth of contributory workmen's insurance schemes, they, too, relied far less heavily on patient payments than similar hospitals in the United States. American hospitals seemed to be far more mercantile in their general outlook—more like hotels than hospitals in some respects—and more luxurious in their facilities.[48]

Journals like *Trained Nurse and Hospital Review* criticized special inducements by hospitals to attract the patronage of the wealthy classes at the turn of the century. This journal criticized Roosevelt Hospital in New York in particular for advertising, "just as Wanamaker advertises a store opening and a new stock of goods." The hospital trustees had distributed a circular to the medical and nursing professions, describing the rooms in the new private patients' pavilion as designed to appeal to "those of the most cultivated tastes." They had offered an open day on which visitors might come to inspect. The process, said the journal, "all through savors of a modern business advertising proclamation."[49] Nevertheless, in some form or other, hospitals' awareness of what we would now call marketing was quite common, even before the turn of the century. Methods ranged from low initial pricing of private rooms, in order to tempt both the public and physicians to use them, with the hope of making a profit later on that would be used for other hospital purposes (as at Wilkes-Barre Hospital, Pennsylvania), to establishing subscription programs, whereby employers and workers could be eligible for specified service benefits (as at German Hospital, Philadelphia).[50] One New York charitable hospital, reported the *New York Medical Journal* in 1911, sent out a bill for two weeks' board and service (amounting to $21) to every charity patient or his family immediately after admission, even when it had been determined that the patient could not pay. Others charged $35, $50, or even $100 a week, outrageous prices even for service in an "affair of domes and vast central halls, with its hotel charges and tips, . . . its reproduction of the hotel air of service and 'hustle.' "[51] Such hospitals sent out three clear messages: first, their services were valuable; second, they came at a price; and third, those individuals who were given services (because they could not pay) were misfits and recreants. The more hospitals charged, the more valuable their services seemed. Thus hospital service was structured to be expensive.

The medical profession, disorganized, overcrowded, and, for the most part, poorly paid at the turn of the century, was initially ill-prepared to cope with the exuberance of the hospital pay system, fostered as it was by eager superintendents and building-minded board members; operating rooms were of special interest to trustees and their architects. The urge to found hospitals, it was complained, was a disease, which attacked the "professional philanthropist, the commercial physician, and the social sponger," and involved "lachrymose sentimentalism and philanthropic vanity."[52] A long period of medical resistance to hospital domination was beginning. Laymen, complained the *Journal of the American Medical Association* in 1901, thought hospitals consisted of "admirable buildings, well-prepared food, smart nurses, and the requisite number of patients," but little more.[53] The hospital was criticized as a "very one-sided competition" with private practice, a "monopoly of natural advantages," and a symbol of "economic evolution"; and there were fears that eventually the doctor in individual practice might be wiped out by the hospital, just as department stores were wiping out individual stores. Perhaps the future of medicine would be dominated by "great incorporated hospital companies," organized as "pure business ventures," which would pay large salaries to selected physicians and use the "ordinary mercantile methods of securing business."[54] Concerns about predatory competition by "pompous laymen, who pose as public benefactors and philanthropists"[55] goaded doctors to join their state and local medical societies in order to establish an independent power base from which they could, *inter alia,* press hospitals to open their staffs to all private practitioners.

However, hospital boards, committed to public service (and recognized in the community for this commitment), had no more desire to be labeled "commercial" than had physicians. A possible exception was to build limited, specialized private facilities as money-makers for the hospital as a whole. The superintendent of St. Luke's Hospital in Chicago suggested at the American Hospital Association meetings in 1907 that modern "hotel-hospitals" should be built, placed fully on a commercial basis (including interest on investment and depreciation). The "customer" would pay the full cost of the service plus a "reasonable profit." The hotel-hospital, designed to add to the net income of the larger hospital, would include a dining room that served as a restaurant where patients could get meals whenever they wanted, a telephone within reach of every bed, light switches controlled by the patient without the intervention of nurses, large numbers of private bathrooms, strict privacy, and abolition of irksome hospital rules.[56] But even for moderately affluent people it seemed no more fanciful, in the American context, to design a well-organized hospital with properly paid doctors, nurses, and other workers, than to establish an "intelligently-conducted system of good restaurants, where clean and good food and skillful cooking can be had at little cost," that is, to provide a "self-supporting hospital for self-supporting people."[57]

The idea of the hospital as a medical hotel was intriguing—for the hospital would return to its ancient role of hospitality—although it was scarcely practical to think of such facilities for everyone in a society committed to service for a fee. But in any event, hospital trustees were committed to the idea of hospitals not as business propositions but as charities, an important part of the life of organized community benevolence that distinguished the American town or city. Board members valued their role on the boards because it made them instant humanitarians, not so that they could duplicate their jobs in business. However businesslike the hospital, it remained, for trustees, a place of service.

At the same time, trustees engaged willingly in the transformation of their charities into complex technical organizations. It was satisfying to know that one's charitable endeavors were producing services that were valued by the richest as well as the poorest members of the population. Hospitals were thrilling institutions. It was much more interesting—more "modern"—to discuss the uses and the purchase of the latest equipment than to decide, as board members had in the midnineteenth century, whether to admit one or another lower-class person as a hospital patient. Now the talk might turn to the advantages of incandescent lighting; refrigeration plants for cold storage; vacuum piping systems; silent elevators with safety devices so that the car could not be started until all the doors locked; dumbwaiters for food; adequate toilets for nurses, visitors, and staff; well-appointed floor stations for nurses; huge mattress sterilizers; bed screens to ensure privacy on the wards, and the latest in hygienic metal beds—and all in the name of charity.[58] Hospital boards met comfortably, month by month, with a familiar, self-perpetuating, often self-satisfied cast of characters, whose very presence signified public virtue and social stability. A living ex-trustee, observed a New York practitioner in 1900, was "as rare as a white blackbird," while a dead one was "as scarce as a dead eagle or a dead mule."[59]

The divided domain of hospital responsibility into medical and administrative services, evident well before World War I, represented recognition of the mutual dependencies of hospitals and doctors, the parallel ideologies of scientific charity and scientific medicine, the growing authority and power of the medical profession, and, not least, the expanded reach of hospital administration itself. Large hospitals employed engineers, pharmacists, cashiers and stenographers, storekeepers and chefs, scrub girls, bellboys and kitchen maids, laundrymen and sewing girls, firemen, carpenters, window washers, and painters; one-tenth of a hospital's budget might go to engineering alone in 1915.[60] Boards of trustees, their sponsoring churches, and community organizations, along with administrators, had little interest in controlling the private practice of medicine; this was the realm of experts. The hospital was a household in which the chief income producer, the doctor, could come and go like a paterfamilias. Both physicians and trustees saw themselves as fulfilling altruistic rather than commercial roles, the former as professionals, the latter as community representatives who were holding public resources in trust. Both had a vested interest in the success and structuring of the pay system.

The ties of charitable allegiance confirmed the hospital as a local institution despite major shifts in demography, institutional expansion, and medical specialization in the early twentieth century, and even though automobiles and rapid transit systems released staff and patients from using the hospital nearest to them. The suburbs, with grass, trees, and open spaces, were now within a few minutes' travel of crowded city centers. In praising Cincinnati's new city general hospital in 1911, built in a suburb on an elevated plateau with an unobstructed view, the chairman of the city's Board of Hospital Commissioners emphasized the new autoambulances, "large and powerful, easy-riding." Surgeons were to be available in transit, "to stop hemorrhage, or give stimulants in shock, or antidotes in poison cases."[61] The new hospital was also of easy access by several car lines. But this model of a regional hospital or "hospital city," however rational in theory, was unappealing to the average private charitable institution, with its vested local network of doctors and charity-givers. The success of the pay system—and, of course, of hospital medicine itself—gave the charitable hospital the freedom to grow as an autonomous institution. The American hospital was grounded in the local marketplace of volunteers and physicians.

The Public Role of Private Hospitals

Not surprisingly, the behavior of both the private nonsectarian charities and the ecclesiastical hospitals—expansionary, charitable in intent, autonomous, charging all possible patients, locally focused, and uninterested in consolidation—raised serious political and philosophical questions in the early twentieth century, as since, about their "public" and "private" roles. Interest focused in particular on accountability, public subsidy, tax exemption, and the general social efficiency of hospitals as a whole. Private charitable hospitals had recognized, but unspecified, public purposes. They were organized by members of the public to provide services to the public; they were open to the public (with facilities graded by ability to pay); they collected funds from the public, particularly for new buildings; and they were often aided with tax funds from state, county, or city.

The term "public," generally applied to charitable institutions, was both independent of such aid and a rationale for its provision. In this vein the State Board of Charities in Connecticut could remark quite naturally in 1906, "There is now public hospital provision in each of the 18 cities of the state." Considered "public" were many hospitals we would now call "private"; for example, Grace and New Haven hospitals in New Haven, the Hartford Hospital, and St. Vincent's Roman Catholic Hospital in Bridgeport. Each of these hospitals, along with others, was regularly aided by the state.[62]

There was little serious pressure for abandoning the voluntary ideal, so central to the production of social institutions in the flowering of industrial capitalism, in favor of a governmental system. The utilitarian function of voluntary association for charitable purposes, including hospitals, was evident both to proponents and to critics. Progressive criticism focused on tidiness, that is, on clear roles, responsibilities, and efficiencies, rather than on rejection of private benevolence itself. Steel baron Andrew Carnegie captured a generational philosophy in his famous "Gospel of Wealth," a declaration of the individual and social merits inherent in the production of wealth and the sacredness of property. The gospel recognized the wealthy, rather than government, as society's agents and trustees, protecting the community from socialists and anarchists, "so that the ties of brotherhood may still bind together the rich and poor in harmonious relationship."[63] The issue was the "proper administration" of wealth as a public function, through charity, without harmful intervention by government agencies—harmful, that is, both to the free enterprise of public charity itself and to general acceptance of capitalism (with private benevolence as its necessary affiliate) as the political alternative to socialism. Indeed, this is *still* the issue. How is American society to mobilize most effectively in support of a system of hospital services based on voluntary hospitals without making them quasigovernmental institutions on the one hand, or having them become socially irresponsible on the other?

In the United States the transmutation of wealth into charity did not mean no government involvement at all—quite the reverse. The role of government was to support both the production of wealth, in all areas of enterprise, and its complementary and supporting structures, including charities—then, as since. The recognized importance of private benevolence as a public function also sustained charitable hospitals, even in their most entrepreneurial forms, as public charities in the courts of law. Charitable hospitals were legally distinguished from hospitals organized as profit-making corporations. The latter, as businesses, could, for example, be sued for negligence. In contrast, under the doctrine of "charitable immunity," voluntary hospitals, like government agencies, could claim immunity from tort liability, even when hospital employees injured paying patients. The doctrine was upheld on grounds both of public policy, which assumed that charitable hospitals served the general good, and on the narrower argument that the funds embodied in a charitable hospital were a public trust, which should not be diverted to extraneous purposes such as court awards to patients.[64] Charitable immunity for voluntary hospitals lingered in some states up to the 1960s, and for local government hospitals to the 1970s.

Charitable hospitals were also exempt from local property taxes in many states in 1900, even though the hospitals made profits on at least some patients or services. Peoria County, Illinois, for example, unsuccessfully brought suit to tax a hospital run by the Sisters of the Third Order of St. Francis where only 5 percent of the hospital's patients were charity patients in 1907.[65] Through the courts, the private charitable hospital, nurturing its increasing market of paying patients, was given public sanction to expand its plant, services, equipment, and endowments.

The courts supported the principle of private benevolence as a public good, *sui generis*. Trustees did not have to offer services necessarily, or even primarily, to serve the poor; nor did they have to demonstrate that the hospital's services were actually needed. It was assumed, rather, that the act of benevolence itself—the administration of wealth to create social ties across the community—should be recognized. It also assumed that trustees knew what they were doing (better, at least, than government), and that what they were doing was for the public's general benefit.

Yet at the same time, the hospitals were vulnerable to criticism. The rush to construct hospitals in the 1890s and early 1900s led to a substantial—and recognized—oversupply of beds; nearly half of all hospitals had a 50 percent or lower occupancy rate in 1910.[66] About 3,000 hospital beds lay vacant in Pennsylvania alone. A journalist criticized the Pennsylvania Hospital, Philadelphia, at state tax hearings in 1910 as a "refuge for the rich," although it had originally been founded for the poor. "When Socialism comes into power," he said, "then, perhaps, the poor and the rich will be taken care of alike."[67] Pennsylvania's system of state aid to charitable hospitals was run virtually as a private venture, through a network of individuals in the hospitals, on the State Board of Charities, and in the legislature. Nevertheless, government aid brought all hospitals, willy-nilly, into politics. (This was one good reason why government subsidies were avoided by the well-endowed voluntary hospitals in London.)

The economic structure of hospital service in the United States meant that available beds were not routinely made available for free patients; quite the reverse, for hospitals discouraged charity care where they could. Neither doctors nor charity-givers wished to engage in "indiscriminate charity," with the dual risks of establishing a permanent underclass of paupers and having people who could afford to pay cheat the system. These two activities were called "pauperization" and "charity abuse." The problem was that the shift of surgery to hospitals created a new category of obviously "worthy" patients: people who were medically needy but not necessarily indigent in other respects, that is, who increasingly had no choice except to go to the hospital but who could not afford the charges of a private room. The largest single occupational group supplying inpatients to the Pennsylvania Hospital in 1910 was of schoolchildren (22 percent of all admissions), typically admitted for tonsillectomies and adenoidectomies, followed by housewives (19 percent) and laborers (17 percent).[68] Hospitals were systematically inegalitarian in the facilities they offered, but they appeared to be particularly inhospitable to society's new consumers, that is, to working families with moderate incomes.

There was no question of the services for rich and poor being assimilated to a common mean; that would subvert the entire purpose of the enterprise, because the rich would most likely stay at home or take their services to private sanatoria if the privacy and luxury of private hospital care were not available. In support of socially privileged clients, some of the largest hospitals duplicated practically all facilities and support services in order to serve paying patients and ward patients independently. Germs were not to climb the social ladder. The *American Journal of Nursing* ran a series of articles on laundries in its first volume in 1900, showing how complete segregation of clothes could be maintained between public and private patients, from separate sanitary washing to drying chambers. Taking the logic one step further, the superintendent of Macon Hospital in Georgia recommended color-coding to insure that articles be kept rigorously separate even after laundry; he suggested cream and white blankets for private rooms and white wards, slate-colored blankets for colored wards, and red blankets for ambulance services.[69] But there was no obvious intermediate range of services between private rooms and wards.

Instead, boards of trustees and administrators went out of their way to encourage a democratic image for their hospitals—listing, for example, the occupations of patients in their annual reports: silk-weavers, cigarmakers, baseball players, stenographers, physicians, teamsters, actresses, housewives, brakemen.[70] Nevertheless, hospitals were obvious targets for socialist criticism. Private hospital pavilions and charity balls suggested aristocratic social influence, privately held accounting books whispered of unfair privilege, and tax subsidy, where this existed, sounded suspiciously like class legislation.[71]

Local tax subsidies provided one-eighth of the income of nonsectarian, private charitable hospitals across the United States in 1904 (table 2.1). The availability of government aid depended on the strength of local interest groups; the relative availability of tax funds; the ability of voluntary and religious hospitals, profit-making hospitals, and almshouses to meet apparent needs without additional tax expenses; the taxing structures which obtained in different states; the inertia of policy-making; and an accretion of tradition. Government aid was most common in the East, but was evident in scattered communities in all regions; one study found some government subsidies to private hospitals in thirty-five states and the District of Columbia in 1909, with examples ranging, alphabetically, from Birmingham, Alabama, to Sheboygan, Wisconsin.[72] Since, by definition, tax-subsidized charitable hospitals were public-private hybrids, debates over tax support concentrated more general criticisms of the "privateness" of "public" hospitals.

Between the 1890s and World War I, tax subsidy of charitable hospitals came under fire from several directions. A critical report from the National Conference of Charities and Correction in 1901 listed eight problems of philosophy and strategy, problems echoed by other reformers, legislators, and journalists. First, once subsidy began, the costs of the private institutions or charities often grew rapidly and beyond expectations, because tax money fueled the expansionary predilections of private agencies. (For the hospitals this principle was to be demonstrated again and again in the future.) Second, public encouragement of private institutions

allegedly encouraged families of ample means to offload their dependents—parents and children—on institutions, rather than caring for them
at home. Third, the subsidies were said to weaken private benevolence
while in some cases bringing people into charitable work from the "most
mercenary motives." (The report cited a case in California where orphan
asylums had been established as business enterprises, and children were
nearly starved to death while the managers reaped a profit on the per capita
payment for their support. Again, there are echoes up to the present.)

Fourth, subsidy of private institutions undercut the potential role of
government institutions, for a policy signifying that government's role was
limited to sustaining private interest was also a denial of direct government
responsibility to provide those services itself. (Whether one viewed this as
good or bad depended on one's political and social views.) Fifth, the
subsidy system prevented the introduction of better methods of organization, since it created a body of vested interest in continuing without
change, and sixth, prevented the growth of a unified system of public
philanthropy, since the subsidized charities, as private organizations, stood
outside the system of state-controlled institutions. Seventh, the system
promoted lobbying and special influence. In Pennsylvania, indeed, political
lobbying, log-rolling, back scratching, and trading of votes were an accepted part of the extensive system of state subsidies to voluntary institutions, which ran at $2 million to $3 million per year in the early twentieth
century.

Eighth and finally, government subsidies to private institutions were
in conflict with "sound American political principles, as well that of the
separation of church and state, as that of no special favors to any body of
citizens."[73] Others believed quite simply that public services should be
provided in government institutions, and that voluntary and religious
institutions should be strictly private. Amos Warner, in his influential
book on American charities, recommended "consistent opposition to any
and all public subsidies to private charities."[74]

Determining the proper relation of the state to privately managed
charities was, wrote a major critic in 1914, the "sore thumb of public
administrative policy."[75] On the plus side, by making use of voluntary
agencies already established, the public benefited from the cooperation of
private funds and the use of a valuable plant already devoted to a worthy
purpose. Meanwhile, hospitals received a dependable source of income
which did not shrink, necessarily, in an industrial depression. Public subsidies had the advantage of avoiding the American distrust of governmental
machinery; private hospitals were free of the machine politics of local
government agencies; there was greater public accountability for charitable

organizations where government agencies required their records to be open to inspection; and through a tax system everybody was forced to contribute to charities, including the stingy. Some claimed, too, that in private institutions the stigma of pauperism was less likely to attach to the inmates, and "thus the moral effects are better."[76]

New York and Pennsylvania, the most visible and important exemplars of the public-private mix, accounted for more than 60 percent of all tax payments to voluntary and religious hospitals in the early twentieth century. New York City initiated a system in 1899 whereby it contracted for service based on per diem payments for specified patients at standard rates; the surgical rate was $1.10 a day in 1909. These payments were accompanied by regulation, accounting systems, inspections, and other controls over which patients would count as proper charges against the city and by publication of the amounts received in the hospitals' annual reports. Here was one clear message about the quid pro quo of government aid. New York's program was also clearly one of *purchase;* the city bought almost 1 million days of care from private hospitals in 1906.[77]

In Pennsylvania, where state, county, and municipal appropriations provided over 30 percent of the income of private charitable hospitals in 1910, the chief channel of subsidy was a block-grant system from the state, with each hospital lobbying the legislature independently. Once given, funds were largely unsupervised, although it was clear that substantial government controls could, in theory, be imposed through the system. Consolidation of hospitals through government pressure was a recurring theme at tax hearings in Pennsylvania in 1910, for problems of hospital service, lack of coordination, and waste of resources were there for all to see. "Isn't it a fact," asked one of the panel members, Judge Edwards from Scranton, "that there are too many hospitals in Pennsylvania?" There was general complaint, he said, that no one had any authority to decide whether anyone had a right to go ahead and build any kind of hospital.[78] Suggestions for reform included setting up organized hospital systems via county governments; refusing to give any new hospital state aid; moving to a per capita purchase system (like that in New York); consolidating Philadelphia's five medical schools into one and consolidating the hospitals as well; encouraging patients to stay at home rather than go to hospitals, a direct slap in the face to hospital entrepreneurship; and providing better administration of state funds.[79]

In Philadelphia, reform Mayor Blankenberg set up a committee on municipal charities which recommended, in 1913, a comprehensive plan for hospitals along "modern and scientific lines."[80] Under this the charitable hospitals would be licensed, inspected, and audited as "quasi-public institutions" and subject to a rational citywide plan: each hospital would act as a receiving hospital for a specified service district of 50,000 people. But whatever the logic for bureaucratic regulation, municipal efficiency, and public accountability, the private charitable networks were too entrenched for major systemic changes, even in New York City. Charity-givers and doctors worked together to overcome the threat of government domination. The relationship between doctors and hospitals was thus both cozy (for some purposes) and confrontational (for others)—a not untypical marriage.

The ideal role for the hospitals, from their own perspective, was government subsidy (or purchase of service) with little or no government supervision. This was the situation that largely existed for charities in the midnineteenth century. Voluntary and religious hospitals had everything to gain by asserting that they were public institutions, so long as they could justify their "privateness" and autonomy on this basis. Roman Catholic organizations took the most consistent position of all charitable groups, holding to it for decades to come, that the proper separation of church (or charity) and state required minimal interference by government agencies. The general supervisor of Catholic Charities in New York stated this position nicely in 1902: "The state, as a universal provider, must leave autonomy to the institution, which is the moral family of the dependents."[81] However, this did not mean refusal to take government money. Numerous religious hospitals were receiving government aid in the early twentieth century: sixty-six in Pennsylvania alone in 1919.[82] The ambiguity and dilemmas inherent in the public-private questions—really a question of control—have woven through the twentieth-century history of American hospitals in a continuing dialectic to the present.

The Hospital as an Instrument of Progressive Ideas

The success of the hospital pay system, upheld as it was by government subsidy, the existence of almshouse hospitals, charitable immunity, and tax exemption, was a powerful statement of public policy in itself. Governments supported private charitable interests, if not directly then indirectly. Without the existence of charities, including the religious hospitals, there would have been either a predominantly profit-making system or, more likely, a system of predominantly government institutions. Several states, including Michigan, Iowa, Indiana, North Carolina, and Texas, passed enabling laws between 1909 and 1913 so that counties might establish their own hospitals just as they might establish schools. However, there was no major shift toward government responsibility. In none of the major cities, including Cincinnati, were public hospitals the norm of care for members of the paying population before World War I—or after. The charitable hospital was a signal achievement of American culture. Indeed, it appeared to have succeeded *because* it appealed to paying patients. Business, technology, and charity were linked.

Grudging, if not punitive, attitudes toward the indigent were strengthened in three respects by the increasing ease with which hospitals offered their services to paying patients, backed in many instances by government aid. First, where it existed, government subsidy of services for the indigent encouraged hospital boards and superintendents to keep ward care as inexpensive as possible, so that it was clearly differentiated from services for which patients paid even a modest fee. Relief was on no account to be viewed as a right. Establishment social critic Amos Warner advised that this issue could be dealt with "by making the pauper somewhat less comfortable than the man who is self-dependent."[83] In the American system the baseline of service for the indigent could only be increased if all levels above this line were increased in addition, so that the hospital's class structure stayed in alignment.

Second, free care seemed, increasingly, an annoying and unnecessary *loss* to the hospital; certainly not the central purpose of the enterprise. Hospitals with names such as St. Mary's, Baptist, or Beth Israel, as well as those with nonsectarian affiliations, subscribed to the general theory that it was "not the hospital's mission to ease the financial burdens of people."[84] Third, the availability, or even the potential, of government purchase of care for the indigent allowed hospitals, paradoxically, to reduce, not increase, the amount of charitable care, if they so wished, because now the indigent were by definition the government's, not the hospital's, problem. Hence the low proportion of free days in charitable hospitals in states like Illinois.

As the percentage of private patients rose rapidly in hospitals everywhere in the United States, the poor increasingly became a nuisance, even though if a "free" patient could be charged to government, even partially, the patient was no longer "free" as far as the hospital was concerned. As David Rosner has observed, older patterns of moral decision as the rationale for hospital admission, based upon social and personal criteria, were replaced by monetary surrogates as a means of sorting patients in a hospital system which was shifting from a basis of charity (free care) to a basis of purchase.[85] The stigma of low caste remained. The antiforeign sentiment that swept America in the early twentieth century joined the traditional concerns about pauperization and charity abuse, that is, the fear that free services would be inappropriately sought, by those who could afford to pay, thus undermining the assumptions on which charity was built: of bountiful giver and worthy recipient. Where worth was defined by patient payment, charity-giving was much easier.

In stratifying both inpatient and outpatient services, hospital trustees and superintendents supported the interests of private medical practitioners, on whom they depended for paying patients. But it would be misleading to conclude that trustees were pushed into this position over their own rather different inclinations. The tradition of charity-giving was well designed for the needs of the medical profession. Scientific charity, like private practice, encouraged patients to be self-supporting (that is, to pay); reduced free services to a minimum (in order to avoid pauperization); focused on individual and specific causes of disease rather than on the general environment from which diseases sprang, including poor housing, malnutrition, and unemployment; and encouraged scientific expertise.

In turn, scientific medicine suggested that medicine's greatest social benefits in the future might well come from the laboratory—that is, from "science"—rather than from massive social reorganization. Brilliant laboratory demonstrations of the causes of tuberculosis, Asiatic cholera, various types of pneumonia, tetanus, influenza, bubonic plague, and other diseases—and the success of salvarsan (for syphilis) and commercial diphtheria antitoxin—promised a golden age of medical treatment. (It was impossible to know at the time that this promise would be largely unfulfilled until the discovery of the sulfa drugs in the 1930s.) Medical research, wrote eminent physician Richard M. Pearce in 1913, echoing an appealing and generally held belief, was a "vitalizing, reforming, uplifting factor, not only for the practice of medicine but for the good of the community at large."[86]

In the meantime, there were two well-recognized problems with hospital services to patients: the problem of providing affordable inpatient services for the working-class family, and the vexing problem of outpatient care. In the vernacular of the time, hospitals were best able to treat patients in first class and steerage, with enormous variety in the middle, but outpatient care was definitely steerage—and indeed, the typical outpatients were immigrants. Hospital inpatients were classified by their accommodation and pay status, from single room to small ward, to wards where some would pay and some would not, to charity wards. However, the social test for dispensary (outpatient) care was simple acceptance or rejection, according to local definitions of indigence. Outpatient departments were, in theory at least, for those too poor (or ignorant) for private practice. Some outpatient staff maintained a moral stance by adding qualifications such as "honest," "ignorant," or "deserving" to just "poor" well into the twentieth century, while some hospitals limited access by charging a fee, with the aim of driving all but the truly desperate away.[87]

The problem was that many of the destitute, unemployed individuals who thronged to outpatient departments before World War I were suffering from conditions that were as much social as medical in their origin—diseases of work, of overcrowding, and of ignorance, from tuberculosis to rickets—and they had nowhere else to go. Michael M. Davis, a leading advocate of organized medical services before and after World War I, estimated in 1916 that the number of freestanding and hospital dispensaries had multiplied by about sevenfold in the previous fifteen years.[88] Most patients attended hospital clinics rather than freestanding dispensaries. It made little sense, as Davis and others stressed for years, to view outpatient departments as purveyors solely of "snap judgments," based on a technical view of medicine. Yet most outpatients received drugs and X rays, were given other diagnostic tests, and were then sent on their way, usually not returning. Dr. Richard Cabot, founder of the first social-service department for outpatients (at Massachusetts General Hospital in 1905) observed: "Our patients shoot by us like comets, crossing for a moment our field of vision, then passing out into oblivion."[89]

One result was a critical division between inpatient and outpatient hospital care: in the social class of patients, in the array of disease seen, and even in the medical staffing of the two types of unit. In the old charitable tradition physicians served outpatients on a voluntary basis. A position as outpatient physician was usually taken as a stepping-stone to something higher, that is, to the prospect of a prestigious inpatient appointment which in turn might lead to an enhanced private practice. It was not surprising that the lack of pay, the frustrations, and the temporary nature of outpatient work made the care often cursory, unfriendly, and superficial. But for all the chief players in hospital policy, doctors, administrators, and trustees, outpatient services were a problem without an obvious solution. The outpatient department was useful to the teaching hospital in providing teaching material and as a "feeder" to the inpatient units. Elsewhere, "outpatient abuse" was watched vigilantly by both charity-givers and private practitioners, lest it affirm free (or inexpensive) care as a right *and* divert potential pay patients from private practice. Private patients saw their doctors in their own homes or, increasingly, in specialists' offices.

In stratifying inpatient hospital care by income, the pay system also sanctioned other forms of social segregation. Charles Rosenberg describes in telling detail the exquisite patterns of stigmatization among categories of patients, a holdover from earlier, paternalistic assumptions about moral worth. Not only were wards for black patients in predominantly white hospitals in the least desirable facilities; so were wards for venereal diseases for indigent whites, thereby defining their role as social outcasts.[90] Hospitals, as social institutions, carried (and enhanced) prevailing assumptions about social class and racial divisions in the United States, not only legitimizing written rules but also making informal practices visible—and thus sanctioning them in turn.

Supported by Jim Crow laws, which allowed legal segregation of services for blacks in the South, only 60 percent of all hospitals in the southeastern states reported receiving "colored" patients at all in 1910.[91] In several cities white benefactors or groups established hospitals specifically for the black population: for example, the Good Samaritan Hospital in Charlotte, North Carolina, and the Sarah Goodridge Hospital in New Orleans. Kansas City, Missouri, established a separate city hospital in 1908—Kansas City Hospital Number 2 (Kansas City Colored). Across the country there were an estimated 63 black hospitals and nurse-training schools in 1912; 118 by 1919.[92] Racial segregation was taken for granted, South and North. Jefferson Medical College Hospital in Philadelphia, for example, reported with pride in 1918 the introduction of "colored volunteer workers" into its "colored clinic," which was under the direction of a "colored physician," with social investigations undertaken by "colored social workers."[93] Formal desegregation of hospitals, North and South, was not achieved until the middle and late 1960s, under the double force of the Civil Rights Act of 1964 and the Medicare legislation of 1965. Informal practices of discrimination have, as yet, received little attention but undoubtedly continue, to an unknown extent.

In all of these respects hospitals reflected and fostered the views of the "community"—the views of community elites, at least—in ways that might have been impossible in a governmental system. The American private benevolent hospital, progressive, expansionist, and ill defined, occupied the middle ground between commerce and government while also being supported by both. Organizationally, the charitable hospital was in a strong position. It avoided the rigors and excesses of the marketplace through the privileges of tax exemption, government subsidy, and charitable donations, while also avoiding the leveling, regulation, and political scrimmages of government administration.

The hospital system of the early 1900s was thus an assemblage of local units. As social institutions the charitable hospitals were valuable chameleons: monuments to good intentions, workshops for physicians, public services, medical hotels, definers of social class, symbols of community pride, temples of science, and factories for treatment. The principles of scientific charity and scientific medicine were natural partners at the local level; if both principles were successfully refined and applied, there would be no paupers and no untreatable diseases. Indeed, the hospital movement and the professionalization of medicine grew together. But while hospital charity was a local affair, medicine was professionalizing as a *national* force. It was to be medical organizations, not charitable groups, which were to provide a national frame for depicting the role and purpose of the "hospital" as a generic institution.

3

A National Enterprise: Setting Basic Rules

THE FORMAL RULES that were made for hospitals between 1910 and 1917 were written almost entirely by national groups of physicians, largely medical-school professors. The new standards proclaimed that hospitals were a national *medical* enterprise, subject to medical oversight and inspection. How and why was hospital standardization achieved? I will suggest that this "medicalization" had two distinct aspects and implications. The hospital was to be seen, first, as an institution with standard functions and expectations based on ideas about medical science that were generated in leading U.S. medical schools. But, second, the three major standardization schemes—the American Medical Association's policies for medical-school affiliations with hospitals, its lists of approved internships, and the standardization of hospitals by the American College of Surgeons—also defined the hospital as the workshop of a responsible profession of practitioners. In so doing, standardization upheld the organizational separation of hospitals and physicians, ratified the role of the small community hospital, and supported private practice.

From the medical point of view the standardization movement was thus both aristocratic (or elitist) and democratic (or all-inclusive). Hospitals were to be brought up to "scientific" standards, but these would not be set so high that some hospitals would be forced to merge or some local practitioners would be excluded. From its beginnings to the present, hospital accreditation has embodied mixed messages.

Scientific Medicine as a Basis for Authority

The American medical profession, overcrowded and disorganized before World War I, represented a motley collection of talents, education, behavior, and skills. The census report of 1910 reported over 150,000 physicians: one doctor for every 609 members of the population! There were more physicians per 1,000 population in every U.S. state than in any of the major countries of Europe.[1] Even the most adventurous medical graduates, traveling to new settlements in the West, often found other doctors there before them. In two areas there was evident need for reform, both affecting hospitals. The first need was to upgrade medical education for all new practitioners, including postgraduate internship training. The second was to control standards of surgery, particularly the surgery being done by unethical, unsafe, moneygrubbing practitioners who saw surgery in the expanding hospitals as a wonderful new source of income.

Surgery could be controlled by individual hospitals through the enforcement of a closed-staff system, that is, by only allowing reputable operators to use the operating room. This was standard practice in hospitals controlled by university medical schools. In Britain, too, closed-staff arrangements for surgery (and for other specialties) were strengthened between 1910 and 1917, with the general practitioner largely excluded from hospital practice. But the tide was in the other direction in the United States. The average practitioner in an overcrowded profession wanted the privilege of a hospital appointment for reasons of income, knowledge, and prestige. Closed-staff hospitals were also often chauvinistic institutions, making their appointments on the basis of favoritism rather than skill. The trustee's family doctor, wrote the prolific Dr. S. S. Goldwater, was "forever bobbing up as a hospital candidate, seeking surgical or other important appointments."[2] As local medical societies became effective pressure groups at the local level, they pressed hospitals to become more "democratic" and less "elitist" in their appointments, that is, to open their staff to all local practitioners.

How, then, was surgery to be upgraded? There seemed to be three practical avenues for reform: first, some way to specify (and ideally to enforce) surgical educational requirements so that surgeons would at least have specified training; second, regulating hospitals directly by specifying minimal standards of staff and facilities and basic operating procedures; and third, encouraging some form of collective responsibility for standards among the "open staff" itself. The latter was to be known as medical staff

organization after World War I. All of these policies were to be pushed—
successfully—by an elite group of U.S. surgeons, while the AMA was
pressing for radical reforms in the medical schools. Indeed, the cast of
characters overlapped. Arthur Dean Bevan, chairman of the AMA's powerful Council on Medical Education, set up in 1904 to inspect, monitor, and
standardize the medical schools, was a surgeon, as were many of the early
leaders of the AMA, including Dr. William Mayo.

Surgery could be dangerous when left in ill-trained hands—or in
hands that were overly ambitious or mercenary. The elite surgical journal,
Surgery, Gynecology and Obstetrics, established in 1905, reflected the concern of
leading surgeons, as well as pride in hospital-based technique. There was
an "appalling increase" in the number of gastroenterostomies.[3] Unwar-
ranted operations had become a "curse"; the principal sufferers were
women, through the "dishonest," "ignorant," and "misguided" enthusiasm of (male) gynecologists. Arthur Dean Bevan estimated in 1906 that 30
percent of the gynecological operations being done were unnecessary.[4] The
vogue for cesarian sections promised to become a "serious menace," while
operative statistics for radical approaches to cancer of the uterus "must
dampen the enthusiasm of even the most ardent optimist."[5] In short,
technological laissez-faire did not work—either for the benefit of the average patient or for the professional reputation of American surgeons.

Far from being in the forefront of discovery, innovation, and publication of results, American doctors were forced to consult foreign literature,
because there was little or no "clerical work" done in the United States;
that is, no patient records.[6] Over and above this, the dubious practice of
fee-splitting was widespread. This was a private arrangement between
practitioners and surgeons, undisclosed to the patient, whereby the
surgeon kicked back part of his fee—a direct invitation to unnecessary
referrals.

Criticism of such practices jangled discordantly against two concurrent professional and hospital goals: the creation of a unified, prestigious
national medical profession based on university education, and self-con-
gratulatory and public approval of hospitals as the epitome of modern
science. The public showed signs of disillusion. The Illinois legislature
introduced a bill to license surgeons in 1913; and in 1914 Wisconsin made
it illegal for surgeons to give commissions to practitioners who referred
cases to them. George Bernard Shaw's scathing comedy *The Doctor's Dilemma*
had a successful run in New York in 1915. In the play's preface Shaw
ridiculed surgeons as fee-hungry butchers.[7]

Some of the criticism of surgery might be discounted as overly alar-
mist or as the views of leading surgeons in academic centers, whose skills

could not possibly be duplicated outside major cities. But concerns were both general and widespread. H. D. Niles's criticism in 1902 remained valid for years: "It is not enough that our hospital authorities provide and equip rooms where a promiscuous assemblage of physicians may be permitted to occupy their leisure moments trying to sustain the scientific reputation of their institution by unsystematic and irregular work."[8] Science, it seemed, needed systemization.

The association of medicine with observation, precision, perfectability, and engineering—central values in American medicine to this day— served well as the basis for major reforms in surgery and in American medical education in the early twentieth century. Observations in research laboratories provided the certainty of knowledge that was aspired to, in other contexts, by management experts and social engineers, looking for the "one best way" of designing machines, organizing work, or reforming the administration of cities. The same year that Röntgen discovered the medical applications of the X ray (1895), Frederick Winslow Taylor published his first paper on what was quickly known as "scientific management": the application of rational principles to industrial processes, designed to produce optimal efficiency.[9] The discovery of the bacteriological origin of relapsing fever, anthrax, and gonorrhea in the 1870s, of malaria, diphtheria, pneumonia, typhoid fever, tetanus, and other diseases in the 1880s, and of influenza, bubonic plague, and dysentery in the 1890s, laid the base for a well-justified optimism about "scientific medicine" as a form of mechanics, in which there were clear rules of cause and effect. Surgery was also "science" in these terms, although much of it had developed empirically. Science and progress seemed interchangeable. For medicine, the university medical school and the hospital were their major organizational manifestations.

The AMA and its constituent societies created a joint platform for professional enhancement: recognition of medicine as science, and rejection of any taint of commerce. "One of the demoralizing tendencies in this commercial age," said Dr. Mayo, in his presidential address to the AMA in 1906, "is the money standard of success."[10] But it was difficult for AMA leaders and professors in the elite medical schools—their ranks interlocked—to espouse a doctrine of the purity of science and altruism over commerce when most doctors were ill-paid. Resentment was readily incurred among honest, conservative practitioners when they saw unscrupulous colleagues dressing well and driving fancy automobiles—including slick city specialists admitting women into hospitals for unnecessary hysterectomies or cesarian sections. For those without hospital appointments for private patients, the hospital was a potentially alarming economic threat. "The old physician waits and waits for work while the hospital eats up his bread and butter," complained a New Jersey doctor in 1910 at a symposium on the economic influence of hospitals.[11] In some areas, because of the oversupply of hospital beds, hospital superintendents and registrars competed not only for paying patients but for charity ones as well, in order to maintain their hospital's census and thus not lose their own positions.[12]

A variety of contractual and salaried arrangements between other organizations and doctors kept medical incomes in many areas at an unsatisfactorily depressed level—and divided medical interests even further. Medical concern about contract practice between industrial corporations and hospitals was widespread. Mayo gave as an example the arrangement in Pittsburgh, where steel companies paid one dollar a day for the care of their injured men at hospitals, while paying the surgeons at those hospitals absolutely nothing; and similar conditions existed with many of the large railroad and streetcar companies and other public corporations.[13] Resistance to the "corporate practice of medicine" became a central tenet of organized medicine, although opposition to organized-practice arrangements was by no means total. There was no objection, for example, to members of the Mayo Clinic practicing medicine as a group, nor to doctors operating their own profit-making hospitals. As James Burrow has argued, the medical profession was engaged in much the same battle as conservative business interests; it was fighting for "limited competition strictly controlled."[14] But opposition to various forms of organized practice, with their suggestions of commercialism, exploitation of doctors, and loss of professional dignity, was also a rallying cry for the creation of consensus in a very diverse profession. Before World War I, as later, organized political opposition to outside threats served to unify and strengthen the profession of medicine. For a brief, heady period, 1900 to 1920, the aims of upgrading education and standards of entry to medical practice coincided with the scientific, social, and economic interests of the majority of the medical profession. Hospitals were in the middle of all these concerns.

Standardizing Medical Education

The medical teachers on the AMA's Council on Medical Education began to inspect, criticize, and classify medical schools in 1905. Medical licensing boards in each state tightened their requirements for a license to practice, in line with AMA standards; and new philanthropic foundations, founded by banking, oil, steel, and railroad magnates, notably Rockefeller, Harkness, and Carnegie, made money available to upgrade selected schools and their associated hospitals. Some of the excess profits of industrial capitalism were thus shifted, through the vehicle of private charity, to improve the efficiency of scientific medicine.

In 1910 a candid, critical report on American medical education was published by the Carnegie Foundation for the Advancement of Teaching, written by foundation executive Abraham Flexner, who had toured medical schools with members of the AMA Council on Medical Education. This report, published by a source apparently independent of the medical profession, became both the bible and the symbol of medical reform.[15] Flexner became a significant figure in educational reform. Through his supervision of expenditures for medical education at the Carnegie Foundation, and later at the General Education Board (a Rockefeller endowment), he pushed for the reorganization and consolidation of medical schools around laboratories and hospitals, and for the development of full-time medical teachers, both for basic sciences and clinical teaching. An intrinsic theme of "scientific medicine" was linking medical schools with hospitals.

The educational-reform movement and the parallel movement to reform surgery had different implications for the organization and control of hospitals. Medical schools needed, ideally, a few large hospitals with specialized facilities for research and teaching, perhaps no more than one or two hundred across the country, if they were specially designed as teaching hospitals. Surgery, in contrast, was the mainstay of four thousand local hospitals, mostly small, with all the community interest this represented.[16] Surgery was the economic lifeblood of these hospitals and of many, if not most, practitioners. And open-staff hospitals were being pushed by local medical societies—whose support the AMA needed. Thus the two movements ran in parallel. They had the same basic goals of professional upgrading, but different agendas, opportunities, and constraints.

For research-oriented physicians on medical-school faculties, hospitals had scientific value by providing clinical laboratories in which the results of examinations of sputum, stools, tissues, blood, and urine could

be coordinated with the patient's symptoms; by offering an array of patients sick enough to be in bed, on whom systematic case histories and
differential diagnoses could be developed, and who could be observed
during the course of their hospital stay; and by providing, in outpatient
departments, a ready pool of lower-class patients on whom new drugs and
procedures could be tested. The epitome of the research hospital was the
hospital officially opened in 1910 as an intrinsic element of the Rockefeller
Institute in New York; a whole floor of the hospital was devoted to
laboratories. This hospital became, *inter alia,* a major research center for the
early study of poliomyelitis.

Modern medical schools also needed hospitals for clinical teaching.
For Flexner, hospitals and dispensaries, as "laboratories in the strictest
sense of the term," were places for students to collect and evaluate the facts
from which deductions could be made for diagnosis and treatment.[17] The
twentieth-century teaching system, based on observation of patients and
the case method, required medical-school faculties to relinquish the high
drama of the old teaching amphitheater, where the physician or surgeon
was the star of a dramatic demonstration.[18] Teaching was now accomplished by small-group instruction on the wards, where students could see
and talk to patients at close range. Besides discussions of the patient as a
"case," good patient records and a close relationship between the wards
and the laboratories were expected. Otherwise, in Flexner's words, "the
clinical end is not rooted."[19]

On the wards in a well-organized teaching hospital, a student could
study a disease's progress and the impact of therapeutics during the patient's two- or three-week stay. In the outpatient department the student
could learn to do initial physical examinations and see a wide variety of
cases that did not enter the wards, such as minor surgery, trivial medical
complaints, and conditions involving the eye, ear, nose, throat, and skin.
The two types of setting conveniently recapitulated the major work settings of physicians in private practice outside the hospital: the office, where
the patient sought out the physician, and the sickroom (usually in the
patient's home), where the physician attended the bedfast patient. In these
ways the medical student would, in Flexner's words, become part of the
"hospital machine."[20]

In 1906, 94 of the 162 medical schools then in existence had no access
to hospitals.[21] The Flexner report (1910) revealed enormous disparities
even among those that did. At one end of the scale was the medical
department of Johns Hopkins University, providing 385 beds and clinical
laboratories under the complete control of the medical-school faculty. At

the other end were dismal proprietary schools, such as the Ensworth Medical College, St. Joseph, Missouri, with a faculty of 40 and an adjoining hospital with only 6 free beds. (Private patients in general were not subjected to teaching.) A basic problem was medical economics. In Knoxville, Tennessee, private practitioners on the faculty of the medical college were siphoning fees from the medical students to subsidize their private hospital next door.[22] The community hospital's focus on surgery, with few nonsurgical cases, was a common problem for teaching throughout the country.

The interests of the average practitioner in the use of hospitals were different from those of elite medical teachers. Only a few schools were in the fortunate position of Johns Hopkins, the University of Michigan, or the University of Pennsylvania, with their own university-owned hospitals. Typically, clinical education was "put together of scraps."[23] Students might have access to a medical clinic at one hospital, obstetrics at a second, or dermatology at a third, with little continuity of teaching and much time wasted in travel. Teaching depended on the whims and preferences of hospital attending physicians and hospital policies toward teaching. At the Los Angeles County Hospital, for example, a major clinical facility for the University of California, students were not permitted to handle surgical patients, in deference to the surgeons.[24]

At many hospitals, including those used by most of the southern schools, there were no clinical laboratories. Even where there were, these, too, might be closed to teaching—as were those connected with the municipal hospitals in St. Louis, Chicago, and Minneapolis.[25] Some schools, such as Mississippi College in Meridian, remained without hospital connections at all. In Nebraska it was claimed that "there are no poor in Lincoln."[26] As a result, since teaching was confined to charity cases, medical students had no regular hours in the hospital but had to wait, hopefully, for indigent patients to be admitted.

The needs of medical education spurred interest in hospital regulation, for it was difficult for students to learn in places where there were no patient records and thus no account of a patient's problem, history, or treatment. Even in hospitals used by medical schools, private practitioners tended to keep the patient's history in their heads. Increased surgery, increased use of medical specialists, and the mobility of the American population provided the impetus for *all* hospitals to have clinical records, so that at the very least doctors could consult patient records for previous surgery or drug treatment, or send the patient's records to doctors elsewhere. Otherwise, one surgeon might have no idea what another had done. A 1902 editorial put this point succinctly, claiming that "abdominal operations are so numerous, various organs may be extirpated with apparent impunity and others may be transposed or sutured in abnormal situations, leading to considerable confusion about anatomic relations."[27]

The problem with the hospital's requiring records on patients was its assumption of an organizational role that cut into the practitioner's domain. Who was going to make this demand? A local businessman who happened to be president of the Board of Trustees? An upstart superintendent? A doctor admitting his own patients had no incentive to create records that others might use or that served the hospital as a whole—unless he was interested in the scientific potential of the hospital for studying patterns of care across a group of patients or unless professional organizations required it. Doctors could claim that they owned their own records and that the hospital, as a physician's workshop, had no separate, legitimate interest in recording or monitoring patient care. Implementing "scientific medicine," as defined by the leading schools in the early twentieth century, thus came down, strategically, to questions of physicians' attitudes and hospital control.

For the mandarins of educational reform, medical records were *de rigueur*. The physician with a "scientific" cast of mind demonstrated institutional allegiance, saw the hospital as a teaching and research laboratory, and supported record systems and discussions of cases; the university teacher was an ideal type, dedicated to research and teaching without any thought of personal gain. The ideal hospital, in turn, served medical science, benefited the indigent patients who provided case material, and was neither profit-oriented nor dominated by surgery.[28] It followed that the average private practitioner, attending to the care of individual patients and primarily interested in hospitals for private accommodations and operating rooms, was de facto "unscientific."

Unfortunately for the reformers, it was these practitioners who were the mainstay of teaching in most of the medical schools and the backbone of AMA membership.[29] Flexner estimated that there were almost 4,000 part-time clinical professors in the United States and Canada who were local doctors (for fewer than 24,000 medical students). He described them as "contentedly non-productive."[30] The problem here was that if a school dropped an inadequate teacher on the grounds of quality, it might be worse off than if it retained him, since he would continue to use the hospital but the school would lose access to his beds. The medical school could only push so far, because boards of trustees and administrators of teaching and voluntary hospitals were obviously sympathetic to surgeons who brought in private patients. Kenneth Ludmerer has shown that these problems were exacerbated where schools brought in outsiders to improve the quality of the faculty—men on the nationally elite network of clinical science who did not mix readily with local society and were thus doubly resented by local practitioners.[31] The uneasy tensions inherent in relations between medical schools and hospitals were to mark undergraduate teaching hospitals until at least the 1960s, and still exist to some extent. But at the same time, the threat of aristocratic university dominance brought local surgeons and hospitals nearer together through mutual, democratic interest.

The chairman of the AMA Council on Medical Education, Arthur Dean Bevan, urged universities and hospitals to establish links with each other. The hospital's best interest, he wrote, demanded that they be conducted as scientific institutions, that is, under the control of teachers and investigators. Bevan's model of affiliation was the great clinics in Vienna and Munich that served indigent patients in the service of research.[32] However, in Germany the major teaching hospitals and universities fell under the same governmental control, whereas in the United States the schools and the hospitals were for the most part institutionally independent.[33] Each tended to be insecure, organizationally and financially, and suspicious of each other's motives.[34]

In the American system complete control of hospitals by medical schools was rarely possible, nor did men like Bevan see it as necessary. Such a system would have required the complete control of the practice of medicine by professors and would have fanned town-gown hostilities. Nor could medical schools in general afford to build their own hospitals, even considering the relatively modest level of hospital care in 1910 or 1920. The most visible successes either had major endowments, like Johns Hopkins, or state aid, like the University of Pennsylvania, or were state-run affiliates of state university medical schools—as in Michigan, Texas, Missouri, Colorado, Iowa, and Kansas by 1910. The general pattern was for the schools, as they reformed and strengthened their curricula in the first two decades of the century, to seek clinical opportunities in local government and charitable hospitals, wherever these were available. This required tact, clout, and negotiation, and preferably also money.

Affiliation of medical schools with hospitals grew rapidly after 1910, when three affiliations took place between already prestigious institutions: the College of Physicians and Surgeons (Columbia University) with Presbyterian Hospital in New York, Harvard Medical School with Peter Bent Brigham in Boston, and Washington University Medical School with Barnes Hospital and St. Louis Children's Hospital in St. Louis.[35] Most hospitals, however, were not affiliated. In 1916 it was estimated that about 20 percent of American hospitals participated directly or indirectly in the undergraduate teaching of medicine, and many of these participations were often loose or very modest.[36] Education was thus not a form of systemwide standardization for all hospitals. Indeed, the expansion of medical-school teaching in hospitals served to create new divisions: between large teaching complexes based on university medical schools (the forerunners of what we now call academic health centers) and the mass of community hospitals. But medical-school affiliation did enhance the prestige of hospitals as a whole, with ripple effects through the entire system.

Foundation grants spurred formal links between schools and large urban hospitals in cities throughout the United States between 1910 and 1930. By 1920, for example, Yale University had achieved complete medical and surgical control of its affiliated hospital.[37] In Cincinnati, clinical teachers at the University of Cincinnati controlled the large municipal hospital. In Cleveland, Western Reserve University affiliated with Lakeside Hospital, and in Chicago, Rush Medical College affiliated with Presbyterian Hospital. Arthur Dean Bevan, who was a professor at Rush, described the latter arrangement as "very satisfactory."[38] At Harvard a fourth-year medical student published a small book on the medical school and its clinical opportunities in 1916, stressing that the clinical facilities of the school were equal in importance to its laboratories. Harvard then reported links with seventeen independent hospitals.[39]

Where possible, medical school and hospital moved or rebuilt on one site, forming a university-based "medical center" in which the medical school stood in an array of monumental buildings. In St. Louis, for example, where Barnes Hospital and Children's Hospital were rebuilt and entwined with the medical school, the design was so unified that, it was claimed, "it would be practically impossible ever to separate it into its constituent parts."[40] That, of course, was the idea. In city after city the pattern of the modern university medical center was set: a conglomeration of medical school and hospitals on a single site, unified through walkways, bridges, and tunnels. These visible signs of the wealth and importance of medicine provided persuasive architectural and functional analogies between the medical complex, producing knowledge, and industry. Flexner described Cook County Hospital in Chicago, for example, as a "clinical mine of enormous wealth."[41] Scientifically trained physicians were the engineers and producers of this wealth.

Indigent patients were valuable cogs in the teaching-hospital machine. Within a large county or municipal hospital there were numerous cases of tuberculosis, pneumonia, rheumatic fever, Bright's disease, cancer, heart disease, and other common and uncommon medical conditions, as well as the opportunity for the student to learn surgery and to gain extensive clinical experience through being given responsibility for indigent patients. In contrast, a large pay ward "afflicted with ailments already well understood" was, in research terms, an "obstacle" to research and education.[42]

In turn, the teaching hospital could be a terrifying, unfriendly place for patients. The patient, said Chicago reformer Jane Addams, was not the chief concern of these hospitals at all. Training the intern appeared to come first; next, the visiting staff of physicians; third, the training of the nurse; and only fourthly the comfort of the patient. Woken up at inconvenient times to be bathed, the patient's comfort was "sacrificed to the hospital's looks."[43] Nurses had developed their own rituals, such as a special way of unfolding and refolding laundered sheets, and they treated patients with condescension, usually calling them by their first or last name, with no prefix.[44] Patients were expected to follow orders meekly—just as student nurses followed the directions of their superiors in a profession committed to hierarchy and discipline. On the coattails of physicians, nurses assumed an elevated position of authority over patients, justified by moral superiority (their commitment to duty) and by nursing technique.

The immigrant, with the added unfamiliarity of a foreign language, was doubly oppressed. Few hospitals had interpreters. The Americanization movement discouraged perpetuating foreign languages, even in a hospital setting; and comparatively few foreign girls took nurses' training. Lower-class immigrants were isolated from the mainstream hospital system by barriers of language, class, and income, as well as by the aloofness of hospital routine. This impersonality lingered for years. A student of immigrant health wrote in 1921: "Most hospitals give even the sophisticated visitor a sense of being surrounded by very busy, presumably very efficient, doctors, nurses, and employees, who are passing rapidly from one duty to another and have little time for *him.*"[45]

But even in the more cozy, comfortable rooms of paying patients, and in hospitals where private practice was the norm, the cult of efficiency and scientific expertise encouraged deference to medical authority on the part of patients; the patient was a "medical subject," presenting a specific medical "condition."[46] In the medicalized model of hospital care, patients were part of the production system of scientific medicine. Surgery provided the ultimate model for medical ascendance and patient dependency, for at the critical point of treatment the patient was asleep.

Rapid changes in medical education between 1900 and 1920 seemed to justify public confidence in physicians. In 1900 less than 10 percent of practicing physicians were graduates of genuine medical schools; about 20 percent had never attended medical-school lectures. By 1920 the medical schools had been consolidated and transformed—there were only eighty-five schools in 1920, about half the number that existed in 1906. Educational standards had been raised significantly and curricula remodeled to include basic science and clinical education. The medical profession had also created an effective national consciousness that was an essential ingredient for seeing hospitals, too, as a national enterprise. By 1920 well over half of all physicians belonged to the AMA and three-quarters reportedly read its journal.[47] In turn, as hospitals received increasing national attention, the ideal model of a "hospital" was derived from hospitals affiliated with the university medical schools: a model of medicine as applied scientific knowledge that was to appear again and again throughout the century.

The image of scientific medicine, based on the successful identification and cure of infectious diseases on the one hand, and successful surgical intervention on the other, served well as a stimulus for reforming medical schools, placing them within universities, and associating them (and their ideas) with hospitals. Through analogy to parallel developments in science and industry, "scientific medicine" ratified the hospital as a short-term, successful curative workshop. The "bed day" was the unit of work, wrote one medical editor, comparable to the foot-pound in dynamics and the volt in electricity.[48]

The American public, as well as its experts, liked instant mobilization and immediate solutions rather than slow approaches to apparently intractable social problems, such as malnutrition, tuberculosis, or infant diarrhea. After the San Francisco earthquake of 1906, lamented one public health officer, there was an outpouring of $15 million in less than two weeks and a national government vote of $2.5 million without debate; yet the loss of life was only one-third the city's *annual* death rate from tuberculosis. The *Titanic* disaster stimulated similar observations in 1912. Instant action by governments (in this case on both sides of the Atlantic), private aid, massive publicity, and a general sense of shock and national grief for 1,500 lives lost at sea, contrasted vividly with public apathy about the needless waste of life on land.[49] Then as now, American social policy was charged by dramatic response to crisis—and to a different valuation placed on "lives" according to visibility and social class.

Most hospitals were untouched directly by changes in the medical schools. Nevertheless, building on the ethos of scientific medicine, a national medical consciousness for standardizing hospitals as acute medical centers was also being built, which was to be realized in the associated movements for the education of interns and the standards of surgery. Hospital administrators, too, were beginning to design and articulate their own mutual interests at the national level—setting themselves apart, in the process, from both physicians and boards of trustees.

Hospitals and the Internship

Acute hospital medicine required ongoing medical supervision of patients and the twenty-four-hour availability of physicians to treat accident and emergency patients. In small hospitals, attending physicians served such functions on a rota or on-call basis. However, in the urban hospitals in major cities like New York, the house staff had become, by 1900, the "real staff of every hospital in the city."[50] Attending surgeons sought out promising surgical interns by guaranteeing them large numbers of operations. Medical students eagerly sought internships to provide a period of clinical experience following the M.D. degree as preparation for passing state licensing examinations. The first survey by the AMA Council on Medical Education in 1904 estimated that 50 percent of graduates were then going on to hospital training, and many more tried to do so.[51]

Large urban hospitals which were affiliated with medical schools were particularly attractive to prospective interns because of the availability of cases and the opportunity to learn from pioneering clinicians, and because of the prestige inherent in the emerging professional networks of scientific medicine. It was evident by 1910 that the next generation of teachers and prominent specialists would include graduates of well-equipped and well-known schools who had experience in a recognized teaching hospital. A competitive internship provided entry to an important professional network (provided that the physician was also a presentable white male, and preferably Christian). Less favored graduates took internship positions in hospitals with little or no connection to university-based medical schools. Most local-government teaching hospitals appointed their interns by competitive examination, as did prestigious voluntary teaching hospitals such as Massachusetts General, Lakeside in Cleveland, and Jefferson in Philadelphia. In New York, Eliot's quiz, a special late-evening course for prospective interns which ran from 1890 to 1913, claimed success not only in sending students through these fiercely competitive examinations, but in the outcome of this experience for their future careers as well. The quiz was later credited with helping to produce six deans of medical schools and sixty-one full professors.[52]

When the AMA undertook its first survey of internships in 1914, interns were a major presence in large city hospitals throughout the country. Bellevue in New York had the largest number (64), followed by Cook County (60), St. Louis City Hospital (54), Boston City (52), and Johns Hopkins (42). In all, 508 general hospitals provided opportunities to 2,667 interns in 1914, the majority on a one-year basis.[53] Most of the hospitals offering internships were not affiliated with medical schools—thus another stratification of the hospital system emerged, between hospitals with and without interns. To add to the confusion, hospitals offering internships were (and are) known as teaching hospitals even if they had no medical-school affiliation. In the large hospitals interns were an essential aspect of hospital routine and a major presence, living in the hospital on a twenty-four-hour basis. They rode the ambulance, staffed the laboratories, acted as surgical assistants and anesthetists, were available on call to deal with emergencies, and provided general aid to attending physicians. In so doing they took over many of the technical functions that were otherwise performed by nurses, thus distinguishing hospital jobs as "male" (technique) and "female" (care).

Interns in the most competitive hospitals, undergoing a common, difficult, often stressful experience, relieved by beer-drinking, noisy parties, and childish pranks, formed a strong, cohesive alliance within the major hospitals—the basis, in many cases, for lifelong friendships. But the interns also changed the character and power structure of the large hospitals. Where teaching-hospital services were run by full-time faculties who were also heads of major hospital departments, as at Hopkins, the interns were an extension of the medical school's role. Where hospital services were under part-time practitioners, as was most usual, the interns challenged the authority of the practicing physician. The intern, a graduate with recent exposure to the latest research, too often assumed an arrogance about medical technique in relations with older attending physicians. The establishment of hospital records systems and institutional expectations about the ordering of laboratory and X-ray tests enhanced the intern's authority, for he could always claim that "here this is the way things are done." The intern might proceed with patient care when the attending physician was absent—and sometimes challenged the latter's judgment. The presence of large groups of interns thus represented a further incursion of "scientific medicine" into the traditional domain of practitioners.

In two broad respects the wide acceptance of internships demanded some general rules of play. First, although they had increasing power, interns typically had no systematic training for hospital work; they gained experience at the expense of indigent patients. Fresh from medical schools, with little or no practical experience, interns could be found in sole charge of hospitals, treating accident cases and performing life-and-death operations. As the *Journal of the American Medical Association* remarked, "No one would take a young man just graduated from a technical school and put him in charge of a great electrical manufacturing plant."[54] If internships were to be recognized as an increasingly necessary practical training experience for all new graduates, some organization would have to be responsible for their duties and their role: a medical school, a state medical licensing board, a hospital organization, or the AMA Council on Medical Education. By 1913 the council was viewing the whole question of hospital teaching as the most important question in medical education.

The second, related aspect of the internship was its widespread dissemination beyond the major undergraduate teaching hospitals—and thus beyond medical school supervision. In 1914, even relatively small institutions reported interns: hospitals like Southern Infirmary, Mobile, with one intern for the hospital's 40 beds; Robert Burns Hospital, Chicago (32 beds, 2 interns); Copper Range Hospital, Trimountain, Michigan (25 beds, 1 intern); Southern Pacific Benefit Association Hospital, Glendive, Montana (45 beds, 2 interns); or Mid-Valley Hospital, Peckville, Pennsylvania (34 beds, 1 intern). Surgical work was particularly important at hospitals like Mid-Valley, where two-thirds of the beds were allocated to surgery and where the intern was allowed to charge fees. The presence of an intern also allowed for the immediate treatment of accident cases, often at the site of the accident itself. The hybrid role of the intern, part student, part employee, made the position difficult to regulate. Either all internships would have to be regulated by medical schools, or rules would have to be set for all employing hospitals.

The AMA Council on Medical Education flirted briefly, in 1913, with the idea of requiring all internships to be affiliated with medical schools, but there was little support for a movement that would give medical schools more work, antagonize the community hospitals and physicians, and prove difficult to supervise and administer. Instead, moving toward hospital regulation itself, the council put together a provisional list of hospitals regarded as "apparently acceptable" for internship training. It sent the list to trusted physicians in each state to check whether hospitals of "shady reputation" had been inadvertently included.[55] Council members hoped that the Carnegie Foundation would finance a more thorough investigation, but the foundation, embarked on funding scientific medicine in the universities, showed little interest in the practical elements of hospital apprenticeship.[56] The council issued its first list of internships in 1917. Thus the AMA, already pressing medical schools to affiliate with hospitals, became involved in a more general scheme of hospital accreditation for graduate apprenticeships.

Regulating Hospitals: A Posse of Players

The AMA Council on Medical Education, focusing on medical education
and the internship, viewed hospitals as laboratories for teaching. Its reports
rang with phrases such as "clinical material deficient," "facilities for maternity cases and post-mortems very limited," or "serious dearth of children."[57] The organization representing medical schools, the Association of
American Medical Colleges, was also interested in the educational function
of hospitals and the possibility of requiring a fifth year of medical education to be taken as a hospital internship. However, neither the council nor
the AAMC wanted to confront local medical societies or community
power structures by having medical schools attempt to rank their local
hospitals.[58] Both organizations considered the state medical examining
boards (which were in large part responsive to medical-society interests)
as the most appropriate regulatory force over hospital standards for the
internship. But two other groups of physicians were also interested in
hospital regulation by 1917: reform-minded surgeons and medical superintendents of the large teaching hospitals.

By 1917 the male medical superintendent was well on the way to
establishing his authority in the large teaching hospitals, wresting power
from the boards of trustees through the argument that hospital administration was itself scientific. Most of the smallest hospitals were run by nurse
administrators, and the remainder by individuals with a wide variety of
backgrounds, including business and the church. A group of medical superintendents established their own Section on Hospitals within the American Medical Association in 1911. The minutes of the short-lived AMA
section (it died in 1916) are instructive. The hospital, it was stressed,
should be run by a physician hospital executive because the hospital was
a "first class hygienic machine." Physician-superintendents of hospitals
had no desire to see nurses in positions of control over medical work.
Nursing was "only a differentiation of domestic duty," and the nurse
herself a "half-baked social product, thrust into the fulfillment of an
uncertain social need." Nurses were not, reportedly, interested in the comfort of the patients, but only in the order and symmetry of the ward.[59]
Different groups were, in effect, jostling for position at the national level,
in order to strengthen their positions locally—physicians battled with
nurses, physician-superintendents with other physicians, and medical
superintendents with nonmedical superintendents.

Hospital administrators, caught between clinicians and trustees, were a potential source of national influence over hospitals. Although medical organizations were rapidly seizing power over hospital standards, administrators—medical and nonmedical—were well aware of their emerging but ambivalent role as managers of scientific medicine. The growing organization of the medical profession stimulated administrators to band together as a national force. Initially brought together by the superintendent of Lakeside Hospital in Cleveland, ten administrators of large urban hospitals (nine males, one female) had paid dues to the new Association of Hospital Superintendents of the United States and Canada (later the American Hospital Association) in 1899, although most of the original members drifted away in the next year or two. But by 1912 the association reported a membership of 922. Of these, 235 were medical superintendents (i.e., doctors), and 421 were females (predominantly nurses).[60] The association was soon, however, dominated by the medical superintendents. Men like Drs. Henry M. Hurd, superintendent of the Johns Hopkins Hospital in Baltimore, Frederic A. Washburn of Massachusetts General Hospital in Boston, and A. R. Warner of Lakeside Hospital in Cleveland were visible hospital experts on the national scene by World War I.

The medical superintendents, like the medical educators, embraced the idea of hospital inspection and regulation, for the standards of the large hospitals would thereby be extended to the small ones. One suggestion was for the appointment of state inspectors to review every hospital admitting charity patients to its wards, another for an independent national body so that interstate comparisons of hospitals could be made.[61] Again, there was hope that one of the great foundations, such as Carnegie, would be able to support such a scheme. The American Hospital Association agreed in principle in 1913 to the inspection, classification, and standardization of hospitals. However, like the AMA Council on Medical Education, it lacked both the power over hospitals and the resources to launch a major program of national regulation. In the same year, leading surgeons established the American College of Surgeons, with hospital standardization as one of its aims—and it was the surgeons, of all groups, who were ultimately to be successful in hospital accreditation.

In this jostling cast of characters, however, it was members of the New Jersey Medical Society and the Pennsylvania medical licensing board who made the most important inspections of hospitals before World War I. The New Jersey Medical Society appointed a committee on the standardization of hospitals in 1914, which visited each hospital in the state and developed minimal requirements for what it called a "standard hospital" for internship education, in terms of hospital size, diagnostic facilities, and records systems. Pennsylvania's first inspection by the state's Bureau of Medical

Education and Licensure was reported in 1916 and publicized by its director, Dr. J. M. Baldy. Outside the major teaching hospitals in Philadelphia and Pittsburgh, hospital standards were "woefully deficient." Few hospitals had laboratories or postmortem facilities. X-ray equipment was frequently out-of-date—"generally of antiquated type," wrote Baldy, "set aside as an heir-loom, giving evidence of some former spurt of scientific ambition."[62] Patient records were largely unknown, hospitals were open to all practitioners irrespective of demonstrated competence or training, and the general dominance of surgery meant a relative lack of medical and obstetric cases from which interns could gain experience.

Pennsylvania, like New Jersey, established standards for internship approval and enforced them across the state, ranging from standards for equipment in the pathology laboratory to those for financial and clinical record-keeping. But there was little action in other states. Most state licensing boards were subject to local medical and political influences, including hospital interests. There was, in short, an enormous difference in perception between the scientific (elite) model of the hospital espoused by medical teachers and the idea of the hospital as an entrenched local community institution, responding to the expressed needs of its local practitioners and to the pride of its supporting networks.

The question of national hospital regulation centered on the relative power of the different players, each of whom had their own motives. The AMA and the state licensing boards were reasonably safe, within the politics of medicine, in pushing for upgraded standards of licensing for entry to the profession. They were on weak ground in trying to challenge the position of physicians already practicing in the community, for these were the mainstay of medical-society membership. Foundation grants helped to build university-centered medical complexes. But in small communities the open-staff hospital, where all local doctors could take patients, offered the greatest good to the greatest number of physicians. Increasingly, the community hospital was a center for diagnosis and treatment, a resource for practitioners to learn about new techniques, and a potential center for preventive medicine. If hospitals were doctors' workshops, upgrading standards in most hospitals meant upgrading the standards of the average physician. Not surprisingly, then, the wish to set rules proceeded simultaneously in several different directions. The AMA struggled to define the internship as a connected element of scientific medicine. However, this task did not help directly to upgrade standards of hospital surgery. Medical superintendents and other administrators, meanwhile, were embarked on their own reform agenda.

Hospital Administrators and Scientific Management

Just as physicians in the medical schools captured "scientific medicine"—leaving nurses, incidentally, with no separate "science" of their own—administrators and surgical reformers rallied in turn around enthusiasm for prevailing doctrines of "scientific management." In theory, running a hospital was like running any other business. Leading surgeon Dr. (Professor) Edward Martin, asked rhetorically in 1917, "You know of the great shop of Mr. Henry Ford. Does it run itself?"[63] The expected answer was obviously no.

Doctors joined administrators on the bandwagon of efficiency. The movement for efficiency in industry before World War I stressed the role of the expert in measuring and understanding input and output, and productivity. Time and motion studies, cost-benefit analysis, and organizational analysis were to lay the foundations of modern business administration; the emphasis was on measurement, standardization, performance, coordination of operations, and motivating workers. In Philadelphia the County Medical Society, pushing for open staff appointments, set up a committee on hospital efficiency in 1913 and urged every hospital in that city to adopt a uniform system of hospital records and reports, including both financial and clinical records, so that comparisons among hospitals could be made. Although there was little serious interest among either hospital administrators or physicians in providing detailed information of what they were doing, the rhetoric of scientific management was useful in establishing relative positions and asserting control.

Two organizational characteristics of hospitals made hospital administration, however, a very different enterprise from business management. The first was the nature of the larger hospitals as either private charities or governmental organizations; the second was the peculiar relationship of doctors and hospitals. A third major problem for the administrator was that hospitals lacked a readily definable product. Their success was measured largely in process rather than in outcomes; that is, the hospitals gave so many days of care and produced so many surgical operations, but most of what they did was an act of faith, not thought to be readily susceptible to measurement. The administrator had an important role in balancing budgets, but profitability was a means to an end, not an end in itself in an institution with complex social and professional agendas. Unlike their counterparts in industry, therefore, hospital administrators could not demonstrate their success—and advance their own roles—through product innovation and profitability. Not only did the charitable hospitals have no shareholders, trustee interests lay in maintaining (and expanding) their own institutions rather than merging or consolidating services with their neighbors. Hospital administrators, therefore, could not identify themselves directly with managers in other fields, who were rising in strength and importance in this period.

There was a negative ring in many of the meetings of the American Hospital Association, as administrators attempted to establish some independence from trustees on the one hand and attending physicians on the other. The superintendent needed tact, good sense, and judgment just to keep things going; that is, to bring about conditions which would prevent things being done which were bad for the hospital, and to bring in improvements in a way which did not set members of trustees and heads of departments against one another. The role of the administrator was one of "harmonizer," attempting through his or her personality to command the respect of all participants.[64]

The role and rewards of board membership were also quite different from those of a board of a business corporation. The aggressive, chiseling, driving businessman put down his cudgels at the hospital's doors and became, in an instant, a philanthropist who no longer acted like a businessman, however businesslike the internal operation of the institution or however much money the hospital gained from private fees. Board membership was most useful to the hospital in establishing institutional prestige, for external relations, and for fund-raising, and useful to the members as an exercise of benevolence and as a demonstration of social position. Hospitals, like surgeons, gained their expanded clientele by reputation and self-assertion. For those interested in the principles of scientific management, with its rhetoric of efficiency, it seemed illogical for hospitals to be run through this "estimable-gentlemen-men-of-affairs" tradition, with board members contributing only a little of their spare time to the organization. Few bankers or lawyers would expect department stores or theaters to be run successfully on this basis.[65] But trustees liked the role they played.

Hospital administrators, caught between the trustees and autonomous visiting physicians, were faced with a role of considerable difficulty, even before World War I. One observer of medical superintendents of large hospitals complained that they were under "almost heartbreaking strain."[66] Maud Banfield, administrator of the Polyclinic Hospital in Philadelphia, warned that women had to be especially careful not to make mistakes in a masculine world, since any failure was a "double failure"—

not only as a superintendent but as a female.[67] Hospital management had become a juggling act of keeping up a smoothly functioning organization; ensuring a steady flow of funds from patients, governments, and gifts; maintaining and flattering the trustees; deflecting external criticism; and retaining the most powerful and productive physicians, whose private admissions brought in revenues. The trustees' general lack of involvement in medical reform or day-to-day management left a lacuna in power that was filled by the increasing authority of physicians. But trustees remained the "fountain of authority," the custodians of funds, and the final arbiter in approving the employment of workers.[68] Administrators struggled, in the middle, and kept a low profile in controversial areas.

By concentrating on internal housekeeping and hotel management techniques, accounting and public relations, administrators could present themselves, concurrently, to trustees as experts in scientific management and to medical staff as experts in areas outside the clinical domain, thus avoiding potential clashes of interest. No doctor was threatened by groups of administrators meeting to discuss methods of working with local industries for fund-raising, the appropriate composition of floors, or training courteous telephone operators. The division of responsibility was convenient: doctors left funding to trustees and administrators, while the latter ceded to doctors all questions concerning the care of patients, including medical records. There was, in John Thompson's phrase, a "gauze curtain" drawn between them, by wary, unspoken agreement.[69]

Hospital administrators organized, then, around the hospital's hotel-management and financial concerns rather than in relation to its medical function—the entire purpose for which, in theory, the hospital existed. In New York, for example, trustees and administrators organized a conference of over twenty hospitals in 1905 to counter newspaper attacks of extravagance, abuse, favoritism to certain doctors, and unnecessary secrecy in their administration. No voluntary hospital wanted to inhibit private giving. One writer put this problem succinctly: "An uninformed public is a fickle friend."[70]

One of the most successful joint administrative efforts was the establishment of a hospital bureau of standards and supplies for joint purchasing in New York in 1910. In its first six months the bureau made twenty-one joint purchasing agreements—including agreements for ice, coal, meat, towels, gauze, incandescent lamps, and drugs, and by 1916 the bureau served forty-one hospitals, including twenty-four outside New York City. However, the general need to raise funds and justify patient fees put accounting systems at the top of the administrators' priorities. A published handbook, setting out uniform charts of accounts and statistics, by the treasurer of Presbyterian Hospital, New York, was in its fourth edition in 1918.[71]

The wide variety of backgrounds of hospital superintendents and the enormous range in the size of institutions made it difficult to say there was one general administrative role. Over half of the superintendents who belonged to the AHA in 1916 were graduate nurses. The first formal hospital administration and nursing-school administration teaching program, in hospital economics, was established (for nurses) at Columbia Teachers College in 1900. This stressed uniform accounting, advertising, government aid, and, very sensibly, "political pull."[72] Interestingly, present-day hospital administration textbooks do not mention this program in presenting the history of management education. Nursing administration has indeed rarely been viewed fully as "administration," for reasons which go far beyond the role itself and include strong elements of gender prejudice. Instead of building on the experience of nursing administration, medical superintendents and other (largely male) administrators sought to establish themselves as a new profession.

There were, in short, schisms within the broad field of hospital administration. Within the AHA there was an implicit stratification of hospitals as "large" and "small," with different constituencies and agendas, and different types of administrators.[73] Lack of unity as well as lack of power inhibited the creation of a strong national organization for hospital administrators. Not until 1917, after eleven years of discussion about the need for centralized information, did the AHA established its own permanent headquarters, in Philadelphia (later in Chicago). Throughout this period, the association remained a diverse, heterogeneous club without a strong common purpose and with little national influence.

At the institutional level, administrators who attempted to redefine hospital care in terms of broader definitions of public health rarely received the backing from trustees which would enable them to overcome the resistance of physicians. The exceptions proved the rule. Michael M. Davis, for example, the authoritative head of the Boston Dispensary, successfully extended the role of the outpatient department there by starting a pay clinic for middle-income workers in 1913, beginning with an eye department. Brooklyn Hospital followed in 1915. A third pay clinic was established in Chicago in 1916, and a fourth at Lakeside Hospital, Cleveland, in 1917.[74] However, as the superintendent of Johns Hopkins Hospital observed, there were enormous difficulties in starting a pay clinic, because of the need for "educating the rank and file of physicians to appreciate this need and to give their support."[75] Extending the economic base of the hospital into ambulatory care was not part of the accepted ideology of private practice. Nor was extending the social role of the hospital part of the ideology of trustees—directed, as it was, toward a limited paternalism toward the indigent.

Coming to Grips with Standards in Surgery

In the event, surgeons took over the rhetoric of efficiency. Surgery was, after all, the central craft in most hospitals between 1910 and 1917. And surgical considerations were intrinsic to good general management of hospitals in the days before antibiotics, since it was imperative that the hospital be clean in order to avoid infections. A Pennsylvania report remarked, with double entendre, "Slovenliness is infectious."[76] Surgery also made it possible to think of hospitals in terms of standard definitions, because surgical methods were being internationally standardized through the consensus being formed in studies published in medical journals. The vehicle for reform was the new American College of Surgeons (ACS).

Chicago surgeon Franklin Martin, founder of the ACS, launched the first Clinical Congress of Surgeons in the operative clinics of Chicago in 1910—the year the Flexner report on medical education was published, and the year in which Frederick W. Taylor's congressional testimony on railroad efficiency popularized scientific management to a general audience. Analogies with industry abounded as the second Clinical Congress of Surgeons was held in Philadelphia in 1911 and the third in New York in 1912. Each provided the opportunity for surgeons from far and wide to study surgical technique by watching it in leading centers. Participants in the third congress expressed enthusiasm for standardizing both surgery and hospitals, and these goals became an intrinsic element in the establishment of the American College of Surgeons, which obtained its charter in 1912 and first met in 1913.[77] The ACS's central purpose was to create a category of Fellows of the College, who would be of sufficient skill that they would be recognized as superior surgeons by patients, hospitals, and other practitioners—and also as noncommercial surgeons, since fellows had to take an oath that they would not split their fees with doctors who referred patients to them. Hospital standardization took the process one step further by specifying the desirable hospital environment of the surgeon.

The ACS set up a committee on the standardization of hospitals in 1913. The president, Professor Edward Martin of Philadelphia, invited Dr. E. A. Codman of Boston, an enthusiast for efficiency and evaluation techniques, to be chairman. Codman's was one of the few persistent voices pressing for defining hospital quality in terms of the actual outcome of care to the patient—and on behalf of the patient. Hospital surgeons, Codman wrote, should be judged by ability, not prestige or reputation. Now that the latest operation had become a topic of dinnertable conversation, a "considerable part of the entertaining news among all classes," trustees should accept the responsibility for overseeing "the quality of the Product which their Hospital factories give to the Public."[78] Codman remarked that a factory which sells its products takes pains to ensure itself that the product is a good one, but a hospital which gives away its product seemed to regard the quality of that product as not worthy of investigation.[79] The only firm ground for evaluating a hospital was by actual results.

Codman developed his own "end results" system, designed to evaluate whether a given patient had actually benefited from a given surgery, and he berated trustees for ignoring the results that their institutions were actually obtaining. Under the system, hospitals could find out whether the patient improved or not by installing a detailed system of patient records, which recorded each diagnostic judgment and therapeutic intervention, and by instigating a system of reviewing patients one year after discharge and comparing the results against the charts. In so doing, hospitals would also find out who were the best and worst surgeons, irrespective of their general reputation. Codman also suggested that patients should have access to the results of treatment and should be able to study the reports of large hospitals in order to learn where specific branches of surgery were well done. He was, in short, that unusual combination of professional reformer and consumer advocate. But as Susan Reverby has observed, he was also eccentric, assertive, and difficult—and he challenged the medical profession's hard-won unity with a system that would expose the variety of standards within the practice of medicine, and that would change the balance of power between physicians and hospital trustees. Everyone in authority knew, Codman said, that nobody was responsible for examining the results of treatment at hospitals, and that the "reason was MONEY; in other words that the [medical] staff are not paid, and therefore cannot be held accountable."[80] This comment was, of course, correct.

Discussions of objective criteria for evaluating surgery were part of a wider interest in hospital, industrial, and social efficiency. Michael Davis at the Boston Dispensary and Richard Cabot at the Massachusetts General Hospital, for example, stressed the value of follow-up visits in outpatient care, while several enthusiastic Taylorites, including Frank Gilbreth, were interested in applying the efficiency methods designed for the shop floor to the evaluation of surgical techniques. Robert L. Dickinson, a Brooklyn gynecologist who worked with Gilbreth, wrote prolifically on efficiency. He advocated, along industrial lines, time and motion studies, standardized hospital charts of organization, and one-man committees to oversee the routines of the operating room, medical records, wards, and dispensaries: a system, in short, of efficient management.[81] But surgeons were no more eager to be managed by surgeons than by anyone else.

Meanwhile, the American College of Surgeons established criteria for training programs for surgeons. At the first convocation of the college in November 1913, fellowship was conferred on 1,059 surgeons who were selected as being recognizably competent. The following year, success in an examination became the portal of entry, following specified types of training. This system of standardizing surgeons assumed that knowledge, appropriately transmitted and certified, led to acceptable methods of practice. In theory, by certifying the *surgeon* as competent, certifying the *surgery* was unnecessary. (This has been the traditional British view.)

Standardizing the surgeon emphasized professional authority. Standardizing the work suggested the surgeon was a mere craftworker, or even a mechanic working in an organization. Scientific management in industry ranged from time and motion studies to sweeping organizational analyses—activities that surgeons did not want. Codman's methods would put trustees and administrators as policemen over medical work, while in the sphere of health reform Davis and Cabot advocated widespread organizational change in medicine, from group medical practice to compulsory health insurance. Surgeons, as a group, were willing to upgrade standards but not to lose their professional prerogatives to individuals they did not trust. It was not surprising, in the event, that neither the ACS nor individual hospitals pressed for quality-assurance systems along Codman's lines.

Lack of interest in hospital standardization by the Carnegie Foundation put the final damper on the conclusions of Codman's committee. The American College of Surgeons merely appropriated five hundred dollars to establish a minimum hospital efficiency record (i.e., a patient record), building on Codman's work. Although the Carnegie Foundation revised its position in January 1916 following the appointment of John G. Bowman, one-time secretary of the foundation, as the ACS's new director, the momentum for an end-results system was lost.[82] The foundation's gift of $30,000 to the college for a hospital standardization program was to launch, for the first time, a major set of national hospital inspections. By then few were taking the end-results system seriously.

Instead, the ACS decided to press for minimum standards for hospitals which would cover all branches of medicine in a general hospital; and the American Hospital Association agreed to cooperate. Essential steps to ensure good-quality surgical care in hospitals would include a system of certifying surgeons, provided by fellowship in the American College of Surgeons; adequate case records for teaching and research; pathology and X-ray departments; and an organized (but not necessarily a closed) hospital medical staff, which could develop its own efficiency committees to supervise standards within each institution. Through such measures local physician autonomy would be maintained. ACS representatives aired these practical ideas at a conference in Chicago in the fall of 1917, at which sixty hospitals were represented. Arthur Dean Bevan, still chairman of the AMA Council on Medical Education, was there to offer his support—although the AMA was to show some reservations later. Thus the ACS's great program of hospital standardization was established, the forerunner of the present accreditation system.

Throughout the long debates about standardization between 1910 and 1917 the ideology of scientific medicine prevailed, that is, the assumption that knowledge could be developed by observation and research, and applied to the population by individual practitioners—like the antisyphilis drug salvarsan, for example, or diphtheria antitoxin or a new surgical operation. Two major patterns of authority over hospitals had been established: control of hospitals at the community level through a negotiated balance of charitable, administrative, and medical interests, and national specification of hospital standards by the AMA and the American College of Surgeons. Meanwhile, calls for health insurance were appearing in different states and hospitals were increasingly visible. John Hornsby, editor of the journal *Modern Hospital,* estimated in 1917 that $1.445 billion was then invested in hospital land and buildings, and that hospitals accounted for annual expenses of over $578 million a year.[83]

In the event, the success of national medical standards for hospitals was a double-edged sword for the medical profession. In establishing national rules the American College of Surgeons and the American Medical Association proclaimed that hospitals were of more than parochial concern. The community hospital was confirmed as the factory or workshop of *physicians,* held in trust by its board of bankers and businessmen and maintained by an assiduous superintendent. Major teaching hospitals were *sui generis.* However, the more successful hospitals became as technical centers (largely surgical centers), the greater the case for their organization into mass-distribution networks, where specialized services could be made more efficient, and for the organization of medical specialties into coopera-tive groups.

The hospital of the future, it seemed, could serve one of two quite different functions: either as a supporting framework for the work of autonomous private practitioners, or as a controlling center in the health-care system, where doctors might, perhaps, be employed and where com-munity services could be extended. The most likely nucleus of such an empire was the university-affiliated teaching hospital. Local battles for open-staff hospitals carried the weight of these wider questions, while assuming that the hospital was the practitioner's domain. Nevertheless, there was rising public and medical concern by 1917, when the United States entered World War I, that hospital services were inefficiently orga-nized for the growing throng of middle-class consumers.

4

The Case for Cooperative Medicine: World War I

War, for all its horrors, often leads to innovation in medicine or accelerates tendencies that were proceeding slowly in the previous period of peace; and World War I was no exception. The American College of Surgeons' program of standardization developed in the shadow of the war. The same surgeons who were pushing for hospital upgrading at home were simultaneously planning for the development of mobile base hospitals for the European theater, where war began in 1914.

Yet the war itself, fought by Americans on a distant continent, was only part of the broader socioeconomic environment of medicine at home. There was a curious dichotomy between the experiences, brief but dramatic, of U.S. physicians and surgeons in the battlefields of Europe in 1917–18, and concerns at home about compulsory health insurance, the "Americanization" of immigrants, and the rational organization of medicine and public health. On both fronts, organized or cooperative medicine made intuitive sense. But the conclusions reached were varied—and, ultimately, contradictory.

The surgeons, physicians, administrators, and nurses who were involved in setting up streamlined, specialized base hospitals and field units for the European theater readily appreciated the efficiency of large-scale organization. These base hospitals were designed as short-term, acute, highly efficient technological systems for the injured or suddenly sick. At home, however, other models were available: models which emphasized a strong preventive and community role and in which technology was secondary. In St. Louis, for example, the Stix, Baer & Fuller Dry Goods Company, a department store, provided emergency and outpatient services as a "splendid preventative of the employees becoming incapacitated."[1] In Detroit the Michigan Workmen's Compensation Mutual Insurance Company opened the Manufacturers' Hospital in 1916, to take care of men injured in industrial work, and services included home inspections by a social-service nurse.[2] Railroads and large manufacturing concerns, moreover, had demonstrated that just as good results could be obtained in plain and unostentatious buildings as in elaborate and expensive hospital facilities. Frederick Hoffman, well-known insurance statistician, told the American Hospital Association convention in 1916 that hospitals were only "at the beginning of their field of broad public usefulness." He predicted: "They will soon be used far more for the treatment of the half-sick and to-be-sick than for the already sick and the half-dead. We should have hospitals where people may go at the beginning rather than the end of their sickness."[3] This was clearly not the military model—nor, significantly, the model of major teaching hospitals at home.

Whatever might have been the outcome otherwise, World War I ratified the model of the acute medical center. The efficiency of the military base hospitals was obviously an important reason for this. However, it was surely not enough to explain the continuity of their image in the postwar period. A critical factor, I suggest, was rather that the army base hospitals were, uniquely among Allied medical services, clones of leading hospitals and medical schools. For its military medical services the U.S. government drew upon private institutions. More than any other medical or hospital organization in the United States, it was the medical schools that mobilized for war. In the stress and camaraderie of war, the army units set up emotionally powerful professional links among those involved. It was these individuals, high-ranked surgeons and administrators, rather than the public-health and industrial experts who stayed at home, who were to stamp their image on postwar medicine. Proposals for health insurance paled against the rich drama of national emergency. Two powerful prewar themes, the authority of American medical schools and hospital leadership by surgeons, were thus strengthened. After the war imaginative (and low-cost) alternatives for acute hospitals were conspicuous by their absence, even in providing for the rehabilitation and long-term care of stricken veterans.

Organizing Medicine for the Service of Patients

In October 1916 surgeon George Crile's unit from Lakeside Hospital in Cleveland (Western Reserve University faculty) provided a stirring demonstration of American organizational genius by constructing a completely organized, 500-bed temporary hospital in Fairmount Park in Philadelphia during the ACS meetings in that city. Such developments were thrilling both to the medical profession and to the general public. Thirty-three base hospitals were organized or underway when President Wilson declared war on Germany in April 1917. By December 1917, when the ACS completed its initial questionnaire on standardization, to send to the 2,711 largest hospitals in the United States, most leading surgeons were already commissioned. Altogether, approximately one out of every four American physicians—30 percent of those of service age—served in some capacity in the military. Half the fellows of the American Surgical Association who were of service age went "over there."[4] American medicine was caught up in an outpouring of patriotism.

The disruptions of war and the inevitable increase in national planning in all economic spheres were joined by the leadership of surgeons in policy-making for war, for traditional warfare is overwhelmingly a surgical affair—requiring imaginative removal of the wounded from battle, well-organized distribution systems, and prompt and ingenious operative techniques. "Patients come in volleys," Crile wrote from France in his wartime diary. "The surgeon is barraged with fractures; shelled with broken heads; bombed with bellies; gassed with wounds."[5] Orthopedic and plastic surgery developed in particular; the phrase "physical medicine and reconstruction" came into general use; and knowledge about surgical shock, blood transfusions, splints, and operating techniques boomed. A contemporary described the European battlefront as a "tremendous vivisection experimental laboratory."[6] War required organization, streamlining of medical and hospital services, the cooperation of different specialists, and a sharing of skills, medical records, and experiences. War defined medical efficiency in terms of hospital-based group practice mobilized for rapid, lifesaving care. Before the war the Mayo Clinic was the classic example of cooperative physician organization: a group of specialists working together, with diagnostic and operative services available in a well-run hospital. However, the Mayo Clinic was in many ways unique. War brought into general prominence the vexed question of how medicine should ideally be organized and how hospitals might fit into a rationally organized health-service system.

Leaders of the hospital standardization movement, focusing before the war almost entirely on physician education, had largely avoided the problem of how physicians, as specialists, would be organized so that the combined result of specialist care would be a well-coordinated service for the individual patient; the university teachers leading the ACS had enough on their plate without further antagonizing the part-time surgeon or general practitioner. Yet "group medicine" was widely recognized—by the academics, at least—as the rational modern alternative to the old general practitioner and as the only efficient way to arrive at an accurate diagnosis. A good example is a thoughtful article by distinguished physician Hugh Cabot of the Harvard Medical School and Massachusetts General Hospital, published in 1915. Cabot, like others, recommended "group medicine with the hospital as its center"—although he also expressed concern lest medicine become a profit-making trade, run by physicians who were business-oriented "big men."[7] It was difficult to shake the taint of commercialism.

The problem was, where would the initiative and capital for organized medical systems come from if not from physicians? And what would motivate physicians to set up cooperative practices—risking the displeasure of their local colleagues and competitors—unless they expected to make money? The Mayos seemed a special case, products of an earlier generation and hallowed by their nationally recognized skills. Industrial medicine was a possibility, in theory—that is, the establishment of well-organized health systems within the framework of major industrial corporations as a cost of doing business. New state workmen's compensation laws put responsibility for industrial accidents on business; industrial medicine was growing as a field, stimulated by research on occupational diseases by Dr. Alice Hamilton and others; and industrial clinics were popping up everywhere. But there were problems here, too. Notably, not everyone was a worker in a large corporation. Corporations had little interest in providing a major service beyond their own responsibilities. Moreover, the average doctor was antagonistic to anything smacking of "contract practice," in which the doctor's income could be pared to the bone.[8]

But disease was, after all, only partly the business of business. State health-insurance commissions, seeking to assign reasons for sickness, tended to ascribe it to three sources, with industry the least important; industry was blamed for hazards ranging from toxic dusts to other poisons, poor lighting, and industrial fatigue. A more important villain of ill health was the community, which could be blamed for failures in social organization which led, in turn, to the community's unwillingness to prevent tuberculosis, which was (and is) a disease of poor housing and poverty. The community also aided and abetted disease by failing to provide proper sanitation, sewage, milk inspection, and housing codes. A third, further responsibility for disease was placed on the individual, for his or her carelessness, recklessness, and addiction to tobacco, alcohol and drugs, and "vice." An estimated 16 to 18 percent of hospital admissions in Boston and St. Paul, for example, suffered from syphilis, which was usually sexually transmitted.[9] For advocates of cooperative medicine the only practical alternative sources of capital to start organized schemes seemed to be the hospital and the state, or the two in combination.

Through health insurance, organized by the states, hospitals might become the center for the practice of medicine. The potential link between health insurance (prepayment) and the organization of medicine (group practice), evident before the war, was pushed by social reformers like Hugh and Richard Cabot and Michael M. Davis. Parallel discussions of hospital-based group practice as an element of medical efficiency and discussions of health insurance in the states made such connections virtually inevitable. A well-organized hospital group practice might have two major advantages for patients: first, one physician could be responsible for a patient, coordinating the service of different specialists; and second, accurate diagnosis could be assured by the availability of advanced technology in the hospital and by a system of referral and consultation.

The Health-Insurance Movement

The movement for compulsory (state) health insurance between 1915 and 1920 was built on ideals of the social efficiency to be achieved by guaranteeing a healthy population. Healthy workers are productive, the argument went. To maintain health is therefore, in theory, a form of collective conservation. Numerous sickness surveys between 1910 and 1920 demonstrated that sickness and poverty go hand in hand and that care of the poor is socially expensive. Wage earners were estimated in 1919 to lose $600 million each year in lost pay because of sickness—a sum, it was pointed out, that was greater than the U.S. national debt before the war—while

American families spent more than a $1 billion a year on medical and hospital care. In New York alone workers were thought to receive free treatment worth $10 million from private and public hospitals, with another $12 million in free medical care.[10]

At the same time, many individuals received no care, or care only at an advanced stage of disease. Surveys done by the Metropolitan Life Insurance Company before the war found that a third of specific cases of sickness received no medical care whatever; and where care was given, it was often inadequate.[11] A prudent industrial state might well build a health-insurance program to safeguard against such heavy losses. A progressive society, expecting individuals to serve their fellow citizens in peace as well as in war, sought social-insurance schemes as a matter of course. There was, therefore, considerable discussion of the pros and cons of a state-supported system before and during the war. There was also considerable confusion as to what exactly health insurance meant—for any of the participants: hospitals, doctors, employers, or beneficiaries.

Workmen's or accident compensation, with the direct encouragement of President Theodore Roosevelt, was the first form of social insurance to come into prominence in the United States. By 1919, thirty-seven states and three territories had passed workmen's compensation laws, explicitly imposing upon industry the cost of injury and other damage to workers.[12] The American Association for Labor Legislation, established in 1906, considered health insurance the logical next step after workmen's compensation. Its model bill for health insurance was introduced in three states in 1915; in 1917 twelve states were contemplating bills. Ten states appointed special commissions to investigate social insurance—and six of these were still at work at the beginning of 1919.

Advocates of health insurance tended to draw, turgidly and at length, on European illustrations, rather than develop plans specifically suited to the United States, as if the legislative success of workmen's compensation had exhausted the creative possibilities. The AMA's committee on social insurance, apparently favorable to the general notion of health insurance, produced a report on foreign schemes for its annual meeting of 1916 that ran into thirty-four closely printed pages in the AMA *Journal.*[13] Only the enthusiast can have read this report, full of arcane details of different programs, with any care or even interest. Would, for example, any American state follow Leipzig's example of compulsory commitment of patients to hospital in certain cases, including illnesses requiring serious operations, when treatment in the home was considered to be unsuitable?

The British National Health Insurance Act of 1911 appeared, intuitively, to be the most comprehensible. This may have been because of the bond of a common language, or because American wartime sympathies were, on balance, with the British. But in fact the British system was not directly relevant to U.S. conditions. The British scheme was limited to general practice, while American doctors saw specialization as the way ahead. It is also extremely unlikely that Americans would have supported Britain's exclusion from health insurance of hospital care, X-ray diagnosis, pathological and bacteriological examinations, or major surgical operations. From the U.S. perspective England was considered to lack adequate hospital accommodation.[14]

The insurance committee of the California Medical Society noted with some frustration in 1917 that although they were heartily in favor of the principle of health insurance, no plan of medical organization had yet been produced that the committee could endorse.[15] But there was also something odd about considering health insurance at all in countries that were plunged in war. It was perhaps with some relief that with America's entry into World War I compulsory health insurance, developed initially in Germany, could be conveniently attacked as "un-American" or dismissed as the "Teuton" conception of the state.

By 1918 the medical profession and some employers' associations, organized labor, commercial insurance companies, and other groups were rising in opposition to compulsory insurance. But at the same time, the various state reports on health insurance marked a general uneasiness about health services as a whole. There was distrust on all sides about how well insurance schemes would work, given the disorganization of the American system and the rapid disappearance of general practitioners. Doctors were a very mixed bag of individuals, ranging from eminent professors and highly paid city specialists (sometimes topflight experts, sometimes organized into affluent private groups which offered the latest fads to well-heeled patients) to poorly trained and marginally paid hacks, looking for all the practice they could get. At hearings before the social insurance commission in California in 1917, a labor representative reported that doctors earned less than the average organized working man in that state—and California medical fees were supposedly higher than those in the East.[16] Ordinary practitioners were wary of both the surgical professors who were seeking to clean up surgery, and of medical schools and major hospitals which were expanding their clinics. Hospitals were notoriously varied; hence the drive for standardization. At the beginning of World War I both hospitals and physicians were also only beginning to appreciate the potential effect of the new workmen's compensation schemes; and many were taken by surprise.

In California, for example, where workmen's compensation took ef-

fect in 1914, physicians found themselves locked in battle with the commercial insurance companies which administered the program. Sometimes
physicians were tricked into accepting fees that were even below the
official (low) thirty cents a visit. The companies complained, in turn, that
some doctors were squeezing them for exorbitant fees. The medical profession, reported a special committee of the California Medical Association
in 1917, "suddenly realized that without even being consulted, its practice
of surgery was being radically altered."[17]

In Pennsylvania, where workmen's compensation legislation took effect in 1916, the act brought physicians into conflict with hospitals, as well
as with insurance companies. There the superintendents of the large Philadelphia hospitals had the foresight to organize a system where they, rather
than the physicians, had first call on the limited funds allowed for each
case: $25 per case for treatment, limited to services given within two weeks
of injury, or $75 in the case of a major surgical operation; both to include
both doctors' fees and hospital bills. Spokesmen for the hospitals claimed
that reimbursement was a simple matter of hospital management and that
the physician had no right to "dictate policy," indeed that the average
physician was in the hospital's debt by being honored with a staff appointment.

This practice led, not surprisingly, to accusations by physicians that
hospitals were selling the charitable services of physicians for a profit. In
return, hospital administrators claimed that the same physicians were
keeping patients out of hospitals for the first two weeks of care and then
dumping them in hospitals as charity cases after the workmen's compensation payments ceased.[18] Such squabbles, in a program that was of relatively minor financial importance to hospitals, cast doubts on what the
behavior of providers would be like in a much larger health insurance
system.

The generally opportunistic outlook of hospital administrators and
medical staffs, drumming up the market for paying patients, together with
the growth of outpatient departments in the large hospitals as a basis for
teaching and a source of "interesting material" for the wards, created other
tensions between hospitals and physicians. These tensions were exacerbated as outpatient practice increased during the war as a necessary response to the absence of so many American physicians. The alleged
"abuse" of outpatient clinics by middle-class patients and huge teaching
hospitals was a ready target for medical society criticisms. Charity Hospital
in New Orleans, for example, which was a major teaching center, refused
to introduce a means test until 1926. Small-scale experiments in outpatient
practice for pay patients before the war, even when credentialed by Massa-

chusetts General Hospital or Johns Hopkins, ran into trenchant opposition by local doctors as deliberate attempts at unfair competition.

Hospital superintendents regarded workmen's compensation cases primarily in terms of income. But the monetary standard prevailed in all aspects of the hospital system. It was generally accepted by both hospitals and physicians that care was better when a fee was paid.[19] But unfortunately for the hospitals, the per diem charges for workmen's compensation generally did not match the hospital's posted charges for paying patients. As a result, workmen's compensation cases did not fit readily into the stylized class system of hospital care; superintendents tended to regard workmen's compensation cases as charity patients while still collecting a fee from the workmen's compensation program. None of this augured well for compulsory health insurance. It was entirely likely, as one speaker remarked before the San Francisco County Medical Society in 1916, that: "Probably a good deal of the opposition to any sort of socializing change in medicine, such as the adoption of the hospital and dispensary system, has risen largely from the feeling against such institutions as they are now."[20]

A fundamental criticism of hospitals under workmen's compensation was their apparent lack of initiative in providing services tailored to the needs of injured employees, ranging from acute treatment to rehabilitation back to full employability. Even the hospitals which had been established in the nineteenth century primarily to care for accidents had succumbed to the narrow glamour of surgery, the shortened length of stay, the acute medical focus, and the lack of interest in postoperative care or long-term conditions that distinguished twentieth-century "scientific medicine." A careful postwar review of the national industrial picture by state officials in Missouri concluded that there were few adequate facilities for industrial accident cases in hospitals anywhere in the United States. The average hospital organization, geared to undertake "careful and daring surgery," was just not attuned to effective reconstruction (rehabilitation) work, including the "unremitting aftercare" of massage, exercises, electrical treatment, education, and appliances. Indeed, hospitals had "never desired this sort of work particularly."[21] Some hospitals established industrial clinics. However, the central core of treatment—the continuous care of an injured worker, both as inpatient and as long-term outpatient—was generally unavailable. The organizational and social rift between inpatient and outpatient services in hospitals made even the notion of comprehensive hospital-based care alien to institutional expectations.

Nowhere was it clear what, exactly, hospitals would be expected to do under any proposed system of health insurance, nor how they would be controlled by the states, if at all. Would hospital outpatient departments expand into hospital-based group practices, serving all social classes? Would their physicians be put on salary? Would general medical care be given at home but all specialist care be concentrated in hospitals? What would be the relationship between the fees of general practitioners and specialists? What would be the arrangement for paying for special services such as X rays? It scarcely needed special wisdom to agree with the AMA committee that such questions contained "serious possibility of dispute."[22]

The visibility of Progressive academicians in the health-insurance debates, as well as leading hospital superintendents with well-known reform views, emphasized a growing division of interest between reformers and rank-and-file practitioners. Reformers such as Michael M. Davis (the Boston Dispensary) and S. S. Goldwater (Mount Sinai Hospital, New York), were described by critics as "men who played a prominent part in the development and extension of free hospitals and dispensaries."[23] On occasion, it seemed as if the reformers wanted to take over the medical profession, flawed as it was by the inclusion of an unknown number of incompetent doctors and those marked by graft and greed. Dr. A. R. Warner, the reform-minded superintendent of Lakeside Hospital in Cleveland, stated bluntly at the AHA meeting in 1917, that the medical profession in the past had "too often" exploited hospitals. Now, he said, it was time to reverse the trend. It is "past time, and never will come time again, for the American physicians to feel that they can control and should control the hospitals of this country."[24]

However, it was one thing to look in the distant future to the probability of free dispensaries and hospitals, "in which the staff are paid by the state and where service is open to rich and poor alike,"[25] and quite another to advocate such an abrupt and massive change as an immediate possibility. The health insurance bills were weak on practical details. Not until 1918 did the AHA officially endorse compulsory state health insurance, urging AHA members and state hospital associations to solve the remaining problems. By then it was far too late. An informed report on debates on health insurance at the AHA meeting in Cincinnati in 1919—four years after the original model bill for health insurance—described members as coming away "more confused as to its ultimate value than they were before."[26] A Massachusetts expert on industrial accidents, addressing the topic of medical competence and hospital efficiency the same year, began his speech with an apposite jest: "Many people might suggest that it would be better to speak of medical incompetence and hospital inefficiency."[27] The health-insurance movement was rapidly running out of steam. By 1920 it was dead.

Hospitals at War

Perhaps, without the war, some states might have adopted compulsory health-insurance schemes and addressed issues of hospital function, reimbursement, and control; perhaps not. In the event, the removal from the scene of powerful spokesmen for surgery and hospital administration divided national hospital policy-making into two camps: those "over there" in Europe and those left at home. Spokesmen in both camps considered hospitals to be short-term repair shops rather than centers for preventive medicine or long-term care. However, wartime conditions sparked increased public interest in the nation's health status and imposed unusual pressures on the home-front hospitals, whose staffs were seriously depleted. Conditions were strained to the point of breakdown in the virulent outbreak of influenza in 1918. The war period was one of striking contrasts for the hospital world, most notably between the military efficiency and multispecialist organization of the large army bases, which were held in high regard, and the pervasive sense of muddle, inefficiency, and diversity of interests that marked hospitals of widely varying size at home.

The divisions were emphasized by the role of leading surgeons as the obvious medical experts on military planning. Franklin Martin, founder of the American College of Surgeons, was one of the seven members appointed to President Wilson's advisory commission as a counselor on national defense in 1916. (Hospital administrators tried to get their own representatives on the Council of National Defense, but failed; thus the surgeons outgunned the superintendents.) Another leading surgeon, George Crile of Cleveland, visited France to observe medical needs before American entry into the war. He pushed strongly for medical-school/teaching-hospital sponsorship of mobile surgical units on three grounds. First, the privately-organized base hospital could build upon established teams. Second, the best surgery was likely to be found in large hospitals, particularly the teaching hospitals. And third, a teaching-hospital system would avoid the embarrassing need for the formal screening-out of large numbers of incompetent and dangerous surgical operators, whose practice was based in the smaller hospitals.[28]

The formal ideology of scientific medicine was endorsed both by university medicine and the success of wartime surgery. As a consequence, the fundamental characteristics of that ideology—technological efficiency, impersonality of treatment, regimentation of patients, dependence on diagnostic tests, importance of records, and focus on immediate results—

were forcibly imprinted on the medical profession as the ideal basis for the practice of hospital medicine. Shell shock and tuberculosis posed rather different long-term problems, but these were to be seen, significantly, as outside the domain of general hospital care.

America's largest teaching hospitals and their associated medical schools entered enthusiastically into the complicated logistics of cloning themselves into two organizations, one of which had to be completely mobile. In all, fifty base hospitals were established, plus nineteen smaller hospital units; minimum hospital capacity was initially 500, later 1,000, beds. Most of the hospitals were mobilized in the spring of 1918—chiefly to France, although six were set up in Great Britain. One unit stayed behind in recognition of its peculiarly "foreign" origin: that organized by the German Hospital in New York.

Local Red Cross chapters provided materials, and volunteers collected, knitted, and sewed. The supplies for Base Hospital No. 20, organized in 1917 by the University of Pennsylvania Hospital, filled thirty-four railway boxcars. This hospital, like others, had complete medical and surgical capabilities, including orthopedics, neuropsychiatric care, neurology, ophthalmology, contagious diseases, dentistry, and other specialties. The unit provided trained nurses and female volunteers to act as nurses' aides, a chaplain, and a complement of enlisted men and appropriate civilian employees.

The base hospitals were strongly directed, productive, and cohesive professional villages. Base Hospital No. 20, for example, treated over 8,000 patients in France between May 1918 and January 1919, in over 1,400 beds scattered among twelve hotels; and only sixty-five patients died. The unit fielded its own sports teams, including, so they said, the best hospital baseball team in France, and had its own plays, orchestra, and jazz band.[29] There was an enormous difference between the drama, danger, inconveniences, and "esprit de corps" of such endeavors and the mundane trials and jealousies of hospital care in the United States.

The fifty base hospitals were organized by eighteen medical schools and forty-two teaching hospitals across the United States, sometimes in combination, creating a national wartime hospital elite: from centers like the University of Oregon; City Hospital in Indianapolis; Milwaukee County Hospital; Youngstown Hospital in Ohio; and Emory University in Atlanta. The New York area provided nine hospitals, while four each were drawn from the great medical centers of Philadelphia, Chicago, and Boston. But the epitome of base-hospital provision was the Harvard medical teaching complex, supporting no less than three bases, one sponsored by the school itself, a second by Boston City Hospital, and the third by

Massachusetts General Hospital (MGH); the latter two were Harvard teaching hospitals. The experiences of these units in Europe in World War I entered the folklore of Harvard medical history, and the social bondings made in war were to affect numerous postwar careers. The European experience urged, on all concerned, the advantages of well-organized hospitals and high-technology specialization.

The Harvard and MGH network could look with pride on their wartime contributions. Harvard faculty, together with former faculty and MGH residents, were in influential positions all over Europe. The huge MGH Base Hospital No. 6, still growing after the armistice, had 100 wards with nearly 5,000 beds, all occupied. Its success testified to the administrative skills and iron will of its commanding officer, Dr. (then Colonel) Frederic Washburn, a prominent force in national hospital affairs, who was on leave from directing MGH. Washburn had evacuated a French hospital and expanded it from its original 500 beds by scattering wards and walkways among trees which the French would not allow to be removed, thus producing, according to Surgeon General Merritte Ireland, the complex architectural scheme of a "Chinese ideograph." Others, like Dr. Paul Dudley White, the eminent cardiologist, recalled the mud and chill of winter, the dullness of the daily grind, the enormous efforts required to cope with wounded and gassed American troops arriving by convoy or ambulance train, and the heavy impact of influenza when it hit France in September 1918, dividing the hospital into two halves, one dealing with the wounded and one with flu victims, scores of whom died. The MGH later credited its alumni and staff with providing 238 commissioned officers, including two brigadier generals, 228 female nurses, and 80 male nurses and employees.[30]

America exported the cream of its medical and nursing professions to the war in France. Back at home the depleted hospitals coped as best they could. Although some schools, like the University of Pennsylvania Medical School, refused to release departmental chairmen (keeping Dr. Edward Martin, a strong supporter of hospital standardization, at home), other staffs flocked abroad. George Crile of Lakeside went to Rouen; Harvey Cushing of Harvard to Étaples; and J. M. T. Finney of Johns Hopkins to Bazoilles-sur-Meuse. Dean W. H. Welch of Hopkins advised Surgeon General William Crawford Gorgas of the army on health matters in the United States. All such activities took obvious precedence over concurrent calls, stateside, for hospital upgrading, multispecialist group practice, and state health insurance. Retired physicians were brought back to work and, for the duration, women physicians, married nurses, and volunteers were welcomed.

At MGH, for example, the great physician Frederick C. Shattuck, who had been professor of clinical medicine and visiting physician at the hospital until his retirement in 1912, was called back to active duty—"resurrected" was how he put it. Shattuck's recollections of this experience speak volumes about the rapid changes in major teaching hospitals that immediately preceded World War I, which in turn affected the base hospitals and were then fed back after the war as the predominant professional model of care. Not all changes were, he felt, for the good. In tribute to generally better hygiene, nutrition, and education in the population, diseases of filth, such as typhoid, were far less evident in the MGH of 1917, compared with that of 1912. There was also less enthusiasm for open-air treatment of pneumonia and less general therapeutic use of alcohol. But at the same time, he remarked, there was an increased inclination to *study* the patient and his or her disease. Shattuck expressed concern about overreliance on X rays (in, for example, cases of gastric ulcers among males, which were admitted to MGH more frequently in 1917 than 1912), and about the danger that the patient might be forgotten "in his disease." Medical records had become "so voluminous and minute that it was hard to see the wood by reason of the trees."[31] Here, then, was the "scientific" institution.

Influence of Wartime Practices at Home

In Europe the base hospitals gave thousands of physicians the opportunity to obtain a crash course in continuing education and to see the advantages of cooperative multispecialist groups. Colonel Richard C. Cabot of the Army Medical Department—the same Cabot who had started social services at the MGH—described the base hospital, in a speech in Paris, as ideal in its attainment of the best results, because all specialties were represented there, working without rivalry, without a spirit of gain, for noble ends. Influential leaders at home, including Arthur Dean Bevan, who was president of the AMA in 1919, and Dr. John Dodson, acting chairman of the AMA's Council on Medical Education, believed that the wartime patterns marked a new mode of delivery and that those who returned from war, having experienced the advantage of accurate scientific work in groups, would shift to multispecialist group practices, preferably hospital-based.[32] In the event, it was the technology and specialization that would stick, rather than new forms of organization.

Meanwhile, the draft revealed enormous deficiencies in the basic health of Americans. One-third of the applicants were rejected for physical reasons and an estimated 60 percent of these owed their impairments to ignorance or neglect. Not only had the great development in scientific medicine not led, evidently, to improvements in the general health, but the hospital as a central institution of this movement appeared to be irrelevant to social needs, and showed no sign of changing. A unanimous AHA resolution proposed the belated appointment of a war service committee for hospitals in 1917 and urged cooperation with the government in the care of sick and injured soldiers and sailors, as well as in the conservation of the "health of our people."[33] But the main purpose of this seems to have been to prod the military to make use of civilian hospitals rather than to establish their own separate system.

The immediate concern of most hospitals in the war was merely to keep going; there was little actual change in purpose or direction. The price of drugs quadrupled between 1914 and 1918 as the European war cut off drugs made abroad under German patents. New domestic sources of supply also had to be created for surgical needles, imported from England before the war but reassigned to U.S. sewing-machine and jewelry companies, and for thermometers and syringes, previously imported from Germany. For construction materials and furniture, hospitals competed with other industries for short supplies. Centralized supervision of medical supplies was provided through a national committee, consisting of leading hospital superintendents, and supplies continued to come through. Hospitals appeared to have listened to their leaders, who were, in turn, subject to the War Industries Board. All were exhorted not to hoard supplies and to purchase as little as possible in order to help the war effort.[34]

Although hospitals in the U.S. did not have the strategic importance of armaments, steel, or railroads to the wartime industrial machine, the war experience provided hospitals with a boost in national self-consciousness and solidarity. Hospital representatives could not yet speak with the national authority and unity of the medical profession, which was represented with ever-increasing effectiveness by the American Medical Association and the American College of Surgeons, but slowly a common purpose was beginning to be achieved among numerous, diverse hospital interests. In 1917 the American Hospital Association had over 1,300 members, of whom about a third were physician-superintendents. Roman Catholic hospitals now also had their own separate organization, the Catholic Hospital Association, established in 1915 as a response, in large part, to the standardization movement. (Catholic hospitals were usually run by members of religious orders with ultimate obedience to the bishops.) But hospital administration as a field continued to be dominated by the large university teaching hospitals, usually run by physicians—men such as Washburn (MGH), Winford Smith (Johns Hopkins), Warner (Lakeside), and Goldwater (Mount Sinai, New York).

Commissioned service for teaching-hospital superintendents and leading surgeons in the war strengthened the idea of hospital administration as a province for male physicians, while at the same time furthering the idea of hospitals as a national community of emerging interests. All of these movements strengthened the supremacy of the teaching hospital as a primary model for the postwar hospital. Meanwhile, across the country, hospital superintendents and trustees, calling on patriotism, urged their workers and volunteers to give the best work and longest hours they could.

Nursing as Patriotism Made Visible

Nurses, too, embraced the doctrines and ideology of wartime scientific medicine. Just as the war had a profound effect on the medical profession, it also altered the status of the nursing profession—but in rather a different way, because prewar nurses had excelled in areas which were conspicuous by their absence from the base hospitals. Nursing was fractionated into different domains: public health, private-duty nursing, and hospital work. Before the war public-health nursing was the elite area; nurses had been instrumental in the campaigns against tuberculosis and for infant welfare, and in other aspects of public health. In contrast, the war emphasized the supremacy and glamour of hospitals. In 1920, 70 to 80 percent of all graduate nurses worked in private duty, about half of these in patients' homes, and half on special assignment to private patients in hospitals.[35] Nursing education and the movement to professionalize nursing was also squarely centered on the hospitals; about half of all general hospitals reported nursing schools in 1920. Students in the schools, who staffed the hospital floors, were socialized into daily hospital work. Thus nurses, like physicians, were trained—and ready—to perform in an increasingly specialized, acute-care medical environment rather than to expand their interests in social medicine and public health.

The war created an immediate need for additional nurses to staff the military base hospitals. It also provided a unique, heroic, and deserved image for nursing as a symbol of patriotic fervor and of the spirit of national dedication and efficiency. The picture of a Red Cross nurse on a recruitment poster patriotically urged enrollment in the Red Cross Nursing Service, the reserve force for both army and navy. The *American Journal of Nursing* exhorted nursing educators to create in their pupils the "proper professional spirit" to do so; fifty percent of the graduates of the spring of 1918 could, it was thought, be spared for the service.[36] Florence Nightingale's wartime leadership (in the Crimea) was flourished as an example to nurses. Sacrifice and toughness were stressed: "Ours is not a profession for women who are looking for soft places in life and this is not a time when pampered girls are wanted in nursing. It is a field for a woman looking for an opportunity to give service and calls for self-denying character and strength."[37] The journal encouraged its readers by heartwarming personal vignettes of the decisions of individual nurses to join up and published long lists of the names of nurses assigned to the Army and Navy Nurse Corps and Reserve. Later it published lists of wounded nurses and those killed.

There were thought to be 79,000 registered nurses in the U.S. in May 1917, together with another 120,000 rendering some form of nursing care. By March 1918 the Red Cross had over 6,000 nurses already assigned to duty out of its total enrollment of over 18,000. In sixteen states 10 percent or more of the registered nurses had signed up for duty; in North Dakota the figure was 20 percent.[38] Their war record rings with heroism and personal sacrifice. Seven of the nursing alumni from MGH, for example, died in the war, including one woman, Mrs. Jaggard, who "left her home, husband and child" to serve at the front. The extent of service offered by nurses and the resulting gaps left in civilian hospitals can be illustrated in the experience of New York Hospital. In late 1917, 135 of the hospital's nurses were overseas, 222 more were working with the Red Cross and army nursing services in the United States, and 31 were waiting to be called to active duty.[39] Such hospitals were doubly hit by the influenza epidemic—when senior pupils were in charge of the wards.

Immediate national efforts were made to increase the supply of nurses. Annie Goodrich of Yale became dean of the Army School of Nursing, overseeing the general supply of nurses. Across the country regular classes were enlarged, extra training sessions added in the summer, and nonresident students were admitted to nursing schools, which had previously been strictly residential. There was deliberate encouragement of specialized training for nurses in fields such as contagious diseases, psychopathology, tuberculosis, pediatrics, and ophthalmology, in order to provide more room for pupils in the pipeline. College and high-school graduates were told that as nursing students they would automatically displace women of "lesser education and culture" and thus graduate in the shortest possible time.[40] After years of neglect of nursing by women's colleges, Vassar announced a preparatory course in nursing for college students as a contribution to national preparedness. Patriotic appeals for students were reinforced by publicity in magazines and newspapers across the country. As a result of all these efforts the number of nursing pupils increased by about 25 percent by the spring of 1918. Indeed, so successful was the campaign that after the war there was to be immediate concern about a nursing surplus and confusion about the future of nursing as a whole.

The weight of traditional roles proved a heavy burden to the nursing profession: angels and heroines at war, but confined by the iron discipline of hospital rules and social expectations. Even on the western front, nurses, who had no proper military rank, found themselves in an ambivalent position between officers and enlisted men, with no clear basis for authority, subject to misunderstanding and humiliation with respect to their rights and privileges. Nurses were open to harassment by doctors, orderlies (who would not take orders), and other officers and enlisted men. The smiling, baby-faced nurse did best, wrote one veteran, but a "strictly business woman" was "up against it"—and off duty "we were treated as kindergarten pupils."[41] Not until the spring of 1918, when the essential contribution of nurses in the base hospitals was obvious, was a bill introduced in Congress to grant nurses military rank, ranging from second lieutenant to captain. (The bill was attributed to the interest of Franklin Martin of the American College of Surgeons, who was also prominent in the Council on National Defense.) After vigorous lobbying, nurses finally achieved the rank of officer in June 1920, long after the war was over—the year women's suffrage was finally achieved.

By then the army nurses were back as civilians. Unlike their medical colleagues there were few new or exciting pathways open to them, as the country subsided into postwar recession, political conservatism, and traditional roles for women. Many ex–army nurses left nursing altogether, gravitating instead to other careers open to women, including business, secretarial work, social work, anesthetics, X-ray and laboratory technology, and dental hygiene, or into "matrimony and tea rooms."[42] Their exodus from the profession left a significant gap in nursing leadership in the 1920s and 1930s.

But the war experience also sanctified the nurse as a dedicated acolyte to hospital science. Leaders of those who remained in the profession were determined to upgrade nursing around high-quality hospital nursing schools, preferably based in universities. In these ways the nursing profession, like medicine, solidified the role of the acute, short-term "scientific" hospital as a central institution of the major health professions. Similarly, nursing, like medicine, caught up in the drama of surgery and other specialist fields, gave only a passing glance to issues of health insurance, social conditions, and public health services in the wartime period. Even when they had the opportunity—as in meetings of the American Hospital Association where nurse members were in the majority—nurses were noticeably silent and markedly absent from the power structures of the health-care system.[43]

The nursing profession might have shifted its sheer weight of numbers behind the parallel maternal and child health movement, which was spurred on by forceful women leaders of the Children's Bureau and buoyed up by the successful women's suffrage movement. Indeed, the suggested curricula for nursing schools continued to include the literature of feminism and social reform through the 1920s. However, by buying into prevailing notions of scientific medicine, nursing chose not to try for an independent role from that of doctors. The heroic wartime role of the nurse probably made this choice inevitable. The idealized nurse, dedicated and deferential, belonged with the physician specialist, in a hospital.

Military Men and Civilian Institutions

What, however, was to be the general hospital's future role at home? However excellent for the short-term treatment of thousands of accidents, and however necessary these services in war and peace, repair-shop care alone was a narrow and negative role for hospitals, at best. In some senses it was a reversion to the idea of the old almshouse hospital—sweeping up the physical misfits of society and recycling them back into the social system where possible. One speaker at the AHA annual meeting in 1917 described hospitals, in this vein, as human repair shops, without which the cities would be choked with human scrap heaps and the whole social fabric would deteriorate.[44] This was certainly their role on the western front. However, it was a critically flawed role without the underpinning of preventive and rehabilitation services.

Physicians in the well-run military medical services looked with despair at the mishmash of hospital services available in the United States and the lack of aftercare for wounded soldiers—the wartime equivalent of industrial-accident cases. Army policy was to avoid civilian hospitals wherever possible. The problem of controlling unruly soldiers allegedly required that they be kept under military discipline (although some patients were assigned to civilian hospitals; the navy paid a relatively generous reimbursement rate of $3 per patient day). U.S. Public Health Service hospitals were meanwhile overwhelmed by a bureaucratic anomaly. Men suffering from tuberculosis and other chronic conditions, who had been accepted by the draft board but who were found physically or mentally unfit when they reported to the camps, were eligible for care paid for by the military. Thus, curiously and inadvertently, the federal government found itself providing "socialized medicine" to a large body of recruits who were neither in nor out of the military.

There was an ostrichlike unwillingness by Congress, as well as by the hospital and medical associations and individual institutions at home in 1917–18, to consider the need for veterans' rehabilitation, including hospital services, after the "War to end all wars." Congress established a War Risk Insurance Program in legislation of 1917 and 1918, designed by nationally eminent, social-insurance experts. Under this program government agents toured the trenches, signing up American soldiers for life insurance. But although this program also provided guarantees of medical care, it was not clear what this would mean with respect to hospitalization.

Suddenly, more than 4 million U.S. servicemen became eligible for potentially long-term services, to take effect on the cessation of hostilities. This new influx of veterans would overwhelm in number the 785,000 veterans who were living in 1914, the majority of whom had seen service in the Spanish-American War. There was no possibility of fitting them into the preexisting military system. (The army, for example, operated only thirty general hospitals and eight embarkation hospitals in the U.S. by the armistice in 1918.) Should a major government service now be planned? If not, how would veterans be served? If so, what would be the reaction of civilian institutions?

The removal of 4 million young Americans from private medical practice would obviously be resisted by the major medical and hospital organizations. Not surprisingly, the AMA was to keep a careful watch on veteran services through the 1920s and 1930s. However, neither private practitioners nor hospitals came up with a promising alternative. As the experience of workmen's compensation clearly indicated, the civilian hospitals were not geared to deal with physical rehabilitation, nor were they interested in the two other primary medical needs of veterans, care of tuberculosis and psychoneurotic conditions, including shell shock. Indeed, the acute general hospitals usually specifically excluded such conditions.

Congressional hearings in 1918 expressed general confusion as to what kind of hospitals would be needed after the war, where they would be located, and who should decide on their location. Senators and congressmen began gearing up to push for the (pork barrel) construction of federal veterans' hospitals in their own districts. No firm action or decision about the postwar care of soldiers was taken before the signing of the armistice agreement in November 1918. Unproductive discussions, alternative measures, and a patchwork of services by the various federal agencies (army, navy, and U.S. Public Health Service) continued until 1920. In the event, the army's decision not to use civilian hospitals for the rehabilitation of soldiers—on grounds both of quality of care and military control over hospitalized soldiers—was to create a schism between services to civilians and services to veterans that continues, uneasily, to this day.[45]

A "Negative Instrument of Evolution"?

World War I confirmed that the United States was now one nation. It had become possible, in parallel, to think of its hospitals, even those originally set up by very different groups of immigrants, as one set of institutions, espousing a common set of principles, rather than as the local outcroppings of competitive, sometimes alien communities. Local elites on boards of trustees continued to represent business and religious interests, but the old ethnic, religious, and national identities of hospitals had blurred. The overtly chauvinist, antiforeign sentiment of the war and postwar period probably hastened the identification of hospitals as "all-American" institutions. At the same time, the social role and prestige of physicians, with the powerful associated images of surgery, nursing, and scientific medicine, created new sources of local community control, and with it institutional autonomy for hospitals as private doctors' workshops.

If there had been well-organized local public health services, including prevention, rehabilitation, and coordinated systems of specialists, most hospitals might have been confirmed as limited-function doctors' workshops, rather like the private nursing homes in England, where doctors could perform tonsillectomies and conduct deliveries free from broad considerations of public health. With the major exception of the large teaching hospital, American hospitals might have developed at the fringe rather than at the center of medical care. Instead, they concentrated with increased dedication on the acute care they did best. Where there were organized health services, as at Creston, Iowa, where a coalition of organizations in six rural counties built a system with public health nursing at its core, the hospital was indeed a "repair shop, necessary only where preventive medicine has failed."[46] But such a system was unusual. It was the ambivalence about the future organization of the *entire* health system that created such confusion in contemplating compulsory health insurance between 1915 and 1920.

The influenza epidemic emphasized that, lacking a well-organized health system, hospitals were necessarily frontline institutions—at home just as they were at war. Spanish influenza was first reported in the United States in March 1918, although its full implications awaited its virulent return in September of that year. The hospital at the army's Fort Devens, thirty miles west of Boston, reported over 1,100 flu admissions by September 1918. By the end of October 17,000 men, one-third of the camp, had had the flu and 787 were dead. The epidemic rapidly spread. Influenza and its associated pneumonia killed half a million Americans in 1918–19—and there were almost 22 million deaths worldwide.[47]

The epidemic struck health facilities and professions that were already weakened by war, but influenza also struck at the basic tenets of modern scientific medicine. Like AIDS today, the epidemic seemed a terrifying throwback to the great, unmanageable scourges of the nineteenth century like smallpox and cholera. Scientific medicine could do little for influenza except provide good nursing, control the body temperature, and "wait it out." Influenza temporarily jolted the public out of any complacency about medical progress or uncritical accolades to hospital-based medicine in somewhat the same way the *Titanic* disaster had jolted faith in technology six years before.

Across the United States, hospitals were besieged with influenza cases in the fall of 1918. The depleted nursing services came close to breakdown. Military-type authority was often necessary. In Philadelphia, for example, the local Council on National Defense divided the city into seven districts, assigned doctors to the districts, and set up an emergency flu hot line in Wanamaker's department store. At the height of the epidemic in September-October 1918, schools, theaters, churches, and other public places were ordered closed. Patients, overflowing from hard-pressed hospitals, were housed in armories, schools, and other buildings. Thus for a national emergency, organized health services were achieved. In San Francisco the city's San Francisco Hospital, a teaching hospital that was considered the best hospital in the state, and well known as a center for treating pneumonia, was filled beyond capacity with 1,100 patients, nearly all pneumonia cases. Mortality among respiratory cases admitted to the hospital was over 25 percent. When the epidemic passed its peak, this hospital, like others, was on the verge of collapse. More than three-quarters of the nurses had been ill with the flu.

One incidental result of the epidemic was that hospitals throughout the country opened their doors to infectious diseases, relying on good nursing practice and management techniques to contain infection within the institutions. Among its many other effects, the epidemic took attention away from concurrent debates about compulsory health insurance. In some cases the connection was direct. For example, by public order there was no audience to hear the testimony given at the California Health Insurance hearings in Sacramento in the fall of 1918. Those testifying wore the masks that were required by law during the epidemic, despite complaints from civil libertarians and from the police, who were concerned about the appearance and apprehension of masked criminals. In East St. Louis, meanwhile, the Illinois Health Commission canceled its hearings.

The epidemic also emphasized the entrenched place in American society—and the enormous success of door-to-door marketing strategies—of commercial life insurance, whose policies were suddenly collected by millions of families of flu victims. In a single day one company, Prudential, paid out $506,000 in claims, the largest total ever to be paid, until then, in a twenty-four-hour period.[48] Such payouts, however financially debilitating to the life insurance companies, gave them an unexpected political advantage in the ongoing debates about compulsory health insurance, which the companies generally opposed. These various scattered events, overlaid on a health system in collapse, aided the general disintegration of the movement for compulsory health insurance.

At the same time, the militarylike mobilization of social forces to combat influenza at the local level—a mobilization that was undoubtedly more readily achieved in wartime than in peace—emphasized that there was no communitywide organization of health services under normal operating conditions. The inevitable question was how far, as social institutions, hospitals should cooperate in larger health-care systems, parallel in efficiency to the base-hospital system with its multispecialist groups, hierarchical organization, and regional distribution network of first-aid and casualty clearing stations.

Calls for closer coordination of medical care rang through the medical

and hospital journals between 1916 and 1920. The organization of medicine seemed to be "inevitable"; high distinction in medicine, epitomized
in the university teaching hospitals, required organized rather than independent efforts; medical experiences in public health, medical research,
and industry stressed the value of organization; the decrease in infectious
diseases reduced the apparent demand for family doctors working independently, as did increased state and local government involvement in
managing tuberculosis and other infectious diseases through specialized
public health clinics; and wartime regulation and the general dependence
on "man-made groups" rather than on individuals, as the "vital entity" of
social organization, suggested cooperative endeavors at home.[49] One editorial in *Modern Hospital* in 1918 even suggested the formation of a voluntary federation of hospitals under government supervision, analogous to
voluntary federal banking regulation.[50] Would-be American reformers
pored over a British book, by Benjamin Moore, who recommended a
national hospital service with hospitals under state control. Moore justified
this as the only rational response to the demands and progress of modern
medicine. Voluntary hospitals, he wrote, were a "great national nuisance,"
signifying "puling sentimentality" and a "spurious air of decency" while
preventing public exposure of what was wrong in medicine.[51]

It was unclear in 1918 what forms of leverage were to produce these
cooperative changes—barring a quasi-military national structure for
health care in the United States or compulsory health-insurance systems
in the states. There seemed a lack of fair play in what the president of the
American Surgical Association called the "agitation for the legalizing of
socialized medicine," a German innovation, while the surgical heroes were
overseas fighting the Germans.[52] But in fact much of the debate over
cooperative medicine and health-care coordination in the wartime years
was abstract. The words had a rhetorical utility, useful for bonding diverse
interests, like the debates about "efficiency" which immediately preceded
them. Just as there was no single strategic meaning for efficiency, calls for
"cooperation" and "coordination" suggested change without inconve-
nience; allowing hospitals and physicians to do only what seemed—to
them—to be essential.

Apart from the lingering debates about compulsory health insurance,
three major hospital themes claimed the attention of the thousands of
physicians returning from war: organizing specialist practice; upgrading
the standards of hospital care around the ideals of scientific medicine; and
considering the appropriate place of the hospital within the full spectrum
of medical care—should the hospital be at the center or at the periphery
of medicine? The first issue was problematic. The second and third were

based on different assumptions about the hospital's utility, the one positive, the other negative. Standardization assumed that the major problem faced by hospitals was lack of identifiable services and procedures. These could be assured through inspection and upgrading, given the cooperation of individual institutions. However, the role of the hospital in the health-care system raised larger, much more difficult questions of hospital function and control. Attempts to place hospitals within organized health-care systems challenged the autonomy of the voluntary hospital as well as that of private practitioners.

Physicians and hospital trustees applauded hospitals as the center for advancing medicine between 1916 and 1920. But the fact that there were also negative views of the hospital needs to be stressed, for in the 1920s the acute general hospital rose to new heights of social respectability that were to make the acute model seem inevitable. An influential report for the Rockefeller Foundation, by Ernst Meyer, put the negative case nicely in 1919:

> The school is a positive and the hospital a negative instrument of evolution. The school serves for constructive development. The hospital serves to salvage certain by-products of development. It is for this reason that our ideal of life would be no hospitals and many schools.
>
> Every activity which reduces the need of providing hospitals serves a distinct constructive purpose, just as every activity in the operation of hospitals represents an effort on the loss side of evolution. Hospital service from this point of view partakes of much the same character as does refuse and sewage disposal.
>
> The hospital represents this negative feature of human service on that side of its work which involves the care of those who are already sick and who need the sort of care required by the bedfast. Only as its preventive features develop does it assume a position of positive rather than negative service. . . . In so far as the hospital is a building erected for the care of the bedfast sick, the question may be asked whether such a building is in all cases necessary?[53]

The question was rapidly becoming moot. Superintendents and clinicians of the base hospitals returned as heroes, bringing their experienced staff, their new knowledge, and their war stories back home with them, to rejuvenate teaching hospitals across the country—and to dominate the postwar hospital scene.

5

Hospitals in the 1920s: The Flowering of Consumerism

WORLD WAR I had demonstrated the efficiency of specialized medicine and the importance of hospitals. In the 1920s hospitalization became an accepted consumption good. The American hospital became a middle-class institution concentrating on three diagnoses with highly successful outcomes: obstetrical deliveries, appendectomies, and tonsillectomies and adenoidectomies. Standardization, too, shifted in focus—from a program primarily designed for organizational efficiency to one of consumer protection, public image, and building the hospital as a workshop for practitioners. Hospitals, offering their services to an increasingly receptive, consumer-oriented population, were stations for the diffusion of medical technique.

As power was transferred from the semimilitaristic federal authority of wartime government to private local interests, influential hospital administrators, like other leading Progressives, dropped their identification with the social-insurance movement, now tarred with allegations of bolshevism and socialism, and embraced the new rhetoric of "normalcy": conservative politics, self-help, consumerism, voluntarism, and decentralization of decisions to local communities. Shucking off its earlier identification with relatively small, segmented cultural groups, the American hospital became—and was to remain, at least until the early 1980s—an icon of American mass perceptions.

Constructing the Consumer Institution

The movement to standardize surgery was also a movement to hospitalize surgical and obstetric patients. In the early 1920s, in cities like Cleveland and San Francisco, two-thirds of the patients in nongovernmental general hospitals were surgical or obstetrical patients.[1] By the late 1920s four diagnoses provided 60 percent of all hospital admissions: tonsillectomies and adenoidectomies, deliveries and abortions, accidents, and appendicitis. Tonsillectomies and adenoidectomies represented well over a quarter of all admissions, bringing children to the hospital in droves, although their stay was comparatively brief (table 5.1).

TABLE 5.1

Admission to Hospitals, Excluding Mental and Tuberculosis Hospitals, by Major Diagnosis, as Reported in a Household Survey of 8,758 White Families, 1929–31

	Percentage of Hospital Admissions
Tonsillectomies and adenoidectomies	27.5
Deliveries and abortions	16.1
Accidents	9.0
Appendicitis	8.3
Digestive diseases	5.9
Pneumonia, tuberculosis, and other respiratory diseases	5.7
Female genital diseases and pregnancy complications	5.5
Degenerative diseases	5.4
Communicable diseases	3.1
Diseases of bones and joints and related conditions	2.5
Nervous diseases	.9
All other	9.9
Total	100.0

NOTE: Table adds up to 99.8 percent in original source, presumably due to rounding.
SOURCE: Selwyn D. Collins, "Frequency and Volume of Hospital Care for Special Diseases in Relation to All Illnesses Among 9,000 Families, Based on Nation-wide Periodic Canvasses, 1928–1931," *Public Health Reports* 57 (September 25, 1942), table 8, p. 1447.

The rapid growth of hospital obstetrics was largely a postwar phenomenon. Operative gynecology, including cesarian sections and hysterectomies, had been a central element in the rise of abdominal surgery, providing a model for intervention in normal deliveries. Medical students were taught about the advantages of the hospital over the home as a matter of safety and technique because every delivery was potentially pathological or dangerous.[2] Forceps deliveries and cesarian sections seemed as rational an intervention as the excision of tonsils for infected throats. Puerperal septicemia was a "wound infection"; and labor, complicated by a moderate degree of pelvic contraction, "quite as serious as a case of appendicitis."[3]

Obstetrics, like surgery, emphasized the hospital as a place where the individual temporarily relinquished responsibility to experts. The die was cast with the discovery and campaign for twilight sleep by upper- and middle-class women—a drug regimen (from Germany) that was popularized in the United States in 1914.[4] In offering childbirth without the memory of pain, twilight sleep promised to liberate women from the very fears of delivery that were fanned by hospital-based obstetricians. As a carefully controlled procedure in which mothers-to-be were heavily drugged, twilight sleep required hospital supervision. Thus drug treatment and surgery went together. By 1930 it was unusual for a woman in comfortable circumstances in a large city to be delivered at home, anywhere in the United States. Ward patients remained, on average, for two weeks after birth, and private patients might remain for three.[5]

Obstetrics provided hospitals, as modern consumer service centers, with an unrivaled product: the newborn baby. The image of uniformed nurses with babies (rather than mothers and babies) became a popular subject for hospital annual reports and publicity materials. There seemed almost a guarantee that in the modern hospital the best possible results would be achieved. There was, in short, a revolution in social expectations. With an average rate of hospital admission for all diagnoses of 6 percent a year, hospital care became an essential backdrop to the "good life" of America.

Surgery and obstetrics were the fields that paid doctors best and produced the most dramatic results and the most grateful patients: a child whose throat was no longer swollen from inflamed tonsils; an appendicitis victim brought back from expected death; a patient with a mended bone; a healthy mother with a new baby. Patients were happy to pay for the privilege. In San Francisco in 1922, for example, 77 percent of the patient days in voluntary hospitals were incurred by full-pay patients; another 14 percent were for patients who paid part of the bill, while only 9 percent were free.[6] This kind of distribution was possible for voluntary hospitals in cities which had major government hospitals to care for indigent patients. (In San Francisco one-quarter of all the individuals who were hospitalized were scooped up by the city hospital.) The greater the proportion of private patients, the more desirable voluntary-hospital care became as a consumer good, and the higher the social status of the hospital's patients.

Gone was the earlier association of hospital service with struggling immigrants—in voluntary hospitals at least. In Cleveland in 1920, for example, two-thirds of the adult patients in hospitals were American-born, a larger proportion than existed in the general population of the city; and two-thirds of these American patients paid at least something for their care. Table 5.2 shows both the obvious attractiveness to hospitals of American-born over foreign-born patients as a general class of prospective patients in that city—they were richer—and the continuing social stratification of all patients by income. Where you were treated—in which kind of hospital, in which kind of bed—affirmed your social status in the general population. If you were rich, hospitals made your stay as easy as possible, tempting you with special meals and allowing a generous supply of visitors. If you were poor, the experience could still be frightening or mystifying. In Cleveland no hospital made any regular provision for interpreters despite the many foreign-language speakers in the population, while the city hospital, with 785 beds, continued to serve the lowest classes, including large groups of tuberculosis, alcoholic, venereal disease, and contagious disease patients who did not appear in any other hospital in the city.

Paying patients were tempted in the 1920s with equipment such as incubators; with specialized medical services such as ophthalmology, neurology, orthopedics, and ear, nose, and throat surgery; and with specialized technical support services, including those given by nurse-anesthetists and X-ray and laboratory technicians. Large hospitals employed dietitians

TABLE 5.2

Adult Hospital Patients in Cleveland by Pay Status and Parentage, 1920

	Total		American-born		Foreign-born	
	Number	Percent	Number	Percent	Number	Percent
Pay	1,340	33.5	989	39.2	351	23.8
Part-pay	1,179	29.5	735	29.1	444	30.1
Free	1,364	34.1	733	29.1	631	42.8
Unknown	114	2.9	66	2.6	48	3.3
Total	3,997	100.0	2,523	100.0	1,474	100.0

SOURCE: *Cleveland Hospital and Health Survey* (Cleveland: Cleveland Hospital Council, 1920), pt. 10, *Hospitals and Dispensaries,* p. 851.

(products of the new domestic science colleges); physical reconstruction aides (physical therapists), who received training for the first time during World War I; and social workers. The hospitals provided special rooms for anesthesia, ultraviolet radiation, sunlamps and shortwave diathermy, diet kitchens, large laboratories, X-ray rooms, and hospital pharmacies. Hospital administrators strove for a bright, clean, and restful environment, decorated in creams and greens, and for attractive, hygienic food, like canned peaches; the food itself might be prepared in central kitchens, with steaming pressure-cookers and automated dishwashers. Radios and telephone completed the image of modern service and made hospital convalescence a real rest. The paying patient recuperated in the hospital rather than at home, surrounded by flowers and get-well cards, and able to press a call button for attendance.

As hospitals assimilated their image to the consumer-oriented society of the 1920s, they engaged in increasingly sophisticated marketing techniques, including offering lines of credit that enabled Americans to purchase surgical operations or supervised deliveries as easily as they purchased dishwashers, refrigerators, or automobiles. Announcement of the discovery of insulin (in Toronto) in 1922 provided powerful new evidence of the promise of research. A new rush of optimism about the possibilities of medical science rapidly replaced unhappy memories of the influenza epidemic; American medicine appeared to be rising in effectiveness as successfully and rapidly as American business.[7] Even the negative criticisms of hospitals by public-health advocates were turned to advantage by stressing the value of the very characteristics for which hospitals were berated: acute, dramatic, specialized inpatient care provided in luxurious, sometimes monumental buildings. A cartoon on the front of the monthly journal, *Hospital Management*, in October 1920, described hospital superintendents who emphasized public health as "putting the cart before the horse." Another (February 1920) exhorted hospital executives to relate to the community: "Advertise to them all."

Minneapolis General Hospital commissioned a public-relations movie in the early 1920s which is a good example of the exciting, "modern" images of the day; not for nothing were hospital-based dramas to become a staple of American entertainment. The film began with a telephone ringing urgently to summon an ambulance driver. The ambulance speeds off to pick up a child wounded in an automobile accident, then transports him to the hospital's receiving ward, where he is treated by a white-coated doctor and nurses. Scenes follow in an X-ray room and a laboratory, where workers are seen performing tests. After consultation between doctor and parents in a hallway, the scene shifts to the operating room, where a specialist operates; then to a children's ward, where the child is surrounded by nurses. These images of technique and efficiency are balanced by others conveying the ease of hospital life: movies of Charlie Chaplin and Mary Pickford shown to patients on Wednesdays in the hospital auditorium, and the hospital information desk issuing passes to visitors. Other images appear almost as an afterthought and do not fit the prevailing vision: pictures of a dental department, and at the end a curiously old-fashioned image of a social worker visiting a patient's home on a snowy day.[8] The main message of this movie, as in all of the numerous hospital public-relations campaigns of the 1920s, was to stress that the hospital was a safe, scientific, and friendly place.

The move to honor hospitals across the country through a National Hospital Day emphasized the centrality of the hospital to American culture and expectations. Indeed, the superintendent of Mercy Hospital in Chicago suggested a National Hospital Day pageant in 1921 that would have linked the hospital with another venerable American institution, the parade—led by "Florence Nightingale" as the lady with the lamp and including *inter alia* Uncle Sam, Columbia, sisters of religious orders, soldiers, Louis Pasteur, Lord Lister, nurses from each training school, and representations of the modern hospital, including X rays, laboratories, surgery, and an autoambulance.[9] National Hospital Day itself, May 12, the anniversary of Florence Nightingale's birth, was established in 1921 through the leadership of the journal *Hospital Management* in order to focus attention on the service and problems of local hospitals. It was endorsed not only by the American Hospital Association and other hospital groups, but also by successive U.S. presidents, governors, church leaders, and local elites; and it was instantly successful.

The day became, in a sense, a showplace for the hospital as a middle-class community institution, but an institution which was organized, nevertheless, for all classes, races, organizations, and religions. Hospitals held "open house" for the public, set up special displays in X-ray departments and laboratories, held "reunions" of babies born in the hospital, and sponsored essay contests for schoolchildren, radio programs, and lectures. Local stores displayed hospital exhibits in their windows, clubs were invited to lunch at the hospital to learn about the institution, and clergymen mentioned the hospital in their weekly sermons. By 1930 about 2,500 hospitals observed Hospital Day. This day and related activities organized by hospitals throughout the year enabled administrators and boards to educate their communities about the rising costs and values of hospitals, and to celebrate both consumer service and voluntary effort. By making the day a gala event, the hospitals' success was also signaled. In the idealized experience the visitor toured the hospital, admired the marvels and costs of X-ray and operating rooms and the efficiency of the institution, from its records room to its business office and patient-identification systems, and was relieved of any lingering fear of hospitals, including those caused by several sensational articles in the press about "baby mix-ups." At the end of the tour the visitor would be guided to an attractive reception room where music wafted in from an orchestra (provided as a therapeutic benefit to patients) and where the wife of the chairman of the board of trustees and the superintendent of nurses presided over a "charming tea table."[10] What could be more delightful and uplifting than this?

The volume of hospital care was impressive, even in the early 1920s; it was to become more so under a rush of construction throughout the decade. Patients spent over 53 million days in general hospitals in 1922, the equivalent of one day for every two members of the population.[11] Year by year a larger proportion of the population had some connection with the hospital as a patient. Hospital construction boomed in the 1920s, buoyed up by successful hospital fund-raising efforts and by an increasing number of bequests. Between 1925 and 1929, $890 million was spent on the construction of hospitals and related institutions, almost 80 percent more than was spent between 1921 and 1924. When prices are held constant, the real value of hospital construction in the late 1920s was not to be reached again until the 1950s. Total capital investment in hospitals was estimated at over $3 billion by 1930, including $2 billion in general hospitals. This investment made hospitals one of the largest enterprises in the United States, outstripped only by the iron and steel industry, the textile industry, the chemical industry, and the food industry. In 1930 a single hospital in a major city could represent a capital investment of $10 million and employ a permanent work force of 1,500 professional, skilled, and unskilled workers.[12] In many smaller towns and cities the hospital was the largest employer in terms of monthly payroll. The more successful hospitals were, the more they appealed to paying patients.

In turn, the huge infusion of construction funds allowed hospitals to rebuild and/or redesign their internal arrangements. Particular attention was paid to two areas: shifting from large wards to small inpatient rooms; and establishing new diagnostic facilities, labor and delivery rooms, and other technical spaces. Privacy was the new commodity, the American's due. Ward beds represented only 7 percent of the total beds designed for American hospitals in 1928; in contrast, 21 percent of the new beds were in small wards, 23 percent in semiprivate rooms, and 48 percent in single rooms.[13]

Small rooms were a direct response to the marketing of hospital care to the working- and middle-class populations. The successful hospital could respond to cases such as Mrs. X, a sensitive, nervous stenographer, who was described in a national magazine as being filled with dread about lying next to someone brought back from the operating room, "perhaps dead."[14] But upwardly mobile citizens, seeking income and status in America's melting pot, also wanted the best amenities they could pay for. They had little desire to be treated as one of the "bread line" or to be thrown in with people of different economic, occupational, and racial groups, with whom the middle-class patient would "scarcely ever associate in his daily life."[15] Consumerism thus enhanced the preexisting patterns of social stratification of patients by income. There was little of positive value in the wards to attract patients who could pay, even in the newest buildings: little privacy; restricted time for visitors; lack of choice of physician; attendance by student nurses even where graduates were available elsewhere in the hospital; and a general awareness that ward patients were second-class citizens, whether or not they contributed to the costs of their care.

Hospitals could, of course, have changed the rules and made the wards more attractive to paying patients. Father Edward F. Garesche, a Jesuit priest, argued forcefully that hospitals allowed, perhaps even encouraged, patients to be extravagant beyond their means. People who demanded an expensive room, he wrote, ought to be told that in the ward they would have company, friendliness, and quick attention; and he depicted hospitals as hard, grasping institutions which charged the poor too much for services.[16] But the class structure of the hospital was ingrained. Hospitals, doctors, and patients all contributed to the consumer ethos.

As a result, the large hospital was like a multiclass hotel or ship, offering different facilities for different prices. The grade of semiprivate patients, tucked in between private patients and the wards, seemed the logical development of a new "cabin class" between "first class" and "steerage." There was a vast social gulf between the top and the bottom of the social structure, with the white-collar worker in the middle. A telling image was drawn from the dairy: "If we could visualize the four divisions of the social strata as cream, milk, skimmed milk, and water, we could designate the private patient as the 'cream,' the semi-private patient as the 'milk,' and the pauper or indigent patient as the 'water,' " wrote a hospital administrator. Together, he continued, the cream and the milk "furnish figuratively the actual sustenance of the average physician."[17] All hospitals wanted a good dollop of the cream. The successful hospital, attuned to the marketplace, hewed to powerful American themes: the symbolic value of money in attesting social position, even among the sick; the assumption that individuals should get what they pay for, by way of services and professional courtesy; contempt for, and fear of, the poor; and abhorrence and isolation of minority populations.

The general shift to private or two-to-four-bed rooms (at least outside the largest city-owned hospitals) also belittled the idea of the ward—and perhaps also of the patient—as the hospital's organizational and symbolic center, that is, as the reason for the hospital's existence. The focus now was on equipment. While the old ward was a bustling center of attention, where something was always going on, the private or semiprivate room was peripheral to more dramatic events happening elsewhere: the appendectomy in the operating suite, the birth in the delivery room, the baby in the newborn nursery. Patients were wheeled from their rooms to treatment centers: physical therapy, diagnostic and therapeutic X ray. Coffee shops, surgical anterooms, and dayrooms added to the architectural and organizational complexity.

Administrators, doctors, and board members took pride in the new, technological, consumer-oriented institution. It was estimated in the early 1930s that in a compactly built American hospital only a fifth of the entire floor space was devoted to accommodations for patients, a much lower proportion than in hospitals in Europe. Construction costs for hospitals in the United States were three times those of Germany. The superintendent of Beth Israel Hospital in New York, visiting Europe in the late 1920s, encapsulated the American enthusiasm for equipment, privacy, and expense. One of the most striking features of London hospitals, he reported, was their "appalling poverty"; Beth Israel Hospital had, in contrast, just erected a new seventeen-story building.[18]

The shifts also had lasting implications for medical and nursing roles in hospitals. As the pattern of small rooms was extended, working-class patients found it difficult to meet the additional costs of private-duty nurses, for whom private patients traditionally paid a special fee; and hospitals responded by extending their regular nursing service to provide better care for patients in the smaller units, through the growing employment of graduate nurses. However, it was more difficult to supervise nurses when patients were scattered over small rooms, rather than concentrated in large wards. In a system of small rooms, too, the medical specialist might find his or her patients scattered across the hospital, rather than concentrated in one area.[19] There was thus less chance for the physician to forge a close allegiance with the nursing staff of one unit, where all of his or her patients would be treated, and little incentive to feel any innate responsibility for hospital service as a whole. In all of these respects, hospital consumerism thus served, oddly, to enhance the depersonalization of hospital care.

Standardization Is Achieved—Within Limits

The American College of Surgeons began inspecting hospitals in 1918. The standardization system was well designed for three purposes in the consumer environment of the 1920s: to certify the hospital as a well-equipped local surgical and obstetrical center; to enlarge the authority of doctors in hospitals, by assuming that the hospital was a doctors' workshop and by providing an acceptable enabling mechanism to make it so—the organization of medical staff; and to prod the medical staff in local hospitals to police avaricious and inappropriate behavior by the hospitals' surgeons. This was to be done by having pathologists check unnecessary surgery through analysis of tissue removed at operation, and by checking unethical behavior (notably fee-splitting) through the force of peer (physician) pressure. Surgery, wrote a journalist in *Harper's Monthly Magazine* in 1924, "must be sterilized morally," through effective medical-staff conferences, if patients were to feel safe; the ACS was cutting the "greed glands" out of surgery.[20]

Gone now was the prewar, producer-dominated focus on scientific management as the basis for hospital reform. The ACS presented itself in the 1920s as a private organization engaged in establishing voluntary standards for hospitals in the interests of patients. Certification under the standardization plan was conveniently analogous to a "Good Housekeeping Seal of Approval," another voluntary program for producers and consumers that was developed in the 1920s.[21] The program's major scientific success lay in focusing surgery on pathological findings, thus emphasizing both the place of the laboratory in hospitals and accuracy in diagnosis, even in small community institutions.

The ACS implemented the standardization program through trial and error. Standardization could not be imposed on any hospital; and local physicians could be touchy. ACS inspectors criticized doctors in parts of the West, in particular, as self-centered, dogmatic, egotistic, and intolerant of criticism, and as being uninterested in medical records, pathology, radiology, and staff meetings. Less than one-seventh of the first group of hospitals of over 100 beds, reviewed in 1918, could meet the standards, even though these were designed to be minimal. The primary weaknesses lay in hospital organization and lack of good case records, but one-third of the hospitals had inadequate pathology and X-ray departments.[22] Hospitals of fewer than 100 beds were not included until 1922 because of the even greater difficulty for smaller hospitals in equipping and staffing these departments—as well as other problems, ranging from lack of interest to outright hostility. The ACS had a "selling" job to do.

John Bowman, the ACS's director, traveled all over the country between 1918 and 1920, speaking to surgical and hospital groups about standardization. He presented the program as one designed to bring a sense of responsibility to hospitals so that they might seek the goodwill and support of their communities and thus, in turn, attract private patients and community donations. But even appealing to enlightened self-interest, his message ruffled feathers at the local level, where any form of outside intervention was suspect. Community standards were assumed to be a local responsibility, not a matter for national pacesetters.

At the national level, too, the American Medical Association began to look askance at the growing authority of the College of Surgeons.[23] Nevertheless, the ACS was gaining support from powerful constituencies. The most salient pressure in favor of standardization was growing recognition of the mutual interests of doctors and hospitals at both the local and national levels. Particularly important was the support of the Catholic Hospital Association, whose organizer, Father Moulinier, was a regent of the Marquette School of Medicine. Roman Catholic leaders were concerned that their hospitals, which were mostly small community institutions, were falling significantly behind the prevailing standards of medical education and scientific medicine, and were in danger of becoming second-class institutions.[24] In turn, Father Moulinier's presence on the ACS standardization committee and his role as an active hospital inspector provided a useful safeguard for Catholic hospitals against any strong external control.

Success was assured in May 1920, when the Carnegie Foundation gave the American College of Surgeons a five-year matching grant of $25,000 a year: strong affirmation of the medical model of standardization—and of leadership by the surgeons. This money enabled the ACS to implement the program on a more intensive basis, becoming the most important medical organization in hospital regulation. The ACS bore sole responsibility for hospital accreditation until 1951–52, when the program was turned over to the Joint Commission on Accreditation of Hospitals (now the Joint Commission on Accreditation of Health Care Organizations).

A congratulatory article in the magazine *World's Work* in June 1920 set the tone for the decade. Standardization was the "ideals of the profession visualized," a basis for ferment in the development of hospitals across the country, involving the "best men" in the surgical field.[25] Community hospitals hung their certificates in visible positions and announced their success through local newspapers. The ACS stressed its commitment to protection of the public, to the values of community, and to local coopera- tion. The standards were designed to safeguard patients against errors in diagnosis, "lax or lazy treatment," surgical commercialism, unnecessary operations, and operations by unskilled surgeons. In addition, standardiza- tion educated the layman about the functions of the hospital and provided for the surgeons a "subtle strengthening of esprit de corps."[26]

Appointment of Dr. Malcolm MacEachern, superintendent of Van- couver General Hospital, to replace John Bowman as director of the ACS's standardization program in 1921, speeded its success and solidified the college's position as a major force in hospital affairs. MacEachern, a power- ful figure in hospital administration (and later, author of its major text), remained at the college for twenty-eight years. By 1929 over 90 percent of the largest hospitals were approved and smaller hospitals were coming into line. The AMA also pushed for the establishment of X-ray and pathol- ogy departments, compiling in 1926 a list of approved clinical laboratories and in 1928 one of X-ray departments.[27] All of these standards affirmed the place of the small, independent hospital as a base for the local practice of medicine by a responsible profession. One of the major attractions of standardization was acceptance for approval of small hospitals of 25 to 50 beds—a base for doctors in small towns and rural areas.

Standardization also supported the model of open-staff hospital orga- nization in the 1920s, at the very time practitioners were clamoring for hospital connections. Open-staffs were to be made "scientific" or "effi- cient" through being "organized" according to ACS rules and expectations. Medical-staff organization meant the formal association of the private practitioners who used a particular hospital into a self-administering vot- ing unit, rather like a private club, with a president and other officers, bylaws, staff meetings, and committees, all adhering to formally agreed regulations about hospital practice and physician behavior. Through the rules and regulations of the medical staff, all physicians who wanted to use the hospital could be required to attend organizational and educational sessions of the staff, to discuss cases, and to complete proper patient records. Thus basic medical standards could be attained (in theory, at least) without limiting the hospital medical staff to an elite group of practitioners in a given area.

Eventually, admittance to the medical staff would be made through formal credentials committees of the staff, whose decisions about "hospital privileges" could be tailored to an individual's special training and to specialized departments—so that the doctor without surgical training would no longer have unlimited access to operating rooms. In these ways standardization upgraded the average level of surgery while also strengthening the autonomy of doctors in their dealings with administrators and trustees.

Through its standardization program the ACS also provided surgeons, administrators, and trustees with a forum for debate on hospital issues. It was at ACS meetings, rather than those of the American Hospital Association or the AMA, that critical management questions were raised in the 1920s. What, for example, were the pros and cons of employing X-ray technicians rather than having nurses or doctors take X rays? Were males or females to be favored in these roles? (Boston City Hospital, for example, preferred males, even though they were allegedly less amenable to discipline than females.) How could a hospital design a physical therapy department as a money-making proposition? ("With variety and equipment" was the answer—such as that in Grace Hospital, New Haven, which offered hydrotherapy, massage, an infrared-ray room, a "bake" room, and a gymnasium.)[28] These kinds of questions engaged a growing network of administrators in the 1920s.

But the ACS's program was not without its difficulties. The relative youth and inexperience of the hospital inspectors, who had been deliberately chosen from among recent (better-trained) medical graduates, raised the hackles of older practitioners—one can easily imagine the local confrontations. Within the ACS there were complaints that the minimum standards were too low; they had been pitched at a level most hospitals might attain. And there was no consensus about an extended or future role for standards in national hospital regulation. At the ACS's meetings in 1924, for example, the president, Dr. Albert J. Ochsner, recommended—unsuccessfully—that the ACS launch an attack on waste in hospital operations, including nursing practice, operating rooms, food service, and pharmaceuticals. Another brave speaker called for standardization of members of boards of trustees, presumably through trustee selection, specified responsibilities, and trustee education.[29] In the event, Progressive expectations of standardization as a force for general hospital reform gave way to the primary goal of upgrading local practice standards and hospital facilities, while not going beyond what practitioners would accept.

In other ways, too, Progressive ideals of expertise and planning based on high academic standards and organizational efficiency gave way to the democratization—and the politicization—of the medical profession around the idea of the patient as a consumer of private practice in a local marketplace. The AMA's policy was similar to that of the surgeons. It, too, supported hospitals as local, medically democratic institutions (with open staffs), which were professional centers (workshops) for private practitioners.

Arthur Dean Bevan had announced in 1918 that the AMA Council on Medical Education would broaden its role to include hospital standardization beyond the certification of internships, although the success of the ACS left this option hanging. In the event, the council published formal standards or "essentials" for internships in 1919, and staked its claim by changing its name to the Council on Medical Education *and Hospitals* in 1920. The council also started its own program of hospital registration, which was much broader than the ACS's program. By 1930 the AMA reported over 6,700 registered hospitals, sanatoria, and related institutions of all kinds, of which fewer than 3,000 were certified by the ACS.[30] The difference in numbers partly signified the inclusion by the AMA of the smallest hospitals.

Publication of detailed hospital statistics, published annually in the AMA *Journal* from 1921, provided an invaluable data base for hospitals and physicians while underlining the AMA's own interests. The Council on Medical Education and Hospitals also began to investigate hospitals offering specialized residencies in 1924, publishing its first list of residencies in 1927, and the first "essentials" in 1928. In so doing, the AMA challenged the educational monopoly of the medical schools by backing the development of residency training programs for specialties in hospitals which were unaffiliated with medical schools. By 1930 there were over three hundred hospitals on the approved residency list, offering more than two thousand positions.

Nevertheless, throughout the decade the AMA Council on Medical Education and Hospitals struggled to define its own vision and authority in hospital affairs. Should the council be described as primarily interested in the hospital as an educational environment while the College of Surgeons was primarily interested in patients? This distinction was obviously not satisfactory to the AMA's wish to serve all local doctors; and it was their associations at the county level which were the constituents of the state associations, which formed in turn the federated structure of the

AMA. Regular telephone calls between staff of the council, the college, and, by the end of the 1920s, the American Hospital Association, helped to smooth out interorganizational difficulties. But the field of hospital oversight was fraught with politics, as each organization jostled for position.[31]

Outside of medical education the AMA's chief impact on the emerging hospital system in the 1920s lay in its policies for local autonomy and hospital distribution. Despite an apparent abundance of beds nationwide, over half of all U.S. counties had no hospital of any kind, a major concern to physicians and their patients in these areas. Throughout the 1920s the AMA reverberated with the anxiety and unrest of rural general practitioners, who were under the simultaneous pressure of overwork, lack of prestige, lack of access to new technology, and the loss of paying patients to hospitals and specialists in the cities. For these practitioners, hospital provision seemed essential. AMA policy was simply that every doctor should have a hospital within his or her local territory. The more hospitals there were, the more chance the individual practitioner had of an appointment in at least one institution. The smaller the hospital, too, the greater the possibility of physician control, the less chance of a strong superintendent, and the less bureaucratic interference. Spreading hospital services conveniently over the whole country, it was thought, would also encourage doctors to practice in country areas, enhancing the distribution of physicians, as well as hospitals, across the whole population.

The AMA and its constituent societies, like other contemporary advocates of rural community development, were thus more interested in the number of *hospitals* than in the overall supply of *beds* (which could be provided, alternatively, in a few large regional institutions). They were also committed to decentralized rather than regional control of hospital service. It was not surprising, then, that alternative proposals for regional medical networks had a lukewarm or chilly reception. For example, a 1924 report for the General Education Board, a Rockefeller philanthropy, recommended organized health-care systems radiating out into the country from local market towns. Similar notions of an organized health-service system, based on specified norms of need and demand for care, were also developed by the university-sponsored Commission on Medical Education, organized by the Association of American Medical Colleges in 1925.[32] Such schemes were practicable, for by the mid-1920s telephones and automobiles were commonplace, even in rural areas. Town-based physicians and district nurses could provide services in patients' homes across a wide rural district, with buses, automobiles, and ambulances to transport patients to a town-based, regional hospital when necessary. Under such a system, however, relatively few hospitals would be needed. Unfortunately for the planners, both doctors and.small towns which did have tiny hospitals wanted to hang on to them—and not be dictated to by "foreigners" or "townies."

But for almost everyone there was the implicit assumption that medicine should be hospital-based. This dogma was already so well entrenched that it was rarely questioned whether medical care should necessarily be centered on a hospital. British feelings about more or less similar problems, for example, saw the answers in voluntary or municipal community care. In the United States, hospitals and medicine were mutually dependent. Thus while hospitals were standardized as recognizable facilities with medical records, pathology labs, X-ray facilities, and an organized staff of physicians, the hospitals were also being standardized (or legitimized) by the national policies of major medical associations, as autonomous local units that were central to the practice of American medicine.

The values of the marketplace, though clearly evident in hospitals in the 1920s, were thus tempered in two ways: first, by the interest of the medical profession in independent hospitals and by their special position as the real "consumers" of hospital care (since without doctors admitting them, there would be no private patients); and second, by the values ascribed to hospitals as social instruments of their communities. In many other spheres of consumer service in the 1920s construction and expansion transformed and consolidated businesses into new patterns and organizational shapes: networks of gas stations, radio networks, regional electric grids, chains of shopping centers and national marketing and distribution systems for consumer goods. For hospitals, entrenched in local power structures, imbued with ideals of local service and serving as workshops for local physicians, power was diffused and interests disaggregated among more than 4,000 autonomous institutions.

Consumers and Communities

The term "community hospital," in increasing use in the 1920s, carried general connotations of community betterment and social action. These were drawn, in turn, from contemporary social surveys and well-publicized studies of how communities worked and how they should be planned; from increased concerns about the quality of rural life and rural health, as Americans flocked to towns and cities; and from the emotive idea of community enterprise as an American tradition, mythologized from the frontier, as the older ties of ethnicity, language, social class, and religion were eroded. Voluntary organization assumed, in President Hoover's phrase, that "probity and devotion in service which no government can ever attain."[33] These values came together in the rural hospital movement.

Widespread concern about the prevalence of sickness and the importance of community medicine in agricultural areas after World War I made the rural hospital a natural center for rural public health and community development—and an important community organization in its own right, rather like the 4H Club. "Growing the Hospital from the Hearts of People" was the way a Rockefeller Foundation spokesman put it.[34] In the absence of an organized health-care system, with good transportation to local centers, there was a strong case for reinventing the small rural hospital. Well-equipped local hospitals were useful in emergency cases of typhoid, acute rheumatism, and pneumonia, as well as for appendicitis and maternity care. They reduced the burden of sickness on the family by transferring responsibility to known professionals and allowed the patient to be cared for near to home, avoiding the cost and the anxiety of travel to a distant city along snow-clogged, waterlogged, or muddy roads. Hospitals brought the use of X rays, pathology, and other modern techniques to rural America, distributing the country's technological wealth.

Unfortunately, though, many of the small rural hospitals for paying patients were tiny, inadequate proprietary facilities. Individually owned hospitals represented more than 30 percent of all hospitals in the Pacific, West South Central, and West North Central regions in 1922. Even in the mid-Atlantic states, where a much stronger voluntary tradition prevailed, 11 percent of all reported hospitals were individually owned. As physicians, like other members of the population, chose more and more to live in cities, rural hospitals threatened to disappear altogether, like the little red schoolhouse. Unless immediate action was taken to retain them—and to provide for their upgrading—rural communities might lose both hospitals and doctors; and new doctors would be hard to attract, for they wanted hospital affiliations.

Three examples of new rural hospitals in the early 1920s illustrate the idealized elements of community effort; technology was to be brought to the rural community by dint of the hard work and initiative of its citizens. These hospitals were listed, with others, in a U.S. Department of Agriculture publication in 1926, designed to stimulate imitations. "If hospitals are good for city people, why not for country people?" the report began.[35]

Each of the examples was described as springing, spontaneously, from an outpouring of practical community concern and each, by implication, praised the innovation of rural communities and the strength of rural life. In Washington County, Iowa, an area of over 500 square miles, a scattered rural population voted to authorize its county government to build a splendid modern hospital, complete with terrazzo floors, telephone and electric fan connections, indirect lighting, and an electric call system. The hospital offered X rays, a sunlamp, high-frequency equipment, a sterilizer, and a laboratory that was a branch of the state system. Operating costs were covered primarily by patient fees.

In Hutchinson, Minnesota, a town of only 3,300 people, a hospital was funded by selling stocks at $10 per share. The hospital organizers solicited gifts from individuals to pay off its debts and received special help from the Up and Doing Club of farm women, together with gifts of canned fruit and vegetables. In Addison, Michigan, the farm community advertised for a doctor in a national journal and raised $1,700 toward the cost of a small hospital. The new doctor put forward the majority of the money. He was also able, of course, to charge fees. All of these hospitals were locally sponsored, designed to appeal to paying patients while also representing community cohesion. The most vivid example was Hutchinson. Impressive opening ceremonies were held for the new hospital in 1922, attended by the governor of Minnesota, Dr. William Mayo, and Flying Earth, a trained nurse in a Minneapolis hospital. Flying Earth was there to express regret for the action of her grandfather, the Indian leader Little Crow, in burning down the earlier settlement in the 1860s. The hospital was, she said, a place "to heal all wounds."[36]

These examples, and others like them, show the importance of locally raised capital as a defining force for hospital ownership in the United States. Pragmatism in money-raising resulted in some of the new hospitals of the 1920s being county-owned, town-owned, or organized under special tax districts, some voluntary not-for-profit, some owned and operated by physicians, and some proprietary corporations. Irrespective of ownership, the community hospital assumed and symbolized community allegiance; hospitals continued to attest, in the 1920s as in earlier years, to the wider values of community success. It followed that the hospital which was built by local fund drives and community contributions was viewed as a community endeavor in spirit, even if it sold all of its services to paying patients.

Consumerism did not, in effect, mean the formal growth of hospitals as businesses or the rejection of "community" as a primary theme. Less than a sixth of all general hospital beds were in profit-making hospitals in

1929. For-profit hospitals were irrelevant to the balance of power among city hospitals anywhere in the country. More than half the general hospital beds were in private nonprofit hospitals, almost equally divided between independent and church-affiliated institutions, while the remainder were in government hospitals.[37] The hospitals, organizing into new state hospital associations in the 1920s, were well aware of the importance of the community image, if only to sustain donations and fees.

At the same time, hospitals were visible expressions of broad, non-monetary, community expectations about social virtue and moral worth, to be set against the crass materialism of business. The essential nature of any profession (and its institutions), it was claimed, was to be "socially victorious over selfish interest."[38] By defining professional altruism and commercialism as in direct contradiction, the professions elevated their status above that of trades—and encouraged clients' trust. In widely read works, including R. H. Tawney's *The Acquisitive Society,* organizations were also seen to have an important character and ethos of their own, embodying larger social values and community aspirations.[39] Voluntarism itself was an inherently conservative tradition, with a strong mythological or folk element.

The "real hospital," the editors of the *Modern Hospital Yearbook* wrote in 1919, is "an idea." This idea excluded bickerings and unworthy aims, provided the energy to drive the nation forward for the "betterment of the human race," demanded an uplifting "vision of service," and encouraged a cooperative community spirit. "To work, to fight, to die if need be to make the vision come true—that is the hospital idea," wrote the editors.[40] Dr. Ray Lyman Wilbur, who became chairman of a new, distinguished Committee on the Costs of Medical Care in 1927, expressed a related sentiment: "The quality of medical care is an index of a civilization."[41]

This idealized, even mythic social role gave the hospital an identity different from that of a commercial enterprise, even though its services and facilities were expanding rapidly in a mass culture of middle-class consumers. At the heart of public and private policy-making for hospitals in the 1920s (and later) was the overriding belief that hospitals were "good." The community hospital was assumed to be both a center for medical technique and a responsible and able social institution.

The goodwill—indeed the good *feelings*—associated with hospitals sustained voluntary hospitals through renewed legal tests of tort liability and tax exemption in the 1920s and 1930s, as these larger values were codified, strengthened, and interpreted in the courts. (Indeed, the body of legal materials affecting hospitals was large enough to fill a 540-page book on hospital law in the 1920s.)[42] Exemption from liability for injury to patients in charitable hospitals is a striking case in point. Only in the case of a profit-making hospital was the public told, for example, about the negligence of a student nurse (in Oklahoma) who had allowed a patient with pneumonia to lie in a wet bed under a leaking roof for two hours; or of the (North Dakota) patient burned by a hot-water bottle; or the (Mississippi) child with appendicitis who, unattended, fell out of bed; or the (Indiana) surgeon who left a piece of gauze in a patient's sinus. Despite consumerism, then, the old notions of charity, embodied in hospitals, were cherished as a positive social good. Voluntary hospitals acquired the mystique and the silence of professionalism—and the unspoken assumption that their service was better than either governmental or profit-making hospitals. The combined imagery of community, professionalism, and voluntarism—patriotic, vague, and flexible—would serve them well in the years ahead.

Major national philanthropic foundations also supported the establishment of hospitals as intrinsic elements of their communities, particularly in rural areas. The most sustained practical effort of this kind in the 1920s was in the Carolinas, through the Duke Endowment (established in 1924), a private philanthropy funded from a tobacco fortune. The foundation's hospital section, under health reformer Dr. Watson Rankin, encouraged the establishment of nonprofit community hospitals in North and South Carolina. By 1939 only 12 percent of the general hospital beds in the Carolinas were in proprietary institutions, compared with 51 percent (of a much smaller bed supply) in 1925.[43]

A second program was developed by the Commonwealth Fund, a Harkness philanthropy based in New York. The Commonwealth Fund backed into its hospital program when it discovered that its child health demonstration in Rutherford County, Tennessee, in the early 1920s, was hampered by a "retarded" medical environment and a declining number of physicians in the area. Although fund executives said that they harbored no delusion that the building of a hospital would "convert any given area into a paradise of health,"[44] a hospital seemed a necessary base for organized health care in the area. The Rutherford Hospital opened in 1927; its major service to inpatients was surgery, with maternity care coming second. However, from the beginning the hospital was designed as a community center for prevention and health education, coordinating its services with the new county health department. By the end of 1930 the fund had created three other rural hospitals along similar lines in Virginia, Maine, and Kentucky, and two others were on the way. Among other things, doctors were required to admit all patients, regardless of income.

Despite some physician resistance, this program, like the Duke program, was an acknowledged success. The Duke Endowment virtually took over responsibility for the hospitalized poor in the Carolinas, using its financial clout to improve hospital care (in segregated services) for blacks and whites of all incomes. Both programs attracted young, well-trained physicians, built up-to-date clinical facilities, and provided guidelines for development. Both foundations fulfilled functions that might elsewhere— or later—have been performed by government. But both programs were limited in geographical scope.

Nevertheless, a national policy, of sorts, existed for hospital distribution in the 1920s, agreed to by the professional associations and foundations, and supported by government and the courts. The policy was that small-town and rural hospitals should be maintained—indeed, that they should be strengthened. Both the ACS's standardization program and AMA efforts took this policy as a given, confirming the hospitals as doctors' workshops. The philanthropies and the Department of Agriculture encouraged hospitals as elements of community development and public health. Both sets of policies presented small-town hospitals as ideal American institutions—institutions which simultaneously demonstrated community initiative, professional altruism, and diffusion of medical technology to consumers (paying patients) throughout the population.

As policy, the emphasis on independent local hospitals, rather than on hospital networks or regional systems, was successful. Despite a steady shift in population and of doctors from rural to urban areas in the 1920s, the proportion of counties without hospitals diminished from over 50 percent to 40 percent by 1930. The hospital was affirmed as a local institution.

The Public Power of Private Interests

Throughout the 1920s government agencies and the courts supported hospital policy-making through private organizations as a matter of course. Support came in two main guises: providing hospitals with practical support, ranging from encouragement by the Department of Agriculture through the continuance of tax payments for the indigent, tax exemption, and exemption from tort liability; and establishing new services under government auspices in spheres in which existing hospitals were uninter-

ested, notably services for psychiatric and long-term illness and for dis-
ability. The most striking instance of the latter was service to veterans of
World War I, whose conditions did not fit the model of the successful,
surgically-oriented, consumer institution.

No general hospital worth its salt—standardized or unstandardized—
wanted to treat the long-term conditions presented by the majority of
veterans. The prospect of halls filled with swearing men carrying sputum
cups, shell-shocked patients in pajamas and cigarette-smoking paraplegics,
challenged the image of a refined, controlled, and homelike "community"
institution being projected by the general hospitals in their wooing of
private obstetrical and pediatric patients. And long-term treatment was
expensive: who would pay? Since something clearly had to be done about
veterans on a national basis, the veterans' program provided a major federal exercise in national hospital planning in the United States. The result
was a separate national system of hospital service, organized and financed
by the federal government for veterans (and no one else), the beginning
of the system that exists today. It exists because no one else wanted to
provide veterans with care.

After a series of makeshift efforts in government hospitals and contracted services for veterans in other hospitals, and after bitter congressional debates, Congress finally appropriated $18.6 million in 1921 to build
special-purpose institutions for ex-soldiers.[45] As one of his last official
acts, President Wilson appointed five men as consultants on hospitalization to advise the program. Among the five was John Bowman, who had
launched the hospital standardization scheme, had left the American College of Surgeons the year before under criticism that he pushed too fast,
and was now chancellor of the University of Pittsburgh.[46]

The consultants' actions, summarized in their report in 1923, made a
lasting mark on veterans' hospital care.[47] Echoing the wartime philosophy
for the care of sick and wounded soldiers, the consultants took the position
that veterans should be cared for in government institutions without regard to the availability of beds in local civilian hospitals. There would, in
short, be an independent, national system for veterans which would not
have to take into account the problems, political rivalries, and medical
culture of a given region. However, the report went further, for the consultants recommended that there should be continuing federal oversight of
all hospitals in the United States, government and civilian, in order to
further the goal of "uniform care of the citizens of the United States." This
goal was consistent with the movement toward hospital standardization.
But by 1923 the prospect of potential federal control raised the hackles of
organized medicine. From this time on, the specter of "socialized medicine"

in medical debates implied federal regulation, set against the ideals of local medical autonomy.

The consultants' proposal for a national information center for hospitals was the easiest to counter by those in the field. The American Hospital Association had discussed the need for a national clearing house of hospital information before World War I. The case was reiterated by the multiorganizational American Conference on Hospital Service which met in 1919. The resulting Hospital Library and Service Bureau, established in Chicago under the aegis of the conference in 1920, became part of the AHA in 1929, after that organization opened its new headquarters. Funded by the Rockefeller Foundation, the Carnegie Corporation, and the Commonwealth Fund, with smaller contributions from professional and hospital associations that made up the American Conference, the bureau was immediately successful; in 1926 alone, it reported nearly 3,000 information packages in almost constant circulation.[48] The center also gave advice on request and conducted studies. Since in parallel, the AMA Council on Medical Education and Hospitals began to collect and report national hospital data, there seemed no further need for a government information center. But there were actually no teeth in the consultants' recommendations for federal regulation of the hospital system. Expectations about systemwide rationality conflicted with power structures all down the line.

The consultants' decision to establish a hospital for black veterans at Tuskegee, Alabama, demonstrated, only too clearly, the difficulty of national hospital planning in a system dedicated to the ideals of private initiative, local community control, and local customs—including structured inequality by class and race. In World War I, as in other wars, southern blacks in disproportionate numbers flocked to service in the armed forces. White politicians from southern states were faced with the prospect of veterans' hospitals in their areas in which blacks would be at least a substantial minority of patients, possibly the majority, overshadowing the place of white patriots. Even though these hospitals might legally provide separate accommodation for patients by race, there was substantial southern opposition to veterans' hospitals which would accept black patients as of right. It was this unwillingness that led to the Tuskegee decision: the abandonment, for blacks only, of the national policy of local care, in favor of a national hospital for black veterans.

In a telling vignette of public decision-making by private groups and individuals, the consultants on hospitalization built their consensus for Tuskegee after consulting with President Harding, Secretary of the Treasury Andrew W. Mellon, and representatives of the Rockefeller Foundation and the Carnegie Foundation for the Advancement of Teaching. They also consulted with southern politicians, who were anxious to avoid antagonizing the white establishments in their states, groups of "colored leaders," and committees from the railroads. The philanthropists argued for black institutions as a means of providing for the training of black physicians and nurses. The Tuskegee Institute was chosen because it would accept the veterans' hospital, after numerous white-dominated communities throughout the South had refused. The hospital, dedicated by Vice President Coolidge in 1923, provided a symbol of government concern for the care of black veterans; but in terms of power politics, the Tuskegee decision was clear recognition of the federal government's inability, as well as unwillingness, to confront southern politicians, a phenomenon that would reappear in the Hill-Burton legislation of 1946.[49]

As far as broader issues of hospital policy were concerned, too, federal health forces retreated in the early 1920s before a coalition of private interests. After the publication of the consultants' report in 1923, the location of veterans' hospitals became a bureaucratic function, under a new Federal Board of Hospitalization which represented the various federal agencies then involved in veterans' affairs. A new medical council of distinguished academic physicians was appointed to advise the veterans' program in 1924, but this group stuck to the safer realms of medical research, pushing in particular for relationships to be established between veterans' hospitals and medical schools—an affiliation finally achieved after World War II.[50]

In other respects, too, the early, earnest spirit of postwar reform quickly faded, spurred on by AMA opposition to the veterans' program, which became intense starting in the mid-1920s. One reason for AMA opposition was competition. Veterans' hospitals initially limited their services to medical conditions attributable to the veteran's period of wartime service. However, legislation in 1924 extended veterans' benefits to cover nonservice as well as service-connected disabilities, wherever services were available. Conditions to be treated were thus extended from tuberculosis, psychiatry, and rehabilitation as the predominant cases, to all aspects of acute care. Between June 1924 and June 1933, 62 percent of all hospital admissions under the veterans' program were for nonservice conditions.[51] The program, designed as workmen's compensation, had become a form of compulsory health insurance.

A second reason for AMA opposition was organizational. Focusing on government programs as enemies made good tactical sense. The AMA rose in strength in the 1920s, using federal programs as a rallying cry to consolidate its role as the constituency of the average, local private practitioner. Although the number of beds in veterans' hospitals represented only 3 percent of hospital beds of all types in 1930, the service was presented as the thin end of a wedge of a government-dominated health-care system. In a resolution in 1928, the AMA House of Delegates resolved to make every effort to "prevent the extension of socialized medical practice by the government through the veterans bureau and similar organizations"; and in 1930 it described policies to extend the veterans' hospital system as "unsound and communistic."[52] The politicization of hospitals had begun. Instead of joint public-private arrangements—the model in war—government and private interests were polarized as mutually opposing forces.

State legislatures, too, watched closely by state medical societies and fledgling state hospital associations, had little interest in extending their authority over what appeared to be a successful mix of charitable, proprietary, and local-government general hospitals—and certainly no interest in providing them with the additional tax funds that would probably accompany regulation. After the flurry of state interest in compulsory health insurance before 1920, the states drew back from health and welfare issues. Throughout the 1920s the states followed a general policy of noninterference, although laws in at least thirty states in the mid-1920s regulated the care of the sick poor in county hospitals or infirmaries.[53] The most striking incursion of the state into hospital regulation in the 1920s was the licensing of independent maternity hospitals. But since these included deplorable and dirty "baby farms" which had no real claim to be called hospitals at all, such regulation barely impinged on hospitals overall; indeed, it served general hospital interests as these hospitals became growing centers for obstetrics.

The voice and the money of the large philanthropic foundations rather than of government rang through the shifts in hospital policy (as in other medical fields) in the 1920s: funding hospital standardization, consulting on a black veterans' hospital, organizing rural hospital demonstrations, developing urban medical centers, and providing a forum for consensus building. In terms of hospital policy, the foundations largely served the interests and the role of academic (aristocratic or elitist) medicine. They put their funds, judiciously, behind mainstream developments in professionalism, notably into university medical centers, and into the establishment of blue-ribbon committees on special issues, including medical and nursing education, where visible, short-term change might be achieved. The Rockefeller Foundation, for example, considered—and rejected as controversial and unfeasible—a major program of multispecialist pay clinics (group practice); another to build social-service departments as a central, unifying focus for hospitals to correct what one conference speaker called the "dehumanizing tendency of modern scientific medicine among

physicians"; and a third to establish training programs for hospital executives, to prepare them to organize services not only for the hospital but for
the whole community. A training scheme was established at Marquette
University by leaders of the Catholic Hospital Association, but most administrators continued to be hired on the basis of apprenticeship and
through personal networks.[54]

Rural hospitals affirmed foundation interest in health, but it was the
glamour of science in the cities that offered the most spectacular (and
noncontroversial) opportunity for philanthropic giving. Expenditures on
medicine by one hundred foundations totaled a massive $172 million
between 1921 and 1930, of which almost $23.7 million was earmarked
specifically for hospitals, particularly those in the large cities.[55] Columbia-
Presbyterian Medical Center in New York, originally formed by joint
activities between Columbia University and Presbyterian Hospital in 1911,
was formally established in 1921 and became an important symbol of
affiliations between hospitals and medical schools. The Carnegie Corporation, the Rockefeller Foundation, and the General Education Board each
donated $1 million to Columbia University in 1921 to enable the hospital
and the school to be joined; and the medical center opened on a single site
in 1928. Its total cost, including land, buildings, and equipment, was estimated at a whopping $25 million. But the movement toward medical
centers was rapid and general. Indeed, so successful was the movement to
unite medical schools and hospitals that a new Commission on Medical
Education, organized with foundation support in 1925, barely touched on
clinical facilities as an issue at all.[56]

Common interests sparked temporary organizational coalitions in
different cities: the city of Augusta, Georgia, built a teaching hospital for
the state-run University of Georgia; the University of Oregon, also a state
institution, gave Portland land for the construction of a county hospital;
and in Pittsburgh, stimulated by the enthusiasm of faculty members from
the University of Pittsburgh, who had staffed a base hospital in World War
I, seven hospitals were brought together, remaining autonomous but under
a joint administrative board of the university and the hospitals. However,
it was the philanthropic foundations, by providing capital and a national
educational policy, largely influenced by Abraham Flexner at the General
Educational Board, which were the major vehicles for change.[57] Teaching
hospitals and schools were brought together largely through the policies
of private institutions.

Both locally and nationally, the medical profession was the most
powerful influence on the structure and character of the hospital enterprise
as a whole in the 1920s, through the American College of Surgeons and

the American Medical Association. The American Hospital Association, a potentially important participant, was relatively ineffective for most of the 1920s. But although it was rather like a club, marked by cliques and dominated by leading medical superintendents, with members chosen largely on a personal basis, change was in the air. Hospital representatives from more than thirty-five countries attended the AHA annual meeting in 1929 and greetings were sent to the banquet from world figures, including President Hoover and the Prince of Wales.[58] Slowly, hospital administrators were realizing their common interests and potential political power—a power that would be exercised in the 1930s.

Nursing organizations, embarked on upgrading a troubled profession through the establishment of prestigious university programs, were significantly absent from the power structures nationwide. Organizations of the democratic process—that is, government—were supportive rather than directive, as were members of boards of trustees. It was the absence of alternative leadership, as much as medical dominance, that upheld the authority of private organizations in general and medical organizations in particular in the 1920s.

Two striking conclusions emerge from hospital policy-making in the 1920s. First, all of the organizations involved saw hospitals as institutions that were of national importance, for which some form of national action was appropriate: national standards, national norms for the number of beds, and national policies for hospital distribution. Yet none of these policies was to conflict with a pattern of service based on local control; indeed, all served to enhance it. Second, the emerging ideologies of rural and urban hospital service were curiously incompatible. The former spoke to community solidarity and professional cohesion, the latter to community stratification and professional hierarchies. Rural ideology stressed the hospital as a center of practice, urban ideology as a center of science. Philanthropic foundations sat on both sides of the fence, responding to both ideologies at once.

Problems and Limits of a Marketplace Ethos

Behind broader hospital planning concerns of the 1920s were notions of national mobilization left over from the war: national resource planning, an offshoot of the conservation movement; national planning for the supply of physicians, an extension of Progressive, foundation-supported national planning for medical education; and ideas spilling over from industrial mass-marketing and distribution networks, essential elements in America's growing prosperity. The analogies of hospitals to industry were persuasive. Dr. W. H. Welch remarked in 1925 that the health field had a "woefully ineffective distribution service, as compared with its marvelously effective production service in the laboratories of the world." Edward Filene, of Filene's department store in Boston, expressed a similar sentiment. Medical science, he wrote, "travels by airplane in an age of aviation, while medical organization lumbers along in a stagecoach."[59]

Despite their many successes, then, by 1930 hospitals were targets of increasing criticism. Why, for example, should cities like Omaha, Detroit, Grand Rapids, and Wilmington have a relatively low supply of hospital beds, while others, like Akron, Memphis, St. Paul, and San Francisco, were very well supplied? Why should the average length of stay in general hospitals, which was sixteen days, nationally, in 1923, be much lower in cities like Milwaukee, Detroit, and Chicago? Wilmington and Omaha had a short length of stay and a low supply of beds, but St. Paul, with hospital beds in generous supply, also had a relatively short length of stay. There appeared to be no direct association between length of stay and supply of beds, and geographical patterns were inconsistent and diverse. Across the regions, the South was relatively undersupplied and undercapitalized, the Far West had the highest ratio of beds to population, the Northeast the greatest hospital investment, and the central Northwest the smallest reliance on government facilities (table 5.3). However, there were also great variations within the regions.

Although the local, idiosyncratic history of hospitals made such diversity easy to understand—indeed, inevitable—there was an unquestioned sense that there *ought* to be norms for hospital service. Hospital consultants like Michael M. Davis recommended five acute hospital beds per 1,000 population (and preferably six) as the appropriate number for a large American hospital in the 1920s; this figure became a useful benchmark for hospital planners throughout the 1920s and 1930s. (This compares to an accepted norm of 4.4 in the early 1980s.) It followed that cities like Detroit

TABLE 5.3

*Nonfederal General and Special Hospitals Registered by the American Medical Association,
by Region of the United States, 1928*

	Percent of the Population	Percent of All Hospitals	Percent of All Capital Investment	Beds per 1,000 Population	Investment per Person	Investment per Bed	Percent of Beds in Each Region Under State or Local-Government Control
North and Middle Atlantic	29.9	26.7	46.9	4.1	$25	$6,051	25.4
South and South Atlantic	29.1	24.5	11.7	1.9	6	3,416	22.1
Central West	20.8	18.0	21.0	3.1	16	5,062	25.4
Central Northwest	11.1	14.9	9.5	3.1	14	4,308	18.5
Far West	9.2	16.0	10.9	4.3	19	4,356	28.9
Total	100.0	100.0	100.0	3.2	16	4,993	24.5

NOTE: Percentages may not add up exactly, due to rounding.
SOURCE: Calculated from C. Rufus Rorem, *The Public's Investment in Hospitals* (Chicago: University of Chicago Press, 1930), tables IX and X, p. 49.

were "undersupplied" with hospital beds. Detroit, indeed, had little more than half the beds, per capita, of Boston.[60]

But there was no generally agreed plan of campaign in the 1920s in the shape of a model design for hospital care, even in the cities; and there were two problems in the citywide hospital surveys that were undertaken in several major cities. The first was the assumption that a "bed" was an interchangeable unit, without taking into account the institutional, economic, class and racial divisions that influenced the use of beds within cities across the country. The second was lack of interest among hospitals in pooling services and facilities. In San Francisco, for example, both the city hospital and the University of California Hospital, funded from state taxes, continued to care for the poor or chronically sick in disproportionate numbers. Nevertheless, there were too few beds for chronic-disease patients, and for those with tuberculosis, arthritis, and fractures. It was difficult to find hospital accommodation for patients with pneumonia, for drug addicts and the handicapped, and posthospital (convalescent) care was virtually nonexistent. Yet San Francisco had a huge supply of beds overall—7.3 general hospital beds per 1,000 population in 1922, more than twice the number per 1,000 in New York.[61] Throughout the country pay beds stood empty, while unappealing patients were neglected.

A third problem was disagreement among the experts. One group stressed the advantages of the big-city skyscraper hospital, with its wards and treatment units stacked upon each other vertically, with an optimal size of 500 beds for efficient, economic, and medical administration. Another favored small hospital units scattered throughout the urban area, designed for improved accessibility by patients. More critically, then as now, it was much easier to talk about improving distribution when what was meant was rectifying obvious deficiencies in buildings and service, than to make readjustments in areas where the bed supply was sufficient. The former suggested additional funds; the latter, cutbacks, controls, mergers, and/or crimping.

It was only too evident, however, that the exuberant growth of autonomous hospitals had led to considerable waste in the system. On average, 123,000 beds in general hospitals—over a third of all the beds—were empty in 1929.[62] What was happening was a continuing expansion of capacity in acute general hospitals, paralleled by an expansion of patient days, but with demand unable to expand fast enough to meet the additional supply of beds year by year. Although eleven cities formed health federations, councils, or leagues to survey health needs, sponsor new programs, and address the more general problems of cooperation between public health agencies, private practitioners, hospitals, and other private health activities, these agencies had little influence.

High inpatient costs created further problems by 1930. There was a running joke in the late 1920s that there were two classes of people in hospitals, those who entered poor and those who left poor.[63] Patients were often confused, angry, or upset by unforeseen charges on their hospital bill, represented in the growing practice of itemizing the bill into a hospital daily room rate, graduated by type of accommodation, and a menu of special charges. Room costs represented, on average, only 60 percent of the costs billed to patients in 1930. The new image of hospital service as serving private and semiprivate patients (including nursing, meals, and general support services), plus technical services in different parts of the hospital, made expansion of the charge system irresistible—from delivery-room fees through fees for ultraviolet radiation. (Private and semiprivate patients usually also had to pay separate physician fees and sometimes private nursing fees.) Criticisms about overcharging made administrators receptive to ideas for all-inclusive, flat-rate charges and for insurance against hospital costs as answers to the problem of the patient of moderate means, even before the harsh lessons of the Depression.[64]

The success of consumerism also seemed to suggest that hospitals were major "producers" of medicine—and not just the empty shells in which doctors did their work. But rising room rates created friction between hospitals and physicians, making it difficult to make any changes. Since patients were usually expected to pay their hospital bill first and their doctor second, rising hospital charges cut directly into what patients on limited budgets could pay their physicians. In 1929, 23 percent of the nation's entire medical bill was flowing to hospitals, with 30 percent to physicians and the remainder spread across all other fields.[65] Administrators and physicians entered the Depression with conflicting views as to the future of the hospital as the doctors' workshop.

Such problems existed independently of parallel concerns about social equity. Nevertheless, as a final problem, the very success of the consumption credo challenged the assumptions of social inequality within the system. By the late 1920s, Americans in the highest income brackets, who were presumably healthier, on average, than those who were poor, used hospitals much more frequently. The rich "consumed" more surgery, had many more diagnostic tests, and received the overwhelming amount of care given by special private-duty nurses; indeed, they may have received too *much* surgery (table 5.4). In contrast, the average hospitalization rate still seemed far too low for most conditions, especially for families with moderate and low incomes. This pattern seemed intrinsically unfair.

In this vein, a new, blue-ribbon Committee on the Costs of Medical Care, established (with foundation support) in 1927, began by assuming that each member of the population ought to have access to medical care, including hospital services. The committee was to conclude in its final report, published in 1932, that the costs of services were "inequitably distributed."[66] This concept of equity assumed a basic entitlement to modern scientific medicine for all members of the population—counter to a strict market ethos of distribution of services by ability to pay.

But the criticism struck, too, at the heart of consumerism. While the mass-consumption society of the 1920s celebrated workers' affluence, in the case of hospitalization it was the workers who were hurting. White-collar workers, including teachers, were finding it difficult to meet expensive hospital bills. The problem of the "patient of moderate means" thus grew in the 1920s as the marketing of hospital care became more effective and as hospitals expanded in staff, amenities, and equipment. If a government ("socialist") system was to be avoided—and medical and hospital

TABLE 5.4

Hospital and Diagnostic Services by Family Income, 1928–31

Family Income	Hospital Cases per 1,000 Individuals	Surgical Cases Hospitalized per 1,000 Illnesses	Cases Having X ray per 1,000 Illnesses	Cases Having Laboratory Service per 1,000 Illnesses	Hospital Cases Having Special Nursing per 1,000 Hospital Cases
Under $1,200	59.4	44.2	23.8	51.7	67.0
1,200–2,000	52.4	42.0	25.2	61.6	125.0
2,000–3,000	59.4	49.6	27.0	68.8	164.0
3,000–5,000	63.1	48.1	31.0	82.8	251.0
5,000–10,000	79.3	58.6	48.5	120.3	379.0
10,000 and over	98.0	62.6	75.4	132.3	685.0
Services needed, according to expert opinion	107.0*	51.3	186.4	581.7	578.0*

*Excluding care in tuberculosis sanatoria and mental hospitals.
SOURCE: *Medical Care for the American People,* Final Report of the Committee on the Costs of Medical Care (Chicago: University of Chicago Press, 1932), p. 8.

leaders were united on this point—the problem was one of tailoring consumer expectations to the producers' bill or vice versa, or, alternatively, working out some acceptable method of consumer payment by insurance or by credit.

The failure of the health system to serve the middle class, wrote Boston businessman Richards Bradley, was "just plain *bad business,* committed by good business men befogged by the tradition that charity is their main duty."[67] Leading hospital administrators agreed. The aim of the American Hospital Association, its president, the administrator of the Leland Stanford Hospital in San Francisco, said in 1927, should be to foster any movement that offered a reasonable solution to the problem of the patient of moderate means—an estimated 80 percent of the entire population; the logical answer was insurance against sickness, just as people bought insurance against financial loss or automobile insurance.[68] Hospital insurance had a triple appeal: it was a way of easing the relationship between hospitals and patients who were faced by large bills; it brought hospitals needed income; and it provided financial protection and peace of mind for consumers, who could now share the expense of high-cost sickness with large populations of contributors, most of whom were not sick.

In 1929 there were no clear or simple approaches to the questions of hospital costs and financing. When the stock market crashed in October of that year, hospitals were investing heavily in construction while expressing some uncertainties about direction and the need for readjustment. Numerous examples of group financing existed, ranging from long-established insurance schemes, such as the Southern Pacific system or the hospital-insurance associations in Washington and Oregon, or community-wide arrangements like the Endicott Johnson scheme in Binghamton, New York, to a new scheme in Dallas, started in 1929, whereby the Baylor University Hospital offered its services to white public-school teachers and other employee groups for a fixed annual fee. The fee was collected in monthly installments, with a choice of subscribing for care in a ward or in a private room; and the hospital's special charges were included. It was from this latter plan that interest in what is now Blue Cross was to be sparked in the coming economic crisis.

But ingrained cultural attitudes lurked beneath the surface of the new consumerism at all levels. Old notions of charity abuse were translated into the lasting suspicion that poor Americans are as economically manipulative and organizationally clever as other consumers, and that if free services are available they will automatically be abused.[69] Large urban local-government hospitals proved useful to medical schools for testing new diagnostic machines and drugs—electrocardiographs were introduced at Boston City Hospital in 1920 and at Cook County in 1923—but city government hospitals remained stepchildren of the hospital system, with an average cost per patient day half that of voluntary hospitals. A survey by the American College of Surgeons in 1927 found the wards in Cook County Hospital to be dirty, crowded, in ill repair, short of essential supplies such as bed linens, understaffed, and lacking in standard equipment.[70]

Pay beds for black Americans were largely nonexistent, and where they existed, in all-black hospitals, service was often poor and sometimes dangerous. Almost a quarter of all general hospitals in the United States in 1922 reported that they limited their services to "whites"; 1 percent (42 hospitals) reported that they received "Negroes" only. Hospitalization of blacks was rare in smaller towns, as well as in larger cities which had no teaching hospitals to offer service to blacks as "clinical material." In Atlanta, for example, the major source of hospital care for blacks was a 200-bed "colored unit" at Grady Hospital, a major teaching unit for Emory University.

But even in teaching hospitals there was no guarantee of service. In St. Louis, for example, the Washington University dispensary (outpatient department) reported "too many" black patients admitted in 1929–30 for the type of work the institution wished to pursue, leading the dispensary to impose a charge of 50 cents a visit in order to reduce the number of patients. As an exception, black obstetrical patients were encouraged to attend without charge, because they offered a "high percentage of pathological clinical material."[71] Such high-handed practices did little to assuage anxiety about medical care in the low-income areas where teaching hospitals were located.

Throughout the 1920s and 1930s, arguments for and against the racial segregation of hospitals raged among black leaders, local medical communities in cities like Chicago, and within the major philanthropic foundations. In Illinois, Pennsylvania, California, and some northeastern states, black physicians were permitted to attend patients in the mixed wards of major, white-controlled hospitals, but these cases were sporadic and were in no sense the general rule. New York was reported in the early 1920s as having only 10 beds available for black patients attended by black physicians; by 1930 it had 100. A few cities, including St. Louis, Kansas City, New York, and Washington, housed special, "Class A" hospitals for black physicians and black patients. However, the general pattern for black patients was care in basement wards of city hospitals, attended by white physicians.[72] Through the educational system white medical students were socialized into a profession whose model of quality was the white (preferably WASP) male, whose model of medicine was in-hospital technology rather than community service, and whose model of society was racist and class-ridden. It was also sexist; black women physicians, on two counts, were virtually barred from internships.

Meanwhile, the university medical center provided a continuing source of competition and anxiety for the local medical profession. There was particular concern about the exclusion of local practitioners from teaching-hospital staffs, the alleged poaching of private patients by teaching hospitals, and the huge growth of urban outpatient departments. At the University of Wisconsin at Madison local doctors criticized the establishment of a university-run student health service as a step toward socialized medicine; in Chicago the Cook County Medical Society forced the University of Chicago to abandon a proposal to fund a pay clinic. In turn, the availability of foundation and local funds gave the medical centers an aristocratic aloofness and high expectations about expenditures and prestige. All major teaching hospitals had two groups of faculty by 1930, with the first having better access to beds, laboratories, and assistants than the second.[73] The large teaching hospital was indeed a threat to the autonomy of community physicians—and to the idea of the hospital as the physician's domain.

The concurrent growth of national specialist organizations, also led by leaders of academic medicine, offered a further threat—this time from within the profession—and fanned hostilities between academic physicians and community practitioners. When the American Board of Otolaryngology, formed in 1924, suggested that only board-certified physicians should be allowed to do nose and throat operations, this was a challenge to the flourishing market for tonsillectomies and adenoidectomies, as well as criticism of the skills and judgment of other practitioners.[74] These rifts within the medical profession echoed the dichotomy in hospital policy in the philanthropic foundations: exclusive, specialized expertise in major city teaching hospitals versus open-staff hospitals in local communities.

A consumer, market-oriented label for hospitals in the 1920s is thus both an accurate and a misleading description of the complex forces that were in play. The label fits the tenor of the times. It suggests the salesmanship of hospital surgery and obstetrics, the rapid expansion of hospital work, the focus on fee-paying patients, technology and equipment, and the huge program of hospital construction. But patients had little or no rights as consumers. They could usually not choose whether to go into hospital or not. They could not sue most hospitals and were expected to comply with the wishes of experts without question. Charitable hospitals were also cushioned from market forces by their ability to raise capital through donations when they needed it—and not have to pass the capital costs along to patients. Most hospitals did not even include interest, depreciation, or other capital charges on their books until the 1960s.

By 1929 the costs and financing of medical care were open to criticism, while the question of "equity" was charged with emotive—and potentially political—meaning. More immediate problems were managerial. The tripartite division of authority in hospitals—between boards of trustees, superintendents, and attending physicians—made any management decision a process of suspicion, friction, and often protracted negotiations. In the event, accepting the hospital as the doctors' workshop, hospital trustees and administrators tried to provide a mass-consumption service in the 1920s without a mass-financing or a mass-distribution system. It was at this point that the Depression intervened.

6

The Political Creation of the Voluntary Ideal: Hospitals During the Depression and the Early New Deal

U_{NTIL} the 1930s the ideas of voluntarism and community as organizing principles for hospital service had more to do with the mobilization of resources at the local level than with broad public policies for the receipt of care. In the 1930s the balance shifted. The major national hospital and medical associations used voluntarism as a major, unifying rhetoric, allowing them to present a common front against the threat of increased government intervention. The language of the "voluntary way" became the antithesis to "socialized medicine."

At the same time, acceptance of hospitalization and medical care as a necessary human service—which ought to be available to everyone—raised questions about the organization and financing of hospital services for individuals as a basic form of social welfare. General consumer expenditures dropped by 37 percent between 1929 and 1933. The failure of the stock market led, in rapid succession, to widespread unemployment, huge increases in the welfare rolls, and a sharp drop in savings and charitable donations. As more individuals became impoverished, more patients flocked to hospitals as ward rather than private patients and to government rather than nongovernmental institutions. Hospitals were caught in a double bind. The demand for free care rose, while hospital income declined. A contemporary hospital analyst wrote: "[H]ard times are clutching the hospitals like a giant pair of pincers."[1]

Which hospitals would survive? What were hospitals to do? For the voluntary hospitals the answer was to organize. For the first time hospital groups, rather than medical associations, took the lead in defining national hospital priorities and goals. Irrespective of their history as religious, ethnic, or nonsectarian foundations, private nonprofit hospitals dusted their public-service image, disassociated themselves from "proprietary" (for-profit) hospitals, and joined together under the banner of voluntarism. In turn, the voluntary hospitals, with two-thirds of all general hospital admissions, mobilized as a national force. Voluntarism became both an organizing theme and a political idea.

How voluntarism—an antipolitical idea—became an organizing and a political ideology for a disparate group of hospitals (and ultimately for their associated Blue Cross plans) is the first theme of this chapter.[2] The second, intertwining theme is that voluntary hospitals as a group, while claiming their imminent demise, and despite the very real trials and traumas of the Depression, emerged strengthened and unified in the late 1930s. In the process, they avoided the perils both of government regulation and of a destructive confrontation with organized medicine. Organizations and ideology rose together. With suggestions of spontaneous community activity, romanticism, and a sense of nostalgia for the vanished (if mythical) past, the voluntary ethos promised the best of both public and private worlds: public responsibility without government compulsion; private initiative untainted by selfish gain.

Hard Times

For patients and their doctors the lessons of the 1920s had been well
learned. Because hospitals were now recognized as providers of an essential service, it was difficult to cut this service to the bone. The number of
admissions to general hospitals fell from 6.3 million in 1931, the first year
the AMA collected these data, to 6.1 million in 1933, the nadir of the
Depression, a loss of 3 percent. But admissions then began to rise again,
so that the years 1931–33 became, in retrospect, only a temporary setback
for those institutions able to weather the worst of the storm. These were
generally the largest institutions. No major hospital closed its doors in the
Depression. Admissions to general hospitals rose from 51 per 1,000 population in 1931 to 54 in 1935, and on to 70 in 1940 (table 6.1)

The momentum of the 1920s carried through in obstetrics, too. Even
though the overall birth rate declined in the 1930s, the number of hospital
births continued to rise.[3] Less than 29 percent of all births took place in
hospitals in 1929; 56 percent in 1940. Hospitals were prisoners of increased
demand—both from doctors seeking to hospitalize patients and from a
growing group of patients who could not pay. In New Jersey, for example,
61 percent of the patients admitted to general hospitals in 1933 went into
the wards.[4] Hospitals competed with each other, with new concern, in the
collapsed market for paying patients.

The rapid shift of working-class patients to local-government hospi-

TABLE 6.1

General Hospital Admissions, 1931–53, Selected Years

	Admissions (thousands)	Admissions per 1,000 Population	Average Length of Stay (days)	Average Hospital Size (beds)	Occupancy Rate
1931	6,322	51	14.3	89	64.5
1935	6,875	54	13.9	95	64.3
1940	9,219	70	12.9	104	70.3
1945	15,228	115	15.9	194	72.1
1950	15,830	105	10.0	125	73.6
1953	18,693	118	9.3	129	73.0

NOTE: Admissions per 1,000 population are calculated using figures for total population residing in the
United States, excluding armed forces overseas.
SOURCE: Calculated from U.S. Department of Commerce, Bureau of the Census, *Historical Statistics of the United
States, Colonial Times to 1957* (Washington, D.C., 1960), pp. 7, 35, 37. Original hospital data are from the AMA
Council on Medical Education and Hospitals, which stopped publishing its annual statistics in 1953.
Admissions data were published only from 1931.

tals caused particular alarm among private nonprofit institutions. In the spring of 1933 private nonprofit hospitals in New York City reported that their private rooms had a 35 percent occupancy rate, semiprivate rooms 55 percent, and wards 81 percent. Whole floors of nonprofit hospitals stood empty, while the hospitals run by the City of New York were operating at 110 percent of their rated capacity. At Bellevue Hospital extra beds and cots were squeezed into the wards and placed in corridors to cope with the excess. Government hospitals in major cities were swamped with long lines of patients for outpatient care, as the new poor avoided fees and debts to private practitioners. City hospitals like Philadelphia General and Boston City Hospital were triply burdened: by the sudden increase in patients; by urgent, competing demands on public-welfare funds from the masses of unemployed; and by tax critics who sought to limit the expenditure of public funds on grounds of political corruption and public waste.[5]

The primary problem of government hospitals was that demand increased without increased tax budgets, but the problem for the nongovernmental hospitals, which depended on patient revenue, was of plummeting income.[6] There was no hope of raising additional gifts or donations to match expansions in charity care. Gifts for current hospital expenditures declined by 54 percent nationwide between 1929 and 1933, and gifts for capital by 85 percent.[7] Problems for administrators and their boards were compounded by not knowing, in the early 1930s, whether the Depression was a temporary, short-term shift in the business cycle or a lasting economic catastrophe. The *Journal of the American Medical Association* urged hospitals not to sell their property or equipment; rather, plans for the future should be based on growth, and not designed as a "financial promotion" or as a response to the "present abnormal situation."[8]

But the shift in clientele to low-income patients could not be ignored. A survey of working-class families in the poorest districts of Baltimore, Birmingham, Cleveland, Detroit, New York, Pittsburgh, and Syracuse found that physician calls declined by one-sixth between 1929 and 1933, but hospitalized illness *increased* by almost one-third. The highest incidence of disabling illness among wage-earning families was among the "new poor"; that is, families who had been in reasonably comfortable circumstances in 1929 but were now reduced to poverty or relief. Even among those who merely dropped from a "comfortable" to a "moderate" working-class income, a substantial amount of hospital service (62 percent) was now given free.[9] People went to hospitals expecting to be taken in.

Like other major employers, hospitals responded to the fiscal crisis by salary and wage cuts, reductions in the number of working hours, delayed maintenance work on buildings, and increased efficiency. Nursing salaries were cut across the board—largely without complaint. Many hospitals closed their nursing schools, relying on reduced wage levels to employ trained nurses rather than student nurses to staff the wards. In the early 1930s there were more nursing students than professional nurses in hospitals; by the late 1930s there were more professional nurses than students.[10] Pride and employee loyalty helped hospitals maintain essential services, but employees also worked hard in hospitals, as elsewhere, because they were thankful to have a job. Young doctors, like nurses, were loath to leave the shelter of the hospital. Even though half of all interns received no monthly allowances from hospitals or any other form of pay in 1933, they did get food and lodging, and house staff positions were eagerly sought.

Local-government hospitals had three basic avenues for attempting to ease the financial crunch: pushing for additional government appropriations, limiting service by tightening eligibility levels, and competing more aggressively with voluntary and proprietary hospitals in the market for paying patients. Enormous calls on local governments for basic income assistance made the first method usually irrelevant, but both of the other courses were open. The Philadelphia General Hospital (PGH), for example, reported decreased expenditures in 1932 and 1933, despite a large increase in utilization. In response, in 1935 this hospital set up a program to limit admissions, through special checks on eligibility for free care and through screening patients to keep out of the hospital anyone who could plausibly be cared for at home. Parallel efforts were made to ride hard on collections from all who could possibly pay. Further retrenchments were achieved the following year by excluding nonresidents of Philadelphia, by lowering the number of psychiatric admissions and by deflecting nonacute sick and elderly patients to boarding homes. PGH also reduced the number of outpatient visits between 1933 and 1937.[11]

Nor was PGH alone. In the old tradition of "charity abuse" Morrisania Hospital in New York had a credit service bureau run a check on 1,000 persons applying to the hospital and found a substantial proportion able to pay. Similarly, Paterson General Hospital, New Jersey—whose outpatient visits jumped by 65 percent between 1929 and 1933—took its own steps to discourage patients from becoming "clinic-minded." Social workers made home visits to check out social and income status, while the hospital posted an enlarged copy of chapter 141 of the *Laws of New Jersey, 1932,* in English, Italian, and Yiddish, which made charity abuse a misdemeanor, incurring a $1,000 fine or three years of hard labor, or both.[12] City hospitals were, in short, unenthusiastic about taking on additional burdens and were only reluctant competitors with voluntary institutions. But there were obvious limits as to how far tax-supported hospitals could retrench, since they were the hospitals of last resort for the destitute population.

The most promising means of improving a local government hospital's financial position was by increasing the number of paying patients—and here the hospitals ran, full tilt, into head-on competition from voluntary hospitals. Hospital expert Michael Davis estimated in 1934 that 90 percent of government hospitals received paying patients, and that most of them allowed doctors to bring in their private patients, so that physician fees could also be charged. Virtually all tax-supported hospitals in small cities admitted paying patients, and these patients in turn provided most of the income of these hospitals—a direct threat to any competing voluntary institution.[13]

Administrators and trustees of nonprofit hospitals in the cities walked a fine line: attempting to dump indigent patients on local government hospitals, while expressing alarm about the loss of paying patients (or potentially paying patients) to these same institutions. In Cleveland, for example, the voluntary hospitals limited free and part-pay care to cases of the "most emergent nature." Fortunately, perhaps, for these hospitals, the degree to which they actually turned away patients from their doors was difficult for outsiders to assess, as indeed is true today. An officer of the Cleveland Welfare Federation remarked with some frustration: "The thing which cannot be measured statistically is the extent to which persons needing hospital care are having it refused."[14] This was the negative side of the coin. On the positive side, hospitals and their associated doctors and nurses, throughout the country, stretched their efforts, often heroically, to treat everyone they could. In Westchester County, New York, for example, attending physicians in fifteen general hospitals gave away services conservatively valued at over $1.8 million in 1933, with the hospitals donating another $1.8 million.[15]

Administrators welcomed the opportunity to exert their authority, using economic conditions as a rationale for increased prestige. Aggressive systems of bill collection and unremitting public relations helped to maintain income in the face of an increasing flow of charity patients, while hospital journals described new opportunities by which hospitals could become more efficient through the purchase of technology, from steam trays for centralized food services to investment in modern laundry equipment. Hospitals able to maintain their income at a time of falling prices might even come out of the Depression ahead of the game. In New Jersey, for example, hospital costs per patient day fell from $5.30 in 1929 to $4.26 in 1933, a decrease of 20 percent.[16] Since salaries and wages represented only 30 percent of the average hospital budget in the early 1930s, general price cuts, as well as cuts in wage levels, could be significant to a hospital's financial position. Large, lavish buildings already in the works in 1929 continued to be built, benefiting from the windfall of lower prices.

Offering credit and riding hard on bad debts were two ways of keeping income up. In Detroit, for example, arrangements could be made in the early 1930s for a bank to pay hospital bills, charging 6 or 7 percent interest, with the hospital credit investigator acting as the bank's agent. The Cleveland Hospital Council started a hospital finance corporation (in 1933) to determine credit ratings and to make individual financial arrangements. In its first four and a half years, the scheme financed over 4,600 accounts in twelve hospitals, for more than $382,000, and collected $220,000.[17] Unfortunately, the publication in hospital journals of standardized dunning letters and numerous forms designed to collect bad debts did little for the hospitals' public image. The more positive—and practical—approach available to hard-pressed hospital administrators was to abandon credit as a major means of financing middle-class hospital care in favor of hospital *pre*payment (insurance). Through prepayment, a large army of healthy workers could contribute a small amount each month, so that they would have money available when they were sick. The hospital, in turn, would be assured of payment. But such schemes took time to develop. Prepayment gained momentum in the late 1930s (chapter 7).

Generally, the larger hospitals had the most freedom to reorganize their management and finances, to post significant savings, and, sometimes, to get away with reducing unprofitable patient services. Some hospitals sold off part of their real estate or equipment, or closed floors, wards, or even outpatient departments in order to cut down on expenses. Others opened up new ambulatory services, to follow up patients who might otherwise reappear at their free clinics. Social-service departments came under special scrutiny, although for the most part they were retained. Administrators, physicians, and trustees played varying roles in different hospitals, some seeking to expand patient care to serve the enlarged poverty population, others curtailing services to preserve the institution. Nonprofit hospitals had pragmatic as well as humanitarian and traditional grounds for maintaining services to the middle class, even where they could not pay, for these individuals might one day become paying patients again. But the sheer volume of demand was often overwhelming. Where they could, all types of hospitals moved to reduce the number of unprofitable patients, to increase their market position through aggressive competition with other institutions, and to search for alternative sources of income.

Small profit-making hospitals were particularly hard hit. The number of hospitals owned by individuals or partnerships dropped from 1,600 in 1929, to 1,400 in 1933, to 1,200 in 1939; and their occupancy levels were consistently lower than those of other types of institutions. Many of the "proprietaries" were small, inefficient urban institutions which were already generally outdated. Also, for-profit hospitals were much more likely than private nonprofit hospitals to enter the Depression with outstanding debts. While religious or voluntary hospitals usually prepaid their building costs by raising funds in advance, through gifts and donations, profit-making hospitals were responsible for the full obligation on outstanding loans. As their clientele of paying patients fell away, they ran a serious risk of bankruptcy. Nor were state legislatures or city governments eager to save them. In Oklahoma, for example, a bill was proposed to exempt from taxes private hospitals with 10 percent or more charity cases; but it was unsuccessful, as were similar attempts in Maryland and Pennsylvania.[18] The proprietary hospitals had the fewest friends.

A survey done in 1936 estimated that more than two out of every five hospitals owned by individuals and partnerships closed between 1928 and 1936—a much higher proportion than for other groups (table 6.2). (Some of the reported hospital closures may, however, have represented mergers with other hospitals or a change to nonprofit status.) Almost one out of every five government hospitals closed between 1928 and 1936, one out of six hospitals run by corporations (profit and nonprofit), and more than one out of ten of the hospitals owned by churches and fraternities. The general patterns were repeated at the local level. In New York City, for example, one municipal hospital and five voluntary hospitals closed between mid-

TABLE 6.2

General and Special Hospitals Reported as Closing Between 1928 and 1936 as Percentage of All Hospitals Listed in that Period

Hospital Control	Percent Closed	Total Listed Between 1928 and 1936
Churches and fraternities	11	3,435
Not-for-profit and for-profit corporations	17	
Individuals and partnerships	43	1,870
Government	19	1,039
		6,344

NOTE: Figures are drawn from comparing the names of all hospitals that appeared on the AMA register of hospitals in 1928, 1930, 1932, and 1934 with those for 1936.
SOURCE: Joseph W. Mountin, Elliott H. Pennell, and Kay Pearson, *Hospital Facilities in the United States, part II: Trends in Hospital Development 1928–1936,* Public Health Bulletin no. 243 (1938), pp. 40–42.

1930 and mid-1935 (and another six voluntary hospitals merged or combined their facilities), compared with twenty-six proprietary hospitals.[19]

Within these various categories, the experience of individual hospitals was mixed. Both locally and nationally the number of hospital *beds* increased. General hospitals which were large and visible in the community, had a relatively solid capital base, and could compete successfully as specialized technological centers, were in the best position for growth. The number of full-time medical specialists grew by almost 50 percent between 1931 and 1940.[20] The most successful specialists were those associated with multispecialty general hospitals in urban areas; these, in general, were the larger institutions.

Single-specialty hospitals, many of which were small, joined the small proprietary general hospitals as the major casualties of the Depression. Despite the increase in hospital births, the number of specialist maternity hospitals dropped by one-third during the Depression, from 178 hospitals in 1927 to 118 in 1939. Although those that remained increased in average size, over 90 percent of all hospital births took place in general hospitals throughout the 1930s. There was, likewise, a drop in the number of industrial hospitals (by 96 percent), hospitals for the eye, ear, nose, and throat (by 47 percent), isolation hospitals (by 39 percent), children's hospitals (by 17 percent), convalescent homes (by 12 percent), and tuberculosis hospitals (by 6 percent).[21] Orthopedic hospitals were one notable exception among specialty hospitals, increasing in number from sixty-two to eighty-two between 1927 and 1939. These were stimulated by a growing interest in crippled children in the 1930s, incorporated in special federal grants to states under the Social Security Act of 1935.

A far more important exception to the growing dominance of general hospitals was the rapid growth in admissions to hospitals for nervous and mental diseases during the Depression, typically to huge, state-run psychiatric hospitals located outside of the cities. The number of beds in psychiatric hospitals ballooned by 62 percent between 1927 and 1939. (In comparison, the number of beds in general hospitals rose by 29 percent.) Depression conditions were hard on the psyche—poverty, downward mobility, helplessness, homelessness, humiliation, anxiety, failure, and the abandonment of dreams.

Overall, despite the increased burden of free care, hospitals fared less badly than many other sectors of the economy. To some extent, the Depression provided a shake-up and consolidation of the hospital system, emphasizing the advantage of concentrating the fixed costs of radiology, pathology, and other technical services in larger institutions; the average general hospital grew from 84 beds in 1929 to 104 in 1940. And although patient payments to nongovernmental hospitals and sanatoria (of all types) declined by 17 percent between 1929 and 1933, this was less than half the decline in consumer expenditures as a whole. Patient payments to governmental hospitals of all types actually *increased* by 21 percent between 1929 and 1933, as local general hospitals and state and local psychiatric hospitals sought fee-paying patients. None of these figures, moreover, includes adjustments for declining prices.[22] Even under Depression conditions, then, there was a promising market for new forms of consumer financing, including prepayment or hospital insurance. Such schemes might also stem the apparent shift of paying patients to government institutions and bring them all back to the voluntary hospitals.

Defining Hospital and Medical Interests Against the Threat of Government Domination

It was in the context of the apparent shift of patient payments and construction capital away from voluntary to government hospitals that Paul Fesler, president of the American Hospital Association, spoke in 1932 of the "possible breakdown of the voluntary hospital system in America."[23] His words fell on ready ears. The AMA Council on Medical Education and Hospitals took special note in 1933 of a "considerable shift of patronage from the private to the tax-supported hospitals." Claims about the resulting "loss of revenue" in the private not-for-profit sector made these hospitals the alleged victims of creeping government influence which pushed them into a precarious financial condition.[24] Thus local governments, rather than the economy, could be blamed for the financial difficulties of voluntary hospitals. Neatly, government also could be pressed for a solution: that is, to pay voluntary hospitals adequately for indigent care.

These issues, as well as the shaky economic climate and the expanding demand for free care in the early 1930s, encouraged hospital associations and administrators to work in the political arena, and to understand and manipulate their immediate environments in very different ways from the 1920s. In turn, voluntary hospital administrators throughout the country became aggressive seekers of local government funds for charity patients, proponents of hospital insurance for patients of moderate means, lobbyists for federal funds, and earnest advocates of the value of voluntary institutions as an alternative to government provision. For the first time, the national hospital associations became a single, articulate lobby, presenting a combined front in debates over the federal programs of the Hoover administration and the Roosevelt programs of the New Deal.

Doctors and nonprofit hospitals also forged closer ties. In contrast to the consumer ethos and the expanding hospital organization of the 1920s, which pushed doctors and hospitals apart, the common pressures of the Depression reminded them that private practitioners and voluntary hospitals had mutual interests. The watchwords were now "harmony" and "cooperation."[25] Voluntary hospitals still had clear advantages over local-government hospitals for private practitioners. They classified the largest possible number of patients as being able to pay their hospital bills—and thus, by definition, as being eligible for separate physician billings; and they allowed doctors maximum freedom from bureaucratic rules.

In the 1930s, then, physicians and voluntary hospitals were natural allies, with a common set of goals and a common need to present themselves as having a special, private, altruistic mission. The more that contemporary reports critical of the medical-care system emphasized the drawbacks and gaps of American medicine, the closer the alignment between the two groups, if only to maintain the status quo.[26] State and national hospital associations, growing as articulators of the voluntary ideal, took care not to offend the American Medical Association and its state and local affiliates, and not to confront private practitioners by ruthless competition with them.

Taking hospitals as a whole—that is, lumping general, psychiatric, and all other hospitals together into one set of statistics—there was indeed a clear shift toward government-hospital provision between 1929 and 1933. The broad patterns are shown in table 6.3. The *overall* occupancy rate for government hospitals of all types was over 90 percent in 1933, compared with only 55 percent for nongovernmental hospitals as a whole. Such differences suggested alarming changes in the system and, perhaps, a permanent loss of clientele. If these patterns continued for a number of years, government would eventually, it seemed, be the dominant force in the hospital field; and voluntary hospitals would deteriorate. The "wise development of voluntary hospitals"[27] became an agenda item for both hospital and medical associations in the 1930s as a bulwark against state-controlled medicine.

But in fact, these statistics masked (and distorted) the actual experiences of *general* hospitals, since much of the government expansion in the early 1930s lay in areas in which voluntary hospitals had never been interested and were not now, that is, in psychiatric and chronic diseases.

TABLE 6.3

Average Daily Census in All Types of Hospitals—General, Special, Psychiatric, and Chronic Disease—by Ownership, 1929 and 1933

Ownership	1929 (Thousands)	1933 (Thousands)	Percentage Change, 1929–33	Occupancy Rate in 1933
Federal government	46	57	+23	75.0
State government	364	436	+20	94.8
Local government	107	134	+25	84.1
Total government	517	626	+21	90.2
Church-related	76	64	−16	54.9
Fraternal and industrial	7	6	−16	54.0
Independent associations	106	101	−5	58.5
Individual or partnership	21	14	−33	41.2
Total nongovernment	210	184	−12	55.4
All hospitals	727	810	+11	78.9
General hospitals	234	232	−1	59.9
Psychiatric hospitals	395	475	+20	95.2
All other	97	104	+7	73.4
Total	727	810	+11	78.9

NOTE: Figures are calculated from the original statistics; discrepancies are due to rounding.
SOURCE: "Hospital Service in the United States," *Journal of the American Medical Association* 102 (1934), pp. 1006–9.

There were almost twice as many patients in psychiatric hospitals as in general hospitals in 1929. Obviously, the fast growth of federal-, state-, and local-government psychiatric beds affected overall public-private trends. Neither these patients, nor the rising number of chronic disease, alcoholic, and tuberculosis patients entering local government and veterans hospitals in the Depression, were a loss to voluntary hospitals, since they would not usually have been treated in them in the first place. In short, the reported shift to government-hospital provision was, in part, a statistical artifact; it signified the rising proportion of psychiatric and chronic patients rather than a major switch of general hospital patients from voluntary to government institutions. No matter; the statistics provided powerful propaganda for the voluntary general hospitals. The hospital associations could—and did—decry government expansionism, evidenced in the overall statistics, while fighting local-government general hospitals on the issue of private patients.

The most striking differences between the experiences of government and nongovernment *general* hospitals lay in their relative rates of construction. Government general hospitals increased the value of their total capital investment by 51 percent between 1928 and 1935, compared to only 12 percent for church-related and other nonprofit hospitals, while the total value of proprietary hospitals dropped by almost 50 percent, reflecting numerous hospital closings.[28] But even here, rates of increase should not be confused with market position. Religious and other nonprofit hospitals, collectively, entered the Depression as the dominant providers of general hospital care. They retained this dominant position, reporting 66 percent of all capital investment in general hospitals in 1928; 65 percent in 1935 (table 6.4).

Despite the Depression, despite hospital closings, and despite decreasing prices, the total value of voluntary hospitals *increased* in these economically troubled years, from $1.2 to over $1.3 billion. In part, at least, the clarion call for voluntary hospital preservation in the early 1930s was a rhetorical device for organizational unity and an expression of more general fears of government domination. There was a useful gap between rhetoric and experience.

Clear lines of mutual interest began to be drawn among different groups of hospitals after the stock market crash. The church-affiliated and the nonsectarian nonprofit hospitals had vital common interests as "voluntary hospitals" that distinguished their immediate goals from those of government hospitals on the one hand and proprietary institutions on the

TABLE 6.4

Changes in Total Capital Investment of General Hospitals Registered by the AMA, by Type of Control, 1928 and 1935

| | ($ millions) | | Percent change | Percentage Distribution | |
	1928	1935		1928	1935
Governmental	416	628	+51.0	22.5	29.8
Federal	123	226	+83.7	6.7	10.7
Other governmental	293	401	+36.9	15.8	19.0
Church-related and other not-for-profit	1,224	1,369	+11.8	66.2	64.9
Proprietary	209	113	−45.9	11.3	5.4
Total	1,849	2,110	+14.1	100.0	100.0
All reporting hospitals, including general hospitals	3,090	3,218	+4.1		

NOTE: The amounts exclude endowment capital, estimated at $437 million for all types of hospitals in 1928, $519 million in 1935. Totals may not add up exactly, due to rounding.
SOURCES: C. Rufus Rorem, *Capital Investment in Hospitals,* Committee on the Costs of Medical Care, Publication no. 7, 1930 (pamphlet), calculated from tables 1 and 3, pp. 23, 19. Elliott H. Pennell, Joseph W. Mountin, and Kay Pearson, *Business Census of Hospitals, 1935,* General Report, Supplement no. 154 to *Public Health Reports* (Washington, D.C.: Government Printing Office, 1939), p. 38.

other. These interests included, first, an articulation and general acceptance of the unique character of voluntary hospitals as a group, a character that must be maintained, it seemed, against the increasing encroachment of tax-supported institutions; second, the enunciation and publication of a sense of crisis and imminent doom from which voluntary hospitals should be saved; third, an immediate search for additional income. As a fourth factor, all the voluntary nonprofits had a natural interest in dissociating themselves from the profit-making sector, not only because of the poor performance of profit-making hospitals as a group, but also to maintain voluntary hospital tax exemption where this existed. Exemptions were challenged in the courts by tax-hungry local governments looking for additional revenue.

To maintain tax exemptions voluntary hospitals had to show that they were distinctly different from hospitals that were legally organized as businesses. Representatives of the voluntary hospitals presented them as offering flexibility in role and administration, particularly important at times of rapid change, and as inspiring the hospital administrators of government hospitals toward higher grades of service—a clear statement of relative position.[29] Perhaps they did. But the hospitals were also carving out for themselves a special mission in the middle ground between for-profit and governmental agencies.

In the early 1930s the champions of voluntary hospitals described them, variously, for different audiences and purposes, as public utilities, as part of an industry, as producers dealing with consumers, and as an essential social service.[30] The implication of the term "social service" in this context was a claim on government money, as a right, for reimbursement for the care of indigent patients. Another useful word was "community," meaning "tax-supported." Hospital administrator Dr. N. W. Faxon (of Massachusetts General Hospital) put it this way: "The American public owns the hospitals. . . . The United States has developed a social philosophy, one principle of which is that the care of the sick is the concern of the community. Caring for the unemployed and for the indigent members of the community is not the responsibility of the voluntary hospital trustee or superintendent. It rests upon the community as a whole."[31]

Simultaneously, voluntary hospitals and physicians launched a major campaign against local government hospitals in California, seeking to restrain them from "unfair competition." There were tax-supported hospitals in forty-two of California's fifty-eight counties. Although county hospitals in California had long been limited by state law to services for the indigent, from 1932 several county boards of supervisors decided to open their hospitals to the paying patients of local practitioners. The test case was in Kern County (Bakersfield), where the board of supervisors opened a hospital for subsidized care for paying patients in order to improve access to hospital services by Kern County farmers. Doctors in the state brought suit through the California Medical Association. They were joined by hospital administrators in the newly established Association of California Hospitals (1934). Both groups lobbied vigorously—and won. In 1936 the California Supreme Court ruled that county hospitals could render care only to indigent patients, with certain special exceptions for part-pay patients in limited instances.[32] This ruling would hold until broken by Medicaid in the late 1960s. It showed clearly the power of organized (voluntary) hospitals and organized medicine.

But the California decision was also significant for the relative roles of voluntary and local government hospitals across the United States; it made a clear statement of preference for voluntary over governmental institutions. The decision affirmed that tax-supported hospitals had a different, lesser mission than voluntary institutions. Thus the courts conveniently removed county hospitals from competition with voluntary institutions (and also with the small, physician-owned hospitals that were scattered across California). Further, the decision recognized the paramount interests and autonomy of physicians in private practice. In voluntary hospitals doctors could work independently, charging private patients whatever they liked, while the hospitals continued to underwrite the capital for medical work. Medical associations watched to make sure the voluntary hospitals stayed in line, while both groups were allied against government encroachment.

Publication of the final report of the Committee on the Costs of Medical Care in 1932 fanned medical concerns about bureaucratic intervention into private practice,[33] for the committee's majority recommendations came out squarely for hospital-based group practice. If the proposals had been implemented, the American health system would have been reorganized around—and perhaps by—community hospitals. The hospitals would, in turn, be coordinated by local and state planning boards. This group organization would also be matched (and perhaps implemented) by group purchase; that is, by private and/or government prepayment arrangements. Although the report recommended achieving this new system through voluntary, evolutionary change and private-public cooperation, the report carried the strong suggestion of universal (if not compulsory) health insurance. What, moreover, was to stop selected groups of doctors from working with hospitals to form new systems that would compete with independent private practitioners? The very idea of group practice was a challenge to the idea of the hospital as a workshop, that is, as the place where all qualified doctors could admit their private patients.

There were approximately 150 private group clinics in the early 1930s, with 1,500 to 2,000 affiliated physicians. These doctors showed a marked tendency to direct their patients to specific institutions; that is, to set up a relatively closed-practice system. Physician enthusiasts for the group-practice idea—like Rexwald Brown, who argued eloquently for this form of organization as a means of helping patients, while also providing doctors with economic security—thus seemed just as dangerous a threat as social-ized medicine.[34] Throughout the 1930s the AMA and its local societies waged war against group practice and other organized medical systems under the rubric of the "corporate practice of medicine."[35] The AMA passed a resolution in 1934 requiring that medical staffs of hospitals ac-credited for internships include only members of the local medical society: doctors were expected to toe the party line. The AMA already had a resolution on the books (of June 1930) that the practice of medicine by corporations was "detrimental to the best interests of scientific medicine and of the people themselves," on grounds of impersonality, coldness, and the "automaticity of the machine."[36]

In the absence of group practices, however, hospitals needed individ-ual practitioners as much as the practitioners needed hospitals, and not only to bring in patients. As local medical societies variously supported and opposed private hospital prepayment (insurance) plans around the country during the 1930s, hospital administrators learned quickly that no scheme of group hospitalization prospered without the support of the local medical profession. The goodwill of doctors was the key to hospital in-come. Voluntarism was thus further defined as an organizing ideology: as hospital provision that encouraged the maintenance of autonomous, fee-for-service practice by physicians.

Although journals like *Modern Hospital* stressed the central (enlarged) position of hospitals in the recommendations of the Committee on the Costs of Medical Care,[37] hospital representatives also had other reasons not to embrace the report enthusiastically. First and foremost, hospitals had no wish to be regulated against their will. The proposed state and local planning arrangements in the committee's report suggested powerful ex-ternal forces that might threaten the autonomy of individual institutions. The report also presented the committee's recommendations as if they were a natural, rational evolution of health-care organization, so that the solutions appeared preordained, with no other alternatives being plausible. Government health insurance was not specifically recommended, but the European compulsory health-insurance programs were presented in committee publications as ones that had "moved on" from voluntary insurance. Logic might suggest an eventual progression, in the United States, too, to a government-sponsored health insurance system—at the very time that hospital administrators were beginning to pin their faith on private, voluntary hospital-insurance plans. Finally, the recommendations coincided with the new push for hospital policy-making within and among the major national hospital associations. These, like the AMA, had a vested interest in preserving for themselves the right to promulgate new policies and ideas.

Voluntary hospitals, like doctors, were also concerned about "unfair competition," both from tax-supported hospitals and among themselves. A code of ethics developed by the AHA Committee on Public Relations in 1933 was frankly anticompetitive on the subject of hospital advertising. Hospitals were urged not to compete with private practitioners through outpatient care and not to "steal" doctors from other institutions.[38] All these movements suggested that hospitals and doctors had overriding mutual interests that would make it foolish to rock the boat.

Morris Fishbein, editor of the AMA *Journal* and a clever exponent of the uses of rhetoric, used the report of the Committee on the Costs of Medical Care to identify mutual alliances and to crystallize political issues, both right and left. The proposals for hospital-based group practice and prepayment would, he said, both "commercialize" medicine, making doctors "cogs of great machines," and, at the same time, "socialize" it. Voluntarism, as an intrinsic aspect of professional ideology, was polarized against "socialism and communism—inciting to revolution."[39] By this Fishbein meant, loosely, any compulsory governmental action. The old Progressive doctrines, which the report most closely reflected—belief in benevolent social change through knowledge, and free cooperation—were thus transmuted into a political philosophy of the "left." Now only voluntarism was "American." Hospitals and physicians were on the same team.

Hospital Administration as a Profession

The increasing authority of administrators in voluntary hospitals during the Depression was, nevertheless, a potential threat to private practitioners. An ambitious breed of hospital administrator was emerging, young men without medical degrees who would later rise to power in the American Hospital Association: George Bugbee, for example, who graduated from the University of Michigan in 1926 and went to work at the university's new hospital as an accountant; he became assistant director in 1938. Or James A. Hamilton, who graduated from Dartmouth College in 1922, followed by graduate work and then a position on the industrial engineering faculty of Dartmouth's Amos Tuck School of Business. From there he moved to become superintendent of the Mary Hitchcock Memorial Hospital in Hanover in 1926; in 1936 he became superintendent of the Cleveland City Hospital. Or Gerhard Hartman, who became an administrative statistician at Presbyterian Hospital in New York in 1932 while finishing his master's degree at Buffalo in business administration, then went on to work on his doctorate at the University of Chicago. Or John Mannix, born in 1902, who started working at Mount Sinai Hospital in Cleveland while still in school, became superintendent of Elyria (Ohio) Memorial Hospital in 1926, and returned in 1930 to Cleveland as assistant director of the newly merged University Hospitals.[40]

These and other young idealists sparked enthusiasm for a new American College of Hospital Administrators, independent of the American Hospital Association. The college was established in 1933 to provide a professional association for nonmedical (as well as medical) administrators, offering fellowships on a basis similar to that of the American College of Surgeons. Paul H. Fesler, superintendent of Wesley Memorial Hospital in Chicago and then president of the American Hospital Association, underlined the dominant status of voluntary over government hospitals by suggesting as admissions criteria at least five years' experience in a "private and acceptable hospital," as well as examination on the basis of a thesis.[41] Malcolm MacEachern supported the idea for a new college on behalf of the American College of Surgeons; he became an honorary charter fellow. Thus the college and administrators demonstrated their joint interests, interests which the AMA might not always share. (It was by no means incidental that surgical patients represented more than 60 percent of hospital patients in both urban and rural areas in the early 1930s.)

Despite some criticism from physician-administrators of large eastern hospitals, who claimed that the new college was trying to preempt hospital administration for nonphysician managers, the College of Hospital Administrators was immediately successful. It provided an important identification and bonding, primarily for well-educated male administrators. Of the 102 charter fellows, only 16 were women; and only 32 of the men were physicians.[42] Professionalization was spurred on the following year (1934) with the establishment of the first graduate program in hospital administration, by Michael M. Davis, at the University of Chicago. In these and other ways, leaders of the professionalization movement provided a core group, pressing for the values of voluntary hospitals as the standard-setters for hospital quality in the United States—and as institutions that might have interests that were separate and apart from those of organized medicine.

A growing, parallel interest in group hospitalization insurance as a means of raising much-needed hospital income sparked further cohesion among administrators. A paper by Justin F. Kimball, founder of the Baylor hospital plan, was presented (in his absence) at the AHA conference in Toronto in 1931 and stirred considerable interest among the participants. The timing was right for rediscovery of an old idea: hospital insurance, or prepayment. Beginning with the 1932 AHA convention in Detroit, voluntary hospital insurance excited enthusiastic discussion within the association. The American College of Surgeons, with an eye toward hospital prosperity, formally endorsed group hospitalization schemes in 1934. The American Medical Association withheld its approval for another four years, fearing incursions by hospitals into the private practice of medicine; but then it, too, recognized the mutuality of interests.

All groups agreed on the central importance of the voluntary hospital as an institution. Indeed, in retrospect it is striking to note how hard each group worked to accommodate the others' point of view. The AMA moved toward endorsement of voluntary hospital insurance; the surgeons and other hospital-based specialists endorsed the AMA's condemnation of salaried hospital practice; and hospital administrators and boards chose not to extend hospital services (or those of associated prepayment schemes) to include medical fees as well as hospital maintenance charges. But this is looking ahead. Even in the early 1930s, voluntary hospital administrators, surgeons, and other physicians had a common, overriding bond. For all, voluntary hospitals represented a bulwark against the increasing power of government.

Carving Out the Middle Ground: The Voluntary Sector

The first step in defining a voluntary hospital *sector* was to provide it with appropriate rhetoric. The second was to give it an effective power base. The third was to describe it through the production of statistics at the national level. Rhetoric was all-pervasive. In a subtle about-face, spokesmen for voluntary hospitals disengaged themselves from the private sector, spoke of their hospitals as "public," realigned them with public service, and distinguished them from proprietary institutions.

A suggestive report on hospital management written for an AHA Committee in 1930 by the (physician) superintendent of Grace Hospital in Detroit criticized the misuse of the designation "private hospital" to cover both for-profit hospitals and nonprofit institutions. Only the former, he said, were properly private; the latter were best described as public institutions.[43] Spokesmen for the voluntary hospitals took pains to link them with local government hospitals when both sought limited tax funds; voluntary hospitals, it was argued, relieved the local tax burden since without these hospitals taxpayers might be called upon to meet the full cost of hospital services and hospital capital. Meetings of the American Hospital Association rang with claims that hospital care for the poor, wherever given, was "just as legitimate a burden for our taxation as our schools, police and fire protection"; and it was pointed out that the average nonprofit hospital recovered only 42 percent of the costs of services rendered to the indigent, whereas government hospitals were fully subsidized.[44] In the new scenario voluntary hospitals were quasi-governmental agents—noble community institutions which government was unfairly spurning.

The AMA Council on Medical Education and Hospitals helped this movement by making a significant revision in the ordering and presentation of its hospital statistics, clearly distinguishing nonprofit from profit-making institutions for the first time. From 1934 the AMA classified hospitals into three major sectors: government, proprietary, and nonprofit (voluntary). The revision made an important statement. The AMA, as well as the AHA, legitimated the existence of voluntary hospitals as a third sector, occupying the middle ground between the tax-supported and the profit-making institutions.

Table 6.5 shows the power of this middle sector once the statistics (and the rhetoric) are rearranged. Under the earlier AMA classification, hospital services seemed to be provided predominantly by corporations

TABLE 6.5

*Reordering the Statistics: Admissions to Private and Local-Government, General,
Special, Psychiatric, and Chronic Disease Hospitals, by Ownership Category, 1934,
with Update to 1940*

	Thousands of Admissions 1934	Percentage 1934		
Initial AMA Classification:				
Local government	1,360	21.4		
Church-related hospitals	1,787	28.1		
Fraternal	35	0.6		
Corporations and associations (nonprofit and for-profit)	2,801	44.1		
Individual and partnership	366	5.8		
Total	6,349	100.0		
			Update to 1940	
Revised Classification, 1934:				
Local government	1,360	21.4	1,729	19.3
Church-related hospitals	1,787	28.1	2,680	30.0
Fraternal	35	0.6	—	—
Nonprofit corporations and associations	2,343	36.9	3,575	40.0
Total nonprofit	4,164	65.6	6,255	69.9
Individual or partnership	366	5.8	500	5.6
Corporations (unrestricted as to profit)	458	7.2	464	5.2
Total proprietary	825	13.0	964	10.8
Total	6,349	100.0	8,948	100.0

NOTE: Totals may not add up exactly, due to rounding.
SOURCE: "Hospital Service in the United States," *Journal of the American Medical Association* 104 (1935), p. 1081, and 116 (1941), pp. 1060–63. The figures for the initial classification have been recalculated into the categories used between 1921 and 1933. Federal and state hospitals have been omitted in order to exclude admissions to veterans' hospitals and state psychiatric and tuberculosis hospitals.

and associations, with church-related hospitals and local-government institutions providing a significant minority of care. But no type of hospital was in the majority. Under the revised AMA classification of 1934, a very different structure emerges. By dividing the figures for corporations and associations into separate nonprofit and for-profit categories, and by combining church-related hospitals and other nonprofit institutions into one sector, a dominant voluntary (nonprofit) hospital sector appears. In 1934, excluding federal and state hospitals, two-thirds of all hospital admissions were to voluntary nonprofit hospitals, barely more than one-fifth to local government hospitals, and only one out of eight to proprietary hospitals.

Between 1934 and 1940, admissions to the voluntary hospitals rose by 50 percent, much faster than those of the other two sectors.

How did voluntary hospitals achieve this remarkable success? The combination of medical and hospital interests was obviously one ingredient; the high public faith in hospital service another; the identification of high-quality hospital care with voluntary hospitals a third. However, probably none of these factors alone would have been sufficient. Of great importance was the fact that the voluntary hospital leaders became politically well-organized, visible, and articulate during the Depression. Group cohesion was fostered by uncounted meetings of administrators: at the annual institutes for hospital administrators sponsored by the AHA from 1933, at meetings of the American College of Hospital Administrators, at formal and informal gatherings of sponsors of prepayment plans, and at other meetings around professional, political, and economic agendas. The federal programs of the 1930s increased the sense of organizational unity by providing a common target of interest for the hospital associations. Finally, the experience of the financial crisis, like the earlier crisis of World War I, glamorized and uplifted hospitals as symbols of all that was best in America.

Like the lavish new movie palaces, temples of the silver screen, with their oriental rugs and Gobelin tapestries, hospitals played a psychologically important, sustaining social role in the 1930s. One article in *Literary Digest* in June 1933 praised hospitals as "typically American" trailblazers and as "depression cures," important in promoting general confidence and public morale—a prerequisite, in turn, for the recovery of the financial markets.[45] Movie houses promised romance, illusion, and adventure. Hospitals promised cure and care. Hospitals were also important examples of the clean, functional lines of modern technology and modern architecture. Numerous new (expensive) buildings spoke of simplicity, sunshine, sanitation, science, rationality, modernism, and common sense. These, too, were images of promise, success, and of better things to come. The prominent social image of hospitals gave them good reasons to maintain a high level of construction expenditures where they could, rather than cut back to the bone.

Social-welfare experts like I. M. Rubinow complained of hospitals' extravagance to no avail—the "marble and granite, the brass and bronze, and carved woods, the tiles and frescoes, and the hallways and restrooms, and piazzas and private bathrooms and the remaining jim-cracks, gewgaws and gadgets. . . ."[46] Hospital architects, trustees, superintendents, and medical boards were doing more than expressing their own cupidity, vanity, and rich imagination (the reasons suggested by Rubinow); they were tapping into the American dream, as indeed they had in earlier periods.

This visible demonstration of success was virtually monopolized by the voluntary hospitals and their associated physicians. In the large cities (though not elsewhere) local-government hospitals remained for the most part second-rate. The voluntary hospital offered a "brand image" of heroic workers, willingly toiling for the public good. A major new textbook on hospital organization and management by Dr. Malcolm MacEachern (1935) emphasized not only the complexity and importance of hospital operations, but also the hospital's idealized role. The book carried illustrations of the hospital as a shining, scientific citadel, standing on a hill, beaming out rays of glory to patients and serving as a "haven of relief."[47] Voluntarism gave the hospital associations a slogan and a mission as they consolidated their power in the political arena.

Hospital Associations as Political Lobbies

There were three major national hospital organizations in the 1930s. The American Hospital Association represented 1,532 hospitals and 2,760 individuals in 1933, including administrators, board members, members of hospital medical and nursing staffs, and heads of major hospital departments. The Catholic Hospital Association was also rising in strength, having weathered a serious crisis of purpose and leadership in 1929; there had been criticisms within the church that the association was too much under Jesuit control, poorly managed, and too provincially midwestern. The new president, Father Alphonse Schwitalla, a diplomat and canny politician, became a persuasive national spokesman in the 1930s for the moral superiority, privileges, and liberties of private voluntary hospitals compared with governmental institutions. Father Schwitalla brought to the political debates on voluntarism an important reminder of the religious and charitable roots of nonprofit institutions, as they corrected their twentieth-century course from the consumerism of the 1920s to the political realities of the New Deal. The third major national hospital association, the American Protestant Hospital Association, represented a far smaller, less influential and heterogeneous group of hospitals with Episcopal, Presbyterian, Methodist, Baptist, and other sectarian roots. However, this group, too, rallied in the 1930s around both economic and religious interests. The association reported that Protestant hospitals were "doing an annual business of $85 million" in 1936, excluding buildings and bad debts.[48]

The interests of the American Hospital Association and the religious associations were virtually identical. Both needed to project a caring, responsible image for the voluntary hospital that allowed them to be included in any new federal program, without public takeover or regulation. All were concerned about possible competitive expansion of the veterans' hospital system.[49] All sought government funds for their members, provided these came without strings attached, and all insisted that government, not the hospitals, should be financially responsible for the indigent. All meant by this that the care of the indigent should be subsidized by government in voluntary as well as tax-supported institutions. The Catholic Hospital Association provided the best phraseology for this, claiming that the indigent American was the "ward of society" rather than merely a "ward of state."[50]

Links between the national hospital associations were firmly established on a personal level in the early 1930s. Monsignor Maurice Griffin, a prominent Catholic, active in the Ohio Hospital Association, and an AHA trustee, was a moving force for joint activities. By the end of 1932 the joint rhetoric of voluntarism was in place, ready for use in lobbying wherever this seemed to be desirable or necessary. Thus the executive secretary of the AHA was able to write forcefully to the chairman of the new Federal Reconstruction Finance Corporation in December 1932 that federal support should be available to the "voluntary hospitals of this country," not only because they were under serious financial stress, but because they were organized to provide care for "all classes of our citizenry," and for Protestants, Catholics, and Jews.[51] Without the assistance of the voluntary hospitals, it was claimed, government hospitals could not cope, and there might be widespread epidemics.

Three new federal programs, created at a special session of Congress convened in 1933, provided hospitals with major opportunities for political activity: the Civilian Conservation Corps, designed to put the unemployed of the cities to work in the national forests; federal grants to the states for relief; and a program of public works legislated through the National Industrial Recovery Act (NIRA). If federal grants were available for employment and for relief, it seemed reasonable to claim some of this money for care of federal beneficiaries in voluntary hospitals. Public works and relief programs also raised the specter of a potentially massive buildup of government hospitals. Harry Hopkins, the Federal Emergency Relief administrator in the Roosevelt administration, consistently opposed the inclusion of voluntary hospitals in federal relief programs, perhaps because of his previous experience of the successes and entrepreneurial activities of hospitals in New York.[52] Voluntary hospitals rallied quickly to defend their interests.

At the same time, voluntary hospitals needed to be officially recognized as public rather than private agencies in order to escape new, unwanted business regulation. Employees in commercial organizations participating in New Deal programs were guaranteed the right to collective bargaining, and employers were required to meet codes for minimum and maximum hours of work. (Government organizations were exempt from such requirements, on the grounds that they were already acting for the public good.) Since voluntary hospitals everywhere paid their employees less than locally prevailing wage rates and were flexible in assigning hours of work, the requirements for "private" organizations under NIRA filled their boards of trustees with dismay. Hospital workers were not usually unionized, and administrators wanted to keep it this way. Here was a potent argument for claiming that voluntary hospitals were quasi-governmental institutions. Hospital spokesmen argued eloquently that voluntary hospitals had a special role—indeed, that their low pay was a virtue, since it attracted staff who were motivated by the "right values," putting the care of patients above high wages and cherishing job satisfaction and the privilege of service.[53] Organizational association between the religious and nonsectarian hospitals aided in this process, because it extended, by analogy, the dedicated service of Roman Catholic nuns to the jobs of all hospital workers. There were indeed thousands of dedicated workers in hospitals throughout the United States. But such claims successfully held down hospital wage levels and unionization until well after World War II. Hospitals did not become unionized to any great extent until the 1960s.

The inclusion of voluntary hospitals in a federal code designed to regulate commercial and industrial establishments (NIRA) was probably, in fact, inadvertent. Congressional staff had paid little or no attention to the meaning of the code for voluntary hospitals, which competed directly with government institutions. There was little union interest in hospitals in the 1920s and most of the 1930s, and there was thus little awareness, outside the hospital world, that in numerous categories hospital employees were now part of the regular national labor force, occupying jobs similar to those in industry. Hospital elevator operators, janitors, dishwashers, watchmen, porters, maintenance workers, laundry workers, and window cleaners were all expected to buy into the voluntary ethos of dedication and low pay. There was a good case for including voluntary hospitals under NIRA, as administrators of large hospitals were aware.

However, the NIRA experience was probably most important to hospital administrators in providing a practice run for organizational cohesion and effective lobbying. The legislation brought administrators together in local associations and national meetings to discuss, ad nauseam, the implications of the code, whether there ought to be a special code applying only to hospitals, and/or whether voluntary hospitals were to be exempt from the requirements altogether, on the grounds that they were unlike other businesses. Spokesmen for nonprofit hospitals claimed that they deserved exemption because of their degree of social commitment and their efforts to keep service deficits as low as possible despite large overhead expenses. In such meetings the voluntary ideal developed, strategically, as a means of avoiding government regulation.

To combat the potential threat of the new code, the AHA called a meeting of its board of trustees in the summer of 1933, and the board in turn appointed a committee to present the hospitals' case. Urged on by Monsignor Griffin, the Catholic Hospital Association and the Protestant Hospital Association joined with AHA representatives to provide a common political front in order to fight—or at least to negotiate with—the federal government. At its first meeting in August 1933 this new joint committee agreed to ask for exemption from the code, arguing the hospitals' inability to obtain the funds necessary to comply with the act. The joint committee was able to claim an instant victory, for the head of the federal division of reemployment, a General Hammond, readily agreed that the act did not apply to nonprofit hospitals. Subsequently, a ruling from the NRA legal department to the presidents of the three associations ratified this decision.[54]

This experience was important to the political agenda and the organizational power of voluntary hospitals in three respects. First was the evident success of lobbying: the federal government had apparently capitulated to organized interests. Second, the incident distinguished the voluntary hospitals clearly from commerce, including profit-making hospitals. The committee argued that the voluntary hospitals were not "competitive" organizations within the definition of the act; that is, they were not industries but charitable institutions. It was only a step from here to claims that voluntary hospitals should be recognized by the federal government as relief agencies rather than as commercial enterprises. Third, the joint committee of the three national hospital associations became the focus of national lobbying by voluntary hospitals. Between 1933 and 1942 members of the joint committee participated in almost all congressional hearings on legislation that had a bearing on health and hospitals.

The joint committee provided a consistent, unified voice arguing for the maintenance of the voluntary hospitals of America through recognition of a dual "public" hospital system: that is, of a public sector which included both hospitals run by government agencies and hospitals run by nonprofit corporations and associations. The committee was an effective force in developing a common political consciousness among hospitals across the country. (In 1933, for example, the committee gained a useful ruling from the Treasury Department exempting hospitals from the 5 percent tax on dividends for securities held in trust.) Voluntary hospitals also gained a useful foothold in federal programs in becoming eligible, in the winter of 1933–34, for treatment of injured employees among the 4 million workers employed by the Civil Works Administration. Most hospital work under the CWA program was handled by nongovernmental hospitals, with government reimbursing them for their services. A "splendid cooperative spirit" was reported between the AHA and government, with few hitches or complaints.[55]

In 1934–35 the joint committee fought against the inclusion of voluntary hospitals in the massive new Social Security program, proposed in pending Social Security legislation. Claiming that the provisions for Social Security taxes on employers (as well as employees) would "adversely affect every hospital in the United States," the hospital lobby moved rapidly and successfully to exclude voluntary hospitals from any requirement in the Social Security Act of 1935. The joint committee's testimony before the House Ways and Means Committee described nonprofit hospitals, eloquently, as "truly public service corporations," which had a "partnership with the government in providing for the general welfare"; they were not industries but charities, organized and operated for the commonweal. At the close of the session several members reportedly came down from the platform to congratulate the joint committee on its presentation and to assure them of their votes.[56] An all-American glow surrounded such debates. These and other efforts consolidated the associations around single national hospital goals; gave them a common agenda; and, where government aid was not made available, provided them with a justification for any inadequacy in the hospitals' treatment of charity patients. Hospital employees were denied the benefit of Social Security until at least the 1950s, depending on where they were employed. Legislation enacted in 1950 permitted nonprofit hospitals (and other nonprofit institutions) to participate in the Social Security Program on an elective basis, with the concurrence of their employees. Participation was made mandatory under Public Law 98–21, in 1983.

The Political Utility of the Voluntary Ideal

Out of the Depression and the New Deal the hospital associations developed, in turn, a major, two-plank political platform for government aid. They asked first for government reimbursement of hospital care given to the indigent, which would supplement new private programs of voluntary hospital insurance for the middle class, and second, for federal aid for hospital construction. Neither of these proposals was immediately successful. Federal aid for hospital construction was finally achieved in the Hill-Burton Act of 1946, and federal grants to states for "vendor payments" to hospitals and other providers in 1950. But the policies gave the associations an assertive stance—and a lasting base for negotiations with successive congressional committees and government agencies. Hospitals wanted their "fair share" of federal funds.

At the same time, the lobbyists made clear that government aid was only acceptable if it came with no strings. The Catholic Hospital Association was particularly adamant that any federal aid must be given free of any danger of federal control.[57] The goal was subsidy without regulation. A government reimbursement system—a system of purchase—for care of the indigent was preferred over a more general system of government grants, because it appeared to offer less of a threat to hospital autonomy.[58] AHA delegates in 1934 opposed, in principle, any system of federal direct grants to individual hospitals. Hospitals were not so down and out, even then, that they needed to accept federal money on any terms. Unfortunately, perhaps, they never had a chance to test this fortitude.

The AHA protested the exclusion of hospitals from the programs of the Federal Emergency Relief Administration (FERA) in 1933. Hedging its bets, in the same year the association endorsed the principles of voluntary group hospital insurance, to stimulate funds for hospital care for working-class patients. The association also recommended the establishment of local hospital councils to develop private community support. Nevertheless, the exclusion from FERA rankled; the program was serving 18.9 million needy individuals by December 1934.[59] Although hospitals were not included under FERA before its demise in 1935, the experience encouraged hospitals to join ranks behind the principle that government—that is, federal, state and/or local government—ought to be responsible for charity care. It followed that expecting voluntary hospitals to cope with poverty without government aid was intrinsically unfair.

Common political and economic interests brought hospitals together at the local as well as the national level. As local relief funds dried up under the strain of increased unemployment, state and local hospital organizations became assiduous watchdogs of public aid. The Hospital Association of Pennsylvania, for example, lobbied the state legislature vigorously for a relief-fund bond issue in that state. The association produced thousands of posters, leaflets, letters, and cards and urged each board and hospital to mobilize its influential friends and its community by meetings and radio announcements and through churches, universities, women's clubs, physicians' groups, and other organizations. At the election, uniformed nurses and other hospital representatives manned the polls in scores of counties across Pennsylvania. Despite initial expectations that the bond issue would not go through, it was passed by a vote of four to one, and the cost to the hospitals was negligible.[60] The value of united action was clearly demonstrated, together with the hospitals' ability to provoke public sympathy.

At one and the same time, then, the spokesmen for voluntary hospitals were simultaneously declaring their imminent demise and mobilizing effectively to encourage their individual and organizational survival and success. By presenting hospitals as cooperative rather than competitive organizations, hospital superintendents avoided at least some of the hostile criticisms arising from their rollback in wages, limitations on charity care, and stringency in bill collection. Growing interest in hospital-insurance schemes provided a further opportunity to stress cooperation of voluntary hospitals for the community good, as well as to increase hospital income. Group hospitalization schemes were begun by hospitals in Sacramento in 1932; in Essex County, New Jersey, and St. Paul in 1933; and in Washington and Cleveland in 1934.

Local-government hospital expansion slowed down (or even waned) across the United States after the worst years of the Depression, 1931–34, partly because of organized medical pressure against their admission of private patients and partly because local taxpayers had little desire to expand tax-supported services. However, the question of construction continued to vex, because of the exclusion of voluntary hospitals from New Deal construction programs, which focused on building government institutions. The two major programs were that of the Public Works Administration (PWA) and the Works Progress Administration (WPA). PWA was created in the spring of 1933 and rolled into gear in 1934. It based its construction goals for hospitals on the inflated hospital construction figures of the late 1920s (which in fact had led to an acknowledged oversupply of beds), and it limited its funds to government institutions. According to PWA estimates, there was an accumulated deficiency of about $550 million in hospital construction by 1937, because of a general lack of building between 1929 and 1933.[61] Hospitals provided a golden opportunity for getting the construction industry into full operation and the agency swung enthusiastically into action. In Boston, for example, PWA provided funds to the city general hospital to finance construction of a modern ten-story building.[62]

The WPA spent more than $77 million on public charitable, medical, and psychiatric institutions between the time of the passage of the Emergency Relief Appropriation Act of 1935 and December 1938. Almost all of this amount flowed to tax-supported (government) hospitals, but as with PWA funds most went to psychiatric and tuberculosis institutions.[63] Traces of the well-built WPA projects are still to be seen—for example, the fine mosaic in the lobby of the old local-government hospital (Hillman Hospital) in Birmingham, Alabama, now part of the University of Alabama Medical Center.

The PWA and WPA programs were actually a mixed blessing to the voluntary sector, adding to concerns that government hospitals would shortly sweep the decks. But they also provided political ammunition to voluntary hospitals, by demolishing any argument that might be made that hospitals were part of a bloated industry. Given the federal drive for building, voluntary hospitals could claim openly that their own capital needs were critical and that needed modernization was being delayed because of the increased burden of the indigent sick.

Hospital leaders were well aware that at least some hospital cost problems in the Depression arose from inappropriate capital investment in the 1920s: overbuilding, poor planning, an inappropriate mix of accommodations, facilities which were expensive to maintain, and the destruction of older plants in favor of larger, more flamboyant, more expensive institutions. The journal *Hospital Management* warned its readers in 1934 that ready availability of federal funds for hospital construction increased the likelihood of adding to the surplus of over 155,000 unoccupied hospital beds and urged national, state, and local hospital associations to contact state planning commissions, where they existed, and to warn officials against the danger of providing more hospital facilities in the majority of communities. But there were limits to what voluntary hospitals might do when confronted by "this sort of thing."[64] An AHA committee in 1935 suggested that a "certificate of necessity" be required for any proposed increase in beds, matched by a scheme for closing down uneconomical and unneeded hospitals.[65] But this idea was uncomfortably near to proposals for state and local planning, as suggested by the Committee on the Costs of Medical Care. Present-day (state) certificate-of-need legislation was reinvented in the 1960s.

In terms of federal policy, the hospital associations had learned that the time to press for inclusion of voluntary hospitals in federal legislation was in the writing of the bill itself or at least in the initial development of regulations, not when the legislation was being implemented. This was a lesson that was to stand them in good stead. Thus, although voluntary hospitals were not by any stretch of the imagination major economic beneficiaries of the early New Deal, they gained in political know-how and authority.[66] Most voluntary hospitals not only survived the Depression, they added technology, such as X-ray machines, fluoroscopes, and anesthesia equipment (at depressed prices), built up their services, gained in prestige, and honed their collective political skills.

As organizational rhetoric in this expansionary, unifying process, voluntarism had great virtues. It served to cement national cohesion among 4,100 heterogeneous, geographically scattered nonprofit hospitals. It also allowed for spillover analogies in contiguous fields. Most notably, group hospital insurance (Blue Cross) became "voluntary" insurance: signifying not only the nature of the organization itself, organized by volunteers, but also its clientele: individuals (or groups of individuals) who were free to engage in insurance on a voluntary basis. The meaning of "voluntarism" was usefully slippery. Another virtue was more frankly political. Voluntarism allowed nonprofit hospitals to strengthen their alliance with the medical profession in favor of voluntarism as a generic, heroic political ideology, set against any incursions of "socialized" medicine. Beneath the rhetoric, hospitals went on much as before.

To doctors toiling for hours with little hope of recompense, to nurses coping with low salaries, to administrators struggling to stay within the budget while not cutting back on outpatient care, and to newly impoverished patients taken into hospitals for free care, the sense of altruism was immediate, real, necessary, and widely shared. But beyond this, voluntarism evoked wider social meanings. In the depths of the Depression, hospitals were beacons of hope, science, faith, and caring. Extended into the realm of collective action, voluntarism stressed the central importance of private institutions in the United States. These messages were not ignored by the hospitals' representatives. The idea of voluntary enterprise provided the glue to hold autonomous institutions together as their managers mobilized in the political arena.

7

Technology and the
Workers:
The Genesis of Blue Cross

THE SIZE and complexity of the large hospitals of the 1930s stamped them as technological bureaucracies in which experts prescribed ideal treatments and behavior, even for the richest patients. If the basic goal was to spread the benefits of modern medical technology across the entire population through an organized system of distribution, the hospital enterprise might have been organized into a network of corporations that were regulated as public utilities, like gas or electricity. Alternatively, hospitals might become segments in a government-controlled health-care system, either through direct control by state or local government agencies, or through the indirect influence of a massive scheme (or schemes) of government health insurance. Logically, doctors would become employees.

A third possibility was to leave the existing network of local hospitals and private practitioners alone and to focus instead on ensuring access to hospital technology through fostering private prepayment (insurance) arrangements—primarily targeting the middle class, who were most in need, but backed up by government support of the poor. This was the private, "voluntary" approach. By no means incidentally, it avoided the questions of systemwide reorganization.

The resulting Blue Cross plans were a major organizational innovation of the 1930s. By protecting workers against the high costs of hospital technology, the plans improved hospital access without resorting to government (compulsory) health insurance for everyone. They provided voluntary hospitals with needed income, and they gave large employers the opportunity to support or to guarantee services for employees who might otherwise seek "socialist" solutions (i.e., a governmental scheme). From the choices made in the late 1930s came patterns of health insurance centered on the workplace—the patterns that we still have today. From these choices, too, came a balancing of power between doctors and hospitals, locally and nationally, which avoided control by either group.

The Necessary Institution

Hospitalization was commonplace for a wide variety of conditions by the mid-1930s. In 1935–36 almost a third of all cases of pneumonia were hospitalized. In the larger cities one out of every twenty-four children was a hospital patient—over half for surgery, with a continuing predominance of tonsillectomies and adenoidectomies. With improvements in the national economy in the late 1930s, utilization of hospitals expanded further. Occupancy rates for general hospitals rose from 64 percent in 1935 to 70 percent in 1940—rates much higher than those in the late 1920s—while the average length of stay decreased.[1] By 1940 general-hospital admission rates represented seven admissions for every hundred persons.

The social importance of hospital-based technology, including hospital nursing, was reinforced by the fact that there was often no alternative by the mid-1930s. The child with the acute pain of mastoiditis, scheduled for surgery, could not be operated on at home. Scarlet fever, unless carefully nursed, might leave permanent damage in its wake (hence my own hospitalization in the 1940s). Patients could die of a "burst appendix." Pneumonia demanded careful regulation of the body temperature, a daily salt or soapsuds enema, sometimes alcohol sponges, strapping of the chest, sedatives, aggressive administration of specific serum treatment after careful laboratory diagnosis, and often oxygen therapy. Thus, even more than in earlier periods, hospitals embodied and monopolized technique.

For most medical conditions there was no specific therapy, no effective drug, before sulfanilamide (1937). Instead, there was a battery of examinations and procedures designed to keep the patient alive through the crisis of disease. Consider, for example, the pneumonia patient, typically a man of about thirty years of age, who was subject to daily examinations to detect changes as he ran the gamut of shaky chills, drenching sweats, stabbing chest pains and sometimes throat rattles, vomiting, nausea, emaciation, incontinence, euphoria, hallucinations, and dehydration. Or take typhoid fever. Lewis Thomas has observed that if a case of typhoid fever had to be managed today by the best methods of 1935, it would run to staggering expense, with a hospital stay of perhaps fifty days, "requiring the most demanding kind of nursing care, with the obsessive concern for details of diet that characterized the therapy of that time, with daily laboratory monitoring, and, on occasion, surgical intervention for abdominal catastrophe."[2] Thomas contrasts these methods with the present-day ability to provide a bottle of chloramphenicol and to limit the disease to a day or two of fever. However, from the perspective of the 1930s, detailed treatment in hospital was often the only successful form of treatment.

Medical specialization also encouraged hospitalization. By 1940 almost one-fourth of all American physicians in active practice were working as full-time specialists and many more had part-time specialist interests.[3] Specialists looked to the hospital as a technological center: for diagnostic services (X ray and pathology) as well as for surgery, anesthesia, and skilled round-the-clock nursing care. Medical specialization and the increased expense of hospital technology also seemed to suggest, as a necessary corollary, larger, more bureaucratic patterns of organization within the hospitals themselves.

Meanwhile, Americans had become accustomed to having the problems of disease removed to the nearest treatment factory. By the late 1930s home care of all kinds was far less significant than in previous decades, even though there was an increased amount of chronic disease in the population, and despite the views of experts that an increasing percentage of older people could be cared for at home more economically and more satisfactorily than in institutions or in clinics.[4] Patients looked to hospitals with hope even when hope was unrealistic; hence, paradoxically, the rising number of hospital deaths. More than a fourth of all American deaths took place in general hospitals in the mid-1930s, rising to almost a third by 1940, with the highest rates usually in the richest states. In six western states— Wyoming, Colorado, Montana, Washington, California, and Nevada— over 45 percent of all deaths took place in hospitals in 1943.[5]

As both the demand for hospitalization and hospital costs seemed launched on an ever-rising trajectory, the question of distribution became more intense. Obstetrical service was a case in point. In 1935 over a third of all U.S. births were in hospitals. However, that rate was almost doubled for white women in U.S. cities, and was even higher for affluent women in this group. Yet in rural areas of the South deliveries rarely took place in hospitals at all.[6] Such distinctions signified more than distinctions in social amenities by geography, race, and social class, for clinical treatment also varied significantly across the social variables. The rates for forceps-assisted deliveries, for example, rose with the patient's income, signifying, presumably, a higher level of technique. For hospitalized women with family incomes of $2,000 or more the chance of a forceps delivery was well over 40 percent in 1935, but the average rate for all women was only 18 percent.[7]

It was not, then, just the place of care but the *technology* that was differentially spread. Given that forceps deliveries were more "technological" than unassisted care (whatever we may now think about the use of forceps), wealth appeared to be providing privileged access to basic technological benefits; and conversely, poverty seemed to be depriving millions of these same benefits. Yet in other important social realms technology was being shared throughout the population as an accepted element of national policy; rural electrification projects were a prime example. Denial of access to basic medical technology seemed somehow un-American.

Even more un-American was the fact that individuals on relief often received more hospital care than ordinary workers, because of the availability of local-government hospitals and charity care. Those on relief were more likely to be hospitalized when they had pneumonia, for example, than were those with moderate incomes.[8] Again, the bias toward hospitalization made this seem intrinsically unfair. And what about the relatively large use of hospitals by children and the unfairness of rationing their care by family income? Children between the ages of five and nine had the second-highest hospitalization rate of any age group in the 1930s—62.6 cases per 1,000 population per year, compared with 68.1 for persons sixty-five years of age and over. And children had the highest rate of surgical operations of any age group.[9] Why should tonsillectomies not be freely available to all first-graders?

The social problem that accompanied medical technology was not necessarily one of equality of provision but of providing access to basic services for everybody, so that they could call upon the organization to help them in need—just "plug into the system," as they drew on electricity. Low-income workers did not necessarily aspire to private rooms. But it did seem reasonable in the American system, with its general association of technology and wealth, that they should have services at least as good as those for persons who were on public relief; that they should be treated in different surroundings from the indigent; and that the tragedy of serious sickness should not be compounded in working families by the tragedy of debt.

The question of access was not, then, of itself "socialistic." Although compulsory health insurance was one potential means of providing everyone with access to hospitals by removing financial barriers to admission, even this did not imply a uniform system for everyone. There was still little concern about the relatively heavy distribution of poorer patients in the municipal hospitals of large cities, while the striking racial distinctions in clientele between different types of institutions in the cities were accepted as a matter of course.[10] (More than one-fifth of all U.S. general hospitals formally excluded "Negro patients" in 1940, with proprietary hospitals being the most exclusionary in formal terms.)[11] The primary political issue of hospital financing in the mid-1930s was affordability of care to the majority of those with low incomes, who were the backbone of growing productivity, that is, to working-class white Americans.

On the other side of the equation was the hospitals' interest in avoiding potential patient debt, as general hospital admissions soared: from 6.9 million in 1935 to 9.2 million in 1940, and on to 15.2 million by the end of World War II. There was no question that the demand ought to be met, but how was the rising demand to be met without bankrupting the whole system? By limiting services to those who could pay? A major survey of hospitals in New York in 1936 found ninety-four voluntary hospitals setting limits on free care, despite subsidies for the indigent from the city. Most of these hospitals left day-to-day control to the administrators' discretion, thus saving the boards from a major headache.[12] Was an increasing proportion of the population to be excluded from service as costs rose? Organized prepayment schemes—hospital insurance—seemed the most obvious answer on all counts. But before looking at the growth of prepayment plans, let us look first at the hospital itself.

The Technological Bureaucracy

The large hospitals of the late 1930s were marvels of engineering, with their air-control systems, refrigeration plants, centralized kitchens, and central supply rooms comparable to retail stores. An estimated $34 million a year was spent on hospital pharmacies alone in the late 1930s.[13] Paging systems, using loudspeaker, flashing lamps, or mechanical sound, provided drama and a sense of a supraordinate organization. Long corridors were covered with linoleum, synthetic tile, or rubber. Large hospitals were involved in blood collection and the development of blood banks. Blood transfusions were given much more frequently in the 1930s than a generation earlier, although occasionally, it was claimed, "merely to impress the patient or the relatives."[14] Radiology offered an impressive array of diagnostic and treatment procedures, including "deep therapy," radium therapy, fluoroscopy, dental X rays, and stereoscopy. Oxygen therapy and some helium therapy were available, while resuscitation techniques and artificial respiration fed public fascination with the hospital as an institution replete with machines.

Intravenous therapy expanded enormously in the 1930s, effectively tethering the patient to machines. A surgeon on the staff of Harper Hospital, Detroit, estimated that between 1935 and 1940 Harper Hospital used 20,000 liters of intravenous and hypodermoclysis fluids a year: "Some flood!" Routinely, he reported, the postoperative patients received intravenous injections. So many tubes, bottles, and suction machines now dangled about the patient, in contrast to the early 1930s, that the wards "sometimes look like Christmas trees."[15]

Fever therapy attracted considerable attention between the late 1920s and the late 1930s, primarily to treat gonorrhea, but it was also considered a useful treatment for syphilis, chorea, and undulant fever. The patient was enclosed up to the neck in a specially designed fever cabinet, and body temperature was raised by radiant heat to induce fever. During the treatment, hypodermic medication and intravenous therapy were frequently administered. As in pain-free obstetrical deliveries, the treatment itself disabled the patient temporarily, while the dangers of both the high fever and the medication made careful supervision essential. Large hospitals constructed special fever-therapy rooms and provided trained personnel; the departments were designed to pay for themselves through private patients' fees. Elsewhere in the hospital the electrocardiogram was well established, its pens tracing the rhythmic contours of the heart. Metabolism tests, used with increasing frequency, further confirmed the notion of medicine as a battery of measures and devices—a system in which more technology suggested more accurate or better treatment—fanning the demand for hospital technique.

True to contemporary utopian visions, the patient's psychological condition was also regulated: in the decor (quiet colors muted and conducive to a restful mode, now emphasizing greens and grays—white walls were considered psychologically negative; yellows, reds, and oranges too stimulating; and blues and orchids too subduing); in occupational therapy (to focus the patient's mind on positive activities); in provision of suitable entertainment; and even occasionally in "bibliotherapy," where a skilled librarian chose books suitable to the medical condition of the patient.[16] Babies were isolated in separate nurseries for the newborn. If they were premature, they were housed in incubators. Technology emphasized the patient's dependence on the organization: a passive cog in an active machine.

But the technology of medicine seemed to promise more each year. A landmark event was the lifesaving administration by researchers from Johns Hopkins University of an experimental sulfa drug to President Roosevelt's son in 1936, when he was suffering a dangerous streptococcal infection. This striking success was in sharp contrast to the well-publicized death of President Coolidge's son only twelve years before, as a result of "blood poisoning" brought on by a tennis blister.[17] For years, reported one reviewer, the term "blood poisoning" had struck terror in the heart of the patient, the family, and the doctors. Now the development of effective chemotherapy brought a refreshingly optimistic clinical picture. The modern drugs provided "magic in a bottle"; they were a "growing miracle"; and the drug firms were "merchants of life."[18]

The first major American clinical reports on the new wonder drug, sulfanilamide, were published in 1937, providing a clearly effective, dramatic treatment for pneumonia. Virtually overnight pneumonia patients ceased being among the most difficult cases to treat. By the late 1940s pneumonia had become "one of the simplest examples of therapy a hospital intern meets."[19] By 1943 over 3,600 derivative sulfa compounds were synthesized and under study, providing for the first time effective medical treatment of infectious diseases; between 1936 and 1945 the death rate from pneumonia dropped by 40 percent. Septicemia, meningitis, gonorrhea, dysentery, and chronic bladder infections were vanquished by the new drugs. A great period of chemotherapy was beginning that was to be furthered by the widespread production of penicillin and other antibiotics during and after World War II.

Like serum therapy, an alternative treatment for pneumonia of certain types, treatment with sulfa drugs in the 1930s required careful medical and nursing supervision, best provided in a hospital. There was a narrow margin between an effective and a toxic dose of sulfapyridine and related drugs developed for other diseases, including dysentery, and there were risks of unpleasant side effects, including nausea and vomiting. Careful patient monitoring was required, including measurement of urinary output, strict patient compliance to the drug regimen, and observation by nurses for toxic reactions.[20] Thus in medicine as in surgery very real advances in efficacy required an increased commitment to technique at this period. The dramatic reductions in mortality accompanying the introduction of sulfa drugs—the very successes of treatment—also reinforced the image of the doctor as a figure of authority, the hospital as the seat of this authority, and the patient as a compliant, even credulous, participant.

The idea of the hospital as a necessary bureaucracy had, however, uncomfortable connotations in the mid-1930s, particularly for physicians. It was difficult to reconcile two competing images: of the hospital as a technological system in its own right, and of the physician as a heroic individualist, for whom the hospital was a workshop. Doctors had little wish to see themselves as experts who were also bureaucrats, subject to the demands of the hospital machine—like the dehumanized factory workers in Charlie Chaplin's *Modern Times* (1936). Suggestive connections between technology, power, large-scale organization, and denial of individualism spilled over into jumbled fears of unionism, big business, communism, and totalitarianism. Self-perpetuating bureaucracies were the stuff of science fiction, arousing fears from both the political right and left. Socialist writer Kenneth Fearing, in his novel *The Hospital* (1939), described nursing students—uniformed, disciplined, and docile—as trained to be "brainless automatons." All hospital employees, including technicians and unskilled workers, were "pretty well cowed" by administrators who were backed up by the community (business) power structure represented in the hospital board, and there was a prevailing fear of what an unspecified "They" would do to anyone who refused to conform to the rules.[21] The wary, sometimes hostile positions of organized medicine toward hospitals, insurance, and government in the 1930s (and later) have to be seen in the context of these wider fears of institutional control.

Rapid technological change in all spheres of life—from typewriter to airplane—was only too clear to anyone who had lived through the tumultuous period 1900 to 1935. Equally evident were the cultural changes that accompanied the new technology: within corporations, households, occupations, and in morals, gender roles, and behavior; indeed, the whole monetary structure of society—the economy—had failed. Technological change seemed rapid, social adjustment relatively slow. Current theory suggested a "cultural lag": a period of maladjustment in society in the face of new technological conditions.[22] Technology, in short, seemed a force of its own. It followed that aggressive efforts should be made to bring social institutions into their proper alignment with technological change. But what was proper? And by what means? Was technology a juggernaut that would roll over cherished professional ideals?

Reformers of the health-care system, like reorganizers of contemporary public-utility systems into regional networks, could draw on the notion of cultural lag to justify building large-scale organizations. Thus health insurance and systemwide planning could be presented as goals that were both necessary and inevitable. It was not clear to anyone, however, whether any new (presumably large, consolidated, more powerful) health-care organizations would inevitably be large-scale bureaucracies, or whether they would be subject to corporate or to governmental domination. But it was quite clear that *both* forms of domination threatened doctors by challenging their professional autonomy and their relationships with hospitals.

An immediate threat, from the perspective of organized medicine, was the prospect of compulsory health insurance. Government-sponsored health insurance attracted wide support in the late 1930s—more general public attention than in any previous period.[23] Fighting compulsory health insurance became a major activity of organized medicine. Physicians were not simply fighting insurance, or even socialism; they were also reacting to the larger specter of organizational control and technological determinism.

The working conditions of hospital employees stood as a salutary object lesson for doctors of the potential power of the organization over the individual. Hospital workers were generally barred from organizing into unions. John L. Lewis, the feisty head of the Congress of Industrial Organizations (CIO), told a cheering crowd in Madison Square Garden in March 1937 that industrial democracy (worker participation) was the best guarantee against Hitler-type fascism in the United States. Maybe it was, but not easily for hospitals.

The very same day Lewis made this speech, Local 171 of the Hospital Workers' Union called a sit-down strike at Brooklyn Jewish Hospital, New York, calling for union recognition, higher wages, and reinstitution of a telephone operator who was thought to have been discharged for union activity. Fifty police officers broke up the strike with drawn pistols, blackjacks, nightsticks, axes, crowbars, and an operating table used as a battering ram. A second strike of kitchen workers, elevator operators, orderlies, maids, and laundry workers was called two days later when the hospital refused to reinstate the eighteen employees who were fired for striking, resulting in further lay-offs of sixty-three strikers. Further disruptions followed. The hospital's staffing was maintained, significantly, through the traditional charity-givers—the Women's Auxiliary Voluntary Service and other volunteers—and by student nurses, who regarded themselves as occupationally distinct from other groups of workers. The hospital board reacted to the strikers with outrage. The Hospital Conference of the City of New York, representing seventy-two member hospitals, unanimously condemned the strikers, while a leading Roman Catholic spokesman described them as "savages."[24] In the event, the hospital directors, arguing (paternalistically) that the strikers were misled by outside organizers, dropped legal charges against their former employees.

The strikes left a clear indication of the power of established hospitals in the social hierarchy. Trustees were lauded in the press as "public benefactors" who served hospitals willingly, without salaries. Labor law (the right to unionize under the Wagner Act) was held not to apply to charitable institutions on grounds of public policy. Hospitals, meanwhile, were quite free to organize (collude) among themselves in order to press for greater contributions from the City of New York for charity patients—as one aggrieved worker noted at the time.[25] Indeed, because of their voluntary heritage, hospital boards had more power over employees than did industrial corporations, which were also fighting sit-down strikes—but where workers had the right to organize. In short, the voluntary hospitals incorporated the new characteristics of technological bureaucracies into the established organizational advantages of voluntarism: consolidated expertise, organizational autonomy, and associated power over employees. It was not surprising that organized medicine was suspicious of any move to make employees out of doctors.

Since hospitals needed doctors in private practice to bring in hospital patients, the doctors had a strong power base of their own. Nevertheless, the traditional relationship between private practitioners and hospitals, with the hospital as the private doctor's workshop, was difficult to justify and sustain by the late 1930s, for hospitals had obvious technologies of their own. Laboratories, X-ray machines, and anesthesia equipment could be operated by technicians and/or nurses, with or without the direct supervision of medical specialists.

Anesthesia, often bitterly contested in a three-way tussle for control among surgeons, nurse-anesthetists, and medical anesthesiologists, was the most dramatic case in point. But the question applied to radiology and pathology as well, and later to physical therapy, another hospital-based field where activities could be delegated, in large part, to nonphysician therapists. To physicians in each of these fields, as to physicians in other specialties, the surgeon, kingpin of hospital operations and prestige, provided the idealized professional image: an individual clearly in control of the workplace, wielding power within the hospital by virtue of his ability to bring in paying patients, and undertaking interventionist procedures whose results were evident in satisfied patients. Moreover, without the presence of the surgeon the equipment of the operating room would not be used.

The employment status of hospital-based specialties became a major battleground for hospitals and doctors in the 1930s. These fields were the most centrally connected to the technology of machines: oxygen tanks and breathing equipment, large laboratories and huge X-ray units. Yet these specialists were low on the totem pole of medical prestige and felt generally underappreciated. A leading anesthesiologist pressed for a propaganda campaign in the media in 1940 because he was tired, he said, of watching movies where dramatic operating scenes focused on the heroism and authority of the surgeon and represented the anesthesiologist only in images of filling rubber bags and jiggling valves.[26] In the same vein, hospital publicity materials and annual reports represented hospital science through photographs of white-coated technicians peering into microscopes and implied, by omission, that the medically trained pathologist was not central (or perhaps even necessary) to the laboratory.

The AMA, representing private practitioners in all fields, saw general dangers in identification of the hospitals' burgeoning technology with the bureaucracy, rather than with the individual physician. Meanwhile, the number of technical staff in hospitals was rising rapidly. Between 1936 and 1942 the number of laboratory technologists almost doubled. X-ray technicians and pharmacists increased by more than two-thirds, and there were smaller but still significant increases in the number of dietitians and physical therapists.[27] Physicians specializing in radiology were outnumbered by technicians by over seven to one; pathologists twenty to one; and anesthesiologists (by nurse-anesthetists) seventeen to one.[28]

The growing authority and professionalization of hospital administrators also threatened the autonomy of physicians. Over 80 percent of male administrators were college-educated in 1935.[29] Despite the urge to cooperate under the political banner of voluntarism, tussles were commonplace between doctors and administrators. The rules of the hospital game had changed, provoking wary watchfulness from private practitioners. In turn, the sensitivities of hospital-based specialists—and more general concerns about corporate medicine—had to be taken into account by any hospital considering a hospital insurance scheme.

Beginnings of Group Hospitalization

From the practical point of view, there were two major approaches to providing access to hospital technology via means of purchase. The first was a system of health insurance organized by government. Voluntary hospitals and physicians, the largest and most effective lobbying forces in the health-care field in the 1930s, were obviously more interested in the second, mixed approach: out-of-pocket payments by relatively wealthy patients, voluntary group hospitalization (prepayment) for middle-income patients, and tax support for the indigent. Group hospital-insurance schemes, developed in different areas simultaneously, supported the interests and customs of doctors and voluntary hospitals—as independent, interconnected fiefdoms. Prepayment schemes gave voluntary hospitals a strategic response to the market for technological care.

In 1935 voluntary hospitals received 71 percent of their income from patients (table 7.1), but there was a continuing struggle to collect from patients who were unemployed or struggling to regain a viable family income. Prepayment plans generated a ready, guaranteed source of patient income; and they offered a politically plausible alternative to compulsory health insurance, with its potential for government intervention. By 1937 more than 600,000 Americans were enrolled in twenty-six independent plans and the idea was spreading rapidly. There were seventy-one plans in 1940, with 4.4 million enrolled. The plans had a major impact on hospital payment in some areas. In Rochester, New York, for example, over one-fifth of the population was enrolled in mid-1937. In Cleveland more than one-fifth of the income of member hospitals came from group hospitalization in 1940.

One speaker at a conference of plan representatives called by the American Hospital Association in 1940 described group hospitalization plans as the "greatest publicity agent for hospitals that has ever been devised."[30] Plan executives had a strong group consciousness, their own ideology, and their own professional lingo. They talked about "selection," "reciprocal benefits," and "preferential rates." They saw themselves, too, as leaders of community organizations which preached self-help, encouraging Americans to stand on their own two feet, to pay their own way rather than drift toward government handouts. Plan representatives toured factories, businesses, schools, and other organizations all over the country, extolling the value of hospital care and urging workers to join. Through prepayment, hospital technology could be brought to the people—or at

TABLE 7.1

Estimated Total Income and Percentage Received from Specified Sources,
General and Special Hospitals, 1935

	Federal	Other Governmental	Nonprofit	Proprietary	Total
No. of hospitals	289	684	2,857	2,502	6,332
No. of beds (thousands)	53	106	262	57	478
Percent of hospitals	4.6	10.8	45.1	39.5	100.0
Percent of beds	11.0	22.3	54.8	11.9	100.0
Percent of income	11.3	17.9	60.0	10.8	100.0
Percent of income from					
Patients	7.5	16.7	70.8	91.4	56.2
Taxes	92.4	81.1	10.2	4.1	31.5
Other	0.1	2.2	19.0	4.5	12.3
	100.0	100.0	100.0	100.0	100.0

NOTE: Percentages are calculated using unrounded figures.
SOURCE: Elliott H. Pennell, Joseph W. Mountin, and Emily Hankla, "Summary Figures on Income, Expenditures, and Personnel of Hospitals," *Hospitals* 12 (April 1938), p. 16. Based on original data from the 1935 Business Census of Hospitals.

least to those employed in business corporations and government bureau-cracies, which provided a solid enrollment population.

Group hospitalization schemes were prepayment plans, typically founded by strong administrators of voluntary hospitals or hospital councils, which offered subscribers the opportunity to receive specified hospital services, without cost at the time of need, for a small, ongoing monthly payment. Following Baylor Hospital's example, groups of subscribers were generally sought through large local employers; Baylor had forty groups in 1932, most with more than fifty members.[31] Access to business was facilitated where leading businessmen were on hospital boards. In Chicago, for example, the plan was pushed by Charles H. Schweppe, a principal owner of the Marshall Field department store. Schweppe was also chair-man of the board of St. Luke's Hospital in Chicago and became an early organizer of the local hospitalization plan.

Plans that made the greatest initial headway were in areas with strong, well-organized voluntary hospitals, embedded in the hierarchy of business, government, and community prestige. Such communities, distinguished by a high degree of organization and industrialization and a relatively high per capita income, tended to be the large cities of the Northeast and the Midwest. It was here that the new schemes were most successful; they made least headway in the West, notably in California, Washington, and Oregon. Many of the plans were started with very little capital. Voluntary hospitals provided seed money for planning, solicited subscribers, and guaranteed that services would be available as needed. Of thirty-nine plans surveyed in 1944–45, hospitals contributed to the starting capital in twenty-two cases.[32]

As a result, although Blue Cross became a national movement, it was also one which was geographically skewed. The concentration of voluntary nonprofit hospitals (relative to other types of hospitals in different areas) obviously affected the environments in which prepayment plans were established. In industrial states like Illinois, Massachusetts, New York, Pennsylvania, and Ohio, where more than 60 percent of all general hospitals were nonprofit in 1939, unified voluntary policies for prepayment were easier to achieve than in states where there were relatively more government or proprietary institutions (table 7.2). For any group hospitalization plan that developed in Georgia, Nebraska, Oklahoma, or Texas, where proprietary hospitals comprised more than half of all hospitals in the state, it had to be decided whether to include proprietary institutions, assuming it was possible to get a scheme going at all. In the South and West, multihospital voluntary prepayment schemes tended to be limited to the few cities that had both an established pattern of interhospital cooperation, at some level, and a predominance of voluntary institutions.

Texas, in particular, remained a slow and reluctant participant in the Blue Cross movement (Texas was also the only large state where the number of proprietary hospitals increased between 1934 and 1940, and increased again in the following decade). In Dallas, for example, where the Baylor plan had begun, two other competing hospital plans soon arose, including a commercial plan, the National Hospitalization System. This firm also worked with hospitals in Fort Worth, Texas; Louisville, Kentucky; and Shreveport, Louisiana. Memphis reported four separate plans in the late 1930s, each promoted by a different hospital. Two employed a private promoter who worked on a commission, receiving one-third of the enrollment fees. However, for the most part commercial insurance companies expressed little interest in the uncertainties of hospital insurance in the 1930s, while hospitals usually found paid solicitors unsatisfactory and unnecessary. An early experiment in Essex County (Newark), New Jersey, was jettisoned as "disastrous."[33] Instead, plans with large enrollments trained their own representatives and developed their own organizational identity and image, building on the voluntary ethos.

Group hospitalization plans were businesslike from the beginning, targeted to the budgets of the voluntary hospitals and designed for the technology-conscious working population. The men subscribing to Blue Cross plans in 1940 were predominantly in clerical work or sales (40

TABLE 7.2

*General Hospitals in the United States
by Type of Control
in States with 100 Hospitals or More, 1939*

	Percentage				
	Governmental	Nonprofit	Proprietary	Total	Number
California	21.7	29.1	49.2	100.0	327
Georgia	22.3	24.1	53.6	100.0	112
Illinois	12.7	69.2	18.1	100.0	237
Indiana	33.9	41.3	24.8	100.0	109
Iowa	15.8	38.2	46.1	100.0	165
Kansas	17.1	55.3	27.6	100.0	123
Massachusetts	13.6	61.7	24.7	100.0	154
Michigan	27.4	43.3	29.3	100.0	215
Minnesota	15.2	41.6	43.1	100.0	197
Missouri	16.2	45.6	38.2	100.0	136
Nebraska	7.1	27.6	65.4	100.0	127
New York	15.0	61.7	23.3	100.0	373
North Carolina	15.3	62.8	21.9	100.0	137
Ohio	18.1	68.1	13.7	100.0	182
Oklahoma	19.4	20.1	60.4	100.0	134
Pennsylvania	6.6	79.8	13.6	100.0	242
Texas	14.8	26.7	58.5	100.0	337
Washington	25.0	38.4	36.6	100.0	112
Wisconsin	11.7	54.3	34.0	100.0	162

NOTE: Percentages may not add up exactly, due to rounding.
SOURCE: Calculated from U.S. Department of Commerce, Bureau of the Census, *Vital Statistics—Special Reports: Hospital and Other Institutional Facilities and Services 1939,* vol. 13, *State Reports,* nos. 3–51, 1941.

percent), in business or professional jobs (27 percent), or blue-collar occupations (30 percent). Women subscribers were generally professional and clerical workers or in sales (66 percent and 18 percent respectively).[34] Here, socially, was "Middle America": hard workers, prudent managers, aspirants to the silk-stocking life, moviegoers, believers in the necessity of hospital care and the technological promise of the future. They were attracted to the plans by upbeat publicity campaigns in newspapers and by radio spots in music programs and variety shows. Monthly enrollment fees were compared to the cost of a pair of silk stockings every other month or of a package of cigarettes a week. Posters and newspaper advertisements featured storks carrying babies labeled "Prepaid," or advising in cartoon form: "You never know what jolt is around the corner."[35] Thus the technology of hospitals was linked to the expectations of middle-class workers.

The model preferred by the hospital establishment within the American Hospital Association was the multihospital (noncompetitive) prepayment scheme, organized as a nonprofit corporation and supported by local voluntary hospitals. The first such plan, in Sacramento (1932), was soon overtaken in scope by rapidly successful undertakings in St. Paul, New York, and Cleveland, each a city with a strong voluntary-hospital presence. It was from St. Paul that the Blue Cross insignia was taken as a symbol of the entire prepayment movement. Multihospital support encouraged voluntary hospitals not to compete with each other for patients and consolidated their interests at the local level.

Blue Cross plans, like their supporting hospitals, lacked endowments to give free or subsidized care. They were designed to alleviate workers' budgets at times of sickness and to produce more paying patients, not to provide hospital access to everyone. Quite the reverse; for plan executives took pains not to make their members second-class citizens in a hospital system that was already multiclass. Benefits were designed to give members access to patterns of private, high-technology care, with reimbursement to hospitals providing a similar operating margin to that of self-pay private and semiprivate patients, thus avoiding any criticism that Blue Cross was a "class proposition," carrying the odor of charity or philanthropy.[36]

Nor did any plan want its initial membership flooded with expensive hospitalizations. Eligibility for obstetrics usually began ten to twelve months after initial enrollment. Mental health was almost universally excluded, and coverage for chronic diseases was rare. Enrollment was targeted, as far as possible, on groups of workers who formed a relatively healthy population, in order to avoid "adverse selection" or "bad risks" (that is, people who were already sick), as well as to tap into a ready market niche and to reduce the administrative costs involved in enrollment. In twenty-eight of thirty-seven Blue Cross plans surveyed in 1940, members were asked to sign a health pledge before receiving their membership certificate.[37] Structurally, the Blue Cross schemes were corporations founded by corporations (the voluntary hospitals) which responded to the needs of other corporations (employers). As a result, Blue Cross was a "community" scheme but not a "social-welfare" scheme; notably, it excluded the unemployed, the elderly, and the disabled, as well as agricultural, domestic, and other ad hoc or part-time workers who had no affiliations with the organized workplace.

As new (typically nonprofit) corporations, prepayment schemes were a potential threat to local physicians, suggesting hospital control at one remove. However, the physicians were able, in large part, to mold the structure and direction of the plans in ways that served physician interests and encouraged a sense of solidarity between voluntary hospitals and physicians. The question was, what should be covered? Were the new plans to cover, for example, outpatient care, the services of attending physicians, or even the services of the hospital-based specialists in radiology, anesthesia, and pathology? Doctors rallied initially to oppose prepayment. However, as the success of local hospital-medical negotiations rapidly indicated, the plans—as written—actually enhanced physician autonomy and reduced the danger of hospital-dominated medicine.

Notably, the new prepayment schemes did not usually cover doctors' fees, only the hospital's basic services. They thus proclaimed, in effect, that hospitals were not "practicing medicine" as medical corporations (since the financing excluded medical fees). Thus the hospital remained, formally at least, the practitioners' workshop, not their employer, and there was no hidden agenda in the plans in favor of group practice or bureaucratic control over medical work. Hospital experts C. Rufus Rorem (of the AHA) and I. S. Falk (of the Social Security Board) started a long-standing disagreement about the wisdom of this policy of splitting hospital insurance and medical fees, in terms of its far-reaching effects—reaching, indeed, up to the present. Rorem's view was that a pragmatic strategy was necessary in order to get the job done. Falk, on the other hand, saw the formal demarcation of the hospital and medical domains, institutionalized in Blue Cross coverage, as an out-and-out rejection of the policies set out in the Committee on the Costs of Medical Care, that is, as inimical to the future establishment of a rationally organized health system, including organized, hospital-based group medical practices.[38] In the wisdom of hindsight, both views were correct, but Rorem's was the one that was implemented.

Each local plan negotiated its own menu of services to be covered, depending on local custom and medical power structures. Subscribers generally received twenty-one days of acute hospital care in any contract year, as well as operating-room services (but not the surgeon's fee), routine laboratory services, drugs and dressings, X rays, and anesthetics. Plans paid, on average, three-fourths of the entire hospital bill.[39] Following the established custom of separate hospital and medical bills, the plans excluded the service of attending physicians. By this move hospitals effectively ruled out the alternative of hiring their own staff physicians to provide complete medical care.

Some plans covered outpatient care, ambulance service, professional services for anesthesia and radiology, and the service of osteopathic physicians. However, these services were fraught with controversy. Indeed, disagreement with the local medical profession about coverage for hospital care given by substantial numbers of osteopathic physicians delayed implementation of Blue Cross in Kansas City, in Maine, and in Rhode Island. Coverage of physician services for anesthesia, radiology, and pathology sparked bitter disputes in California, in Philadelphia, and elsewhere, implying, as it did, that these specialists were not like other private practitioners and that the hospital bureaucracy was "practicing medicine."[40] For the most part, disputes were negotiated between local medical societies and hospitals. The organizational genius of Blue Cross was that it was a national movement whose strength derived from its ability to adapt to local conditions. It was, in short, both a radical and a conservative undertaking—radical in providing a new vehicle for hospital financing, but conservative in hewing to traditional relationships between hospitals and physicians at the very time that these were threatened.

The plans linked, in a unique way, the prevailing ideologies of hospital technology and of voluntarism. Early Blue Cross leaders like John Mannix—who was influential in starting schemes in Cleveland, Akron, Youngstown, Toledo, Columbus, and Cincinnati, and who also met with people in Rochester (New York), Chicago, Des Moines, and Indianapolis as their schemes got off the ground—saw voluntary hospital prepayment plans as an idea whose time had come; that is, as a grass-roots American movement, rather like the cooperative movement, which also flowered in the 1930s.[41] Both movements were middle-class movements. Local voluntary hospitals could capitalize on their commitment to technology by demonstrating their interest in protecting individual workers' incomes, through their participation in Blue Cross. Hospital participation was twofold: hospitals were prime organizers in the new schemes and guarantors that services would be provided to beneficiaries.

Not surprisingly, then, Blue Cross plans adumbrated, in patchwork form across the country, the ideals of interventionist medicine and private service. Annual hospital admission rates of Blue Cross enrollees in the late 1930s were 50 percent higher, on average, than for the country as a whole, while more than 80 percent of the beneficiaries occupied private or semi-private rooms. Although a number of plans included coverage for ward service, all beneficiaries had the right to choose their own physician, for whose services they were billed directly. For the subscribers Blue Cross made hospital technology purchasable. The most common demand was for surgery; in the late 1930s the majority of Blue Cross beneficiaries were surgical patients, both male (55 percent) and female (56 percent).[42] The plans reinforced the prevailing image of hospitals as acute, high-technology centers. By providing coverage for laboratory tests and X rays, the plans stimulated the use of diagnostic tests, feeding in turn the growth in the number of hospital technicians. The plans also gave attending doctors

a greater chance of collecting their own fees—a question of some importance in the 1930s—since the patient no longer had also to pay a large
hospital bill. It was not surprising that the plans were soon endorsed by
the physicians.

Local plans were free to develop specific organizational and distribu-
tional policies, as well as coverage decisions, and these decisions, too, are
telling. In Minneapolis and St. Paul, for example, the standards were
exceptionally explicit, requiring member hospitals to be nonprofit if they
wished to benefit. This rule encouraged local proprietary hospitals to shift
to nonprofit status and led to an unusually rapid decline of proprietary
hospitals in the state; from eighty-five in 1934, to sixty-one in 1940 and
twenty-six in 1950. The Minneapolis–St. Paul plan, unlike many others,
also voted not to permit group hospitalization outside the limits of the two
cities, through concern that "everyone in the state would run to the Mayos
[that is, the Mayo Clinic] for their hospitalization."[43] In such ways voluntary hospitals maintained their local autonomy, allowed for local variations, and stressed their public service. The result, by the late 1930s, was
an array of plans across the country, enormous enthusiasm and missionary
zeal among Blue Cross organizers, and pride in Blue Cross as a national
movement.

Blue Cross and National Policy-making

The American Hospital Association, following its approval of hospital
insurance in principle in 1933, appointed C. Rufus Rorem as its national
consultant on group hospitalization and catalyst for expansion. Rorem had
previously worked for the Committee on the Costs of Medical Care. In
1936 he became director of the AHA's Committee on Hospital Service,
forerunner of the national Blue Cross Association. Rorem developed national standards or "essentials" for Blue Cross plans in 1933.[44] These
stressed the quasi-public role of the plans, both as public-service agencies
organized on a nonprofit basis, and as cooperative local forces that were
to avoid competition among hospitals and clashes between hospitals and
the medical profession. The essentials went out of their way to build
bridges between hospitals and private practitioners, noting, for example,
the opportunity presented by group hospitalization for hospitals to work

in harmony with physicians. Common threats, such as compulsory health insurance and other major federal proposals, encouraged such cooperation. Thus the AHA's national political agenda fed back into local plan development.

Rorem was a brilliant and effective leader, carefully attuned to strategic possibilities. His success in forging Blue Cross as a national movement lay in anchoring this movement to the mainline ideologies of both voluntary hospitals and the medical profession, thus building the reputation of the AHA and tying it more closely to the American Medical Association. Approved Blue Cross plans were required to exclude the attending physician's fees. They were also required to cover services given by *all* physicians and voluntary hospitals in each area. Through both moves the Blue Cross movement allayed physician fears about hospitals as autonomous technological bureaucracies engaged in the "corporate practice of medicine." Blue Cross asserted the control of hospital technology by physicians, rather than by managers or politicians.

Separating hospital and physician services through the new prepayment arrangements imposed a major structural division into U.S. health services that created long-lasting ripples in American hospital practice, hospital reimbursement arrangements, and competitive proposals for health insurance. The playing-out of major themes in hospital reimbursement in the 1930s also set out long-term patterns of private, rather than governmental, insurance for the middle-class working population. By defining hospitalization, rather than general doctors' services, as the first major service which ought to be covered by collective action (i.e., prepayment), Blue Cross also made an indelible statement about priorities in American medicine, building on the hospital's technological image. Physician organizations began to establish health-insurance schemes for physician bills (Blue Shield) from the late 1930s. But the central place of hospitals, ratified through prepayment arrangements, was to remain part of the culture and organization of American medicine. In the United States the brave new world of medicine was specialized, interventionist, mechanistic, and expensive—at least as interpreted, through prepayment, for workers in major organizations. (In Britain, in contrast, National Health Insurance emphasized general practitioner care.)

In four other ways Blue Cross, which offered the major prepayment arrangement of the 1930s, had lasting implications for hospital policy-making in the United States. The first derived from the contractual arrangement between Blue Cross and the hospitals. Each plan acquired services for its beneficiaries through per diem reimbursement and whatever special charges were covered by the different plans; that is, the plan purchased care as it was used. Blue Cross was a "third party": a new, potentially powerful organization that was not part of the practice arrangements of physicians. Where a Blue Cross plan covered a substantial segment of the population it could, in theory, wield the authority of a major purchaser.

However, none of the initial participants in Blue Cross arrangements wanted the plans to become *too* successful; that is, to develop an independent power base. Otherwise, as one prescient observer remarked in 1938, the control of voluntary hospitals might eventually "pass from the hands of trustees into those of the insurance associations."[45] Although any such development was a long way off, both hospitals and physicians were nervous about the prospect of well-funded, local prepayment associations which might branch out into other forms of health insurance—and which might seek powerful organizational alliances with local employers, who provided their major pool of subscribers.

These were not empty concerns. In 1939 hospital groups were reportedly considering expanding into physician insurance in at least five cities (Cleveland, Cincinnati, Rochester, Buffalo, and Ithaca). Frank Van Dyk, at Blue Cross in New York, was also attempting to develop a combined ward program which would include physician fees as well as hospital charges. This was killed by organized physician opposition, but small voluntary hospitals were also concerned that any such moves might turn the partnership between Blue Cross and hospitals into a Blue Cross dictatorship. The increased size of the plans and the success and professionalization of the plan directors made it important for them to emphasize that their central purpose was different from that of either hospitals or physicians, and that they would not expand their domain. The plans were, in the words of one director, "essentially in the business of contracting and insuring a commodity."[46]

It was a major triumph of the AHA, representing the collective consciousness of voluntary hospitals, that the plans continued to accept the constraints built into the AHA essentials; notably, that there would be no competition between plans and no discrimination among hospitals for reimbursement at the local level. Such agreements stopped the plans from becoming mutually competing insurance agencies; even now this territoriality largely remains. Operationally, the relationship of hospitals and plans could be (and was) compared to the relationships between oil companies and their affiliated gas stations.[47] The plans provided an outlet for the delivery of goods or services from hospitals to consumers.

As a second lasting result Blue Cross offered a new pattern of hospital standardization, based on the ideology of the voluntary sector. The Blue Cross movement represented, by 1940, a useful political and philosophical alternative to proposals for socialized medicine at the national (as well as the state) level. Rorem was explicit in linking the values of group hospitalization with those of voluntary hospitals in general. He stressed its "non-profit, non-political nature"; its "public responsibility without the necessity of public compulsion"; and its "private initiative without the objective of private gain." He was probably right in his claim, in 1940, that the future of voluntary hospital insurance would determine the future of the voluntary-hospital system.[48]

As a third legacy Blue Cross schemes confirmed the right of all physicians to have hospital appointments; by the late 1930s the local plans were reportedly "breaking down the closed hospitals" because of the insistence on free choice of physicians in hospitals which participated in Blue Cross schemes.[49] Fourth and finally, the plans forced the issue of reimbursement for hospital-based physicians in anesthesiology, radiology, and pathology. Indeed, the issue of authority for the hospital-based specialties became readily identified with how the patient's bill was paid. Radiologists, with a specialty certifying board established in 1933, expressed early concern over the "intolerable conditions" that existed between business-minded hospital administrators and radiology departments, with the administrator allegedly "bargaining for X-ray business." Hospitals which included the services of staff radiologists in their charges were attacked as "practicing medicine."[50]

Tensions between hospitals and hospital-based medical specialists were mitigated by an AHA statement in 1939, which set out principles of financial relationships between hospitals and radiologists, anesthesiologists, and pathologists.[51] This statement was approved by other professional groups. It stressed that every hospital should have competent departments in these fields under the direction of physician-specialists, and that specific financial relationships between hospitals and these specialists should be appropriate to local conditions. Payment might therefore include arrangements as diverse as employment of the physician on salary, payment by commission (varying with the amount of work generated), and privilege rental.

Given the growing volume of service in radiology and the capital vested in radiology departments, agreement had also to be reached as to who owned what equipment, and how far the radiologist should benefit financially from the expanding market for hospital X rays. Since these were not easy questions to address, hospital-specialist relationships continued to be ambivalent, varied, and fraught with conflict. But Blue Cross schemes, by allowing for local variations, also eased the resulting tension. Not until Medicare (1965) was a single national solution made explicit. Medical specialists in these fields are now typically organized as medical groups, with their billing separate from the hospital's fees. Meanwhile, Blue Cross reaffirmed the assumption that hospitals were physicians' workshops, at the very time that the hospital-based technologies—and the doctrine of cultural lag—were questioning its validity.

In all of these respects long-lasting hospital policy was made through the machinery of reimbursement. Through Blue Cross, voluntary hospitals influenced the patterns of coverage and the way in which the hospital's income was made available—favoring operating room fees, for example, but often excluding outpatient care. By targeting hospital care to workers in organizations, hospital prepayment schemes defined hospitalization as a necessary, desirable, and purchasable service for the typical working man and woman of the 1930s. The plans further defined the stratification, along class lines, of private, semiprivate, and ward services in the hospitals, and they stimulated AHA and local hospital interest in pushing local governments to provide similar forms of reimbursement for the poor. In fact as well as rhetoric, Blue Cross, like the voluntary hospital sector itself, was thus the ideological antithesis—simultaneously—of egalitarian, big-business, socialist, fascist, and totalitarian approaches to the provision of medical care.

How Should Hospital Technology Be Distributed?

Blue Cross was successful, strategically, because it did not threaten established interests and, in fact, served them. Specific ties between the AHA and Blue Cross were further cemented in 1940 by an AHA decision that its member hospitals should engage in preferential service contracts only with approved nonprofit agencies. However, the new schemes did not address broader questions of hospital care as a collective social good that, everyone seemed to agree, ought to be available to the whole population. The very successes of voluntary prepayment as a national movement emphasized the gaps and discrepancies in hospital distribution. Proponents of both compulsory health insurance and Blue Cross thus found themselves, willy-nilly, involved in the question of hospital supply, as well as demand.

On average, there were 3.5 general and related special hospital beds per 1,000 population in the United States in the late 1930s. But these figures masked enormous regional variations; six southern states reported less than 2 beds per 1,000. For people in areas without a hospital there was little use in establishing prepayment schemes, either under government or private promptings, if hospitals were not available; and in many rural parts of the country they were not. A strong case for rural hospital construction was made when the federal Farm Security Administration developed a medical program in 1938 as an extension of its general rural rehabilitation work, adding medical and hospital prepayment arrangements to preexisting plans for the purchase of farm equipment, livestock, fertilizer, and seed. A federal program for migrant workers was established in California the same year.

Regional linkages could improve the technical quality of care for the whole population—in theory at least—as well as extend the range of potential specialties from the cities to the rural areas. At the very least, a well-equipped hospital of 1940, even if it served only 10,000 people, required good laboratory and X-ray services; but a radiologist needed a population of 60,000 to earn a living, and a pathologist 100,000. Half of all hospitals had fewer than 50 beds—too small to offer a full range of care in the specialties—and there were marked disparities in the receipt of hospital care by geography and size of the area. But it was difficult to see how hospital service, specialized, capital-intensive, and technologically based, could be reorganized without government initiative. Without a major scheme of government health insurance or external control of hospital capital, there were no effective levers for systemwide changes.

Major organizational models for federal hospital planning, distribution, and construction were available in the late 1930s: not only in federal farm policy, designed to transform agriculture from small-scale farms to large-scale businesses and relocate farmers in new areas, but also in the massive alliance of government and technology in the huge, regional Tennessee Valley Authority (TVA) project and in the federal planning and construction of local post offices throughout the country. If the federal government could uproot and relocate thousands of people, dam rivers, commandeer and flood huge tracts of land, and assume an effective national system for mail distribution, why was there not a government program for hospital services?

For political purposes the beauty of voluntarism as an ideology was that it allowed for acceptance of the notion that hospital services ought to be generally accessible to the whole population, without expecting collective responsibility by hospitals for implementation of these ideals. Trustees still kept a proud, private control of the individual hospital, as if it were their own domain—and it was, as the strike at the Brooklyn Jewish Hospital made quite plain. The charitable structure was not designed for industrywide organization.

One southern radiologist reported of the hospital in his community: "The plant is obsolete, there is no endowment, the location is very bad, and generally it is about comparable to the Model T Ford."[52] But he went on, as did others, to note the difficulty of closing down many hospitals even if they were not needed, because of community allegiance and support. In this sense hospitals were unlike gas stations, which opened and shut according to prevailing market conditions. Trustees, volunteers, administrators, and doctors had a strong allegiance to their hospitals. A great advantage of local Blue Cross plans to trustees and to other business leaders in the same elite networks was that the plans met local employers' and employees' needs without requiring changes in the hospital system, that is, without threatening the autonomy of the individual institution.

Nor was the power of the dollar a major incentive for systemwide change. Paradoxically, profit-making hospitals were most evident in the poorest, not the richest, states. The reason was, of course, that many of the proprietary hospitals that survived the Depression were in areas where there were few voluntary hospitals: states like West Virginia, Oklahoma, Arkansas, Texas, Georgia, and Mississippi (tables 7.2, 7.3). And there were relatively few voluntary hospitals in these states because there was an insufficient population base, insufficient income, and/or insufficient interest in founding a hospital and in supporting it with gifts and donations for charity care. It was evident by the late 1930s that widespread distribution of services would not be achieved in such states (or for that matter in other states with large rural populations) without massive external aid for capital construction and, ideally, also for hospital operating expenses. Thus policies for filling in the gaps in hospital construction joined policies for filling in the gaps in ability to pay.

Two major reports set out the wide variety of suggestions for influencing, if not reorganizing, the American hospital system in the late 1930s. The first was a survey of largely reformist opinion collected in a foundation

TABLE 7.3

States in which 20% or More of General Hospital
Admissions Were to Proprietary Hospitals in 1939

	Total Admissions	Admissions to Proprietary Hospitals	Percentage
Alabama	121,071	32,842	27.1
Arkansas	62,700	19,000	30.3
Georgia	157,060	39,182	24.9
Idaho	38,886	9,651	24.8
Mississippi	81,200	19,676	24.2
Oklahoma	113,075	39,853	35.2
Oregon	93,043	21,362	23.0
Texas	358,079	100,703	28.1
Virginia	150,942	35,957	23.8
West Virginia	121,114	56,236	46.4
Wyoming	24,939	5,042	20.2

NOTE: The state with the largest *number* of proprietary hospital admissions was California (108,040), but this state also had an extensive county hospital system and strong nonprofit institutions. Proprietary hospital admissions represented 17.3 percent of general hospital admissions in California, a rate much higher than in states like New York (6.3 percent) or Pennsylvania (2.0 percent) but well below the states in this table.
SOURCE: Calculated from U.S. Department of Commerce, Bureau of the Census, *Vital Statistics—Special Reports: Hospitals and Other Institutional Facilities and Services 1939*, vol. 13, State Reports, nos. 3–51, 1941.

report, *American Medicine: Expert Testimony out of Court* (1937); the second, the proceedings of the National Health Conference organized under the aegis of the Roosevelt administration's Interdepartmental Committee to Coordinate Health and Welfare Activities, in 1938.[53] An array of testimony in both asserted that medical care ought to be organized around the hospital: first, because of the central place of hospitals in American medicine; second, because the hospital was a natural organizational base which could be amplified to cover other aspects of care. But planning hospital care now appeared a necessary corollary of medical technology, with all hospitals organized and coordinated locally into a single service system.

As an alternative, or in addition, some commentators envisaged teaching hospitals supervising hospitals within university-centered regional networks. The suggestions could be described, variously, as hospital-based group practice, the hospital as a community health center, areawide hospital organization, and regionalized hospital services. All were ideas that were to recur, in various guises and proposals, from the late 1930s through the 1960s.

Policies and Politics in the Late 1930s

Neither organized medicine nor organized hospitals in the late 1930s were likely to press for any proposals, governmental or otherwise, that promised multi-institutional organization or external control. Voluntary hospitals were in a strong position to rally support for their interests, since only 3 percent of the U.S. population lived in areas served solely by government hospitals in the late 1930s.[54] In two areas, however, the hospitals were actively interested in government support: first, in increased subsidy for indigent patients, and second, in subsidy for construction—provided it came without strings, of course.

A joint statement from the American Public Welfare Association and the AHA in 1936 recommended that public funds for welfare medicine should go first to government hospitals where these were available, but they might also be used to pay voluntary hospitals for care of the indigent where government hospitals were unavailable or insufficient.[55] This statement was tantamount to approval by the welfare establishment of the position already adopted by the AHA: that is, of government responsibility for the indigent and government reimbursement for their care in voluntary hospitals.

In describing care of the indigent sick by voluntary hospitals as treatment of the "overflow" from government hospitals, it was also neatly suggested that voluntary hospitals performed a function that was not only essentially governmental, but for which the voluntary hospitals should be adequately paid.[56] Since local-government reimbursement rates were generally much lower than Blue Cross rates—sometimes lower, even, than hospital costs—the voluntary hospitals could now produce evidence that they were not getting a "fair deal." This policy put the hospitals on the offensive, in opposition to compulsory health insurance. By the end of the 1930s the hospitals had a two-pronged platform for hospital financing: a system of Blue Cross hospital insurance for those who could afford it, backed up by government reimbursement for services to the indigent.

Both the AHA and associated Blue Cross schemes also supported limited federal aid for construction—a policy that also appealed, more widely, to a broad configuration of interests by the late 1930s. Farmers' groups, politicians from rural and southern states, and organized medicine were arguing for rural hospital construction as a basis for better distribution of medical technique; most rural hospitals had no outpatient departments, and facilities and equipment were often outdated. Powerful states, including California, Illinois, and Michigan, had a strong commitment to rural communities.[57] And southern politicians sought federal subsidies to redress the low bed-to-population ratios in their areas.

Unlike other identifiably deprived groups, including rural blacks in the South and the poverty-stricken in major cities, farmers were well-organized. Speakers representing the Grange and the American Farm Bureau Federation and its associated women's group at the National Health Conference emphasized that farm people were as entitled to proper medical care as anyone else, and entitled to such care near to their home. It was "poor comfort to the expectant mother in the farm home to know that in a distant city there is an elaborately equipped maternity hospital with specialists in obstetrics in attendance."[58]

Recognizing the coalition of interests in favor of construction grants, President Roosevelt sent a message to Congress in January 1940, singling out construction of hospitals in a modest legislative proposal—fifty hospitals, at a total cost of less than $10 million. Although the subsequent "Hospital Construction Act" of 1940 died in Congress, the idea of special legislation for federal grants for hospital construction entered the legislative arena. The idea appealed to legislators who were seeking federal funds for their own areas, and was independent of much wider proposals for a comprehensive national health program. Specific proposals for federal aid to construction were to follow two time-honored principles: the role of government in stimulating the private (voluntary hospital) sector, and the independence and autonomy of hospitals as local, community institutions. But these broader issues of accessibility to hospital service, including regional planning, remained unresolved as the United States entered World War II, in December 1941.

Through all of these debates, the voluntary and professional organizations, not government or industry, captured the technological dream for medicine. The AMA, and voluntary hospitals and their associated prepayment plans, stressed the power of voluntarism as a force for change in America, setting against it, as alternatives, regimentation, compulsory health insurance, and government regulation. Hospital politician and administrator S. S. Goldwater, for example, who had been a supporter of compulsory health insurance in 1920, was now an enthusiastic convert to the "voluntary way."[59] At the National Health Conference he called for a vigorous offensive by Blue Cross leaders, criticized federal officials for ignoring the totality of voluntary efforts, and praised self-help over government planning and control. Protecting the other flank of voluntarism, AHA President Robert Neff said he favored hospital licensing and voluntary, coordinated hospital planning, but drew a firm line between voluntary and profit-making organizations. The public, he said, needed protection against "designing agencies who have only a proprietary interest in care of the sick."[60] Those who favored compulsory health insurance within a national health program spoke of unmet needs, the importance of health care as an economic good for the whole population, and the inability of private insurance to cover groups such as farmers, day laborers, and domestics. Those who favored the voluntary approach expected government to play a major role in health care, but one which shored up the system of nonprofit hospitals and medical practitioners.

The terms of debate had shifted, almost imperceptibly, from the language of technology to that of politics. Arguments over cultural lag—what kind of organization (or organizational system) was required to bring modern technology to the people—were polarized into political statements of the right and left: voluntarism versus socialized medicine. From the point of view of the medical profession, however, the critical question was the threat of bureaucratic control. Control of medicine by hospitals was just as alarming as government health insurance.

8

Consolidation Without Jeopardy: Planning in the Shadow of World War II

IN THE SECOND WORLD WAR, as in World War I, federal agencies, business corporations, universities, and other private groups pooled their efforts for the short-term goal of winning the war, with the federal role largely that of banker and facilitator of private initiative. Dramatic examples of this cooperation were the development of the atomic bomb through the Manhattan Project and the large-scale production of penicillin. Business corporations, fueled by the massive war production program, had little interest in dabbling in large-scale, continuing social programs like hospital services, though they were obviously concerned about the productivity and health of their own growing army of workers.

Meanwhile, in Congress a general backlash against the increased power of the federal government in the 1930s made any new federal program suspect. Senator Robert Taft, the most articulate and eloquent spokesman for individual liberty, decentralized control of public functions, and states' rights in the 1940s, remarked of the abortive 1940 hospital construction legislation: "[W]e wrote it with a great deal of care to be sure we weren't starting a Federal hospital system."[1] With the Japanese attack on Pearl Harbor in December 1941, the New Deal came to an abrupt halt.

This chapter will show that the decentralist, proindustrial, and public-private collaborative policies of World War II were tailor-made for the voluntary hospitals as a sector. As Daniel Fox argues in his work on the history of regionalism, the idea of regional hospital organization was captured and molded by the hospital associations.[2] Between 1940 and 1946 voluntary hospital representatives worked with the federal Public Health Service and state health officers to map hospital services in regional patterns across the country. In so doing, they laid the basis for the successful passage of a major program of federal grants to states to aid construction of local hospitals, the Hill-Burton Act of 1946. Further cooperation between the federal government and the voluntary sector was achieved through the postwar policy of linking veterans' hospitals and medical schools. Justified by the political identification of voluntarism as an antithesis to socialism in the 1940s and by a growing national commitment to science, the hospitals were to emerge from the war as American institutions for which coercive planning seemed unnecessary.

Hospital Medicine as Medical Science

War coincided with the advent of effective chemotherapy, driven by the success of the sulfa drugs and the promise of penicillin. Because of the sulfa compounds, acclaimed as the new "miracle drugs," not a single limb was lost from posttrauma infections at Pearl Harbor. The medical aftermath of the attack was described succinctly in a headline in *Science News Letter:* "Sweeping Victory for Drugs."[3] In World War I the major medical successes lay in the recognition and development of surgical technique and in first-class base hospital organization. By the 1940s these were givens. World War II affirmed the importance of medicine as a science based on careful laboratory techniques.

Penicillin, a British discovery, could initially be produced only in minuscule quantities. Early in 1942 there was only enough penicillin available *in toto* to treat one case, and between March and June 1942 only enough for ten cases. Federally supported research into penicillin production was approved in October 1941, following the organization of the wartime Office of Scientific Research and Development and its Committee on Medical Research (CMR). The CMR stimulated, funded, and coordinated penicillin development in the United States, linking the activities of investigators in universities, government laboratories, and the pharmaceutical, chemical, and distilling industries—with ultimate success.[4] Penicillin treatment of military casualties began in April 1943, allowing for wounded men to be evacuated from military zones to the United States by air, immediately after surgery, with little fear of major wound infection. By the spring of 1944 the increased supply allowed for allocations of penicillin to 1,000 civilian hospitals and by the summer, to 2,700 hospitals. At the end of the war in the summer of 1945, penicillin was an acknowledged success, soon to be available to the entire population. Other antibiotics were under development. By 1947, it was claimed, over half of the drugs in use had been unknown ten years before.[5]

Production of penicillin was the outstanding example of the success of organized national medical research in World War II, but it was by no means alone. The research emphasis spilled over into all aspects of medicine. Resuscitation therapy (for the prevention and treatment of shock) and better blood replacement techniques, including the development of blood plasma supply, further aided treatment of the wounded, and focused on the medical as well as the surgical importance of treatment. In World War II less than 5 percent of wounded Americans died, compared with an estimated 10 percent on the German side between 1939 and 1943.[6] Surgical technique was being integrated into nonsurgical medicine to a greater degree than ever before, and vice versa. From explorations of cerebral blood flow to research on liver conditions, the accelerated, federally sponsored research programs of the war placed scientific research at the center of medicine. Research on gamma globulin, adrenal steroids, cortisone, and other drugs and techniques stimulated the expansion of internal medicine and its subspecialties. Never before, said A. N. Richards, the CMR's chairman, had there been "so great a coordination of medical scientific labor." An eminent British investigator drew on a medical metaphor: war had "done good like a hormone."[7] Spectacular research results fused the images of basic and applied science, and more widely of science and medicine, as if there were no lines of demarcation between them, laying the basis for the enormous upsurge of federal grants for biomedical research in the 1950s and 1960s.

It was easy to overlook the fact that in this war, as in World War I, major health defects in young Americans registering for the draft stemmed from a basic lack of education, income, and medical care rather than a lack of "science."[8] It was also convenient to avoid the sickness experience of soldiers themselves, such as the study of 17,000 patients admitted to the nonsurgical service of general hospitals in the North African and Mediterranean theaters, where 45 percent of the admissions were for neuropsychiatric conditions and 26 percent for infectious diseases. These were two major areas where the problem was to apply existing knowledge and to ensure continuity of care rather than to search for new, fundamental scientific principles.[9] Instead, medicine was reduced to a single goal: the "struggle against nature for more knowledge."[10] For medical schools, knowledge production became an end in itself, with an increasing number of faculty holding Ph.D.'s (rather than M.D.'s) in the basic research fields of anatomy, physiology, biochemistry, pharmacology, and bacteriology. Research, said one dean, had become the "life blood of a teaching institution."[11]

Hospitals were caught up in the research emphasis in three ways: as symbols of the success of scientific medicine; as potential knowledge centers around which community and regional health-care-service networks might be organized; and as institutions whose clientele was changing under the impact of new pharmaceuticals. On the one hand, the new drugs and procedures allowed for early treatment of potentially life-threatening infections outside the hospital, suggesting a reduced hospital role. On the other, they encouraged bold and extensive surgery, buttressed by antibiotics, blood plasma, and shock-prevention techniques, and the admission to hospitals of seriously ill patients with diseases that might respond to sulfa drugs and antibiotics.

The demand for hospital care thus rose in some areas of sickness and declined in others. Mortality from childhood infectious diseases and their sequelae declined virtually to the vanishing point in the 1940s. The overall rate of death from pneumonia dropped to 1 percent in 1944, compared to 24 percent before the sulfa drugs, while the death rate for meningitis, which was 38 percent in World War I, was less than 5 percent in World War II.[12] By 1945 more than two-thirds of all deaths were attributed to chronic diseases, including heart disease, cancer, and stroke; only twenty-five years earlier two-thirds had been from infectious diseases.[13] The overall hospital population was aging, both because of a declining demand for the admission of children and an increased demand for admission for acute illness among those who were old and/or chronically ill.[14]

Infectious diseases were largely associated with the poor; but chronic illnesses were often diseases of affluence, striking those who lived well and lived long. The hospital was becoming increasingly necessary as a treatment station for the upper classes, and it was not surprising that one of the major postwar phenomena was a massive emphasis on coronary care. Science was a peacetime weapon: a way of combating disease, buying health, and delaying death. Borne along on a wave of optimism as to what science could do, Americans looked to doctors and hospitals increasingly (and often unrealistically) for instant cures for all conditions.

Rapid growth in the medical specialties and subspecialties in the 1940s and the expansion of laboratory tests underlined the scientific model for diagnosis. By 1946 routine diagnostic procedures included not only clinical and microscopic analyses of blood, tissues, and gastric and other bodily secretions, but also basal metabolism tests, electrocardiograms (EKGs), and electroencephalograms (EEGs). Not surprisingly, the number of medical technologists employed by hospitals continued to rise rapidly in World War II. Both the Army and the Navy developed special programs for training WACs and WAVEs as laboratory technicians in order to increase the available supply.[15]

The net result of the conjunction of science and treatment was a steady expansion of hospital service throughout the war years. Between 1941 and 1946, admissions to general hospitals rose by 32 percent (table 8.1). Voluntary hospitals held their own with over 60 percent of all general

TABLE 8.1

Admissions to General Hospitals by Type of Hospital
Control, 1935–52, Selected Years

	Admissions (thousands)			
	1935	1941	1946	1952
All general hospitals	6,868	10,646	14,052	17,760
Federal	358	1,220	1,836	1,400
State	260	344	305	397
Local government	1,253	1,633	1,865	2,645
Church	1,906	2,885	4,033	5,318
Other nonprofit	2,228	3,606	4,763	6,594
Individual or partnership	377	507	761	734
For-profit corporations	486	451	489	672
All governmental	1,871	3,197	4,006	4,442
All nonprofit	4,135	6,491	8,796	11,912
All for-profit	862	958	1,250	1,406
Percent governmental	27.2	30.0	28.5	25.0
Percent nonprofit	60.2	61.0	62.6	67.1
Percent for-profit	12.6	9.0	8.9	7.9

SOURCE: "Hospital Service in the United States," *Journal of the American Medical Association,* selected years.

hospital admissions, and increased this share after the war ended. A major report on hospital care, published in 1947, attributed improved hospital care explicitly to the "progressive evolution of medical knowledge."[16] The linked ideas of medical science, hospitals, and quality of care suggested that the hospital's future success would lie in improved medical knowledge and technology rather than in an expanded medical-service role (into ambulatory care, for example) or expanded social functions such as home health services or health education.

A Knowledge-Based System?

The new emphasis on scientific knowledge, accompanied by medical specialization, changed and focused discussions of regionalizing hospital care. If a primary purpose of regionalism was to distribute knowledge, the ideal regional model was one based on a university medical school, where knowledge was produced. What was needed, then, were organizational mechanisms that allowed for the flow of knowledge outward, through larger to smaller hospitals and private practitioners. Since medical centers were also the focus for superspecialized techniques, mechanisms could also be developed for patients who would benefit from these services to be transported from small towns at the periphery to the center of the system. The model was of a distributory network. One such model already existed in the Bingham Associates Plan between Tufts University of Boston and hospitals in Maine. Patients requiring diagnostic study were referred from local hospitals to a specified district hospital center and, when necessary, to Boston. After consultation, they were referred back to the local hospital. Pathologists and radiologists from district centers also visited subsidiary hospitals on a regular basis. The basic assumption behind the Bingham Associates Plan was to regionalize medicine as both diagnosis and management through a flow of knowledge, specialists, and patients.

There was a recognized need for coordinated efforts to make up-to-date diagnostic services available to all geographical areas. In Mississippi, it was reported at congressional hearings in 1943, there were only five physicians able to "take a piece of tissue from your body and tell you if it is malignant."[17] Linking hospitals together into information and service networks could optimize the use of such scarce resources. In theory, regionalism could be achieved, as in the Bingham Plan, through voluntary, cooperative participation of hospitals and physicians, without loss of authority by individual institutions or even interference into their administration. The beauty of this type of coordination was that it focused on regional medical *information* and *consultation* systems. Apart from the availability of advanced diagnostic consultation, there was no attempt to reorganize the health-care system and thus no need to control individual hospitals.

At the same time, the success of the new pharmaceuticals weakened arguments for organizing local health-care systems into multispecialty groups based in hospitals. Improved sulfa compounds, as well as antibiotics, brought the benefits of science to all practitioners. The average rural general practitioner of the late 1940s could do more for a patient with influenza, meningitis, or pneumonia than the most sophisticated specialist in internal medicine in a hospital in 1935. Suddenly, then, the role of the individual practitioner was reaffirmed. Postwar Americans could rely on their personal physician as a fount of cures, expecting a pharmaceutical solution for practically every ailment.

As office practice flourished and medical incomes rose after the war, group organization of specialists and hospital bureaucracies became, in turn, less threatening as competition to the average practitioner. Curiously, then, while medical centers were affirming their aristocratic (meritocratic) importance as the center of medical research, the new pharmaceuticals were democratizing practice. Local practitioners were not even totally dependent on the medical centers for information about new treatments. Pharmaceutical information was readily available to them through medical journals and through visits from aggressive detail personnel from the major pharmaceutical houses. The role of the office-based practitioner was further strengthened by the advent of other powerful chemicals, including tranquilizers, in the 1950s. Connections with hospitals did remain important in establishing informal networks, the doctor's legitimacy, and a pecking order within the profession, and of course the hospitals were important to physicians as places to admit patients. One study of white male general practitioners in Maryland, the District of Columbia, and Georgia in 1942 found them seeing, on average, six to eleven patients in hospitals a week, depending on location (table 8.2). But it was no longer quite so clear that the hospital was the only possible professional base for the future organization of the health-care system.

Dr. Thomas Parran, the surgeon general of the United States Public Health Service, was—nevertheless—a powerful advocate for hospitals as

TABLE 8.2

Average Weekly Patient Load of White Male General Practitioners, Maryland, Georgia, and the District of Columbia, 1942

		Average Weekly Number of Patients Seen			
	Number of Physicians	All Locations	Doctor's Office	Hospital	Patient's Home
Baltimore	288	119	82	6	31
Maryland, exclusive of Baltimore	262	132	96	7	29
District of Columbia	156	115	86	8	21
Urban Georgia	170	112	78	11	23
Rural Georgia	436	111	79	6	26

SOURCE: President's Commission on the Health Needs of the Nation, *Building America's Health* (Washington, D.C.: Government Printing Office, 1951), vol. 3, *America's Health Status, Needs, and Resources*, pp. 148–49.

the key component in a broader health-care system. Parran expressed concern, in particular, about the danger of any program of compulsory health insurance being unleashed upon a disorganized and unregulated hospital system, thus stimulating purchasing power among low-income groups without providing them with hospital beds. Presenting proposals for a regionalized system during hearings on wartime health and education in 1944, Parran urged the development of a coordinated hospital-service plan, linking hospitals with public health agencies, provision for psychiatric care, tuberculosis treatment, chronic disease services, and health centers. Planning and control of the system would be accomplished by an official state agency and directed toward defined service districts. At the center of concentric circles, he proposed, there should be a superspecialized base hospital; at least one of these was envisaged for each state. At the periphery was a health center, providing a base both for public health services and for private physicians.[18]

Under the Parran model, hospital medicine could only partly be seen as the articulation of a freestanding "science." Taken to its conclusion, this scheme would have led to an organized health system, consolidated at the local level, in which hospitals played only one part. This was, in theory, a major challenge to the idea of local autonomous hospitals and indeed to the hospital associations, as they attempted to incorporate prevailing ideas of medical science into debates about federal construction of hospitals. But such discussions were on an academic level as long as there was no compulsory health insurance to provide the economic and regulatory lever for change. As it was, proposals for government health insurance continued to simmer in the background.

Wartime Programs and Their Implications

The immediate stimulus for collective action during the war was the necessity of providing hospital services to workers in the burgeoning war-
production industries. The buildup of the arms industry began well before
Pearl Harbor. War contracts worth $14.2 billion were let by the spring of
1940, two-thirds of which flowed to sixty-eight corporations. Business
corporations consolidated their interests and worked closely with government agencies, creating an army of new jobs. An estimated 1.5 million
civilians were expected to move into encampments adjacent to military
bases and into newly developed industrial areas during the emergency,
including temporary "duration factories" producing TNT and other high
explosives in the prairie. Government figures suggested an estimated need
for 6,300 new hospital beds at a total cost of $25 million.[19]

From the end of 1941, however, existing hospitals were hard-pressed,
even in major cities, because of staff losses to the war effort. For example,
in Detroit the automobile industry expanded through conversion to tanks
and other military equipment and the population rose rapidly, while staff
shortages led to the closing of beds in major hospitals. Both Harper Hospital and Henry Ford Hospital were forced to reduce their bed complement
significantly by 1943. Particular problems of access to care were reported
among the 5,000 black families who migrated to Detroit to provide additional manpower for war production.[20]

Thousands of migrants moved to new communities which had no
established organizational infrastructure. Among the first thirty-three
government-priority areas for hospitals were towns in nine southern
states, but defense establishments were scattered across the United States.
In Saginaw, Michigan, an additional 15,000 or 20,000 people were expected, increasing the population by 20 to 25 percent. Ypsilanti, Michigan,
a college town with 12,000 people, was braced to absorb the additional
22,000 people who were expected to build army bombers under an $18
million national defense project. Small towns such as Charlestown, Indiana, mushroomed; 15,000 workers joined the original community of
1,000.[21] Across the country, from San Diego up to Seattle and across to
Virginia, industry created a new, selective process of migration—together
with potentially explosive social problems in the new and enlarged communities.

There were strong and immediate pressures in Congress to establish
a public-works program which would provide necessary services in war-

production areas: schools, hospitals, and sewage systems; organized enter-tainment; and other services that would alleviate boredom, prevent crime and illness, and stimulate productivity. Hospital construction was now too costly for the available local capital of small-town migrant populations; a new 100-bed hospital cost at least $400,000 in 1941.[22] Business corpora-tions looked instead to Uncle Sam, on whose behalf they were producing.

The Lanham Act, a public-works program dominated by the practical politics of national defense (and named for its sponsor, Congressman Fritz Lanham of Texas), passed with little difficulty in 1941. Administered by the Federal Works Agency, the act provided immediate federal assistance for creating a community infrastructure in defense areas, including hospi-tals and health centers. Grants or loans were provided to nonfederal hospi-tals which remained in nonprofit or local government hands. (There were 100 percent subventions available for any community that wanted a fed-eral hospital.) Between 1941 and 1946, when the Lanham program was terminated, 874 hospital and related projects were undertaken, at a cost of $121 million.[23] Hospitals received one-fourth of all funds under the Lanham Act, more than was spent on schools or water systems.[24]

The Lanham Act was passed as a pragmatic, focused response to national emergency: to provide services rapidly, and to establish and main-tain social order. Nevertheless, by committing federal funds to hospital construction, the act opened a Pandora's box of questions about the philos-ophy of federal intervention and the precise form of hospital planning in the future. Speakers at the hearings on the Lanham bill in 1941 raised the question of whether such aid was necessary at all, or alternatively, if so, why federal aid to hospitals should be limited to areas that happened to have defense workers.[25] Members of congressional committees expressed concern, too, about concentration of power in the federal government. Congressman Lanham soothed away potential confrontation on this issue by stressing that any hospitals built by federal funds would be controlled at the local level.[26] As part of the emphasis on the local community, the Lanham Act established the important precedent of allowing federal aid to private nonprofit hospitals as well as local-government institutions. Indeed, the House bill left open the possibility of grants to profit-making hospitals as well, a question of some importance in areas such as Hampton Roads, Virginia, where both a black hospital and a white hospital were owned by individuals. (At the conference stage, profit-making hospitals were in fact excluded.)

There was further concern in Congress over how a federal program, once started, would be limited and regulated. Several speakers at the hear-ings made it clear that the legislation applied only to emergency (war) conditions. Legislators were concerned that the act not provide "frills," encouraging hospitals to engage in lavish buildings. One speaker described the Lanham bill as having the "earmarks of a perfect unadulterated pork barrel bill," which would indulge the interests of certain "starry-eyed boys," presumably the health-care experts.[27] But these concerns were expressed in the spring of 1941, before Pearl Harbor. In fact, shortages of raw materials after the United States entered the war led to stringent controls over construction in the Lanham program, and limited both its scope and the architectural imagination of its builders. Federal regulations cut frills to the bone, requiring a minimum of four patients per room in buildings constructed under the program, together with hand-operated elevators and dumbwaiters, and reduction or elimination of services such as call bells, signal systems, paging systems, telephones, and hall lights. Regulations also limited new construction to areas where the welfare of patients in existing hospitals was jeopardized because of overcrowding.

Before Pearl Harbor, leading spokesmen of the American Hospital Association were on relatively safe ground in opposing the "general philosophy of government"—that is, increased centralization of power in federal agencies—in favor of a partnership between government and "private charitable agencies."[28] But it was becoming clear that voluntary hospitals would be well advised to have a plan for postwar hospital development, over and above mere adherence to the voluntary ethos. Otherwise, as the president of the AHA, Fred Carter, warned in 1940, there were dangers of inimical legislation that might tear down the "great system of hospitals" (i.e., the voluntary hospitals) that had been built up over the past two centuries.[29] Thus relatively early in the war the AHA and the other hospital associations began to think and to plan for postwar development.

Meanwhile, a second wartime program highlighted the other major deficiency in hospital care in the 1940s: the lack of adequate hospital insurance, in this case for young servicemen and their wives. By late 1941 areas around military camps and installations were badly congested. Babies were born in substandard conditions because of inadequate family funds to pay the hospital and the physician. The problem was particularly evident in obstetrics, because this was a population of young families and the proportion of births in hospitals was rapidly increasing (to almost 80 percent by the end of the war). As an emergency wartime program, therefore, a federal emergency maternity and infant-care program (EMIC) was launched officially in March 1943, run by the states, to provide for obstetrics, hospital, and pediatric care around military camps and installations.[30] Altogether, EMIC served 1.1 million maternity cases before the program was terminated in November 1946. In 1946 the program covered one out of every seven births in the United States.

The American Hospital Association endorsed the principle of direct payment to hospitals on a cost basis. By paying full cost for an otherwise largely uninsured population and covering pediatric hospital care (together with other pediatric care up to one year of age), the program also gave its beneficiaries experience with a program of hospital insurance entitlements, thus helping to pave the way for the general expansion of voluntary and commercial hospital insurance after the war. But EMIC might also have been the thin end of the wedge of nationally controlled hospital insurance. Such connections were made explicit in legislative proposals which rein-troduced into Congress a proposed national health program in 1943, the year EMIC was established.[31]

With respect both to capital acquisition (Lanham) and reimbursement policy (EMIC), then, the American Hospital Association, as the major representative of voluntary hospitals, was well advised to develop its own independent program if it wished to present itself (as it said it did) as the advocate of comprehensive, good hospital care. Graham Davis of the Kel-logg Foundation urged the AHA to provide leadership and to work toward a comprehensive hospital program for the postwar period by forming a planning commission: such a commission would mobilize voluntary hospi-tals as a group, express the values of voluntarism at a time of increasing federal planning, and work toward eliminating the more obvious weak-nesses in the hospital system. Some hospitals, he said, were an "actual menace to the health of the communities in which they are located."[32] Many of these were in the group of 2,500 or more hospitals that the AMA refused to register.

Laying the Base for Postwar Planning

It seemed likely to AHA leaders and other interested observers that a large public-works program would be launched after the war, even if compul-sory health insurance were not enacted. A massive construction program could be used, as in the Depression, to avert or to attack economic reces-sion, such as had occurred after World War I. If money were not made available to voluntary hospitals in any postwar program, local-government hospitals (perhaps even federal or state hospitals) could forge ahead, buoyed up by massive construction subsidies. There were no major congressional proposals for a national health program or national health insurance in 1940 or 1941, but the coalition of liberal, farming, and labor interests was holding firm. In 1942 Representative Thomas Eliot introduced a new bill (HR 7534) that heralded formal renewal of interest in federally subsidized hospital construction, independent of the Lanham program.

The American Hospital Association established its Committee on Postwar Planning the same year. The major outcome was a recommendation for a comprehensive study of hospitals by a specially appointed commission, which would include estimates of future national needs for hospital care.[33] The following year the committee obtained funding from the Commonwealth Fund, the Kellogg Foundation, and the National Foundation for Infantile Paralysis to underwrite the project. An editorial in the journal *Hospitals* reported in May of that year (1943): "People are indulging in postwar planning these days as if it were an indoor sport."[34] It was a sport with serious political, economic, and organizational connotations. Estimated national investment in hospitals was over $4 billion in 1942–43. Meanwhile, a new congressional bill in 1943 proposed compulsory health insurance, federal aid to hospitals for construction, and other elements of a comprehensive national health program.

The election of James A. Hamilton, director of the New Haven Hospital, as president of the American Hospital Association in the same year provided hospital administrators and trustees with a sense of urgency and direction. Hamilton brought in George Bugbee, superintendent of Cleveland City Hospital, as the AHA's executive director, with the specific purpose of transforming the association. Both men envisaged an organization with broad responsibilities in the hospital field, including representation (lobbying) before government and other audiences. One of Hamilton's first tasks was to work with Graham Davis of the Kellogg Foundation to create the new Commission on Hospital Care. The superintendent of the University of Chicago Hospitals and Clinics, Dr. Arthur Bachmeyer, became the commission's director, backed by Maurice Norby, Rufus Rorem's associate at the Blue Cross Commission. Thus a strong body of effective leaders was emerging, forming the nucleus of a renewed, more powerful hospital association.

In September 1943 the AHA formally announced its own national political position in a three-point resolution: federal grants-in-aid to states, to assist in providing hospital care for public assistance recipients and other medically indigent patients; federal grants-in-aid to states for hospital construction, in areas requiring assistance because of generally low incomes or critical shifts in population; and federal stimulation of voluntary hospital insurance (Blue Cross) through permission for payroll deductions for federal employees. The major caveat was that construction funds should be designed to protect and enlarge existing hospitals rather than to establish new ones. The three-point program and the work of the commission were designed, Hamilton said, to preserve the "best of the past."[35]

The positive tone of these proposals spoke for a measured conservatism as a matter of public policy, designed to uphold American ideals (voluntarism), with change seen as incremental. This policy stood the hospital leaders in good stead. By asserting the need for hospital planning, they avoided charges of self-interest, while being able to guide the program's direction. The American Medical Association's consistent opposition to the national health bills appeared, in contrast, reactionary and self-serving. Although leading Blue Cross and hospital spokesmen accurately read the mood in Congress as not ripe for passage of national health insurance in 1943 (nor did they see a need for direct lobbying in opposition to it), there was much to be learned from the legislative experience. The AHA spoke confidently about the hospital's role as a "civilizing influence" in twentieth-century America, through performing "miracles of modern science."[36]

Hospital Planning: Consensus from Within

The Commission on Hospital Care first met in 1944 and produced its report in 1947. Its membership provided a microcosm of what voluntarism meant in American society: cooperation among major foundations, service providers, industrial and university leaders, and representatives from other walks of life, who were supported by government but who worked together to develop a program that would obviate the necessity of government control of major enterprises.[37] The study itself was based on painstaking analysis by the commission's staff and technical advisers, who included experienced hospital administrators, staff from the Commonwealth Fund and the Kellogg Foundation, and a senior member of the U.S. Public Health Service.

A major outcome of the commission's work was to establish and to influence hospital study groups in the states. By the fall of 1945 twenty state hospital surveys were in progress, usually conducted by state health departments or special commissions created by the governors; interest in such surveys was reported in all forty-eight states.[38] Thus the commission generated widespread interest in hospital planning across the country. State planning was facilitated by the presence of a staff member assigned to the commission by the U.S. Public Health Service and by assistance from federal officers in the seven U.S. Public Health Service regional districts. Quantitative guidelines were also established, following a special study of hospital resources and needs in Michigan, which was sponsored by the Kellogg Foundation. In this and other ways, government and foundation resources were made available to buttress the position of the major hospital groups. By focusing on *hospital* care, not on health-care planning as a whole, the commission stimulated interest in hospitals in the states that was largely independent of the concurrent calls for a comprehensive health-care system or national health insurance.

That there was a general lack of *acceptable* hospital beds, particularly in the southern states, was well accepted. Hundreds of hospitals were regarded as obsolete, either because they were too small and ill-equipped or because of a reported lag in capital investment. The real annual value of new hospital construction (for all types of hospitals) had surged between 1936 and 1939 under the impact of government programs and general improvements in the economy. However, even with the stimulus of the Lanham program, construction plummeted between 1940 and 1944, driven down by lack of strategic materials and rising inflation.[39] Surgeon General Parran estimated in 1944 that at least 25 percent of existing facilities were obsolete or obsolescent—and this, he said, was a conservative estimate. But construction, he stressed, was not enough. Needed also was a "coordinated hospital plan."[40] The message was to modernize, link and (perhaps) consolidate the system through huge capital expansion. The American Hospital Association and its associates in foundations and government, including Parran, moved to direct and mold this expected expansion.

The consortium position was clearly stated by Dr. Claude Munger, speaking for the American Hospital Association at congressional hearings in 1944, the occasion on which Parran outlined his estimates. The basic problem of health care, Munger said, was to improve the quality of hospital care and make it more readily available to every citizen. There should be a national definition of "need" for beds, based on specific quantitative criteria. Hospital programs would be determined by the states, subject to review by the U.S. Public Health Service, but as far as possible voluntary efforts would be encouraged as the vehicle for the actual distribution of hospitals in the future. The AHA recommended this program before any attempt was made to finance hospital benefits through compulsory health insurance.[41]

An emerging consensus on regionalism between the U.S. Public Health Service and the hospital associations was reiterated in a detailed design for Michigan, reported from the special Kellogg Foundation study in 1946.[42] In that state, it was assumed, there would be base hospitals at the University of Michigan and Wayne State University. Beneath them would be twenty-one defined regions, each containing regional hospital centers of at least 100 beds, which would provide specialized services to a further array of small hospitals with 50 beds or more. At the bottom would be a network of public health and medical-service centers in small towns and villages. The focus was on the dissemination of big-city medical techniques *outward* and on the closing or consolidation of tiny units, encouraging patients to move to hospitals in larger towns or cities for their care. In Michigan, for example, the surveyors recommended maintaining only 118 out of the 292 hospitals in the state. The plan was to close down substandard or possibly dangerous facilities rather than to create a new system of local community hospitals or comprehensive health centers.[43] A regional *hospital* plan had the strategic advantage of leaving physicians largely alone, while providing them with enhanced hospital and diagnostic facilities. Neither the U.S. Public Health Service nor the hospital associations were willing to fight physician opposition to local health centers where curative and preventive medicine might be integrated.

On the assumption that there would be extensive hospital construction after the war, with or without federal aid, the Council of State Governments sponsored and distributed a model state hospital survey act in the fall of 1944.[44] Virtually all of the pieces for the coming legislation were now in place: continuation of interest in federal hospital construction in rural states, particularly among legislators whose constituencies had benefited from the Lanham Act and from construction of veterans' hospitals; growing interest in hospital planning in the states; well-organized support by hospital interests, provided construction funds were given to voluntary hospitals; norms and background data from the Commission on Hospital Care; and general support of hospital construction by the medical profession and by hospital trustees.

The joint committee of the three major hospital associations, American, Catholic and Protestant, reached general agreement among themselves about the desirability of legislation for federal support of hospital construction during 1944. By the fall of that year they had reached a formulation that was generally acceptable. For the first time the hospital associations would have a bill, sponsored and developed by themselves, that was to lead to major plans for a hospital system. Three circumstances made timing critical. First, there was the coming end of the war; without special legislation there was no guarantee that a public works program would be passed which would include voluntary hospitals on equal terms with tax-supported institutions. Second, there was the rising possibility that legislation for national health insurance would be passed. (During the election campaign of 1944 President Roosevelt appeared to be moving toward an endorsement of such a program, reiterated in his budget message in January 1945.) Third was the continuing watchfulness by voluntary hospitals of their status as public institutions, for the general purposes of charitable immunity, tax exemption, and public image.

The Hill-Burton Act: Expansionism and Independence

The instigating force for the hospital construction bill was George Bugbee, the AHA's executive director, who registered in Washington as a lobbyist. Bugbee knew Senator Harold Burton from his days in Cleveland, where Burton had been mayor; and Burton agreed to introduce the AHA bill provided Senator Taft, who was the other senator from Ohio, was in agreement. Taft, running for president, was strongly opposed to national health insurance, which he called "very Socialistic."[45] However, he had been involved in the passage of the Lanham program and he needed a health bill in his presidential platform. Thus from the beginning, major Republican support was achieved. Burton also suggested the sponsorship of Senator Lister Hill of Alabama, in order to insure bipartisan support in the Senate. The resulting Hill-Burton bill was introduced in January 1945.

The Hill-Burton bill provided for federal aid to states under the Public Health Service Act for surveying hospitals and public health centers, for planning construction of additional facilities, and for authorizing grants to assist in such construction. The bill's writers were careful to specify that construction should apply to both governmental and private nonprofit hospitals. The Catholic Hospital Association pressed, unsuccessfully, for further weighting of the funds to reflect the relative proportion of service rendered by public, tax-supported hospitals and other nonprofit hospitals, so that voluntary hospitals might get maximum value from the program.[46] However, the bill did include the establishment of a new Federal Hospital Council, consisting of private citizens, that might act as a check to any attempt at central federalized control. Under the legislation, as signed in 1946, federal aid was apportioned among the states by a formula designed to take into account greater deficiencies in hospitals in the poorest states. In each state, local or private applicants for federal aid were to be required to put up two dollars for each federal dollar assigned. It was the state's problem to establish priorities. However, the state was not required to finance the project from state tax funds; different mechanisms for nonfederal funding were to be established in different states.

Senator Burton was appointed to the Supreme Court before the bill came up for review. However, Hill and Taft were inspired choices. Lister Hill, as a small boy, had been taken by his father, who was a doctor, on trips to watch the great surgeons in Chicago and Rochester, Minnesota. He had firsthand knowledge of the problems of rural hospital service in his own state of Alabama and successful experience, too, as a congressman in lobbying for a veterans' hospital in Montgomery in the late 1930s.[47] (The Hill-Burton Act, too, would bring federal dollars to local areas.) In his opening remarks at the Senate hearings on federal aid for hospital construction in February and March 1945, Hill described the lack of hospital facilities as a problem of great national significance. In the wealthiest country of the world, he said, we "have not yet organized our efforts to the end that scientific health care is readily available to all our people."[48] Both Hill and Taft favored control through the states rather than the federal government, and strongly endorsed the inclusion of voluntary nonprofit hospitals as eligible for aid.

Senator Taft initially objected to giving federal financing to the richest states. The medical-care system was, he said, "inadequate in spots," not overall, and it was on these spots that the government should concentrate, filling gaps rather than subsidizing the entire system. Otherwise, powerful individuals from rich communities would leap forward for federal aid: "Every hospital in Cincinnati, Ohio, would be here with a tremendous crowd of influential people wanting to double the size of their hospitals."[49] Nevertheless, it was Taft's understanding of the complicated formula by which Hill-Burton funds were eventually allotted, favoring the poorer states, while continuing to include the richer, that expedited passage of the legislation.[50] The decision to administer the new program at the federal level through the U.S. Public Health Service rather than through the Social Security Board also smoothed the way, for the board was the main administrative agency for the compulsory

health-insurance proposals that were being considered concurrently in
the Wagner-Murray-Dingell bill.

There was little action on the Hill-Burton Act until the new president,
Harry Truman, sent a health message to Congress in November 1945, after
the Japanese surrender, along with a redrafted Wagner-Murray-Dingell
bill. But then the president singled out the hospital grant program as a
separate, independent proposal. And the hospital lobby fought for the
legislation, drawing on the wider rhetoric of voluntarism. The AHA voted
unanimously to approve a multimillion-dollar education fund, to "explore
the benefits of free enterprise" and combat government control in the
operation of the nation's hospitals. Most of the money, spent on newspaper advertising, was designed to promote the successful service record of
voluntary institutions and voluntary Blue Cross plans. (The director of
Massachusetts Blue Cross explained that advertising was to be used not
to sell a product but to create understanding of an American philosophy,
the "voluntary approach to living.")[51] Columnist Drew Pearson described
the federal construction proposals, not unfairly, as "private" legislation,
designed to siphon off $375 million from the federal Treasury and put it
largely under control of the "hospital crowd."[52]

The voluntary rhetoric was persuasive. At the hearings Surgeon General Parran spoke admiringly of the hospital's community tradition of
sacrifice and service, and the AMA representative, Dr. R. L. Sensenich,
described the nonprofit voluntary hospital as "really the purest form of
democracy."[53] Arguing for a wide-reaching program of federal grants, he
painted a picture of community self-sufficiency, harking back to the archetypal voluntary tradition of an institution built up in a community by a
board made up of outstanding community citizens, people with confidence
and ability who gave their time willingly, without pay, outside of any
connection with any political group, and provided services to rich and poor
alike. The Senate quickly passed the Hill-Burton bill in December 1945
and the House in July 1946. Hill-Burton was signed, as Public Law 79-75.
As a fitting tribute to Lister Hill's leadership, the first project approved for
federal aid was for an 87-bed general hospital in Langdale in his own state
of Alabama. When he dedicated this hospital, Hill praised the cotton
workers in the region for signing up for voluntary prepayment insurance,
thus providing themselves with medical care "without compulsion or
reliance upon a socialized system."[54]

The Hill-Burton legislation is a major landmark in American hospital
history. In its first twenty years 4,678 projects were undertaken, almost
half directed to communities with under 10,000 population.[55] Major federal responsibility was assumed for hospital expansion across the country,

but with a specific bow to the politically important southern states; these qualified for the program preferentially, both on grounds of rural needs and relatively low per capita income.

Hospital Planning and the Voluntary Ethos

Hill-Burton was designed as a partnership between the voluntary hospital system and the states. The federal government set overall guidelines, including 4.5 general hospital beds per 1,000 population as a measure of adequacy of hospital provision. However, the program reflected the desires of its shapers to limit federal control as far as was practical. Hence the creation of the Federal Hospital Council, composed of members of the health-care establishment and others. The council was designed to act in a semijudicial capacity, with the ability to veto actions by the federal administrator of the program, the surgeon general of the U.S. Public Health Service. A related provision allowed any applicant, including a state or local government, or a private nonprofit organization, to appeal any action of the Public Health Service in denying it a construction grant. President Truman objected to these two administrative provisions of the legislation, which did, after all, weaken government responsibility and accountability in favor of private interests. Nevertheless, he signed it just the same, citing the urgent need for a prompt start on hospital surveys and postwar planning. In other respects, too, the legislation downplayed centralized administration.

Once again, as in the earlier veterans' program, a major opportunity was lost for including racial desegregation as a condition of federal funding.[56] Nor were hospitals seeking funding required to provide specific amounts of charity care or to modify their functions in other directions. As in the tax-exemption cases, there was an underlying expectation that voluntary and local-government hospitals could be trusted to further the public good. Hill-Burton provided a federal enabling framework through which this mission could be achieved.

An essential characteristic of Hill-Burton was its explicit purpose of expansion in the name of hospital science. The modern hospital, said Surgeon General Parran, is a "complex technical machine, employing the latest scientific diagnostic aids, preventative and curative measures, and professional skills."[57] The underlying commitment to the idea of hospital medicine as science suggested that the more hospital services there were, the better. Hill-Burton was indeed a direct parallel to federal support for biomedical research. Both increased the production of science and—presumably—made science more accessible (and useful) to the U.S. population. Hospital administrators, trustees, and attending staff enthusiastically embraced the expansionary ethos. General hospital admissions rose by 26 percent between 1946 and 1952, continuing the expansion of the wartime years (table 8.1). The expansion of hospital inpatient services—a trend that continued until the early 1980s—was perceived as an unambiguous social good.

An important innovation was the requirement that every state wishing to participate in Hill-Burton must develop a survey of its facilities and a plan for implementation. The goal was to create a program of hospital care that was "scientifically planned."[58] States were required to plan for general hospitals on a regional and area basis, in accordance with the concept, if not the reality, of a coordinated hospital system. This "concept" was the pattern of regionalism laid out in congressional hearings by Surgeon General Parran and in the Kellogg Foundation's survey in Michigan, that is, the identification of one or more regional networks of hospitals in each state, each emanating from a superspecialized base hospital, which was usually affiliated with a medical school. State planning required states to define general hospital service areas, to make an inventory and appraise existing facilities and beds within these areas, and to calculate the number of hospital beds needed. States also rated the acceptability of existing beds. Of the total of approximately 475,000 general hospital beds in 1948, 84 percent were rated acceptable, producing a ratio of 2.8 beds per 1,000 population—well below the federal figure of 4.5. Calculations suggested the need for 255,000 additional beds, with a priority for rural areas. The state plans thus further legitimated the general policy of hospital expansion. Planning, as actually implemented, was the creation of opportunities for construction, with federal subsidy concentrating on areas of designated need.

The Hill-Burton program stimulated enormous interest in the role of state health departments as central elements in health-care planning within each state. State legislatures, seeing an opportunity for new services and new dollars, began to gear up for Hill-Burton even before the act was passed. Hospital administrators pressed legislators in states which lagged behind to pass enabling laws quickly, so that they could qualify for Hill-Burton funding. In Michigan the superintendent of Hurley Hospital in Flint urged in 1947: "Four million dollars in subsidies is at stake for this next fiscal year, and six million more during the succeeding three years."[59] By the end of 1948 all states and territories except Nevada had submitted plans to the surgeon general for hospital construction, priorities, administration, and standards.[60] A total of 375 hospital regions had been designated in the United States. Within these regions there were 2,323 defined service areas, 104 of which were base hospital areas.[61]

On paper, at least, these plans were impressive. For the first time, the United States had a nationally defined, regionally organized network for hospital provision—a grid of lines of coordination across the country. The hospital plans, taken together, looked like plans for the national distribution of electricity. The thinking was remarkably similar to that of the consultants on hospitalization after World War I. Hospitals were regarded as a national resource which should be organized rationally as a national system.

This apparent commitment to a hospital system based on science and centered on universities spilled over, too, into postwar planning for the veterans' hospital system. Again there was a sense of déjà vu, harking back to the debates of the early 1920s. As after World War I, community hospitals were noticeably uninterested in caring for returning veterans. They were also wary of being involved with the Veterans Administration. Few medical schools or hospitals showed much interest in community health services, prevention, or rehabilitation for veterans.[62] And the system of veterans' hospitals, as it had grown in the interwar period, staffed by civil servants, was marked by poor quality and administration.

The establishment of a separate medical corps, independent of the civil service, was one major plank for reform of the VA medical system after World War II. The second plank, affiliation of VA hospitals with medical schools, was designed to attract better physicians, raise scientific standards, and have the full resources of a medical center available. With a sophisticated grasp of postwar rhetoric, the VA's new chief medical adviser, Dr. Paul Hawley, posed the problem of raising scientific standards to the American Medical Association as a job for American *medicine*—with no interference from Washington. Hawley created a plan for 166 new buildings near or adjacent to medical schools, and moved toward implementation through the cooperation of the deans of the seventy-seven Class A medical schools. Although the AHA accused the VA in 1947 of establishing a large, unwieldy system of hospitals to the detriment of the private sector, the new program was a success.[63] The reorganized veterans' system recruited almost eight hundred new physicians in its first six weeks of operation in 1946, while moving at the same time to establish university-affiliated specialist residency training programs in the VA hospitals.[64]

Both the VA and Hill-Burton programs were national, governmental programs. Both embodied national policies: upgrading hospital services to veterans and supporting regional hospital systems. Both, at the same time, decentralized control to the local level. In a reprise of the general policy after World War I, the revised VA arrangements removed decisions about locating new veterans' hospitals from the domain of congressional logrolling; the *Washington Post*, for example, referred to the affiliation of VA hospitals with medical schools as a "no-pork" policy.[65] In effect, the VA hospital system shifted from the old political and geographical patronage system—for good or ill—to the patronage of the medical schools.

As a result, although veterans' hospitals were a national system, their placement and administration were dependent on local conditions, that is, on the role of the various deans' committees and on local customs. For example, of ninety-seven VA hospitals surveyed in 1945, seventeen accepted no black patients except in emergencies and twenty-four had separate wards for blacks, while the Tuskegee Hospital accepted only blacks. Black physicians might be appointed to VA hospitals subject to "local custom." Director Hawley was reported in 1946 as considering promoting all-black units (doctors, nurses, and patients) in a number of the VA hospitals.[66] But for the most part, as under Hill-Burton, federal policies were held subservient to policies in the states. At the same time, VA hospitals were placed outside the state hospital planning system being set up under the Hill-Burton legislation.

Like the VA program, Hill-Burton affirmed the values of scientific medicine embodied in the universities. As in the parallel growth of federal grants for biomedical research, designed for rapid expansion of scientific investigation in the medical schools, the goal was to stimulate individual and institutional initiative.[67] The state programs did not impose regional planning on anyone; rather, they pointed out opportunities for funding in areas which appeared to be underbedded, or where existing beds were unacceptable. Any hospital could continue to build, whether or not it had Hill-Burton funds. Federal funds, however, were made available only where need was formally specified in the state plan.

In the VA and Hill-Burton programs, then, the dual prewar national policies of the medical organizations and philanthropic foundations—providing for strong urban medical centers on the one hand and rural community hospitals on the other—were strengthened and reaffirmed by the federal government. Hill-Burton shored up the idea of voluntary hospitals across the country by providing federal support of local initiative. Kenneth Williamson, assistant director of the American Hospital Association between 1943 and 1950, remarked later: "Hill-Burton is one reason we still have voluntary hospitals."[68] Borne along by the joint promise of medical science and federal subsidy, trustees, physicians, local politicians, and other community leaders launched massive fund drives to raise the matching funds required.

Nevertheless, as in earlier periods, there was a continuing vein of criticism of the "charitable" role of voluntary enterprises. Notably, by the 1940s the idea that charitable hospitals should not be held responsible for negligence—charitable immunity—was increasingly hard to sustain. Indeed, voluntary hospitals were generally availing themselves of public liability insurance.[69] The courts continued to be generally favorable to hospitals in tax-exemption cases, but this, too, was by no means a foregone conclusion; hospital concerns were fanned by a decision of the Treasury Department in 1942 to obtain a financial report on each hospital, in order to make some distinction between the bona fide voluntary hospital and the institution "masquerading under the cloak of charity."[70] In most cases the public status of voluntary hospitals was reaffirmed by the courts, but the challenges were ever-present.[71]

It was much more difficult now than in the 1920s or 1930s to see voluntary hospitals solely as "good" institutions which ought to be supported just because they existed. Increased government involvement in all areas of social policy suggested, instead, that where government favors were sought there should be some demonstrable quid pro quo. There was even talk—bravado, no doubt, but nonetheless significant—that if a low rate of local-government reimbursement for the indigent was the exchange for tax exemption, voluntary hospitals might be better off changing their status to profit-making hospitals and billing government at full rates.[72] If the scale tipped away from tax exemption and/or toward national health insurance, voluntary hospitals might lose their favored role and dominance in the health-care system.

To counteract such possibilities, voluntary-hospital administrators linked the language of voluntarism to prospects for democracy in the postwar world. Thus the AHA president, James Hamilton, described voluntary hospitals in 1943 as an "intricate part of the democratic course of life," at a time when, in his view, government welfare was headed toward state socialism. In suggesting that political power was shifting to the lower working class, away from the middle-class property owner, "whose respect for the doctor was maintained by intimate and frequent contact in common social endeavors,"[73] he identified voluntarism overtly with middle-class interests. Roman Catholic spokesmen took the loftier road, linking local initiative, voluntarism, democracy, and freedom. Voluntary hospitals were "agents of society," fulfilling a "prime and indispensable duty." They were to be set against the lesser functions of "agents of government." Voluntary initiative strengthened the sense of responsibility of the individual, affirming the "infinite worth of human personality." Voluntary associations encouraged the individual to enter into associations and organizations of his own choosing, encouraging the individual to provide health protection for his family through his own effort.[74] Thus voluntary hospitals were tied in not only with democracy and American initiative but with other traditional structures of American life.

The identification of voluntarism with spontaneous community action carried over into the idea of the hospital itself—as spontaneously evolving toward better scientific medicine for the public good. Today's health-care system, said the president-elect of the American Hospital Association in 1946, is a "living, growing organism which is instantly adaptable to the latest scientific discoveries, to the needs of the community or to the individual patient."[75]

Planning as a Process, Science as a Mission

By the late 1940s, then, there were elegant hospital plans, coupled with acknowledgment in federal policy of the even greater importance of planning by independent local hospitals and university medical centers. Shored up by federal funding, the hospital system was moving along the pathway of decentralization rather than toward industrial consolidation or regional integration of services or facilities. Scientific research gave the university centers the sanction to ignore both their local communities and the services given in other hospitals, for "science" suggested a more global relevance—the production of knowledge for the whole of humankind. The philosophical commitment to scientific progress seemed a plausible alternative to socialized medicine.

Over and above this, for doctors World War II military experiences of government medical organization had been mixed; there was no general experience similar to that of the pride in base hospitals in World War I. Effective early evacuation of patients now made frontline medicine an episodic, often frustrating experience for surgeons; not until Korea, with further advances in technique, would mobile surgical units return some of the glamour and increase the efficiency of frontline surgical intervention.

Instead, in World War II men like Dr. Perrin Long of Johns Hopkins chafed under administrative restrictions. Administrators, Long said, were limited in outlook and perspective and embodied other "undesirable attributes" which ran counter to the individualistic, peacetime practice of medicine— namely, lack of consideration of the needs of doctors. The experience, he said, was a "lesson learned."[76] What was the lesson? That socialized medi- cine threatened to bring bureaucracy, rudeness, and inefficiency.

Older doctors, too, were battle-weary from the long, fruitless debates about compulsory health insurance over the previous thirty years—while, nevertheless, medical science forged ahead. The pursuit of science, like voluntarism, was the "American way." Indeed, for an uncounted number of Americans, medical science had indeed demonstrated remarkable prog- ress: their lives had been saved or improved through pharmaceuticals and/or surgery. It was easy to link American private enterprise and medical organization with American success in medical science.

To many the reverse associations seemed even clearer. The eminent Dr. Edward H. Ochsner, whose life was a microcosm of changes in the medical profession through the century, made the connection between compulsory health insurance and lower medical quality (that is, poor sci- ence) explicit, when he spoke on behalf of the Chicago Medical Society at the Wagner-Murray-Dingell hearings in 1946. Ochsner's first direct con- tact with the "problem of social insurance," he said, was in 1896, when he was an assistant in a nose and throat clinic in Leipzig, Germany; and there the care was "mediocre."[77] The implication was that under government control it always would be. If the United States had done so well in medical science *without* compulsory insurance, why not drop the whole idea?

Exchanges at the various congressional hearings on postwar planning and on Hill-Burton put hospital construction subsidies squarely in the realm of "science," rather than "socialized medicine." The president of the Florida Medical Association put the case nicely in 1944. Socialized medi- cine, he said, was where government was "pointed toward taking over the practice of medicine." However, he went on, the state should care for the indigent as a duty, while the federal government could make a "construc- tive contribution" by providing rural hospitals. Federal grants-in-aid for hospitals were not objectionable: "There is nothing of socialized medicine in it. That is just progress."[78] The essential question was one of control.

For both hospitals and doctors, then, the identification of science with American progress and American democracy (in health as in other fields) was well suited as the basis for hospital policy in the wartime and postwar years. By 1949 the economy was in deflation, unemployment had risen, and anticommunism was becoming a national preoccupation. The American Medical Association had launched a successful lobbying effort against compulsory health insurance, but this proposal was becoming a tired issue.[79] By 1950 government health insurance was politically dead. There were few calls for a "welfare state," and private health-insurance schemes were expanding rapidly. Business corporations appeared to be well served by these new ventures—without embarking on an expensive system of national health insurance, with concurrent tax increases. The climate of labor-management cooperation rather than conflict further stressed the importance of private insurance, as all parties sought to win the war. Thus health-insurance provision went along its own separate pathway, too, tied to the workplace.

The state Hill-Burton plans, developed with enormous care and enthusiasm, often by visionary young entrants to health-care administration, provided a permissive framework for institutional expansion.[80] Without a major national or state health-insurance scheme, there were no fiscal incentives to push for government control over the hospital system. The incentives were in the opposite direction, toward maintaining hospitals as local units. The concept of a regional health system was also narrowly defined. The state Hill-Burton agencies, providing an organized framework for hospital expansion, accepted the definition of the hospital as an autonomous, scientifically-based treatment center. Comprehensive, primary health centers were a casualty of the Hill-Burton interests.

The beauty of the model of scientific knowledge (rather than, for example, a model of technological diffusion or management efficiency) as the primary rationale for regionalism, from the hospital point of view, was its basic assumption that knowledge was an end in itself. It followed not only that there was a major need to create centers where knowledge could be produced, but also that the distribution of knowledge transcended (and was largely irrelevant) to service organization. The role of the federal government was not to control but to facilitate these ends.

Voluntarism, as political rhetoric, claimed the partnership and trust of government by supporting freedom, the selfless service of religious organizations, and the "finest attitudes in our society."[81] These "attitudes" assumed cooperation between major producers (the hospitals) and government (the U.S. Public Health Service), with hospital associations influencing, if not creating, governmental policy. From the 1940s to the present, hospital lobbyists have been a visible presence on the national scene.

9

Pillars of Respectable
Independence: The 1950s

THE BELIEF that the hospital could be both a technological and a community institution, with little conflict between the two goals, reached its zenith in the fifteen years after World War II. After this war, as after World War I, a general shift toward conservative and traditional values was marked by nostalgia for the ideal community, with its network of supportive institutions. Hospitals responded simultaneously to three powerful themes of postwar life: the belief in the techniques of science as a liberating, rational solution to the problems of everyday existence; the importance of a sense of belonging, with growing emphasis on human relations; and "togetherness," fostered through membership in organized groups, activities, and rituals.[1] Working as a hospital volunteer in an unpaid job in the hospital joined the traditional voluntary roles of board membership and fund-raising in tying hospitals into local social networks. One of the unique characteristics of American life, indelibly stamped "Made in the U.S.A," boasted the report of a new commission, *Health Is a Community Affair*, in 1966, was the participation of "independent, individual citizens" and "associations of individuals linked by a common purpose" in local, state, and national affairs. Here lay the twin virtues of "voluntary leadership and service."[2]

Between 1946, when the Hill-Burton Act was passed, and 1965, the date of the Medicare legislation, American community hospitals embarked on a new wave of expansion, sustained by the belief in their social utility.

Public fascination with both the efficacy and the drama of specialized, high-technology medicine upheld this expansion and fueled a massive drive for private hospital insurance. The most pervasive image of hospital technology in the 1950s was the hospital intensive care unit. Except for the smallest hospitals the great majority of American hospitals established intensive care units between 1950 and 1965. Specialized coronary care units also began to flourish in the early 1960s; and by the mid-1960s there were premature nurseries, special respiratory units and, in the larger hospitals, units dealing with postoperative care after open-heart surgery and neurosurgery.[3] Television, the new vehicle of mass culture, celebrated the hospital as the center of crisis and drama, filled with flashing lights, glass, chrome, and stainless steel. In the 1962 television season, for example, Americans could watch the ABC serial *Ben Casey* on Monday evenings (the experiences, struggles, and triumphs of a chief resident in neurosurgery in a hospital in California); and on Thursday evenings they could choose between NBC's *Doctor Kildare* (the experiences and struggles of a young intern) and the CBS drama *The Nurses* (the experiences and struggles of staff at a hospital in New York City).[4]

For the first time, the federal government became an important force in sustaining the hospital as a local institution, through direct subsidy (via the Hill-Burton program of federal grants to states) and through federal tax incentives.[5] In the 1950s federal hospital policy assumed organizational growth, institution-building, and decentralization; endorsed general principles of individualism and local control over collectivism; and encouraged the establishment of voluntary coalitions.[6] Yet despite the prevailing belief in community control and the enormous success of the hospitals as medical institutions, there were inconsistencies between the idealization of the community hospital and its actualization in the 1950s.

High social expectations of what hospitals could do were sometimes, in the words of a contemporary critic, "so extreme as to be somewhat difficult for the individual institution to realize."[7] Local hospitals duplicated services unnecessarily. And major population groups, notably the elderly and the poor, suffered systematically from inability to pay rising hospital bills—hence the political drives toward Medicare and Medicaid. In the 1970s and 1980s the managerialist credo of the technological system was to succeed both the voluntary and the community ethos as the major organizational rhetoric for hospital policy. What happened between World War II and the mid-1960s is an essential backdrop to this shift.

Government Policy-making by Incentives

In the flowering of community hospital construction, the assumptions of Hill-Burton were fully vindicated. Voluntary hospitals added $2.5 billion to their assets between 1947 and 1955, doubling their overall capital worth from $2.7 to $5.2 billion. Their assets doubled again between 1955 and the early 1960s. Local-government general hospitals grew at an even faster rate, with local governments matching federal Hill-Burton funds through local taxes and capital bond issues.[8] Between 1946 and 1960 the overall (net) number of voluntary hospitals increased by 707, and state- and local-government general hospitals by 475 (table 9.1). The rate of hospital admissions in 1960 was double that of 1935: 129 compared with 54 admissions per 1,000 population.[9]

Many of the new hospitals were quite small, as befitted locally focused institutions. Hill-Burton supported the small-scale hospital, creating and transforming small community units into well-equipped, acute hospital centers. The number of very small hospitals (under 25 beds) declined between 1946 and 1960. But the number of hospitals of between 25 and 50 beds held firm, and the number between 50 and 100 beds increased. Thus the American hospital system continued to be distinguished by a large number of small units and to stress the importance of the hospital to local communities. In 1955 almost two-thirds of all American short-term hospitals had fewer than 100 beds (table 9.2). There were relatively few large hospitals; less than 400 out of 5,237 short-term

TABLE 9.1

Changes in the Number of Nonfederal Short-term General and Allied Special Hospitals, United States, 1946–65, by Hospital Ownership

	Not-for-Profit	State or Local Government	For-Profit	Total	Total Number of Hospitals
1946 total	2,584	785	1,076	4,445*	4,445
Net gain or loss					
1946–50	+ 287	+ 157	+ 142	+ 586	5,031
1950–55	+ 226	+ 178	− 198	+ 206	5,237
1955–60	+ 194	+ 140	− 164	+ 170	5,407
1960–65	+ 135	+ 193	+ 1	+ 329	5,736

*AHA total figure given for 1946 is 4,444.
SOURCE: American Hospital Association, *American Hospital Statistics,* 1987, table 1.

TABLE 9.2

General Hospitals by Size (Number of Beds), 1928–65

| | Percentage of Hospitals in Each Size Category | | | | |
	1928	1938	1946	1955*	1965*
Less than 25 beds	36.9	28.3	22.6	17.3	9.8
26–50 beds	23.3	24.6	22.8	25.8	25.2
51–100 beds	19.5	20.1	21.2	23.1	25.8
101–200 beds	12.1	15.8	17.3	18.8	19.3
201–300 beds	4.4	5.6	7.0	8.1	9.4
300+ beds	3.9	5.6	9.2	6.9	10.6
Total	100.0	100.0	100.0	100.0	100.0
Number of hospitals	4,538	4,286	4,523	5,237	5,736

NOTE: 1928 figures are for 25 beds and under, and so on. Also, percentages may not add up exactly, due to rounding.
*Short-term nonfederal general and special hospitals.
SOURCES: C. Rufus Rorem, *The Public's Investment in Hospitals* (Chicago: University of Chicago Press, 1930), p. 235; E. H. L. Corwin, *The American Hospital* (New York: Commonwealth Fund, 1946), table VII; "Hospital Statistics in the United States," *Journal of the American Medical Association*, reprint, May 9, 1953, table B2; "Hospital Statistics," *Hospitals* 30, pt. 2 (August 1, 1956), table 2; and *Hospitals* 40, pt. 2 (August 1, 1966), table 2.

nonfederal hospitals reported 300 beds or more. Federal policy, like foundation and medical policy before World War II, was, in short, a policy of diffusion and dispersion of hospitals rather than of centralization.

The new hospitals, like those before them, concentrated on short-term cure, with no major shift to long-term treatment or rehabilitation. The local hospital was a place for obstetrical deliveries, respiratory conditions, accidental injuries, and fixing malfunctions. More patients were in the hospital for hemorrhoids than for heart disease in 1957–58; more for hernia repair than for cancer.[10] There was only a small parallel system for long-term conditions. Set against the approximately five thousand short-term general hospitals were a mere three hundred hospitals for long-term care.

Short-term hospitals which did attempt to change their function were heralded as major experiments—and provided the exceptions that proved the general rule. The Lankenau Hospital, for example, became a much-cited model for a new type of hospital when, after moving from central Philadelphia to the suburbs in 1953, it opened a health education department, a health examination and diagnostic service for outpatients, and an inpatient unit of 52 "self-help" beds.[11] A major attraction of the hospital's health museum was the model, "Pandora," the talking, transparent woman. The average community hospital prospered without such innovations.

Approximately 60 percent of all patients in general and special hospitals were there for surgical and obstetrical conditions in the mid-1950s, with higher rates in voluntary than in government institutions, which continued to see more chronic diseases. In 1960 virtually all births (97 percent) and half of all deaths took place in hospitals. Although tonsillectomies, adenoidectomies, and appendectomies were much less frequent than in the 1930s, other operations were on the increase: particularly for hernias, hemorrhoids, and gallbladder conditions, and hysterectomies.[12] Surgery was becoming a matter of excellence through routine; one observer called it a "religion of competence."[13] For the most part, the authority of the doctor was unquestioned.

For both health professionals and patients it was hard, in the optimistic scientific climate of the 1950s, to accept that there were still diseases for which there were no effective medical or surgical therapies. One student of the hospital scene remarked: "When the doctor has to tell a patient that there is no specific remedy for his condition, he is apt to feel affronted, or to wonder if his doctor is keeping abreast of the times."[14] The expectation that each patient—or at least each patient who could afford to pay for it—had a right to a cure had become an intrinsic aspect of American medicine.

It followed that hospitals should be accessible and well equipped, doctors well paid, and specialists' services readily available. Staff, machinery, and equipment proliferated. By 1960 virtually all short-term hospitals had clinical laboratories, diagnostic X ray, and electrocardiography; over half had a postoperative recovery room and a blood bank; over one-third provided X-ray therapy; and one-fifth had a radioisotope facility. The more specialized the technology used, the greater the intensity of hospital care. The average length of stay declined from 9.1 days in 1946 to 7.8 days in 1965, while treatment became increasingly aggressive.

Hospitals were also highly visible in the community because they were major local employers. In 1960 American short-term hospitals employed over 1 million people, twice as many as in 1946 (the figure topped 2 million in 1972). These numbers did not include the thousands of doctors in private practice who attended hospital patients nor an army of hospital volunteers; nor, of course, the many other individuals who came to hospitals as visitors. The hospital was not only an institution in which critical life activities took place (birth, illness, death), but also an important economic and social hub for those who were not sick.

Hill-Burton favored voluntary and local-government institutions over profit-making hospitals (whose numbers declined in the 1950s), but idiosyncratic patterns of ownership continued to prevail. In some areas the profit-making form was still a natural choice, particularly in the South and

West. Eight states reported more for-profit than voluntary not-for-profit hospitals in 1950: Alabama, Arkansas, Georgia, Louisiana, Oklahoma, Tennessee, Texas, and West Virginia. In the rapidly growing San Fernando Valley (Burbank), California, the number of general hospitals soared from 1 in 1950 to 11 ten years later, most sponsored by physicians. Nine of the 11 were under proprietary ownership and operated on a profit-making basis. However, despite the heterogeneity, voluntary hospitals as a group maintained their overall national dominance. Through the 1950s voluntary hospitals consistently reported 70 percent of all short-term general hospital admissions, over 70 percent of hospital expenses and personnel, and over 75 percent of hospital assets. Of the 1.4 million employees in short-term hospitals in 1965, 1 million worked in the voluntary sector.

Throughout the 1950s hospital policy focused on hospital construction—on investment per se—rather than on areawide planning or system coordination. There were general norms for hospital bed supply and state hospital plans, to be sure, but although state Hill-Burton agencies set priorities, they had little power over either voluntary or local-government hospitals, except in approving new construction for funding under the federal program. Federal government policy actually encouraged hospitals to develop as autonomous institutions, each unit doing what it thought fit. Later, federal policy would stimulate hospitals to increase services to the elderly (through Medicare), and more recently to behave as economically driven, competitive units. In the 1950s, as later, hospital boards, administrators, and affiliates responded to federal financial incentives with alacrity. As the total number of hospitals increased, and as the "community" ideology became more firmly vested in the persona of each institution, voluntary planning became more difficult to achieve. This, too, was an outcome of federal policy, however undesired or unanticipated.

The Community Institution

What, however, was a "community hospital" as distinct from just a plain "hospital"? What was the "community" supposed to do? And what, or who, was it? There was clearly more at stake than power politics and vested interests, however important these might be—including the belief that change could be accomplished in the hospital system at the local level (given appropriate incentives) through the good-faith efforts of responsible citizens. The aim was not to provide equal services to everyone (that was socialism) but to extend access to services as far as possible without jeopardizing technological progress *and* to rationalize services, where possible, through improved quality and avoidance of waste.

Robert M. Sigmond, who began his professional career in health administration after World War II and has been one of the most effective national spokesmen for community planning from the 1960s to the present, put it this way: "Community programs generally involve an *inequitably large* contribution of time and money, by the most interested and fortunate, to assure some minimum *(not equal)* benefit to the less fortunate. That is the essence of a community program, as contrasted with a government program."[15] The unique strength of the ideal American community hospital in the 1950s and 1960s, he continued, was its pluralistic financing; its control by community leadership; its commitment to the disadvantaged; its shared responsibility among the medical practitioners for quality; a close linkage of the hospital with the community's physicians; a commitment to take care of community crises and disasters such as epidemics and natural disasters; and an informal process of regionalization, reflecting a willingness to share medical staff members and other services on an ad hoc basis.

In short, support of local hospitals upheld the traditional American values of social stability, of community building, and of charity-giving, in its broadest sense. As with the early models of hospital charity, this was a supply-side, even a paternalistic vision of social welfare. Charity was a voluntary gift from the relatively affluent to the disadvantaged—with no essential right to this gift among those in need.

These ideas about community obviously worked best, in terms of actual planning, in areas where the population was relatively small, homogeneous, and stable, where community elites were powerful and oligarchic, and/or where a few large corporations controlled hospital capital financing through private gifts (as in Rochester, New York, or in Pittsburgh). But there were problems with the idea of private, local initiative as a central ideology for hospital services throughout the United States. President Truman had proclaimed in 1944 that Americans should have the right to adequate medical care. But this right translated strategically, in the American political context, into the ability to *pay* for medical care through voluntary prepayment, and/or government insurance or assistance. There was no right to expect institutions to provide services without cost to those in need—as government-owned hospitals did, for example, in the nationalized hospital service developing at the same time in Britain (under the

National Health Service Act of 1946). American voluntary hospitals claimed, as they had for decades, that it was not their job (but government's) to pay hospital expenses for those without funds. However, community hospitals were also committed collectively to the voluntary idea as a preferred political alternative to compulsory health insurance. Thus they could not ignore the question of access to hospitals by all local residents, irrespective of income; if they did, national health insurance might seem the only avenue for population coverage.

Traditional notions of voluntarism as charity-giving by benevolent elites also seemed to be breaking down in favor of a looser, more democratic association between voluntarism and community representation. The slippery rhetoric of "community" in the 1950s suggested a commitment to community residents as recipients of service; a sensitivity to community needs; and the involvement of the "community," however defined, in a common effort to achieve progress through its social institutions. In the 1960s new "community leaders," representing minorities in particular, were to challenge traditional hospital paternalism directly in different cities. But in the 1950s the challenge was to see how far hospitals could come together and work with other agencies to create a reasonably fair service for a defined local population.

Demographic changes after World War II were creating communities that were filled with contrasts. The flight of relatively young and affluent white, white-collar families to new suburbs left disproportionate numbers of elderly and minority Americans behind in inner cities. Who was to provide *them* with caring communities? Broader questions of social equity thus wove through the commitment to community throughout the 1950s and into the 1960s. Any goal of federal policy to support the successes of the community hospital would, it seemed, also have to alleviate deficiencies in access, service, and means of payment, particularly for the old and poverty-stricken. These policies were to lead, in 1965, to Medicare and Medicaid.

At the local level the strength of "community" as a policy in the 1950s should not, however, be underrated. The small size of many of the hospitals encouraged intimacy and allowed for treatment near the patient's home, with care often given by neighborhood residents. Paid and unpaid hospital workers formed potent local networks of institutional loyalty and community interest. There were thought to be 1.2 million members of hospital auxiliaries in 1961, adults and teenagers, a number not far short of the total number of paid employees. Over half of all hospitals, including psychiatric hospitals—and more than three out of four voluntary hospitals—reported auxiliaries. The highest participation was in the Northeast, where there was the highest percentage of voluntary hospitals; the lowest was in the southeastern states.[16] Volunteers in pink smocks or candy stripes welcomed visitors to the hospital, provided library service to patients, escorted them to specialist departments and back to their rooms, acted as messengers and nursing assistants, and ran gift shops, canteens, and cafeterias. For relatively affluent married women in particular, voluntary hospital work took the place that paid work had held during the war—and would hold again in later decades. In some respects the volunteer work done by women in the 1950s was a training ground for the women's movement.

The American Hospital Association praised the dual role of volunteers: providing service and promoting "community understanding."[17] In many towns the hospital was viewed as an integral part of the community around it. Volunteers, like physicians, developed a fealty to "their" hospital, accentuating its individual identity and binding its ties to local networks.[18] Hospital auxiliaries were more frequent in nonchurch voluntary hospitals than in church institutions, suggesting that volunteering had a particularly important role in forging social ties in the absence of alternative religious networks. But the strong role of hospital volunteers was a general phenomenon, virtually unique to the United States. Attempting to explain it, sociologist William Glaser concluded that general ideologies about voluntary "good works" by the ordinary citizen existed in few other countries; that American economic conditions provided the leisure and class structure needed for unpaid work; that business corporations and other organizations believed that voluntary services by employees and their wives would be valuable public relations; that voluntarism was imbedded in the values of religious and other group beliefs in the United States; and that the communitywide hospital, serving all social classes, attracted individuals who wanted to serve the community as a whole.[19]

The small or midsize hospital in a socially cohesive community, with its high obstetrical rates and a reputation for medical competence and successful surgery, was a relatively cheerful institution in the 1950s and early 1960s. Its organizational character was often in stark contrast to that of the large, impersonal teaching hospital in major cities, where the commitment to science and technology as an organizational ethos overshadowed any attempts to restructure the hospital as a community institution. A contemporary description (by my younger self) of two contrasting hospitals gives the flavor. A community hospital (Manchester Memorial Hospital, Connecticut) is described first:

> Little touches such as magazines (not tattered) in the foyer, friendly faces everywhere, neat nurses, a glimpse of really loving care being given to a patient in the recovery room, a lack of rush and an atmosphere of quiet confidence . . .

In contrast, a nearby university teaching hospital (Grace–New Haven Hospital, Connecticut) seemed:

> a noisy neurotic barracks . . . the nurses' uniforms looked crumpled, their hair messy, their manner casual, the environment also unkempt, e.g., everyone pushes into the elevator without thought even when a patient on a stretcher is being carried. Perhaps large hospitals have to function as machines? . . . Are we all to die to Muzak?[20]

The Industrial Model of Organization

The old split in perception between the local community model and the teaching model of a "hospital" became more marked in the 1950s. But forces other than models or theories gave the large urban hospitals of the 1950s organizational features that were if anything *anti*community. The national rhetoric of community was failing in the cities.

Concern about the impersonality of large hospitals pervaded discussions of hospital administration and policy by the early 1960s. In the large teaching hospital there was a greater social distance between patients and staff than in the hospital in a socially homogenous small town or suburb. And striking differences among the clientele of hospitals obviously affected their institutional personality. With the affluent middle-class well served by community institutions in urban and suburban areas, teaching hospitals continued to attract two quite different kinds of individuals: the very rich, who served on its boards and committees and who came into the hospital as the private patients of eminent physicians, and the very poor, the traditional recipients of "charity care."

The successful institution wanted its patients to conform to the informal code of hospital behavior by looking as prosperous, appreciative, and curable as possible. The "good" patient was the one who accepted the sick or dependent role, followed doctors' and nurses' orders without complaint, and made every attempt to get well or—if there was no choice—died with cheerfulness and dignity.[21] Such expectations were difficult to fulfill on the medical floors of large city institutions, coping with the chronic and indigent sick, whose lives were often remote from those of their care-givers. But for all patients the large hospital was a daunting institution.

In the cities, too, there was usually little incentive to draw hospital workers and patients together. The ideology of scientific medicine after World War II upheld the authoritarian role of the doctor as expert, with the patient as the body on which the doctor worked and little real communication between them. Hierarchical structures and distancing rituals marked the hospital at all levels. Labor conditions, too, militated against harmonious workplace arrangements. Although hospital employees might be better paid in cities than in small towns, city hospitals were more likely to attract transient workers as orderlies, craftsmen, housekeepers, laundry and clerical workers, who took the work only because they could not find anything better paid elsewhere. Blue-collar wages continued to be low. At Montefiore Hospital in New York, the center of a new wave of hospital unionization beginning in the late 1950s, staff turnover rates in some departments were 300 percent a year.[22]

There were now general and open tensions—and an essential ambivalence—between the traditional ideology of the hospital as a quasi-public "charity," in which workers as well as board members were dedicated to ideals and in which benevolent employers protected their workers, and the quasi-industrial character of the large institution. Voluntary hospitals were specifically exempted from the Taft-Hartley Act of 1947 on grounds of their quasi-public role, allowing them the privilege of not recognizing collective bargaining agents and firing union sympathizers at will.[23] As a result, workers in large voluntary hospitals had neither the job protection of workers in profit-making hospitals nor the benefits and job security of civil servants. Legal arguments in favor of the hospital as a "public" institution thus reduced its potential to be a "community" institution in which everyone pulled together.

Yet blue-collar workers were learning that they wielded power. An action filed by the New York Hospital to restrain union organization in the 1940s noted that the hospital then employed 2,500 workers and that since it was totally dependent on its power plant, a strike by power plant workers could quickly shut down the hospital.[24] The reluctance of most hospitals to accept unions in the 1950s, together with the slow modernization of labor practices, added to the sense of alienation among workers in the largest hospitals. In small communities competitive jobs were often unavailable and hospital work enjoyed greater status.

The nursing profession had problems of its own, each more noticeable in larger institutions. In the 1950s many of the menial tasks previously performed by nurses were being done by aides and practical nurses, who began to be employed in large numbers during World War II. But these new workers were engaged in constant jurisdictional disputes with registered nurses (and vice versa), and the RNs were not always supported by doctors. Nurses expressed defiance through private jokes among themselves about particular doctors, through withholding information, and in subscribing only to the outward forms of deference to doctors, thus creating further tensions on the nursing floors.[25]

Nurses, like doctors and administrators, were caught in the middle of a battery of institutional changes, as well as in occupational conflicts and in stereotypes of gender roles. Antibiotics reduced the nurse's vital management role as the guardian of the hospital's cleanliness, since local infections could now be fought with drugs. At the same time, head nurses were inevitably becoming administrators, even though they were often unwilling to delegate. The role of the head nurse on a floor which consisted of multiple rooms, together with facilities for treatment, physicians' offices, and the nursing station, was sometimes unclear, often confusing, and always complicated. Additional problems were created for nurses by the rapid rise in the proportion of paying patients because of the spread of hospital insurance. Patients with minor illnesses were less willing to accept dependency (doing what they were told) and more critical of the services given than those who were seriously ill. Patients also often asked nurses rather than doctors to explain their diagnosis and prognosis, leaving nurses uncertain what to do, given the strict hierarchy of doctor-nurse relations.

The great increase in medical house staff in the 1950s and 1960s compounded the nurses' difficulties. Hospitals expanded the number of specialty residency positions from under 10,000 in 1945 to over 25,000 in 1955, and over 30,000 by 1960.[26] Each July a new wave of neophyte doctors enter the teaching hospitals, including a large minority of foreign doctors. Nurses had an important role in the successful assimilation of each batch of newcomers.

House staff expansion was impelled both by the demand for specialist training by new medical graduates and returning World War II veterans, and above all by the hospitals' own perceived institutional needs. House staff had two important advantages for hospitals. First, they provided twenty-four-hour, in-house coverage of patients. Second, house staff provided the hospital and its specialist departments with the cachet of having a teaching function, and also (perhaps) enhanced the quality of care. Virtually all of the large hospitals were teaching hospitals in 1960; "teaching" meant that they had house staff training programs, not that they necessarily had any formal affiliation with a medical school.

It was easier to cope with interpersonal negotiations, compromise, and institutional changes in small hospitals, that is, with the informal mechanisms and the give-and-take that are necessary to make any complex organization work. The organization of a small community hospital was not only less complicated, but doctors, nurses, and patients were much more likely to know each other outside the institution.

However, even the smaller hospitals of the 1950s were complex. Students of industrial organization compared hospitals in the 1950s with American industrial plants, churches, universities, business firms, and government, seeing hospitals as generic "institutions." This eagerness to identify hospitals with other organizations, both for-profit and nonprofit, seems to have been peculiarly American, as was pointed out at the time.[27] In its organizational behavior and social functioning, the modern hospital was already one of the most complicated organizations in American society: a multipurpose institution, lacking a single product and acutely responsive to its various environments, which in turn the hospital helped to create. Inevitably, the hospital would be compared to that central U.S. institution, the business corporation. Hospitals were also complex organizations because they formed a theater for shifting balances and conflicts among major American occupations, each of which was striving toward increased authority and prestige.

Two astute contemporary critics, Herman and Anne Somers, suggested that the "technical facts" of modern medicine made the industrial model of organization inevitable. They cited the increased use of equipment and technical procedures, the institutionalization of medicine, particularly in hospitals, and the complexity of medical and paramedical relationships. These were, they said, "steadily transforming a highly individualized profession into a vast and intricately interdependent industry."[28] American willingness to see hospitals (and other aspects of medical care) in industrial as well as community terms drew on the pervasiveness of industrial imagery in American culture; on the history of American hospitals as mixed technological and welfare institutions, which had long been described as "workshops" with "products" and "clinical materials"; on the acceptance of science and technology as innovative, invaluable social activities; and on the availability of capital and the economic drive of third-party payment after World War II.

Foreign visitors to the United States in the 1950s were struck by the high technical level of U.S. hospitals compared with hospitals elsewhere, by the importance of surgery, and by the relatively greater use of the laboratory.[29] Members of a British study tour in 1960, for example, showed particular interest in complete air-conditioning and artificial-lighting systems, adjustable electrical beds, carpets in corridors and private bathrooms for private rooms, pass-through refrigerators in the kitchen, central milk kitchens and central sterile supply services, automatic X-ray processers, autoanalyzers in the laboratory, plastic bags for blood, identification bracelets for patients, pneumatic tube systems for communications, and (of course) massive power plants. The power plant at the Grace–New Haven Hospital (666 beds) provided steam to the whole of Yale University.[30]

In terms of human relations, goals, and power structures, the hospital of the 1950s was not, however, quite like other industrial organizations. It was difficult to "fix" the hospital in the analytic scheme of things and fascinating to observe its inbuilt conflicts. Sociologist Robert N. Wilson pointed out, for example, in a study of the hospital's social structure, that the two most significant actors on the scene, doctor and patient, were both guests of the organization. "The patient, who has the distinction of being simultaneously the hospital's client and its product is, hopefully, just passing through," but the attending doctor, visiting the hospital from a base in private practice, also used the organization without fundamentally belonging to it. These two chief figures were "in the organization but not of it." Without them, wrote Wilson, "there was no meaning in the medical process," yet with them came a "disturbance" with which the institution had to cope.[31] Hospital administrators joked that the hospital would run well if only it had no patients.

Charles Perrow, in a notable case study of changing patterns of hospital authority, described an emerging pattern of hospital management by multiple leadership in the 1950s, as administrators, medical staff, and trustees saw the benefits of accommodation in the interest of their larger mutual concerns. Decisions which might expose conflicting interests were avoided: only a "something for everyone" plan could succeed.[32] However, all parties agreed on the value of technology, represented in up-to-date equipment. Thus administrative gridlock joined other factors in promoting the hospital's technological image. The primary characteristics of hospital operations were conflict avoidance and expansionary drift. Neither the community model nor the technological model was an ideal base for rationalizing the hospital "industry" as a whole.

Hospital–Medical-Staff Relations

In nearly every other country, hospital physicians worked full-time as part of the hospital hierarchy. They were thus an essential part of the organization and part of its decision-making and its power structures. But even though hospital employment of physicians increased in the 1950s, only one of every sixteen practicing physicians in the United States received any income as hospital salary in the early 1960s. Another one of the sixteen worked in hospitals under some other form of contractual reimbursement.[33] Private practitioners were centering more of their activity in hospitals, but the role and authority of organized hospital medical staffs was unclear. One critic remarked with some understatement: "It seems that doctors, because they act like doctors, are hard to fit into hospital organization."[34]

The attending-physician system was set up for conflict in the 1950s, as the hospital ceased to be plausibly described as merely the workshop for the local profession; it was an institution with its own goals, character, and momentum. Inside the hospital the authority of hospital administrators rose with the rise in hospital budgets and managerial complexity, emphasizing the old tensions among the three primary power structures: trustees, physicians, and administrators. Administrators saw physicians as resentful of "lay" control and direction, including enforcement of policies, rules, and regulations.[35] Lack of communication and lack of understanding marked both sides of the complaints, and each sector guarded its ascribed turf, assigning activities as "administrative" or "medical." A key role for the board of trustees now was to mediate between administrators and physicians—if only passively, by being there.

Hospital administrators tried to assert themselves as the new managers of an organizational age. The American College of Hospital Administrators focused on the field of human relations in the 1950s, recognizing both the importance of this field to the hospitals and the emergence of human relations as a specialized professional field. The growth of graduate programs for educating hospital administrators after World War II gave them a new claim to special competence. In the 1940s eight new university graduate programs in hospital administration joined the early program at the University of Chicago (1934); nine more followed in the 1950s, many established with the assistance of federal grants, and fifteen more in the 1960s. The program at the Sloan School of Management, Cornell University, begun in 1958, started a new trend toward a two-year graduate program.[36]

Teachers of hospital administration split on the question of whether hospital administrators were sufficiently like business managers to warrant concentrating all their education in business schools (with the uncomfortable notion that hospitals were "businesses") or whether schools of public health were the more appropriate bases. In the latter, hospitals might be placed more squarely in the context of community health, as befitted their role as community institutions. Yale's hospital administration program, which I entered in 1961, included biomedical statistics, epidemiology, and health education, but not finance, management accounting, or marketing, which were not considered central to the running of nonprofit or government organizations at the time; the hospital administrator was presented as the advocate of the patient and as a professional catalyst of community activity.

Hospital–medical-staff relations were a further, central aspect of the curriculum, since local medical hierarchies of private practitioners effectively ran the American medical-care system. Informal networks of physicians, often organized along ethnic and religious lines, could effectively exclude newcomers (by informing them, for example, that there was no room for another doctor in a particular specialty or hospital staff), build up dominant positions for elite physicians, ascribe and maintain status, control conduct, and minimize medical competition and conflict.[37] These networks had, however, no formal structures of their own with which hospital administrators or board members could deal in furthering community-hospital and -health policy, no clearly designated leaders speaking for the networks as a whole. As a result, much of the conflict between hospitals and doctors was displaced to arguments about abstract concepts, such as the "corporate practice of medicine," and to constant crises over specific cases. Administrators always seemed to be "putting out fires."

At the national level the medical profession fought its battles against hospital authority by defending the way doctors were paid, as it had before World War II. In its *Manual of Hospital Standardization* of 1946, for example, the American College of Surgeons, in cooperation with the AMA, stressed the importance of the direct financial relationship between the individual physician and the individual patient: the doctor sent a bill and the patient paid it. A "third person" was not to enter into this relationship. It followed that hospitals "should be discouraged from determining or collecting fees for doctors."[38]

A string of resolutions against corporate practice marked AMA meetings: affirming in 1950 that pathology, radiology, anesthesiology, and physical medicine were an integral part of the practice of medicine, on a par with surgery, internal medicine, and other fields; approving a statement in 1953 that the hospital-based specialists should have the professional status of other members of the medical staff, and that they should only be evaluated professionally by the medical profession; restating in the early 1960s the AMA-approved principles of hospital-physician relations, including the policy that physicians should not dispose of their professional skills to any hospital corporation or other body which permitted the sale of these services for a fee. The AMA also condemned the practice of requiring physicians who used hospitals to pay a percentage to the hospital as a user fee, calling such practice a "compulsory donation."[39] Private practitioners were, in short, fighting to maintain their traditional prerogatives of independent practice, free use of hospital facilities, and absence of administrative regulation. More and more, this appeared as a rearguard action, representing uncreative, untenable vested interests.[40]

In the long debates about the "corporate practice of medicine" in the 1950s, hospital payment of pathologists and radiologists received the most scrutiny, because of their pivotal position as diagnosticians within the institution, their supervision of hospital staff, and their reliance on hospital-based equipment—each spurred on because of the great rise in diagnostic tests during and after World War II. A new element in the debate was that the average hospital expected to make substantial profits on its radiology and pathology services, for diversion (cross-subsidy) to other parts of the institution, thus fanning medical fears of administrative duplicity.

The widely read book on hospital medical staffs by T. R. Ponton painted a bleak occupational picture. The average salaried specialist, he wrote, "faces a constant fight with himself if he is to avoid getting into a rut and deteriorating."[41] This suggested that pathology and radiology were repetitive and boring, that these fields appealed to physicians who were uninterested in improving their work, and that the best rewards were monetary. Both Ponton and Malcolm MacEachern, in his standard textbook on hospital administration, recommended that hospital-based physicians be paid on a system based on departmental earnings; that is, the more work done, the more the physician would be paid.[42] These debates labeled the doctor as driven by business incentives. The stage was being set for widespread criticism of physicians from the late 1960s as the villains of rising medical expenditures.

Echoing much earlier assumptions about the "purer" motivations of scientifically oriented physicians, Ponton assumed that physicians who wished to carry out research were relatively unconcerned about income levels, while physicians outside these hallowed halls, who were "not so deeply imbued with the scientific spirit," were much more money-oriented.[43] In effect, the hospital-based specialists were seen as entrepreneurs, working within the overall framework of an organization. It was only a step from here to recognizing the entire function of radiology and pathology as separate fiscal or corporate units—the system largely prevailing today.

Although the daily dealings between physicians and hospitals in the mid-1950s were outwardly polite and pleasant, underneath, it was reported, there was often "smoldering distrust, antagonism, resentment and even hatred."[44] These were scarcely the ingredients of good human relations. A particular criticism was a tendency for hospital administrators to call hospital-based specialists' services "ancillary services," thus downgrading their prestige. It was difficult to conceive of the local hospital as a friendly, unified institution in the face of such evident and frequent rifts. Instead of one community of charity-givers, doctors, administrators, and volunteers, there were often, instead, fractured interests. Doctor-hospital conflicts created serious problems for the idea of "community" as an organizational ideology for the hospital system.

Firm opposition by organized medicine to prepaid group practice (what are now called health maintenance organizations) in the 1950s also halted any major attempts by reform-minded administrators to extend the outpatient department to cover services to all income groups and for all conditions—despite general agreement in the hospital establishment that hospital-based or hospital-linked group practice was the logical pattern of the future.[45] Models of organized practice by groups of medical specialists existed in major new schemes established during and immediately after World War II—notably the Kaiser Permanente plan on the West Coast; the Health Insurance Plan in New York City; Group Health Cooperative of Puget Sound; Community Health Center in Two Harbors, Minnesota; and Labor Health Institute in St. Louis. But although AMA opposition to group practice eased in the late 1950s (and was reversed in the early 1960s), there was no large, continuing movement for group practice in this period.[46] Hospitals and doctors continued in uneasy tension.

Not surprisingly, then, there were few major efforts in the 1950s by boards of trustees (or by administrators, for that matter) to control medical practice by changing the basis of selection of medical-staff members at the local level, although the possibility of doing so was widely discussed. The right of hospital boards of trustees (rather than the medical staff) to admit physicians and choose their attending staff had been upheld by the courts before World War II.[47] But in fact, the credentials or executive committee of the hospital medical staff was (and has remained) the real controlling body for decisions about new members of the medical staff, with recommendations going to the board of trustees for (largely) rubber-stamp ratification. Hospital boards had, for the most part, no say (and apparently little interest) in whether the medical staff had, for example, too many neurosurgeons for the workload (and quality) of the hospital as a whole (or for the good of the community), or too few specialists in rehabilitation. And this was so despite the fact that decisions on qualifications for attending privileges were a more important aspect of medical staff operations (and bylaws) after World War II, as hospital staff appointment became more clearly restricted to practice in one or more specific specialty departments. Not every hospital, for example, allowed every surgeon to practice every type of surgery, or general practitioners to do surgery at all.

But the role of the hospital medical staff itself was also ambivalent, for its organization was often loose and minimal. The standardization program of the American College of Surgeons, continued by the Joint Commission on Accreditation of Hospitals (JCAH) from the end of 1952, insured that most hospital medical staffs were organized in the formal sense: they had meetings, voted in a president, officers, and committees, and were responsible for the promotion and development of medical and scientific policies in the hospital, subject to the approval of the governing board.[48] However, the attending staff (which might include several hundred doctors in a large hospital) did not work as an executive arm of hospital administration and the actual responsibilities were often unclear. The staff was particularly vulnerable to criticism where it did not adequately police its members (more or less everywhere), was lax in enforcing standards of quality, allowed "ghost" surgery, and/or failed to guarantee up-to-date medical records.

The organization of the medical staff (with a president, officers, and hospital committees) and its separate division into specialty departments created a complex matrix of relationships. Even small hospitals were expected to have at least divisions of medicine and surgery in the 1950s. But the large teaching hospital was becoming segmented into virtually autonomous specialist units. The division of medicine might, for example, now include sections of general medicine, cardiology, communicable diseases, dermatology, endocrinology, gastroenterology, metabolism, neuropsychiatry, pediatrics, and tuberculosis. Surgery included, similarly, an array of surgical subspecialties. And there were separate departments for anesthesiology, pathology, physical therapy, and radiology, which served the entire institution. Department chairmen in the largest teaching hospitals were becoming the controlling czars of substantial domains. If hospital medical staffs had been effectively organized in community hospitals in the 1950s and 1960s, they might have become an important source of influence and policy-making, not only for hospitals but for medical services in local communities.

In the tradition of minimal hospital interference with medicine, collective professional standard-setting, however, was weak. Clinicopathological conferences, tissue committees, and the like suggested a renewed commitment to the appraisal of quality and the outcomes of hospital care, but these functions were distinguished by their mildness of criticism, production of data without analysis or follow-up, and infrequency of meetings. There was thus little critical introspection about the performance of hospitals as a whole—even after the advent of computer systems in hospitals in the late 1950s and 1960s and with reams of data being produced by standardized hospital discharge abstract services, which analyzed the performance of hospitals through review of a sample of patient records. The overriding ethos of the medical staff was maximum autonomy for the individual physician, with little standardization of procedures across the board and little criticism from peers.

In a one-hospital town with open-staff policies, the two sets of medical organizations, hospital staff and local medical networks, were largely identical. But even here distrust of the hospital's potential authority over medical practice mitigated against effective communitywide planning. In a large city different hospitals drew on different sectors of the medical profession; there was little community of interest between and among the hospital medical staffs of different institutions, just as there was little cooperation among their boards of trustees or volunteers. Meanwhile, two new developments emphasized that hospitals had public roles to play in a wider forum than their local communities: the establishment of the Joint Commission on Accreditation of Hospitals and the growing body of law on hospital quality.

Hospitals and the Quality of Care

In 1950 the American Hospital Association approached the American College of Surgeons inquiring about the possible transfer of its hospital standardization program to the AHA. Not surprisingly, the AMA's Council on Medical Education and Hospitals immediately also entered the fray. Was standardization—the very symbol of national medical control over hospitals for so many years—to be usurped by the hospital administrators? There was wariness on all sides as to what the relative roles of standardization and registration of hospitals ought to be in the postwar decades. Here was a replaying of hospital-medical conflicts on a larger field.

The AMA was particularly concerned to maintain its responsibility for approving residency training; it was in the process of creating joint residency review committees with the various specialty organizations, to bring order to the accreditation of house staff education. In June 1950 the AMA board of trustees appointed its own committee to confer with the American College of Surgeons on the broader question of hospital standardization. Shortly afterward, a multiorganizational committee was formed of representatives of the AMA, the AHA, the American College of Surgeons, and the American College of Physicians. And in October 1950 the American College of Surgeons agreed to continue its program, but with the prospect of cooperative effort among the four organizations.

After some stress and misunderstanding among organizations that had been in competition on the hospital question for decades, agreement was finally reached for a joint program of hospital standardization, ratified in December 1951. The activities of the Joint Commission on Accreditation of Hospitals began in 1952. In 1954 the AMA dropped its program of hospital registration (and the annual statistics that went with it), although it continues to be closely involved in accrediting internships and residencies through its participation on residency review committees. As of 1954, the JCAH, a private not-for-profit organization, became the single general organization concerned with hospital standardization.[49] Meanwhile, the responsibility for the basic numbers and statistics on hospitals fell to the American Hospital Association, which has produced annual statistics on hospitals since 1946.

In the event, the new commission made little initial difference to the process of hospital standardization. In part this was perhaps because of the AMA's participation; but inertia also played a role. Malcolm MacEachern, whose term as director of hospital activities for the American College of Surgeons lasted until 1950, observed that so closely were the old general policies and ideals of hospital standardization retained under the new commission, that the two programs were virtually one, except for sponsorship.[50] The commission represented an accommodation of the system to established interests—and a reflection of the large cost of the program itself—rather than any major changes in direction.

The new sponsors had little interest in forcing hospitals to take new roles, although there was concern among organized physician groups that the commission might become a tough policing body, acting independently of their wishes. In 1954, for example, the AMA voted a halt to any "attempts by hospital accreditation authorities to propose, recommend and by threat of reprisal force the adoption of rules, regulations and various and diverse requirements which would look to the most minute and detailed overlordship in every phase of our hospital practices."[51] The AMA also pressed the commission to send the results of its surveys directly to the chairman of the governing board of the hospital and to the chief of the medical staff, as well as to the administrator, thus emphasizing the tripartite system of hospital control—and avoiding the possibility of administrative authority over clinical issues.[52] Unease and dissatisfaction with the JCAH, expressed at AMA meetings in 1955, led to a special AMA committee to review JCAH functions. The resulting Stover report of 1956, although generally in favor of the accreditation system, came out against any extension of accreditation to change patterns of practice or control over physicians, except in ways which extended the authority of the medical profession.[53]

More broadly, the general commitment to local autonomy and community initiative as hospital policy in the 1950s raised questions of how far hospitals should, in any event, be regimented through the machinery of national accreditation. The JCAH itself, in its *Bulletin* of August 1956, stressed local responsibility for the composition of hospital governing boards and a disinclination to make any statement as to whether physicians should or should not be formally represented on these boards.[54] The coalition of interests on the commission's board suggested a balance of hospital and medical interests. But the commission was also carried along by its own momentum. Standardization had become an accepted bureaucratic process. Although there was criticism of the system, and concern that smaller hospitals were not even subject to accreditation,[55] it was difficult to say what any broader goals of the JCAH should be in a system which had reached a state of stability. Accreditation was a voluntary process as far as hospitals were concerned; no one involved in it wanted to rock the boat.

The commission's chief usefulness in the 1950s was probably its continuing concern about organized hospital medical staffs. The JCAH produced model bylaws for hospital staffs in 1955, revising them as experience dictated. These included procedures for granting and withdrawing privileges, including review of credentials and right of appeal. Hospital staffs were reminded that the granting of privileges was of "vital importance" and should be "carefully guarded at all times."[56] Nevertheless, the JCAH did not attempt to enforce effective hospital committees in areas where it had a historic mandate: appropriate hospital utilization, patient-care outcomes, and other internal medical audit procedures. The commission provided instead a framework for assessment of a hospital's administrative structure and resources.

Nor was there much collective responsibility for quality of care elsewhere within the health-care system. It was assumed, not unreasonably, that Veterans Administration hospital services were improved as they became affiliated with medical schools; that medical schools and their affiliated hospitals passed on to patients the higher knowledge achieved through research done as a result of the rapid infusion of federal grants in the 1950s and early 1960s; and that the growth of medical technology outside the major teaching hospitals reflected major advancement in the care of patients. But although research studies of the time suggested that better care was given by specialists than general practitioners and by teaching hospitals than by nonteaching institutions,[57] standards of quality were slippery at best. Moreover, if a hospital attempted to exclude a practitioner on grounds of "quality," it might lay itself open to charges of restraint of trade.[58]

Was the hospital a mere theater for medical practice or an industrial-type enterprise with products of its own? As in many other areas of American social life, it was left to the courts of law to adjudicate and to proclaim a new consensus about where responsibility for standards should be placed. A landmark decision in 1957 in the New York Court of Appeals, in the case of *Bing* v. *Thunig,* put responsibility for the quality of hospital service squarely on the hospital itself. In this case a patient, Isabel Bing, was severely burned during the course of an operation. Not only was her private doctor involved, but also hospital nurses and a hospital-employed anesthetist. The court concluded: "The conception that the hospital does not undertake to treat the patient, does not undertake to act through its doctors and nurses, but undertakes instead simply to procure them to act upon their own responsibility, no longer reflects the fact."[59]

The hospital's legal responsibility for patient care was confirmed and extended by the *Darling* case of 1965.[60] This case involved an eighteen-year-old college football player, who fractured his leg during play. Deficiencies in his treatment eventually led to amputation of his leg eight inches below the knee. In this case the Supreme Court of Illinois held hospitals legally and financially responsible for the medical care given by all employees and all affiliated health personnel, including attending physicians. No longer could hospitals disclaim responsibility for the actions of their professionals or the care given within their walls, nor could physicians claim complete, authoritarian freedom from the hospital's jurisdiction. In theory, hospitals and doctors could no longer justify the division of the hospital into two separate domains, administrative and clinical, although they have attempted to do so to the present.

Whatever the calls for "community," then, all was not calm in the autonomous institution. For the most part, in the 1950s hospitals continued on their way as if no massive changes in demography, medical practice, and social expectations were occurring. Only as long as decisions did not have to be made could the hospital present itself, at one and the same time, as the instrument of the community, the workshop for physicians, and a complex bureaucracy with its own agenda. But hospitals could not be entirely oblivious to the long-term implications of rising rates of chronic disease in the population, the rising proportion of the population that was elderly, the social inequities that continued in the system, and the increasing use and cost of hospital care.

For individual hospitals, change had been rapid over the previous generation. Table 9.3 shows as an example the enormous rise in hospital use between the 1920s and the 1950s in Hagerstown, Maryland. Although the relative number of doctors in Hagerstown was stable in this period, the ratio of hospital beds to population had more than doubled, while the rate of inpatient admissions increased sixfold. There were particular increases in the use of hospitals by the elderly, for conditions ranging from hernias through pneumonia to cataract surgery.

But for patients the most critical issues were costs and availability.

TABLE 9.3

Hospital Use in Hagerstown, Maryland, 1921–24 and 1955–57

	1921–24	1955–57	Number of Times Increased
Hospital admissions per 1,000 persons	18	105	5.8
Under 5 years of age	9	67	7.4
5–14	21	58	2.8
15–24	23	115	5.0
25–44	21	139	6.6
45–64	19	87	4.6
65+	10	134	13.4
Average length of stay (days)	12.5	7.6	
Number of beds per 1,000 population in Washington County	1.4	3.4	
Physicians per 100,000 population	99	104	

SOURCE: Margaret D. West and Ruth M. Raup, "Hospital Use in Hagerstown," *Public Health Reports* 74 (October 1959), pp. 861–69.

Room rates in general hospitals more than tripled between 1945 and 1960. The average annual increase in hospital costs, almost 9 percent, was greater than any other item in the consumer price index. "What do you think about the hospital rates charged in this area?" asked a Gallup poll in 1962. "Too high," reported 64 percent.[61] Although the value of hospitalization was accepted without much question, questions of quality of care were increasingly linked with those of costs, organization, and efficiency. Should each hospital offer X-ray therapy, a blood bank, or intensive care? And how should gaps in care be filled?

Emergence of Larger Community Interests

Cooperative planning seemed an obvious answer. However, the jealous autonomy of individual hospitals, each with its own constituencies of interest, made planning extremely difficult. When voluntarism was embodied as a controlling force in a large-scale, complex system (the hospital system), it acquired transcendent, troubling social connotations. It was much easier to praise the voluntary principle at work in the operation of a single hospital than to see it as the motivating force for the operation of an entire service system for a major city or larger region. Blue Cross plans, with their interweaving systems of hospital contracts, raised the chimera of conflict of interest; voluntary hospital planning agencies, however benevolent in intent, suggested a conspiratorial coalition. The problem was that voluntary and community activity could be seen at one and the same time as inherently disinterested (that is, as a socially desirable exercise of influence by public-spirited citizens) and as narrowly self-serving (as antisocial activity by powerful constituencies). Much depended on one's assessment of the motivations of those concerned and on the importance ascribed to their activities.

In the event, there was little questioning of the superspecialist image to which all hospitals aspired. In his study of the "hospital-support game" in a multihospital city, sociologist Ray Elling found the highest status lodged in the hospitals with the highest degrees of technology. These hospitals also attracted the most prestigious community leaders to their boards. Elling saw the medical schools acting as umpires or referees, passing down standards and judgments to the elite public, who were organized in competing teams, each team representing the board and other supporters of a hospital.[62]

Hospitals responded to the rise in chronic diseases in the classic way, by providing radiotherapy departments, coronary care units, and surgical subspecialties rather than programs for community education and prevention. It was becoming obvious by the late 1950s that community planning was not a technical process, appropriately relegated to experts, but a politically charged process, subject to the power of vested interests. The idea of community thus had to be modified to include the rough and tumble of practical politics; it was more than the expected norm of selflessness, benevolence, and each-for-all. By presenting themselves as community institutions, hospitals raised the issue of community service without necessarily being able to deliver.

Simultaneously, the shift of population from cities to the suburbs sharpened divisions within the American population by social class and race. Classes and ethnic groups were redlined by place of residence. Inner-city populations were left with a high proportion of elderly persons, who were more likely to require hospitalization and care for chronic illnesses as well as for acute conditions, and were less likely to be insured. Inner-city "ghettos" were appearing; that is, areas with a relatively large, growing population of members of ethnic and minority groups. The social stratification that had always distinguished American hospital provision was thus emphasized, both between different institutions and within individual hospitals. Although some hospitals relocated to suburban sites, the new suburban hospitals were not usually connected in any way with the older institutions in the cities. What happened in the postwar period, then, was a stultification of hospital social structures, through a period of rapid transformation in hospital technique.

The clientele of different hospitals was strikingly varied in the 1950s. In New York City, for example, black and uninsured patients were far more likely to be found in municipal hospitals than in voluntary hospitals—just as they were in the 1930s, and earlier. Scientific change was not, in short, matched by social egalitarianism (table 9.4). Voluntary hospitals encouraged these differences by referring or transferring patients expected to have a prolonged stay to a municipal institution.[63] But the facilities of tax-supported hospitals in major cities also kept their historic place; they were often dreadful. Journalist Jan de Hartog described Jefferson Davis Hospital in Houston in the early 1960s: "overcrowded, understaffed, its accreditation had almost been withdrawn after a staph infection in its maternity ward during which 16 babies had died; but it was probably no

TABLE 9.4

Social Class, Race, and Hospital Care, New York City, 1957

		Hospital Accommodation		
	Proprietary	Voluntary Private and Semiprivate	Voluntary Ward	Municipal
White, excluding Puerto Ricans	97%	96%	66%	42%
Nonwhite	3%	3%	19%	38%
Puerto Rican	1%	2%	15%	20%
	100%	100%	100%	100%

NOTE: Totals may not add up exactly, due to rounding.
SOURCE: Herbert E. Klarman, "Characteristics of Patients in Short-term Hospitals in New York City," *Journal of Health and Human Behavior* 3 (1962), p. 48.

more backward, politics-ridden or neglected than similar institutions of charity all over the country."[64]

Thoughtful students of the American health scene, such as Anne and Herman Somers, suggested that the class differences observable in hospitals in the 1950s might be due to an institutional time lag, that is, to the notion of cultural lag, updated. There was, they posited, a slow shift away from the old dichotomy between private patients and wards, which reflected much earlier patterns of treatment, to a realization of the potential of modern medicine—which was, by implication, egalitarian.[65] Herbert Klarman, in a major study of hospitals in New York City, also assumed that the future of medicine was toward more equality in patient mix. He argued that any attempt to coordinate municipal and voluntary hospitals in New York City—as was then being suggested—should rest on the premise of equitable social distribution of patients between them.[66] This sense of needed equality of access to care was to translate in the 1960s into calls to bring everyone into the "mainstream" of medicine through Medicaid and Medicare. However, the social divisions were deeply entrenched and have continued, to some extent, to this day.

Despite the equation of science, voluntarism, and democracy, then, and despite belief in the superiority of American innovation and technology over the supposed rigidity of foreign, governmental health-care systems, American hospital service was both inegalitarian and structurally rigid. Indeed, in the 1950s insurance coverage divided the middle class clearly from the indigent. The latter's care was covered by public assistance (in whole or in part), by cross-subsidy within the hospital, or occasionally by free care from hospital endowments or gifts. The postwar building boom allowed hospitals to provide hospital care, wherever possible, to private patients in single rooms, 2-bed rooms, or at most 4-bed rooms—but not for everyone. And there was still little questioning of the medical desirability or the preference of patients for these accommodations. One study in the 1950s found that, contrary to professional belief, patients in Montefiore Hospital in New York were actually happier in multibed rooms than in single rooms.[67]

Sanctions for social stratification, built into the private voluntary hospital system, were endorsed (and furthered) by federal legislation. Through its policy of decentralization, Hill-Burton allowed for the segregation of patients by race and for the continuation of the multiclass system. Hill-Burton had a general nondiscrimination rule, but it allowed for "equitable provision" to be made through separate but equal hospital facilities. Since no individual hospital applying for aid had to agree not to discriminate, hospitals in the South were able to continue white-only policies where they wished.

Such was the case in two hospitals in Greensboro, North Carolina, in the 1950s, the Moses H. Cone Memorial Hospital and the Wesley Long Community Hospital. The former excluded all but a select few "Negro" patients. Both hospitals refused to appoint black physicians and dentists to their staffs, thus denying patients the possibility of being treated by these physicians. Not until 1964, when legal action by black physicians, dentists, and patients against these two hospitals was upheld on appeal, was the general policy of white-only hospitals successfully challenged, and in this case only for hospitals that were Hill-Burton recipients.[68] General compliance awaited the double impact of the Civil Rights Act of 1964 and the Medicare legislation of 1965.

In the meantime, despite landmark court decisions, notably *Brown* v. *Board of Education of Topeka* (1954), that suggested a policy of equal opportunity in American public institutions, many American hospitals continued to discriminate by race—formally in the South, informally in the North. The general availability of small rooms allowed for de facto segregation, for single rooms could be used to avoid potential complaints by patients about the mixing of races, as well as social classes.[69] There was an obvious gap between the theory that American medicine was the best in the world (and ought to be available to everyone) and the practice of exclusion and differential treatment.

For the hospitals of the late 1950s, there was a basic and growing dissidence between the increasingly troubled external environment and the self-absorbing world of the individual institution. The individual, autonomous institution did not see itself as part of an "industry," or for that matter as part of a "welfare state." The hospital was a "community" institution, a building through which members of the community passed daily, some well and working, others sick. On the other hand, it did not expect to shoulder the entire burden of medical care in its local community. In some respects, the hospital was, as one observer noted, "a special kind of public utility designed to serve the total community."[70] Yet it had none of the legal expectations or protection (or the monetary incentives) that any such status might suggest. There were increasing calls to make hospitals both more efficient (individually and as a system) and more equitable, that is, to make them more like an industry in some respects, while expecting them also to carry more general responsibility for public service. But it was often impractical, if not impossible, for the individual hospital to do both at once, however community-oriented it might be.

During the 1950s, too, although the voluntary hospital became a center for community aspirations writ large, these aspirations were varied and conflicting. Americans wanted unlimited technology, access to it by the whole population, and a service that was affordable to all—all without recourse to a governmental system. It was not possible to achieve all these goals simultaneously. The policy of community, vague though it was, conflicted with social expectations about equity of access, with the cherished prerogatives of local doctors who saw the hospital as their workshop, and with the autonomy of the local voluntary institution as a center for private charity-giving. "Community" might have carried the day if what hospitals did had remained stationary through the twenty-year period after World War II. Instead, technological expansionism drove the system. Beneath the rhetoric of community were powerful twin economic incentives—capital formation and booming patient income.

10

The Drive for Reimbursement

B Y THE EARLY 1960s hospitals were the reluctant objects of public scrutiny: by state commissioners of insurance, through the criticisms of a growing body of health-service experts, in congressional hearings, and in the press. Major cracks were appearing in the system. American medicine, claimed *Harper's* in a special supplement in 1960, was in "crisis."[1] Millions of Americans were dissatisfied; some hospitals were reportedly on the brink of bankruptcy; expensive services were unnecessarily duplicated and employees were underpaid. There were renewed calls for recognizing hospitals as public utilities. Problems associated with the large, uncoordinated, and scattered system of individual hospitals were echoed by the tensions imposed on the voluntary ethos within Blue Cross plans, as they competed against the parallel rise of third-party coverage by commercial and mutual insurance companies.

American voluntary hospitals continued to be praised for being "private"—that is, nonsocialistic or nongovernmental—but they were increasingly castigated for behaving as entrepreneurs. Critics might complain about the "menacing prospects" of rising hospital expenditures, but hospitals continued to respond to the promise of income—as indeed they always had. The pot of gold held out by third-party payers encouraged hospitals to respond to the market incentives of increased demand by providing more, more expensive, and better care, in areas that were most likely to be reimbursed. Total expenditures of short-term nonfederal hospitals rose steadily from $2.1 billion in 1950 to $5.6 billion in 1960 and on to $9.1 billion in 1965, the year of the Medicare legislation—a more than fourfold increase in fifteen years.

For individual hospitals, the availability of insurance provided the opportunity for a natural extension of their traditional mission: to provide excellent service to as many patients as possible and to provide well-equipped facilities for physicians. But widespread insurance also allowed hospitals, by analogy, to castigate government agencies for chiseling on welfare reimbursement. "Present-day voluntary hospitals," proclaimed an AHA-sponsored Commission on Financing of Hospital Care set up in 1951, "are becoming nonprofit community agencies financed almost entirely by earned income for services rendered to paying patients. Consequently, hospitals are not able to provide care for patients who cannot pay without finding sources of reimbursement."[2] In 1953, government agencies reimbursed hospitals at only 57 percent of average hospital costs in the Northeast, 58 percent in the mid-Atlantic states, and 66 percent in the Pacific states; indeed, the only states in which welfare payments and costs seemed to be in line were Georgia and Virginia.[3] Without adequate payments, the commission claimed, hospitals could not render high-quality hospital care; and the "vital services hospitals provide to the community will suffer."[4]

Just as hospital insurance removed individual anxieties about paying large hospital bills, it removed considerations of cost constraints from hospital billings. Hospitals could pass increased costs on to insurers, who could pass them on again to millions of subscribers, sick and well, in small increases in hospital insurance premiums. The potential of a third-party payment system unleashed an unprecedented demand for hospital services. It was a demand that could be stimulated by the suppliers, that is, by the doctors and hospitals themselves. Hospital expenditures and reimbursement mechanisms drove each other, in an expansionary spiral.

In turn, the sources and the mechanics of hospital reimbursement assumed central importance in hospital behavior. From the 1960s through the present, hospital policy-making has been dominated by the contractual relationship between third parties and the hospitals. Even in the 1950s, as this process began to get under way, uneasy questions of hospital mission, governance, and control rode on how American hospitals were financed— and how they should be paid. Medicare and Medicaid were logical responses to years of debate over the question of providing adequate levels of reimbursement for hospital services for the elderly and poor and years of experience with private health insurance.

But Medicare was also a watershed in hospital policy-making. Before

the legislation hospital policy was influenced by thousands of reimbursement decisions by diverse agencies, acting on accepted insurance principles. Medicare concentrated funding sources for services to a substantial
group of patients. Through Medicare the federal government was to
become a major payer, and thus a potentially powerful source of regulation. The rules are still volatile, evolving, and unsettled.

Hospital Financing: Largesse and Limitations

By 1960 almost two-thirds (63 percent) of all nongovernment expenditures
on hospital services were met by Blue Cross plans or by other insurance
schemes. About half of those covered by private hospital insurance were
enrolled in Blue Cross or similar plans, the other half by commercial
companies (table 10.1). Blue Cross and other forms of hospital insurance
rose in tandem, forming a huge multimillion dollar enterprise. The combined total insurance benefits for all types of health-care expenses rose
from $772 million in 1948 to $8.7 billion in 1964.[5] The health insurance
trade association, the Health Insurance Council, referred to these activities
collectively as "voluntary health insurance," both to emphasize the individual's (or the employee group's) choice as a consumer in the private
marketplace, and to distinguish private health insurance from the political
alternative of "compulsory health insurance" proposals. But in turn, the
use of the word "voluntary" for both Blue Cross (and Blue Shield) and
commercial carriers blurred the lines between not-for-profit and profit-
making insurance activities in the postwar years. If commercial hospital
insurance was "voluntary," how were Blue Cross plans to distinguish their
own special niche from that of profit-making organizations? How were
they different from insurance companies?

Although short-term hospital services were overwhelmingly available
through voluntary not-for-profit hospitals in the early 1960s, insurance
coverage was much more mixed. In 1964, for example, of the total of $5.1
billion paid out for hospital expense benefits, $2.3 billion flowed through
insurance companies, $2.5 billion through Blue Cross, Blue Shield, and
medical society plans, with the remainder going to an array of health plans
sponsored by industrial corporations, unions, physicians, and coopera-
tives.[6] In the early 1960s, voluntary or private health insurance—the an-

TABLE 10.1

*Persons Holding Some Type of Private Hospital Insurance,
United States, 1940–86*

	U.S. Population* (Millions)	Percent With Hospital Insurance	Percent of Persons with Hospital Insurance Covered by Blue Cross, Blue Shield and Medical Society Plans
1940	132.5	9.0	50.3
1945	133.4	24.0	58.9
1950	152.3	50.3	50.7
1955	165.9	61.1	50.0
1960	180.7	67.8	47.4
1965	194.3	71.4	45.7
1970	205.1	77.5	47.2
1975	216.0	82.5	48.5
1980	227.8	82.3	46.3
1986	241.6	74.4	43.4

*Population includes armed forces abroad.
SOURCES: Population from U.S. Department of Commerce, Bureau of the Census, *Statistical Abstract of the United States,* 108th ed., Government Printing Office 1987, table 2, p. 7. Percents calculated from Health Insurance Association of America, *1988 Update: Source Book of Health Insurance Data* (Washington, D.C., 1988), table 1.2.

tithesis of compulsory, government schemes—meant the combination of Blue Cross and Blue Shield plans, commercial and mutual insurance companies, and independents. Indeed, in many ways their function had become indistinguishable.

Private health insurance expanded rapidly as a result of government policies in the 1940s, gained momentum in the 1950s, and was leveling off in the early 1960s in terms of individuals covered for basic hospital insurance. The encouragement of health insurance as a fringe benefit by large corporations during World War II, stimulated by the decision of the War Labor Board in 1942 to approve fringe benefits of up to 5 percent of wages in an otherwise controlled wages and employment situation, was further boosted in the Inland Steel case of 1948, which found that welfare bargaining was covered within the phrase "other conditions of employment" on which management negotiated with unions.[7] After this, hospital and medical insurance took off. By mid-1950 all the major automobile companies, for example, had labor-negotiated health insurance coverage. The same year, the massive U.S. Steel contract also came into effect. Employment power was launched as the fulcrum of hospital-insurance benefits.

Commercial and mutual insurance companies were in many cases already selling other lines of insurance, including lucrative life and automobile insurance, to organized working populations. By offering multiline insurance, the companies were able to tailor their product to special circumstances and to balance out expected profits between one type of insurance and another. By the early 1960s well over seven hundred insurance companies were selling some form of health insurance. As with other forms of insurance, the contracts were experience-rated, that is, adjusted to the risk (the expected cost) of each insured group.

The entry of commercial companies into health insurance on a wide scale challenged Blue Cross's role as a communitywide, quasi-public service. Early Blue Cross philosophy stressed community rating, that is, a single rate paid by all members of a local population who were enrolled in group policies in the area. In this way the risk of hospitalization was shared across a relatively large population, including individuals with high and low medical risks. Blue Cross representatives talked of community sponsorship and were proud of the *service* approach that distinguished Blue Cross benefits from the traditional *indemnity* coverage of insurance companies.[8] Pure service benefits specified the types of services that would be given to the person covered, with no mention of the cost of these services, while indemnity programs specified fixed dollar benefits; under indemnity, as hospital costs went up, patients were liable for greater out-of-pocket costs. Community rating also reflected a distinct social philosophy: that all employment groups enrolled in the particular Blue Cross plan ought to share equally in the total costs experienced among all members. It was a form of social insurance.

As long as Blue Cross schemes held a special status as hospital insurers in different areas, both community rating and service benefits could be maintained, and local Blue Cross plans, with their agreed-upon injunction not to compete with each other in the same area, could be seen as quasi-public institutions. Public support engendered by Blue Cross spoke to their acceptance as socially responsive institutions. One official, replying to a question as to why Blue Cross should continue to have a tax exemption, remarked: "In some states it would be like trying to put a tax on the Social Security Program."[9] However, neither community rating nor service benefits could survive effectively against the policies of the commercial carriers, which were under no similar constraints. Insurance companies were able to provide specialized insurance packages for specific groups of employees, offering lower rates than Blue Cross for groups of young healthy workers. There was concern that the Blues might become weighed down by the older, sicker, much more costly members of the insured population, while the commercial carriers prospered by skimming the cream.

Blue Cross plans had various potential options in the 1950s. They could stick to their principles and perhaps risk sinking and eventually going out of business. Alternatively, they might find themselves with sicker patients and those with more chronic conditions, and perhaps eventually be maintained with government support, as a kind of analogy to tax-supported hospitals in the cities, that is, as the lower half, socially speaking, of a two-class system. They might compete with the insurance companies on the latter's terms. Or they might press for federal subsidy of Blue Cross as a basic form of national health insurance for the whole population, thus extending the association's role as a quasi-public social institution. The most promising development, from the Blue Cross perspective, would have been the successful passage of the Flanders-Ives proposals (1949–1955), which would have provided a voluntary national prepayment program for the whole population, building on existing nonprofit plans and subsidized by federal government grants to states.[10]

In 1955 the American Hospital Association proposed a system of federal grants to states for paying premiums of recipients of public assistance in voluntary nonprofit plans. A related AHA proposal recommended a similar system of prepayment for older persons, with benefits of at least thirty days of hospital care provided on a service basis.[11] However, none of these schemes was adopted. Indeed, they were hobbled by appearing as self-serving attempts by the AHA and Blue Cross, both to counter rising pressures for compulsory health insurance and to strengthen their own positions vis-à-vis the insurance companies.

By the early 1960s, Blue Cross plans were under pressure to shift from community rating to experience rating as the dominant method of establishing rates. Although most plans continued to hold the line on community rating as a general policy into the 1960s, it was not uncommon for plans to offer experience rating (i.e., lower rates) for special (relatively healthy) groups of employees who might otherwise choose commercial companies. Service coverage largely continued. In 1961 approximately three-fourths of the persons covered by Blue Cross had full-service coverage of room and board costs in participating hospitals, usually in semiprivate rooms. The number of days covered ranged from 21 to 365 days a year, depending on region of the country.

Competition thus led to diverse packages of Blue Cross benefits, with special arrangements negotiated for different groups and sometimes special limitations on the number and types of service covered, in order to keep premium costs in line with the amounts offered by different companies. Under Connecticut Blue Cross, for example, local employees of General Motors were eligible for a generous 485 days of consecutive hospital care in the early 1960s, and for relatively wide insurance coverage in other respects, under a contract paid for by the company. In contrast, local telephone company employees who paid their hospital premiums out of salaries and wages were eligible for only twenty-one days of hospital care.[12] The combined result of the hundreds of policies written by almost eighty Blue Cross plans and almost eight hundred insurance companies was a complex mosaic of coverage patterns which subscribers did not often fully understand—until perhaps faced with a hospital stay. Health insurance became a well-known butt of jokes; for example, the joke by comedian Phil Leeds: "I have health insurance. If a giraffe bites me on the shoulder, I get $18, provided I am pregnant at the time."[13] The foreign visitor could only be amazed.

Blue Cross on the National Scene

Once again, lack of a clear federal policy put the onus for national policy-making on the collective decisions of nongovernmental organizations. Blue Cross plans faced criticism whichever way they turned. If their coverage expanded, additional hospital services were made available and thus hospital expenditures went up. Thus Blue Cross could be criticized as the cause of rising hospital expenditures. In turn, as hospital rates rose, Blue Cross plans paid out more in benefits and sought ever-higher premium rates. The Commission on Financing of Hospital Care described Blue Cross plans as a "logical extension of the voluntary hospital's community function" and an "indispensable part of community organization."[14] But such functions were difficult to measure.

Hospital expenses per patient day more than doubled between the mid-1940s and the mid-1950s, and almost doubled again in the next ten years (table 10.2). Although expense per inpatient day was a crude measure—not allowing, in particular, for the increasing amount of outpatient care being given in these years, nor for changes in hospital productivity—such figures offered dramatic evidence of the increased cost of hospitalization. Average expenses per patient day rose from less than $10 in 1946 to over $44 in 1965.

Cost increases moved in tandem across all types of hospitals, including state and local government institutions, many of which continued to rely largely on tax support. What seems to have happened is that the

TABLE 10.2

Finances of Nonfederal Short-term General and Allied Special Hospitals, 1946–65, Selected Years

	1946	1955	1965
Total expenses ($ billions)	1.2	3.4	9.1
Expense per patient day ($)			
All hospitals	9.39	23.12	44.48
Nonprofit	10.04	24.15	45.40
State and local government	7.39	20.62	41.84
Proprietary	10.13	21.25	43.74
Patient income (including private and government third parties) as percent of total income			
Nonprofit	83.5	91.4	93.6
State and local government	57.1	NA	NA
Proprietary	96.9	96.9	96.1
Difference between reported revenue and expenditures for nongovernmental hospitals ($ millions)			
Nonprofit	+37	+38	+227
Proprietary	+12	+18	+42
Percentage difference between revenue and expense for nongovernmental hospitals			
Nonprofit	+4.4	+1.5	+3.4
Proprietary	+12.5	+10.6	+8.2

SOURCE: American Hospital Association, *Hospitals,* Annual Guide Issues.

availability of insurance allowed the voluntary hospitals, as flagships of quality for the entire system, to increase their staffing, equipment, and facilities, including intensive care units. Then these standards, accepted as essential elements of good medical care, were duplicated in other types of hospitals in turn through the network of medical professionals, with the teaching hospital as the model. Staffing was a particularly important element. The number of personnel per 100 patients rose steadily in all types of hospitals between 1946 and 1965. There were 150 full-time (equivalent) personnel for every 100 patients in 1946; up to 250 in 1965.

Blue Cross plans came under attack for their rising rates in many parts of the country from the late 1950s. State Insurance Commissioner Francis Smith of Pennsylvania was a particularly outspoken advocate for greater oversight of hospitals and better information about hospital utilization rates. But commissioners were not the only critics. In New York, protesting against an average increase in Blue Cross rates of 37.4 percent in 1960, labor organizations picketed the building where public hearings on the petitions for rate increases were being held. Associated Hospital Service of New York was then America's largest Blue Cross plan.[15] The same year,

Cleveland's City Council passed an emergency resolution requesting a special committee to study hospital costs in the Cleveland area and called for deferment of a proposed 27.4 percent Blue Cross rate hike until the study was completed.[16] A special report for *McCall's* magazine in January 1963 observed that the then seventy-seven Blue Cross plans, collectively, were spending over $2 billion a year nationwide, an amount larger than the budget of any state except New York.[17]

But although it might appear that the Blue Cross network had a major national power base of its own, in fact Blue Cross was decentralized. Built from the ground up in local communities, Blue Cross plans and local hospitals had mutual interests in sticking together and were sensitive to local rather than to national issues. Some areas were distinguished by relatively low Blue Cross coverage, including states such as South Dakota, Montana, Oregon, and Idaho, and the cities of Seattle, Durham, Columbus, and Baton Rouge. (Blue Cross plans reportedly included 52 percent of the population in metropolitan areas in 1963, 45 percent in rural non-farm areas, and 36 percent in rural farm areas.) The idea of Blue Cross as a *national* voluntary movement imbued with its own special, all-encompassing American "spirit" was a myth.

In areas where Blue Cross covered the majority of subscribers, chiefly in the Northeast and Middle West, Blue Cross and the hospitals could work out mutually reinforcing policies. Striking examples of heavy Blue Cross coverage were in plans covering Allentown, Pennsylvania; Washington, D.C.; Rochester, New York; New York City; Cincinnati; Cleveland; Philadelphia; Delaware; Rhode Island; and Connecticut. In these areas Blue Cross plans covered over half of the population as subscribers—and thus, including dependents, a great majority of the entire population. In such areas there was at least a possibility of developing joint hospital service planning and of thinking more broadly about service needs.

In Allentown, for example, the hospital staff of a 400-bed hospital (Sacred Heart) decided in the 1950s to tackle the hospital's high waiting list by setting up a system of stiff review of admissions, leading to general recognition that there was a trend toward overutilization of hospital facilities and, by selective admissions, to the end of the problem within two years.[18] This case triggered a diatribe from Pennsylvania Commissioner Smith against overutilization of hospitals and a call for Blue Cross to undertake utilization studies. In Rochester, New York, meanwhile, backed by strong corporate interests as well as heavy Blue Cross participation, the Hospital Council was receiving publicity by having one of the few effective planning mechanisms in existence. One study in the early 1960s found

23 percent of the patients unnecessarily occupying acute general beds in the Rochester region, leading the council to direct private local capital funding away from acute-care construction to extended care units for rehabilitation and convalescence.[19] However, local oversight of hospital utilization was relatively rare.

Blue Cross did not begin to become a centralized organization with strong national interests until the 1960s.[20] In 1960 the older Blue Cross Commission was disbanded and the Blue Cross Association, essentially a trade association, became the national arm, formally separate from the AHA. With the appointment of a young professor of health-service administration who had substantial experience in hospital utilization studies, Walter McNerney, as president in 1961, the Blue Cross Association acquired an expanded role. McNerney's intention was, he said, to strengthen the authority of Blue Cross interests, nationally, in negotiations with the federal government, and as a power able to deal with the insurance industry, and also to develop the association as an organization that would be closer to hospitals at the national level.[21]

One early step was to launch a hospital-utilization study (under a federal research grant) which compared the experiences of federal workers enrolled by Blue Cross in different types of health services, including comprehensive group-practice plans. This study, confirming other studies, suggested marked reductions in hospital use when patients were members of comprehensive group practices (health maintenance organizations) such as the Kaiser plans on the West Coast.[22] There appeared, in short, to be considerable waste in the hospital system, represented in substantial overutilization of hospital facilities. Although there was some doubt at the time about the general applicability of such findings, the growing body of material on hospital utilization by the mid-1960s—the product, in large part, of the professionalization of health administration and the availability of federal research grants—added to a pervasive uneasiness about the role of private health insurance in providing effective and efficient benefits and the role of hospitals and doctors as potential exploiters of hospitalization.

Taking all medical and hospital services together, only one-fourth of all private expenses for health services were met by insurance in 1960.[23] But hospital coverage was relatively generous. Insurance benefits represented, for example, 48 percent of all nongovernmental payments for hospital care in 1955, 64 percent in 1960, and 67 percent in 1963; and under some policies the proportion was over 90 percent.[24] An example of one hospital's experience (St. Luke's Hospital, New Bedford, Massachusetts) is

TABLE 10.3

A Community Hospital in the Pre-Medicare Period:
St. Luke's Hospital, New Bedford, Massachusetts,
1958 and 1964

	1958	1964	Percent 1964
Average daily census	264	313	
Admissions	13,685	15,902	100.0
Private	1,571	2,606	16.4
Semiprivate	7,236	8,256	51.9
Ward	2,455	2,452	15.4
Newborn	2,423	2,588	16.3
Operations	6,872	7,678	—
Outpatient visits	13,166	14,393	—
ER visits	7,425	14,989	—
Income	$3,421,807	$5,160,842	100.0
Patients	3,281,501	5,012,122	97.1
Endowment	83,567	105,361	2.0
United Fund	46,627	43,000	0.8
Gifts	10,112	359	*

*Less than 0.01%.
NOTE: Percentages may not add up exactly, due to rounding.
SOURCE: Robert H. Goodwin, "The Community Hospital," in Leslie J. DeGroot, ed., *Medical Care: Social and Organizational Aspects* (Springfield, Ill.: Charles C Thomas, 1966), pp. 112–13.

given in table 10.3. Over 97 percent of this hospital's income was raised from patients in 1964, and almost 75 percent from third parties (private and governmental). Third-party coverage offered a direct incentive for care to be given inside rather than outside the hospital.

The private third-party system was also inherently conservative, in the scientific and organizational sense, at a time when medicine was rapidly changing. By paying for high-cost services, third-party payments crystallized and exaggerated the preexisting emphases of hospital care on high-technology medicine; thus the patient was encouraged to enter the hospital as an inpatient even for diagnostic tests. Insurance covered the immediate medical response to a heart attack but not long-term management of cardiac conditions—or their prevention. Hospitals were encouraged in turn to develop special units for cardiac care—indeed, to make them as lavish and expensive as the market would bear. Endorsement of high-cost medicine was further emphasized by the rapid development of major medical insurance from the early 1950s, to protect patients against the cost of long and serious illnesses when ordinary benefits would be rapidly exhausted; by the end of 1964, forty-seven million persons held major medical coverage.

But as hospital costs went up, those outside the organized workplace found it difficult to afford insurance of any kind. The elderly, rising in political strength, were the major case in point. A joint report from the Blue Cross Association and the AHA in 1961 found more than 7 million persons age sixty-two or over who had no health insurance, less than $5,000 in savings, and annual incomes for themselves and their spouse of less than $3,000.[25] Here was a large group of people who were the new poor—or would become so rapidly when they were sick. The National Catholic Welfare Conference described them evocatively as "widows, orphans, disabled and dependent aged."[26] As with other such groups in the past (including veterans), there was little disagreement that government, rather than private institutions, should be responsible for them. The disagreement lay in how this responsibility should be met.

Blue Cross continued to enjoy one major competitive advantage vis-à-vis the companies: its relationship with hospitals. Not only were the majority of Blue Cross board members hospital representatives, but hospitals offered the Blues services at cost, while charging the companies (and individuals) on the basis of scheduled charges, that is, at higher (sometimes much higher) rates. Although hospitals justified the difference by their endorsement of Blue Cross as a community venture and as an extension of the hospital's own operation, from the companies' point of view the system was unfair. A knowledgeable insurance executive estimated that Blue Cross plans enjoyed at least the equivalent of a 10 percent discount in prices compared with other carriers in the Federal Employees Program.[27]

Selling Hospital Services to Government

By the early 1960s private insurance was clearly unwieldy (and perhaps unworkable) as a vehicle for covering the whole population. But advocates of a government insurance program, too, had abandoned the goals of 100 percent population coverage and insurance for comprehensive services. With the abandonment of optimism among liberal reformers that a system of compulsory health insurance would be achieved through federal legisla-

tion in the late 1940s, the attention of the major protagonists—in the
health associations, in federal agencies, and on the staffs of congressional
committees—shifted to the obvious gaps in insurance coverage: that is, to
the elderly and the poor, particularly to those who were both elderly and
poor. From 1950, proponents of compulsory *health* insurance turned to the
much more limited goal of a national *hospital* insurance program that would
be targeted to those sixty-five years of age and over and financed through
the Social Security program.

Numerous legislative proposals were made for different approaches to
hospital insurance in the 1950s. These included various methods of encouraging private ("voluntary") health insurance, stimulating prepaid
group practice, providing federal or federal-state subsidies of health services through private carriers, providing national voluntary insurance for
those with low income, and providing compulsory health insurance
through the states. But none succeeded. Reliance on private insurance,
backed by proposals for federal aid to the states to provide services for the
poor, was the official Republican position. In theory, this joint public-
private policy could cover everyone, rich and poor, making broader government intervention unnecessary.

It was as a politically acceptable alternative to compulsory health
insurance that federal responsibility for the sick poor was finally firmly
established in 1950, when Congress approved a system of so-called "vendor payments." Under this system federal grants were made to states for
direct third-party payments to hospitals, doctors, and other health-service
providers for care given to public-assistance recipients. However, this
program remained relatively small, with substantial variations from state
to state. And it failed to achieve its goals in two critical respects. First, it
was irrelevant to those who were above the local assistance level but who
might be unable to afford medical care when they needed it; and second,
it excluded those who did not wish to apply for aid because of the ancient
stigma of "indigence." Public *assistance,* repackaged as vendor payments,
continued to suggest moral failure, degradation, and lack of social worth.

The position of those supporting the extension of vendor payments
as the solution to universal hospital coverage was that of the old advocates
of scientific charity. Social *insurance* suggested services by right (in return
for contributions to the Social Security system) and membership in the
category of the "productive" or "deserving" population. Those who sponsored compulsory hospital insurance opted for an egalitarian point of view:
everyone over sixty-five would be covered without regard to income. The
movement for hospital insurance for the aged through Social Security
gained momentum with the Forand bill of 1957, introduced by liberal

Democrats. This bill was to develop, through various manifestations, into Part A of Medicare in 1965.

In the long debates over paying for hospital care for the elderly in the late 1950s and early 1960s, the interests of Blue Cross and the hospitals were politically joined. The AHA leaned toward a scheme of federal subsidy of voluntary health insurance. Under this, the needy elderly might be brought (and bought) into the "mainstream" of Blue Cross and perhaps of commercial hospital insurance by having their premiums paid for them. However, the technical and political difficulties of defining an actual plan to implement the program stymied this approach at the discussion stage. The AHA's official position on the Forand bill was guarded concern and expressions of the "real dangers" in this approach to the future of voluntary hospitals and Blue Cross. Nevertheless, equally concerned about hospital funding for the elderly, the AHA supported congressional hearings on the Social Security proposals, thus opening the way, with other organizations, for hearings on the Forand bill in 1958.

Meanwhile, the advent of vendor payments, with their direct assumption of government purchase of care from hospitals as "vendors," made a strong statement about "charity" within the hospital system. The various congressional proposals assumed, in effect, that private charity-giving to the poor—by hospitals and physicians—ought to be unnecessary. The ideal American system was to cover everyone through third-party (insurance or assistance) payments, either through a mix of private insurance for the upper and middle classes and government reimbursement for the indigent, or through compulsory health insurance for the whole population. Both approaches were consistent with the evolution of hospital policy in the previous five decades.

Even in the 1950s relatively little care was actually given away, deliberately, by private nonprofit hospitals. Charity by voluntary hospitals, where it did exist, was often inadvertent. Hospital administrators talked of the percentage of charges to patients that were "uncollectible" or, matching income from patient fees against total hospital expenses, would claim a posted "deficit"—sometimes conveniently ignoring other income, from endowments, donations, or any local tax subventions. Uncollectibles represented 3.5 percent of the total charges of voluntary hospitals in 1953; 5.9 percent for proprietary hospitals, and 6.2 percent for government hospitals.[28] Exactly how many patients were arriving at voluntary hospitals without funds and being treated free, with no government reimbursement, was unknown. Hospital representatives argued that their earned income from patients in short-term general hospitals averaged $18.10 per day while their expenses averaged $19.55, creating a total national disparity of approximately $140 million.[29] But this amount did not necessarily reflect the provision of charity care; it could just as well mean undercharging those who could pay, inefficiencies, or both.

Lack of standardized accounting or reporting systems for hospitals made it difficult to assess the financial situation of hospitals at all. But there was also an intrinsic difficulty in talking about "hospital charity" when well over 90 percent of the voluntary hospital's income came from patients, either directly or via private or government third parties (table 10.2). Actually, it was not the hospitals themselves (through endowments or donations) which were making up for any deficits in "charity care," but other patients—through cost-shifting from one part of the budget to another. Hospital endowment funds were minuscule, probably less than 2 percent of the hospital's average income in the 1950s,[30] so that there was little or no "free money" for giving away services at the hospital's discretion.

Following the establishment of the federal-state program of vendor payments, local government officials in major cities began to reinterpret their traditional commitments to hospitals, thus further confusing the question of services to the poor. In Denver, for example, a report from the planning board in 1962 suggested five alternative courses of action for the Denver General Hospital, including closing the hospital altogether.[31] At the same time the contribution of local government funds to voluntary hospitals seemed now to make less sense.[32] Declining local government interest in hospital provision for the indigent was to become fully evident in the 1970s.

Hospital administrators were also troubled that state and local government fee schedules were almost invariably targeted to pay less than full costs, leaving voluntary hospitals to cover deficits incurred by services to the indigent from limited endowments and gifts (which might otherwise be used for capital) or from profits made elsewhere in the hospital— notably from radiology and pathology. A pamphlet issued by the Hospital Association of Pennsylvania in 1951 complained that hospital care of "charity inpatients" cost nearly $16 million a year while the state paid hospitals only $7.2 million, leading to a "total loss" to the hospitals of nearly $8.8 million, with further losses of $8.4 million in treating needy persons in hospital dispensaries.[33]

For the first time, hospital associations and administrators began to grapple with the larger political issues of hospital financing and to think of the budget more consciously as a management tool. Under the combined influence of increasing third-party payments and administrative vigilance, the margin of income over expenditures for voluntary hospitals rose from a bare 1.5 percent in 1955 to 3.4 percent ten years later (table 10.2). Hospitals had entered the world of collective economics. At the center of a spider's web of government and private reimbursement, administrators worked in the 1950s with their counterparts in the local and national hospital associations and Blue Cross, although many of them were neophytes on the political scene. The American Hospital Association published its first *Principles of Payment for Hospital Care* in 1953. This was an attempt to establish consensus about contract reimbursement between hospitals, federal and state government, and insurers. Two revisions of this statement were made in 1962 and further revisions in 1963 and 1965.[34] Reimbursement principles for hospital care were slowly being standardized at the national level through a continual process of tinkering.

Since well before World War II, estimates of the cost per patient day had been accepted as a reasonable rule-of-thumb measure for reimbursement of indigent care by governments. The federal government had developed a formula for "reimbursable costs" per patient day, under the maternal and child-care program (EMIC) in the 1940s, and this concept was adopted, with modifications, by various Blue Cross plans. The concept of hospital cost reimbursement grew, incrementally, into a set of principles for payment by Blue Cross that formed the basis for negotiating reimbursement contracts as a whole. These principles assumed that the appropriate basis for cost reimbursement was the patient day.[35] Such a figure was unsatisfactory in many ways, because it did not allow for cost comparisons to be made between hospitals with different functions or case mix. It was difficult, for example, to compare a hospital with a large teaching program to a nonteaching hospital, or a hospital with sicker patients with one that served a healthier clientele. Nevertheless, cost per patient day was a useful—and simple—shorthand approach for hospitals bargaining with third-party payers. It was also a necessary shorthand since hospital cost accounting was amateur and idiosyncratic in the early 1960s. Few hospitals used standardized charts of accounts. And computers were just beginning to enter the picture; Baylor University Medical Center made a big splash by installing a computer in the late 1950s. The AHA *Principles* were a practical effort to provide some standardization, under the association's leadership.

Leading the American Hospital Association between 1954 and 1972 was Edwin L. Crosby, a devout believer in hospitals as major agencies for social good. From a Salvation Army background Crosby went into public health in New York State; he went from there to Johns Hopkins for training in public health, and from there into hospital administration. Subsequently, he became director of the Johns Hopkins Hospital, then director of the new Joint Commission on Accreditation of Hospitals, from which he moved to head the AHA.[36] The development of principles of cost reimbursement stemmed from five regional conferences that were held in the early 1950s, before Crosby's appointment. But Crosby continued the process on the assumption that adequate standards were necessary for hospitals, both for themselves, as quasi-public agencies, and for the public and quasi-public agencies with which they contracted—namely, government and Blue Cross plans. The principles were supposed to provide hospitals with an adequate level of payment for hospital care of recognized quality and maximum efficiency. This required general agreement among hospitals and third parties about what should be covered in areas such as clinical research and education, allowances for maintenance and improvement of facilities, allowances for the services of members of religious orders who worked without pay—and inclusion of at least some capital costs. What, in short, was "hospital service"?

Congressional debates over hospital-insurance proposals for the aged, sparked by the Forand bills of 1957 and 1959, supported the idea of hospital-specific, per diem, cost reimbursement as the basis for funding third-party care under a greatly enlarged federal program, rather than paying hospitals their posted charges or some negotiated rate. Also in the King-Anderson bills of 1961, successors to the Forand bills, it was assumed that hospitals would be reimbursed on a per diem, "reasonable cost" basis. By 1965, when the Medicare legislation was passed, reasonable cost reimbursement appeared preordained. Hospitals presented themselves as responsible, quasi-public institutions, whose costs ought to be met by government and private insurers. In turn, the hospitals would (presumably) behave responsibly in increasing only such costs as were actually necessary, both for individual patient care and for total social spending.

New Elements in the Public-Private Mix

The political debates leading up to the passage of the Medicare legislation in 1965 have been well documented: the development of philosophically diverse proposals for covering the costs of health care for the elderly and poor; the political compromises that were made under Congressman Wilbur Mills's leadership; and the emergence of a three-part program, each part of which developed from independently sponsored legislative proposals.[37] Medicare Part A derived from proposals for health services for the elderly under Social Security; Medicare Part B, from originally alternative proposals for federal subsidy of private health insurance for the elderly; and Medicaid was a much enlarged, corrected version of vendor payments. From the hospital point of view, however, what was important was not so much the political philosophies but the developing strategic assumptions being built into government programs and their reimbursement. These were incremental responses to continuing changes in reimbursement arrangements, from World War II through the early 1960s.

Before Medicare was passed, the vendor payment system (of federal grants to states for medical services for the needy) was greatly increased, through the Kerr-Mills legislation of 1960.[38] For the hospitals concerned, Kerr-Mills was a partial transition from the older system of underfunded welfare care to their enlarged expectations about cost reimbursement. The vendor payment system varied by state, so that the actual benefits to hospitals depended on where they were located. New York State, for example, had a generous program, as did Massachusetts, Michigan, Illinois, California, Connecticut, and Pennsylvania, while some other states had none at all. And even in states which did have programs there were huge differences in the hospital service that was covered, and in the implicit, underlying assumptions about charitable care. Kentucky, for example, provided hospital care of up to ten days per admission but only for acute emergency and life-endangering conditions.[39] Nor was it clear whether the care was to be provided only in the wards, as specified in Pennsylvania, or whether it was to be regarded as a form of third-party reimbursement, assuming semiprivate care. The issue, of course, was whether the indigent patient was to be patronized on the old paternalistic welfare model, or whether the new program was more akin to insurance.

Reimbursement mechanisms and levels under Kerr-Mills also varied widely state by state. Hospitals and their associations watched the massive New York program in particular, because the New York State Department of Social Welfare issued rates for per diem payment for hospitals based on items of cost reported to that agency. However, in New York as elsewhere local welfare departments were not required to adopt these rates with respect to their own city and county programs. Through these various experiences hospital associations were learning of the potential advantage of federal specifications for coverage and reimbursement—and the importance of specifying reasonable levels of reimbursement from the hospitals' point of view.

Fortunately for the hospitals, Kenneth Williamson, the chief of the

AHA Washington Service Bureau, served as an informal adviser to the influential congressman Wilbur Mills in the early 1960s. In a critical meeting with Mills, Williamson pushed successfully for reasonable cost reimbursement in the extension of the Kerr-Mills program into Medicaid in 1965. This move had two important implications. First, it would release billions of additional dollars in reimbursement to hospitals, which would now theoretically be given the full amount of what they spent on care of the indigent. Second, Medicaid recognized reimbursement for the poor as having the same legitimacy for reimbursement as services for other members of the population. Williamson was later to remark, "I often think that, in terms of money, there probably isn't anything I ever did that earned my pay more than that one day's work."[40] The idea of full cost reimbursement was thus accepted—at least for a year or two.

In other respects, too, the coming of Medicare and Medicaid changed the rules. First, since hospital service was now something to purchase through third parties, it followed that social equity would be attained once third parties covered *everyone* on an equitable basis. Second, Blue Cross and the insurance companies appeared, as third parties which might act as Medicare's agents, as parts of an undifferentiated "private sector." Third, with the enormous changes and shifts taking place in the hospital world in the early 1960s, there was a general groping toward hospital standards: standards for reimbursement, utilization studies, consensus about cost accounting, attempts to assess the degree and the desirability of cost-shifting within hospitals, increased concern about quality appraisal (but few useful tools to examine it), and attempts to bring physicians and hospital staffs together into closer examination of such issues.

Walter McNerney, president of the Blue Cross Association, later remarked of the endless discussions about controls on costs, negotiating formulas, strengthening areawide planning, and other forms of regulation in the early 1960s: "The state of the art differed. We didn't know as much [then as we did later] about how to exercise controls."[41] But even though ideas about reimbursement mechanisms were evolving and incomplete, and there was little reliable, cross-institutional information, the idea of control was already present.

Medicare represented the art of the possible—familiar patterns—in terms of program implementation, too. Compulsory hospital insurance for the elderly under Social Security was designed as if it were an extended Blue Cross program. Medicare, like the King-Anderson and Forand bills before it, assumed a basic division between hospital and medical insurance; Part A was to cover hospitals, Part B, physicians.[42] Moreover, as in Blue Cross, the focus was on acute inpatient hospital care, even though most of the health problems of the aged were chronic conditions that did not necessarily require hospitalization; thus hospitals were not initially encouraged to enter new fields. Again like Blue Cross, Medicare included some deductibles and limited, rather than comprehensive, benefits. Reimbursement was on a service rather than an indemnity basis, with beneficiaries covered for so many days of care irrespective of the actual cost. Hospitals, in turn, were to be paid on a per diem basis.

In line with the developing AHA principles, Medicare reimbursement included some elements of capital costs, opening up a Pandora's box of hospital capital expansion. There were no direct requirements in the reimbursement system for control of capital development or for community-wide hospital planning. Similarly, there were no attempts in the initial Medicare regulations to control hospital costs; indeed, there was little idea about how to do it, or even how to measure them. AHA President Crosby remarked at congressional hearings in 1965 that hospital costs would probably keep going up anyway, because of overdue raises in hospital wage levels, as hospital employees were brought up to the income levels of comparable employees elsewhere, and because of the increased development of hospital technique.[43]

For a combination of reasons, then, the process of contracting for hospital services by government agencies and Blue Cross, developed well before Medicare, encouraged expansion of services in individual hospitals, with little or no incentive for joint efforts. Once again, voluntary hospitals were assumed to serve the public good by virtue of their very existence. How, then, would costs be moderated under an expanded federal reimbursement system?

Is Voluntary Planning Feasible?

In theory, the concomitant to voluntary institutions, under cost-based reimbursement, was voluntary hospital planning. The former provided incentives for expansion; the latter offered cooperative restraints on unnecessary growth. Regional or areawide planning seemed the obvious, "community" answer to questions about hospital efficiency in the early 1960s, based on an assumed partnership between responsible community leadership and representatives of hospital, medical, and other professional groups. In 1961 the Hill-Burton program was extended to provide money for areawide health planning—voluntary planning at the local level.[44]

There were only fourteen local hospital planning agencies throughout the United States in 1961. Notable examples were in New York City, Baltimore, Birmingham, Buffalo, Chicago, Cleveland, Columbus, Detroit, Kansas City, Los Angeles, Pittsburgh, Rochester (New York), and Scranton.[45] But almost all actual planning through the mid-1960s concentrated on planning for facilities—bricks and mortar—rather than on planning for community health *services.* Yet the hospital still seemed a natural organizational focus for community health services. Leading AHA spokesmen praised the structure of the Medicare proposals, for example, for their primary emphasis on the hospital "as the center, or hub, of health affairs."[46] It was in this vein that the U.S. Public Health Service, implementing the new Hill-Burton planning program, called on communities to establish local hospital planning agencies. "What Can You Do as a Community Leader?" asked a government pamphlet. The answer was to form a community organization for hospital planning, to improve patient care, efficiency, and economy. Thus you would "Help *Your* Community Meet Its Total Health Needs."[47]

Hopeful discussions of voluntary planning in the early 1960s—vague, laudatory, nostalgic, and harking to the old themes of voluntarism, charity-giving, and community—clashed oddly with the immediate realities of hospital financing. The former was urging joint, altruistic efforts, while the latter was encouraging institutional competition.[48] But voluntary hospital planning clearly did change the system in some instances. In New York City, for example, agreements were made in 1961, under the leadership of Dr. Ray Trussell, for the affiliation of municipal hospitals with voluntary hospitals. The affiliations were designed to upgrade the standards of the municipal hospitals by providing them with medical and technical staff.[49] Fifteen municipal hospitals were affiliated with voluntary hospitals in New York by 1967. In Columbus, Ohio, the planning agency had launched a successful fund drive for construction that had added a total of 400 new beds and supporting facilities by the early 1960s. In Pittsburgh, following a survey done by the Hospital Council in 1957, a hospital planning association was established in 1960 that was strongly backed by the county medical society and by industry.

These and other arrangements formed the backdrop to the establishment of a National Commission on Community Health Services by the American Public Health Association and the National Health Council in 1962, after four years of discussion and planning. Marion B. Folsom, a previous secretary of the Department of Health, Education, and Welfare, a director of Eastman Kodak, and a strong supporter of the Rochester hospital planning system, was named chairman, and funding was provided by the U.S. Public Health Service and by private foundations. Its final report was published in 1966, after the passage of Medicare.[50] In the meantime, frustration with existing planning arrangements, increased tensions in inner cities, the lack of services available to inner-city and minority groups, and the availability of Hill-Burton funding led to a flurry of local activity. By 1965 there were fifty planning agencies covering most of the major cities in the United States. The question now was what they would (and could) do.

The question was complicated by the reappearance of the idea of *university-based* regionalism—this time as a framework for developing a network of federally supported regional medical complexes for heart disease, cancer, and stroke. Then as now, these were the three most important causes of death. In effect, Medicare, representing the social-insurance approach to health services, assumed that the major problem for the elderly was financing expensive hospital care, while areawide planning represented a move toward efficiency through voluntary community organization. Regional medical programs focused on the dissemination of technological knowledge out from the university medical centers to other institutions and practitioners. Hospital policy was developing through a scattershot philosophy of "Let's try everything that might work."

The new regional proposals arose from the Commission on Heart Disease, Cancer, and Stroke established by President Johnson early in 1964 and headed by Dr. Michael E. De Bakey, distinguished Houston heart surgeon. The commission, with its membership heavily weighted toward university research interests, exemplified American successes in biomedical research by the early 1960s, the strong biomedical research presence in medical schools throughout the United States, and the enormous changes in the specialized treatment of heart disease, both in cardiology and in cardiovascular surgery. Not least, heart disease was President Johnson's special interest. The reports of the commission, issued in 1964 and 1965, expressed the same underlying optimism about progress through technology that infused the space program and major approaches to warfare and domestic issues in the mid-1960s. Through the invention and application of science and technology, produced in America's burgeoning academic medical centers, the health status of the population would be improved.[51] In essence, areawide planning assumed a community model and regional medical programs a technological model of medical care; but neither model was defined strategically—or given the funds to make major changes.

Cardiology, with its dramatic and symbolic connotations of American know-how and surgical heroism, offered a strong case for celebrating American knowledge and disseminating it far and wide across the country. The De Bakey Commission's reports noted with pride that research in high blood pressure had resulted in the development of drugs to lower blood-pressure levels. Atherosclerosis of major arteries was being "attacked surgically with gratifying results" and artificial arteries had been invented. Cardiac pacemakers were now available, implanted in more than 5,000 living adults. Anticoagulant drugs were in use. The recent transplantation of human hearts affirmed the model of the body as a machine, with the surgeon as a master technician, and research was underway to develop an artificial heart.[52] Although, as future years would show, the prevention and treatment of cancer and stroke were much more problematical than was then assumed, prevailing optimism about biomedical research and biomedical technology spilled over into these diseases, too. Imaginative and aggressive treatment of cancer and recognition of the importance of early diagnosis and morbidity reporting suggested the potential for considerable progress. The average "cure rate" for cancer in the early 1960s, as measured by the five-year survival rate, was estimated as approximately 33 percent; National Cancer Institute statistics from large hospitals found an average "cure rate" of 43 percent within these major institutions.[53]

In a telling analogy to the space program, Houston was becoming a major national center for the excitement, the glitter, and the success of medical technique—and for the relationship between modern medical technology and high-powered communications. Electronics, said Senator Edward Kennedy, much of it pioneered in his own state of Massachusetts, had "eliminated much of the guesswork and trial and error of diagnosis and therapy."[54] The organizational logic suggested, as a natural corollary, regional medical centers and diagnostic and treatment stations "wired into our medical university complexes," conveying basic information, for example, over thousands of miles from Houston to experts in Boston and other large cities.

The De Bakey Commission recommended a network of regional centers concerned with heart disease, cancer, and/or stroke which would conduct clinical investigation, teach local practitioners, and provide patient care. These would be linked with a network of diagnostic and treatment stations, bringing medical skills within the reach of every citizen. Medical complexes based on university medical schools would incorporate advanced medical equipment, and provide teaching and research activities to doctors affiliated with the regional centers and diagnostic and treatment stations.[55] The expansion of academic medical centers through federal research grants in the 1950s and 1960s made them scientific and technological resources—tertiary care centers—to which patients with complicated problems were referred for study and treatment. The medical schools, through their Association of American Medical Colleges, supported the idea of regional medical centers as a logical extension of a process that was already underway.

The American Hospital Association supported regional medical programs, as a means of focusing national attention on heart disease, cancer, and stroke and for providing a "bridge" between the science of medicine and its full application to the care and treatment of patients. However, the AHA was cautious about supporting major changes in the health-care system. Potentially, the eighty U.S. medical schools, with their two hundred affiliated hospitals, could become authoritarian regional medical complexes under any legislation which followed the De Bakey proposals, exerting unwanted power over six thousand smaller hospitals.[56] Neither hospitals nor physicians, who were demonstrably reluctant to engage in even voluntary planning at the local level, could be expected to jump enthusiastically into a federally organized, university-dominated, hospital network.

In the event, the regional medical program legislation of 1965 (PL 89-239) was, like most legislation, a compromise. Medicare was in the process of passage and the Johnson administration was keenly aware of the need for the cooperation of physicians and hospitals in order to get Medicare going. Rules regarding federal grants under PL 89-239 barred construction of new buildings and the establishment of patient-care programs, and encouraged voluntary regional planning and cooperative arrangements between medical schools, hospitals, and other institutions or agencies. Specific programs depended on local initiative and local possibilities. As with the voluntary areawide planning efforts being stimulated through Hill-Burton funds, the legislation opened a tentative window for organizational cohesion. In both of these instances the federal government acted as if it were a private foundation; it offered funds to those who sought grants, on the basis of national goals and guidelines, but with considerable leeway for local initiative. This was indeed a common pattern in the numerous federal grant programs of the 1960s. The federal role was more permissive than prescriptive.

What was new was not the principle of federal aid—filling in gaps of care, stimulating private enterprise—but the sheer volume of programs streaming out of Washington in these riot-torn, war-torn, and prosperous years, sometimes programs with conflicting goals. The Great Society programs were proposals dusted off the shelf, legislated, and poured into the attack on major social problems: health, education, housing, poverty.

Major social and organizational problems would, it was hoped, be solved by goodwill, by planning techniques, and by the availability of money to stimulate individual and collective opportunity. Federal policy was a crucial influence on the health-care system in the 1960s and 1970s, but its influence was largely indirect; only in the 1980s did the wheel turn toward strong federal intervention.

Federal legislative proposals through 1965 were unqualified endorsements of private initiative. Hospital planning was to be achieved through spontaneous, locally organized altruism; hospital services would be provided, for the most part, through the market for insurance; and inequality in provision would be addressed through federal programs for the elderly and poor. An enormous onus was placed on largely inchoate organizational structures at the local level. Yet experience of the past suggested, only too convincingly, that voluntary participation in hospital affairs among leading citizens, while encouraging social stability, community cohesion, and public virtue, only rarely resulted in communitywide services.

In the early 1960s, moreover, the very structure of leadership in communities across the country was challenged by a reservoir of grievances among nonelite residents, including the residents of inner-city "ghettos." The Kerner Commission report, a prestigious national report on civil disorders published in 1967, described the race riots of the previous few years as reflections of intrinsic social failure. The commission pointed to the perceived failure of American social institutions, including health-care institutions, the widening gap between needs and public resources, and a "growing cynicism regarding the commitment of community institutions and leadership to meet those needs."[57] Large voluntary teaching hospitals in the inner cities in the 1960s, protected by armed guards, with their windowless walls sheering up out of low-income areas, were dangerously isolated from their immediate communities. What was the "community," and who should speak for it?

Areawide planning was an attempt to form new community-based structures of voluntarism, springing beyond individual institutions. But by 1965 there was still relatively little such planning experience. Although areawide planning was furthered by new federal legislation in 1966 (PL 89-649) which provided funds for the establishment of "comprehensive health planning agencies," these, too, had little actual control over the system, nor did *their* successors, the health systems agencies, established by legislation of 1974 (PL 93-641). Throughout the 1960s there were endless grass-roots meetings, with the emergence of new community leaders and struggles for power over new federal programs in major cities. Discussion about hospital trusteeship in the health-administration literature focused on community representation on boards rather than on what the hospitals actually did, let alone what they should do. Meanwhile, hospital-reimbursement principles presaged major changes in the control of capital investment throughout the hospital system. Medicare was enacted in 1965 in a climate of diverse planning principles, evolving responses, and unfinished agendas.

Medicare: The Watershed

Medicare Parts A and B, which became effective (under PL 89-97) in 1966, provided members of the population sixty-five years and over with substantial hospital and medical benefits; in 1972 the disabled and kidney dialysis and transplant patients were also included. Basic benefits initially included up to ninety days of inpatient hospital care per illness, outpatient care, posthospital care in a skilled nursing home of up to a hundred days per illness, home health services, and physician services, with various deductibles and coinsurance imposed upon patients. Hospitals were guaranteed payment by the program on the basis of "reasonable costs," and Medicaid was initially developed under the same system.

Nationally, the program was administered by the federal Social Security Administration. However, payment of hospitals on behalf of Medicare patients was organized through fiscal intermediaries. These third parties provided a buffer mechanism between the government and voluntary, for-profit, and local-government hospitals. In the negotiations surrounding the legislation the AHA fought for the concept of intermediaries, arguing that the hospitals "needed protection" from the potential iron hand of government agencies.[58] The ideal intermediary, from the hospital perspective, was Blue Cross, with its commitment to the strength and goodwill of the voluntary approach. Under Medicare, hospitals were allowed the privilege of picking their own intermediary; 90 percent chose Blue Cross. In another bow to the existing system, hospitals were guaranteed participation in the federal program by virtue of accreditation by the Joint Commission, as an alternative to government certification.

Thus with a stroke of the pen the elderly acquired hospital benefits, the hospitals acquired cost reimbursement for these benefits, the Blue Cross Association was precipitated into prominence as a major national organization (since the national contract was to be with the association, with subcontracting to local plans), and the Joint Commission was given formal government recognition. Simultaneously, through the implementation of federally subsidized Medicaid programs in the various states, the poor, like the elderly, were brought into the "mainstream" of medicine. In theory, at least, most Americans might now be fully insured.

But what was the "mainstream" as far as hospitals were concerned? From the perspective of 1965, hospitals seemed to be marked by flux: in reimbursement arrangements; in responsibility for the quality of care; in the question of racial integration of facilities; in acceptance of private patients as "teaching material"; in consideration of the hospital's role in the community; in shifting sources of funds for indigent patients, with recognition that now almost all the hospital's income came from earned income; and in reappraisal of capital financing. Blue Cross reimbursement mechanisms were also in flux, becoming, in some plans at least, more similar to those of its commercial competitors.

With more than twice as many workers in 1965 as in 1950, hospitals attracted the attention of labor economists as a source of new jobs in an expanding economy, of union leaders looking for new fields to organize, and of educational institutions as an outlet for expansion in training. More Americans were working in hospitals in 1960 than for the interstate railroad, the automobile industry, or in basic steel. Yet at the same time, major social issues of the early 1960s played across the hospitals' facades: questions of access to care, of equity, of planning, and of public responsibility.

Medicare was a catalyst, testing the organizational resilience and the social altruism of the voluntary enterprise—testing, that is, its essential character. But some lines of development were already evident. Medicare and Medicaid together were to support the voluntary over the governmental hospital system. They affirmed the central importance of the hospital in American medicine, but left to individual hospitals the translation of this importance into networks and systems. There was little to push hospitals much beyond their exciting space-age image on TV. The altruistic aspects of voluntarism remained appealing, as did the continuing strategic connotations: freedom of action, political immunity, local initiative, and noninterference of government in caring for the sick. But maintaining voluntarism carried the paradox of voluntary controls, if strong government controls were to be avoided, as well as opportunities for voluntary initiative.

In Medicare, Congress recognized the central importance of hospitals over other types of health-service organizations. Yet voluntary hospitals, borne along over the years by public approbation and increasing revenues, were marked by a series of unresolved tensions: the division between the hospital as an institution and its medical staff of attending physicians; the perplexing role of hospital governance by voluntary trustees, whose business acumen in their individual and several professional roles often vanished in the hospital board room; the maintenance of voluntary hospitals, legally, as tax-exempt, while their role was increasingly as a seller of services; the importance of buildings to demonstrate purpose; the lack of interest in patient-outcome measures; the fact that the hospital was not at risk for bad investment decisions because, increasingly, its costs were reimbursable; the tension between local community involvement and national standards and expectations; the division between acute care and long-term care; and, last but not least, the ambivalence between seeing the hospital as a cog in a major distribution system (with large units and regional networks) and seeing it as a local community institution.

Medicare responded to the prevailing questions, trends, and apparent needs of the early 1960s. Its great expansion made possible by the dollars available for reimbursement was to lead, first, to a rapid expansion in hospital services and expenditures, but along preexisting lines; and second, in sequence, to a focus on capital expansion, an overtly profit-making nexus, huge industrial growth, and federal regulation. The fruits of this process are the hospital system we have today: opportunistic and unsettled; ebullient and nervous; politically attuned and market-oriented.

11

Pragmatism in the Marketplace: 1965–80

MEDICARE gave hospitals a license to spend. The more expenditures they incurred, the more income they received—until the system was changed in the early 1980s. Medicare tax funds flowed into hospitals in a golden stream, more than doubling between 1970 and 1975, and doubling again by 1980. Medicaid, though smaller, was equally expansive. In 1980 the two programs combined spent $35.5 billion on hospital care of all kinds. This was the equivalent of almost half the total expenditures of nonfederal short-term general hospitals.[1] One major result of Medicare was to distinguish further the role of government as purchaser from that of hospitals as sellers of services in the marketplace. Another was a great increase in government power, through recognition of the power of the purse. Later, there was recognition of the similar power vested in major, nongovernmental purchasers, that is, employers.

The most obvious phenomenon of hospital history since 1965 is the overwhelming force of national government policy. This was expressed first in governmental pressures on hospitals from the 1970s to seek "private sector" (that is, business) solutions to perceived problems in hospital service. Under the basic (though untested) assumption that economic competition is more efficient than nonprofit enterprise, incentives pushed hospitals toward an industrial model of organization. From the late 1970s through the mid-1980s, the success of for-profit hospital chains on the national stock exchanges seemed to justify this policy of "privatization" and the "coming of the corporation."[2]

The three major hospital sectors—voluntary, governmental, and profit-making—became, oddly, both more alike and more sharply delineated in the fifteen years following the Medicare legislation. All responded to the same signals from the federal government in the shape of Medicare reimbursement regulations, but each had a special challenge to its mission. Profit-making hospitals had to demonstrate that they were benevolent, voluntary hospitals that they were efficient, and local-government hospitals that they were necessary. Although profit-making hospitals, with less than 8 percent of all nonfederal short-term hospital beds in 1980, continued to be a relatively small part of the overall hospital system, they became the bellwether institutions of the 1970s, buoyed up and swept along by the political and economic conservatism that distinguished the Nixon, Ford, and Carter years.

Medicare and Medicaid—social programs which were designed to maintain the incomes of the elderly and poor—fed the market enthusiasms of the 1970s. It was now permissible (indeed admirable) for voluntary hospitals to post a surplus, indicating effective management. These hospitals were renamed, by the American Hospital Association, to suggest a subtle change in goals: formerly "nonprofit," they were now "not-for-profit." Proprietary, or profit-making, hospitals became "for-profit" or "investor-owned." Articles in major law journals in 1980 suggested that the major distinction between the not-for-profit and for-profit forms of organization was their formal difference in tax status, rather than any necessary difference in role or purpose.[3] However, by stressing their parallelism with for-profit institutions, the voluntary hospitals opened themselves up to being judged by the free-market values of the profit-making system and to having their tax exemption seriously threatened. They were to face, too, the same kind of detailed federal and state regulation that distinguishes American business enterprise, but which voluntary institutions had long been able to avoid under the claim that they were autonomous, moral, "public" institutions.

What happened between the mid-1960s period with its mainstream, egalitarian political rhetoric and 1980 with its strong market stance? How did the hospital complex shift so rapidly to market expectations? Three themes stand out. First, the Medicare legislation exposed the weaknesses of traditional vendor payment systems as a vehicle for government entitlement programs. Second, decisions made about capital were key to the profit-oriented direction of all hospitals. And finally, Medicare supported

voluntary hospitals as private institutions without giving them counter-
vailing responsibilities—or the money—to operate as public agencies.

Medicare and Medicaid Are Implemented

The act setting up Medicare specified that there should be "prohibition
against any federal interference" with the practice of medicine or the way
in which medical services are provided.[4] But this statement was in part
wishful thinking, in part legislative boilerplate, for a program as large as
Medicare, even as initially envisaged, could not help but affect the health-
care system. The experience of Blue Cross and commercial health insurance provided the precedent for the potential influence of governmental
third parties on hospitals. From the beginning the inflationary potential of
Medicare's payment policy was evident to officials in the Bureau of Health
Insurance, set up within the federal Social Security Administration to run
Medicare. Immediate federal concerns were to implement the program as
quickly and efficiently as possible, and this meant insuring hospital cooperation, irrespective of cost. In retrospect, the hospitals, too, had little
choice. It would have been foolish to repudiate the certainty of short-term
gains for some nebulous expectation of long-term freedom from federal
control, which might (or might not) be the consequence of presenting
themselves as frugal, quasi-public agencies. Nevertheless, the hospitals put
themselves into a box. Medicare, a federal program, would only survive
without strong federal regulation as long as it remained relatively small
(and thus of politically low visibility) and as long as it could be justified
as effectively serving public needs. Neither of these conditions was to be
met.

From the beginning Medicare expenditures grossly outran federal estimates. In 1965, for example, it was estimated that the hospital insurance
part of Medicare (Part A) would cost $3.1 billion in 1970; this figure was
steadily revised upward to $5.8 billion in the latter year, an increase of 87
percent.[5] Although hospital utilization by the elderly increased more rapidly than expected, these figures could not be attributed entirely, or even
in the main, to increased inpatient admissions. One study of factors contributing to the increase in total hospital costs between the mid-1960s and
early 1970s, including both Medicare and non-Medicare patients, at-

tributed less than 10 percent of the increases to expanded utilization and growth of population. Another 23 percent was attributed to the rapid inflation in the economy in this period. The remaining two-thirds represented massive expansions in hospital payroll and nonpayroll expenses—including "profits."[6] The average cost per patient day more than doubled, in real terms, between 1966 and 1976, that is, even after allowing for inflation.[7] The total assets of short-term hospitals rose from $16.4 billion in 1965 to $47.3 billion ten years later, with all three sectors gaining in strength (table 11.1).

Changes in treatment contributed to rising costs. Anne Scitovsky's studies of patients at the Palo Alto Clinic, for example, found marked rises in the costs of treatment for heart attack patients who were treated in intensive care units between 1964 and 1971. Similarly, coronary bypass surgery in the 1970s was a much more expensive, more intensive type of treatment than more conservative forms of care, costing almost $48,000 per case in 1981, as against $10,000 for the older methods. New treatments of breast cancer by chemotherapy and radiotherapy, with or without mastectomy, were more expensive than mastectomy alone. And deliveries by cesarian section increased from fewer than 6 percent of births in 1971 to over 18 percent in 1981; this procedure was twice as expensive as a vaginal delivery. But at the same time, hospital technique was becoming impres-

TABLE 11.1

*Assets of Nonfederal Short-term General and Allied
Special Hospitals, United States, 1947–77,
Selected Years*

	$ Millions			
	Voluntary Nonprofit	State and Local Government	For-profit	Total
1947	2,697	612	129	3,439
1950	3,350	861	138	4,349
1955	5,223	1,614	148	6,985
1960	8,422	2,193	243	10,858
1965	12,476	3,474	414	16,364
1970	20,502	5,301	871	26,674
1975	35,827	8,890	2,538	47,256
1977	46,686	10,953	3,494	61,133

NOTE: Totals may not add up exactly, due to rounding.
SOURCE: *Statistical Abstract of the United States,* selected years, from original data from the American Hospital Association. Comparable figures are not available for later years.

sively efficient. Scitovsky shows the length of stay for myocardial infarction among the patients studied dropping from 19.7 days in 1964 to 10.6 days in 1981, and for breast cancer from 10.5 to 3.3 days. (Vaginal deliveries dropped from 3.8 to 1.9 days, barely time for a good sleep after the delivery.)[8] Hospitalization was now often an *incident* in illness, not coterminus with the illness itself. The hospital seemed less a health center than ever before, and more and more a mechanical treatment station.

Nevertheless, voluntary hospitals continued to operate on a good-faith basis, providing little evidence that the *value* of hospital services had increased in tandem with the costs. Charity-giving in its modern guise of providing expert medical care was assumed, in itself, to be enough, although arguments about increased value could certainly be made: dollar figures assigned, for example, to the value of the executive brought through a major heart attack or the elderly woman walking after a total hip replacement. As it was, almost all of the figures flying about after Medicare's implementation referred to dollar *expenditures* rather than to individual or social *benefits*. By the late 1960s, Medicare hearings in Congress rang with concern about "rapidly rising hospital costs," and there were increasing criticisms of program administration. Figured solely in dollar terms, hospitals and fiscal intermediaries (Blue Cross, overwhelmingly) appeared to be gaining at least as much from the program as were the elderly patients who were saving money on hospital bills. What actually happened to them in the hospital (and afterward) seemed curiously irrelevant, just as it had in previous decades. Hospitals were caught without a defense.

In 1966, however, when the Medicare legislation was implemented, the mood of all those concerned was bullish. The first priority was to get the program going by enrolling all those eligible, issuing Medicare cards, selecting fiscal intermediaries (for hospitals) and carriers for physicians, and developing basic guidelines for services, reimbursement, and administrative procedures. The channeling of federal funds through nongovernmental agencies, as well as government hospitals, followed the American pattern of the public-private mix. Officials from the national associations and Blue Cross worked successfully with federal officers to implement the program by the target date of July 1, 1966. By federal regulation Medicare would now pay hospitals the "reasonable cost" of providing services on behalf of virtually everyone in the United States sixty-five years of age or older, a total of 20 million persons in 1970—almost 10 percent of the entire population. However, as with the initial negotiations between hospitals and local Blue Cross plans in the 1930s, decisions had to be made as to exactly what would be paid for, and on what basis.

The existence of principles of payment for hospital care that were based on cost-based reimbursement per patient day made this task easier. All parties in 1965–66 wanted to conform with payment practices already followed by third-party payers.[9] Agreement on what should legitimately be included as reimbursable "costs" (and what not) within the Medicare reimbursement formula was hammered out in meetings between HEW officials and lawyers, Blue Cross, and other private representatives—meetings that Walter McNerney, president of the Blue Cross Association, was to describe as "gutsy and protracted."[10] This process of accommodation was eminently successful in launching the huge new program with maximum cooperation. However, intractable problems were not faced, including the ambivalent role of Blue Cross as an intermediary between hospitals and government. Medicare transformed Blue Cross, which became the dominant carrier for hospital reimbursement. By 1969 45 percent of the entire operating income of community hospitals was flowing to hospitals via Blue Cross/Blue Shield plans. Half of this represented their private insurance coverage and half represented Medicare.[11]

To the Social Security Administration, the federal agency administering the Medicare program, Blue Cross was its administrative arm or agent, that is, it had a delegated government function. But Blue Cross had a long historical allegiance to the hospitals and, in the absence of strong federal ground rules, thus inevitably had a dual accountability—actually, a triple accountability, if one includes a general responsibility to the public. What was Blue Cross to do when the interests of government and the hospitals conflicted? The initial answer was obvious: favor the hospitals. Indeed, the Blue Cross Association required good relationships with hospitals, both to get Medicare implemented and to maintain Blue Cross plans' market share. After the Medicare legislation was implemented, it was difficult to see Blue Cross, embarked on a wave of expansionism, either as an extended branch of government or as a community-sponsored agency of member hospitals.

It is interesting to speculate what might have happened if Blue Cross had become a quasi-public hospital-insurance scheme at the national level in the 1960s, with its own public-policy agenda. Perhaps it would have blossomed into a national public service corporation, administering new forms of national health insurance. But this is idle speculation, for Blue Cross was (and remains) a collection of largely autonomous local plans, which were riding their own wave of prosperity in the late 1960s. Moreover, even if Blue Cross had been unified and standardized on a national basis, it is not at all clear that it would have sought to strengthen its public role. The trend had been, rather, toward commercial competition. In the event, under Medicare, Blue Cross acted as if it were selling insurance administration services to government rather than acting as government's agent.

As sellers in a new, government-driven marketplace—with cost reimbursement—Blue Cross plans opened themselves up to direct competition from commercial insurers for Medicare business, and to challenges of their special, not-for-profit status. Senate hearings on the high cost of hospitalization in 1971 criticized Blue Cross plans as businesses. Concurrently, a suit brought by the Travelers Insurance Company against Blue Cross of Western Pennsylvania (Pittsburgh) accused the plan of violating antitrust laws and engaging in unfair competition.[12] Although the final decision by the Supreme Court in this case was ultimately favorable to Blue Cross, the handwriting was on the wall. Blue Cross plans were, for example, to lose their exemption from federal taxes in November 1986.

By 1970 voluntary hospitals, too, were under attack, although from two strangely conflicting perspectives. On the one hand, they were blamed for managerial inefficiency, but on the other, they were blamed for expert exploitation of the new market conditions. Either, it seemed, they were Machiavellian institutions poised to take advantage of any loophole in federal regulations *or* they were part of an outmoded system of "charity" that had no place in the late twentieth century. In fact, most voluntary hospitals probably did little differently in the early 1970s than they had done before Medicare, working under institutional objectives which assumed that ever more technology and more staff were in the public's interest—provided, of course, that money was available. And administrators were reluctant to make a conceptual leap in mission: from being public-spirited to market-driven corporations. Nevertheless, the traditional middle ground of voluntarism was insecure: that safe zone between government and commercialization, where autonomous organizations were left to function unmolested.

Were the voluntary hospitals to be able, any longer, to sit complacently, like medieval manor houses, on a rich and rightful social domain? The domain itself was being reconsidered—as a no-man's-land between two warring factions. For the first time, both government and private enterprise were becoming seriously interested in hospital control. Congressional committees eyed hospitals in the 1970s with a view to more effective regulation, while entrepreneurs saw Medicare's cost-plus system as a bonanza for profit-making.

As a result, there was no longer always an a priori argument for voluntary organizations as social institutions that were necessary because private enterprise was uninterested *and* because government enterprise was regarded as inappropriate. Voluntary-hospital lobbyists, administrators, and trustees uneasily contemplated the reasons for their existence— reasons that had previously seemed self-evident, if unspecified—and did so in an atmosphere of self-defense. What was a "voluntary" hospital? The shift was gradual, but seemingly inexorable. Paul Starr expresses the discouraged mood among hospital leaders in the early 1980s through his phrase the "decomposition of voluntarism,"[13] as if the very notion were rotting away. Hospital lobbyists began to grope for clearer, or at least more plausible definitions of "voluntarism" and "community," while they were castigated for ignoring "charity care."

Throughout the 1970s the hospitals responded to the main, initial messages of Medicare and Medicaid: to bring the poor and the elderly into the "mainstream" of medicine, while continuing to improve the services available to the upper- and middle-class population. These goals were unabashedly expansionist. By the early 1970s, however, the mainstream approach was politically dead, victim of the new federal commitment to "cost containment." Hospitals were caught out by the speed of this change. In an era of management rhetoric there was as yet no management ideology for voluntary institutions.

As economist Karen Davis pointed out in 1972, little attention was given in the first five years of Medicare to the motivation of those who controlled major decisions in the voluntary hospitals—either managers or physicians. (Similarly, little attention was initially given to the economic motivations of decision-makers in Blue Cross plans.) Hence the expressions of surprise mixed with outrage in congressional hearings and the media, by 1970, at galloping hospital expenditures. The average cost per patient day jumped from an annual 7.4 percent increase between 1963 and 1966 to 13.3 percent during the period 1966–69, to 15.7 percent in the year 1969–70. Net hospital income for voluntary hospitals rose from $227 million in 1965 to $400 million in 1969.[14] However, standard economic theories of behavior for nonprofit voluntary hospitals in the mid and late 1960s held that profit maximization was not a primary goal of such institutions, and perhaps not a goal at all. It was assumed that "public opinion opposes profit" and that the typical short-term hospital, as a "voluntary and charitable institution" was "not interested in making a profit as such," but was merely content to cover its costs.[15]

Under this model, charges were a derivative aspect of costs, while costs in turn derived from some hypothetical standards of reasonable utilization of services and reasonable patterns of admission—set by responsible doctors. This model was obviously useful to hospitals, if only because administrators could turn around and claim that pricing was a mere technicality, or, alternatively, blame physicians for rising costs. The hospitals appeared to be doing nicely. But it was not clear how well hospitals *should* do financially under contracts with federal programs. Nor was it clear how far the federal government should rely on autonomous, private not-for-profit organizations to set and achieve public goals.

A direct outcome of the historically weak, generally supportive federal role was the lack of any overarching philosophy of regulation. In the Johnson administration alone Congress enacted fifty-one pieces of health legislation, administered through four hundred different authorities, and often representing quite different health-care goals and administrative approaches. In some instances the Small Business Administration and the Hill-Burton program made grants and loans to competing hospitals in the same communities, with resulting overexpansion and waste of facilities.[16] It was difficult to praise the autonomous local institution in light of the lack of effective hospital planning. Although following the federal health-planning legislation of 1966, local comprehensive health-planning agencies appeared across the states—fifty-two at the state level and ninety-seven at the local level by mid-1969—these agencies had little authority to change the system. They had no money to give to hospitals for capital investment, no powers to curtail expansions, and none to enforce redirections. Like the university-based regional medical programs being set up at the same time, the health-planning agencies, which were federally funded local coalitions, succeeded (and often failed) on the basis of voluntary interinstitutional cooperation.

Trust in voluntary compliance also marked hospital utilization review. Under the Medicare legislation, participating hospitals were required to have utilization review committees. These committees were supposed to review patient care as a controlling safeguard against unnecessary and excessive hospital use. But hospitals, confident in their own autonomy, largely ignored utilization review. There had been little action in most hospitals since the early enthusiasm for scientific management and "efficiency committees" well before 1920; hospitals and their medical staffs were largely ignorant and generally uninterested in patient-care appraisal. A federal study undertaken in 1968 found that almost half the hospitals were not reviewing any admissions at all, even though this was a basic statutory requirement.[17] Nor were the fiscal intermediaries (largely Blue Cross) performing their legally mandated function of enforcing utilization review at the hospital level. In short, expectations about voluntarism conflicted. The hospitals' own assumptions of voluntarism continued to stress institutional autonomy (a general philosophy of "we know what we are doing") well into the Medicare period. Meanwhile, federal legislation assumed that national goals could be voluntarily achieved. There were no strong external controls to counter the incentives for institutional expansion built into hospital reimbursement mechanisms.

But Medicare was also a story of success, and these early experiences were, perhaps, a reasonable trade-off for the enormously successful implementation of the program. The initial impact of Medicare was increased utilization of short-stay hospitals by the elderly population. Expansion continued from the late 1960s through the 1970s. By 1979 America's elderly, those sixty-five years and over, were receiving, on average, 4.1 days of care in nonfederal short-stay hospitals per person per year. This rate was well over twice the rate of patients in the next-lowest age group (45 to 64 years of age). Hospitals in the South reported more discharges per 1,000 Medicare enrollees each year than any area, with the Northeast having the fewest, but the surgical rate was highest in the West. Almost one-third of all Medicare patients who were hospitalized had surgery in the first ten years of Medicare. The equivalent of 12 percent of the Medicare population were operated on in 1979 alone.[18] Hospitalization for cataract operations (now more usually done on an outpatient basis), the provision of artificial hips, and heroic measures in the later months of life encouraged acute medical intervention as part of the expected care of the elderly.

If such figures were seen as a part of a phenomenal success story, then rising expenditures on hospital services were the necessary cost built into the equation. However, Medicare did more than stimulate rising costs and focus congressional interest on national regulation. Through the reimbursement system the structure of the hospital system was also radically changed, despite the pious expectations of the Medicare legislation. The key here was hospital capital, and specifically, the mandated links between capital development and operating income.

Capital: The Keystone of the Arch

Medicare made hospital managers and entrepreneurs acutely aware of the games that could be played to maximize hospital income by including the costs of borrowing money in third-party reimbursement rates. The availability of Medicare reimbursement accelerated the preexisting trends toward borrowing funds for hospital capital projects and deemphasized the role of government grants and private gifts as the base funding for new buildings. Voluntary-hospital administrators, as well as for-profit hospital managers, began to view their budgets in terms of the institution's entire financial requirements, including operating expenses and capital as one package. Demands for capital were increasing—from the working capital necessary to keep an institution going pending delays in reimbursement, through funding for the development and start-up costs of new projects, to money to replace buildings and equipment and to add new services and facilities.[19] Far from making hospitals more "socialized," Medicare encouraged them to be more "capitalistic," in the most fundamental sense of this word.

This was not merely a matter of institutional self-interest. Hospitals had a public mandate—even a social duty—to expand, rebuild, and re-equip. President Johnson, in his health and education message of March 1965, claimed that one-third of the nation's hospital beds were in "obsolete condition."[20] A federal conference on medical costs estimated in 1967 that $10 billion was needed for hospital modernization, irrespective of the additional demands required to meet the expanded market of Medicare patients, and despite the enormous increases in hospital assets. Hospital services in the major cities were allegedly reaching a point of breakdown.[21] Rebuilding was expensive. By the end of the 1960s, existing plant assets in community hospitals, as recorded, averaged over $20,000 per bed;[22] and new construction cost much more than this.

If hospital or health-care planning had been a major focus of Medicare, Congress would have been well advised to make a clear division between the funding of capital projects and the reimbursement of services for Medicare patients; that is, to control the future direction of the hospital system by controlling capital expenditures. But Medicare was not designed to improve health services across the board; its prime purpose was to protect the incomes of the elderly against catastrophic hospital bills (and to do so without rocking too many boats).

Over and above this, the federal government's major incursion into hospital construction, the Hill-Burton program, was now being roundly criticized. Despite shifts in the program over the years, including grants for hospital modernization and urban services from 1964, Hill-Burton had a minimal impact on hospitals in the inner cities, which were not a program priority; nor did Hill-Burton funds come anywhere near the total cost of the massive construction programs of the 1960s. Hill-Burton provided less than one-fifth of the overall construction costs in voluntary not-for-profit institutions in 1965 and less than one-fourth in state and local government institutions (table 11.2).

Voluntary hospitals were still heavily dependent on private contribu-

TABLE 11.2

Reported Construction Costs of Selected Nonprofit and Governmental Hospitals and Source of Funding, 1965

	Percentage	
	Voluntary Nonprofit	State and Local Government
Hill-Burton	19.2	23.4
Bonding Indebtedness by Taxing Agency	3.2	56.9
Long-term borrowing	21.0	8.1
Private contributions	40.7	0.9
Hospital reserves	11.1	6.8
Other	4.8	3.9
	100.0	100.0
Number of hospitals surveyed	78	27
Total construction for these hospitals ($ millions)	158	35

SOURCE: Jeffrey Lynn Stambaugh, "A Study of the Sources of Capital Funds for Hospital Construction in the United States," *Inquiry* 4 (June 1967), pp. 14, 17.

tions. But increasingly—and significantly—they were also entering into long-term debt and building up their own capital reserves. These latter sources together represented over one-third of estimated voluntary non-profit construction costs even in 1965. Table 11.3 shows the declining role of both government funds and philanthropy—and the increasing role of debt in capital formation—as hospitals entered the 1970s.

Planning goals were also in conflict. A problem with Hill-Burton as a tool for consolidation of the hospital system stemmed from its overt support of the capital-intensive, local institution. Two-thirds of the Hill-

TABLE 11.3

Funding Sources for Hospital Construction, 1968–81, Selected Years

	Percentage			
	1968	1973	1978	1981
Philanthropy	21	10	6	4
Government	23	21	16	12
Internal reserves	16	15	17	15
Debt	38	54	61	69

NOTE: Figures for 1968 add up to 98 percent rather than 100 percent in original source.
SOURCE: "American Hospital Association Surveys of Sources of Funding for Hospital Construction," Reported in AHA *Hospital Capital Finance,* Fourth Quarter 1985, p. 4.

Burton funds to general hospital projects between the mid-1940s and the mid-1960s were given to smaller towns and rural areas, greatly strengthening the role of the rural hospital. These same institutions scrambled to upgrade their facilities in the late 1960s and 1970s in order to incorporate the latest in hospital technique—passing the cost along to private third parties and to Medicare. Between 1962 and 1975, for example, almost half of all hospitals of under 100 beds adopted respiratory therapy, one-fourth added diagnostic radioisotopes, and a fifth acquired electroencephalograph equipment. By 1969 over half of the not-for-profit hospitals reported intensive care units, compared with one-seventh in 1961.[23] Each hospital, however small, was becoming a well-equipped technical center.

Without any effective local coordination or regional assignment of specialist services—and with reimbursements tied to what the market would bear—overlap and duplication were inevitable. Meanwhile, hospitals did a roaring trade. The average occupancy rate was over 75 percent in 1980; and there were two surgical operations for every three admissions.[24] The rate of surgical operations in short-stay hospitals rose from 77 per 1,000 population in 1965 to 109 per 1,000 in 1980 (in comparison the rate was 62 per 1,000 in the period 1928–31).

The significant aspect of funding capital from debt and internal reserves is that both draw—continuously—from the hospital's operating income. Borne along on a wave of expansionism, hospitals supplemented Hill-Burton funds and private gifts by building up reserves from operating surpluses. (Reserves may also include proceeds from sales of replaced assets and, for investor-owned facilities, from stock sold to investors.) It was not surprising, then, that the inclusion of reimbursement for borrowing capital was a major item in negotiations for Medicare reimbursement regulations. As Anne and Herman Somers observed in their careful study of the implementation of Medicare, the hospitals' drive to increase funds for capital formation "colored and complicated every major dispute on payment."[25] Medicare reimbursement from the beginning included a specified allocation for the funding of depreciation. For every patient bill there was a small addition targeted for hospital reserves, although hospitals were not initially required to set up specific depreciation funds.

This welcome sweetening was further enhanced by redefining the depreciation formula. Before Medicare almost all of the third parties that paid depreciation based the amount on the original or historical costs of specific assets. However, the American Hospital Association revised its *Principles of Payment* in August 1965 to define depreciation in terms of *current* replacement costs. (A contemporary estimate suggested that the average replacement costs of a hospital capital investment of $600,000 in 1945 would be almost $1.3 million in 1965.)[26] An additional 2 percent of reimbursable operating costs was added to the original Medicare formula, an item described by the American Hospital Association as a "capital improvement payment."[27] In a marked break from tradition, for-profit hospitals received in turn a "reasonable return on equity capital" as part of the allowable costs to be reimbursed under Medicare. Thus both types of hospitals were encouraged to spend.

Implementation of Medicare—and its further modification—required voluntary-hospital administrators to develop skills in two vital areas: financial management and practical politics. Marketing was to be added as a "must" by the early 1980s. With the wide adoption of the new mainframe computers in hospitals during the 1960s and 1970s, data-processing centers for billing and management became as ubiquitous in hospitals as intensive care units. However, only gradually, through the 1970s, did hospital financial management come into its own as a specialized field. Berman and Weeks' textbook *The Financial Management of Hospitals* first appeared in 1971 and was in its fourth edition in 1979. By then it was obvious, as the authors stated, that "hospitals are big business. In fact, hospitals are one of the biggest industries in the country." Depreciation had become "an expense of doing business, whether in a supermarket or in a community hospital." And decisions involving capital investment choices were likely to be the "most crucial" decisions for a hospital manager throughout his or her professional career.[28]

Organizations (and individuals) that were already oriented toward capital development and profit maximization had a head start in the early years of Medicare. The rapid expansion of proprietary nursing homes from the early 1960s, when the Kerr-Mills legislation was enacted, attested to the potential profitability of health-care institutions, once income was virtually guaranteed by government; of 22,000 nursing homes in 1971, 17,000 were profit-making. Medicare and Medicaid, guaranteeing full-cost reimbursement for expensive and financially risky hospital patients, suggested a similar bonanza in the hospital field. Through the new programs (and through Medicare's ripple effects on private health-insurance schemes) profit-making firms could accumulate capital for the acquisition and construction of new facilities, passing on their costs—and generating profits—via accepted patient-reimbursement procedures.

In the late 1960s, as a direct result of Medicare, investor-owned hospital chains appeared as a new presence on the hospital scene.[29] By 1970 there were twenty-nine such chains, each owning two or more hospitals, the largest then being American Medicorp Inc., with thirty-one hospitals, and Hospital Corporation of America with twenty-three.[30] For the most part, the growth of chains occurred through the acquisition of existing proprietary hospitals in exchange for stock in the chain. Proprietary hospitals as a whole (those in chains and those remaining independent) represented only 13 percent of all nonfederal short-term hospitals in 1970. Nevertheless, their sudden visibility on the national scene was initially shocking to voluntary-hospital representatives, both with respect to their operating assumptions—the language of capitalistic profit-making—and in their phenomenal success.

"Your Company," reported Humana to its stockholders in 1976, "is a major participant in one of the fastest growing industries in the country." No other industry listed in *U.S. Industrial Outlook,* it was reported, including the computer and business-machine industry, soft drinks, and electronic components, could match the hospital industry's 13.8 percent annual growth rate.[31] The language of the chains was the language of business: of operating revenues, net income, dividends, and shares; of descriptions of hospitals as "profitable" and of overt discussion of significant competition. Hospital Corporation of America, which billed itself as the "world's largest hospital management company," pronounced its "fundamental belief that private enterprise can deliver a superior quality of health care at a reasonable cost using private capital, paying all property and income taxes and providing the finest facilities and equipment available."[32]

Investor-owned hospital chains had a phenomenal success on the U.S. stock market in the 1970s. Although the overall number of for-profit hospitals remained relatively stable during the decade—there were 769 such hospitals in 1970, 730 in 1980—the advent of the chains implied substantial rearrangements within the profit-making sector. The chains raised capital not only through long-term debt but also through issuing common stock and through the purchase and immediate reevaluation of preexisting hospitals. (This latter practice was also available to not-for-profit chains.) Reevaluation allowed both for the raising of additional capital through debt financing and for higher cost-reimbursement rates for depreciation. One chain (unnamed) was reported by the federal Bureau of Health Insurance in 1970 as claiming for one hospital a book value of approximately $277,000 but a sale price of $4.8 million. The chain hoped to claim the amount as a cost basis for depreciation reimbursement under Medicare.[33] However, the value of a hospital was difficult to determine in the early years of Medicare, because voluntary not-for-profit hospitals had rarely, if ever, had to think of "value" in terms of a potential sale price in the marketplace. Figures on hospital assets reported to the AHA from the late 1940s were useful in establishing relative growth and relative position for the various hospital sectors, and they did indeed record the phenomenal growth of the for-profit sector, from $.4 billion in 1965 to $3.5 billion in 1977, a much greater rate of growth than the voluntary and governmental sector.[34] But these figures became meaningless in an era of massive long-term debt and stock market speculation.

The growth of for-profit enterprise in the hospital sector provoked two immediate reactions: widespread concern about the appropriateness of profit-making in the health-care system and entrepreneurial behavior in the voluntary sector. Specific concerns were expressed about the soliciting and selling of stock in proprietary hospitals to local doctors, with its implicit conflict of interest; the possible cream-skimming of "desirable" (i.e., income-producing) patients by for-profit hospitals, leaving the indigent as dead financial weight on voluntary institutions; the lack of interest by for-profit hospital chains in teaching and research in the early years of Medicare, although the balance was to shift as the chains matured; and broader philosophical issues about the use of a major federal program as a vehicle for stimulating profits in the private sector.[35] Were doctors and hospitals of the future to be seen as overtly profit-making entities? Was the assumption of trust in professionals and in their associated nonprofit institutions to be jettisoned in favor of caveat emptor? The answer appeared to be "yes." But if so, voluntarism could no longer claim its old, vague meanings of private charity and public benevolence.

The importance of federal policy in stimulating a capitalistic hospital system cannot be overstated. Nor was Medicare the only target, for Hill-Burton fell out as a casualty. In the spring of 1969, heralding the new trends toward private enterprise, HEW Secretary Robert Finch proposed a "radical redirection" of the Hill-Burton program to one of guaranteed loans to stimulate private capital.[36] As the Hill-Burton program came under fire from the Nixon administration in the late 1960s and was folded into the National Health Planning and Resources Development Act of 1974, federal hospital construction funds faded from the scene. Now as earlier, hospitals (and associated hospital chains) were responsible for their own capital formation. The difference was that now capital costs were regarded as a reasonable element of the cost to be reimbursed for patient care.

Capital signifies power and influence. A hospital which derives most of its capital from local donations may truly say that it is a community institution. But one which borrows from the bank or sells bonds acquires new partners, with their own agendas. A gift-giver may get, in exchange, a feeling of duty done and pride in a local institution, but a bondholder looks for financial return. By going into debt the voluntary hospitals thus jeopardized their independence. Voluntary hospitals increased their debt levels from approximately 40 percent of their total capital financing in the late 1960s to 80 percent in 1981. Approximately 80 percent of all debt financing was through tax exempt bonds. By 1981, as table 11.3 shows, government controlled only 12 percent of total funding for hospital construction.

Investor-owned hospitals reported a mix of debt and equity funding (the issuance of stock). Government-owned hospitals also greatly increased their debt level so that their funding patterns, too, shifted radically between the late 1960s and the early 1980s—from primary reliance on government subsidy to primary reliance on debt. By the 1980s, then, all short-term hospitals in the United States were attuned to borrowing, meeting the expenses of borrowing through rises in reimbursement rates or from other sources, including for some the issuance of stock.

The search for additional capital (and income) also prompted hospitals to develop new, profit-making businesses—including management companies, parking lots, and the selling of computer software. In order to spin off profit-making enterprises, voluntary hospitals restructured themselves into an array of corporations, some of which were not-for-profit while others were overtly businesses. Thus another result of Medicare and its aftermath was to muddy the definition of the "voluntary" institution by weakening its nonprofit nature. Voluntary institutions were behaving pragmatically in their search for income. But if the for-profit form was appropriate for some voluntary-hospital subsidiaries, it could be argued—and it was—that the non-profit form itself, including tax exemption, was a matter of convenience rather than mission.

In terms of generating capital the Medicare policies were enormously successful. Overall capital expenses are approximately 6 or 7 percent of hospital operating revenues, on average. The higher the revenues, the higher the amount of capital that may be raised. Thus capital and operating expenses rose together in a symbiotic relationship. The total expenses of nonfederal short-term general and related special hospitals were on an apparently unstoppable trajectory—rising from $5.6 billion in 1960, through $9.1 billion in 1965, to $77 billion in 1980, and on to $140 billion in 1986.

However, the proprietary ownership of capital—that is, the responsibility of hospitals for raising capital through the markets and through payment for services given—took voluntary hospitals across a critical conceptual bridge. No longer heavily dependent on community gifts and fund drives, voluntary hospitals were no longer gaining capital from "public" sources on a voluntary basis, that is, from their local communities. Instead, in their capital formation voluntary hospitals were now similar to major business corporations. By emphasizing technology rather than the rapid expansion of community service, for which reimbursement was largely unavailable, hospitals also bought into the technological conception of capitalism. The president of the Blue Cross and Blue Shield Association, Walter McNerney, was to capture the new image of the hospital nicely in the early 1980s when he called it a "technological emporium."[37]

Reactions against the egalitarian (welfare) assumptions and profligate spending of the Great Society programs of the 1960s furthered the ethos of market competition over the extension of the welfare state. By the late 1960s the federal government appeared to be an intrinsically inefficient institution, unable to win wars on communism abroad or poverty at home. The successive domestic policies of the Nixon, Ford, Carter, and Reagan administrations stressed the primacy of private enterprise as a force for innovation and attacked big government on principle. Competition justified the denigration of equal opportunity, while public roles were implicitly less valuable than private endeavors. Now it was private (business) organizations that were intrinsically "good"—supposedly more imaginative and efficient than other types of institution. From the discovery, in the Nixon administration, of the supposed superiority of the free-market model as a means of reorganizing the health-care system, to the decentralist political policies of the Carter administration—and beyond—"competition" was valued as the alternative to "regulation."

This broader set of shifts made it even less plausible for voluntary hospitals to present themselves as "public" institutions. In the early 1970s phrases such as "laissez faire" and "regulation," applied to health services, were regularly presented as if they were alternatives (which they are not), somewhat along the lines of capitalism versus socialism. Either, it seemed, the health-care system was doomed to a socialized, highly regulated future or it could be "saved" by American know-how and vigor in the private sector. Hence the Nixon administration's "health maintenance strategy" of 1970 was presented as a means of restructuring the "medical marketplace" around decentralized, private, competitive institutions—the newly conceived health maintenance organizations (HMOs).[38] There was an implicit assumption that governmental institutions were bogged down, uncreative, and inefficient. Sheltered by the new rhetoric of the 1970s and lured by Medicare's financial incentives, the voluntary hospitals rushed to redefine themselves as private, efficient, market-oriented corporations.

Direct attacks on not-for-profit institutions from the mid-1970s completed the bombardment of the voluntary hospital. In 1975 the Federal Trade Commission began investigating the medical profession on grounds of suspected antitrust activities. The informal professional pact against physician advertising, for example, was now criticized as unacceptable collusion by doctors for business reasons rather than as part of a profession's long accepted principles of medical ethics. Accreditation of medical schools by professional groups (and by analogy, accreditation of hospitals) became anticompetitive devices to protect monopolistic groups. The slow growth of HMOs was attributed, in part, to "anti-competitive conduct engaged in by practitioners of fee-for-service medicine."[39] And physician influence over Blue Cross and Blue Shield suggested further conspiratorial activities. With the spotlight on physicians, who were the FTC's main focus of attack, hospitals had much to gain in stressing, in contrast, their own entrepreneurial, aggressively competitive behavior. Hospital marketing began to flourish. It was not surprising that the voluntary hospitals, instead of attempting to fight the engulfing tide of competition, looked to the investor-owned chains as models for their own organizational justification. It was difficult not to, in any event. Investor-owned companies had become heroes of the leading financial journals.

By 1980 hospitals seemed obsessed with the language of management. Instead of an increased emphasis on chronic care and social services after the advent of Medicare and Medicaid—not an unreasonable expectation in programs dedicated to the elderly and poor—hospital administrative-training programs began to require courses in financial management. Administrators became managers, presidents, or CEOs; and the hospital journals rang with news of "product lines" (patient care), of capital financing, of diversification and innovation, and of the "bottom line." Sparked by the potential economic demand for care represented by Medicare and Medicaid, hospital management companies grew rapidly, offering private investors some of the hottest stocks in the market. As a result, although the number of for-profit hospitals declined (partly through consolidation) between 1965 and 1980, the number of beds and of patient admissions in them increased, largely within the investor-owned systems, with particular expansion in the traditionally strong proprietary areas in the South and West. Admissions to profit-making hospitals almost doubled—from 1.8 million in 1965 to 3.2 million in 1980.[40] Their organization, the Federation of American Hospitals, with its own journal, became a visible presence on the national scene. (It is now the Federation of American Health Systems.)

From the practical point of view, the growth of the for-profit hospital chains showed the value of large-scale mobilization of resources and centralized support services, including capital fund-raising and consulting, while no one could deny their phenomenal success. A Standard & Poor's report on the "fundamental position" of Hospital Corporation of America for 1975 showed that net income had advanced 32.8 percent over the previous year, while future revenues were expected to benefit from the addition of new equipment, increasing occupancy at newer hospitals, and increased outpatient revenues; 30 percent of its entire revenue was drawn from Medicare. Most of the "company facilities" were said to provide general medical and surgical care for short-term patients and included operating rooms, recovery rooms, X-ray and electrocardiograph facilities, medical laboratories, and pharmacies. Of the sixty-two hospitals owned by HCA at the end of 1975, fifty-six were already accredited by the Joint Commission on Accreditation. Fifteen new projects were under construction and long-term debt of over $270 million had already been incurred.[41] With other companies rising in tandem, voluntary-hospital administrators could only be worried and confused—and impressed.

But the climate of competition in general, and the investor-owned sector in particular, also gave the voluntary hospitals the go-ahead to do what they wished: that is, to continue to expand in services and equipment, to present an ultramodern image, to be seen as emblems of American success, to exclude unprofitable patients and services where possible, and to oppose government regulation. Most significantly, the establishment of major not-for-profit *systems* heralded a significant change in the voluntary-hospital sector and its power structures in the 1970s, a change which was largely overshadowed by the growth of the profit-making chains.

One of the earliest examples of not-for-profit chains was the Kaiser hospitals, together with their associated medical groups and prepaid insurance plans, after World War II. Another early example was Great Plains Lutheran Hospitals Inc. of Phillipsburg, Kansas, established in the 1950s to provide management services for small community hospitals built under Hill-Burton. Others followed quickly. Indeed, the evolution of multiple hospital management was sufficiently advanced that Duke University sponsored a national forum on the subject in 1965. A follow-up conference ten years later described a steadily evolving movement, emerging in response to the conflicting demands being placed on hospitals: pressures from the federal government through Medicare; comprehensive health-planning legislation; the erosion of Hill-Burton; the impact of economic stabilization programs; the emergence of state rate structures for hospitals; and amendments to the Taft-Hartley legislation (in 1974), bringing unionization to hospitals with a vengeance. Employee attitudes in voluntary hospitals were changing, it was claimed; now hospital work was "just a job."[42]

Church-related hospitals were also beginning to perceive their mutual interests. By the mid-1970s the Roman Catholic Sisters of Mercy were in the process of organizing multiunit corporations. Eight of the nine regions

or "provinces" of the Sisters of Mercy in the United States sponsored
hospitals, a total of 125 hospitals in all. Historically, these hospitals had
never been unified; indeed, there were recognized jealousies among different branches of the order. But external factors were now stimulating
these hospitals, as well as others, to cooperate. In the Detroit Province of
the Sisters of Mercy, for example, five multiunit corporations were established between 1965 and 1975, at Detroit; Grand Rapids; Lansing; Hammond, Indiana; and Dubuque, Iowa.[43] Similarly, Intermountain Health
Care was founded by a group of Morman hospitals in Utah, and other
major systems were developing as well.

Out of these efforts, as well as the drives of the investor-owned
systems, would come the huge hospital systems we have today. By 1982
one of every three U.S. hospitals, with nearly 36 percent of the nation's
hospital beds, belonged to a multihospital system.[44] By 1987 not-for-profit
chains with more than 4,000 hospital beds in the United States (some also
ran hospitals overseas) included the Adventist Health Systems (administered from Arlington, Texas), Sisters of Charity Health Care System (Cincinnati), Sisters of Mercy of the Union (St. Louis), Catholic Health Corporation (Omaha), and Sisters of Charity Health Care System (Houston).[45]

Paradoxes and problems accompanied all of these new trends. While
seeking an aggressive market stance, voluntary hospitals experienced a
weakening of their historical base as local community institutions, jetti-
soning traditional reliance on local gifts and donations, and forming affiliations with hospitals outside their immediate areas. At the same time,
the hospitals were setting up new dependencies on outside financing and
regulatory agencies. Hospitals which had long been proud of their ability
to respond rapidly to changing conditions locked themselves into a huge
burden of debt that would obviously constrain their future operations.
Capital expenditures were linked to complicated reimbursement for-
mulae—and these were in turn managed by Medicare, Medicaid, and Blue
Cross, in the main. The more money hospitals borrowed, the more vulnerable they became to external expectations (including those of the federal
government). The more businesslike the hospitals, the more dependent
they were on a new army of experts: tax and bond advisers, corporate
lawyers, software specialists, management experts, politicians. Voluntary-
hospital administrators had not (yet) fully faced the fact that the business
model comes with a price: that business corporations are more closely
regulated than government or nonprofit agencies, if only to provide the
basic rules for effective competition. Hospitals, too, would be standardized
and regulated in the 1980s, with respect both to "process" and to
"product."

A basic element of market competition was missing, however. Although the capitalist model in its purest form assumes selling to individual consumers, by 1980 more than 92 percent of hospital expenditures were flowing through organized third parties: government, Blue Cross, and major insurance corporations. Continued hospital growth depended on the willingness of these and other powerful external groups to fund services at wished-for levels—including major employers, who contributed to private health-insurance premiums as a cost of doing business. Hospital policy in the 1970s, and later, thus rang with contradictory claims. Side by side with the free-market drives for untrammeled institutional competition, Medicare costs (and taxes) rose—and so did public complaints, accompanied by calls for the elimination of fraud and waste, for more effective planning, and for cost containment. The development and implementation of Medicare forced voluntary hospitals simultaneously—and ironically— into the ethos of the marketplace and the glare of public criticism—to be, in short, both more "private" and more "public."

Planning and the Politics of Debt

Left out of the marketplace equation were the powerful themes of access and availability, that is, the opportunity for all Americans to avail themselves of medical technology where needed, without difficult barriers of cost or distance. In the early 1970s some form of national health insurance seemed inevitable. A major report (the Perloff report) submitted to the board of trustees of the American Hospital Association in 1970 asserted that health care was "an inherent legal right of the individual and of all the people of the United States."[46] The American Hospital Association wrote its own national health insurance plan, Ameriplan. Under this scheme state-regulated health-care corporations would be set up, either not-for-profit or for-profit, with most services provided on a capitation basis and financing drawn from both federal and private sources.

However, the first, enthusiastic wave of national health insurance proposals in the early 1970s failed in 1974, victim of the post-Watergate elections and of the cycle of recession, inflation, and backlash against Great Society programs that distinguished the mid-1970s. The imposition of wage and price controls on hospitals in 1971—an attempt to stem spiraling inflation—angered hospital representatives, who fought unsuccessfully for exemption from wage and price controls. (States attempted an alternative form of regulation through state rate-setting programs, analogous to rate-setting for public utilities.) Although the American Hospital Association did not rescind its support of rate review and universal health insurance, its active advocacy ceased. The evident fact that the federal government did not trust hospitals to regulate themselves as responsible, quasi-public agencies thrust them more deeply into a political stance that was antigovernmental and procompetitive, giving them the green light to proceed, with political impunity, in the direction of the marketplace. Nevertheless, government controls of some sort were inevitable, in order to match the social goals of Medicare and Medicaid with the obvious inequalities of the unregulated marketplace.

At the same time, the urge to democratize the planning process meant the demise of many preexisting voluntary areawide planning agencies. Comprehensive health-planning (CHP) agencies, set up under legislation of 1966 (PL 89-49), provided federal funding to states for statewide planning, for the establishment of areawide or metropolitan health-planning agencies at the local level, and for training a new type of professional in health-care planning. But it took two to four years to organize an areawide planning agency, and an enormous amount of time was spent in defining the specific mix of consumers and providers who would be members of the boards. Although there were at least 150 such agencies by 1974, many were still organizing themselves.

Over and above this, there was the intractable difficulty in expecting local hospitals and other health agencies to plan their services cooperatively, for the good of the community, while the fiscal incentives for capital pushed hospitals, the dominant health-care institution, in the opposite direction. The working assumptions behind the CHP legislation assumed, once again, that knowledge of problems would build consensus and that this in turn would lead to action. This philosophy was expounded in the 1968 report of a major committee set up by the U.S. Department of Health, Education, and Welfare to review hospital effectiveness (the Barr Committee). It was easy to specify the problems:

> Two new hospitals, both half empty, within a few blocks of each other in one city neighborhood; half a dozen hospitals in another city equipped and staffed for open heart surgery, where the number of cases would barely keep one of the centers busy; empty beds the rule rather than the exception in obstetric and pediatric services across the nation; aged chronically ill patients lying idle in $60 a day hospital beds because no nursing home beds are provided;

overloaded emergency rooms, and under-used facilities and services that have been created for reasons of prestige rather than need.[47]

However, the Barr Committee, composed of major figures within hospitals and associated health-care fields, stopped short at how planning should be achieved—even what it should do. The report merely urged that the hospital service remain "complex and pluralistic" without any "simplistic solution," and endorsed comprehensive health planning as a panacea. Sociologist Robert Alford described hospital planning aptly as a form of symbolic reassurance.[48] In the event, the health planning agencies were primarily important in testing consensus in the 1970s. They brought together various local constituencies, and they proved that there was no effective consensus for a voluntary program of hospital regionalism. Actual planning decisions were being made through financial markets.

The American Hospital Association, although strongly supporting voluntary health planning in the late 1960s as a means of achieving a middle position, pushed for controlled competition of new construction through state-mandated certificate-of-need (CON) legislation. New York was the first state to adopt a certificate-of-need law, in 1964, requiring state approval of construction through investment controls. And certificate-of-need laws took off rapidly from 1968. By 1972 twenty-three states and the District of Columbia had adopted CON legislation with specific arrangements varying among the states. All of these states required certification (i.e., permission) for new construction over a specified investment. Most of the CON statutes in effect in the early 1970s stated explicitly that decisions should be based on state or areawide plans. Thus CON was linked with the emerging comprehensive health-planning program, giving it one clear focus.

During the 1970s endless discussions took place at the local and state level on specific hospital requests for building, accompanied by overt and behind-doors bargaining as each hospital sought success. Even here, however, the effect was equivocal. A widely circulated study by David Salkever and Thomas Bice in the late 1970s suggested that controlling one channel of expansion merely diverted capital into another—in short, that the CON laws did not significantly affect total investment by hospitals, although there was change in the type of investment.[49] CON programs appeared to lead to a lower growth of bed supply than might otherwise have been achieved, together with a higher growth of plant assets per bed, but as a form of total capital expenditures control, CON had obvious limitations. There was game-playing at every level.

An important effect of the shifting policy environment of the 1970s was that quantitative criteria assumed great significance—indeed, standardization became as important a theme for hospitals in the 1970s and 1980s as it had been in the 1920s. New health systems agencies (HSAs), set up under PL 93-641 (1974) to replace the comprehensive health-planning agencies, were required to develop plans for health-resource and health-status needs for the population residing within each of 205 designated health-service areas, based on specified national goals. A goal was set, for example, of 4 acute beds per 1,000 population for the country (a figure lower than the norms circulating in the 1920s). Since approximately 20 percent of the HSA areas fell below this federally mandated goal in the late 1970s, this form of standardization was inherently expansionist; thus once again federal policy was contradictory, pushing toward expansion while proclaiming cost containment. Although the purpose of "scientific" standards was generally applauded, a storm of protest erupted in 1977 when the Department of Health, Education, and Welfare issued guidelines that appeared to mandate hospital closings, particularly in rural areas, by providing funds to enable closings to take place; and local champions rose in wrath. In this respect, as in other ways, experience demonstrated that planning is a highly political endeavor.

The HSAs lost even on their most visible effort: to limit the supply of computed tomographic (CT) scanners, which first appeared in the United States in 1973. By 1978 there was one CT scanner per 100,000 population in Indiana—compared with one per 1 million population in Canada (which had a national health insurance scheme) and one per 2 million population in Great Britain (with a national health service).[50] There were strong arguments for the value of CT scanning as a major diagnostic improvement over conventional X-ray techniques; money was available through third-party reimbursement; hospital administrators and boards manipulated local HSA hearings; and groups of doctors, who, like the hospitals, were effective entrepreneurs in the 1970s, readily subverted the planning system by buying CT scanners outside hospitals, where they were not subject to HSA regulation. Canny hospital administrators contracted for CT with a group of radiologists, sometimes leasing them hospital facilities.

By 1980 HSAs were limping along toward elimination. Norms, it was clear, were not enough; the only effective norms were those that were enforceable through effective regulation or made irresistible through fiscal incentives. But by 1980 effective regulation had not been achieved. President Carter, abandoning a major fight for hospital cost-control legislation in 1978, blamed the "selfish concerns" of the hospital and medical lobby for its failure.[51] But from the hospitals' point of view government regulation piled on additional costs and harassment. Government and the hospitals were now antagonists.

Meanwhile, major health insurance schemes (including Blue Cross), HMOs, and major local employers began to see that they, too, had a potentially important long-term role to play in hospital control, including control of hospital facilities, because they controlled the purse strings. As hospitals responded to Medicare, therefore, and hospital expenditures escalated, groups of third-party payers began to see their own interests more clearly and to recognize their emerging power and status. In the late 1970s, congressional staff, Medicare officials, and business executives in major corporations began to criticize the cost of the biases built into a high-technology hospital system. Joseph Califano, who was secretary of health, education, and welfare in the Carter administration and later adviser on health policy for the Chrysler Corporation, put the case succinctly. Rather than being "institutions of last resort," hospitals had become "settings of first choice for treating too many minor ailments, especially when the insurance coverage was good."[52]

This rethinking of the hospital's mission echoed much earlier criticisms of its role—but now the driving force was cash. In 1982 Chrysler found it was paying more than $300 million a year for health care but "didn't know what it was buying or from whom." The response was to collect detailed information, develop audits, screen hospital admissions, control length of stay, and press for outpatient over inpatient services wherever possible. As a result, Chrysler reported health costs $20 million under its original budget for 1983, and $58 million for 1984. Chrysler was by no means alone. The stage was set for major transformations of hospitals in the 1980s, including the rapid development of outpatient surgery, reduced inpatient utilization across the board, controls on individual admissions, and a major restructuring of the incentives built into inpatient reimbursement (via prospective reimbursement schemes).

Federal policy designed to create a competitive market among hospitals thus generated, in turn, new and powerful foci for policy-making that were only in part governmental. Instead of planning for the future organization of hospitals through direct control of capital, Medicare and other third parties, including major corporations and private insurers, were assuming an indirect but powerful control of hospital service through purchase contracts—including the development of standards for participating institutions and specifying what services would be covered. Hospitals were faced by 1980 with the need for boundary negotiations in two areas simultaneously: in the private markets of contract negotiation, finance, and salesmanship, and in the public fishbowl of national politics.

The Death of Charity?

For decades voluntary hospitals had been seeking governmental responsibility for the poor and socially dependent. Medicare and Medicaid, apparently assuming responsibility for these groups, might be seen as a vindication of the hospitals' long-held position. With cost reimbursement, giving services free to patients through "hospital charity" seemed dead; now hospitals were merely—and clearly—vendors. But the apparent death of charity—charity, that is, as free care—also suggested that hospitals were not "charities." Hospitals were now vendors of services, moreover, not to the clients themselves or even to their local governments—people they knew, with offices down the road, whom they might see at lunch in restaurants, and whose activities were reported in the local press—but to organizational abstractions: to the federal Medicare and state Medicaid programs and to other third parties. This distancing of responsibility further weakened the idea of charity in (and by) local communities.

Indeed, so strong was the shift away from local responsibility that it had major spillover effects on the behavior of local government hospitals, too, in cities with a heterogeneous hospital system. Viewing the high cost of their tax-supported hospitals with a jaundiced eye, hard-pressed city governments rushed to argue that the new federal and federal-state programs had made the "public" (i.e., tax-supported) hospital outmoded and unnecessary, since the elderly and poor now had the right to care in "private" hospitals. As an unanticipated by-product, Medicare and Medicaid thus promoted a doctrine of institutional irresponsibility for the poor among both voluntary and city-owned institutions.

The "one class" or "mainstream" ethos of medical care in the 1960s suggested that the largest city hospitals either be abolished or upgraded. City hospitals in the major cities were described by a New York medical school dean in 1967, one year after Medicare was implemented, as "badly run, impoverished, long-neglected fleabags."[53] City hospitals, wrote the New York City health commissioner, would be inferior as long as they remained the residual system for the voluntary hospitals.[54] The director of the University of Michigan Hospital, foreseeing a loss in the traditional clientele, remarked, "Even if the patient feared he would be used for teaching and experimentation, he had no alternative but to come anyway or stay home and suffer."[55] Meanwhile, in Philadelphia, controversy over policemen and firemen treated at the city hospital led to charges that at least four city employees had died because of the wrong diagnosis.[56]

By the late 1960s tax-supported hospitals which were the heritage of the old almshouse tradition were in crisis in Chicago, Boston, New York, and Minneapolis; and their role has continued to be ambivalent. (In contrast, local-government hospitals which have traditionally served all social classes have continued along an independent path.) Harlem Hospital staff severely curtailed services for a month, protesting hospital conditions. Cook County house staff bought a full-page advertisement in the *Chicago Sun-Times,* proclaiming, "The Hospitals Are Dying and the Doctors Are Helpless." The faculty council of Louisiana State University Medical School predicted medical disaster unless more funds were made available for the state's Charity Hospital in New Orleans, and St. Louis City Hospital lost its accreditation. Doctors revolted at Boston City Hospital in the summer of 1968, while 200 of Kansas City (Missouri) General Hospital's 500 beds were slated to be closed and 150 employees dismissed.[57] Meanwhile, rising property taxes, competing city services, and high employment made hospitals less useful political vehicles for city administrations. With high employment there was less call for hospitals as employers of last resort and as sources of political patronage.

In theory, government hospitals are unnecessary in a "contract state." Government agencies specify what needs to be bought, as a matter of public policy. Where they buy goods and services is irrelevant, provided the contract conditions are met. Thus the old almshouse hospitals were left in limbo. Did they have a social mission at all? Do they have a function outside of being teaching institutions? If they are successful as entrepreneurs in the stakes for patient payments, why not "privatize" them, that is, reorganize them as private nonprofit or for-profit agencies? From the late 1960s to the present these hospitals have existed in a climate of tension. Some have closed; some have chosen management by outside firms, usually for-profit companies; some have sought to strengthen their "public" mission. In this latter vein, three attending physicians at a New York City municipal hospital wrote to the *New York Times* in 1987 praising the city's commitment to care for people "abandoned by everyone else," and called it a system to be proud of, speaking to the public conscience.[58] But this is looking ahead. There were difficult philosophical, ethical, and economic questions enmeshed in the relative futures of all kinds of hospitals under the immediate impact of federal spending.

New York City, with its historical commitment to municipal hospitals, was a visible focus for debate. Were its hospitals to be assimilated into the mainstream, shut down, or limp along as second-rate?[59] In the event, a new, quasi-public New York City Health and Hospitals Corporation was created in 1969—in a climate of frustration and hostility—which took over the eighteen municipal hospitals. The corporation was designed to be a managerial buffer between the city and the hospitals, in order to cut them free from the bureaucratic red tape of city government. But fundamental class issues were at stake in removing city-owned institutions from democratic control to an independent board of directors, however efficient and benevolent they might be. Barbara Ehrenreich, of the critical policy organization Health-Pac, summed up the process in New York as "private, elitist and essentially secret."[60] A bitter meeting of corporation members and the public at Bellevue Hospital in June 1971 was marked by the trading of insults, profanity, fist fights, and disruptive chanting: "Hire more workers, lay off the bosses"; "Same enemy, same fight: build for a general strike."[61] Six people were treated at the hospital's emergency room for minor injuries and four were taken into custody by the police. A persistent complaint was lack of participation by client communities. This audience demanded that the Health and Hospitals Corporation take prompt steps to place blacks, Puerto Ricans, and Jews in policy-making positions—which it did. But obvious tensions continued.

The 1960s coalition among health reformers, young doctors working in city institutions, and organized groups representing the poor weakened in the conservative, market-driven environment of the 1970s. The egalitarianism built into Medicaid—turning the poor into middle-class consumers by providing them with free choice of hospital—also proved to be illusory.[62] Hospitals across the country continued to be segregated according to income, which in the inner cities was seemingly correlated to race. Indeed, although much was made of the principle of "free choice" of services for the poor (as for other members of the population), there was no guarantee that voluntary or for-profit hospitals would accept poverty-stricken patients.[63]

Medicaid, like Medicare, was also weighted with mainstream assumptions about "hospital care," drawing on the model of the acute voluntary hospital. Thus, although the character of many city hospitals certainly changed after Medicaid—for example, the majority of patients in Cook County Hospital were not on county aid in 1970—the role of the large city hospitals could still only be defined and explained in terms of what local voluntary hospitals were doing. The old poorhouse hospital was still largely the foil and backstop to the private sector.

By fostering reimbursement for acute care in private hospitals, the new federal programs also ignored the broader medical and social services that large city-owned hospitals traditionally offered their patients, including long-term hospital care. Medicare and Medicaid, concentrating on acute inpatient care, defined the "hospital" in narrow terms and made it easier for tax-supported hospitals (and their affiliated medical schools) to split off services that were not part of the acute medical complex as irrelevant to the hospital's main mission.

The wider role was illustrated in the bitter arguments in Philadelphia in 1976 and 1977 about whether the Philadelphia General Hospital should be closed to save city taxes. (It was.) At the time, the PGH served over 10,000 inpatients a year and accommodated 200,000 outpatient visits and 72,000 visits to the emergency room. But about half of the inpatients could, in theory, be transferred to nursing homes, provided such facilities were available. Many of the others were eligible for Medicare, Medicaid, or Blue Cross, and thus might be shipped to nonprofit institutions. However, there was also a minor but difficult pool of "undesirables": prisoners, chronic patients without insurance, rape victims, and addicts.[64]

The PGH emergency room was closed in April 1977 against a quivering backdrop of racial prejudice—for most of the patients were black. Outpatient services were now to be provided in new, relatively inexpensive city-run health centers; acute care patients were transferred to other hospitals in the area. By mid-June 1977 only about four hundred patients remained on the PGH site: chronic disease patients who would be moved to a separate facility when it was completed. The Philadelphia city administration under Mayor Frank Rizzo released a thirty-page report in July 1977, claiming that closing the hospital was a wise decision and that the city's residents would now receive better care at a better price.[65] But it was significant that no major study was done to see what happened to members of the population who were the hospital's traditional beneficiaries.

For city administrators and local property taxpayers, Medicaid, a state program subsidized by the federal government, was financially and strategically valuable because it suggested a reduced local role. Responsibility was being displaced upward. Paradoxically, though, while tax-supported hospitals were scaling down, the not-for-profit and for-profit hospitals were to become increasingly interested in extending their *own* range of service through purchase of (or affiliation with) other kinds of institutions, including nursing homes; this is known as "vertical integration." Medicare and Medicaid thus had enormous class effects. They served both to upgrade services to the middle class and to stem the rising tide of criticism by the poor, who were now, potentially at least, "in the mainstream." The programs also helped to stratify the system, notably to define some hospitals as financially successful acute centers (successful private hospitals) and others as centers of financial loss (inner-city hospitals with large poverty populations).

In 1978, when a new Commission on Public General Hospitals reported, there were ninety urban public general hospitals located in sixty-three of the hundred largest cities. These hospitals accounted for almost 13 percent of all inpatient admissions, 28 percent of outpatient visits, and 17 percent of all hospital employees in these cities.[66] These hospitals continued to serve patients who had no other source of financing, for Medicaid proved in the event to be an inadequate solution for everybody. These hospitals also provided services to neighborhood residents for whom they were the hospital of choice, and often provided highly specialized and emergency services to a much wider community. Many of the hospitals were also major teaching institutions.

Urban public general hospitals were susceptible to financial problems because they served large numbers of patients who did not have third-party coverage, private or governmental (despite Medicare and Medicaid), and because they also provided services, including a massive amount of ambulatory care, that were not adequately reimbursed by third-party payers. The commission—formed by an organizational affiliate of the American Hospital Association, funded by foundations, and made up of a mix of hospital, medical, and political representatives—urged that these "public" hospitals be retained. But many of them were caught in a vicious cycle: they could not raise needed capital for renovations, which would make them more competitive, because of their weak financial position. They had few effective champions. They seemed set on a path of deterioration.

The politics of capital ensured, in short, the simultaneous rise of successful institutions and the decline of those that were already weak. By the early 1980s it was clear that existing financing arrangements would not lead to anything like a one-class system in the large cities; quite the reverse. At the very least in the American system, given its reliance on service through contractual obligation, egalitarian expectations would require an egalitarian, universal insurance program. But this was a dead issue in 1980; indeed, the signs were in the other direction, with consistent chipping away at Medicare and, in particular, Medicaid.

It was in this context that there was a backlash against *voluntary* hospitals which, it was assumed, had abandoned "free care" (now assumed to be the essence of voluntarism) in favor of institutional self-interest and greed. On the basis of a shaky view of history, free care was now made a requirement for voluntary hospitals by post-factum manipulation of the Hill-Burton legislation. Here was irony indeed—for the voluntary hospitals were not trusted to be caring. The action began in 1970 when eight individual plaintiffs brought suit in *Cook* v. *Ochsner Foundation Hospital,* claiming that ten Louisiana hospitals which had received Hill-Burton funds were not providing a reasonable volume of care to the poor, either free or below cost, as apparently mandated in the legislation of 1946.[67] The result, after a series of charges, cases, and investigations, was a proposed government regulation drafted in 1971, which suggested a standard for "charity" of 5 percent of the hospital's estimated patient revenues, with an appropriate waiver in unusual cases. The "free service" regulation, substantially amended, became effective in 1972, generating a flurry of confusing technical interpretations and general obfuscation, but little enforcement. A similar fate fell to the related "community service" obligation, which supposedly required hospitals which had accepted Hill-Burton funds to act as quasi-public agencies, including participation in Medicaid. Nevertheless, the saga suggested strongly that hospitals would not give away services unless forced to do so.

Although the charity-care regulations, applied retrospectively, were always problematic from the legal and ethical points of view, they also reflected a willingness by the federal government to use the legal-regulatory machinery as a vehicle to protect the interests of social dependents and minorities, extending the body of case law when necessary. However, by the mid-1970s effective interest in civil rights and poverty law had waned. The first wave of civil rights actions—against blatant discrimination in hospitals—had proved, for the most part, successful but the second wave was more difficult. How should a government agency or court deal, for example, with a hospital which decided to move from an unprofitable inner-city site, where it provided vital services to the poor and minorities, out to a relatively affluent (white) suburb? Was a hospital which was situated in a largely black neighborhood practicing discrimination because it treated few black patients? Was the grouping of patients, by race, in semiprivate rooms a question of the patients' or the hospital's preference?[68] Medicare and Medicaid avoided such issues in two ways: by having no direct control of hospital capital, and by acting as insurers in the marketplace rather than as guarantors of care.

Conflicting legal theories of what constitutes a "charitable institution" muddied the waters further. Hospitals seemed an undifferentiated mass of vendors, with little charitable or public intent, and little to choose between voluntary, investor-owned, and governmental institutions. Were any of them charitable at all? Even tax-supported hospitals, playing the game as if they, too, were businesses, came under increasing criticism from the courts. A notable example was when government hospitals' traditional exclusion from tort liability for negligence was overturned in a key Michigan case in 1978, *Parker* v. *Highland Park*. This case reiterated earlier criticisms about the doctrine of charitable immunity for voluntary hospitals: "We have new facts described by old nomenclature."[69] The facts were that all hospitals were charging and receiving money for their services, and seeking profits. The *Parker* case was quite specific: "The modern hospital, whether operated by a city, a church, or a group of private investors, is essentially a business."[70]

New Alignments by 1980

In parallel, the special circumstances of different groups of hospitals under Medicare reshuffled the organizational divisions of hospitals into a complex array of intertwining interest groups. Governmental general hospitals, for example, continued to be a heterogeneous group of institutions. The 357 metropolitan public (tax-supported) general hospitals outside the hundred largest cities functioned much like private community hospitals, as they had throughout the century, and continued to show a variety of forms; some, for example, although owned by government, were operated by voluntary corporations and some by profit-making management companies. Since these hospitals primarily served paying patients, they were in a favored category during the post-Medicare readjustments and in the search for capital; indeed, some had preferential access to capital through general obligation bonds of their government sponsors. The political interests of these hospitals were similar to those of their counterparts, of similar size, under voluntary (and in some cases, for-profit) control and management.

A further major group of 1,413 government hospitals were rural public general hospitals, usually serving as the community hospital for all area residents, and generally quite small. These hospitals shared the increasing problems of *all* rural general hospitals, including prolonged periods of low occupancy, inadequate revenues to meet operating expenses, and, as a result, difficulties in raising capital. These hospitals, like small hospitals in medium-sized cities, were potential targets for acquisition by the for-profit chains. These chains, in turn, were able to raise needed capital on a system-wide basis and had the potential to turn hospitals around financially through improvement of facilities and equipment—moves that elicited support from local medical practitioners, who, in turn, admitted more hospital patients.

A final group of government general hospitals were those owned and operated by forty-five tax-supported universities, that is, by state medical schools and the municipal University of Cincinnati. These hospitals had lobbying interests similar to those of the voluntary teaching hospitals. Indeed, both rural hospitals and major teaching hospitals were building new channels of support by 1980, drawing on old themes: rural hospitals as centers of rural communities, built into the very fabric of rural life—an echo of the rural hospital movement of the 1920s—and university teaching hospitals as centers of "scientific excellence," whose commitment to the poor was based on their willingness to be subjects of research and teaching. All medical schools, including both state-supported and private not-for-profit institutions, had common concerns about the adequacy of Medicare and Medicaid reimbursement in hospitals devoted to research, to teaching, and to tertiary (superspecialized) care.

Medical-school faculties, too, faced a major change after the Medicare and Medicaid legislation. The new programs provided reimbursement for physician care to impoverished teaching patients who previously had been treated on a free, courtesy basis by full-time faculty and by local doctors who had part-time faculty appointments; the quid pro quo for the latter was the faculty position. Now that full-time faculty were paid directly (or as a result of supervising residents who provided the actual care), local clinicians were far less important to the schools as teachers—and so was the maintenance of good town-gown relations. Indeed, the new climate of competitiveness was to pit the medical school's facilities against other local hospitals in an out-and-out struggle for the market share of patients. In these ways medical schools were encouraged—again as a result of federal policy—to downplay any lingering commitment to university-based regionalism.

Formally, too, university-based regionalism was extinguished in the 1970s. The regional medical programs set up by legislation of 1965 (under PL 89-239) were politically on their way out by 1973. The program was folded into the planning legislation of 1974 (PL 93-641) and soon after, the regional medical programs ceased. Specific activities were left to the medical schools requesting grants under the program in different regions—for once again the federal government acted as if it were a private foundation. Programs included such diverse efforts as continuing medical-education programs for local physicians, training programs for nurse-practitioners, high-technology demonstration projects such as kidney transplant or dialysis units, and emergency medical networks and outreach clinics. On a general basis the program forged links between medical schools and affiliated teaching hospitals, prompted the appointment of directors of medical education in affiliated hospitals, and brought medical residencies in all specialties into some kind of affiliation, however loose in practice, with a university medical center. (These affiliations, in turn, made the role of the large city-owned or county hospital less necessary for the teaching of interns and residents, or even medical students. Students could now be sent to affiliated voluntary institutions instead, thus further downgrading the tax-supported hospitals' position.)

By 1980 university medical centers were so authoritative—and so large—that they needed no further (regional) definition. Total U.S. medical-school revenues rose from $2.2 billion in 1972–73 to $8.2 billion ten years later; more than $65 million per school.[71] Nor do these figures include the cost of their huge associated hospitals and clinical facilities, or of other health-professional schools on the medical-center site. Taken together, the complex represented by the academic health center was a formidable array of multimillion-dollar institutions by 1980, with common vested interests. The academic health center (the academic medical center under a new name) had come into its own, as an identifiable organizational entity, with increasing importance in the health-care system. Two-thirds of the centers and the same proportion of their principal teaching hospitals were "public" (i.e., tax-supported) institutions and one-third private in 1980. There were not only larger medical centers in 1980 than in 1965, there were far more of them. Stimulated by federal funding, the number of medical schools rose from 87 in 1965–66 to 127 in 1982–83.

University teaching hospitals were particularly vulnerable to changes in federal policy because they served a relatively large proportion of Medicare and Medicaid patients. These units were also largely unprepared for aggressive competition by other hospitals hoping to "skim the cream" of private patients in the early years of Medicare, and they were administratively unwieldy at a time when speedy responses to the shifting political and economic environment were essential. Tulane University caused a stir by signing a contract in 1972 with Hospital Affiliates International of Nashville, a profit-making company, to develop a new university hospital which was specifically designed to draw private patients (and to make a profit for the university). By the late 1970s alarm was being expressed that the days of traditional support of academic centers by government were now over; the relationship was increasingly confrontational and adversarial.[72] Nevertheless, the academic health centers were becoming powerful actors on the national political scene—politicized via the influence of Medicare.

Given the rapidity of change, hospitals of all kinds made remarkable adjustments to changes in their environments in the years following Medicare and Medicaid. Some hospitals became aggressively profit-oriented, closing their emergency rooms and seeking maximum reimbursement rates. Others, seeking to maintain a traditional social role, became increasingly hard-pressed. Hospital outpatient visits to local-government hospitals expanded rapidly in the early 1970s but dropped in the late 1970s and early 1980s. Taxing agencies, like their private counterparts, looked for ways to reduce demand for care by patients who were unable to pay. The dictates of the market seemed all-pervasive.

Not only did hospitals change in organization, but their rhetoric also suffered a metamorphosis. Notably, voluntarism was brought under the ideological cloak of business and further divorced from ideas of charity. The word "voluntarism" was most forcibly used by hospitals in the 1970s in the political arena, as a response by major trade associations to the threat of government ("socialistic") cost controls. Thus the American Hospital Association, the Federation of American Hospitals and the American Medical Association called for a "voluntary effort" in 1977, pledging that hospitals, irrespective of ownership, would collectively and willingly hold the line of increased costs by keeping their budgets in check. The voluntary effort was initially successful as hospitals clamped down on expansionism, although it soon failed in terms of keeping costs in line. However, it was a major *political* success, since it carried the hospital industry through the years of the Carter administration, which threatened direct controls on hospital budgets and national health insurance, into the smoother, pro-competitive waters of the Reagan administration. The voluntary effort also underlined the common political interests of voluntary and investor-owned hospitals. Through all of these activities in the 1970s, voluntary hospitals lost their exclusive brand image.

In the 1970s, then, market-oriented behavior became public policy, effectively stimulated by the Medicare reimbursement system. Market-oriented behavior was a rational response by hospitals to the structures and incentives built into Medicare, clearly favoring their short-term financial interests. One effect was to bring hospitals into prominence as enterprises motivated by organizational self-interest, by the excitement of the game, by greed. America was confirmed as the home of the "pay system." But there was jeopardy inherent in this response. Embracing the new language of competition in the marketplace with the eagerness and enthusiasm of converts, both voluntary and tax-supported hospitals endangered the very characteristics which differentiated them, historically, from profit-making institutions. "We are being treated like an entrepreneur and, by the way, we're acting like an entrepreneur," wrote a hospital administrator in explaining his role in developing a consortium of hospitals in greater Hartford, Connecticut.[73]

Medicare and Medicaid, supposedly designed to promote egalitarian-ism, fostered sharp inequities in the health-care system while disarming criticism from low-paid American workers and the poverty population. The stage was set for today's struggles to rethink, once again, the American health-care system—and to redefine the relative roles of voluntarism, gov-ernment, and business for the last few years of the twentieth century.

12

Hospitals at the End of the Twentieth Century

ALMOST A DECADE has passed since the events described in chapter 11. During that time there have been enormous changes in the American hospital system. Through the fiscal incentives and controls of Medicare, the federal government has become an overt and forceful arbiter of hospital-service reimbursement. At the same time, important changes have occurred in hospital function and behavior. These include shifting services previously given to inpatients to outpatient service or other treatment outside the hospital, a general drop in hospital inpatient admissions after decades of increase, the diversification of hospitals into new corporations, and a general "urge to merge" hospitals into larger hospital systems. As the power of both the government and the health-care corporations has increased, new stresses have been placed on doctor-hospital relationships. All these changes have been accompanied by further pressures on voluntary hospitals to behave as profit-making businesses.

Hospitals are now undergoing a transformation that may prove as profound as the one they experienced between 1870 and 1920. This new transformation, characterized by the emergence of large-scale systems, corporate enterprises, and an overtly profit-making ethos, has been largely generated by the federal government. But as a result, the United States has created a system of hospitals that is neither a truly private enterprise nor one with efficient government direction. In the process, old questions, still unanswered, have reappeared in new forms: questions of standardization, of quality, of the moral and symbolic attributes of social institutions, of the appropriateness of luxurious services for private patients—and of how to provide basic services to those without funds (the uninsured and underinsured).

The New Standardization: Federal Control

The recent push for hospital standardization has come not from within the hospital and medical power structures, as in earlier periods, but from federal rule-setting, designed to streamline the Medicare reimbursement system (and control its rising costs) and to encourage economic competition and consumer choice—free enterprise—as the key to organizational efficiency in commerce and industry. Stanford economist Alain Enthoven was a persuasive spokesman for the new rhetoric in the early 1980s. The United States, unlike most countries, he asserted, has the opportunity to address the problem of rising health-care costs through a "unique solution based on rational economic incentives and a carefully-designed system of economic competition in the private sector."[1] Assumptions about competition, like assumptions about streamlined purchasing, carry with them notions of fair play—that is, rules. The rules of the game require standardization.

Continuing frustration over rising hospital costs in the U.S. Congress made the idea of a new approach to hospital financing irresistible—as did lack of resolution over alternative approaches to hospital cost containment, the mixed success of state programs in regulating hospital rates, concern about duplicate hospital facilities, an oversupply of doctors, and an overuse of hospital technology.[2] Direct regulation of hospital costs appeared not only to have failed by 1980 but to have been self-defeating. A study by the U.S. General Accounting Office in 1980 found hospitals burdened by a battery of inspections; there were 101 different inspections in three hospitals that were studied.[3]

The cost emphasis of federal policy was underlined from 1980 when the budget reconciliation process in Congress became the main source of congressional decision-making about major federal programs. It was not a piece of health legislation but the Tax Equity and Fiscal Responsibility Act (TEFRA) in 1982 that called for development of "prospective payment" for

Medicare. During 1982 inflation in the hospital sector increased three times faster than the overall rate of inflation; there were reports that the Medicare program could go bankrupt within four years.[4]

President Reagan signed the legislation incorporating prospective payment into Medicare in April 1983, after an unusually fast passage of the legislation through Congress. (The system began in the fall of 1983 with hospitals being included on a staged basis, depending on the timing of their fiscal years.) The idea was to strengthen the hand of government and make it a more prudent purchaser of Medicare services. Instead of reimbursing hospitals on the basis of the costs incurred, Medicare was now to pay a set fee per case, with the fee varying by type of diagnosis; for convenience, diagnoses are arranged in 467 diagnosis-related groups (DRGs). The assumption that voluntary, for-profit, and local-government hospitals were to compete with each other as providers on a "level playing field" suggested a common set of operating procedures. A policy that assumes that all hospitals are businesses in a competitive industry has brought on them all—including the voluntary hospitals—the full force of detailed federal regulation.

In the 1980s, as in the 1920s, standardization was defined by the practical politics of what can be regulated. Interweaving through the new standardization of hospitals by government has been an increased ability to *measure* health-service utilization and financing. Research interests in academia and policy centers, the generation of large-scale sets of data for analysis, and the widespread availability and increasing sophistication of computers have made it easier to describe services in statistical terms. The DRG system is a case in point, based on studies done in the 1970s by John D. Thompson and Robert Fetter at Yale of approximately half a million inpatient records, chiefly from hospitals in New Jersey.[5] DRGs provide standard classifications for fee regulation. In cardiovascular diagnosis-related groups, for example, DRG 103 designates a heart transplant; DRG 119, vein ligation and stripping; DRG 129, cardiac arrest; and DRG 134, hypertension. Without some such measures, there was no way for outside agencies to overcome claims by hospital administrators that hospital service could not be measured, standardized, or compared, that "my hospital is different; my patients are sicker."[6]

From the beginning, DRGs were fraught with the politics of administrative regulation. But DRGs also challenged variety in medicine itself. The assumption that cases falling into each group are relatively homogenous, in terms of medical technology, use of hospital labor, and length of stay, suggests that medical practice can be standardized into defined expectations and procedures. Here was a direct threat to the clinical autonomy of physicians and to the traditional division between medical and administrative responsibilities in the hospital. Patient care could be seen—for Medicare, at least—in terms of standardized "products," reinforcing the image of the hospital as a factory. "Scientific management" was finally to be achieved. The question was, at what cost?

The DRG system gave the federal government the authority, for the first time, to establish the purchase price for identifiable services for over 20 million Medicare beneficiaries. Thus, paradoxically, prospective (DRG) payment for Medicare significantly increased the federal role in hospitals in the 1980s, even at a time of defederalism and deregulation.[7] At the same time, monitoring of services under Medicare has been strengthened through the establishment of tougher peer-review organizations. These may, for example, refuse to authorize Medicare funding to hospitals for patients deemed inappropriately admitted. Legislation in 1986 established additional federal requirements that prevent hospitals from rejecting patients from their emergency rooms or "dumping" them on other institutions solely on economic grounds. In short, although hospitals have been exhorted to behave as competitive, economically motivated institutions, they have not been expected to take this too far, by using money as a primary criterion for admission. Policy is in a constant process of correction.

The managerial and mechanistic assumptions about the hospitals' "product" embedded in the prospective-payment system have potentially far-reaching implications. The old, inflationary reimbursement system paid hospitals as if they were medical hotels, providing bed, board, and routine services on a daily basis, with other special services under special billing arrangements; but the DRG pays a standard fee per "case." The hospital receives one payment according to the DRG category, however long the patient stays or the services he or she receives. The underlying assumption in choosing DRGs as a basis for third-party payment was, of course, that efficient hospitals would treat patients faster, more intensively, and with greater success than their less efficient competitors—and would thus reap profits out of standard payments per case. Weaker hospitals, in contrast, would lose money, because they would be paid the same amounts but require more time to complete their treatments—and waste technology. In theory, there were thus built-in incentives for efficiency in the DRG payment system, at least as measured by length of stay.

However, hospitals naturally responded to DRGs, as they had to other government programs in the past, with an eye to maximizing their own income, to expanding rather than contracting their overall services, and to solidifying their competitive position. Five characteristics of the DRG system soon emerged. First, even before the adoption of DRGs by Medicare, payment according to DRG seemed likely to have unanticipated consequences because of the hospitals' long experience in maximizing their income, whatever its source or derivation. Hospital administrators and associated financial and computer-software experts rose to DRGs as to a challenge. The soon-to-be-well-known phenomenon of "DRG creep" was described in 1981 as a "deliberate and systematic shift in a hospital's reported case-mix in order to improve reimbursement."[8] This process was not much different in principle from an individual looking for loopholes in income tax regulations. DRG creep was the discovery that the choice of the group into which a patient was classified might make a huge difference in the amount received by the hospital for that particular case.[9] For many patients, it was difficult to claim that one diagnosis was truly the principal diagnosis and another only the secondary condition; and physicians could be encouraged (or schooled by hospital administrators) to choose one diagnosis over another.

Second, there was a strong, untested, and naive assumption behind DRGs that medical staff and hospital executives had—and held to—standard definitions of what constituted "finished care," that is, that everyone knew when the patient was well enough for discharge and that this point would be held constant, in more and less efficient hospitals alike. If one hospital were discharging patients with a given diagnosis who were much sicker than another hospital, the basic assumptions of DRG incentives would not work as expected. However, since there was still no standard for the "end results" of hospital service, variations were to be expected. Not surprisingly, complaints soon came from patients and their advocates charging that seriously ill Medicare patients were being inappropriately discharged from hospitals, that many patients were given incomplete information on their rights of discharge appeal and on options for posthospital care, and that some hospitals were denying admission to patients with multiple, serious conditions.[10]

Third, DRGs only applied to services traditionally regarded as "hospital services" in the American context, that is, they excluded payments for the services of attending physicians. This was logical in terms of the prior division of Medicare into Parts A and B, for hospital and physician services respectively. But as a result, the system gave managers the go-ahead to act as if cost was their (and the hospital's) primary justification or mode of operation, while physicians continued to bill patients separately on the basis of their usual and customary fees. Doctors had no organized power base within the new system. Meanwhile, hospital administrators had an incentive to view the medical staff as income-producers or as losses to the institution, in terms of the profitability of their admissions. Since hospitals could keep any differences between the actual cost of services for a given case and the amount received per DRG, the system gave administrators an incentive to press doctors to give minimal service, justified on grounds of fiscal efficiency. Old rifts between doctors and administrators widened.

With the prospective-payment system only ten months old, Health and Human Services Secretary Margaret Heckler was already expressing concern about the way in which the incentives were working. Average length of stay per discharge dropped from 9.5 days in August 1983 to 7.5 days in August 1984 and DRG creep seemed widespread.[11] Was this increased efficiency or less than adequate care? The DRG system provided incentives to discharge elderly patients as quickly as possible, but no equal incentive to provide them with an appropriate place to go, unless it was to a long-term care institution or a psychiatric or rehabilitation facility run by the same institution (for which separate reimbursement could be claimed). In December 1984 the American Medical Association published the results of an informal survey conducted in thirty-eight states, reporting that a majority of the physicians surveyed felt quality had already deteriorated or would deteriorate as a result of the new system. Administrators, it was claimed, were encouraging doctors to discharge patients for a primary condition and then to readmit them for a second, thus being able to charge for two DRG episodes; there was pressure to release patients prematurely, evidenced in rising rates of readmission within seven days; and doctors were being pressured to review the number of tests and procedures they were ordering for their patients.[12]

These observations were confirmed by a preliminary report released early in 1985 by the General Accounting Office, at the request of Senator John Heinz, chairman of the Senate Special Committee on Aging. This report claimed that patients were being released "sicker and quicker" than before DRGs.[13] In turn, the Health Care Financing Administration announced in the winter of 1985 that the new peer-review organizations should focus on protecting the quality of Medicare inpatient services under prospective payment. In full circle, therefore, federal agencies became increasingly concerned about the quality of care. There was a strange, Alice-in-Wonderland logic to all of this.

A fourth effect of DRGs was to enhance preexisting political splits within the national hospital establishment. The new system was, for example, strongly supported by the Federation of American Hospitals, the trade association of for-profit hospitals, and was also supported, though with less enthusiasm, by the American Hospital Association. However, not all hospitals viewed the new legislation with enthusiasm. Notably, the

Council of Teaching Hospitals of the Association of American Medical Colleges, representing academic health centers, opposed the legislation because of its possibly deleterious financial consequences to these institutions.[14] One result of this opposition was to modify the DRG system to include a factor for the cost of medical education. In addition, 5 to 6 percent of total DRG-related Medicare expenditures was set aside to make supplemental payments for atypical cases (outliers), that is, for patients with complex conditions (more likely to be found in teaching hospitals) whose length of stay vastly exceeded the average for a given DRG.

Fifth and finally, DRGs established a strong beachhead for the federal government as an enforcer of further changes in the health-care system, through detailed regulation of prices, hospital policies, regionalization, quality, length of stay, and specific procedures that must be followed. Beginning in October 1987, for example, hospitals around the country have had to identify potential donors of kidneys, livers, hearts, or lungs to people in need of transplantations, and organs are distributed according to uniform federal criteria.[15] Federal standardization through reimbursement is regulation by micromanagement. As a result, the U.S. health-care system now has more central regulation in the clinical affairs of hospitals than is apparent in "socialized" systems such as Britain.

If pushed too far, Medicare regulation may eventually be self-defeating, for it assumes that medical processes can be reduced to standard practices to an extraordinary degree. But the most significant aspect of the new standardization is the involvement of the federal government in areas which have traditionally been the domain of the professional and hospital associations. Present-day debates on hospital quality, on the role of hospitals as businesses, and on the role of doctors as professionals center on an apparent paradox. Competition requires *more* (and more detailed) federal regulation than does a system of trust in medicine's traditional institutions, that is, in the medical profession and the voluntary hospitals.

Quality: A Question of Measurement or
a Question of Trust?

The shift in the governmental role from that of supporter of the private sector—its traditional role—to that of powerful rule-setter has been both profound and unsettling. Eli Ginzberg has characterized the process as destabilization, the "undermining of the existing structure."[16] The cherished autonomy of both voluntary hospitals and the medical profession has not just been challenged, but reinterpreted as the exercise of self-interested monopolies whose primary interests are money and greed. In the mid-1970s the professional associations of medicine began to embark on a major critique of their activities; but the tide was already turning to public distrust. Most notably, the American College of Surgeons and the American Surgical Association published an ambitious, self-critical report on surgery in the United States in 1975, addressing the quality of surgical care, as well as questions of surgical manpower and the organization, delivery, and financing of surgical services and related issues.[17] But major studies of the distribution of hospital services and efforts to quantify the quality of care are no longer the monopoly of the medical profession. They are, rather, in the hands of a network of health-service researchers with access to massive quantities of data. These data focus largely on the *system*, rather than on the effects of medical practice on individual patients. The existence of data thus confirms, in turn, the managerial focus of standardization.

Studies of surgery, for example, following up on the surgeons' own studies, have found that the mortality rates of open-heart surgery, vascular surgery, transurethral resection of the prostate, and coronary bypass decrease, by hospital, with the increasing number of operations.[18] These findings suggest that a prudent payment system should concentrate such services in hospital centers where large numbers of procedures are done. It is not surprising, then, that hospitals seeking to qualify for Medicare reimbursement for cardiac transplantation now have to meet specified conditions. These include preexisting open-heart surgery programs that perform at least 250 procedures a year, at least 12 heart transplants (on persons of any age) in each of the past two years, and specified survival rates (73 percent after one year and 65 percent after two years), together with other criteria. There is an obvious relationship between designating cardiac transplantation centers for Medicare and influencing (if not dictating) where cardiac transplantation will be done in the United States, and who should do it. Thus regionalization of specialized hospital services has reappeared as a national policy—but through the back-door of purchasing regulation.

There are both advantages and disadvantages in this process, in a system that is highly sensitive to the pay nexus. But such regulation may be narrow and limited. For example, the federal government's bureaucratic need to select transplantation centers on the basis of quantifiable rules of operation—in order to be administratively fair and not to be challenged in courts of law—means that survival rates (a measurable product) have been made a primary variable for selection, while other, less measurable questions of quality of care, such as the quality of life in survivors, are ignored. Nevertheless, other prospects for regionalization will undoubtedly appear because of demonstrated statistical relationships between costs and outcomes. A federal report in 1987, for example, concluded that Medicare could achieve large savings on the more than $1.5 billion a year it spends for coronary bypass surgery (DRGs 106 and 107), if it contracted with high-volume heart-surgery centers.[19]

There are also strong bureaucratic arguments, backed up by statistical studies, for encouraging standard patterns of hospital use across the population. A study in Maine by John Wennberg and associates in the early 1980s, for example, found that 90 percent of medical and surgical admissions fell into DRGs with highly variable admission rates from community to community, suggesting great variety in professional practices and choices in different areas. Examples of very high variation were admissions for chest pain, hypertension, peptic ulcer, chemotherapy, knee operations, tonsillectomies, and breast biopsies.[20] If admission rates and length of stay are much lower in one area than another, without measurably different results, it is only a step to characterizing the physicians in the first area as more efficient and to assuming an immediate association between variations in practice patterns and the quality of care. Doctors may, in turn, be exhorted to examine their practice patterns and to alter their practice style if necessary.[21] Defining quality in terms of norms thus extends decision-making beyond traditional practitioners, and beyond their professional and hospital associations, to the realm of mechanistic management decisions.

Whatever the future of the DRG system, the idea of standard patterns of treatment has become accepted to a degree that would have been unthinkable twenty years ago, challenging a variety of groups to define quality in these terms—or to invent new definitions. Coalitions of employers are now using data collected by third-party insurers, as well as Medicare and Medicaid, to review hospital admission and treatment patterns among their covered employees. The question of inappropriate admissions is also being carefully scrutinized through review of large data sets. And there are continuing studies of the effects of surgical volume and hospital volume on quality of care, and other variables which may be associated with surgical outcomes, including death rates, survival rates, and postoperative morbidity.[22] Studies are also being done to refine the basic DRG classification system so that it may account for different levels of severity of illness.[23] Statistical analysis has become the sine qua non of policy-making, standard practices the norm, and regionalization of superspecialist services a politically feasible proposition.

The strong pressures toward standardization are countered and modified in turn by the lobbying of diverse interest groups. Just as the DRG system has fractionated and extended the hospital lobby, defining quality in terms of norms has split the medical associations into splinter interests, each with a different balance sheet of political and economic losses and gains. Medical peer-review organizations, for example, now have their own association with its own agenda, separate from that of the American Medical Association. Teaching hospitals—claiming the triple burden of a relatively large proportion of Medicare and Medicaid patients, expensive teaching programs, and specialized referral services, drawing complex cases—have different interests than urban, nonteaching hospitals. Rural hospitals, which have been receiving lower DRG reimbursement rates than urban institutions, are organizing for their future survival and success. In the political world of the late twentieth century, the AMA, the AHA, and the Catholic and Protestant hospital associations are only four of a much enlarged group of lobbying and representative groups focusing on Medicare regulations. The group also includes powerful representatives of consumer coalitions and business interests.[24] Major effects of the competitive policies of the 1980s have thus been to make hospital care intensely political and to focus policy-making on the very detailed level of regulation-writing and implementation.

A good example is the release in March 1986 by the Health Care Financing Administration (HCFA) of mortality figures of different hospitals under Medicare. Published in newspapers, these showed the general public which of their local hospitals had the highest death rates—hardly a prima facie advertisement of success. Hospitals with relatively high mortality rates rose in protest, claiming that the data did not account for the case mix of different institutions. All else being equal, a hospital which takes a relatively large proportion of seriously ill patients, with a high risk of dying, is likely to have a higher mortality rate than a hospital which takes healthier patients. Here was a good example of available measurements producing crude, perhaps misleading conclusions.

Responding to pressure, HCFA revised the protocol. New data issued late in 1987 included both a general ranking of all hospitals, based on each institution's overall mortality rates, and separate mortality rankings for heart disease, stroke, lung disease, and orthopedic problems, which together account for over a third of all deaths overall.[25] This case illustrates nicely the two outstanding phenomena of Medicare regulation in the 1980s: the focus on measurement (even if what can be measured is difficult to interpret and thus not always very useful) and the role of lobbying in decision-making, even at a detailed level.

But there are critical problems with federal rule-making as a basis for national policy. Standardization as detailed rules of play can only go so far before it founders on the reefs of common sense. Ever more detailed criteria promise to lead to organizational frustration, higher administrative costs, systemwide rigidity, and eventually to absurdity. We may, for example, know more and more about the chances of dying under a given diagnosis in a given hospital, but not much about life after discharge, or whether the treatment did any good.

Federal standardization is also inherently legalistic, suggesting potential confrontation between providers and patients. If you are a Medicare patient who is discharged "too soon," advises a state public-interest group, "You do not have to leave. If you are being pushed to leave, you have the right to request a written notice from the hospital."[26] This is not the language of trust in public-spirited institutions. Consumer protection is obviously important and patients' rights need to be affirmed; nevertheless, a general climate of distrust between patients and providers is an accompaniment of the contract system.

A more serious criticism is the contradiction between a regulatory system based on the idea of medicine as standardized, reproducible modules of treatment and what is actually happening in clinical practice. While Medicare regulation assumes a clear definition of "product," the medical journals have been suggesting instead the importance of uncertainty, indeed variety, in clinical decision-making. In the multifactorial, complex nature of chronic disease, a single line of action is not always evident. Medical organizations are rediscovering the importance of doctors and patients working together for an individually designed (that is, *un*-standardized) health-care outcome, taking into account factors which are difficult to quantify, including the patient's self-esteem, suffering, tolerance of pain, and general preference. It may sometimes—but not always—

make sense, for example, for a ninety-year-old patient to have a cataract operation or even a total hip replacement. The AIDS epidemic is bringing into hospitals patients for whom there is, as yet, no standard cure or course of treatment, and therefore challenges the hospital to be a center for "caring." There remains, in short, an argument for professional *discretion* as a qualitative alternative to standardized rules.

Effective competition in medicine presumably also allows patients a real choice of types of treatment, practice style, and amenities. Some medical groups may, for example, wish to present themselves as favoring a conservative approach to medical treatment, others as aggressive; some as taking a long time to talk to patients, some as stressing sophisticated pharmacology, and so on. Thus standardization of practice collides with basic assumptions about competition as well as with the realities of clinical judgment.

Hospitals as Businesses

Meanwhile, as in earlier decades, hospitals have responded with finesse to shifting incentives in their environments. The notion that hospitals are simply businesses was fueled by their financial success for most of the 1980s, by the financial environment in which they operate, and by antitrust regulations—all directly attributable to federal policy. Federal business policies, including antitrust policy, assume that hospitals are on a par with other businesses as a matter of course. After years of discussing the rhetoric of cooperation, hospitals are now legally barred from cooperating together in many circumstances; hospitals are now villains, to be watched for potentially conspiratorial activities.[27] Meanwhile, business organizations argue that nonprofit organizations represent "unfair competition."[28]

Income maximization has continued. With the widespread establishment of same-day surgery and freestanding ambulatory facilities—stimulated by changes in surgical technology and improvements in anesthesia, as well as opportunities for income—hospital admissions declined; 1981 was the high point. Over 94 percent of community hospitals reported ambulatory surgical services by 1987; and over 43 percent of surgery was then being done on an outpatient basis (up from 23 percent in 1983).

TABLE 12.1

Utilization of Nonfederal Short-term General and Allied Special Hospitals,
1960–87

	No. of Admissions	Hospital Occupancy	Average Length of Stay	No. of Outpatient Visits (Millions)	Total Expenses ($ Millions)
1960	22,970	74.7	7.6	NA	5,617
1970	29,252	78.0	8.2	134	19,560
1980	36,198	75.4	7.6	207	76,970
1981	36,494	75.9	7.6	207	90,739
1982	36,429	75.2	7.6	251	105,094
1983	36,201	73.4	7.6	214	116,632
1984	35,202	68.9	7.3	216	123,550
1985	33,501	64.8	7.1	223	130,700
1986	32,410	64.2	7.1	234	140,907
1987	31,633	64.9	7.2	248	152,909

SOURCE: American Hospital Association, *Hospital Statistics,* 1988 ed., table 1.

TABLE 12.2

Changes in the Number of Nonfederal Short-term General and Special
Hospitals, United States, 1965–87

	Not-for-Profit	State or Local Government	For-Profit	Total	Total Number of Hospitals
1965 total	3,426	1,453	857	5,736	5,736
Net gain or loss					
1965–70	−40	+251	−88	+123	5,859
1970–75	−22	+136	+6	+120	5,979
1975–80	−25	−5	−45	−75	5,904
1980–85	+25	−219	+75	−119	5,785*
1985–87	−75	−74	+23	−126	5,659
1987 total	3,289	1,542	828	5,659	5,659

*AHA published statistics give a total of 5,784, but the detailed tables add up to 5,785.
SOURCE: American Hospital Association, *Hospital Statistics,* 1988 ed., table 1.

Simultaneously, hospital occupancy dropped (table 12.1). The number of hospitals has also been declining, some forced out of business by the dwindling supply of inpatients, some by aggressive competition, some by the tightening of third-party payments (table 12.2).

Through these shifts hospital budgets continued to rise, from under $77 billion dollars in 1980 to almost $153 billion in 1987. Medicare's share of the hospital bill also continued to rise, from 26 percent of hospital expenses in 1981 to 29 percent in 1985. A study by the Office of the Inspector General of the Department of Health and Human Services found that in 1984 hospitals reaped a "net profit margin" of about 15 percent on Medicare revenues and a return on investment of 25 percent.[29] Larger profits were recorded by teaching hospitals compared with nonteaching hospitals, by investor-owned facilities compared with nonprofit hospitals, and by urban compared to rural hospitals. These successes have been followed in turn by constrictions; the present-day picture is much more mixed.

As in earlier decades, hospitals have also adapted rapidly to changes in clientele. Today's hospitals are weighted toward the acute phases of complex chronic diseases. Almost one-third of the patients in short-stay hospitals are aged sixty-five or older, twice the proportion of the mid-1960s (table 12.3). A majority of patients over sixty-five years of age are hospitalized for diseases of the circulatory system or digestive system, for neoplasms, or for diseases of the nervous or sense organs.[30] At the same time, the proportion of inpatients who are children has declined; patients under fifteen years of age now represent less than 9 percent of hospital patients. Thus the age profile of hospital patients is quite different from that of, say, the 1920s.

Technological successes in medicine have also brought sicker individuals into hospitals. Open-heart surgery and other complex procedures have become routine—mundane, even, and huge teams are mobil-

TABLE 12.3

Selected Characteristics for Inpatients Discharged from Short-stay Hospitals, United States, 1965, 1985, and 1987

	1965	1985	1987
Total number of patients discharged	28.8 million	35.1 million	33.4 million
Male	38.8%	40.4%	40.6%
Female	61.1%	59.6%	59.4%
Under 15 years of age	14.8%	8.5%	8.1%
65 years and older	16.0%	30.0%	31.3%
Average length of stay (all patients)	7.8 days	6.5 days	6.4 days
65 years and older	13.1 days	8.7 days	8.6 days
Percentage discharged by U.S. region:			
Northeast	22.5%	20.4%	20.1%
Midwest	29.4%	26.0%	26.1%
South	32.4%	35.0%	33.8%
West	15.7%	18.5%	20.0%

SOURCE: National Center for Health Statistics, "Inpatient Utilization of Short-stay Hospitals by Diagnosis—U.S. 1965," series 13, no. 6, 1970, selected tables; *Advancedata,* no. 127 (September 25, 1986) and no. 159 (rev.) (September 28, 1988).

ized for the care of individual cases. A seventy-member surgical team was reported at the Johns Hopkins Hospital in September 1987, in the surgical separation of seven-month-old twins who were born joined at the head. But the cost of treating many conditions has risen because of changes in the technologies used; good examples are breast cancer and myocardial infarction. And the cost of childbirth rose greatly in the 1970s and 1980s because of an increase in deliveries by cesarian section.[31] But it is still difficult to decide what counterbalancing values should be placed against rising hospital costs to account for such changes. If the primary criterion of a market system is the number of units produced, profits, and some measure of consumer satisfaction, hospitals have been performing well, while their products are constantly changing.

In the early 1980s, the voluntary not-for-profit hospitals engaged in a process of "institutional isomorphism," to use DiMaggio and Powell's useful phrase; that is, they conformed, homogenized, and adjusted their roles to the model of the for-profit hospitals, because of the specific organizational and financial advantages these hospitals appeared to offer.[32] Corporate reorganization was touted in the early 1980s to protect and increase a hospital's revenue, to diversify its activities, to avoid government interference, to compete in the marketplace, and to maintain quality of care. The most prevalent corporate reorganizational structure by the early 1980s was the parent-subsidiary model: the division of a single corporation into a holding corporation with subsidiaries, which might be not-for-profit or for-profit. Freestanding health facilities became particularly popular, including freestanding surgical centers, where patients were admitted and discharged on the same day.[33] Cataract surgery shifted almost entirely from an inpatient to a same-day procedure between 1980 and 1987. Doctors also sponsored the rapid growth of so-called immediate care centers in the early 1980s, placing primary care units in shopping centers and bringing doctors into relatively prosperous neighborhoods.[34]

As not-for-profit hospitals also clustered eagerly into systems and engaged increasingly in joint ventures, including joint ventures with physicians, they strengthened this similarity to investor-owned firms. Among the ten largest hospital systems in the United States in 1987, in terms of facilities and revenues, were not only major investor-owned chains, including Hospital Corporation of America, the largest of all kinds of system (with 471 hospitals), National Medical Enterprises (with 133), American Medical International, Humana, and Charter Medical Corporation, but also governmental and voluntary nonprofit systems: including the New York City Health and Hospitals Corporation and the systems run by the Sisters of Providence, Seattle, and by the Sisters of Charity. Here, in a microcosm, is the pluralism of the American hospital enterprise that has existed throughout the century, transmuted into the corporate strategies and structures of today. The difference now is that within systems the hospitals' scope has expanded, centralized, and gone beyond the local community, and that managers of all types of institutions have embraced the managerial rhetoric as they continue to optimize revenue. Sisters of Charity Health Care Systems reported gross revenues of almost $738 million in 1986; its president, Sister Celestia Koebel, described 1986 as a year to "negotiate for expansion and position for growth."[35]

The great majority of all hospitals now advertise, chiefly in the newspapers, and these advertisements do not usually make clear whether the hospitals are for-profit or not-for-profit. For the most part, patients probably do not know or care. Marketing staffs boomed in the early 1980s as hospitals all over the country embarked on major public-relations campaigns. "Those rooms of empty beds are making hospitals sick," reported the *Philadelphia Inquirer* in its business section in October 1984. Hospital services are indeed now commonly discussed in business periodicals, for a wide variety of reasons. For example, health care, the *Philadelphia Business Journal* reported recently, is a "booming business for interior designers," with hospitals favoring peaches and other pastel shades.[36]

With a strange sense of déjà vu, luxurious accommodations for private patients have once more come to the fore. The objectives are the same as they were at the beginning of the century: to appeal to the rich, build a high-income clientele, and raise the hospital's profile as *the* place to go for hospital care. For "pampered patients," reported the *Chicago Tribune* in November 1986, "VIP suites are good medicine." A new private facility, the Centennial Suites, at the Michael Reese Hospital, a voluntary not-for-profit organization, was described as a "distinctive new environment for medical and surgical patients who desire more than a private room when pulled away from their busy lives and careers."[37] One suite reportedly included a mauve carpet and a two-cushion couch, which can be made into a bed for a guest; luxurious towels; two private-line telephones; a small refrigerator stocked with soft drinks, fruit juices, and beer and wine (if the doctor approves); and a VCR. The old analogies about private rooms have also reappeared. No longer is the talk about first class and steerage (on ships), but about first-class airline tickets and the most expensive hotel suites. The idea of VIP treatment, reports the *Tribune,* "appears to be a master stroke, so to speak, perfectly suited for today, a cycle in our history when being rich is admired and flaunting one's money is considered not at all tasteless."[38]

In the early 1980s the anxious euphoria and institutional isomorphism of hospitals suggested a total reshaping of the U.S. hospital and health-care system into a handful of profit-oriented "megacorporations," accompanied by the closing of numerous hospitals, perhaps as many as 2,000, or one-third. But by 1986, rethinking was being done all down the line, because of the checkered career of for-profit hospitals. Between 1977 and 1984 the number of hospitals in investor-owned (for-profit) systems grew from 414 to 878 and growth seemed set on a steady 10 percent a year. A dollar invested in an investor-owned system returned nearly 40 percent more in earnings than the average for other industries in these years.[39] By the mid-1980s, however, the picture was changing. For the large investor-owned systems the halcyon days of the late 1970s and early 1980s were replaced by retrenchments, internal consolidation, and reappraisals, partly as a result of the new Medicare payment system (DRGs). For both inves-tor-owned hospitals and the not-for-profit systems that rose in tandem, the year 1986, reported the journal *Modern Healthcare,* was a "white-knuckle" year. The journal surveyed 164 hospital systems. Overall, these registered an 11.9 increase in revenues between fiscal 1985 and 1986, but a 47.1 percent decrease in profits.[40]

As investor-owned hospitals reported financial and organizational reappraisals, they ceased to be quite so obvious a target for imitation by the not-for-profits. Diversification, too, has lost some of its allure because of poor planning, a lack of clear objectives, poor execution, and unrealistic expectations.[41] Advertising and marketing strategies are now undergoing reexamination across the country. And the early proliferation of competing home health-care agencies and freestanding primary care units has been replaced by closures or consolidations. The president of the large investor-owned company American Medical International was recently quoted as saying that "health care markets are local in nature and not susceptible to a broad national approach,"[42] suggesting a much more decentralized, flex-ible, variable set of activities in the future, even for the national investor-owned chains. Once again, events have shown how quickly the hospital's environment can shift—and have challenged the assumption that health care is inevitably moving toward consolidation into a few giant, profit-oriented corporations. Dominance by megacorporations now appears a myth.[43]

A sustained murmur of unease about the appropriateness of profit-making—the business ethos—in health care accompanied the rapid changes of the 1980s. The journal *Science* put the question succinctly: "The idea that, from a business point of view, owning a chain of hospitals is not unlike owning a flourishing chain of fast-food eateries took hold in the public imagination—and bothered a lot of people."[44] A major study by the

Institute of Medicine of the National Academy of Sciences, reporting in 1986, found no clear evidence of increased efficiency among the profit-making hospitals, compared with voluntary hospitals. Thus there appeared to be no obvious argument in favor of a commercial system; nor was there quantitative evidence of differences in the quality of care in the two types of hospitals. Moreover, in some areas the voluntary hospitals came out ahead. Notably, the not-for-profits provided more uncompensated charity care, with substantial differences in states where for-profit hospitals were numerous, chiefly in the South and West.[45]

A complete fusion of hospitals into the commercial sector was not, then, a necessary corollary to the market rhetoric of the 1980s. Nevertheless, major changes have been made in the hospital and health-care system which will probably affect their directions for years to come. Of most immediate interest are the political and organizational segmentation of the hospital field along new lines; the long-term implications of debt and other aspects of capital formation on the system; the increased sophistication of (nonhospital) employers in the 1980s, leading large corporations to think of themselves as organized purchasers of care; and the greatly enlarged role of managers in the hospital system.

Meanwhile, a complex matrix of interdependencies has arisen across the public, commercial, and nonprofit sectors, making it more difficult to see any of them independently. In 1986, for example, investor-owned firms managed 131 tax-supported hospitals. In turn, three corporations under secular, not-for-profit control managed 28 investor-owned institutions.[46] A few not-for-profit hospitals have been sold or leased to investor-owned chains. Notable examples are Wesley Medical Center to Hospital Corporation of America, USC Medical Center to National Medical Enterprises, the University of Louisville Hospital to Humana, and Presbyterian–St. Luke's Medical Center to American Medical International.[47] Some not-for-profit corporations have organized for-profit management firms, or subsidiaries selling software, renting medical equipment, or running medical office buildings or parking lots. But for-profit hospitals may run not-for-profit corporations for such functions as community fund-raising. As a result of all of these processes, it is less easy than ever before to distinguish a simple not-for-profit voluntary hospital "sector," with a supposedly charitable role, from a for-profit sector whose primary purpose is to satisfy investors.

Since 1985, voluntary hospitals as a group have been attempting—once again, as in the 1930s (and for some of the same reasons)—to delineate their role from that of investor-owned hospitals: to search, that is, for a definable "mission" that recaptures the old sense of public trust and institutional autonomy inherent in the associations between voluntarism and charity. The reasons for doing so are presented partly as a matter of conscience by hospital representatives (recreating, for example, a sense of the religious service of Catholic hospitals) and partly as good strategy (defining voluntarism as a preferable, quasi-public alternative to commercial hospitals in a potentially tightening economic marketplace and holding on to tax exemption).[48] Two major constraints mold the possibilities: the standardization and purchasing decisions of the federal government and other major third parties, and the heavy obligations of hospital debt.

Most hospitals are already carrying considerable loads of debt, but much more building might take place if financing were more readily available. One projection of desired hospital investment was as high as $145 billion for the 1980s.[49] In 1986 alone, ground was broken for 100 new hospitals with over 12,000 beds, and for 320 hospital expansions with over 11,000 beds.[50] How much building actually takes place in the 1990s depends largely upon government policy, that is, changes in the market for tax-exempt bonds and decisions about capital as an element of Medicare. Even at present levels, high interest payments and depreciation charges, passed along to the payers of care, place a continuing burden on the costs of hospital service and make hospitals, even more, the creatures of third-party payers and of lending agencies. Although hospitals are once again becoming seriously interested in philanthropy as a potential source of capital, philanthropy contributes only about 4 percent of all construction funding.[51]

In one sense the wheel of privatization has come full circle. Hospitals began by serving business and corporate interests in various ways; and one way to interpret present events is to see big business as capturing the control that earlier business leaders exercised through voluntary institutions. Major employers have finally realized that they spend millions (or in some cases billions) of dollars on health insurance over which, in the past, they have had little control.[52] By the mid-1980s many employers were segregating their premium dollars for health services into their own benefit trusts and putting the management of benefit claims processing out to bid, thus bypassing Blue Cross/Blue Shield or insurance companies. Instead, they collect their own premiums and manage their own benefits. Premiums paid to commercial insurance and Blue Cross plans, as a result, represented a declining percentage of the health-insurance dollar by the mid-1980s, while independent plans have surged.

Employers are now an important presence on the health-care scene— redesigning their benefit plans in order to encourage employees to use lower-cost services such as outpatient surgery, home care, and other alternatives to hospitalization; establishing auditing and other oversight activities to police utilization and billing; educating employees to be prudent purchasers of health care; providing work site wellness and health-promotion programs, from alcoholism treatment centers to corporate fitness programs; and becoming involved in a new form of voluntary organization: local business coalitions. By 1985 there were 133 coalitions across the United States, with over 6,000 members representing business, health, labor, and government.[53] Their activities include lobbying, data collection, utilization review, health-benefit-plan design and management, and the development of wellness programs. Business has come to realize the value of health services to the capitalist economy and the importance of involvement of business leaders in health services, if only to avoid unwanted government intervention.[54] It remains to be seen how far (and for how long) major corporations will be willing to substitute their own efforts as health-benefit managers for functions that in most countries are the job of government. In the long term, business enterprises may become the strongest advocates yet for comprehensive government health insurance.

But this is looking ahead. In the short run, as business leaders, controlling the health expenditures of an army of employees, establish their own health-service agendas, they are likely to come into conflict increasingly with the leaders of local hospitals or health-care systems. For example, consolidation of hospitals into local or regional conglomerates may well be resisted by the business community (as major purchasers of care) in some areas, because it reduces effective competition among providers and may create new quasi-monopolies in health, with which business as a purchaser must bargain.[55]

The irony inherent in these events is obvious. Voluntary hospitals are no longer the amiable creatures of corporate capitalism, with business and religious representatives on their boards; they are also big businesses themselves. In this process, there has been a breakdown in the role of voluntary-hospital trustees as benevolent guardians of the larger capitalist ethos—and/or as the altruistic extension of this ethos. The very success of hospitals as entrepreneurial business organizations has called the role of trustees into question.

The most salient result of the role of hospitals as businesses is, however, that the power of managers *within* the hospital system has increased. It is difficult for bystanders, including board members and physicians, to keep abreast of the arcane details of Medicare politics, methods of reimbursement, the role of coalitions, the future of tax-exempt bonds, the measurement of quality, and the latest news on hospital sponsorship of alternative delivery mechanisms: HMOs, PPOs, and CMPs.[56] Virtually all of the recent changes have increased the power of health-care managers within the system. Hospital managers are now paid sums equivalent to their counterparts in industry, are commonly referred to as chief executive officers or presidents, and are clearly accountable to their boards as business experts.

In the process the role of the boards has become increasingly unclear. One recent study found that hospital boards were spending almost two-thirds of their time on questions of financial restructuring, competition, and public policy.[57] Boards of trustees have two basic, alternative futures, leaning either toward a business or a charitable mission: as small boards of corporate directors, possibly paid, and representing financial clout and/or specific areas of hospital-business expertise, or as more outspoken representatives of the traditional, amateur role of community trusteeship, acting as members of local elites.

Redefining the Workshop: Hospitals and Doctors

The growth of managerialism has also changed the balance of power between managers and physicians. For most of the last decade, the mood of professional medical meetings has been glum and dour. Doctors have been called upon increasingly to be "gatekeepers," that is, managers or controllers of specialist care, poised between the patient and expensive services, on behalf of third parties or health-care systems. It is difficult to sustain the role of the physician as the patient's advocate where he or she is expected to police and to allocate expensive services.[58] Expectations about consumer choice have forced hospitals to open up their staffs to other health professions, including chiropractors. Clinical records in hospitals are now monitored on a routine basis, analyzing physician practice patterns as well as patients' length of stay; and DRGs, for the first time, have imposed on doctors responsibility for the cost of the hospital component of patient care. The more drugs and procedures ordered by the physician, the higher the costs to the hospital, and the less the profit made on the DRG. Fiscal incentives push doctors to cut back on hospital services, a direct reversal of the old cost-based reimbursement incentives, which encouraged them to utilize all the technology that was available. The general message seems to be one of restrictionism—loss of the medical dominance over hospitals which physicians have enjoyed through most of the century.

Large hospital and health-care systems have set up major corporate structures—new technological bureaucracies, of a size unimagined in the 1930s—with which the doctor has to deal. Large hospital organizations are a consortium of related businesses, each of which rewards entrepreneurial behavior geared toward financial efficiency. "The name of the game is skimming, and this is no longer frowned upon," one critic wrote gloomily in the mid-1980s. "All providers are involved in this process, and only those who do it best will survive. Skimming will become an art, deeply impregnated with the highest cultural value of success."[59] By skimming is meant neglect of those who cannot pay (for there is no reward for doing so; and even the psychic reward of charity is now questionable) and making do with minimal services.

In university hospitals, too, the money ethos is in the fore. Faculty-practice plans maximize income for the medical center, with many physicians on the full-time faculty earning more fees than they are paid in salaries, and rolling back the profits into the schools. Gone is the credo of the Flexner decades that medical scientists, interested only in research, fall outside the dictates of the money system. A full-time faculty member at Temple University School of Medicine and Episcopal Hospital, Philadelphia, recently criticized the medical schools for "debauching" the concept of full-time teaching faculties, and described medical schools as "not only landlords and accountants but launderers of the money generated."[60]

The flowering of lawsuits by doctors against hospitals has done nothing to improve hospital-physician relations. As more doctors have competed for hospital staff appointments, some hospitals have limited their staffs by denying newcomers staff privileges—and occasionally revoking the privileges of doctors on staff, or granting exclusive arrangements to selected physicians, allowing them sole rights to use hospital equipment. In an echo of the old "corporate practice" debates, excluded doctors have contended that such measures are conspiracies between hospitals and inside physicians to create medical monopolies—clearly an anticompetitive maneuver. The National Health Lawyers' Association estimated in 1984 that 240 medical antitrust suits were then pending across the country. The legal odds were generally in favor of hospitals, as long as they could show that limitation of staff privileges was related in some way to patient care.[61] But suspicion of the mercenary motives and autocratic behavior of the medical profession by federal agencies and in the press has fed in turn the declining morale of the medical profession. "A lot of doctors like to view the hospital as though they have some God-given right to walk in and give services there," a Federal Trade Commission attorney was reported as saying.[62] Here is a direct denial of the role of the hospital as the doctor's workshop—and an apparent transfer of power from doctors to administrators.

At the same time, hospitals have increasingly engaged in regulating and manipulating physician behavior. Some hospitals provide economic incentives to individual doctors to admit "profitable" patients to the hospital, or they reward doctors if, for example, DRG payments received by the hospitals exceed, on average, 75 percent of the hospital's usual charges.[63] How far incentive payments will be allowed in the future depends, as does so much of hospital policy, on legal, political, and other challenges in particular cases, and on the emergence of political consensus. Simultaneously, additional surveillance has been placed on physician decision-making by payers. By 1984, for example, more than a fourth of all employers required preadmission utilization review—that is, a check on a doctor's decision to admit a patient to hospital—and over half the employers paid for the cost of a second surgical opinion.[64] Medical decision-making is now under fire from all directions.

Organized medicine has been distinguished by attempts to retain power within the hospital and health-care system, fighting the battles of the late twentieth century with the defensive rhetoric of the 1930s—presenting physicians, for example, as cogs in the great corporate machine, and talking about the proletarianization, corporatization, and deprofessionalization of the doctor. Recommendations in medical journals range from endorsements of trade unionism in medicine (that is, providing a confrontational source of power for doctors in the battle with managerialism), to infiltration from within, by training doctors as managers themselves (physician executives), who would attempt to take over the entire system.[65]

The patient often seems forgotten in the exciting dynamics of the health-care industry, although this is nothing new. However, increasing clamor from consumers about early discharge of patients under the DRG system, as well as increasing federal regulation, may well force doctors and hospitals to forge new alliances; for there is nothing like a common set of enemies. One interesting development is the identification of an inner group of doctors in some hospitals who are particularly committed to the institution and who can act as a sounding board for medical decision and advice within the hospital as an organization. Another is the chance to establish what British doctors call a "practice," that is, clinical responsibility for a defined group of patients through work in large-scale group practices, backed up by the group's own statistical information systems.

A third opportunity is for doctors to become more heavily involved in the whole spectrum of health services, from health and sickness to rehabilitation, by virtue of working within relatively comprehensive systems rather than in relatively narrow, fee-for-service, independent practice.[66] Despite uneasiness and confrontation between physicians and hospitals, the mutual interests between doctors and hospitals continue to be strong, as they have been in the past, at both local and national levels.

Voluntarism Redux: Charity and Tax Exemption

The special social role of voluntary institutions, like the special privileges of professionalism, was seriously challenged in the 1980s. An article by Robert Clark in the *Harvard Law Review* in 1980 set the tone for the decade of competition. Clark argued for a principle of neutrality between not-for-profit and for-profit institutions—specifically, that both types of institutions should be subject to property taxes on the same basis as other organizations.[67] In effect, the two types of institutions were seen as having identical missions. It followed that any favoring of voluntary institutions, through tax exemption or other privileges, was a form of unfair discrimination against *for-profit* institutions. The basic assumption was that voluntary hospitals are solely private institutions, with no demonstrable public functions distinguishing them from the hospitals run as businesses.

The obvious unfairness to patients of having different consumer rights if they happened to be admitted to a nonprofit or a for-profit hospital made tort cases an early challenging ground for voluntarism as special privilege. A Pennsylvania case, *Flagiello* v. *Pennsylvania Hospital,* established more than twenty years ago that where hospitals function as businesses by charging money for their services, they are also to be regarded as businesses in meeting obligations incurred in running them, including liability for injury.[68] But if there are to be no distinctions with respect to tort liability, why should there still be differences with respect to tax exemption? Such questions became more urgent in the 1980s as hospitals restructured their organization and diversified into nonhospital businesses, such as property management, consulting, hotels, and parking lots—functions readily criticized as "sweetheart contracts," or the kind of "commercial nepotism" found in unfair business deals.[69]

The establishment in the 1970s of quantitative criteria for the amount of "charity care" to be required of recipients of Hill-Burton funding also suggested that charity should be *measured.* In state after state in the 1980s, there were debates about standards for the term "charitable" that might be applied to hospitals and other institutions; that is, some general, measurable community benefit, specifically the availability and accessibility of hospital services.[70] The issues came together in a case in Utah in 1985, *Utah County* v. *Intermountain Health Care, Inc.* The question here was this: what was it reasonable for a community to expect from a not-for-profit hospital which was part of a system or chain, as a quid pro quo for tax exemption? The Utah Supreme Court ruled that hospitals in that state should be eligible for exemption from county property taxes only if they were able to satisfy a test relating to "charitable purpose."[71] Among the factors considered were whether the hospital provided a significant service to others without immediate expectation of material reward, whether it was supported by philanthropy, and whether it was in a favorable net-earnings position.

The removal of federal tax exemption from Blue Cross/Blue Shield in 1986 has further changed the environment of voluntarism. Voluntary health organizations can no longer get by unscathed by simply claiming that they are "good." In the summer of 1986 the U.S. General Accounting Office had reported that exemption from federal income taxes for Blue Cross/Blue Shield put them at an unfair competitive advantage over taxable insurance firms, which essentially provided the same services. The House Tax Reform Act included a clause for repeal of the Blues' tax exemption. An aide to Congressmen Fortney (Pete) Stark, who was behind both activities, reported that the tax-exempt status of Blue Cross/Blue Shield was a holdover from an earlier time, when these organizations performed a unique and essential public service, including offering a community rate under which all enrollees paid the same premium regardless of health-care status.[72] Although Blue Cross/Blue Shield representatives countered by charging that the GAO report was inaccurate and its methodology flawed in the comparisons made between Blue Cross/Blue Shield and commercial insurers, the legislation carried.

It is not yet known what the long-term effects of the change in the federal tax status will be in terms of reduced services or additional health-insurance premiums. Some Blue Cross plans around the country were already working under commercial tax arrangements; moreover, the tax system may bring financial advantages, as well as obligations to individual plans. A Blue Cross/Blue Shield representative, in testimony before the Senate, estimated that federal taxes would cost the government $5 billion in the next five years, because taxes would lead to higher prices for premiums, which would lead in turn to the dropping of supplementary insurance by senior citizens, who would end up on the welfare rolls.[73] For a brief period the Medicare Catastrophic Coverage Act of 1988 (PL 100-360) changed this entire picture, because it moved much of the responsibility for supplementary coverage from private insurance into the governmental Medicare program. (This act broke new ground by establishing a supplemental premium based on the federal income taxes of the elderly, and it was this that led in turn to its demise.) Two facts are abundantly clear, however. First, Congress, state legislators, local governments, and the courts have begun to look critically at the tax-exempt status of hospitals. Second, tax exemption is no longer to be regarded as a self-evident privilege for voluntary organizations.

Legislators—and others—have watched the continuing expansion and apparent prosperity of most hospitals, even though a large number of Americans (37 million at last count) are uninsured and thus not automatically assured of hospital care. Local taxing agencies ask about the specific values brought to a community by tax-exempt organizations. The questions are especially pointed where these organizations are making obvious profits, where competing hospitals in the area are run as tax-paying (for-profit) businesses, and where the not-for-profit hospital is part of a chain with headquarters in a distant city. In the latter instance questions arise as to what extent the hospital has a primary responsibility to its immediate community at all. If profits made in a hospital are removed from the community to help support hospitals somewhere else, why should the hospital be exempt from local taxes?

Traditionally, tax exemption has recognized that voluntary hospitals serve public purposes *sui generis.* Until recently, the legal view of community benefit for the purpose of tax exemption was broad: the provision of an open emergency room and the willingness to take all paying patients, including those whose payments are made by third parties, including Medicaid. Providing health services was regarded as a charitable purpose in itself.[74] In their basic motivations and assumptions about the pay ethos, stratification, and income maximization, the voluntary hospitals themselves have changed very little since the beginning of the century. But at issue now are fundamental assumptions about "charitable purpose" as an in-built, moral attribute of health-care institutions.

In 1983—at the height of the competitive rhetoric—a commission to study ethical problems in medicine set up by President Carter, and continued under President Reagan, concluded that society has an "ethical obligation to insure equitable access to health care for all." But what does this mean? The report ducked the definition of "society"—who is it?—in favor of the old (mythological) road of voluntary initiative. Health care, reported the commission, is a field in which two important American traditions are manifested: the responsibility of the individual for his or her own welfare and the obligations of the community to its members.[75] The commission did not recommend how this rhetoric of "community" should be realized in a system committed to the dictates of the market, but it did observe that the cost of achieving equity should be shared fairly at the national level and not be allowed to fall more heavily on the shoulders of particular institutions, practitioners, or residents in different localities. (The commission also left open the continuation of a multiclass health-care system.)[76] Since community organization by elites seeking to distribute services through voluntary initiative has never fully worked in the U.S. health-care system, the obvious follow-up is a system of nationally mandated basic health-insurance benefits. However, such a mandate lies largely outside the notion of hospitals as "charities" in a "community" setting, since it can only be fulfilled through government. Once again, practicalities are hidden behind vague rhetoric.

Instead, the strengthening of the pay nexus in the 1980s, coupled with cutbacks in government programs, exacerbated the inequalities of the hospital service market. In California, for example, MediCal benefits were terminated for 270,000 indigent adults whose care was transferred back to the county hospital system in the 1980s, but the counties were not required to provide care to these individuals free of charge. In Los Angeles, county health facilities imposed charges of twenty to thirty dollars for an outpatient or emergency department visit.[77] As a result, some patients found themselves in a worse position than they were in before Medicaid was enacted. Class and race biases continue; and there is some discrimination by age. Young adults are more likely to be uninsured than older adults, blue-collar service workers and agricultural workers than white-collar workers. Blacks and Hispanics are more likely than whites to be uninsured. Americans living outside major cities have less coverage than those living in metropolitan areas.[78] Race is also a potentially significant characteristic in determining the intensity of hospital care (that is, the actual services given), as well as access to care itself.[79]

It has been convenient to blame voluntary and for-profit hospitals for these patterns, for "dumping" patients, for not admitting patients without adequate insurance, and for not giving large amounts of charity care. Hospitals should indeed be criticized, now as in the past, for pressing policies which are clearly self-serving rather than lobbying for the needs of patients. In the American system, however, the primary responsibility

for social equity *and* for the incentives built into the health-care system has
fallen on government. Throughout the 1980s it was as if voluntary hospitals, as instruments of the capitalist system, had betrayed the capitalist
system by not performing adequately as an alternative to socialism. The
question of tax exemption has swirled around all of these questions and
is to some extent a proxy for them.

Ironies and Inconsistencies

Debates about health policy-making in the United States often center on
abstractions or money, or both. This chapter has described abstractions
that sometimes appear to have agendas of their own: standardization,
regulation, competition, taxation, incentives. Enormous energy has gone
into defining workable *processes,* as if the process itself is the goal of the
system. Standardization, for example, has been geared toward redirecting
economic incentives in the behavior of health-care providers, rather than
improving standards of service. To some extent standardization is a substitute for direct federal control of the hospital system. It represents, that is,
the unwillingness to tackle problems of health services directly or even to
identify them as concrete issues. Yet at the same time standardization, as
exercised through the prospective payment system, has created a greatly
enlarged vehicle for federal influence, with the managerial rhetoric to go
with it. The central irony of recent federal policy is the heavy hand of
government regulation under the guise of private enterprise and competition.

In a decade devoted to competition and free enterprise, the consumer
of health services, the patient, has been almost invisible in the policy-
making process. The average patient has no direct, controlling stake in the
economic and political process that determines health policy in the United
States. Moreover, patients, when they do organize, are split into different
groups of individuals with different goals: kidney dialysis patients, Medicare beneficiaries, lobbyists for better hospice care, advocates for better
coverage of children. The social stratification and segmentation of American society—its essential lack of social solidarity on welfare issues—has
also made it permissible for individuals to deal with problems of other
individuals at one remove, by creating abstract classifications in which to

isolate and insulate them. If one is well insured, for example, the problem of 30 to 40 million Americans who are uninsured, together with additional members of the population who are underinsured, may not seem terribly pressing; it is easy to see the "problem" as falling into a generic category of "others." The reluctance of federal and local agencies to recognize and to respond to the community-health implications of AIDS in the early 1980s was undoubtedly greater because of the initial classification of AIDS as a problem relating to a defined minority group of homosexuals.[80]

It is individual cases, publicized by the press, that bring home the hardships that may actually be endured. For example, the *Philadelphia Inquirer* recently featured the case of a thirty-seven-year-old man who was admitted to a hospital intensive care unit with an apparent heart attack. Although working, he had minimal health-insurance benefits through his employment. He and his wife may now be faced with thousands of dollars of bills that they will be unable to pay; indeed, they are already in debt for outstanding medical bills for their children.[81]

Meanwhile, the overriding importance of financial incentives in hospital service has centralized and concentrated power over money in agencies extrinsic to both hospitals and patients. Economic power shifted in the 1980s from those who provide health services to the organizations that pay for them. But the interests of those served as patients are not necessarily identical with the financial interests of third-party payers. These include major employers, insurers, and specialists in "managed care," whose role is to identify potentially high-cost patients, such as a patient with AIDS, and organize a program designed for efficient utilization of resources. Individuals are being told, in effect, that doctors, as entrepreneurs, and hospitals, as businesses, are no longer to be trusted as agents and advocates for the consumer; but that the large payers *are* to be trusted, even though their goals are overtly the goals of management efficiency.

Hospital policy-making since 1965 has not been a steady, market-directed movement toward an industrial model for the hospital system. It has been a process of trial and error, spurred by federal incentives and restraints, both of which might easily change again in the future. In two respects hospitals have been enormously successful in the past ten years: in continuing to survive and prosper (for the most part) as major, expensive, visible social institutions, and in broadening the services they offer including, among others, incontinence control, rental of medical equipment for the home, menopause centers, centers for back pain, exercise centers, outreach clinics and primary care services, home care, and post-hospital nursing-home care. As a result, hospitals are now better attuned to broad patterns of health and disease—at least for those who can afford the services and choose them wisely—than in any other decade of this century. The hospital has become a multifunction health-care institution, in a constant search for a new market niche.

Nevertheless, accompanying these changes are troubling questions of social ideals and aspirations. Is American medicine now so routine that it has lost the glow of a higher purpose? Are hospitals primarily useful to U.S. culture as embodiments of the values of money, organizational success, and utilitarianism—and no longer important for suggesting cultural, religious, and altruistic aspirations? Do we need hospitals to articulate social class and to create community cohesion and a sense of common purpose? Are patients purely customers, hospitals machine shops, and doctors mechanics? The commercial model for hospitals, largely a product of the 1980s, has in many ways been a success. But it is no accident that the debates in major hospital groups—and elsewhere—are turning to questions of "quality" and "values" in the last few years of the twentieth century.[82]

13

The American Hospital
System
in Historical Perspective

FEW OF US, in the jaded final years of the twentieth century, would describe hospitals as an idea to "die for," to use the more enthusiastic rhetoric of our predecessors (chapter 5). Nevertheless, community and voluntarism remain powerful themes. While the meaning of the word "charity" has both narrowed and gone out of fashion, its earlier meanings remain subsumed under "volunteerism": the social act of giving. One Gallup poll reported that almost half of the U.S. population over fourteen years of age was active in some kind of volunteer work in 1985; and the trend appears to be increasing.[1] Ideals, it would seem, *are* as important to American culture as the "business of business." And hospitals have symbolized American ideals, combining as they do science, philanthropy, and social obligation with technological innovation and the power of the purse.

The central role of voluntary hospitals has also fostered the impression that the United States has a "private" hospital service. In fact, as this history has emphasized, there has been a long-accepted interdependence of voluntary (and for-profit) hospitals with government institutions and governmental policies. Local-government hospitals in major cities have provided the residual services for the poor without which city voluntary hospitals would not have been able to select their clientele and maintain their income and autonomy. Tax exemption, government subsidy for construction, government purchase of care for the poor and dependent, including Medicare and Medicaid, and, for much of the century, charitable immunity from tort liability have shored up the voluntary hospital's fiscal position and stressed its central social role.

As a result, well before Medicare and the other Great Society programs of the 1960s, the United States could be described as a "welfare state that has acquired a universal reputation as arch-defender of the free enterprise system."[2] A Canadian critic, assessing U.S. national policy on hospital costs in the early 1980s at the height of the procompetition rhetoric, described Medicare, Medicaid, the veterans' program, and other smaller governmental programs as collectively "probably the largest socialized free system in the West." Yet, he observed, it was a system which "has not been allowed to develop the bureaucratic machinery by which a socialist society controls its expenditures."[3]

It is this clashing reality of government policy and fiscal power set against the facade of (and belief in) the morality and efficiency of private institutions that lies at the heart of contemporary unease about the future direction of the entire health-care system. The U.S. hospital enterprise challenges strongly held American myths—about charity, moral obligation, the strength of private organizations, and a minor role for government.

Ideals and Ideology in Hospital Policy

A major conclusion of this book is that the United States has a de facto national health system, expressed through its hospitals, although Americans are unwilling to recognize the fact and will indeed go to enormous lengths to deny it. As a result, we have high costs without concomitant social benefits. Without the commitment to a consistent national health policy and the will to implement it, the hospital system will not work equitably. The complaints of hospital critics fifty or sixty years ago still ring true: American hospitals constitute a production system with an inadequate distribution and financing system.

Hence also the paradox that while the American hospital enterprise has major deficiencies as a public service, as a largely private industry it has been enormously successful. Throughout the century hospitals have responded with great efficiency to the demands of purchasers and to opportunities for income and capital acquisition. The hospitals' essential ambiguity of purpose and adaptability to changing environmental pressures, particularly to monetary incentives, have enabled them to maximize their financial opportunities, expertise, and technique.

To a great extent hospital managers, trustees, and associated doctors have also created the demand for service. Hospitalization of obstetrics after World War I is a good example—as are today's outpatient surgery, rental of equipment for the home, management-consulting, and fitness centers. But these strengths—and they are strengths—are opportunistic. In the absence of financial incentives, hospitals have rarely tried to change the system in directions which would clearly be in the public interest: notably toward comprehensive services for long-term illness. It would of course be foolhardy to expect hospitals to carry the full weight of national policy-making for health care in the United States. But the present situation is one in which federal and state agencies are trying to further public agendas indirectly, through payment regulations, standardized systems, and limits on services, while hospitals are trying to deflect and/or resist them, in order to further their own organizational objectives.

It would be convenient to be able to reduce the tensions in the health-care system to simple dichotomies: to see "solutions," for example, in throwing the whole system to for-profit enterprise or to government. However, such a straightforward choice between alternative political value systems would ignore those other, largely apolitical values that have formed a major theme throughout this history. Although nongovernmental hospitals have been presented by their organizers as an alternative to socialist intervention since the nineteenth century, the history of American hospitals can only partly be explained in terms of a dichotomy between capitalism and socialism. Public and private roles are intermingled.

Voluntarism, for example, has served not only as a form of private entrepreneurship but as a vehicle for mutual responsibility. Yet in many small towns in America the vehicle for this same sense of solidarity has long been local-government and sometimes for-profit organization rather than the voluntary hospital (chapter 5). The actual form chosen has been a matter of local convenience, and/or the availability of local capital, and has had little to do with attitudes for or against "socialized medicine." In the 1920s, as today, a small-town community hospital under not-for-profit auspices may be difficult to distinguish from a for-profit or local-government-owned hospital. In the United States ownership is, as a general rule, less important as an indicator of what a hospital actually does than the clientele it serves and the management policies it pursues.

From the perspective of national policy, distinctions between rural and urban hospitals and between urban community hospitals and university medical centers form more critical dividing lines than ownership—now, as in the 1920s and 1930s. Current American Hospital Association statistics, for example, distinguish urban and rural community hospitals as discrete groups, without further specification by ownership within these categories.[4] Just as hospital statistics were used to delineate a voluntary hospital "sector" in the 1930s (chapter 6), today's statistics identify rural hospitals—almost *half* of all U.S. community hospitals—as an endangered sector—endangered, that is, under the impact of Medicare prospective payment.

American ideals of community, voluntary organization, and charity in its widest sense infuse the history of American hospitals, providing an ethos for social welfare which is largely independent of political divisions into "market" or "government" organization. But these ideals are as difficult to interpret in practical terms today as they were in the 1950s or 1920s. Community is now challenged by the centralization of policy-making in federal and state governments, voluntarism by the shift to a commercial ethos, and charity by the general assumption of third-party payment.

This history has shown that these words have long had vague, emotive meanings. They have expressed a rhetoric of intention—a description of a collective state of mind—rather than any exact program or method. Most hospitals, for example, have given away relatively little service throughout the century; they have not had the endowments to do so. Yet the idea of hospitals as charities has long been a pervasive theme because it has embodied the intentions imputed to hospital founders, the charitable intentions of board members and volunteers, and the general belief that hospitals are "good."

Rhetoric has also been useful as a rallying cry for action, enabling coalitions to be formed among potentially conflicting interests.[5] The political mobilization of the major American hospital associations around the idea of voluntarism in the 1930s is a major case in point; hospital interests are now one of the strongest political lobbies in the United States.

It is the constantly negotiated interplay of intentions and colliding social expectations that has generated the system we have today, with all its strengths, gaps, and weaknesses. Patients with chronic or terminal diseases and the large number of Americans who are uninsured or underinsured are the system's major victims. Hospitals simply cannot meet American ideals of technology, science, expertise, charity, voluntarism, equity, efficiency, community, and the privilege of class all at once, to everybody's satisfaction.

There are thus no simple solutions or obvious, predetermined pathways to the future development of hospital service. Public-policy concerns are acted out whenever too great a success in any one realm appears to be at the expense of others: too much equality, for example, if this means reducing ("rationing") services for those who can pay (or vice versa); too much government intervention if this means a threat to private initiative or local responsibility; too much local autonomy if this means an unacceptable amount of overlap and waste, leading in turn to rising costs, or unacceptable geographical variations. Lacking an agreed policy across the board, American national health policy is made through negotiated consensus among shifting coalitions.

Two other general conclusions emerge from this history. The first concerns the slippery role of the hospital itself, past and present: that chameleonlike, income-maximizing yet idealized institution. The second is a conclusion I did not expect when I began work on this book: a defense of the voluntary hospital, warts and all, as an instrument of social policy in the United States, justified by the historical record—and in the absence of any better alternative.

Coping with Ambiguity

The goals of American hospitals have been ambiguous throughout the century for basically four reasons: the lack of a unified social-welfare policy; the social agendas of hospitals, making them multipurpose institutions (part short-term treatment stations, part educational and professional centers, and part community organizations); the dual role of hospitals as both "charities" and "businesses"; and the symbolic value placed on hospitals as instruments of the wider culture.

Throughout the century U.S. hospitals have been motivated to be expensive not only to encourage the admission of paying patients but also to enhance their role as cultural icons. Today's hospital system is extravagant, visible, flamboyant, exclusive, and money-oriented, just as it was at the beginning of the century. Success in the hospital has helped to balance failures elsewhere in American society. Hence in the 1930s, hospitals could be described as "depression cures" (chapter 6). Large hospitals continue to be cultural palaces, lavish embodiments of the latest in American architecture, wealth, and engineering, even as their role changes and their structure is diversifying.

Yet hospitals, unlike other symbols of cultural pride, carry a central paradox within them, for medical success is intertwined with social failure. Hospitals signify achievements in American science and technology, but they also represent a breakdown in the public's health. In their beds lie, *inter alia,* victims of accidents, violence, poor nutrition, lack of knowledge, carelessness, overindulgence, poverty, and addiction, translated into damaged hearts, babies, lungs, and livers. As Ernst Meyer wrote in 1919, hospitals are at root "negative instruments of evolution" (chapter 4). They are reclamation centers, still more akin to sewage treatment plants than to schools. For most of the century there has been uncritical acceptance of science and technology (and of hospitals) as unalloyed "social goods." The pendulum is only now turning away from this position. (The end of government funding for the development of artificial hearts in 1988 is a good case in point.)[6] Even so, Americans tend to value hospitals, culturally, more highly than elementary or secondary schools—and pay their practitioners far more money.

Throughout the century the American identification of high medical quality with high cost has been legitimated by the central importance of the pay system. The drive to third-party payment since World War II and particularly since Medicare began has accelerated this trend toward market behavior; in the United States, hospital care is a commodity to be purchased. But hospitals have also long stood for "science." Doctors engaged in "scientific medicine" in university settings have long been associated in the professional and popular press with a spirit of dedication and altruism that transcends money.

It was in pursuit of medical science that major national philanthropic foundations poured money into university medical centers before World War II, followed by federal government subsidy after the war. (Foundation money to rural hospitals represented, in contrast, commitment to the ideal of "community," continued in the federal Hill-Burton legislation after World War II.) As Daniel Fox has argued, the identification of teaching hospitals with scientific knowledge was central to conceptions of hospital planning—regional networks or hierarchies centered on university medical complexes—from before World War I to the 1970s.[7] Belief in a science-based hospital system as the "democratic" alternative to socialism in the 1940s (chapter 8) presented a larger variant of this theme.

The idea of medicine as a "science," with hospitals as its major instrument, continues to infuse hospital policy, most recently represented in standard definitions for prospective payment (DRGs) and standard expectations about hospital use. Yet so long as medicine is seen as a system of standardized problems and reproducible results, complex health (and public-health) problems will remain largely unexamined, while incurable diseases, including, notably, AIDS, will remain on the fringes of medical prestige. It remains to be seen whether the impact of AIDS will be so great that it will change the basic attitudes of medicine itself.

Because hospitals have represented science in the United States, they carry important weight in the culture as a whole. If they are to be seen, in the future, purely as technological systems (spare-part factories) with little symbolic importance beyond this, their cultural importance will diminish. We are seeing part of this cultural shift now: the secularization of hospitals as images of science and charity and their relegation to the realm of mammon. Hence the paradox that as medical work in hospitals has become more brilliant and effective year by year, public criticism has increased, not decreased.

In other ways, too, hospitals, like other social institutions, have served the larger interests of the culture, polity, and state. Early in the century hospitals protected the growth of corporate capitalism by providing a charitable device designed to counter its worst effects, including treatment for industrial accidents and services for transient workmen and families crowded in tenements. Charitable hospitals transformed business leaders, in their role as hospital sponsors and board members, from materialists to philanthropists; defined the role of society women and social networks in delineating the emerging social order; emphasized the place of private efforts, organized by volunteers, as an alternative to government intervention; and upheld science, technology, and expertise as valuable attributes of the culture as a whole. Hospitals have been powerful instruments of American ideas (or myths) about community, first strongly articulated in the 1920s (chapter 5), and espoused as federal policy after World War II (chapter 9).

Today's hospitals serve less obviously as forces for social order and for the definition of social class than they did at the beginning of the century. Nevertheless, there is a strong thread of continuity. Membership on prestigious hospital boards still confirms social standing through the privilege of duty. Hospital staffing is still a good reflection of contemporary class, gender, and racial relations—from the cadre of well-paid (still largely male) attending physicians, through the (largely female) ranks of nurses, therapists, and technicians, to the army of blue-collar workers in lesser-paid occupations, who are disproportionately members of minority groups. Indeed, in some ways the occupational divisions are now more important than they were in earlier decades, because of the sheer size of the hospital enterprise. (In the city where I live, Philadelphia, hospitals are the largest category of employer, with the largest annual payroll, followed by colleges and universities, with eating establishments coming third.)

The organizational principle emerging from this history is one of constructive ambiguity. Keeping options open has served hospitals well as a means of surviving and adapting. But a necessary corollary to this principle is an organizational environment in which flexibility can be maintained. And today two salient, connected features of the hospital system are in doubt: decentralized decision-making (institutional autonomy) and voluntary nonprofit organization.

In the past, national standards have consistently been used to encourage local initiative, from the early standardization program of the American College of Surgeons (chapter 5), through the Hill-Burton program (chapters 8 and 9), to the competitive rhetoric of the last decade (chapter 12). The result has been to concentrate the hospital enterprise in a large number of relatively small units (many of which are now formally part of multi-institutional systems), thus meeting the goals of community provision, but to support the provision of up-to-date techniques in each of them, thus meeting the ideals of technological capability. The average community hospital in the United States contains only 172 beds. Yet more than 60 percent of all community hospitals have CT scanners, ultrasound, blood banks, histopathology laboratories, emergency departments and facilities for ambulatory surgery, as well as (relatively new) health-promotion units and, of course, volunteer services.[8] It is not surprising that the hospital system overall is expensive, nor that Medicare should be seen as an opportunity to impose national order on the system. Standardized Medicare regulation, state rate-setting programs, specifications for service by major private payers, including large employers, and other external forces are imposing far more uniformity than did the older professional standardization of hospital accreditation.

But if the U.S. system is becoming simultaneously more standardized, more profit-oriented, and more government-driven, is there still a case for voluntary not-for-profit hospitals, whose traditional strength has been local autonomy and organizational flexibility? My conclusion is that there is.

The Not-for-Profit Sector

Not-for-profit hospitals, like other nonprofit institutions, are valuable in three ways: as a device for containing conflicts of values and diverse social interests; as an opportunity for voluntary effort and for the symbolic meanings attached to this effort (altruism, commitment, pride, stability); and as a means for mobilizing social action where public goals are value-laden and unquantifiable.[9] Today, however, U.S. voluntary hospitals are threatened in each of these three areas of social usefulness. If prospective payment regulations can specify the services to be purchased, hospital care is not "unquantifiable." If there is general agreement that hospitals are businesses, there is no longer a conflict of values. If "charity" has disappeared, where is the rationale for voluntary effort? It is these shifts in perception—coupled with the power of financial incentives to shape the system—that have created, as much as anything else, the sense of instability in the health-care system. Voluntary hospitals are bereft of their claim for existence as public entities.

Apart from the basic irony of federal policy in the 1970s and 1980s—stimulating hospitals to behave like businesses and then chastising them for being successful—two elements in the collapse of the traditional relationship between government and voluntary hospitals after the introduction of Medicare should be stressed, one a question of balance, the other a question of centralization. After Medicare (1965) hospital income shifted rapidly toward government funding, while capital shifted from local donations to debt. Voluntary hospitals were treated as businesses, with their central relationship with government represented by the purchase contract (chapters 11 and 12). But Medicare is dramatically different from a grant-in-aid program such as Medicaid or the old Hill-Burton program or grants for biomedical research, which all rely on local decision-making and decentralized initiative. There is as yet no accepted political and managerial philosophy for hospitals which encompasses the new relations between hospitals and the "state" other than the purchase model, backed by detailed standard-setting.

A mixed public-private system of subsidized service, through relatively autonomous local organizations, has nevertheless been the most consistent approach to hospital policy throughout the century; and it is too early to write it off.[10] The potential of government grants to independent hospitals or health-care systems, as an alternative to the DRG (prospective payment) system, remains a possibility for the future.

Such organizations do not necessarily have to be non-profit organizations. There is a long history of government contracting with business corporations in the United States. I have described voluntary hospitals as being income-oriented, exclusionary, and self-serving throughout the century. All else being equal, the hospital sector might become more efficient, as Regina Herzlinger has argued forcefully, if it were transformed into a for-profit, tax-paying entity, "subject to the intense scrutiny of its owners."[11] However, the history of hospitals is, if nothing else, about constant, often unpredictable change. A decade or so of belief in the values of self-interest and for-profit enterprise may well be followed in the 1990s by a swing toward collective concerns and social obligations and to bolder government initiatives. I think this cycle has already begun.

Five arguments suggest the continuing value of voluntary hospitals in the future. The first is the well-known American axiom, "If it ain't broke, don't fix it." Voluntary hospitals have been successful organizations in the past hundred years because of their chameleonlike adjustments to changing conditions. At times of "privatization," like the 1920s or the early 1980s, the hospitals have stressed their efficiency as businesses. At times when the political pendulum has swung toward a greater role for government, the hospitals, too, have swung toward a more public stance and purpose—as in the 1930s and the 1960s. By being able to present themselves as politically and economically independent, as private charities, as public charities, as public utilities, as businesses, and so on, the hospitals have been able constantly to update their image. Voluntary-hospital representatives are already attempting to differentiate themselves from investor-owned enterprises, if only for political and economic advantage, just as they did in the 1930s, stressing a new mission of altruism and voluntary "spirit."

A second argument stems from the behavior of investor-owned enterprises of any kind. The public responsibility of an investor-owned organization is naturally to its shareholders. If income flowing to hospital care declines substantially, as it may well do, the responsible investor-owned enterprise will divest and shift its resources into other, more profitable fields. There may be short-term public-relations values in investor-owned firms maintaining loss leaders in some communities or for some purposes; for example, a major teaching hospital may bring the corporation valuable prestige. Nevertheless, an underlying characteristic of investment is versatility in the use of *capital.* Voluntary hospitals constitute a relatively permanent form of institution, whose versatility is represented by a shift in *function* and *presentation,* as the environment changes, rather than shifting capital and abandoning ship. They are, in short, both flexible and stable.

Third, it is not in the long-term interests of the business community, locally or nationally, to encourage a hospital system dominated by investor-owned institutions. Hospitals do provide public services—there is no avoiding the historical comparisons of hospital service with electricity, water, and telephones. If the United States had a system where most hospitals were run as private investments, the hospitals collectively would assume quasi-public functions, thus limiting their maneuverability as investments and undermining their ability to appeal to stockholders. Hospitals would become regulated as public utilities. This is indeed one possible road for the U.S. hospital system in the future. The question then becomes, whether the public utility model is better, and in what ways, than the present system dominated by voluntary institutions. My own conclusion is that we see the best of all three types of organization—investor-owned, voluntary, and governmental—when the former is in a small minority, and where there is competitive tension among the different forms of institution. But there is no magic formula as to what the appropriate balance should be.

Fourth, voluntarism begs the question of public and private roles, while assuming that hospitals have responsibilities in both spheres. Voluntary hospitals were established as the natural complement to business in the United States. Even today, if voluntary hospitals did not exist, they might well be reinvented. Indeed, business coalitions, a new form of voluntary organization, are in some respects reinventing the old ideas of community sponsorship and trusteeship. Without a strong commitment to welfare-state egalitarianism or to a government-run health service in the United States—quite the reverse—voluntary organizations will continue to be useful. Voluntary organizations also continue to be the natural alternatives to socialism in the United States: an acceptable form of private enterprise which government agencies may support, regulate, and criticize without accepting full responsibility for what they do or how they do it.

Finally, it has proved impossible—even after a decade of "competition"—to lay the ghosts of social obligation and moral virtue that cling to the powerful American ideals of voluntarism, charity, and community. American hospitals have embodied powerful social ideals in the past. They still do, even if only in the sense of concern about the profit ethos. Voluntary, not-for-profit hospitals are important *because* they carry the burden of unresolved, perhaps unresolvable contradictions—and because they make these contradictions visible.

What Next?

The future of American hospitals is tied to the future of American medicine while medicine itself is undergoing a profound transformation. Older notions of scientific medicine on which the profession and hospitals have been based—grounded in assumptions about infectious disease and surgery at the turn of the century—are no longer adequate. Resolving present problems of uncertainty (and low morale) in the American medical profession requires nothing less than the development of a revised body of theory, targeted to chronic disease, care as well as cure, and a restatement of the meaning of professionalism. These tasks are similar in scope to the creation of the national medical profession at the beginning of the century, with its corollary effect on hospital service.

If medicine takes the road of technological reductionism, hospitals are likely to develop as factories for human repair. If medicine becomes more socially, psychologically, and behaviorally oriented, hospitals will find it easier to grow in these directions. Doctor-hospital relations pose problems for the immediate future. There is a sense among both doctors and hospital managers that they are antagonists engaged in a power struggle, which the managers expect to win. However, as in the past, the strongest institutions promise to be those where mutual accommodations are negotiated.

The speed of technological change must also be emphasized. Cardiology and cardiovascular surgery, for example, emerged as specialties only after World War II. Spectacular changes since the late 1950s have included closed chest massage and defibrillation, electronic monitoring, and major changes in electrophysiology and in pharmacology, from the development of beta-blockers to anticlotting therapies, including streptokinase and aspirin. Pacemakers, prosthetic valve replacement, cardiac catherization, and heart transplantation have become common procedures. A recent editorial pointed out that when President Eisenhower was hospitalized for an uncomplicated heart attack in 1955 he spent seven weeks convalescing in the hospital, but a similar patient may now be discharged in three days.[12] One physician, looking back on his own simpler, beeperless house staff days, remarked: "Comparing medicine then and now is like comparing horse-and-buggy days with interplanetary travel."[13]

Coupled with changes in hospital-based medicine is a fundamental questioning of the uses and future of technique as a central attribute of medicine and the medical profession. The patient with a chest pain, wrote one cardiologist in the early 1980s, does not go to the doctor looking for a stress test or an arteriogram or open-heart surgery; he or she comes for advice and help.[14] The logic of this comment—and there are many such illustrations—suggests a new kind of medicine in which the encounter between doctor and patient is less a matter of technological and scientific absolutes (the ground rules on which the modern hospital was based) and more of discussion and priority-setting.

The idea of medicine as progress, an ideal central to the hospital's twentieth-century image, is also under fire. A recent review of trends over the past thirty years stated flatly, "We are losing the war against cancer."[15] Surgeons are not the heroes they once were. One medical critic, describing coronary-artery bypass surgery, the most common major surgical procedure in the early 1980s, as a "panacea," questioned: "Will it go the way of tonsillectomy, once the most frequently performed operation?"[16] The answer is, quite possibly yes. The high rate of cesarian sections is, similarly, being questioned. Hospitalization is no longer viewed as "safe," the hospital's message in the simpler days of surgery, sixty or seventy years ago. Risks created by the medical procedures themselves can create problems of their own (iatrogenic diseases) and invoke a clinical process that, once started, may develop a momentum of its own—with an outcome not always favorable to the patient.[17]

What hospitals will actually treat—the social individual, the patient's body (the physiological machine), or the cell—is a major question for the future. The average hospital of the future may be little more than an intensive care unit or a collection of specialized workshops. At the other end of the range of possibilities, all hospitals may expand into multifaceted health-care complexes which would include freestanding surgical centers, primary care units, high-technology home care, nursing homes, and other functions and facilities. In this model the basic notion of the "hospital" extends beyond the walls of the institution to the application of medical technology in a wide variety of service centers. The hospital becomes, in effect, the health-care system.

U.S. hospitals will probably continue to affiliate with others in larger local systems; and there may be enhanced identification of hospitals as part of regional and national chains, depending on financial incentives and other messages in the environment, including antitrust regulation—that is, on how far hospitals are allowed to combine, by law, into monopolies or oligopolies. There will probably be a variety of models in the future, as there have been in the past, together with a reaffirmation by hospitals of their functions in local communities, irrespective of ownership or membership in larger systems. The history of hospitals suggests that hospitals will continue to expand wherever possible rather than to contract, and that they will continue to be controlled by shifting coalitions of community interests: business interests, physicians, third-party payers, trustees, administrators, politicians, lobbyists. The key question now, as in the past, is, however, the availability and the channeling of hospital income. Without adequate income, hospital bankruptcies, mergers, and closures will be as commonplace as they were in the Depression of the 1930s.

The question of hospitals as instruments of "charity" is more difficult. Just as the old notion of "scientific medicine" is being reworked within the medical profession and "scientific management" by increasing managerialism, so "scientific charity" also demands rethinking as a strategic social undertaking. The three "sciences" still stand for the roles of doctors, administrators, and trustees, as they did early in the century, although government agencies, lobbying groups, and major purchasers are also major players. Trustees are under special strain. Hospitals may have a future as exemplary social institutions; that is, as institutions where science and humanitarianism, business and ideals are mixed. But trustees have traditionally been conservative (and often uninformed). How far will they wish to (or be able to) define community goals and roles for hospitals? How much influence will they exert? How far will they regain some of the power lost early in the century to doctors and more recently to managers? All these are open questions.

Optimists see trustees emerging as the "rationers of hospital care on behalf of the community" and as the only component of the hospital community "able to achieve a reconciliation of the conflicting demands in a relatively objective manner."[18] We shall see. Out of all the cast of characters within the complex of the hospital itself, the role of managers is at present the most critical in a system whose norms are frankly mercantilist, but the policies which pushed this stance, too, may change—a conclusion which managers may wish to remember.

Two overriding messages come from this history. First, given economic incentives, public support and a strong, prestigious medical profession, hospitals will respond to public policy in ways that protect their institutional survival and ensure, where possible, their prosperity. Ambiguity, adaptability, and income maximization have marked their long success as businesses. The second message is that what hospitals do has never been seen purely as a business; hospitals have carried strong elements of idealism. They are still, to some extent, charities in the early-twentieth-century sense: institutions through which the moral values of American society are expressed. Racial distinctions and disparities in services by social class, type of illness, age, income, and employment are the major challenges to the ideals of hospital service today. Redefining ideals in the late twentieth century means lobbying by consumer groups, hospitals, employers, and others for public policy designed to improve individual insurance coverage; mobilization at the local level to define and meet community needs; and pressures within the system to bring the major players together to work for common goals.

There is no single or obvious direction for the future. As in the past, the hospital system is what we make it, for good or ill, as charity and business. The quality of American medical care is, indeed, an index of American civilization.

NOTES

Chapter 1

1. Unless otherwise stated, I limit the term "hospitals" in this book to mean nonfederal short-term, acute general hospitals (with a few related special hospitals), as distinguished from federal hospitals, long-stay hospitals for chronic disease, and psychiatric hospitals, which have their own, separate histories.

2. American Hospital Association, *Hospital Statistics, 1988 Edition* (Chicago: American Hospital Association, 1988), pp. 4–6.

3. In thinking about the role of hospitals in American society, I have drawn on the literature of American medicine, technology, ideas, organizations, and social history. I am particularly indebted to Sam Bass Warner, *The Private City: Philadelphia in Three Periods of Its Growth,* 2nd ed. (Philadelphia: University of Pennsylvania Press, 1987); Robert Wiebe, *The Search for Order, 1877–1920* (New York: Hill & Wang, 1967), and *The Segmented Society: An Introduction to the Meaning of America* (New York: Oxford University Press, 1975); Alfred Chandler, Jr., *The Visible Hand: The Managerial Revolution in American Business* (Cambridge, Mass.: Harvard University Press, Belknap Press, 1977); Michel Crozier and Erhard Friedman, *Actors and Systems: The Politics of Collective Action,* trans. Arthur Goldhammer (Chicago: University of Chicago Press, 1980); Charles E. Rosenberg, *No Other Gods: On Science and American Social Thought* (Baltimore: Johns Hopkins University Press, 1976), and *The Care of Strangers: The Rise of America's Hospital System* (New York: Basic Books, 1987); David Rosner, *A Once Charitable Enterprise: Hospitals and Health Care in Brooklyn and New York 1885–1915* (Cambridge: Cambridge University Press, 1982); Morris J. Vogel, *The Invention of the Modern Hospital: Boston 1870–1930* (Chicago: University of Chicago Press, 1980); Russell E. Richey and Donald G. Jones, eds., *American Civil Religion* (New York: Harper & Row, 1974); Grant McConnell, *Private Power and American Democracy* (New York: Knopf, 1966); and Harvey Brooks, Lance Liebman, and Corinne Schelling, eds., *Public-Private Partnership: New Opportunities for Meeting Social Needs* (Cambridge, Mass.: Published for the American Academy of Arts and Sciences by Ballinger Publishing Co., 1984).

4. A good account of the way in which the different parts of the American health-care system work together to produce and disseminate technology is Howard Waitzkin, "A Marxian Interpretation of the Growth and Development of Coronary Care Units," in Peter Conrad and Rochelle Kern, eds., *The Sociology of Health and Illness,* 2nd ed. (New York: St. Martin's Press, 1986), pp. 219–31. The rapidity of this diffusion is shown by Louise B. Russell, *Technology and Hospitals: Medical Advances and Their Diffusion* (Washington, D.C.: Brookings Institution, 1979).

Thomas P. Hughes and other historians and sociologists of technology are developing general models of technological systems, their evolution and behavior, and hospitals may be analogous to these models to some extent. My point is that the concurrent values of community service and professionalism form an interweaving counterpoint and provide alternative models for interpretation of hospitals—which constitute, by their very nature, a hybrid system. Thomas P. Hughes, *Networks of Power: Electrification in Western Society 1880–1930* (Baltimore: Johns Hopkins University Press, 1983); and Weibe E. Bijker, Thomas P. Hughes, and

Trevor Pinch, eds., *The Social Construction of Technological Systems: New Directions in the Sociology and History of Technology* (Cambridge, Mass.: MIT Press, 1987).

5.   The best recent example is Henry J. Aaron and William B. Schwartz, *The Painful Prescription: Rationing Hospital Care* (Washington, D.C.: Brookings Institution, 1984).

6.   American Hospital Association, *Hospital Statistics*, p. xxviii.

7.   "Hospital Life in New York," *Harper's New Monthly Magazine*, 1878, p. 176.

8.   In 1984, for example, the equivalent of 15% of the population were served as inpatients in a nonfederal short-stay hospital; the equivalent of 8% had operations as inpatients; and 5% experienced other invasive diagnostic and other nonsurgical procedures. *Health, United States, 1986, and Prevention Profile* (Washington, D.C.: U.S. Department of Health and Human Services, 1986), pp. 144, 148, 150.

9.   For the best descriptions and analyses of this process and its consequences, see Susan Reverby, *Ordered to Care: The Dilemma of American Nursing 1850–1945* (Cambridge: Cambridge University Press, 1987); and Barbara Melosh, *The Physician's Hand: Work, Culture, and Conflict in American Nursing* (Philadelphia: Temple University Press, 1982).

10.   Commonwealth Fund, *Report of the Task Force on Academic Health Centers: Prescription for Change* (New York: Commonwealth Fund, 1985).

11.   Paul Starr, *The Social Transformation of American Medicine: The Rise of a Sovereign Profession and the Making of a Vast Industry* (New York: Basic Books, 1982).

Chapter 2

1.   Alfred Worcester, *Small Hospitals: Establishment and Maintenance* (New York: Wiley & Sons, 1894), p. 1.

2.   U.S. Bureau of the Census, *Benevolent Institutions, 1904* (Washington, D.C.: Government Printing Office, 1905), p. 23; ibid., *Benevolent Institutions, 1910* (Washington, D.C.: Government Printing Office, 1913), p. 22. The comment on hospitals as a "public undertaking" is from the *1904 Census*, pp. 16–17.

3.   Henry James, *The American Scene*, with an introduction by Leon Edel (Bloomington: Indiana University Press, 1968), pp. 187–89, 318–20.

4.   W. W. Keen, "Surgery," in Alfred Russel Wallace et al., *The Progress of the Century* (New York: Harper & Brothers, 1901), p. 254. Keen was professor of the principles of surgery and of clinical surgery, Jefferson Medical College, Philadelphia.

5.   Isabel M. Stewart, "Problems of Nursing Education," *Teachers College Record* 11 (May 1910), pp. 16, 9–10.

6.   The definitive work on the transformation of American hospitals between 1850 and 1920 (and their earlier history from 1800) is by Charles E. Rosenberg, *The Care of Strangers: The Rise of America's Hospital System* (New York: Basic Books, 1987). The best recent account of the growing cultural authority of the medical profession is by Paul Starr, *The Social Transformation of American Medicine.*

7.   Charles Stewart Loch, "Charity and Charities," in *The Encyclopaedia Brittanica*, 11th ed., vol. V (New York: Encyclopaedia Brittanica Co., 1910), p. 886.

8.   S. S. Goldwater, "The Appropriation of Public Funds for the Partial Support of Voluntary Hospitals in the United States and Canada," *Transactions of the American Hospital Association* 11 (1909), p. 243. For the early financial history of the Pennsylvania Hospital, see William H. Williams, *America's First Hospital: The Pennsylvania Hospital, 1751–1841* (Wayne, Pa.: Haverford House, 1976), p. 15 and passim.

9.   Warner L. Wells, "Pioneer Hospitals in North Carolina," in Dorothy Long, ed., *Medicine in North Carolina: Essays in the History of Medical Science and Medical Service*, vol. 1 (Raleigh: North Carolina Medical Society, 1972), p. 283. The lack of local capital—as well as physician choice—as a major reason for establishing proprietary hospitals is cogently argued by J. Rogers Hollingsworth and Ellen Jane Hollingsworth, *Controversy About American Hospitals: Funding, Ownership, and Performance* (Washington, D.C.: American Enterprise Institute, 1988).

10.   The U.S. Census Bureau found in 1910 that there were fewer than 2,000 government, religious, and other nonprofit hospitals. The *A.M.A. Directory* figures for 1909 report more than 4,000 "hospitals." However, both lists must be taken very tentatively because of con-

tinuing problems of differentiating hospitals from clinics and from nonmedical institutions. About 16% of the 692 hospitals reporting to a Bureau of Education survey in 1911 were proprietary hospitals. This proportion, if generalizable, would obviously put the number of proprietary hospitals well below 1,500, but it is not clear what the basis of selection was for this sample—presumably, these were hospitals with nursing schools. Adelaide Nutting, *Educational Status of Nursing* (Washington, D.C.: Government Printing Office, 1912), p. 20.

11. Starr, *The Social Transformation of American Medicine*, pp. 165–66.

12. A survey conducted in 1903 found that seventeen out of twenty major hospitals in the Northeast and Midwest were allowing doctors to charge fees directly to their private hospital patients. "Statistics of Pay Patient Service in Twenty One American Hospitals," Report of Committee on Pay Patients, *Proceedings of the Hospital Association of Philadelphia*, 1903, pp. 38–47. There is now a good literature on the growth of physician billing. The best general accounts of the change from physician donation to charging for these services are Rosenberg, *The Care of Strangers*, pp. 252–58 and passim; Vogel, *The Invention of the Modern Hospital*, pp. 97–119; Rosner, *A Once Charitable Enterprise*; Starr, *The Social Transformation of American Medicine*; and George Rosen, *The Structure of American Medical Practice, 1875 to 1914* (Philadelphia: University of Pennsylvania Press, 1983).

13. St. Mary's Hospital, Rochester, was independent and self-supporting, largely through charging fees for bed, board, and nursing. The hospital made a slight profit in 1904. Lucy Wilder, *The Mayo Clinic* (New York: Harcourt Brace & Co., 1936), pp. 13, 32, and passim.

14. Frances Stuart Hanckel, "American Hospitals in 1910" (Johns Hopkins University, Ph.D. diss., School of Hygiene and Public Health, 1985), p. 359. From original data reported to the U.S. Census Bureau in *Benevolent Institutions, 1910.*

15. Edward T. Devine, *The Principles of Relief* (New York: Macmillan, 1904), p. 48.

16. Nutting, *Educational Status of Nursing*, pp. 14, 18. Hanckel found that half the hospitals in the Far West had nursing programs in 1910, a far smaller proportion than in the Northeast. *American Hospitals in 1910*, p. 268.

17. The phrase "true scientific plan" is from a comment by Arthur Ryerson, president of St. Luke's Hospital, Chicago, at the International Congress on Charities and Correction at the Columbian Exposition of 1893. Ryerson's views were probably commonplace among board members of hospitals established before the 1890s. He said he had had great difficulty in moving from the idea of the hospital as an "institution of charity" in the sense of giving away services free, feeling "that we were in some way violating our pledge to the public by taking pay patients." Now, however, he had become convinced of the desirability of regulating charges according to the patient's economic condition. John S. Billings and Henry M. Hurd, eds., *Hospitals, Dispensaries, and Nursing,* Papers and Discussions in the International Congress of Charities, Correction, and Philanthropy, sec. III (Baltimore: Johns Hopkins University Press, 1894), pp. 127–28.

18. Henry C. Burdett, *Hospitals and Asylums of the World* (London: J. A. Churchill, The Scientific Press, 1893), vol. 3, *Hospitals: History and Administration,* p. 55. Burdett's own studies in the early 1890s found enormous ranges of practice, even in the same cities; for example, income from pay patients ranged from less than 1% at the well-endowed Protestant Episcopal Hospital in Philadelphia to over 70% at the Pennsylvania Hospital in the same city, which catered in large part to the working population. Ibid., pp. 712, 718–19.

19. Henry M. Lyman, in Billings and Hurd, eds., *Hospitals, Dispensaries, and Nursing,* p. 126.

20. Ibid., p. 4.

21. Ibid., p. 126.

22. Joan E. Lynaugh, "The Community Hospitals of Kansas City Missouri, 1875–1912" (Ph.D. diss., University of Kansas, 1981), p. 7.

23. Rosenberg, "Inward Vision and Outward Glance: The Shaping of the American Hospital, 1880–1914," *Bulletin of the History of Medicine* 53 (1978), pp. 346–91.

24. Sidney E. Goldstein, "The Social Function of the Hospital," *Charities and the Commons* 18 (May 4, 1907), p. 161 and passim.

25. Hanckel, *American Hospitals in 1910,* p. 359.

26. Charles P. Emerson, "The American Hospital Field," in Charlotte Aikens, ed., *Hospital Management* (New York: W. B. Saunders, 1911), p. 48. Morris Vogel attributes Boston City Hospital's success to local party politics, to medical rivalry with Massachusetts General Hospital, and to the hospital board's desire to capture all possible revenues. *The Invention of the Modern Hospital,* p. 110 and passim. In turn the city of Boston drew the most receipts

(including patient income) from its general hospital of all large cities in 1916: about $150,000. Cleveland came next ($99,000), followed by Philadelphia ($29,000) and New York City ($20,000). In other major cities the gap between "pay hospitals" and "city hospitals" was more pronounced. Chicago, for example, reported less than $3,000 in receipts from its city hospital in 1916, St. Louis less than $400, and Baltimore a mere $27. U.S. Department of Labor, Bureau of the Census, Special Reports, *Financial Statistics of Cities Having a Population of Over 30,000, 1916* (Washington, D.C.: Government Printing Office, 1917), p. 180.

27.   Emily Dunning Barringer, *Bowery to Bellevue: The Story of New York's First Woman Ambulance Surgeon* (New York: Norton, 1950), p. 145. The best historical account of city hospitals is Harry Dowling, *City Hospitals: The Undercare of the Underprivileged* (Cambridge, Mass.: Harvard University Press, 1982).

28.   Rosenberg, *The Care of Strangers,* p. 324.

29.   Denslow Lewis, "The Management of Our Charity Hospitals," *Illinois Medical Journal* 4 (1903), p. 591. The best reviews of almshouse services in the 1920s are Harry C. Evans, *The American Poorfarm and Its Inmates* (Mooseheart, Ill.: Loyal Order of Moose, 1926); and Estelle M. Stewart, "The Cost of American Almshouses," *Bulletin of the U.S. Bureau of Labor Statistics,* no. 386 (Washington, D.C.: Government Printing Office, 1925).

30.   New York City also spent by far the most tax funds on hospital operating expenses: $3.67 million in 1916. This figure included the cost of the city's own hospital system plus subsidies to charitable institutions. Next in line came Chicago (less than $900,000), Boston (less than $800,000), and Philadelphia ($400,000). U.S. Department of Labor, Bureau of the Census, Special Reports, *Financial Statistics of Cities Having a Population of Over Thirty Thousand, 1909* (Washington, D.C.: Government Printing Office, 1913), p. 170; ibid., *1916* (Washington, D.C.: Government Printing Office, 1917), p. 206.

31.   Cincinnati, with a population of approximately 350,000, reported the value of its city hospital facilities as $3.06 million in 1909—much more than the value of city hospital facilities in Chicago ($2.33 million), where the population was six times larger. Ibid., *1909,* p. 170.

32.   Hanckel, *American Hospitals in 1910,* p. 359.

33.   John Foote, "Hospitals, their Origin and Evolution," *Popular Science Monthly* 82 (1913), p. 491. Hospitals admitted half of all inmates in "benevolent institutions" in 1903, and incurred half of the cost of all such institutions, but drew more than 80% of the income from paying patients. *1904 Census,* p. 23.

34.   Jon Kingsdale, "The Growth of Hospitals: An Economic History in Baltimore" (Ph.D. diss., University of Michigan, 1981), pp. 248, 265. According to the Census Bureau, there were six states in which more than $1 million was spent on hospital care in 1903. Of these, New York reported 29% of its combined government and voluntary hospital revenues from pay patients, Pennsylvania 30%, and Massachusetts 36%, while in Illinois, California, and Ohio the proportions were 63%, 56%, and 42% respectively.

35.   Walter Mucklow Burnett, *Touro Infirmary* (New Orleans: Touro Infirmary, 1979), pp. 67–68.

36.   "Hospital Shortcomings," editorial, *New York Medical Journal* 101 (1915), p. 29.

37.   Joseph J. Weber, "A Survey of Sickness," *The Survey,* October 16, 1915, pp. 65–69.

38.   These points were made by Charles P. Emerson in Aikens, ed., *Hospital Management,* p. 46.

39.   *Report of the Jefferson Hospital for Year Ending May 31, 1916* (Philadelphia, 1916), p. 22.

40.   Keen in Wallace et al., *The Progress of the Century,* pp. 238–39.

41.   J. M. T. Finney, "The Duty of the Family Physician in the Management of Surgical Cases," *New York State Medical Journal* 12 (1912), p. 230.

42.   Frank B. Gilbreth, Jr., and Ernestine Gilbreth Carey, *Cheaper by the Dozen* (New York: Bantam Books, 1984; first published 1949), pp. 76–84.

43.   Henry M. Hurd, "The Relation of the Hospital to the Community," *Teachers College Record* 11 (May 1910), pp. 52–54.

44.   Joel D. Howell, "Early Use of X-ray Machines and Electrocardiographs at the Pennsylvania Hospital," *Journal of the American Medical Association* 255 (1986), pp. 2320–23.

45.   Alexander K. Pedrick, ed., *Charitable Institutions of Pennsylvania Which Received State Aid in 1897 and 1898* (Harrisburg, Pa.: State Printer, 1898), p. 191.

46.   "Report of the Medical Board," in Brattleboro Memorial Hospital, *Sixth and Seventh Annual Reports for the Years Ending December 1, 1910 and 1911* (Brattleboro, Vt.: Brattleboro

Memorial Hospital, 1912), unpaginated. As an example of a larger hospital, Jefferson Hospital, Philadelphia, reported receipts in 1916 not only from the boarding of patients (such fees include care by student nurses) but also from boarding special nurses, operating-room charges, X-ray charges, special charges in the maternity department and in the department of diseases of the chest, ambulance charges, special charges for physiotherapy, charges for telephones, and—most lucratively—charges for the sale of drugs. *Report of the Jefferson Hospital for Year Ending May 31, 1916,* p. 70.

47. Aikens, *Hospital Management,* p. 125.

48. Burdett estimated in the 1890s that the average daily expenditure was at least 20% higher in American hospitals than in English and Scottish hospitals. He attributed this to the fact that American hospitals furnished everything, whereas British patients were often expected to provide food and linens, and to a somewhat higher salary scale in America. Burdett, *Hospitals and Asylums of the World,* p. 720. The 1911 figures are from Robert Pinker, *English Hospital Statistics 1861–1938* (London: Heinemann, 1966), pp. 149–50. The best national study of British hospital history is Brian Abel-Smith, *The Hospitals 1800–1948* (London: Heinemann Educational Books, 1964). The best regional study of the growth of hospitals in Britain is John V. Pickstone, *Medicine and Industrial Society: A History of Hospital Development in Manchester and its Region, 1752–1946* (Manchester: Manchester University Press, 1985).

49. "Public Hospital or Private Sanitarium?" *Trained Nurse and Hospital Review* 18 (January 1897), p. 44.

50. German Hospital, Philadelphia, issued a circular in English and German strongly recommending the advantages of subscribing to the hospital in return for stated service benefits. Working people of both sexes up to the age of fifty would pay an initiation fee of $1 and monthly installments of 50 cents in return for free treatment when sick. "Heads of families and owners of factories," advised the circular, "should particularly recommend their servants and employees to avail themselves of this excellent facility." Edward Jackson, "The Hospital, the Doctor, and the Community," *Proceedings of the Philadelphia County Medical Society* XVIII (1897), pp. 43–44.

51. "Commercializing the Hospital," editorial, *New York Medical Journal* XCIV (1911), p. 1291; "Hospitals and Commerce," editorial, ibid., XCIX (1914), 843.

52. George M. Gould, *Borderland Studies* (Philadelphia: Blakiston & Co., 1896), pp. 175, 177.

53. Editorial, *Journal of the American Medical Association* 37 (1901), p. 114.

54. Jackson, "The Hospital, the Doctor, and the Community," pp. 46–48.

55. Editorial, *Medical News,* December 19, 1896, p. 707.

56. Louis R. Curtis, "The Modern Hotel-Hospital," *Transactions of the American Hospital Association* 9 (1907), pp. 182–84.

57. J. Bayard Clark, "Plans a Self-Supporting Hospital for the Care of Self-Supporting Patients," *New York Times,* Sunday, December 6, 1914, p. 6. Clark's plan was for a hospital of 50 beds, with a charge of $1.00 a day for ward patients, $1.50 for each patient in a double room, and $2.00 a day for single bedrooms. Moderate physician fees would also be expected. He estimated that total daily operating costs would be approximately $110,000, and the total returns approximately $128,000, most of it coming from outpatients, who would attend the hospital on a private fee-paying basis. See also Clark, "A Self-Supporting Hospital," *New York State Journal of Medicine* 16 (1916), pp. 369–91.

58. The examples are from John Allan Hornsby and Richard E. Schmidt, *The Modern Hospital: Its Inspiration, Its Architecture, Its Equipment, Its Operation* (Philadelphia: W. B. Saunders Co., 1913), pp. 93–198.

59. Thomas J. Hillis, "The Hospital Governor and his Staff: Being a Glance at the Personnel of a Modern Hospital and a Plea for a Permanent Resident Staff," *Medical News* 77 (1900), p. 1.

60. Thomas Howell, "Boiler Room Economics," *Transactions of the American Hospital Association* 17 (1915), p. 388. A review of twenty-seven major hospitals in 1906 found that the highest-paid worker was the chief engineer (an average of $88 or $89 a month in 1906)—an occupational field in which hospitals had to compete with other institutions, including factories, hotels, and schools. Next in line came cashiers, bookkeepers, pharmacists, and carpenters, all of whom earned more, on average, than the steward or administrator. At the bottom of the wage-earning class were the bellboys and maids ($16 to $17). Asa Bacon, "The Selection and Management of Hospital Employees—A Comparison of Hospital Payrolls," ibid. 9 (1907), p. 119.

61.   Christian R. Holmes, *The Planning of a Modern Hospital* (Detroit: National Hospital Record Co., 1911), pp. 5, 21. Distinguished hospital expert Henry Burdett recommended the establishment of a suburban "hospital city" as a general plan for future hospitals, particularly in the United States, where the lines of urbanization were more fluid than in Britain. "Hospital," in *The Encyclopaedia Brittanica*, 11th ed., vol. XIII, p. 796. David Rosner, in *A Once Charitable Enterprise*, gives an excellent analysis of the breakdown of the "walking city" and the questions this raised for hospitals in Brooklyn.

62.   Connecticut Board of Charities, *Report 1905–1906*, Public Document no. 28 (New Haven: Tuttle, Morehouse & Taylor, 1907), p. 101.

63.   Andrew Carnegie, "Wealth," *North American Review* 148 (1889), 653–54. This article was reprinted widely under the title "The Gospel of Wealth." For an excellent elaboration of the principle, see Merle Curti, "American Philanthropy and the National Character," *American Quarterly* 10 (Winter 1958), p. 436.

64.   The hospital was obligated, though, to exercise due care in the selection of its agents under a much-cited precedent, *James McDonald* v. *Massachusetts General Hospital*, 120 Mass. (1876), p. 432. I discuss the relationships between the legal and social attributes of "public charities" more fully in "A Poor Sort of Memory: Voluntary Hospitals and Government Before the Depression," *Milbank Memorial Fund Quarterly/Health and Society* 60 (1982), pp. 551–84.

65.   Another 6% were county patients for whom the county paid $7 a week. The county claimed that the hospital was not "public" because it limited its medical staff, excluding local homeopathic and osteopathic physicians, and conducted a nursing school where trainees could receive training for a profitable business (private-duty nursing). The county assessed the hospital at $20,940 for the year 1907, and the hospital appealed. The appeal carried on the grounds that the hospital was a public charity and that all other claims were immaterial. *Sisters of Third Order of St. Francis* v. *Board of Review of Peoria County*, 231 Ill. (1907), 317–24.

66.   Nutting, *Educational Status of Nursing*, p. 18.

67.   The journalist went on to claim, with some justification, that the rich did not pay for what they got in hospital care, for in Pennsylvania the state gave private hospitals substantial appropriations for construction and operation; but in addition hospitals were generally constructed with funds drawn from the working community as well as from the rich. Henry W. Cattell, Pennsylvania Legislature, Joint Committee of the Senate and House of Representatives, *Report upon a Revision of the Corporation and Revenue Laws of the Commonwealth Pursuant to Joint Resolution of May 13, 1909, PL 944* (Harrisburg: State Printer, 1910), pp. 56, 335 (hereafter, Pennsylvania Joint Committee).

68.   Two-thirds of the patients were surgical patients; the largest single diagnostic group was tonsillectomies and adenoidectomies, closely followed by appendectomies. *Report of the Board of Managers of Pennsylvania Hospital for 1910*, pp. 33, 37–41. While Pennsylvania Hospital, like other city hospitals, still served a substantial number of immigrants—in this case primarily Italians, Russians, and Irish—a majority of the hospital's patients were now American-born. Perhaps recognizing the role of government aid, in Pennsylvania as a whole, 57% of the patients treated in the 142 voluntary hospitals aided by the state were treated free in 1910, 28% were paying patients, and 14% were part-pay. Pennsylvania Joint Committee, p. 91.

69.   A. C. Abbott, "A Description of the Proposed New Laundry of the University of Pennsylvania Hospital," *American Journal of Nursing* 1 (December 1900), pp. 224–26; (January 1901), pp. 282–84; (February 1901), pp. 359–62; Eugene B. Elder, "The Management of the Race Question in Hospitals," *Transactions of the American Hospital Association* 9 (1907), p. 128.

70.   These examples are taken from a long list of occupations in the Allentown Hospital Association *Annual Report* (Allentown, Pa.: Allentown Hospital Association, 1914), pp. 107–9. The two largest single categories were housewives and laborers.

71.   Pennsylvania Joint Committee, p. 335 and passim.

72.   S. S. Goldwater, "The Appropriation of Public Funds for the Practical Support of Voluntary Hospitals in the United States and Canada," *Transactions of the American Hospital Association* 11 (1909), p. 243.

73.   "The Division of Work Between Public and Private Charities," statement, *Proceedings of the National Conference on Charities and Correction*, 1901, pp. 128–29.

74.   Amos G. Warner, *American Charities* (New York: Thomas Y. Crowell & Co., 1894), p. 354.

75.   Alexander Fleisher, "State Money and Privately Managed Charities," *The Survey* 33 (1914), p. 110. See also Fleisher, "Pennsylvania's Appropriations to Privately-managed Chari-

table Institutions," *Political Science Quarterly* 30 (1915), pp. 15–36; Frank A. Fetter, "The Subsidizing of Private Charities," *American Journal of Sociology* 7 (1902–3), pp. 359–85.

76. "The Division of Work Between Public and Private Charities," statement, *Proceedings of the National Conference on Charities and Correction,* 1901, pp. 127–28. Warner, *American Charities,* pp. 344–45.

77. Stevens, "A Poor Sort of Memory," pp. 559, 562–64. David Rosner, "Gaining Control: Reform, Reimbursement, and Politics in New York's Community Hospitals, 1890–1915," *American Journal of Public Health* 7 (1980), pp. 533–42.

78. Pennsylvania Joint Committee, p. 934.

79. Rosemary Stevens, "Sweet Charity: State Aid to Hospitals in Pennsylvania, 1870–1910," *Bulletin of the History of Medicine* 58 (1984), pp. 287–314, 474–95.

80. Philadelphia had a Department of Health and Charities, but it was not well organized. There was not even a list of Philadelphia's thirty-five general hospitals, twenty special hospitals, and ten dispensaries, let alone of related sanitaria and private proprietary institutions. The city department, on request, sent the reform committee a page from the telephone book, in which veterinary hospitals, so-called "stammering institutions," and other unrelated organizations were classified side by side with hospitals like St. Agnes, Pennsylvania Hospital, and Jefferson. Philadelphia Committee on Municipal Charities, *Report of the Committee on Municipal Charities of Philadelphia* (Philadelphia: Philadelphia Committee on Municipal Charities, 1913), pp. 103–5 and passim.

81. Reverend D. J. McMahon, "Private Institutions and Public Supervision," *Proceedings of the National Conference of Charities and Correction,* 1902, p. 138.

82. Stevens, "A Poor Sort of Memory," p. 570.

83. Amos G. Warner, *American Charities,* 3rd ed., 1919, p. 367. The same sentiment was expressed, with slightly different wording, in the first edition (1894), p. 307. For an extended discussion of attitudes to pauperization in general, see Roy Lubove, *The Professional Altruist* (Cambridge, Mass.: Harvard University Press, 1968); Walter Trattner, *From Poor Law to Welfare State: A History of Social Welfare in America,* 3rd ed. (New York: Free Press, 1984); Michael B. Katz, *In the Shadow of the Poorhouse: A Social History of Welfare in America* (New York: Basic Books, 1986); and Robert H. Bremner, *American Philanthropy* (Chicago: University of Chicago Press, 1960).

84. Worcester, *Small Hospitals,* p. 68.

85. David Rosner, "Health Care for the 'Truly Needy': Nineteenth Century Origins of the Concept," *Milbank Memorial Fund Quarterly/Health and Society* 60 (1982), p. 357.

86. J. McKeen Cattell, ed., *Science and Education* (Garrison, N.Y.: Science Press, 1913), vol. II, *Medical Research and Education,* p. 72.

87. A survey of sixty-one Philadelphia dispensaries in 1903 found great diversity of opinion as to how poverty should be defined for the purpose of eligibility. Definitions of poverty ranged from "very destitute" to "moderate wage earners." Charges for outpatient care also imposed a barrier to access. In 1903, 90% of New York dispensaries charged for a dispensary card at the patient's first visit. Massachusetts General Hospital made a uniform charge of 10 cents for each dispensary case, and a few dispensaries imposed charges in Philadelphia. Such measures were largely successful in limiting the clientele of dispensaries to indigent patients with urgent conditions. New York, through its Dispensary Law of 1899, also imposed stiff penalties on misrepresentation of income for the purpose of getting free care. *Proceedings, Hospital Association of Philadelphia,* 1903, p. 11; and see S. S. Goldwater, "Dispensary Ideals," *American Journal of Medical Sciences* 134 (September 1907), pp. 313–15.

88. Michael M. Davis, "The Organization of Medical Service," *American Association for Labor Legislation Review* 6 (1916), p. 16.

89. Richard C. Cabot, *Foregrounds and Backgrounds* (Boston-printed by permission, 1906), unpaginated. There was general overdrugging of outpatients. A study of four hundred general dispensaries (of which 63% were hospital outpatient departments) found that over 80% had facilities for urine examinations, blood counts, sputum examinations, bacteriological examinations, and throat and vaginal smears, while approximately 70% had facilities for Wasserman tests (for venereal disease) and X rays. Michael M. Davis et al., "Report of Committee on Out-Patient Work," *Transactions of the American Hospital Association* 16 (1914), pp. 312–48.

90. Rosenberg, *The Care of Strangers,* pp. 286–309 and passim.

91. Hanckel, *American Hospitals in 1910,* p. 111.

92. Vanessa Northington Gamble, "The Black Community Hospital: Contemporary Dilemmas in Historical Perspective," manuscript, University of Pennsylvania, 1986, pp. 14

and passim; and Gamble, "The Negro Hospital Renaissance: The Black Hospital Movement, 1920–1940" (Ph.D. diss., University of Pennsylvania, Department of History and Sociology of Science, 1987).

93. Jefferson Medical College Hospital, *Annual Report for 1918* (Philadelphia, 1918), p. 34.

Chapter 3

1. In England and Wales, for example, there were 55 physicians per 100,000 population compared with America's 164. In Austria and in the German empire—the meccas for scientific research in medicine at this period—there were fewer than 50 doctors per 100,000 population. Council on Health and Public Instruction, Committee on Social Insurance, *Statistics Regarding the Medical Profession,* Social Insurance Studies Pamphlet VII (Chicago: American Medical Association, 1917), pp. 4–8.

2. S. S. Goldwater, "The Hospital and the Surgeon," *Modern Hospitals* 7 (1916), p. 275.

3. M. Milton Portis, "A Plea for Conservatism in Gastroenterology," *Surgery, Gynecology, and Obstetrics* 2 (1906), pp. 445–46.

4. Arthur Dean Bevan, "Unnecessary Operations on Women," ibid. 3 (1906), pp. 591–92. Bevan was professor of surgery at Rush Medical College, Chicago.

5. Editorial, "Cesarian Sections versus Perforation," ibid. 2 (1906), pp. 74–76. John C. Clark, "Has Experience Sustained the More Radical Operation for Cancer of the Uterus?" ibid. 2 (1906), p. 146.

6. Victor L. Schrager, "Surgical Records in the Clinic of Dr. J. B. Murphy," ibid. 2 (1906), p. 315. Murphy, a noted surgeon, kept a surgical record form incorporated into a thousand-page book, which included an index. This system, though unwieldy, provided a record of cases for the surgeon and a basis for surgical statistics. Most doctors did not bother with records.

7. George Bernard Shaw, "Preface on Doctors," in *The Doctor's Dilemma* (Baltimore: Penguin 1974; first published 1911), pp. 7–35.

8. H. D. Niles, "Our Hospitals," *Journal of the American Medical Association* 38 (1902), p. 760.

9. The best general analysis of the scientific management movement (and craze) is Samuel Haber, *Efficiency and Uplift: Scientific Management in the Progressive Era, 1890–1920* (Chicago: University of Chicago Press, 1964).

10. William J. Mayo, "The Medical Profession and the Issues Which Confront It," *Journal of the American Medical Association* XLVI (1906), p. 1739. The question of the "money standard of success" as a principle antithetical to the role of profession in the Progressive era cries out for further work. Between 1905 and 1917, as Schwartz points out, several states declared that corporations could not engage in the commercial practice of medicine on grounds of "sound public policy." How these grounds were defined demands elucidation. Jerome Schwartz, "Early History of Prepaid Medical Care Plans," *Bulletin of the History of Medicine* 39 (September–October 1965), pp. 450–75.

11. William A. Darnall, "The Hospital and the Young Physician," *Bulletin of the American Academy of Medicine* 12 (1911), p. 79, quoted by George Rosen in *The Structure of American Medical Practice, 1875 to 1914* (Philadelphia: University of Pennsylvania Press, 1983), p. 50.

12. Thomas Dixon, "How the Present Hospital Situation Affects the General Practitioner," *New York Medical Journal* XCVII (1913), p. 791. See also Charles Davison, "The Post-Graduate Preparation and Legal Registration of the Surgeon," *Surgery, Gynecology, and Obstetrics* XVI (1913), pp. 439–41.

13. William J. Mayo, "The Medical Profession and the Issues Which Confront It," p. 1739. Over one-fourth of the hospitals in Chicago subscribed to some form of contract practice in 1910, including direct contracts with major corporations as well as contracts with individuals. In Washington and Oregon, meanwhile, employers in the timber and mining industries used for-profit "hospital associations" as intermediaries. Oregon passed a hospital association act in 1917, permitting corporations to provide medical and other related services without a medical license. Starr, *The Social Transformation of American Medicine,* pp. 204–5.

14. Both Burrow and Starr provide excellent analyses of the variety of alternatives to independent private practice in the Progressive period. James G. Burrow, *Organized Medicine*

in the Progressive Era: The Move Toward Monopoly (Baltimore: Johns Hopkins University Press, 1977), p. 122. Starr, *The Social Transformation of American Medicine,* pp. 198–232.

15.   Abraham Flexner, *Medical Education in the United States and Canada: A Report to the Carnegie Foundation for the Advancement of Teaching,* Bulletin no. 4 (New York: Carnegie Foundation for the Advancement of Teaching, 1910). In fact, Flexner worked closely with members of the AMA Council on Medical Education, which had already done substantial surveys of medical schools, and the report was actually a joint effort. See Rosemary Stevens, *American Medicine and the Public Interest* (New Haven: Yale University Press, 1971), pp. 55–74; Kenneth M. Ludmerer, *Learning to Heal: The Development of American Medical Education* (New York: Basic Books, 1985), pp. 166–90.

16.   Philanthropists in New York and Chicago, reported Abraham Flexner, would not give money for hospitals in Philadelphia or Omaha. Rather, "it is held to be the business of every community to look after its own wear and tear in human life." Abraham Flexner, "Hospitals, Medical Education and Research," *Transactions of the American Hospital Association* 13 (1911), p. 363.

17.   Flexner, *Medical Education in the United States and Canada,* p. 92.

18.   It was Dr. William J. Mayo's custom, for example, to wheel the operating table around the room at interesting stages of the operation, to show the students in the "clinic," occupying each side of the room. Hornsby and Schmidt, *The Modern Hospital,* p. 206. In a huge local-government hospital such as Blockley Hospital (Philadelphia General Hospital) the shift in medical-teaching practice was apparent well before 1910. In 1909 medical students paid almost 50,000 visits to Blockley, of which 39,000 comprised small group instruction. Charles E. Rosenberg, "From Almshouse to Hospital: The Shaping of Philadelphia General Hospital," *Milbank Memorial Fund Quarterly/Health and Society* 60 (Winter 1982), p. 142.

19.   Flexner, *Medical Education in the United States and Canada,* p. 119.

20.   Abraham Flexner, quoted by L. B. Baldwin, "Report of the Committee on Medical Organization and Medical Education," *Transactions of the American Hospital Association* 14 (1912), p. 284.

21.   N. P. Colwell, "Progress of the Year in Medical Education," *Report of the Commissioner of Education, 1914,* vol. 1, no. 645 (Washington D.C.: Government Printing Office, 1915), pp. 201–2.

22.   Flexner, *Medical Education in the United States and Canada,* pp. 235, 254, 303.

23.   Ibid., p. 115.

24.   For other patients, teachers were not allowed to conduct bedside clinics when it was possible to remove the patient from the ward for teaching. Ibid., p. 116.

25.   Ibid., pp. 113–14.

26.   Ibid., p. 120.

27.   *American Medicine* 3 (1902), p. 667.

28.   William H. Welch, "Advantages to a Charitable Hospital of Affiliation with a University Medical School," *The Survey* 27 (1912), pp. 1766–70. The man of science, pure, dedicated, and noncommercial, became a recognized American "type." He is best described in the character of Max Gottlieb in Sinclair Lewis's popular novel *Arrowsmith* (1925). Dr. Martin Arrowsmith, the hero, has to make his own career choice among very different models of medicine, including scientific research, rural general practice, politically laden public health, and slick city specialist practice, oriented toward money-making.

29.   A Harvard professor claimed, from a survey at the beginning of the century, that in many places surgeons "who hold clinical material can practically dictate their terms to a medical school." Herbert L. Burrell, "The Teaching of Surgery," *Transactions of the American Surgical Association* 20 (1902), p. 99.

30.   Flexner, *Medical Education in the United States and Canada,* p. 111.

31.   Ludmerer, *Learning to Heal,* p. 215 and passim. Ludmerer notes that at Washington University members of the new executive faculty were dubbed the "wise men from the East," and in New Haven, among other examples, local practitioners boycotted the hospital in open antagonism to faculty domination.

32.   Arthur Dean Bevan, "The Modern School of Medicine," *American Medical Association Bulletin* 7 (March 15, 1912), p. 149.

33.   In England, too, medical school–hospital relationships were simpler than in the United States since the early medical schools developed from within the older voluntary hospitals, including St. Thomas's, Guy's, and St. Bartholomew's in London. See Rosemary Stevens,

Medical Practice in Modern England (New Haven, Conn.: Yale University Press, 1966), chaps. 1 and 2.

34.   The educational reformers were not always tactful. In his usual confrontational style Flexner told a meeting of the American Hospital Association in 1911, "Your hospitals are mothering proprietary and unconscionable medical schools" and did not hesitate to give examples: the Franklin Square Hospital in Baltimore, open to students of the "wretched" Maryland Medical College; or Buffalo Hospital, encouraging the "feeble so-called medical department" of the University of Buffalo; or Grace Hospital, Detroit, offering clinical facilities to the "unspeakable Detroit homeopathic medical college." Abraham Flexner, "Hospitals, Medical Education, and Research," *Transactions of the American Hospital Association* 13 (1911), p. 373.

35.   See Ludmerer, *Learning to Heal,* pp. 220–21.

36.   Even in 1926 only 316 hospitals were directly affiliated with the 79 medical schools then in existence, of which 50 were run and controlled by the schools and another 37 were controlled but not owned by them. Warren J. Babcock, "The Open Hospital, a Factor in Preventive Medicine," *Transactions of the American Hospital Association* 18 (1916), p. 79; *Report of the Commissioner of Education, 1924–26,* p. 48.

37.   *Annual Report of the General Education Board, 1919–20* (New York: General Education Board, 1921), p. 44.

38.   Bevan, "The Modern School of Medicine," p. 49.

39.   Leroy E. Parkins, ed., *The Harvard Medical School and its Clinical Opportunities* (Boston: Ralph W. Hadley Press, 1916).

40.   *The General Education Board: An Account of its Activities, 1902–1914* (New York: General Education Board, 1915), pp. 168–69.

41.   Abraham Flexner, "Hospitals, Medical Education, and Research," *Transactions of the American Hospital Association* 13 (1911), p. 365.

42.   *The General Education Board,* p. 174.

43.   Jane Addams, "The Layman's View of Hospital Work Among the Poor," *Ninth Annual Conference, American Hospital Association, 1907,* vol. 9 (Chicago: American Hospital Association, 1907), p. 57.

44.   Physicians who insisted that each patient be addressed as "Mr. This" or "Mrs. That" were likely to be greeted with jeering and laughing among the nurses. Julia Lathrop, in discussion, *Transactions of the American Hospital Association* 9 (1907), p. 90.

45.   Michael M. Davis, *Immigrant Health and the Community* (New York: Harper & Brothers, 1921), p. 308.

46.   A good example of contemporary criticism of this phenomenon is Sidney E. Goldstein, "The Social Function of the Hospital," *Charities and the Commons* 18 (1907), pp. 160–66, 205–11.

47.   Stevens, *American Medicine and the Public Interest,* p. 73 and passim.

48.   "The Bed-day," editorial, *American Medicine* 3 (1902), p. 626.

49.   Mayzck P. Ravenel, "State and Municipal Control of Tuberculosis," *Transactions of the National Conference on Charities and Correction,* 1906, pp. 182–85; E. E. Munger, "Hospitals and the Health Problem, with Special Reference to the Necessities of Rural America," *Transactions of the American Medical Association's Section of Hospitals,* June 1912, reprinted in *Journal of the American Medical Association* 59 (1912), pp. 1703–5.

50.   Thomas J. Hillis, "The Hospital Governor and His Staff," *Medical News* 77 (1900), p. 4.

51.   By 1914 an estimated 75% to 80% of graduates took an internship. Five colleges required an internship for the M.D. degree and one state licensing board (Pennsylvania) also required an internship. "The Education of the Intern," *Journal of the American Medical Association* 43 (1904), p. 469; Stevens, *American Medicine and the Public Interest,* p. 118.

52.   In addition, during World War I, 176 of the alumni served as officers in the army, nine in the navy, and ten in the Red Cross. Howard Fox, ed., *Eliot's Quiz: A Tribute to a Great Teacher, Ellsworth Eliot, Jr.* (New York: American Books, Stratford Press, 1938), p. 6.

53.   American Medical Association, Council on Medical Education and Hospitals, "Provisional List of Hospitals Furnishing Acceptable Internships, Corrected List, 1914," *Hospitals Approved for Interns 1916–36* [*sic*], AMA Archives, Chicago.

54.   "The Necessity for Reorganization of Our Large Hospital Services," editorial, *Journal of the American Medical Association* 40 (1903), pp. 1360–61.

55. American Medical Association, Council on Medical Education, *Minutes of Business Meeting, Volume I, 1907–1917* (December 27, 1913), p. 79. I am grateful to the council staff for giving me access to these minutes, which I have drawn on for invaluable background material in discussing graduate medical education throughout this book.

56. The foundation's official position was that it would be unwise to embark on another major enterprise—a study of hospitals and their relation to medical schools—until they had completed their work on medical education in the schools. Carnegie Foundation for the Advancement of Teaching, *Ninth Annual Report of the President and of the Treasurer* (New York: Carnegie Foundation, 1914), p. 6.

57. Council on Medical Education, *Minutes of Business Meeting*, I, pp. 72, 448, and passim.

58. A response from the University of Texas reflected a general feeling among the schools about medical-school responsibility for a hospital year. "We are unable to see how this can be done in the South and West, with the antagonism which exists in many hospitals and a lack of affiliation with medical schools." "Uniformity in Standards of Medical Education," Report of Committee on Education and Pedagogy, Meeting of the Association of American Medical Colleges, Chicago, February 25, 1914, p. 23.

59. H. B. Howard (superintendent, Peter Bent Brigham Hospital, Boston), "The Medical Superintendent," American Medical Association, *Transactions of the Section on Hospitals* 1 (1912), p. 76; Richard Olding Beard, "The Trained Nurse of the Future," section minutes reported in *Journal of the American Medical Association* 61 (1913), p. 2149; W. Gillman Thompson, "Efficiency in Nursing," ibid. 61 (1913), p. 2146.

60. American Hospital Association, *Treasurer's Manuscript Records of Membership Dues 1899–1909* (Chicago: American Hospital Association, 1946), box 21, AHA Archives; Proceedings of the American Hospital Association, Fourteenth Annual Conference, 1912. According to Daniel D. Test of the Pennsylvania Hospital, who was member number eleven of the AHA, the first three years of the association were dominated by James S. Knowles, superintendent of Lakeside Hospital, Cleveland, who had called the group together in the first place. Knowles, wrote Test in 1923 (when the latter was the oldest living member of the association) was "chock full of ideas, some good and some ridiculous," but was hampered by not carrying through and by an unspecified "sub-normal moral streak." The first few years of the association were lackluster. But the evident demand for an organization of administrators, from administrators themselves, carried the association through. Daniel Test to A. R. Warner, executive secretary, AHA, July 9, 1923, in Frank D. Hicks, *American Hospital Association History*, no. 1, Notebook, n.d., box 54, AHA Archives.

61. H. B. Howard, president's address, *Transactions of the American Hospital Association* 12 (1910), 123–33; F. Washburn, ibid. 15 (1913), pp. 95–102.

62. J. M. Baldy et al., "Hospital Standardization," *Pennsylvania Medical Journal* 20 (December 1916), p. 215; for New Jersey, see "The Standardization of Hospitals, Adopted by the New Jersey State Board of Medical Examiners," statement, Federation of State Medical Boards, *Monthly Bulletin* 2 (October 1916), pp. 152–56.

63. Edward Martin, "The Hospital and Its Community," *Bulletin of the American College of Surgeons* 3 (1917), 13.

64. See I. Fisher, "Relationship Between Superintendent, Managers, and Staff," *Transactions of the American Hospital Association* 18 (1916), p. 436.

65. William H. Allen, "Hospital Efficiency," *American Journal of Sociology* 12 (1906–7), p. 302. Other good examples are "Standardization of Institutional Accounts," editorial, *American Medicine* 3 (1902), p. 627; and Maud Banfield, "Some Unsettled Questions in Hospital Administration in the United States," *Annals of the American Academy of Political and Social Science* 20 (1902), p. 328.

66. Charles P. Emerson, "The American Hospital Field," in Aikens, *Hospital Management*, p. 68.

67. Maud Banfield, "Some Unsettled Questions in Hospital Administration in the United States," *Annals of the American Academy of Political and Social Science* 20 (1902), p. 351.

68. The role of the administrator in the hospital was a frequent topic of discussion at American Hospital Association annual meetings in the first two decades of the twentieth century. A good example is Henry M. Hurd, "The Proper Relation of the Superintendent to the Trustees of the Hospital," *Transactions of the American Hospital Association* 12 (1910), p. 244. "The fountain of authority" comes from this source.

69. John D. Thompson, "The Uneasy Alliance," in Duncan Yaggy and Patricia Hodgson,

eds., *Physicians and Hospitals: The Great Partnership at the Crossroads* (Durham: Duke University Press, 1985), p. 18.

70.   William H. Allen, "Hospital Efficiency," *American Journal of Sociology* 12 (1906–7), p. 310. Similarly, Philadelphia hospital administrators had organized their own association in 1902 to protect their image and their interests against public criticism and the potential loss or reduction of subsidies from the Commonwealth of Pennsylvania.

71.   William V. S. Thorne, *Hospital Accounting and Statistics,* 4th ed. (New York: Dutton, 1918).

72.   Significantly, by 1910 more graduates had taken jobs as training-school superintendents than as hospital superintendents. Adelaide Nutting, "A Brief Account of the Course in Hospital Economics," *Teachers College Record* 11 (May 1910), p. 5.

73.   At the national level, the most interesting activity in the association before World War I was the lobbying by twelve prominent members (medical superintendents) for a federal bureau of hospital information, which would be organized as part of the U.S. Public Health Service; the surgeon general supported this idea. However, although a bill was finally introduced for this purpose in 1912, by this time the supportive surgeon general had died, and there was by no means unanimous support for a national bureau, either from congressmen or within the AHA. The idea died in 1915. The initial bill number is reported in the AHA Archives as S. 4972 of the 62nd Cong. 2nd sess., and there are only scattered references to its progression through Congress. Walter Wyman, surgeon general, to W. P. Morrill, February 7, 1911, RA960A1, AHA Archives.

The history of the American Hospital Association remains to be written. A good beginning on the general history of the association is Alejandra Laszlo, "The American Hospital Association: Emergence of a Professional Organization 1899–1938," manuscript, University of Pennsylvania, Department of History and Sociology of Science, April 1982. A review of the topics of association meetings up to 1932 is given in Bert W. Caldwell, "American Hospital Association" in James Clark Fifield, ed., *American and Canadian Hospitals* (Chicago: Physicians' Record Co., 1937), pp. 11–35.

74.   Dr. A. R. Warner, at Lakeside, like Davis, also argued strongly for defining the hospital as a focus for community action, in the interests of public health. He described the composition of the average hospital ward in 1915 as a "public disgrace" and a reproach to society. Typhoid cases existed "because we drink our sewage." Diseases such as syphilis and tuberculosis could be ascribed to social organization or behavior, and the wards, too, contained occupational diseases and diseases arising from alcoholism and lead poisoning—all examples of social failure. But Warner was unusual in defining his own role as a public-health advocate. He opened Lakeside's records to a city investigation of venereal disease which led, first, to the mayor's closing down the red-light district in Cleveland and, second, to opening a new 150-bed pavilion for venereal disease in the city hospital. A. R. Warner, "The Possibilities of Future Development in the Service Rendered by a Hospital to a Community," *Cleveland Medical Journal* 11 (1915), pp. 651–56.

75.   Winford Smith, "Relation of the Hospital to the Community," *Journal of the American Medical Association* 65 (1915), p. 1499.

76.   J. M. Baldy et al., "Hospital Standardization," *Pennsylvania Medical Journal* 120 (December 1916), p. 216.

77.   Stevens, *American Medicine and the Public Interest,* pp. 85–92. On the general history of the ACS, see Loyal Davis, *Fellowship of Surgeons: A History of the American College of Surgeons* (Springfield Ill.: Thomas Publishing, 1960).

78.   E. A. Codman, *A Study in Hospital Efficiency as Demonstrated by the Case Report of the First Two Years of a Private Hospital* (published privately, 1914), p. 26.

79.   Codman, *The Second Two Years of a Private Hospital* (published privately 1916), p. 30. See also Codman, "The Product of a Hospital," *Surgery, Gynecology and Obstetrics* 8 (1914), pp. 491–96.

80.   Codman, "A Meeting for the Discussion of Hospital Efficiency at the Boston Medical Library, January 6, 1915," in his preface to *The Shoulder* (Boston, published privately, 1934), p. xxiv. The best accounts of Codman's career are by Susan Reverby, "The Search for the Hospital Yardstick," in Susan Reverby and David Rosner, eds., *Health Care in America: Essays in Social History* (Philadelphia: Temple University Press, 1979), pp. 206–25; and "Stealing the

Golden Eggs: Ernest Amory Codman and the Science and Management of Medicine," *Bulletin of the History of Medicine* 55 (1911), pp. 156–71.

81. An excellent analysis of the various positions and viewpoints is Edward Mormon's introduction, "Efficiency, Scientific Management, and Hospital Standardization," in Mormon, ed., *Efficiency, Scientific Management, and Hospital Standardization* (New York: Garland Publishing Co., in press).

82. Loyal Davis, *Fellowship of Surgeons*, pp. 208–9.

83. J. A. Hornsby, "The Hospital Problem of Today: What is it?" *Bulletin of the American College of Surgeons* 3 (1917), pp. 4–11.

Chapter 4

1. "Complete Hospital in Big Department Store," *Modern Hospital* 1 (April 1916), p. 17.

2. "Underwriters Establish Industrial Hospital," ibid. 2 (September 1916), p. 18.

3. "The Fifth or Hospital Year," ibid. 3 (October 1916), p. 28. See also C. L. Bonifield, "Excessive Expense in Connecticut Criticized," ibid. 1 (June 1916), p. 6.

4. Thomas W. Huntington, "Address of the President," *Transactions of the American Surgical Association* 36 (1918), p. 2. Huntington described the mobilization of so many surgeons as an "inspiration." Regret, he wrote, "finds small place in contrast with our pride in the assurance that from us, as from a family, have gone forth a battalion of strong men, devoted and brave, to do their part unselfishly in the world's great tragedy and to bear a message from American surgeons to bleeding France and our stricken allies." Ibid.

5. Grace Crile, ed., *George Crile: An Autobiography*, vol. 2 (Philadelphia: J. B. Lippincott, 1947), p. 312.

6. Lewis Stephen Pilcher, "The Influence of War Surgery on Civil Practice," *Annals of Surgery* 69 (June 1919), p. 572; and Surgeon General's Office, *The Medical Department of the U.S. Army in the World War–Vol. 1* (Washington, D.C.: Government Printing Office, 1923), pp. 92–93 and passim.

7. Hugh Cabot, "Medicine—A Profession or a Trade?" *Boston Medical and Surgical Journal* CLXXIII (1915), pp. 685–88. Other good examples are M. M. Davis, "Organization of Medical Service," *American Labor Legislation Review* 6 (1916), pp. 16–20; Richard Clark Cabot, "Better Doctoring for Less Money," *American Magazine* 81 (April 1916), pp. 7–9, 77–78; (May 1916), pp. 43–44, 76–81; and Donald B. Armstrong and J. H. Berkowitz, "An Urban Community Plan for Health and Medical Service," *Modern Hospital* 8 (1917), p. 309.

8. A study of industrial medicine in California in 1917 found much interest expressed by employers but little actual worker protection; a major exception was the Scotia Hospital Association of the Pacific Lumber Company, which provided medical, surgical, and hospital services, and sickness payments to employees, but this was actually owned and organized by employees. *Report of the Social Insurance Commission of the State of California, January 25, 1917* (Sacramento: State Printing Office, 1917), p. 103.

9. Ohio Health and Old Age Insurance Commission, *Health, Health Insurance, Old Age Pensions* (Columbus: State of Ohio, February 1919), p. 111. The same joint attribution of blame was made by other commissions, e.g., *Report of the Health Insurance Commission of the State of Illinois* (Springfield: State of Illinois, May 1, 1919), p. 33. On contract practice between 1900 and 1920, see James J. Burrow, *Organized Medicine in the Progressive Era: The Move Toward Monopoly* (Baltimore: Johns Hopkins University Press, 1977), pp. 119–32; and Ronald L. Numbers, *Almost Persuaded: American Physicians and Compulsory Health Insurance, 1912–1920* (Baltimore: Johns Hopkins University Press, 1978), pp. 6–7 and passim.

10. Karl de Schweinitz, "Sickness as a Factor in Poverty," *Proceedings of the National Conference on Social Work* X (1919), pp. 156–64.

11. Ernst C. Meyer, "Hospital Service in Rural Communities—A Preliminary Report," pt. II, *Journal of the American Medical Association* 72 (May 3, 1919), p. 1292.

12. The laws focused on monetary compensation and varied enormously in their coverage of hospital and medical care; Alaska and Arizona made no provisions for medical care. Most other states included monetary or time restrictions on benefits. For example, Delaware pro-

vided two weeks of medical benefits up to a maximum of $25; Oklahoma had a time limit
of fifteen days, Virginia of thirty days. Alexander Trachtenberg, ed., *American Labor Year Book
1919–1920* (New York: Rand School of Social Sciences, 1920), p. 235.

13.   Alexander Lambert, "Report of the Committee on Social Insurance," *Journal of the
American Medical Association* 66 (1916), pp. 1951–85. On the general history of compulsory
health insurance between 1915 and 1920, see Numbers, *Almost Persuaded;* Burrow, *Organized
Medicine in the Progressive Era;* Odin Anderson, "Health Insurance in the United States," *Journal
of the History of Medicine* 5 (Autumn 1950), p. 369; Arthur Viseltear, "Compulsory Health
Insurance in California," *Journal of the History of Medicine* 24 (1969), pp. 151–82.

14.   Lambert, "Report of the Committee on Social Insurance," pp. 1951–85.

15.   "Report of the Committee on Compulsory Health Insurance," *California State Journal of
Medicine* 15 (1917), p. 194. California's bill was defeated, by the voters, in 1918.

16.   "Doctors' Incomes," editorial, ibid., p. 4.

17.   Ibid., p. 196. See also "Report of Committee on Industrial Accident Insurance," ibid.,
p. 198; J. Rollin French, "The Medical Situation of the New Workmen's Compensation Act,"
ibid. 12 (1914), p. 151. An essential ingredient of these complaints was that doctors, in a still
overcrowded profession, were often very poorly paid.

18.   Harry A. Mackey, "Pennsylvania Compensation Law and the Doctor," *Pennsylvania
Medical Journal* 19 (1916), p. 727; William H. Walsh, "The Pennsylvania Workmen's Compensation Act as It Affects Hospitals," ibid., p. 731. I am grateful to Richard Gillespie for bringing
these points and these references to my attention.

19.   One Philadelphia physician put the point explicitly: "It is much easier to forget to visit
or to postpone visiting a wounded man who is not expected to pay a fee than one whose bill
for professional treatment is guaranteed by the state law and the treasury of a mining
company or a successful manufacturer." John B. Roberts, "The Promotion of Surgical Efficiency in Hospital," *Transactions of the College of Physicians of Philadelphia,* 3rd Series, XLIII (1920),
pp. 433–39.

20.   James L. Whitney, "Cooperative Medicine in Relation to Social Insurance," *California
State Journal of Medicine* 14 (1916), p. 435.

21.   *Missouri: Red Book 1920, 1919, 1918,* pt. II: *Wartime Industrial History of a Progressive Commonwealth* (Jefferson City: Missouri Bureau of Labor Statistics, 1920), p. 249 and passim.

22.   Lambert, "Report of the Committee on Social Insurance," p. 1984.

23.   James L. Whitney, "Cooperative Medicine in Relation to Social Insurance," *California
State Journal of Medicine* 14 (1916), p. 432.

24.   A. R. Warner, in discussion, *Transactions of the American Hospital Association,* 1917, p. 195.

25.   James L. Whitney, "Cooperative Medicine," *California State Journal of Medicine* 14 (1916),
p. 432.

26.   "Health Insurance and Coming Legislation," editorial, *American Journal of Nursing* 20
(November 1919), p. 97. See also "Statements of Prominent Persons in Favor of Health
Insurance," *American Labor Legislation Review* 8 (1918), pp. 324–27.

27.   Francis D. Donaghue, "Medical Competence and Hospital Efficiency," *Labor Statistics Bureau–Bulletin 248* (Washington, D.C.: U.S. Department of Labor, March 1919), p.
132.

28.   *The Medical Department of the U.S. Army in the World War,* vol. 1. Prepared under the
direction of Surgeon General M. W. Ireland (Washington, D.C.: Government Printing Office,
1923), pp. 92–93 and passim.

29.   *History of United States Army Base Hospital Number 20* (Philadelphia: E. A. Wright Co.,
1920), pp. 44–93 and passim.

30.   Merritte W. Ireland, "The Place of the Civil General Hospital in the Scheme of
Medical Preparedness," in *Massachusetts General Hospital Memorial and Historical Volume* (Boston:
Massachusetts General Hospital, 1921), pp. 60–61; Paul D. White, "The Hospital in the World
War: Base Hospital No. 6," ibid., pp. 67–69; and "Address of Colonel Frederic A. Washburn,"
report from a reception held at the hospital, June 9, 1919, for those who served in the war,
ibid., pp. 74–75.

31.   Francis Cheever Shattuck, "Cinq Ans Après," *Bulletin of the Johns Hopkins Hospital* 29
(April 1918), pp. 77–79.

32.   John M. Dodson, "Remarks on Medical Education," *American Medical Association Bulletin*
13 (1919), pp. 185–191; Bevan in discussion, p. 247. Cabot is reported by Surgeon General
Ireland in *MGH Memorial Volume,* p. 62.

33. "Resolution Proposing the Appointment of a War Service Committee," *Transactions of the American Hospital Association* 19 (1917), p. 316. The resolution began by reminding any readers that the AHA was composed of administrators of hospitals with combined investments of over $300 million and annual expenses of over $125 million. On health status and the draft, see Eugene Lyman Fish, "Some Lessons from the Draft Examination," *Journal of the American Medical Association* 70 (1918), pp. 300–3.

34. The best general account is Bernard M. Baruch, *American Industry in the War: A Report of the War Industries Board* (New York: Prentice-Hall, 1941), p. 216 and passim.

35. Barbara Melosh, *The Physician's Hand* (Philadelphia: Temple University Press, 1982), pp. 77, 92.

36. "The Nurse's Privilege," editorial, *American Journal of Nursing* 18 (1918), pp. 442–43.

37. "Criticism of Nursing Schools," editorial comment, ibid. 18 (1917), pp. 83–84.

38. Jane A. Delano, "The Red Cross," ibid. 18 (1918), pp. 548.

39. Helene Jamieson Jordan, *Cornell University–New York Hospital School of Nursing, 1877–1952* (New York: Society of the New York Hospital, 1952), p. 50. See also Isobel Stewart, S. Lillian Clayton, and Anna C. Jamme, "Possible Changes to Meet the War Emergency," *American Journal of Nursing* 18 (1918), pp. 541–45. The MGH example is from *MGH Memorial Volume,* p. 90.

40. "The Nurse's Privilege," *American Journal of Nursing* 18 (1918), p. 445.

41. Letter, signed RKH, *American Journal of Nursing* 20 (1919), pp. 241–42. Praise from doctors, too, tended to be sexist. One brigadier general in the medical corps, for example, paid a backhanded tribute to nurses for the "uplifting, stimulating, refining influence" that the women exercised upon officers and men, despite prejudice and concern among old-line physicians about complications and scandals, and despite rumors and gossip carried by "busybodies." W. S. Thayer, "Nursing and the Art of Medicine," ibid., p. 189.

42. Clara D. Noyes, "President's Address to the American Nurses' Association," ibid. 20 (1920), p. 783.

43. "Are our members going to sit back, let the men do all the talking, serve on all the committees, decide all the problems, and vote as the men tell them to?" asked an editorial in the *American Journal of Nursing.* The answer seemed to be yes. "Are Nurses Alive to their Opportunities?" ibid. 20 (November 1919), p. 90.

44. Frederick D. Greene, "Publicity as a Means of Education," *Transactions of the American Hospital Association* 19 (1917), p. 77.

45. See chapter 5. The best accounts are Robert D. Leigh, *Federal Health Administration in the United States* (New York: Harper & Bros., 1927), pp. 165–69 and passim; Robinson E. Adkins, *Medical Care of Veterans* (Washington D.C.: Government Printing Office, 1967), printed for the use of the Committee on Veterans' Affairs, 90th Cong., 1st sess., House Committee Print no. 4, pp. 87, 104–5, and passim.

46. A. E. Kepford, "The Greater Community Association at Creston, Iowa," *Modern Hospital* 12 (1919), p. 347.

47. I draw in this section from Alfred W. Crosby, Jr., *Epidemic and Peace, 1918* (Westport, Conn.: Greenwood Press, 1976); Crosby, "The Influenza Pandemic of 1918," in June E. Osborn, ed., *Influenza in America* (New York: Prodist, 1971); and Richard Collier, *The Plague of the Spanish Lady* (New York: Atheneum, 1974).

48. Earl Chapin May and Will Oursler, *The Prudential* (New York: Doubleday, 1950), p. 179. Life insurance was popularized, too, by the federal government through its war risk insurance program in World War I.

49. A good early example is David Edsall, "Movements in Medicine," *Boston Medical and Surgical Journal* 174 (1916), pp. 891–97.

50. "After the War, What?" editorial, *Modern Hospital* 10 (1918), pp. 272–74.

51. Benjamin Moore, *The Dawn of the Health Age* (London: J. & A. Churchill, 1911), p. 71. References to this book may be found in state hearings on compulsory health insurance.

52. Thomas W. Huntington, "Address of the President," *Transactions of the American Surgical Association* 36 (1918), p. 3.

53. Ernst Meyer, *Relative Value of Hospitals and Dispensaries as Public Health Agencies and as Fields of Activity for the Rockefeller Foundation,* typescript, Rockefeller Foundation, International Health Board, December 1919, RG 1.1, series 200, box 23, Rockefeller Archives.

Chapter 5

1. *Cleveland Hospital and Health Survey* (Cleveland: Cleveland Hospital Council, 1920), *pt. 10, Hospitals and Dispensaries,* p. 831; Haven Emerson and Anna C. Phillips, *Hospitals and Health Agencies of San Francisco 1923* (San Francisco: Council of Social and Health Agencies, 1923), p. 56. Almost 30% of all births were in hospitals by 1930, with a much higher proportion in the urban areas.

Although over 90% of all non-surgical conditions were still cared for at home, by 1930 almost 80% of all surgical cases were hospitalized, including both major and minor surgery. Selwyn D. Collins, "Sickness and Health: Their Measurement, Distribution and Changes," *Annals of the American Academy of Political and Social Science* 237 (January 1945), pp. 153–63; E. H. L. Corwin, *The American Hospital* (New York: Commonwealth Fund, 1946), p. 91. Michael Davis stated that it was unusual for a woman in comfortable circumstances in New York City to be delivered at home in the late 1920s. Davis, *Clinics, Hospitals, and Health Centers* (New York: Harper, 1927), p. 13. In cities like Cincinnati, the cost of a hospital confinement was also reported as less than that at home. Mary L. Hicks, *Hospitals of Cincinnati: A Survey* (Cincinnati: Helen S. Trounstine Foundation, 1925), p. 171.

2. At Johns Hopkins Hospital, for example, the medical graduate of the early twentieth century learned to admit charity patients in order to avoid complications of toxemia and infections. Students were told that confinements in private houses could be conducted with as "rigid and satisfactory a technique as is possible in a well-regulated hospital"—provided the physician was willing to take "sufficient pains" and was "seconded in his efforts by a competent nurse." However, there was little point in taking these pains if even paying patients could be persuaded to go to the hospital. Lack of trained nurses in the war speeded up the general drift. J. Morris Slemons, "The Conduct of a Normal Labor at the Johns Hopkins Hospital," *Surgery, Gynecology, and Obstetrics* 2 (1906), pp. 197–201.

3. J. W. Williams, *Obstetrics and Animal Experimentation: Defense of Research,* Pamphlet XVIII (Chicago: American Medical Association, 1911), pp. 5–19, 189. For a good contextual view, see Grace L. Meigs, *Maternal Mortality from All Conditions Connected with Childbirth in the United States and Certain Other Foreign Countries* (Washington, D.C.: U.S. Department of Labor, Children's Bureau, 1917).

4. In its pure form, twilight sleep included morphine and scopolamine only, without ether or chloroform, for the purpose was to induce amnesia rather than to anesthetize the patient (with potential accompanying dangers for the delivery). Twilight sleep was championed by society leaders such as Mrs. John Jacob Astor, and Edith Wharton's novel *Twilight Sleep* was published in 1927. Marguerite Tracy and Constance Leupp, "Painless Childbirth," *McClure's,* June 1914, pp. 37–51; and see Margarete Sandelowski, *Pain, Pleasure, and American Childbirth, from the Twilight Sleep to the Reed Method, 1914–1960* (Westport, Conn.: Greenwood Press, 1984); and Judith Walzer Leavitt, *Brought to Bed: Child-Bearing in America, 1750–1950* (Oxford: Oxford University Press, 1986), pp. 128–41 and passim

5. Richard W. Wertz and Dorothy C. Wertz, *Lying-In: A History of Childbirth in America* (New York: Free Press, 1977), p. 156.

6. Emerson and Phillips, *Hospitals and Health Agencies of San Francisco,* p. 48.

7. Frederick Gates, who directed the distribution of funds for the Rockefeller Foundation in the 1920s, was an early recipient of insulin, the new wonder drug. He described his new outlook on life following his first dose of insulin as "filled with the glorious autumnal colors," the effect being "simply magical." Frederick T. Gates to John D. Rockefeller, Jr., April 28, 1923, quoted by Ludmerer, *Learning to Heal,* p. 202. Similarly, important research into pernicious anemia underlined the promise of research. The successful treatment of pernicious anemia with extracts of liver in large quantities by mouth was demonstrated in 1926; the production of an injectable extract of liver followed in 1928, and the brilliant suggestion (by Castle) of the existence of an intrinsic and extrinsic factor in 1929.

8. The description of the movie is from Walter E. List, "Minneapolis Hospital Enters the Movies," *Modern Hospital* 18 (April 1922), pp. 347–50.

9. "Suggests Hospital Day Pageant," *Modern Hospital* 11 (1921), pp. 5–36.

10. Malcolm T. MacEachern, "How Are You Going to Observe National Hospital Day?" *Hospital Management* 31 (April 1931), p. 22. See also "Why a National Hospital Day," ibid. 31 (March 1931), p. 62.

11.   Averaged out over the entire country, there was one general hospital bed for every 340 members of the population in 1922; in comparison there was one bed for 225 persons in 1980. The average general hospital, with 71 beds and a budget of $78,000, reported a financial loss of $2,300 in 1922, but deficits were commonly made up by donations—and prospects were good. Less than one-third of the patient days, averaged over all kinds of general hospitals—including local-government institutions, and voluntary and proprietary hospitals—were attributed to free patients. At the other end of the scale, full-pay patients represented about half of all patient days, and patient fees accounted for two-thirds of the receipts. U.S. Bureau of the Census, *Hospitals and Dispensaries, 1923,* tables 1–4. Other hospital statistics for the early 1920s cited in this chapter are drawn from this source unless otherwise stated.

12.   U.S. Department of Labor, *Construction During Five Decades, Historical Statistics 1907–1952,* Bulletin no. 1146 (Washington, D.C.: Government Printing Office, 1953), table 7; C. Rufus Rorem, *The Public's Investment in Hospitals,* Committee on the Costs of Medical Care Publication No. 7 (Chicago: University of Chicago Press, 1930), p. 5 and passim.

13.   Niles Carpenter, *Hospital Service for Patients of Moderate Means: A Study of Certain American Hospitals* (Washington, D.C.: Committee on the Costs of Medical Care, 1930), p. 23. The best historical analyses of the issue of privacy are John D. Thompson and Grace Goldin, *The Hospital: A Social and Architectural History* (New Haven: Yale University Press, 1975), pp. 207–25; and Rosenberg, *The Care of Strangers,* pp. 237–61.

14.   "Why It Costs So Much to be Ill," *World Magazine,* November 28, 1926, p. 6.

15.   Charles F. Neergaard, "Solving the Middle Class Patient Problem," *Modern Hospital* 31 (October 1928), p. 84; Carpenter, *Hospital Service for Patients of Moderate Means,* p. 11.

16.   Father Edward Garesche, "The Extravagant Patient," *Trained Nurse and Hospital Review* 81 (1928), p. 452. Relatively few patients needed separate rooms for medical reasons. It was estimated that less than 15% of ward patients needed isolation because they were dangerously sick, psychotic, infectious, in uncontrollable pain, incontinent, or because their behavior was distracting to other patients. S. S. Goldwater and E. M. Bluestone, "How Many Ward Patients Need Separate Rooms?" *Modern Hospital* 24 (March 1924), p. 197.

17.   Basil C. MacLean, "Dispensary Scope and Responsibilities," *Transactions of the American Hospital Association* 32 (1930), pp. 712–13. On the "cabin class," see Carpenter, *Hospital Service for Patients of Moderate Means,* pp. 70–71; Nathan Sinai and Alden B. Mills, *Philadelphia Hospital and Health Survey, 1929,* Committee on the Costs of Medical Care Publication no. 9 (Chicago: University of Chicago Press, 1931), p. 70.

18.   Louis J. Frank, "What I Found in the Hospitals of Europe—Part I," *Modern Hospital* 30 (February 1928), pp. 67–74. The other comparisons are from E. H. Lewinski-Corwin, "Hospitals and Sanatoria," *Encyclopedia of the Social Sciences,* vol. 7 (New York: Macmillan, 1932), p. 469.

19.   In Philadelphia, for example, in 1928 more than one-quarter of all hospital beds were used interchangeably for medicine, surgery, or obstetrics; most of these were for private and semiprivate cases and most were in small units. Sinai and Mills, *Philadelphia Hospital and Health Survey,* p. 602.

20.   William G. Shepherd, "The New Control of Surgeons," *Harper's Monthly Magazine,* February 1924, pp. 310, 312.

21.   The ACS's standards required participating hospitals to have systematic case records (patient records) and to utilize these records to analyze medical and surgical efficiency, through setting up records committees or regular case conferences. Standards were set for working clinical laboratories, electrocardiography, radiology, intern training (where applicable), nursing, postmortem pathology, obstetrics and pediatrics, infection control, pharmacies, library facilities, dietetics, and administrative and accounting systems. Surgeons were prohibited from dividing fees, secretly, with referring physicians. Added to the standards in 1919 was the requirement that the hospital medical staff be formally organized as a group, with its own rules and regulations. The staff had to have regular meetings, and it had to be restricted to competent and ethical physicians. American College of Surgeons, *Seventh Year Book,* 1920, pp. 16–17.

22.   Ibid.; G. A. Fox, "Some Hospital Problems of the Small Community," *Colorado Medicine* 24 (1927), pp. 23–26. For material on the American College of Surgeons, unless otherwise stated, I have drawn from Loyal Davis, *Fellowship of Surgeons: A History of the American College of Surgeons* (Springfield, Ill.: Charles C. Thomas, 1960).

23.   The AMA Council on Medical Education preferred a joint standardization commis-

sion, organized by multiple institutions. *Minutes of the Business Meeting of the Council on Medical Education,* March 4, 1919, p. 24. In 1919 the AMA brought together seventeen national organizations interested in hospitals as the American Conference on Hospital Service. Participants represented, *inter alia,* the American College of Surgeons, the American Hospital Association, the Catholic Hospital Association, the American Medical Association, and the National League of Nursing Education. This "conference" continued as a cooperative organization through the 1920s, providing a useful, if limited, channel for mutual organizational interests. In 1920, for example, AMA leader Frank Billings was president, while the executive secretary of the American Hospital Association, A. R. Warner, was first vice president, and Homer F. Sanger of the AMA's Council on Education was on the Library Committee; the Rockefeller Foundation provided support. The conference threw its combined support behind standardization, though not necessarily behind the surgeons. "American Conference on Hospital Service," *Monthly Bulletin of the Federation of State Hospital Boards* 5 (1919), pp. 194–97.

24.   Moulinier's discussions with representatives of the American College of Surgeons in 1914 were instrumental to the establishment of the Catholic Hospital Association a year later—and it was the association's pledge to bring six hundred Catholic hospitals into the standardization program that got the ACS's program moving. The most potent criticisms came from the religious segment of the Catholic hospital community, whose authority was threatened. The spiritual director of the Hospital Sisters of St. Francis, which then owned fourteen hospitals in Illinois and Wisconsin, attacked the standards as a direct (medical) menace to the sisters' control of the hospitals—which they were. Robert J. Shanahan, *The History of the Catholic Hospital Association 1915–1965: Fifty Years of Progress* (St. Louis: Catholic Hospital Association, 1965), pp. 20, 32–33, 52–54, and passim; Reverend C. D. Moulinier, "Guiding Fundamental Principles in Hospital Standardization," *Bulletin of the American College of Surgeons* 9 (April 1925), pp. 16–17.

25.   Hawthorne Daniel, "Better Hospitals for Everybody," *World's Work* 40 (June 1920), p. 202.

26.   American College of Surgeons, *Eighth Year Book,* 1921, pp. 31, 33; *Ninth Year Book,* 1922, p. 48.

27.   By 1927 an estimated 4,400 general hospitals reported laboratory and X-ray departments and 2,100 included physical therapy. Stevens, *American Medicine and the Public Interest,* p. 158.

28.   These examples are drawn from the *Bulletin of the American College of Surgeons* 9 (1925).

29.   "Report of the Hospital Conference," ibid., pp. 7, 33. The most imaginative extension of the standards was the "health inventorium" program, developed by MacEachern in the late 1920s. This program was designed to take the idea of the hospital as practitioner's workshop one step further, by specifying and codifying the arrangements under which hospitals would be diagnostic centers, as of right, for the private patients of local practitioners. Participating hospitals would agree to provide examining rooms, diagnostic facilities, and access to consultants, so that local practitioners might offer periodic health examinations to patients. The ACS sent details to approved hospitals early in 1928; 70% of the replies indicated approval of the concept. MacEachern proclaimed in 1930 that the hospital was well on the way to becoming an organized health service for its entire community, a "veritable mecca of health." But he spoke too soon; the rigors of the Depression intervened. In the event, the inventorium program had little long-term effect and was to vanish, finally, in World War II. Malcolm T. MacEachern, "The Hospital as an Organized Health Center," *Bulletin of the American College of Surgeons* 6 (1930), p. 20. I am grateful to Dr. George W. Stephenson of the American College of Surgeons for bringing the health inventorium to my attention.

30.   For local practitioners the AMA hospital registration system was potentially useful as a vehicle for sustaining AMA policy in other areas—notably in defining what was and was not to be regarded as ethical medical practice. Local medical societies could, for example, report hospitals as inappropriate for registration because of locally unacceptable staffing practices. These included having an osteopathic physician on the staff, refusing to require all staff to be members of the county medical society, fostering a pay clinic, or out-and-out fraud. In 1930, 540 hospitals were rejected for AMA registration because of "irregular or unsafe practice." There were also continuing complaints by county medical societies that hospital medical staffs were holding meetings having nothing to do with hospital affairs, thus usurping the medical society's role. The educators on the Council on Medical Education and Hospitals found decisions about registration on political grounds difficult and distasteful, and

tried to avoid taking strong positions. Remarks of Arthur Dean Bevan, *Minutes of Business Meetings of the Council on Medical Education and Hospitals,* February 18, 1929. Registration figures are from "Hospital Service in the United States, 1931," *Journal of the American Medical Association* 96 (1931), p. 1023.

31. The case of osteopathy at the Los Angeles County Hospital is a good example of differences in view among different professional organizations. The State of California set up a board to license osteopathic physicians in 1922 and, not surprisingly, these practitioners claimed the right to practice at the County Hospital. The local medical society took a realistic position and went along with the proposal for a separate building for osteopathic medicine, completed in 1928. However, a bridge connected this building with the main hospital—over which interns, nurses, and physicians with M.D.'s might possibly stray. How was this hospital to be recognized by the national organizations, which then viewed osteopathy as quackery? For a while the American College of Surgeons refused to recognize any part of the Los Angeles County Hospital on the grounds that osteopathic medicine was inferior and unscientific. But the AMA Council favored approval of the M.D. unit, fearing the loss of "clinical material" to osteopathic physicians. *Minutes of the Business Meeting on the Council of Medical Education and Hospitals,* October 28, 1928 and February 18, 1929. "AMA Eyes Hospital Field with Increasing Interest, Members are Told," *Hospital Management* 29 (March 15, 1930), p. 60.

32. Lewis Mayers and Leonard V. Harrison, *The Distribution of Physicians in the United States* (New York: General Education Board, 1924); Commission on Medical Education, *Preliminary Report* (New Haven, Conn.: Office of the Director of the Study, 1927). On a related theme Ernst Meyer of the Rockefeller Foundation took the view that the rural hospital should primarily be an educational institution, "through which the community may be taught the fundamentals of hygiene and right living," but the foundation decided not to fund local institutions. Meyer, "Hospital Service in Rural Communities," *Journal of the American Medical Association* 72 (1919), p. 1135.

33. Quoted in Edith Abbott, *Public Assistance: American Principles and Politics* (Chicago: University of Chicago Press, 1940), p. 660.

34. Ernst C. Meyer, "Hospital Service in Rural Communities," *Journal of the American Medical Association* 72 (1919), p. 1365.

35. Wayne C. Nason, *Rural Hospitals,* U.S. Department of Agriculture, Farmers' Bulletin no. 1485 (March 1926), p. 1.

36. Ibid, p. 32. Much-needed work on the history of hospitals as local community institutions between the two world wars is being done by Barbara Rosenkrantz and Peter Buck, who argue that the rural hospital became in many places a central institution for community activities of many different kinds—just because it was there as a visible social organization. I have benefited from drafts of some of their work in thinking through this chapter.

37. The largest profit-making acute hospital in 1928 was the West Suburban Hospital at Oak Park, Illinois, with 327 adult beds. Other notable urban hospitals included St. Francis Hospital in San Francisco, the Virginia Mason Hospital in Seattle, the Cleveland Clinic Hospital, and Doctors Hospital in New York City. Rorem, *The Public's Investment in Hospitals,* pp. 14, 201.

38. Charles Harris Whitaker, "The Interrelations of the Professions," *Annals of the American Academy of Political and Social Science* CI (May 1922), p. 12. Calvin Coolidge's remarks on business and ideals are quoted at the beginning of this book. A related sentiment is expressed by F. M. Feiker, "The Profession of Commerce in the Making," ibid., p. 207. Feiker remarked that, as Greece left the imprint of its culture in art, and Rome in war, America's civilization would leave as its legacy the link between commercialism and high ideals. There is still no detailed study of how this apparently pervasive rhetoric of commerce and ideals played out for social institutions like hospitals in the 1920s.

39. R. H. Tawney, *The Acquisitive Society* (Oxford: Harcourt, Brace & Howe, 1920).

40. "The Hospital and the Community it Serves," *Modern Hospital Yearbook,* 1919, p. 13.

41. Ray Lyman Wilbur, "Introduction," in *Medical Care for the American People: The Final Report of the Committee on the Costs of Medical Care* (Chicago: University of Chicago Press, 1932), p. ix.

42. This book was written following a study suggested by the influential secretary of the AHA, A. R. Warner. John A. Lapp and Dorothy Ketchum, *Hospital Law* (Milwaukee: Bruce Publishing Co., 1926). Case examples cited here are drawn from this source, pp. 156, 162.

43. The Duke Endowment provided standards for hospital bed supply, provided money

for construction and a dollar-a-day subsidy for the provision of care to charity patients in North and South Carolina, and produced handbooks of information for those interested in the location, building, and equipment of small hospitals. The endowment assisted 149 hospitals between 1925 and 1939 with funds of well over $13 million, mostly for hospital operations. The hospital bed ratio rose in these two impoverished, largely rural states, from 1.4 beds per 1,000 population in 1924, to 2.1 in 1939. Duke Endowment, *Fifteenth Annual Report of the Hospital Section* (Charlotte, N.C.: Duke Endowment, 1940), pp. 9, 34.

44. Commonwealth Fund, *Annual Report the Year 1924–25* (New York: Commonwealth Fund, 1926), p. 69.

45. The best accounts of veterans' services in the 1920s are Robert D. Leigh, *Federal Health Administration in the United States* (New York: Harper & Bros., 1927); and Robinson E. Adkins, *Medical Care of Veterans* (Washington, D.C.: Government Printing Office, 1967), printed for the use of the Committee on Veterans' Affairs, 40th Cong., 1st sess., House Committee Print no. 4.

46. Another member was ex-Colonel Frank Billings, dean of Rush Medical College, an AMA trustee, and twice AMA president. The others were experts on psychiatry and tuberculosis. These consultants were joined almost immediately by a further committee of medical-school stars and base-hospital veterans, appointed by the new president, and the two groups reinforced each other's efforts.

47. *Report of the Consultants on Hospitalization Appointed by the Secretary of the Treasury to Provide Additional Hospital Facilities Under Public Act 384 (Approved March 4, 1921)* (Washington, D.C.: Government Printing Office, 1923). I have also drawn on the minutes and reports of the consultants in the National Archives, RG 121, boxes 220–34.

48. On the American Conference on Hospital Service, see n. 23 above. Influential members of the conference, including S. S. Goldwater, director of Mount Sinai Hospital, latched on to the notion of a library and service bureau as an important, relatively noncontroversial focus for the group—whose members were nervous about the conference's future role. (Notably, the AMA wanted control of the conference while the American College of Surgeons wished not to participate.) Trying to get the AMA and the college together was a "delicate situation," wrote Goldwater to A. R. Warner at the American Hospital Association in 1920, who forwarded the letter to Edward R. Embree, secretary of the Rockefeller Foundation. A. R. Warner to Edward R. Embree, November 26, 1920, RG 1.1., series 100, box 1, folder 13, Rockefeller Archives.

The story of the Hospital and Library Service Bureau in the 1920s, as revealed in the Rockefeller Foundation Archives, is one of continuing friction, for a conflict arose between the bureau's director, Donelda R. Hamlin, who believed that the bureau should have a strong, independent, educational and propagandist function, prodding hospitals to change, and the new AHA secretary Walsh, who wanted the AHA to monopolize hospital information. In a vignette of the pervasive power of the foundations, the conflict came to involve representatives of the Rockefeller Foundation, the Carnegie Corporation, and the Commonwealth Fund, none of whom wanted to engage in controversial activities. The AHA won, and Hamlin resigned. Ibid.; box 1, folder 14; and box 2, folder 19.

49. The opposing views of black veterans, including the National Committee of Negro Veterans, and of the U.S. Public Health Service were largely ignored—namely, that blacks, like whites, should have the right to choose the best hospitals and white physicians, should they so desire, that they and their families should not be expected to travel long distances, and that federal tax funds should not be used to promote segregation.

Since the Tuskegee Institute, founded by Booker T. Washington, had no medical school, the decision to attach a veterans' hospital to it also flew in the face of the development of affiliations between hospitals and medical schools that was a cherished part of the agenda of foundations. The hospital was constructed with two units, one for tuberculosis and one for mental illness, with no unit specifically designed for medicine and surgery, and it was difficult to see how far black physicians interested in general practice or other specialties would benefit from training in such an institution. The various views are reported in the papers of the consultants in the National Archives.

Local white-black conflicts also distinguished the early days of the hospital, because of conflicting expectations. Pete Daniel, "Black Power in the 1920s: the Case of Tuskegee Veterans Hospital," *Journal of Southern History* 36 (1970), pp. 368–88.

50. Ray Lyman Wilbur, president of the AMA, was chairman of the 1924 committee;

Malcolm MacEachern, director of the Surgeons' Standardization Program, was secretary. The ACS surveyed all fifty veterans' hospitals—forty-five of them were fully approved in 1925. Two major diagnostic centers were set up within the veterans' system in the 1920s, at Cincinnati and Washington. Adkins, *Medical Care of Veterans,* p. 138.

51. Veterans Administration, *Annual Report 1933,* p. 11; and see James G. Burrow, *AMA: Voice of American Medicine* (Baltimore: Johns Hopkins Press, 1963), p. 156.

52. *AMA Digest of Official Actions 1846–1958* (Chicago: American Medical Association, 1959), pp. 708–9.

53. Lapp and Ketchum, *Hospital Law,* pp. 402, 495–98.

54. The Rockefeller Foundation's response to group practice was timid and limited. Although it funded a committee on dispensary development in New York in 1920, headed by Michael Davis, which in turn established the pay clinics at Cornell and Presbyterian, foundation support was terminated in 1926. See also "Conference on Hospital Social Service," February 21, 1920, 200 RG 1.1, series 200, box 23, folder 265, Rockefeller Archives; *Principles of Hospital Administration and the Training of Hospital Executives* (Chicago: Committee on the Training of Hospital Executives, 1922). Familiar faces on the committee were John Bowman, S. S. Goldwater, Frederic A. Washburn, and Father Moulinier, among a total of ten members. Michael M. Davis, *Hospital Administration: A Career* (New York: privately published, 1929).

Among successful foundation efforts, the most far-reaching was the Goldmark report (1923), which recommended a three-tier structure of nursing education, including the training of leaders in university nursing schools. As an outcome, the Rockefeller Foundation established the Yale Nursing School, and another endowed school was developed at Western Reserve. A committee on the grading of nursing schools also began to rate the hospital nursing schools, much as the medical schools had been graded twenty years before. By 1932 several hundred of the poorer nursing schools had closed, while the average enrollment per school increased. There was increasing anxiety among doctors about staffing hospitals in small-town areas, which were left without nursing students to provide basic services. Here foundation policies conflicted with the interests of rural practitioners, for whom nursing students were a boon. *Nursing and Nursing Education in the United States: Report of the Committee for the Study of Nursing Education and Report of a Survey by Josephine Goldmark* (New York: Macmillan, 1923); May Ayres Burgess, *Nurses, Patients, and Pocketbooks: Report of a Study of the Economics of Nursing* (New York: Committee on the Grading of Nursing Schools, 1928), pp. 544–45.

55. Eduard C. Lindeman, *Wealth and Culture* (New York: Harcourt, Brace & Co., 1936), pp. 21, 99.

56. Commission on Medical Education, *Final Report of the Commission on Medical Education* (New York: Office of the Director of the Study, 1932).

57. Ludmerer, *Learning to Heal,* p. 198 and passim. The GEB, for example, made major grants to Vanderbilt University ($4 million) to provide for the development of a new medical school with its own hospital as the foundation's flagship in the South, and to the University of Rochester, New York (initial grants of $5 million), which developed another major medical school in the 1920s, in conjunction with Strong Memorial Hospital. In 1921 the GEB also assisted what it called "unpretentious but active institutions," as well as other schools already in the lead. GEB funding, *inter alia,* helped the transfer of Baptist Memorial Hospital, Waco, Texas, to Baylor University, where it became Baylor Hospital; assisted the construction of a general hospital at Emory University in Atlanta; and helped to build a huge new city hospital in Cincinnati, designed to provide better clinical facilities for its municipal university. General Education Board, *Report 1920–21,* pp. 16–17.

58. The AHA began an official publication in 1926, with the printing of quarterly bulletins. The *Bulletin* became the monthly journal *Hospitals* in 1936. A new headquarters building and the acquisition of the Library and Service Bureau shortly afterward further strengthened the AHA's position as did the appearance of state hospital associations as organized constituents; the Ohio Hospital Association was the first to be voted into the American Hospital Association, in 1920. Joseph Doane, "What the Future Holds for American Hospitals," *Modern Hospital* 31 (September 1928), pp. 49–54; Joseph G. Norby, "An Elder Colleague Takes a Look at the Long Path of Progress," *Hospitals* 29 (February 1955), pp. 64–66.

59. W. H. Welch (1925), quoted by Harry H. Moore, in President's Research Committee on Recent Social Trends, *Recent Social Trends in the United States* (New York: McGraw-Hill, 1933), p. 1062; Edward A. Filene, "Autocare versus Medical Care," *Journal of the American Medical Association* 93 (1929), p. 1247.

60.   Michael M. Davis and Gertrude E. Sturges, "Memorandum on the Hospital Situation in Detroit, April 8, 1921," typescript, R362 D29M, AHA Archives.

61.   The Cleveland and San Francisco surveys, cited above, offer a rich mine of material for historians. Figures for hospital beds per 1,000 population are calculated from U.S. Bureau of the Census, *Hospitals and Dispensaries, 1923* (Washington, D.C.: Government Printing Office, 1925), table 9.

62.   "Hospital Service in the United States," *Journal of the American Medical Association* 106 (1936), p. 784.

63.   Although overall cost figures for hospitals are not available for the 1920s, the example of a "well-known hospital" cited by the secretary of the American Hospital Association in 1930 is probably fairly typical. In this hospital the cost of maintaining one patient for one day rose from $2.65 in 1919 to $4.71 in 1928, an increase of nearly 80%. Bert W. Caldwell, "The Cost of Medical Care from the Viewpoint of the Hospital," in *Hospitals and the Cost of Medical Care,* papers read at session of the American Conference of Hospital Service, February 18, 1930 (Chicago: American Hospital Association, 1930), p. 4.

64.   For example, by 1930 all-inclusive charges for obstetrics were offered at Hollywood Clara Barton Hospital of Los Angeles and at Vassar Brothers Hospital at Poughkeepsie, New York, and for tonsillectomies at Delaware Hospital in Wilmington, while a flat charge for hospital diagnostic procedures was available at Madison General Hospital, Wisconsin. A bolder scheme was offered when Massachusetts General Hospital opened Baker Memorial Hospital in 1930 as a unit specially designed for patients of moderate means. The payment schedule covered ward rates, special services, and attending physician fees in one carefully controlled package. This plan, like a similar "middle rate plan" in Keokuk, Iowa, assumed the cooperation and active participation of physicians—not something to be counted on everywhere. The plan also required enormous administrative efforts, special funding, and new organizations. It was much easier to introduce new facilities than graft new methods on to established organizations. Carpenter, *Hospital Service for Patients of Moderate Means,* pp. 38–40; Nathaniel W. Faxon, *The Massachusetts General Hospital, 1935–1955* (Cambridge: Harvard University Press, 1959), pp. 13–14, 160–62.

65.   One study of charges for patients with appendicitis in four metropolitan nongovernmental hospitals in the early 1930s found that hospital and special-nursing charges represented half of the total cost of the illness, physician fees the other half. However, in one of the four hospitals less than half the physician fees were actually collected. Michael M. Davis, "Physicians, Fees, and Hospital Bills," in Davis and C. Rufus Rorem, *The Crisis in Hospital Finance* (Chicago: University of Chicago Press, 1932), p. 95 and passim.

66.   Committee on the Costs of Medical Care, *Medical Care for the American People* (Chicago: University of Chicago Press, 1932).

67.   Richards M. Bradley, "Past Charity, Present Vanity: Medical Service and the Middle Class," *Survey* 66 (July 1931), pp. 348–49.

68.   R. G. Brodrick, "Presidential Address," *Bulletin of the American Hospital Association* 1 (October 1927), p. 27.

69.   One hospital administrator from Mississippi went so far as to claim in 1930 that, even though the laws of that state required a pauper's oath and certificate of indigence from a physician as a prerequisite for admission into the charity hospital, the wards were crowded with patients able to pay for service in a private intitution—and presumably for private medical fees. He did not say why he thought physicians were cutting their own billings in this way, by certifying for admission in the first place. W. Hamilton Crawford, "Discussion," *Transactions of the American Hospital Association* 32 (1930), p. 647.

70.   That poor service was not a necessary corollary of local-government status was demonstrated by the high standards of city hospitals in Cincinnati, where a high-quality hospital continued; in Oakland, where the Alameda County system was regarded as a showplace for centralized health services under official control; and in St. Paul, where the superintendent of the city hospital held that the hospital should be seen as parallel in its municipal functions to public schools. Harry Dowling, *City Hospitals: The Undercare of the Underprivileged* (Cambridge, Mass.: Harvard University Press, 1982), pp. 94, 149, and passim.

71.   Emmet B. Bay, *Medical Administration of Teaching Hospitals* (Chicago: University of Chicago Press, 1931), p. 24.

72.   H. M. Green, "A Brief Study of the Hospital Situation Among Negroes," in Committee on Hospitalization of Colored People, *Report of the City Hospital for the Colored* (Chicago:

American Hospital Association 1930), p. 19; E. H. L. Corwin and Gertrude E. Sturgis, *Opportunities for the Medical Education of Negroes* (New York: Scribners, 1936), p. 256. The statistics are from U.S. Bureau of the Census, *Hospitals and Dispensaries, 1923,* table 1. The best study of the integration-segregation debates over hospitals in this period is Vanessa Northington Gamble, "The Negro Hospital Renaissance: The Black Hospital Movement, 1920–1940" (Ph.D. diss., Department of History and Sociology of Science, University of Pennsylvania, 1987).

73.   A study of nineteen major teaching hospitals in 1930 found twelve with full-time chiefs of the major clinical departments and an increasing bureaucracy of interns and residents. Bay, *Medical Administration of Teaching Hospitals,* p. 39. On the "full-time plan" of medical teaching, see Ludmerer, *Learning to Heal,* pp. 207–13 and passim; Daniel Fox, "Abraham Flexner's Unpublished Report: Foundations and Medical Education, 1909–1928," *Bulletin of the History of Medicine* 54 (1980), pp. 475–96.

74.   I discuss the politics of specialty organizations in *American Medicine and the Public Interest,* pp. 149–71, 198–217.

Chapter 6

1.   Mary Ross, "Crisis in the Hospitals," *Survey Graphic* 22 (July 1933), p. 365.

2.   In thinking through this chapter, I found particularly useful Michael Rogin's "Voluntarism: The Political Functions of an Antipolitical Doctrine," *Industrial and Labor Relations Review* 15 (July 1962), pp. 521–35 (on craft unions); and Murray Edelman, *The Symbolic Uses of Politics* (Urbana: University of Illinois Press, 1967; first published 1964).

3.   From 622,000 in 1929 to 832,000 in 1936, and on to 1.4 million in 1941. Utilization figures in this chapter are from the AMA Council on Medical Education and Hospitals, "Hospital Service in the United States," published annually in the *Journal of the American Medical Association,* selected years, unless otherwise stated.

4.   The comparable figure for 1929 was 52%. Emil Frankel, "Trends in General Hospital Services in New Jersey: 1929–1936," *Hospitals* 11 (December 1937), p. 40.

5.   W. F. Walker, "What the Depression has Done to Health Service," *Public Management* 16 (November 1934), pp. 360–84. The New York figures are from Ross, "Crisis in the Hospitals," p. 364. Admissions to the city hospital in Philadelphia increased by almost 50% between 1929 and 1934 and outpatient visits swelled to 139,000, almost four times as many as in 1928. In Boston, reputed to have the most generous public welfare in the country, welfare expenditures rose from 6% of all outlays controlled by the mayor in 1929, to almost 36% in 1933, and remained close to that figure throughout the decade. Annual Reports of the City of Philadelphia, selected years; Charles H. Trout, *Boston: The Great Depression and the New Deal* (New York: Oxford University Press, 1977), p. 285.

6.   In 1932, for example, the fifty or so hospitals that reported to the United Hospital Fund in New York City showed an aggregate operating deficit of about $4 million. In Cleveland the hospitals affiliated with the Community Fund estimated their earnings for 1933 at $2.1 million, down from $3.6 million in 1929. Their Community Fund allocation of approximately $400,000 was less than half the 1929 amount and their endowment income down by 30%. Ross, "Crisis in the Hospitals," p. 365; "Hospital Work Up, Funds Down," *The Survey* 69 (September 1933), p. 323.

7.   Edward F. Denison, "Consumer Expenditures for Selected Groups of Services, 1929–41," *Survey of Current Business* 22 (October 1942), pp. 25–26.

8.   "Hospitals in 1933," editorial, *Journal of the American Medical Association* 102 (1934), p. 1013.

9.   Over half of the hospital days reported for urban working-class patients in 1933 were spent by individuals whose incomes had decreased significantly since 1929. The investigators estimated that the families received an estimated 50% more free hospital care in 1933 than they would have done if there had been no Depression. G. St. J. Perrott, Edgar Sydenstricker, and Selwyn D. Collins, "Medical Care During the Depression: A Preliminary Report upon a Survey of Wage-Earning Families in Seven Large Cities," *Milbank Memorial Fund Quarterly* 12 (1934), p. 108; Perrott and Sydenstricker, "Causal and Selective Factors in Sickness," *American Journal of Sociology* 40 (1934–35), p. 804.

10. The best account of this switch is Barbara Melosh, *The Physician's Hand* (Philadelphia: Temple University Press, 1982).

11. *First Annual Report of S. Davis Wilson, Mayor of Philadelphia, Containing the Reports of the Various Departments of the City of Philadelphia for the Year Ending December 21, 1936,* p. 209; *Second Annual Report, 1937,* pp. 515–19.

12. Nathan B. Van Etten, "Abuses of Medical Charity and the Free Service of Physicians," in *The Medical Profession and the Public: Currents and Countercurrents* (Philadelphia: American Academy of Political and Social Science, 1934), p. 18; Edna Sproat-Martindale, "Preventing Dispensary Abuse," *Modern Hospital* 44 (January 1935), p. 85.

13. Michael M. Davis, "What the Council Has Been Doing," *Transactions of the American Hospital Association* 36 (1934), p. 533; "Report of the Council on Community Relations and Administrative Practice," ibid. 37 (1935), p. 303.

14. "Hospital Work Up, Funds Down," *The Survey* 69 (September 1933), p. 323.

15. Van Etten, "Abuses of Medical Charity," p. 12.

16. Frankel, "Trends in General Hospital Services in New Jersey," p. 40. Another contemporary writer, looking at the accounts of four illustrative nonprofit hospitals between 1929 and 1931, found that receipts decreased in three, but the decrease ranged from 13% to 45%. Thus while some hospitals fared very badly, others did quite well. Sister M. Robert, "Hospital Economics: Depression and Its Effect on the Hospital," *Hospital Progress* 12 (1931), pp. 319–21.

17. E. L. Harmon, "Cleveland's Credit Plan," *Modern Hospital* 51 (July 1938), pp. 51–53.

18. "Proposed Legislation Affecting Hospitals," *Bulletin of the American Hospital Association* 6 (January 1932), p. 99.

19. *Report of the Hospital Survey for New York,* vol. II (New York: United Hospital Fund, 1937), p. 141.

20. Rosemary Stevens, *American Medicine and the Public Interest,* p. 181.

21. Figures are calculated from "Hospital Service in the United States, 1940," *Journal of the American Medical Association* 114 (1940), pp. 1166–67.

22. Denison, "Consumer Expenditures," p. 25.

23. "President's Address," *Transactions of the American Hospital Association* 34 (1932), p. 147.

24. "Hospital Service in the United States," *Journal of the American Medical Association* 100 (1933), p. 887; ibid. 102 (1934), p. 1011; "Hospitals in 1933," editorial, ibid. 102 (1934), pp. 1084–85.

25. Good examples are Abraham Oseroff, "Two Mutually Dependent Forces—The Hospital and the Doctor," *Modern Hospital* 39 (1932), p. 89; Malcolm T. MacEachern, *Hospital Organization and Management* (Chicago: Physicians' Record Co., 1935), p. 781.

26. The most notable critiques were the Committee on the Costs of Medical Care, *Medical Care for the American People: The Final Report of the Committee on the Costs of Medical Care,* Publication no. 28 (Chicago: University of Chicago Press, 1932); and Commission on Medical Education, *Final Report* (New York: Office of the Director of the Study, 1932).

27. See, for example, remarks of Ray Lyman Wilbur, *Proceedings of the Annual Congress on Medical Education,* 1932, p. 2; S. M. Robert, "Hospital Economics—Depression and Its Effect on the Hospital," *Hospital Progress* 12 (1931), pp. 319–21.

28. The figures are given in table 6.4. A retrospective study of new capital investment by Michael M. Davis, drawing on hospital reports in the journal *Modern Hospital,* estimated that the government share of new construction moved from less than 30% in 1927 to almost 80% in 1932, while private construction rapidly decreased. He estimated that the value of nongovernment construction for all types of hospitals fell from $95.8 million in 1927 to $5.7 million in 1932, with only a partial correction to $28.7 million in 1937. Michael M. Davis, "Who Finances Construction?" *Modern Hospital* 52 (November 1938), p. 57.

29. By asserting a public mission for voluntary hospitals throughout the 1930s, the courts maintained the position that money received by voluntary hospitals from paying patients was to be regarded not as a quid pro quo of purchase but as a contribution toward the maintenance of a charity. See, e.g., Emanuel Hayt, "Tax Exemption of Charitable Hospitals," *Hospitals* 14 (January 1940), pp. 22–26; S. S. Goldwater, "Do American Cities Need Both Voluntary and Tax-Supported Hospitals?" ibid. 15 (February 1940); and Arnold Emch, "Tax Exemption of Voluntary Hospitals," ibid. 14 (April 1940), p. 73.

30. I discuss the background to this language in "A Poor Sort of Memory: Voluntary Hospitals and Government before the Depression," *Milbank Memorial Fund Quarterly* 60 (1982), pp. 551–84.

31. N. W. Faxon, "Half-Empty Hospitals," *Survey Graphic* 23 (December 1934), p. 604.

32. The best analysis is Peter N. Grant, "The Struggle for Control of California's Health Care Marketplace" (Ph.D. diss., Harvard University, 1988). For a contemporary account, see Arthur J. Will, "Relationship Between Public and Private Hospitals in California," *Hospitals* 12 (April 1938), pp. 94–96.

33. Committee on the Costs of Medical Care, *Medical Care for the American People.*

34. Rexwald Brown, "We Believe in Group Medicine," *Survey Graphic* 23 (December 1934), p. 595. C. Rufus Rorem, *Private Group Clinics* (Washington, D.C.: Committee on the Costs of Medical Care, 1931), p. 17 and passim; Harry H. Moore, "Health and Medical Practice," in *Recent Social Trends,* vol. 2, p. 1076.

35. A good account is James G. Burrow, *AMA: Voice of American Medicine* (Baltimore: Johns Hopkins University Press, 1963), pp. 205–27 and passim.

36. *AMA Digest of Official Actions 1846–1958* (Chicago: American Medical Association, 1959), p. 129.

37. See, e.g., Michael M. Davis, "The Committee on Costs of Medical Care Makes Its Report," *Modern Hospital* 39 (December 1932), pp. 41–46. The *American Journal of Nursing* also supported the CCMC: "The Committee on the Costs of Medical Care Reports," editorial, *American Journal of Nursing* 32 (1932), p. 1286. For an initial evaluation of the reception of the report, see Forrest A. Walker, "Americanism versus Sovietism: A Study of the Reaction to the Committee on the Costs of Medical Care," *Bulletin of the History of Medicine* 53 (1979), pp. 489–504.

38. "Report of Committee to Study Methods of Protecting Voluntary Hospitals from Unfair Competition," *Transactions of the American Hospital Association* 36 (1934), p. 217; ibid. 35 (1933), pp. 225, 326; ibid. 37 (1935), p. 839.

39. Editorial, "The Committee on the Costs of Medical Care," *Journal of the American Medical Association* 99 (1932), pp. 1950–52.

40. Brief biographies are given in Lewis E. Weeks and Howard J. Berman, *Shapers of American Health Care Policy* (Ann Arbor, Mich.: Health Administration Press, 1985).

41. Duncan Neuhauser, *Coming of Age: A 50-Year History of the American College of Hospital Administrators and the Profession It Serves, 1933–1983* (Chicago: Pluribus Press, 1983), p. 13.

42. Ibid., p. 65.

43. Warren L. Babcock, "Report of the Committee on Hospital Organization and Management," *Transactions of the American Hospital Association* 32 (1930), pp. 30–40.

44. Lewis A. Sexton, "Presidential Address," *Transactions of the American Hospital Association* 33 (1931), p. 198; "Payment for Care of Indigents," ibid. 34 (1932), p. 169.

45. "Hospitals as Depression Cures," *Literary Digest* 115 (June 17, 1933), p. 34.

46. I. M. Rubinow, *The Quest for Security* (New York: Henry Holt & Co., 1934), p. 202. The phrase "temple of the silver screen" and the description of the movie palace are also Rubinow's. For the point about hospitals being important symbols of modern architecture, I am indebted to Wecter Dixon, *The Age of the Great Depression, 1929–1941* (New York: Macmillan, 1948), p. 271.

47. MacEachern was still directing the hospital standardization program of the American College of Surgeons. Malcolm T. MacEachern, *Hospital Organization and Management* (Chicago: Physicians' Record Co., 1935).

48. James Clark Fifield, ed., *American and Canadian Hospitals* (Chicago: Physicians' Record Co., 1933), pp. 9, 44; Robert J. Shanahan, *The History of the Catholic Hospital Association* (St. Louis: Catholic Hospital Association of the United States and Canada, 1965), pp. 86–87, 93, 120.

49. In 1931, for example, the AHA began active and successful opposition to federal expansion of veterans' facilities, joining the AMA and the American Legion in arguing that veterans should be served in voluntary hospitals near their homes. Both the AHA and the AMA also sought to restrict veterans' programs to service-related disabilities, again protecting the voluntary hospitals' turf, as well as that of private practitioners. Although the "bonus army" veterans' march on Washington in 1932 dramatized veterans' complaints, they were now competing for funds with a new army of younger men who were now unemployed. President Roosevelt tightened eligibility for veterans' benefits, including medical benefits, in 1933. The official view of the VA was that the whole system had "gone too far." Between June 1932 and June 1933, the VA cut back its patient load by 23%, chiefly for nonservice disabilities, and in this group chiefly for tuberculosis and psychiatry. Veterans Administra-

tion, *Annual Report for 1933,* p. 11. Eligibility was eased in 1934, and the hospital lobby continued to be vigilant.

50. Shanahan, *The History of the CHA,* p. 121.

51. Bert W. Caldwell to Hon. Atlee Pomorene, quoted in "The Reconstruction Finance Corporation and Our Hospitals," editorial, *Bulletin of the American Hospital Association,* December 1932, pp. 1–2.

52. Reportedly, the hospitals kept separate sets of accounts, designed to maximize local-government and community income, and these were seen by Hopkins as designed for double-dipping. I. S. Falk, personal communication, October 1983.

53. For a statement of the AHA position, see Richard P. Borden, "The Conference of the Committee of the Association with Mr. Harry L. Hopkins, Director of Emergency Welfare Relief," *Bulletin of the American Hospital Association,* August 17, 1933, pp. 3–4. In this section I have drawn from a wide variety of articles and statements in contemporary hospital journals and transactions. The best account of the joint committee set up by the associations is Shanahan, *The History of the CHA,* p. 118 and passim.

54. Sister John Gabriel, "The Role of the Hospitals in the Recovery Program," *Hospital Management* 37 (May 1934), pp. 36–38.

55. Wherever federal hospitals were unavailable (and this was true in most parts of the country), injured workers were sent to the nearest hospital, with no priority given to state- or local-government hospitals over voluntary institutions. *Report of the Committee on Public Relations* (Chicago: American Hospital Association, 1934), p. 1.

56. Shanahan, *The History of the CHA,* pp. 118–20; Robert Jolley, "Hospitals Must Obtain Exemptions From Pension and Insurance Bills," *Hospital Management* 39 (March 1935), pp. 13–15.

57. "U.S. Aid in Care of Indigents Asked By Catholic Group," *Hospital Management* 38 (July 1934), pp. 34–35; Shanahan, *The History of the CHA,* pp. 120–21.

58. The Civil Works Administration, for example, paid hospitals a standard per diem fee of $3.50 a day plus special charges for services such as operating fees, anesthesia, specialized laboratory services, or unusually expensive drugs, and followed the traditional practice of excluding physicians' fees from its hospital reimbursement arrangements. This type of reimbursement rocked no boats.

59. Under FERA programs state emergency relief administrators were responsible for ensuring that individual income was sufficient to prevent physical suffering and to maintain minimal living standards; allowances were included for medical care in estimating need, but not for hospitalization. The president of the Protestant Hospital Association urged that group to take the hospitals' plight directly to President Roosevelt in order to press for changes in FERA policy. "Report of the Committee on Bed Occupancy of Hospitals," *Transactions of the American Hospital Association* 34 (1932), p. 116; Charles F. Neergaard et al., "Report of the Committee on Hospital Planning and Equipment," ibid. 37 (1935), p. 744.

60. M. H. Eichenlaub, "Pennsylvania Hospitals Successful in Relief Bond Issue," *Hospital Management* 36 (December 1933), p. 32.

61. Federal Emergency Administration of Public Works, Research Section of the Projects Division, *PWA Provides Modern Hospitals* (Washington, D.C.: Government Printing Office, 1937), p. 6. The best review of the PWA, the WPA, and related programs, is Commission on Hospital Care, *Hospital Care in the United States* (Cambridge, Mass.: Harvard University Press, 1957), pp. 529–35.

62. In 1936 the PWA financed hospitals in all but five states and territories, mostly for state hospitals for the mentally ill, to alleviate overcrowding in these institutions. However, 121 projects were for general hospitals, at an estimated construction cost of over $47 million. *PWA Provides Modern Hospitals,* p. 15.

63. Through June 1942, WPA workers constructed 202 new hospitals, provided additions to 143, and were responsible for other types of construction or improvement in 2,069 hospitals.

64. "Is Your State Planning More Hospital Facilities?" editorial, *Hospital Management* 37 (February 1934), p. 37; "Shall More Hospital Beds Be Provided by Government?" ibid. 39 (May 1935), p. 32.

65. An AHA committee on bed occupancy, concerned with declining utilization rates, had also recommended community control of new hospital construction in 1932, in order to shut the door on future hospital expansion. (By this they meant a voluntary, cooperative system.)

"Report of the Committee on Bed Occupancy of Hospitals," *Transactions of the American Hospital Association* 34 (1932), p. 116; Charles F. Neergaard et al., "Report of the Committee on Hospital Planning and Equipment," ibid. 37 (1935), p. 744.

66.   Small federal programs did provide useful aid. For example, well over two hundred voluntary hospitals took advantage of the insured loans made available through the Federal Housing Administration's modernization credit plan. These loans encouraged them to purchase equipment such as X-ray machines, fluoroscopes, and anesthesia machinery in a depressed market; $490,000 had been extended to hospitals under this program by the fall of 1936. "F.H.A. Credit Simplifies Hospital Modernization," *Hospital Management* 42 (August 1936), pp. 30–33.

Chapter 7

1.   The figures on children refer to children under fifteen years of age in cities with a population of 100,000 or more. Children were also frequently seen in hospitals for the acute communicable diseases that were widespread in the 1930s, including scarlet fever, ear infections, mastoid diseases, and pneumonia. Dorothy F. Holland, "The Disabling Diseases of Childhood: Their Characteristics and Medical Care as Observed in 500,000 Children in 83 Cities Canvassed in the National Health Survey, 1935–1936," *Public Health Reports* 55 (February 9, 1940), p. 236. The average length of stay for pneumonia, for all ages, was 19.1 days in 1935–36. Rollo H. Britten, "The Incidence of Pneumonia as Recorded in the National Health Survey," *Public Health Reports* 57 (October 2, 1942), p. 1491. For hospital admission rates, see table 8.1.

Patients stayed in hospitals, on average, for 13.9 days in 1935, 12.9 days in 1940. For whites in urban areas in the mid-1930s the average length of stay was 24 days for those on relief, but only 15 or 16 for those with incomes of $2,000 or more—probably because the latter were healthier and because they entered hospitals in greater numbers for short-term elective procedures. Again, hospital utilization figures are drawn from the annual "Hospital Service in the United States," in the years cited, published in the *Journal of the American Medical Association*, unless otherwise stated. Figures on race are given by Rollo H. Britten, "The National Health Survey: Receipt of Medical Services in Different Urban Populations and Groups," *Public Health Reports* 55 (November 29, 1940), p. 13.

2.   Lewis Thomas, *The Lives of a Cell: Notes of a Biology Watcher* (New York: Viking, 1974), p. 35. And see J. G. M. Bullowa, *The Management of the Pneumonias* (New York: Oxford University Press, 1937).

3.   Stevens, *American Medicine and the Public Interest*, p. 181.

4.   See Mary C. Jarrett, *Chronic Illness in New York City*, vol. 1 (New York: Published for the Welfare Council of New York City by Columbia University Press, 1933), pp. 50–53, 62.

5.   Commission on Hospital Care, *Hospital Care in the United States* (Cambridge, Mass.: Harvard University Press, 1957), pp. 235–37.

6.   In 1935, 35% of births were in hospitals. For white women in U.S. cities the figure was 65%, and for women in this group with family incomes of $2,000 or more, 88%. By 1940 the overall rate for hospital births had risen to almost 56%, but whites were more than twice as likely to enter hospitals as others (60% percent and 27%, respectively). Jennie C. Goddard, "Medical and Nursing Services for Maternal Cases of the National Health Survey," *Public Health Bulletin* no. 264 (Washington, D.C.: Government Printing Office, 1941), pp. 23, 27.

7.   Ibid., p. 45.

8.   Britten, "The Incidence of Pneumonia," p. 1492.

9.   Children aged five to nine reported 50.9 surgical cases per 1,000 population during the year. Selwyn D. Collins, "Frequency and Volume of Hospital Care for Specific Diseases in Relation to All Illness Among 9,000 Families, Based on Nationwide Periodic Canvasses, 1928–31." *Public Health Reports* 57 (September 25, 1942), pp. 40–41. In large cities children under fifteen who were on relief were 50% more likely to be hospitalized than children of any other income level. The difference was negligible, however, between children on relief and those of low-income families in small cities—here the richest children got the most hospital care. Holland, "The Disabling Diseases of Childhood," p. 236.

10. In 1933, 60.8% of the whites treated in New York City hospitals were treated in voluntary hospitals, and 39.2% in municipal hospitals. In contrast, 75.1% of the "Negro" population was treated in municipal hospitals and 69.6% of the population labeled as "other colored." Neva R. Deardorff and Marta Fraenkel, *Hospital Discharge Study* (New York: Welfare Council of New York City, 1942), vol. 1, *Hospitals and Hospital Patients in New York City*, p. 66.

11. In an AMA census done in 1980, 42.9% of the proprietary hospitals reported that they refused to admit "Negro patients." Comparable figures for government hospitals were 15.5%, church-related 19.6%, and other nonprofit 21.6%. The average for general hospitals was 21.5%. "Hospital Service in the United States," *Journal of the American Medical Association* 116 (1941), p. 1066.

12. Haven Emerson, *The Hospital Survey for New York,* vol. I (New York: United Hospital Fund, 1937), p. 227.

13. Edgar C. Hayhow et al., "Report of the Committee on Pharmacy," *Transactions of the American Hospital Association* 39 (1937), p. 173.

14. Alden B. Mills, *Hospital Public Relations* (Chicago: Physicians' Record Co., 1939), p. 69.

15. Harry C. Saltzstein, "Hospital Bed Care Ten Years Ago and Now," *Hospitals* 14 (December 1940), p. 88.

16. Gordon R. Kamman, "The Role of Bibliotherapy in the Care of the Patient," *Bulletin of the American College of Surgeons* 24 (June 1939), p. 183. See also Earl C. Elkins, "Essentials for Fever Therapy," *Modern Hospital* 50 (March 1938), pp. 44–48. On color schemes, see Bertha Mears, "Color in the Hospital," *Transactions of the American Hospital Association* 39 (1937), p. 689.

17. A. McGehee Harvey, "The Story of Chemotherapy at Johns Hopkins: Perrin H. Long, Eleanor A. Bliss, and E. Kennedy Marshall, Jr.," *Johns Hopkins Medical Journal* 138 (1976), pp. 54–60.

18. Harper Richey, "Modern Therapy of Common Bloodstream Infections," *Kentucky Medical Journal* 38 (1940), pp. 32–110; Milton Silverman, *Magic in a Bottle* (New York: Macmillan, 1941); Waldemar Kaempffert, "The Growing Miracle of Sulfa Drugs," *New York Times Magazine,* July 19, 1942; Tom Mahoney, *Merchants of Life: An Account of the American Pharmaceutical Industry* (New York: Harper & Brothers, 1959).

19. Morris F. Collen, *The Treatment of Pneumonoccic Pneumonia in the Adult* (Oakland: Permanente Foundation, 1948), p. 5.

20. Hendrika Vanderschuur, "Nursing Care of Patients Receiving Sulfonamide," *American Journal of Nursing* 45 (1945), pp. 39–41.

21. Kenneth Fearing, *The Hospital* (New York: Random House, 1939), pp. 214–15.

22. See, e.g., William F. Ogburn, "National Policy and Technology," *Technological Trends and National Policy: Report of the Subcommittee on Technology to the National Resources Committee* (Washington, D.C.: Government Printing Office, June 1937), pp. 3–15; Ogburn, *Social Change* (New York: B. W. Huebsch, 1922), pp. 200–13.

23. Joseph Hirsch, "The Compulsory Health Insurance Movement in the United States," *Social Forces* 18 (October 1939), pp. 102–14.

24. *New York Times,* March 21, 1937, p. 8. See also ibid., March 16, p. 1; March 18, p. 3; and March 25, p. 1.

25. Ibid., May 18, 1937, p. 22. See also ibid., July 22, p. 8, and August 10, p. 3.

26. Howard W. Haggard, "The Place of the Anesthetist," *Anesthesiology* 1 (1940), pp. 1–12.

27. "Hospital Service in the United States," *Journal of the American Medical Association* 121 (1943), p. 1020; ibid. 133 (1947), p. 1077.

28. Robin C. Buerki, "The Hospital and the Radiologist," *Modern Hospital* 46 (April 1936), p. 68. For the figures quoted, see Stevens, *American Medicine and the Public Interest,* p. 195.

29. This compares with 35% of the women. Neuhauser, *Coming of Age,* p. 58.

30. Proceedings, Midwinter Conference, Hospital Service Plan Executives, Pittsburgh, January 24–26, 1940, called by the Commission on Hospital Service and the Council on Hospital Service Plans of the American Hospital Association, manuscript, AHA Archives, p. 7; and see Nathan Sinai, Odin W. Anderson, and Melvin W. Dollar, *Health Insurance in the United States* (New York: Commonwealth Fund, 1946), p. 44; and *Committee on Hospital Insurance and Bed Occupancy Report* (Chicago: American Hospital Association, 1937), p. 2.

31. C. Rufus Rorem, "Sickness Insurance in the United States," *Bulletin of the American Hospital Association* 6 (July 1932), p. 26.

32. Louis S. Reed, *Blue Cross and Medical Service Plans* (Washington, D.C.: Federal Security Agency, U.S. Public Health Service, 1947), pp. 29–30 and passim. This is by far the best

account of the early Blue Cross plans and their relationship with hospitals. Most helpful for utilization data is J. T. Richardson, *The Origin and Development of Group Hospitalization in the United States 1890–1940,* University of Missouri Studies, vol. 20, no. 3 (Columbia: University of Missouri, 1945). For a good recent account of the emergence of Blue Cross in the context of other forms of prepayment, see Paul Starr, *The Social Transformation of American Medicine* (New York: Basic Books, 1982), pp. 290–334. For the point on Marshall Field's I am indebted to Robert Cunningham, who worked for the plan in Chicago in the 1930s.

33. Frank Van Dyk, "Oral History," Blue Cross Archives, Chicago. On Dallas, see Starr, p. 295. On Memphis, see *American Medicine: Expert Testimony Out of Court,* vol. II (New York: American Foundation, 1937), pp. 1027–28.

34. Richardson, *The Origin and Development of Group Hospitalization,* p. 79.

35. C. Rufus Rorem, "Hospital Care in the Family Budget," *The Survey* 71 (March 1935), p. 74. See also "Hospital Care at 3 Cents a Day," *Readers Digest* 29 (September 1936), p. 96; Richardson, *The Origin and Development of Group Hospitalization,* p. 50; Associated Hospital Service of New York posters, reported in *Business Week,* March 18, 1944, p. 44.

36. Perry Addleman, "Basis of Compensating Member Hospitals in Hospital Care Insurance Plans," *Hospitals* 12 (April 1938), pp. 37–40.

37. Richardson, *The Origin and Development of Group Hospitalization,* p. 48.

38. I. S. Falk, personal communication.

39. For coverage figures and utilization data I have drawn on Richardson, *The Origin and Development of Group Hospitalization,* pp. 57, 66–67, 73–75.

40. In 1939, for example, only twenty-six out of fifty-six plans in operation provided complete or limited X-ray diagnosis (and none covered radiotherapy); these were mostly in large cities where the X-ray department was closely integrated with the hospital. In cities such as New York, Baltimore, Philadelphia, Chicago, and Oakland, a direct commitment was made to private-physician office practice, for outpatient coverage was rare, and where it did exist was usually limited to emergencies or to providing services which substituted for inpatient care. Reed, *Blue Cross and Medical Service Plans,* pp. 58–60.

41. Weeks and Berman, *Shapers of American Health Care Policy,* pp. 154–55.

42. Average length of stay was little more than eight days—only two-thirds that of general hospitals nationwide. Women stayed in hospitals longer than men (and a prolonged rest after childbirth made maternity units happy places). Besides "female diseases," the most common reasons for admission were for tonsillectomies, adenoidectomies, appendectomies, and respiratory conditions. Richardson, *The Origin and Development of Group Hospitalization,* pp. 66–75; Frank Van Dyk, "Experience as a Guide in Development of Group Hospitalization," *Hospitals* 12 (January 1938), pp. 78–83.

43. Weeks and Berman, *Shapers of American Health Care Policy,* p. 167. Information in this paragraph is from Reed, *Blue Cross and Medical Service Plans,* pp. 30, 47–48. Proprietary figures are from the respective issues of "Hospital Statistics" in the *Journal of the American Medical Association.*

44. C. Rufus Rorem, "Policies and Procedures for Group Hospitalization," *Bulletin of the American Hospital Association* 8 (May 1934), pp. 9–12.

45. E. H. L. Corwin, "The Future of the Hospitals," *Hospitals* 12 (November 1938), p. 14.

46. David Wark, "Hospital Groups May Plan to Offer Physicians' Services," *Medical Economics* (May 1939), pp. 79–84; Wark, "The Prices in Group Hospitalization," *Medical Economics* (August 1939), pp. 28–32, 72–74; Perry Addleman, "Basis of Compensating Member Hospitals in Hospital Care Insurance Plans," pp. 37–40.

47. This metaphor was used by R. M. Cunningham of the Chicago plan. Proceedings, Midwinter Conference, Hospital Service Plan Executives, 1940, p. 74.

48. C. Rufus Rorem, *Non-Profit Hospital Service Plans: Historic and Critical Analysis of Group Hospitalization, a Non-Profit, Non-Political Application of the Principle of Insurance to the Purchase of Hospital Care* (Chicago: American Hospital Association, 1940), pp. 70, 98.

49. Remarks of Malcolm T. MacEachern, "The House of Delegates—Proceedings of the Dallas Session," *Hospitals* 12 (November 1938), p. 84.

50. "Section on Radiology," *Journal of the American Medical Association* 103 (1934), p. 45.

51. Council on Professional Practice, *Principles of Relationship Between Hospitals and Radiologists, Anesthetists, and Pathologists* (Chicago: American Hospital Association, 1939).

52. *American Medicine: Expert Testimony* (see n. 53), vol. 2, p. 723.

53. American Foundation, *American Medicine: Expert Testimony Out of Court,* 2 vols. (New York:

The American Foundation, 1937); Interdepartmental Committee to Coordinate Health and Welfare Activities, *Proceedings of the National Health Conference,* July 18, 19, 20, 1938 (Washington, D.C.: Government Printing Office, 1938).

54. Michael M. Davis, *Public Medical Services: A Survey of Tax-Supported Medical Care in the United States* (Chicago: University of Chicago Press, 1937), p. 47.

55. See Nelle L. Williams, *Public Welfare Agencies and Hospitals* (Chicago: American Public Welfare Association, 1937), pp. 3–6. There were government hospitals in only 43% of the counties in 1935, counties which included 36% of the population. Over $30 million in tax funds flowed to voluntary hospitals in that year. Local governments typically purchased care in voluntary hospitals through per diem reimbursement in the late 1930s, usually in the range of $1.50 to $4.50 a day. Elliott H. Pennell, Joseph W. Mountin, Emily Hankla, "Summary Figures on Income, Expenditures, and Personnel of Hospitals," *Hospitals* 12 (April 1938), p. 16.

56. See, e.g., Mills, *Hospital Public Relations,* pp. 98–99.

57. Nearly half of the hospitals in small-town areas in 1937, for example, were in the six states of California, Illinois, Indiana, Michigan, Minnesota, and Texas. Michael Davis, *Public Medical Services,* p. 41.

58. Fred Brenckman, in *Proceedings of the National Health Conference,* p. 137.

59. Goldwater was commissioner of the Department of Hospitals of New York City in the late 1930s. One can only speculate as to how far his experience of New York's major municipal system, as well as more general considerations, affected his views.

60. *Proceedings of the National Health Conference,* p. 79 and passim.

Chapter 8

1. U.S. Congress, Senate, Committee on Public Buildings and Grounds, *Hearings on H.R. 4545 and S. 1375,* 77th Cong., 1st sess., May 19–20, 1941, p. 15.

2. Daniel M. Fox, *Health Policies, Health Politics: The British and American Experience, 1911–1965* (Princeton: Princeton University Press, 1986). For other general themes on regionalism I draw mostly upon my own earlier work on the federal government, regionalism, and the health-care system; see, e.g., *American Medicine and the Public Interest,* pp. 496–527.

3. "Pearl Harbor Was Scene of Sweeping Victory for Drugs," *Science News Letter* 41 (1942), p. 53; Waldermar Kaempffert, "The Growing Miracle of Sulfa Drugs," *New York Times Magazine,* July 19, 1942.

4. The best account of the organization and work of the Committee on Medical Research is Stephen P. Strickland, *Politics, Science, and Dread Disease* (Cambridge, Mass.: Harvard University Press, 1972), pp. 16–19 and passim. See also Starr, *The Social Transformation of American Medicine,* pp. 340–42.

5. A. N. Richards, "The Production of Penicillin in the United States," *Annals of Internal Medicine* 71 (November 1969), suppl. 8, pp. 71–73. See also Austin Smith and Arthur Herrick, eds., *Drug Research and Development* (New York: Revere Publishing Co., 1948).

6. Perrin H. Long, "Medical Progress and Medical Education During the War," *Journal of the American Medical Association* 130 (1946), pp. 983–90.

7. Edward Mellanby, quoted in Esther Everette Lape, *Medical Research: A Midcentury Survey,* vol. 1 (Boston: Published for the American Foundation by Little, Brown, 1955), p. 65. Richards is quoted by Strickland, *Politics, Science, and Dread Disease,* p. 16.

8. Poor eyes, teeth, feet, and musculoskeletal conditions led the list of conditions observed among registrants; and syphilis, lack of education, and nervous and mental diseases were the primary causes for rejection for service. None of these conditions actually required new knowledge for prevention or treatment. President's Commission on the Health Needs of the Nation, *Building America's Health* (Washington, D.C.: Government Printing Office, 1951), vol. 3, *America's Health Status, Needs, and Resources,* p. 38.

9. Long, "Medical Progress and Medical Education During the War," p. 988.

10. George W. Gray, *The Advancing Front of Medicine* (New York: Whittlesey House, 1941), p. 392.

11. The dean of the Columbia University Medical Faculty, quoted in Lape, *Medical Re-*

search: A Midcentury Survey, vol. 1, p. 327. One count of the 371 men teaching basic sciences at Yale, Johns Hopkins, Chicago, and the University of California between 1946 and 1949 found that 229 did not hold a medical degree. Ibid., p. 217.

12.   Louis I. Dublin, *Health Progress 1936 to 1945* (New York: Metropolitan Life Insurance Co., 1948), pp. 1–2; U.S. Congress, Senate, Committee on Education and Labor, Subcommittee on Wartime Health and Education (chairman, Claude Pepper, Fla.), *Hearings Pursuant to S. Res. 74,* A Resolution Authorizing an Investigation of the Educational and Physical Fitness of the Civilian Population as Related to National Defense, 78th Cong., 2nd sess., July 1944, pt. V, p. 1669. (Hereafter, *Pepper Hearings.*)

13.   In 1900, 24% of all deaths were attributable to chronic diseases and 76% to infectious diseases. By 1920 the proportions were 34% and 66% respectively; and in 1945 68% and 32%. President's Commission on the Health Needs of the Nation, *Building America's Health,* vol. 3 (Washington, D.C.: Government Printing Office, 1951), p. 30.

14.   About half of all cancer deaths occurred in hospitals in the mid-1940s, together with half of all deaths from pneumonia and diabetes, one-third of deaths from heart disease, and two-thirds of deaths from tuberculosis. Apart from tuberculosis, a disease associated with poverty and ignorance, the majority of these deaths occurred in voluntary nonprofit hospitals. (Tubercular patients died, as they were treated, disproportionately in government institutions.) "Number of Deaths from Selected Causes in Institutions, by Type of Service and Type of Control: United States, 1943," *Vital Statistics—Special Reports* 22, no. 1 (February 28, 1945), pp. 14–15.

15.   According to one estimate from the mid-1940s, acute hospitals should have an average of 5 technicians for every 200 beds; these figures produced a "shortage" in 1943 of 21,000 full-time technicians. E. H. L. Corwin, *The American Hospital* (New York: Commonwealth Fund, 1946), p. 126.

16.   Commission on Hospital Care, *Hospital Care in the United States,* pp. 45–46.

17.   *Pepper Hearings,* December 1943, pt. II, p. 959 (Dr. J. P. Wall).

18.   Ibid., July 1944, pt. V, pp. 1785–90 (Dr. Thomas Parran).

19.   See Bernhard J. Stern, *American Medical Practice in the Perspective of the Century* (New York: Commonwealth Fund, 1945), pp. 10–18; and, on the general theme, Robert A. Brady, *Business as a System of Power* (New York: Columbia University Press, 1943).

20.   *Pepper Hearings,* September 1944, pt. VI, pp. 2000, 2003.

21.   *Congressional Record* 87, May 9, 1941, pp. 2849, 3859–60.

22.   U.S. Congress, House of Representatives, Committee on Public Buildings and Grounds, *Hearings on H.R. 3213 and H.R. 3570,* 77th Cong., 1st sess., March 1941, statement of John M. Carmody, administrator of the Public Works Agency, p. 46.

23.   Commission on Hospital Care, *Hospital Care in the United States,* p. 535.

24.   *Annual Report of the Federal Works Agency for Fiscal Year Ended June 30, 1942* (Washington, D.C.: Government Printing Office, 1942), p. 16; *Annual Report, 1945,* p. 27.

25.   *Hearings on H.R. 4545 and S. 1375* (Senator Walsh, Massachusetts), p. 5.

26.   The bill provided that no department or agency of the U.S. government would exercise supervision or control over either hospitals or schools. *Congressional Record* 87, May 4, 1941, pp. 3855–56.

27.   Ibid., May 9, 1941, p. 3846 (Mr. Allen of Illinois) and passim.

28.   Claude W. Munger (American Hospital Association), U.S. Senate Hearings Before a Subcommittee of the Committee on Education and Labor on S. 1620, *To Establish a National Health Program,* 76th Cong., 1st sess. 1939, p. 654.

29.   Fred G. Carter, "Presidential Address," *Transactions of the American Hospital Association* 42 (1940), p. 305.

30.   The EMIC program was run by the states under federal rules and regulations. There was no means test, except that families of commissioned officers were excluded. Benefits were full-service benefits and hospitals were reimbursed on an actual per diem cost basis, with medical bills being reimbursed separately. A minimum stay of ten days in the hospital after delivery was suggested. Nathan Sinai and Odin W. Anderson, *EMIC (Emergency Maternity and Infant Care),* Bureau of Public Health Economics, Research Series no. 3 (Ann Arbor: School of Public Health, University of Michigan, 1948), p. 21 and passim.

31.   On the legislative history of the proposals for a national health program, see Peter A. Corning, *The Evolution of Medicare—From Idea to Law,* U.S. Department of Health, Education and Welfare, Social Security Administration, Research Report no. 29 (Washington, D.C.:

Government Printing Office, 1969); Stevens, *American Medicine and the Public Interest,* pp. 267–89; Starr, *The Social Transformation of American Medicine,* pp. 280–89.

32. Graham L. Davis, "The Committee on Post-War Planning," *Transactions of the American Hospital Association* 44 (1942), p. 96.

33. Ibid., p. 95.

34. E. M. Bluestone, "Post-War Planning," editorial, *Hospitals* 17 (May 1943), pp. 66–67.

35. James A. Hamilton, "The Future of the Voluntary Hospital," *Hospitals* 17 (June 1943), p. 15.

36. E. M. Bluestone, "Post-War Planning," pp. 66–67.

37. The commission was chaired by the president of the University of Pennsylvania, with the chairman of the board of a major steel company (Inland Steel) as vice chairman. Among its twenty other members were the president of a women's college, the president of a black university, a former U.S. president (Herbert Hoover), the director of Catholic charities and hospitals from the Archdiocese of Los Angeles, the vice president of General Motors, a representative of organized labor, two farming representatives, and an array of other academicians and hospital administrators: in all, a melting pot for middle-of-the-road consensus. Commission on Hospital Care, *Hospital Care in the United States.*

38. Minutes of the Commission on Hospital Care, October 16–17, 1945, pp. 13–15, AHA Archives.

39. President's Commission on the Health Needs of the Nation, *Building America's Health,* vol. 4 (Washington, D.C.: Government Printing Office, 1951), table 7.10, p. 274.

40. Parran considered that approximately 66,000 general hospital beds were needed as replacements, together with another 100,000 beds to even up the distribution of hospital care across the country—at a combined cost, in prewar prices, of $996 million. Adding on the perceived needs for additional beds for psychiatric patients and for those with tuberculosis and chronic diseases, and for beds in health centers, he estimated a total needed construction bill of nearly $2 billion. This compared with the annual rate (in 1939 prices) of only $65 million in 1944. *Pepper Hearings,* July 1944, pt. V, pp. 1786, 1788.

41. Ibid., pp. 1809–12.

42. *Hospital Resources and Needs* (Battle Creek, Mich.: W. K. Kellogg Foundation, 1946). A synopsis is given in Commission on Hospital Care, *Hospital Care in the United States,* pp. 359–403.

43. The U.S. Public Health Service had designed four types of centers and these designs had wide distribution. Health centers such as those constructed at Texarkana, Texas, or Fort Smith, Arkansas could form the local outposts of a regionalized system of institutional medical care—always assuming that medicine was envisaged in the future as a collection of groups or teams of specialists. The best account of the politics of health centers and hospital planning at this period is Fox, *Health Policies, Health Politics,* pp. 115–31.

44. Mary M. Guerin, "Legislation on Hospital Surveys, Construction, and Licensing Considered by State Legislatures in 1945," *Public Health Reports* 60, no. 51 (December 21, 1945), p. 1519.

45. Taft is quoted in a transcript of the hearings, "The Wagner-Murray-Dingell Bill," *Journal of the American Medical Association* 130 (April 13, 1946), p. 1022. I am grateful to George Bugbee for discussing his role in these events with me. Bugbee has written his own account in *Recollections of a Good Life: An Autobiography* (Chicago: American Hospital Association, The Hospital Research and Educational Trust, 1987), pp. 59–96.

46. Alphonse M. Schwitalla, "The Catholic Hospital Association's Position on the Hospital Construction Act (S. 191)," *Hospital Progress* 26 (December 1945), p. 393.

47. The *Montgomery Advertiser,* May 27, 1937, allegedly reported that it was "tickled to death" at then Congressman Hill's wresting of the veterans' hospital from competing cities to Montgomery, after the Federal Board of Hospitalization had decided unanimously in favor of Tuscaloosa. Hill had considerable clout with the White House. He was chairman of the House Military Affairs Committee. Minutes of the Federal Board of Hospitalization, June 4, 1937, p. 15, National Archives.

48. U.S. Senate, Committee on Education and Labor, Hearings on S. 191, *Hospital Construction Act,* 79th Cong., 1st sess., February–March 1945, p. 7.

49. Ibid, pp. 67, 77.

50. See oral history of I. S. Falk in Weeks and Berman, *Shapers of American Health Care Policy,* p. 41.

51. Quoted in *Chicago Tribune,* November 6 and 7, 1945.

52. *Washington Post,* November 28, 1945.

53. Senate Hearings on S. 191, *Hospital Construction Act,* Dr. Thomas Parran (U.S. Public Health Service), p. 55; and Dr. R. L. Sensenich (American Medical Association), p. 149.

54. Virginia Van der Veer Hamilton, *Lister Hill: Statesman from the South* (Chapel Hill: University of North Carolina Press, 1987), p. 139.

55. U.S. Department of Health, Education, and Welfare, *Hill-Burton Progress Report, July 1, 1947–June 30, 1966* (Washington, D.C.: Government Printing Office, 1966), pp. 32–33.

56. The Senate rejected an antidiscrimination amendment as part of the bill. This would have denied funds to hospitals that excluded a doctor from the staff because of race, color, or religion. Senator Lister Hill, from the segregated state of Alabama, said administrative rules for hospitals were best left to the states. Congressional Quarterly, Inc., "Hill-Burton Hospital Survey and Construction Act, 1946," in *Congress and the Nation 1945–1964* (Washington, DC: Congressional Quarterly, 1965), pp. 1122–23. This source provides an excellent legislative history and review of the act's extension to the mid-1960s.

57. Thomas Parran, "The Hospital Construction Bill: Statement by Surgeon General Thomas Parran," *Hospital Progress* 26 (March 1945), p. 65.

58. *Senate Hearings on S. 191,* p. 8.

59. Ralph M. Hueston, "What the Hospital Survey and Construction Act Means to the Hospitals of Michigan," *Journal of the Michigan State Medical Society* 46 (February 1947), p. 162.

60. In 1945, while the legislation was in Congress, eighteen states enacted legislation for statewide hospital surveys and/or construction programs; another five states considered such legislation; and fourteen states enacted hospital licensing laws. Illinois, New York, Virginia, and West Virginia had special commissions or committees to study hospitalization and medical care in those states. North Dakota and Wisconsin enacted laws establishing state medical centers, while New Mexico enacted legislation for the establishment of a state general hospital. To qualify for funding, each state had to designate a single state agency to conduct the survey, supervise planning, and make all necessary reports. It also had to provide a state advisory council, including the representatives of consumers of hospital service, as well as other groups, and to establish a plan for conducting the survey. By the end of 1948 all states and territories except Delaware, the District of Columbia, and the Virgin Islands had taken advantage of the provision of federal aid for surveys and planning. Guerin, "Legislation on Hospital Surveys," p. 1519 and passim.

61. Dorothy P. Rice and Louis P. Reed, *The Nation's Need for Hospitals and Health Centers* (Washington, D.C.: Federal Security Agency, Public Health Service, June 1949), p. 15. Initial guidelines were laid out in Joseph W. Mountin, Elliott H. Pennell, and Vane Hoge, *Health Service Areas,* Public Health Bulletin no. 292 (Washington, D.C.: Government Printing Office, 1945), table 1.

62. There was, for example, little response to the VA's willingness to pay for hospital care of veterans with service disabilities in hospitals in their home communities (rather than in remote veterans' hospitals), with reimbursement tied, as nearly as possible, to cost. An editorial in the AHA journal, *Hospitals,* in the spring of 1946 criticized hospitals for their lack of action in most states and lack of leadership. Hospitals, their organizations, and their associated Blue Cross plans were depicted as having a backlog of immediate problems and as overly cautious, if not hostile, to any government approaches. Each "feels obliged to guard its own prestige against all encroachment." "An Urgent Invitation," editorial, *Hospitals* 20 (May 1946), p. 105.

63. The best account of this history is Robinson E. Adkins, *Medical Care of Veterans* (Washington, D.C.: Government Printing Office, 1967), pp. 168–71 and passim.

64. "Veterans Administration Recruitment of Physicians," *Journal of the American Medical Association* 130 (1946), p. 710.

65. *Washington Post,* December 4, 1946.

66. "Veterans to get Three-Way Hospitalization Program," *Journal of the American Medical Association* 130 (1946), p. 955.

67. I have discussed the growth of biomedical research funds through the National Institutes of Health and their impact on medical schools from the 1940s through the 1960s in *American Medicine and the Public Interest,* pp. 348–77.

68. Quoted in Weeks and Berman, *Shapers of American Health Care Policy,* p. 45.

69. Emanuel Hayt and Lillian R. Hayt, *Law of Hospital, Physician and Patient* (New York:

Hospital Textbook Company, 1947), p. 20. See also "Doctrine of Exemption as Influenced by Practical Considerations," *Hospitals* 16 (February 1942), pp. 78–79; and Austin Wakeman Scott, "Tort Liability of Hospitals," *Tennessee Law Review* 17 (1943), p. 838.

70. Basil C. MacLean, "Hospitals Now and After the War," *Hospitals* 16 (June 1942), pp. 13–18.

71. The state of Minnesota, for example, was not allowed to claim property taxes from the Sisters of St. Francis of the Third Order, even though the sisters took a profit from the highly successful Mayo-affiliated St. Mary's Hospital, Rochester, to support other activities of the order; St. Mary's had a net income of over $500,000 in 1942. In another Minnesota case a proprietary hospital owned by three doctors until 1941 and then reorganized as a nonprofit hospital, open to any doctor in good standing, was allowed tax exemption, even though the three original stockholders (who were three of the incorporators) reduced their indebtedness by the new purchase price. Hospital proponents defended charitable status on various grounds. Hospitals provided the general, constantly available contribution of inpatient and outpatient care to community life, it was argued, like a water system or power system. The hospital made essential education and training contributions, and filled a useful role as a research and testing laboratory. Voluntary hospitals were praised for their flexibility in administration, compared with the rigidity of government bureaucracies. It was folly, it was said, to expect the modern hospital to operate at a loss—that is, not to make a "profit"; thus many of the arguments that the hospitals were actually profiting were unsound. It was also argued that it was reasonable to let hospitals derive income from any purpose, as long as this income supported the institution, including, for example, renting part of their property to drugstores, coffee shops, or beauty shops. *State* v. *Academy of Our Lady of Lourdes,* 21 NW (2nd) 617, Minn. 1946; *Fairmount Community Hospital Association, Inc.* v. *State,* 21 NW (2nd) 243, Minn. 1945. Both are reported in *Journal of the American Medical Association* 131 (1946), p. 355. And see Arnold F. Emch, "Tax Exemption for Voluntary Hospitals," *Hospitals* 14 (April 1940), pp. 71–75.

72. Fred G. Carter, in *Hospital Trends and Developments,* p. 3, from "Some Trends of Today That Will Help Shape Tomorrow's Hospital," *Hospitals* 18 (October 1944), p. 35.

73. James A. Hamilton, "The Future of the Voluntary Hospital," *Hospitals* 17 (June 1943), pp. 13–17.

74. Quoted in *Journal of the American Medical Association* 131 (June 29, 1946), pp. 766, 764.

75. Ibid., p. 756.

76. Perrin H. Long, "Medical Progress and Medical Education During the War," *Journal of the American Medical Association* 130 (1946), p. 989.

77. "The Wagner-Murray-Dingell Bill," ibid. 131 (1946), p. 1149.

78. Dr. John R. Boling, *Pepper Hearings,* September 1944, pp. 2078, 2074.

79. Corning, *The Evolution of Medicare,* p. 64 and passim.

80. The states had, in theory, a potent vehicle for hospital regulation through new hospital licensing procedures, designed to provide the minimum standards which were needed for hospitals to participate in the Hill-Burton program; by the beginning of 1948 more than thirty states had adopted hospital licensing laws. But the states were reluctant to interfere and were ill-equipped administratively. Licensing was generally limited to the physical plant of hospitals and general safety, including fire safety, with few attempts at regulating procedures, techniques, or personnel.

81. Donald T. Smelzer, "The Hospital Construction Bill: Statement by Dr. Donald T. Smelzer," *Hospital Progress* 26 (March 1945), p. 71.

Chapter 9

1. The themes were pervasive. For the three-pronged formulation, I have drawn here on William H. Whyte, *The Organization Man* (Harmondsworth, Middlesex: Penguin, 1960; first published 1956), pp. 22–47. Another good example of contemporary rhetoric is Robert A. Nisbet, *The Quest for Community* (New York: Oxford University Press, 1953), p. 23. Nisbet described the quest for community as the dominant social tendency of the twentieth century (p. 45).

2. National Commission on Community Health Services, *Health is a Community Affair* (Cambridge Mass.: Harvard University Press, 1966), p. 151.

3. The best study of hospital technology in this period is Louise B. Russell, *Technology in Hospitals: Medical Advances and Their Diffusion* (Washington, D.C.: Brookings Institution, 1979).

4. One of the earliest TV hospital series was the syndicated *Dr. Hudson's Secret Journal,* a thirty-minute drama which ran for thirty-nine episodes in 1955 and centered on Dr. Wayne Hudson, a neurosurgeon pioneering new treatments. J. S. Harris, ed., *TV Guide: The First 25 Years* (New York: Simon & Schuster, 1978), p. 276; Vincent Terrace, *Encyclopedia of Television Series, Pilots, and Specials, 1937–1973* (New York: Zoetrope, 1986), selected entries.

5. Hospitals were not unusual in this respect. In his book on suburbanization, Kenneth Jackson has shown how federal housing policy supported the suburban dream itself, decentralizing a relatively young, affluent population outward to the periphery of cities and stratifying America's metropolitan populations by social class and race. Kenneth T. Jackson, *Crabgrass Frontier: The Suburbanization of the United States* (New York: Oxford University Press, 1985).

Federal policies encouraged local giving to hospitals in three ways. First, changes in the tax law provided income-tax relief for corporate gifts designed for the improvement of local communities; this encouraged large businesses to contribute to hospitals and to view their local hospitals with greater interest. In 1950 hospitals were the most important of the local health services supported by corporations, with gifts going chiefly for capital construction; major corporations donated more to hospitals than to educational institutions. Confirmation, in 1954, that employers' contributions to health-insurance benefit programs were exempt from federal taxation was in the same line of federal support of private interests.

Second, individuals, too, could claim charitable deductions on their income taxes. The great majority of capital financing for voluntary hospitals continued to come from general fund drives and donations from an appreciative local population. And third, the potential availability of Hill-Burton matching grants encouraged fund-raising at the local level. Starr, *The Social Transformation of American Medicine,* p. 333.

6. Daniel Fox has argued that Americans tended to act as if scientific progress, coupled with economic growth and the intelligent application of goodwill at the local level, would promote equity without the necessity for structural changes in the health-care system. Fox, *Health Policies, Health Politics,* p. 208 and passim. Paul Starr makes a similar argument in *The Social Transformation of American Medicine,* p. 336 and passim.

7. Edith Lentz Hamilton, "Voluntary Hospitals in America," *Administrative Science Quarterly* 1 (March 1957), pp. 444–63.

8. See table 11.1.

9. The figures on hospitals and hospital utilization throughout this chapter are from the American Hospital Association's annual *Hospital Statistics* unless otherwise stated.

10. Herman M. Somers and Anne R. Somers, *Doctors, Patients, and Health Insurance* (Washington, D.C.: Brookings Institution, 1961), p. 65. Although virtually all births took place in hospitals in the early 1960s, maternity stays were kept to a minimum. In terms of overall expense and income, maternity was now barely more important than injuries in the overall hospital balance sheet. Percentage distributions of hospital-care expenditures for nonfederal short-term hospitals in 1963 were as follows: diseases of the digestive system 14.9%, diseases of the circulatory system 12.8%, maternity 10.5%, injuries 10.4%, neoplasms 10.2%. Dorothy P. Rice, *Estimating the Cost of Illness,* Health Economic Series no. 6 (Washington, D.C.: U.S. Department of Health, Education, and Welfare, Public Health Service, 1966), p. 11.

11. Somers and Somers, *Doctors, Patients, and Health Insurance,* p. 63.

12. See Frank G. Dickinson, "Age and Sex Distribution of Hospital Patients," *Journal of the American Medical Association* 157 (1955), pp. 173–82; Frank G. Dickinson and James Raymond, "Some Categories of Patients Treated by Physicians in Hospitals," ibid. 162 (1956), pp. 1546–54.

13. Robert N. Wilson, "Teamwork in the Operating Room," *Human Organization* 12, no. 4 (1954), p. 12.

14. Temple Burling, Edith M. Lentz, Robert N. Wilson, *The Give and Take in Hospitals* (New York: Putnam, 1956), p. 9.

15. Robert M. Sigmond, personal communication, September 18, 1986.

16. American Hospital Association, *Hospital Auxiliaries and Volunteers: Report of a Survey Con-*

ducted by the American Hospital Association in 1962, Report Series no. 3 (Chicago: American Hospital Association, 1963), pp. 2–5.

17.   Ibid., p. 1.

18.   For example, in one town, studied by Burling et al., a hospital which replaced a nurse superintendent who was deferential to the physicians by a professional hospital administrator (who was not), leading to new rules for physician behavior in the hospital, led to a public outcry against the administrator. Burling et al., *The Give and Take in Hospitals,* pp. 21–22.

19.   William A. Glaser, "American and Foreign Hospitals: Some Sociological Comparisons," in Eliot Freidson, ed., *The Hospital in Modern Society* (London: Collier-Macmillan, 1963), pp. 62–63.

20.   I was a graduate student in hospital administration in 1961–62, and was required to keep a diary of observations as part of the course. Student Notes, Program in Hospital Administration, Department of Epidemiology and Public Health, Yale University, March 4, 1962.

21.   The best general study of hospital life in this period is Rose Laub Coser, *Life in the Ward* (East Lansing: Michigan State University Press, 1962). On the relationship between hospital and community, I have drawn throughout this chapter on Burling et al., *The Give and Take in Hospitals.* The best study of differing institutional personalities is Emily Mumford, *Interns: From Students to Physicians* (Cambridge, Mass.: Harvard University Press), 1970.

22.   Leon Fink and Brian Greenberg, "Organizing Montefiore: Labor Militancy Meets a Progressive Health Care Empire," in Susan Reverby and David Rosner, eds., *Health Care in America* (Philadelphia: Temple University Press, 1979), p. 231.

23.   Jack Pressman, "Unionization in America's Non-Profit Hospitals: An Overview," project paper, manuscript, University of Pennsylvania, 1983. The best general published account is Norman Metzger and Dennis Pointer, *Labor-Management Relations in the Health Service Industry: Theory and Practice* (Washington, D.C.: Science and Health Publications, 1972).

24.   *Society of New York Hospital* v. *Hanson,* 59 NYS (2nd) 91, New York, 1945, reported in "Medicolegal Abstract," *Journal of the American Medical Association* 131 (1946), pp. 252–53.

25.   Burling et al., *The Give and Take in Hospitals,* pp. 84, 147, 153.

26.   One-fourth of house staff were graduates of foreign schools in 1960. See Rosemary Stevens and Joan Vermeulen, *Foreign Trained Physicians and American Medicine,* DHEW Publication no. (NIH) 73-325 (Washington, D.C.: Government Printing Office, 1972), p. 112 and passim.

27.   Glaser, "American and Foreign Hospitals," p. 43. See also Mary E. W. Goss, "Patterns of Bureaucracy among Hospital Staff Physicians," in Eliot Freidson, ed., *The Hospital in Modern Society,* pp. 170–94.

28.   Somers and Somers, *Doctors, Patients and Health Insurance,* p. 27. Paul Starr uses a similar formulation in the extended arguments about the industrialization or corporatization of medicine in pt. 2 of his book, *The Social Transformation of American Medicine* (1982).

29.   Glaser, "American and Foreign Hospitals," p. 70.

30.   T. W. Hurst, "International Hospital Federation Study Tour in U.S.A.," *The Hospital* (November 1960), pp. 923–33; "Hospital Planning in the U.S.A.," unidentified communication, ibid. (December 1960), pp. 1041–42.

31.   Robert N. Wilson, "The Social Structure of a General Hospital," in James K. Skipper and Robert C. Leonard, eds., *Social Interaction and Patient Care* (Philadelphia: J. B. Lippincott, 1965), p. 236.

32.   Charles Perrow, "Goals and Power Structures," in Freidson, *The Hospital In Modern Society,* p. 144.

33.   American Medical Association, Council on Medical Service, *Report on Physician-Hospital Relations, June 1964* (Chicago: American Medical Association, 1964), p. 3.

34.   Oswald Hall, "Research in Human Relations in the Hospital," *Hospital Administration* 1 (February 1956), p. 11.

35.   For a good contemporary analysis, see Samuel Levey, "Source of Medical-Administrative Conflict: A Survey Report," *Hospitals* 36 (1962), pp. 60–66.

36.   By the end of 1961 sixteen graduate programs had provided well over 3,000 professional administrators. The great majority of these were not physicians (and few were minorities or women). Duncan Neuhauser, *Coming of Age: A 50-Year History of the American College of Hospital Administrators and the Profession It Serves, 1933–1983* (Chicago: Pluribus Press, 1983), pp. 105–11, 108–9, 174–77.

37. The best contemporary analysis is Oswald Hall, "The Informal Organization of the Medical Profession," in *Medical Care: Readings in the Sociology of Medical Institutions,* W. Richard Scott and Edmund H. Volkert, eds. (New York: Wiley, 1966), pp. 149–63. Originally published in *Canadian Journal of Economics and Political Science* 12 (February 1946), pp. 30–44.

38. American College of Surgeons, *Manual of Hospital Standardization* (Chicago: American College of Surgeons, 1946), p. 19.

39. American Medical Association, *Digest of Official Actions 1846–1958* (Chicago: American Medical Association, 1959), p. 368.

40. The general confusion between the corporate practice rule and the fear by physicians of the growing role of organizations was illustrated in the case of *Group Health Cooperative* v. *King County Medical Society* (1951), when the Supreme Court of the State of Washington held that it was perfectly ethical for physicians to be compensated by salary. Indeed, several members of the King County Medical Society were employed in Seattle hospitals on a salaried basis. But the case also highlighted the fundamental issue—physician opposition to new practice arrangements—by deciding that there was a medical conspiracy to injure the development of Group Health Cooperative. In fact, the grounds on which corporate practice, as a legal position, rested were unclear. Alanson W. Willcox, "Hospitals and the Corporate Practice of Medicine," *Cornell Law Quarterly* 45 (Spring 1960), pp. 433, 438, and passim.

41. T. R. Ponton, *The Medical Staff in the Hospital,* 2nd ed. (Chicago: Physicians' Record Co., 1953), p. 33.

42. Ibid., p. 35.

43. Ibid., p. 31.

44. Frederick B. Exner, president of the King County Medical Society, Seattle, quoted in "The Hospital-Specialist Controversy: Where Does the Solution Lie?" *Hospitals* 30 (October 1, 1956), p. 46.

45. A good analysis of the optimism of contemporary thinking on group practice is Somers and Somers, *Doctors, Patients, and Health Insurance,* pp. 61–72 and passim.

46. The AMA's influential Larson report (1959) found no evidence of lay interference in medical decisions in Kaiser and other prepaid plans, and recommended that patients have free choice of plans as an acceptable substitute for free choice of physician. After this, there was no organized AMA opposition to group practice. In 1962 the AMA cooperated in producing guidelines for physicians interested in forming or joining a medical group. In 1959 there were only 1,546 organized groups of physicians of any kind in the United States, with or without prepayment, including 13,000 physicians; there were 4,289 groups with 28,381 doctors in 1965. In the mid-1960s less than 2 percent of the entire population was insured through prepaid practice groups. Starr, *The Social Transformation of American Medicine,* p. 327; Stevens, *American Medicine and the Public Interest,* pp. 424–25.

47. Despite the fact that most hospitals had staffs open to all eligible practitioners, it was also held in the courts that hospital standards of practice were higher than those in private practice in almost all communities. W. L. Babcock, "The Right of Hospitals to Admit Physicians and Choose Staff," editorial, *Hospitals* 13 (December 1939), pp. 74–75.

48. Other physicians, usually known as the courtesy medical staff, were also allowed to admit patients into private rooms. The active staff was expected to have at least an elected president, an executive committee, a credentials committee, and a joint conference committee. The latter was designed to facilitate discussion between the medical staff, the governing board, and the administrator. Other committees might include a medical records committee, to supervise and appraise records, a tissue committee or medical audit committee, and ad hoc committees as needed.

49. There is still no good history of the establishment of the Joint Commission on the Accreditation of Hospitals. Both the commission and the American College of Surgeons claim to have no records of events that preceded and coincided with the transfer of standardization from the surgeons to the JCAH. I draw here from several sources, including the *Minutes of the Business Meeting of the AMA Council on Medical Education and Hospitals,* selected years. I thank the staff of the Council on Medical Education for access to these unpublished records, which are housed in the council's office at the American Medical Association, Chicago.

50. Malcolm T. MacEachern, *Hospital Organization and Management* (Chicago: Physicians' Record Co., 1957), p. 1180.

51. AMA, *Digest of Official Actions 1846–1958,* p. 364.

52. Ibid, p. 365.

53. It was recommended, for example, that physicians should be on the administrative boards of hospitals, that general practice sections in hospitals should be encouraged, that the Joint Commission should not require attendance at medical staff meetings nor concern itself with the number of hospital staffs to which a physician belonged, and that the commission should not be "punitive" (i.e., act as an effective regulatory body vis-à-vis physicians). However, the committee did recommend that the JCAH study the problems of exclusion from hospitals and "arbitrary limitation of the hospital's privileges" of general practitioners and develop more clearly stated principles about hospital medical-staff privileges. "Accreditation Commission Explains the Action Taken on Recommendations of Stover Committee," *Modern Hospital* 87 (1956), pp. 158, 175–76; Kenneth B. Babcock, " 'Stover' Report," *Bulletin of the Joint Committee on Accreditation of Hospitals* 12 (August 1956), pp. 1–4.

54. Ibid.

55. Somers and Somers, *Doctors, Patients, and Health Insurance,* p. 64.

56. *Model Medical Staff By-Laws, Rules, and Regulations* (Chicago: Joint Committee on Accreditation of Hospitals, 1964), p. 2.

57. See especially O. L. Peterson et al., "An Analytical Study of North Carolina General Practice," *Journal of Medical Education* 31, no. 12, pt. 2 (December 1956).

58. On these issues, see Gladys A. Harrison, *Control of Medical Staff Appointments in Voluntary Nonprofit Hospitals* (Chicago: American Hospital Association, 1963).

59. *Bing* v. *Thunig,* 2 NY 2nd 656, 143 NE 2d 38 (1957).

60. *Darling* v. *Charleston Community Hospital,* 33 Ill. 2d 326, 211 NE 2d 253 (1965). I draw here from Richard P. Bergen, "Darling Case Revisited," *Journal of the American Medical Association* 206 (November 18, 1968), pp. 1875–76.

61. George H. Gallup, *The Gallup Poll: Public Opinion 1935–1971,* vol. 3 (New York: Random House, 1972), p. 1760.

62. Ray H. Elling, "The Hospital-Support Game in Urban Center," in Freidson, ed., *The Hospital in Modern Society,* p. 107.

63. Herbert A. Klarman, *Hospital Care in New York City: The Roles of Voluntary and Municipal Hospitals* (New York: Columbia University Press, 1963), p. 519.

64. Jan de Hartog, *The Hospital* (New York: Atheneum, 1964), pp. 5–6.

65. Somers and Somers, *Doctors, Patients, and Health Insurance,* p. 161.

66. Klarman, *Hospital Care in New York City,* p. 119.

67. John D. Thomson, "Patients Like These Four-Bed Wards," *Modern Hospital* 85 (December 1955), pp. 84–86.

68. See James L. Curtis, "Civil Rights in Medicine," *Journal of Public Health Policy* 1 (1980), pp. 110–20; Paul B. Cornely, "Segregation and Discrimination in Medical Care in the United States," *American Journal of Public Health* 35 (September 1958), pp. 1075–79.

69. A probably typical example, cited by Burling et al., was of a hospital whose practice it was to put a black patient in an empty two-bed private room and then ask a white patient if he or she minded sharing—but not vice versa (p. 207).

70. Edith M. Lentz, "Hospital Administration—One of a Species," *Administrative Science Quarterly* 1 (March 1957), p. 445.

Chapter 10

1. "The Crisis in American Medicine," a special supplement of *Harper's,* October 1960.

2. Harry Becker, *Financing Hospital Care in the United States* (New York: Blakiston, 1955), vol. 3, *Financing Hospital Care for Nonwage and Low-Income Groups,* p. 3.

3. Ibid., p. 104.

4. Ibid., p. 5.

5. Louis S. Reed, "Private Medical Expenditures and Voluntary Health Insurance, 1948–60," *Social Security Bulletin* 24, no. 12 (December 1960), table 9; Health Insurance Institute of America, *The Extent of Voluntary Health Insurance Coverage in the United States as of December 31, 1984* (New York: Health Insurance Council, 1964), p. 5.

6. Ibid., p. 26.

7.   See Raymond Munts, *Bargaining for Health: Labor Unions, Health Insurance, and Medical Care* (Madison: University of Wisconsin Press, 1967), pp. 9–11, 250, 262; Stevens, *American Medicine and the Public Interest,* pp. 271–72.

8.   The service approach was supported by the American Hospital Association requirement that a Blue Cross plan cover, on the average, not less than 75% of the total bill for the usual hospital services received by subscribers, under the most widely held Blue Cross certificate in that plan. Robert D. Eilers, *Regulation of Blue Cross and Blue Shield Plans* (Ph.D. diss., University of Pennsylvania, Department of Economics, 1961). See also Starr, *Social Transformation of American Medicine,* pp. 328–31. Figures relating to Blue Cross come from Eilers, unless otherwise stated.

9.   Quoted by Eilers, *Regulation of Blue Cross and Blue Shield Plans,* p. 279.

10.   Related proposals, incorporated in the Hill-Aiken bills, 1945–53, included subsidy of both nonprofit and other plans.

11.   On these proposals, see Agnes W. Brewster, *Health Insurance and Related Proposals for Financing Personal Health Services* (Washington, D.C.: U.S. Department of Health, Education, and Welfare, 1958).

12.   Don V. Ruck, Connecticut Blue Cross, lecture at the Department of Epidemiology and Public Health, Yale Medical School, Spring 1962.

13.   Quoted in Richard Carter, *The Doctor Business* (Garden City, N.Y.: Doubleday, 1958), p. 96.

14.   Becker, *Financing Hospital Care in the United States* (New York: Blakiston, 1955), vol. 2, *Prepayment and the Community,* pp. 301, 310.

15.   "Labor Fights Blue Cross Petition; Pickets Used to Protest Rate Increase," *Hospitals* 34 (July 16, 1960), p. 121.

16.   "Special Committee to Study Hospital Costs Requested by Cleveland City Council," *Hospitals* 34 (December 16, 1960), p. 113.

17.   Samuel Grafton, "From $9 a Year to $150: Blue Cross," *McCall's,* January 1963, p. 122.

18.   Kenneth W. Taber and Donald E. Stader, "How We Provided 'Active Beds' for New Patients," *Hospitals* 30 (December 16, 1956), pp. 36–38, 93–94.

19.   Statement of Marion B. Folsom, director of Eastman Kodak Co., in U.S. Congress, Senate, Committee on Labor and Public Welfare, Hearings on S. 596, *Combatting Heart Disease, Cancer, Stroke, and Other Major Diseases,* 89th Cong., 1st sess., February 1965, p. 119.

20.   With the great increase of union- and business-sponsored plans after World War II, including those in industries with employees in more than one state, Blue Cross did, however, need some national vehicles, in order to respond to requests for multiplan coverage of employee groups, and a national organization, Health Service, Inc., was established in the late 1940s. In addition, a separate Blue Cross Association was formed, with stock ownership in Health Service, Inc. The association, once formed, developed other joint activities out of its base in New York leading to the development of two national organizations, with the original Blue Cross Commission still connected with the AHA in Chicago. Multiplan coverage was successful, with the steelworkers' plan being the first major example in 1950. Two federal health-insurance programs, CHAMPUS (for civilians working for the Defense Department) and the Federal Employees' Benefits Program, gave Blue Cross plans, collectively, the opportunity to become truly national in coverage. Blue Cross plans carried coverage for CHAMPUS in two-thirds of the states in the early 1960s, with Mutual of Omaha covering the remainder, and Blue Cross became the major hospital carrier for the Federal Employees Program, begun in 1960. Selected plans provided coordination and leadership in these various efforts. This history is told in Odin Anderson, *Blue Cross Since 1929: Accountability and the Public Trust* (Cambridge, Mass.: Ballinger Publishing Co., 1975); and Sylvia A. Law, *Blue Cross: What Went Wrong?* (New Haven, Conn.: Yale University Press, 1974).

21.   Walter McNerney, in Weeks and Berman, *Shapers of American Health Care Policy,* pp. 175–77.

22.   A survey of care given under the steelworkers' contract in 1957–58, for example, found that major group-practice prepayment plans reported only 60% of the average number of hospital days per 1,000 persons incurred by Blue Cross beneficiaries. The plans were Kaiser, HIP in New York, Group Health Association in Washington, D.C., and Group Health Coop-

erative of Puget Sound. *Medical Care Program for Steelworkers and Their Families* (Pittsburgh: United Steelworkers of America, 1960), tables 34, 35.

23. Reed, "Private Medical Expenditures and Voluntary Health Insurance," table 9.

24. Louis S. Reed, "Private Consumer Expenditures for Medical Care and Voluntary Health Insurance 1948–63," *Social Security Bulletin* 28 (December 1964), table 11.

25. Blue Cross Association and American Hospital Association, *A Report on Health Care for the Aged* (Chicago: BCA and AHA, 1961).

26. Quoted in Becker, *Financing Hospital Care for Nonwage and Low-Income Groups,* p. 79.

27. Daniel Pettengill, in Weeks and Berman, *Shapers of American Health Care Policy,* pp. 186–87.

28. John H. Hayes, *Financing Hospital Care in the United States* (New York: Blakiston, 1954), vol. 1, *Factors Affecting the Costs of Hospital Care,* p. 56. See also pp. 77 and passim.

29. Becker, *Financing Hospital Care for Nonwage and Low-Income Groups,* pp. 3–4. Analysis of the changing sources of hospital income for the Commission on Financing Hospital Care cites Philadelphia, scarcely a typical case because of the long practice of state subsidy of hospitals for "charity" care. In Philadelphia 38% of hospital service in nonprofit general hospitals was provided on a full or part "charity basis" in 1928, 25% in 1949. The report states that "many other examples" of reduced charity care could be given, but refrains from doing so. Hayes, *Factors Affecting the Costs of Hospital Care,* p. 56.

30. Hayes, *Factors Affecting the Costs of Hospital Care,* p. 62.

31. See Denver Planning Board, *Responsibilities of the City and County of Denver for Providing Hospital Treatment* (Denver: City of Denver Planning Office, 1962).

32. In 1958 tax funds (from all sources) represented 6% of voluntary hospital income nationwide, but there were substantial variations from place to place. In New York City, still the leader in this respect, tax funds represented about 9% of voluntary hospital budgets in 1957. Herbert E. Klarman, *Hospital Care in New York City* (New York: Columbia University Press, 1963), p. 510.

33. Hospital Association of Pennsylvania, *Costs of Hospital Care Have Sky-Rocketed,* pamphlet, 1951. This pamphlet was part of more general lobbying by the association for increased state reimbursement levels.

34. The best account I have found is Irwin Wolkstein, "The Legislative History of Hospital Cost Reimbursement," unpublished position paper for the Secretary's Advisory Committee on Hospital Effectiveness (Washington, D.C.: Department of Health, Education and Welfare, 1968).

35. In its crudest form the cost per patient day was an average, derived from the total inpatient expenditures of the hospital in a given time period, divided by the number of inpatient days.

36. Weeks and Berman, *Shapers of American Health Care Policy,* pp. 217–18.

37. An excellent analysis is Theodore R. Marmor, "The Congress: Medicare Politics and Policy," in Allan P. Sindler, ed., *American Political Institutions and Public Policy* (Boston: Little, Brown, 1969), pp. 3–66. The best analysis from the point of view of the language used in creating consensus among divergent points of view is Max J. Skidmore, *Medicare and the American Rhetoric of Reconciliation* (University, Ala.: University of Alabama Press, 1970). Excellent studies of the rule-making surrounding Medicare passage and earlier implementation are Herman M. Somers and Anne R. Somers, *Medicare and the Hospitals: Issues and Prospects* (Washington, D.C.: Brookings Institution, 1967); and Judith Feder, *Medicare: The Politics of Federal Hospital Insurance* (Lexington, Mass.: Lexington Books, 1977).

38. The legislation established a new category of potential recipients of welfare medical care, the medically indigent aged. These were persons sixty-five years and over who were judged to be medically indigent according to means-test standards set by each state, but who were not on public-assistance cash-benefit programs. As in the earlier vendor payment program, participation was optional by each state. But Kerr-Mills provided, for the first time, a federal definition of components of medical care, requiring participating states to provide at least some institutional and some noninstitutional medical services. All of the twenty-nine state plans in operation in 1963 covered hospital care. Reflecting, once again, old welfare traditions, only sixteen covered the cost of physician services for hospital inpatients and twenty-one covered physician services in outpatient departments. Of $1.1 billion spent on vendor medical bills in 1963, $451 million (42%) flowed directly to hospitals for inpatient care. (Another $337 million went to nursing homes, providing a direct stimulus to the

expansion of the profit-making nursing-home industry.) *Welfare in Review, Statistical Supplement, 1964 Edition* (Washington, D.C.: U.S. Department of Health, Education, and Welfare, Welfare Administration, 1964), table 6.

39.   When the program was first started in 1961, the coverage was only six days. When asked what happened if the patient was still sick after six days, the Kentucky Commissioner for Economic Security replied, "We pay only for six days. If the patient is in the hospital longer, the care may be paid for by a relative or a charity, or the hospital may discharge him. We do not know what happens after our responsibility is met." Quoted by Robert Stevens and Rosemary Stevens, *Welfare Medicine in America* (New York: Free Press, 1974), p. 40 and passim; and see Alonzo Yerby, "Public Medical Care for the Needy in the United States," in Leslie J. De Groot, ed., *Medical Care: Social and Organizational Aspects* (Springfield, Ill.: Charles C. Thomas, 1966), pp. 382–401.

40.   Quoted in Weeks and Berman, *Shapers of American Health Care Policy*, p. 92.

41.   Ibid., p. 98.

42.   One immediate result was to polarize the issue of hospital-based physicians whose payment prior to Medicare usually came through the hospital bill, whatever the specific contractual or salary arrangements between radiologists and pathologists with individual hospitals. See, for example, Daniel Pettengill in ibid., p. 156.

43.   U.S. Congress, House of Representatives, Executive Hearings before the Committee on Ways and Means, on H.R. 1, *Medicare for the Aged*, 89th Cong., 1st sess., January–February 1965, p. 246.

44.   See *Areawide Planning for Hospitals and Related Health Facilities*, Report of the Joint Committee by the American Hospital Association and Public Health Service (Washington, D.C.: Department of Health, Education, and Welfare, Public Health Service, Division of Hospital and Medical Facilities, 1961), p. 8; Kenneth W. Wisowaty, Charles C. Edwards, and Raymond L. White, "Health Facilities Planning—A Review of the Movement," *Journal of the American Medical Association* 190 (1964), pp. 752–56. The Hill-Burton program had been adjusted over the years: adding grants for research on hospital utilization in 1949, including construction of nursing homes and other facilities in 1954, and providing long-term loans as well as grants in 1958. Construction of out-of-hospital community health facilities was also included in 1961. In 1964 the program was further adjusted to include grants for hospital modernization and for urban services developed through regional, metropolitan, or local area plans.

45.   *Areawide Planning*, p. 13.

46.   Williams in *Medicare for the Aged*, p. 224.

47.   *Rx: A Local Hospital Planning Agency*, Publication no. 877 (Washington, D.C.: U.S. Department of Health, Education and Welfare, Public Health Service, 1961).

48.   The two sets of policies also expressed the different agendas of different federal groups. Voluntary planning was the strategy of those in the U.S. Public Health Service, while extended service was the goal of those in the Social Security Administration. I am grateful to Dr. William Kissick for this observation, but it still seems an insufficient explanation for the two distinct approaches.

49.   The precipitating factor here was when the old Gouverneur Hospital lost its accreditation and most of the foreign medical staff at Harlem Hospital failed to pass the examination of the Educational Council for Foreign Medical Graduates (now the Educational Commission for Foreign Medical Graduates). The affiliation program followed one of the main themes of the 1960s: the encouragement of medical quality.

50.   National Commission on Community Health Services, *Health Is a Community Affair* (Cambridge, Mass.: Harvard University Press, 1967).

51.   Daniel Fox argues that in the mid-1960s, health policy seemed a logical result of the "progress of medicine." *Health Policies, Health Politics*, p. 206 and passim.

52.   Subcommittee Reports of the President's Commission on Heart Disease, Cancer and Stroke, "Report of the Subcommittee on Heart Disease," in *Combatting Heart Disease, Cancer, Stroke, and Other Major Diseases*, p. 171.

53.   "Report of the Cancer Panel," *Combatting Heart Disease, Cancer, Stroke, and Other Major Diseases*, p. 183.

54.   *Combatting Heart Disease, Cancer, Stroke, and Other Major Diseases*, p. 103.

55.   These recommendations came out of a busy nine months of commission hearings and deliberations (there were forty-five hearings and over 7,500 pages of testimony). One available model was the Albany regional hospital program, which began formal activities in

September 1960, supported by the National Heart Institute, one of the National Institutes of Health, and by annual contributions from participating hospitals in the states of New York and Massachusetts. Six general hospitals were directly involved in a program of faculty development and residency training centered on the Albany Medical College. Other examples were the continuing Tufts-Bingham Associates program and programs run by New York University and the Universities of Michigan, Ohio, Wisconsin, Kansas, Iowa, and Rochester. Ibid., pp. 28, 81.

56. The association suggested starting any program as a small demonstration of teaching and research, limiting treatment only to carefully selected places, and the AMA also advised caution in the face of the potentially "far reaching ramifications" of any major development of regionalism for the structure and organization of the health-care system. Ibid., pp. 157–58, 162–63.

57. *Report of the National Advisory Commission on Civil Disorders* (Washington, D.C.: Government Printing Office, 1968), pp. 136–37 and passim.

58. Williamson, in *Shapers of American Health Care Policy*, p. 100.

Chapter 11

1. The $35.5 billion includes all types of hospitals, including those for psychiatric and chronic diseases. Daniel R. Waldo, Katherine R. Levit, and Helen Lazenby, "National Health Expenditures, 1985," *Health Care Financing Review* 8 (Fall 1986), p. 16. However, both Medicare and Medicaid were heavily focused, for hospital care, on short-term general hospitals. In 1980 nonfederal short-term general and other special (nonpsychiatric) hospitals incurred expenses of $77 billion. *Hospital Statistics: 1981 Edition* (Chicago: American Hospital Association, 1981), table 1.

2. Paul Starr uses the evocative phrase "The Coming of the Corporation" as the title of the last chapter of *The Social Transformation of American Medicine* (1982). This enormously success-ful and widely read book suggests a system moving inexorably toward corporate domination of medicine and the "reprivatization of the public household"—major issues in this period.

3. H. B. Hansman, "The Role of Nonprofit Enterprise," *Yale Law Journal* 89 (1980), pp. 835–901; R. C. Clark, "Does the Nonprofit Form Fit the Hospital Industry?" *Harvard Law Journal* 93 (1980), pp. 1417–89.

4. PL 89–97, Title XVIII, section 1801. The best account of Medicare's passage and im-plementation is Judith M. Feder, *Medicare: The Politics of Federal Hospital Insurance* (Lexington, Mass.: Lexington Books, 1977).

5. U.S. Congress, Senate, Committee on Finance, *Medicare and Medicaid: Problems, Issues, and Alternatives*, Staff Report, 91st Cong., 1st sess., February 1970, p. 4. See also Stevens, *American Medicine and the Public Interest*, pp. 445–63.

6. *Trends Affecting the U.S. Health Care System*, Health Planning Information Series, Publica-tion no. HRA 76-14503 (Washington, D.C.: U.S. Department of Health, Education and Welfare, 1976), p. 165.

7. Martin Feldstein and Amy Taylor, *The Rapid Rise of Hospital Costs* (Washington, D.C.: Executive Office of the President, Council on Wage and Price Stability, 1977), p. 7 and passim.

8. Anne A. Scitovksy, "Changes in the Costs of Treatment of Selected Illnesses, 1971–1981," *Medical Care* 23 (December 1985), pp. 1345–57.

9. There was discussion in the late 1960s of the advantages, in an ideal situation, of getting away from cost per patient day entirely as the basis for reimbursement, in favor of reimbursement figures for each patient's stay; and, indeed, there were enormous theoretical advantages in this possibility. (It was eventually to be achieved in 1983, through reimburse-ment tied to diagnosis-related groups or DRGs.) However, the technical difficulties of precise cost-finding for the aged were prohibitive in the 1960s, if only because of lack of standardized accounting and partial adoption of computers and software. The 1965–66 regulations for Medicare reimbursement gave hospitals two options. The first required a new accounting system, to identify what proportion of each hospital department's costs was attributable to the Medicare population. The second was a combination method, which used average per diem rates for room and board and proportional costs for nonroutine or ancillary services.

10. Quoted in Weeks and Berman, *Shapers of American Health Care Policy,* p. 103. For a good description and discussion of the negotiations, see Feder, *Medicare,* pp. 55–57 and passim, and Somers and Somers, *Medicare and the Hospitals,* pp. 154–96.

11. An additional 9% was derived from the new Medicaid programs, which were underway in the states. Medicaid, too, was required under the 1965 legislation to reimburse hospitals on the basis of "reasonable cost," and some states used Blue Cross as their fiscal agents to administer Medicaid. John Krizay and Andrew Wilson, *The Patient as Consumer: Health Care Financing in the United States* (Lexington, Mass.: Lexington Books, 1974), p. 93. On the role of Blue Cross, see Odin Anderson, *Blue Cross Since 1929,* p. 93 and passim; and Sylvia A. Law, *Blue Cross: What Went Wrong?*

12. See, e.g., U.S. Congress, Senate, Committee on the Judiciary, Subcommittee on Antitrust and Monopoly, *High Cost of Hospitalization,* 91st Cong., 2nd sess.; and discussion on the *Travelers* case in Anderson, *Blue Cross Since 1929,* and Law, *Blue Cross.*

13. Starr, *The Social Transformation of American Medicine,* p. 436.

14. *Trends Affecting the U.S. Health Care System,* p. 9.

15. Karen Davis, "Economic Theories of Behavior in Nonprofit Private Hospitals," *Economic and Business Bulletin* 24 (Winter 1972), p. 1. See also Burton A. Weisbrod, "Some Problems of Pricing and Resource Allocation in a Non-Profit Industry—the Hospitals," *Journal of Business* 38 (January 1965), pp. 18–28; Mary Lee Ingbar and Lester D. Taylor, *Hospital Costs in Massachusetts* (Cambridge, Mass.: Harvard University Press, 1968).

16. See Stevens, *American Medicine and the Public Interest,* pp. 496–513.

17. Senate Committee on Finance, *Medicare and Medicaid,* p. 107.

18. Marian Gornick, "Ten Years of Medicare: Impact on the Covered Population," *Social Security Bulletin* (July 1976), pp. 3–21; U.S. Department of Health and Social Services, *Health, United States 1981,* Publication no. (PHS) P2-1232, p. 166.

19. For an excellent overview of hospital capital requirements, see Uwe Reinhardt and Bradford H. Gray, "Financial Capital and Health Care Growth Trends," in Gray, ed., *For-Profit Enterprise in Health Care* (Washington, D.C.: National Academy Press, 1986), pp. 47–73. See also American Hospital Association, *Statement on the Financial Requirements of Health Care Institutions and Services* (Chicago: American Hospital Association, 1969).

20. Presidential Message, *Congressional Quarterly Almanac, 1965,* p. 1256.

21. Robert M. Ball, "Problems of Cost—As Experienced in Medicare," in U.S. Department of Health, Education and Welfare, *Report of the National Conference on Medical Costs* (Washington, D.C.: Government Printing Office, 1967), p. 65.

22. Richard W. Foster, "The Financial Structure of Community Hospitals: Impact of Medicare," in *The Nature of Hospital Costs: Three Studies* (Chicago: Hospital Research and Educational Trust, 1976), p. 65 and passim.

23. Louise Russell, *Technology in Hospitals: Medical Advances and Their Diffusion* (Washington, D.C.: Brookings Institution, 1979), p. 75 and passim. See also U.S. Department of Health, Education, and Welfare, *Hill-Burton Progress Report, July 1, 1947–June 30, 1966* (Washington D.C.: Government Printing Office, 1966), pp. 32–33.

24. *Hospital Statistics,* p. 5; U.S. Department of Commerce, Bureau of the Census, *Statistical Abstract of the United States: 1984* (Washington, D.C.: Government Printing Office, 1983), pp. 115, 117.

25. Somers and Somers, *Medicare and the Hospitals,* p. 177: and see Feder, *Medicine,* pp. 57–70.

26. Somers and Somers, *Medicare and the Hospitals,* p. 173.

27. Ibid, p. 181.

28. Howard J. Berman and Lewis E. Weeks, *The Financial Management of Hospitals* (Ann Arbor: Health Administration Press, 1979), pp. 63, 66, 511.

29. Senator John Williams described the situation in 1969: "Since medicare started there has been a remarkable increase in the number of chains entering the for-profit hospital and nursing home field. These groups, whose stocks have soared to unbelievable price-earnings ratios, are obviously lured by medicare's generous reimbursement. The 1½ percent bonus paid on top of reimbursable costs, the prospect of getting accelerated depreciation allowances and then selling a facility at an inflated price, the fact that medicare will pick up all of the costs of a 100 bed facility even if its total patient load consists of just five medicare beneficiaries, the fact that there is no effective review of the utilization of beds and services in these facilities, and the fact that the nursing home or hospital can choose the Government agent who will determine how much it is to be paid have certainly encouraged the get-rich-quick

operations." *Congressional Record,* May 14, 1969, S. 5202, reported in Senate Committee on Finance, *Medicare and Medicaid,* February 9, 1970.

30.   See Bruce Steinwald and Duncan Neuhauser, "The Role of the Proprietary Hospital," *Law and Contemporary Problems,* Autumn 1970, p. 31.

31.   *Humana 1976 Annual Report* (Louisville, Ky.: Humana, 1976), p. 2.

32.   *Hospital Corporation of America: 1973 Annual Report* (Nashville, Tenn.: Hospital Corporation of America, 1973), frontispiece.

33.   Senate Committee on Finance, *Medicare and Medicaid,* p. 136.

34.   See table 13.1.

35.   Senate Committee on Finance, *Medicare and Medicaid,* p. 136. For the best statement of concern, see Arnold Relman, "The New Medical Industrial Complex," *New England Journal of Medicine* 303 (1980), p. 963.

36.   *Congressional Quarterly Almanac, 1969,* p. 868.

37.   Walter J. McNerney, "The Role of Technology in the Development of Health Institution Goals and Programs," HEW Conference, "Technology and Health Care Systems in the 1980s," January 1972, manuscript, p. 7.

38.   Paul M. Ellwood, Jr., "Alternatives to Regulation: Improving the Market," in Institute of Medicine, *Controls on Health Care* (Washington D.C.: National Academy of Sciences, 1975), pp. 49–72.

39.   Allan K. Palmer, assistant director of the federal Bureau of Competition, quoted in "The Federal Trade Commission Enters a New Arena: Health Services," Sounding Board, *New England Journal of Medicine* 299 (1978), p. 481.

40.   The high mark was 1982, when for-profit hospitals reported over 3.3 million admissions. Since 1982, admissions to all categories of short-term general hospital have declined. *Hospital Statistics,* Data from the American Hospital Association 1987 Annual Survey (Chicago: American Hospital Association, 1987), table 1, p. 5.

41.   Standard and Poor's Corporation, *Standard NYSE Stock Reports* 43, no. 76 (April 20, 1976), sec. 13. See also David A. Stewart, *The History and Status of For-profit Hospitals* (Chicago: Blue Cross Research Series, 1973), pp. 2–9.

42.   B. Jon Jaeger, ed., *The Decade of Implementation: The Multiple Management Concept Revisited* (Durham, N.C.: Duke University, Department of Health Administration, 1975), p. 7 and passim.

43.   May Elizabeth Burns, "Changes in Church-Operated Systems," in ibid., pp. 76–92.

44.   Dan Ermann and Jon Gabel, "Multi-Hospital Systems: Issues and Empirical Findings," *Health Affairs* 3 (Spring 1984), p. 50.

45.   *Modern Health Care,* June 5, 1987, p. 46.

46.   See Gail M. Lovinger, *Market Reform and Regulation in the Hospital Field* (Chicago: American Hospital Association), 1985, p. 4 and passim. See also U.S. Department of Health, Education, and Welfare, *Toward a Comprehensive Health Policy for the 1970's: A White Paper* (Washington, D.C.: U.S. Department of Health, Education, and Welfare, May 1971), p. 1; and Starr, *The Social Transformation of American Medicine,* pp. 379–419.

47.   Secretary's Advisory Committee on Hospital Effectiveness, *Report* (Washington, D.C.: U.S. Department of Health, Education, and Welfare, 1968), pp. 11–12. See also Symond R. Gottlieb, "A Brief History of Health Planning in the United States," in Clark Havighurst, ed., *Regulating Health Facilities Construction* (Washington, D.C.: American Enterprise Institute for Public Policy Research, 1974), pp. 20–24 and passim.

48.   Robert R. Alford, *Health Care Politics: Ideological and Interest Group Barriers to Reform* (Chicago: University of Chicago Press, 1975), p. xiv and passim.

49.   David S. Salkever and Thomas W. Bice, *Hospital Certificate-of-Need Controls: Impact on Investment, Costs, and Use* (Washington, D.C.: American Enterprise Institute, 1979), pp. 4–5, 75, and passim. The Social Security Amendments of 1972 (sec. 1122), specified advance approval for capital expenditures if depreciation charges were to be included in Medicare—although states with CON laws could apply for a waiver.

50.   Victor G. Rodwin, *The Health Planning Predicament: France, Quebec, England, and the United States* (Berkeley: University of California Press, 1984), p. 45; and see Drew Altman, Richard Greene, and Harvey N. Sapolsky, *Health Planning and Regulation: The Decision-making Process* (Washington, D.C.: AUPHA Press, 1981), p. 49 and passim.

51.   *Congressional Quarterly Almanac, 1978,* p. 619. Attempts to enforce federal requirements for hospital utilization review under Medicare through new professional standards review

organizations (PSROs), under the Social Security Amendments of 1972, also appeared to have marginal benefits. In the late 1970s, over two-thirds of all hospitals were undertaking their own review of the appropriateness of hospital admission and length of stay, on behalf of Medicare—hardly a guarantee of service limitation. The fox had been set to guard the chickens.

52. Joseph A. Califano, Jr., *America's Health Care Revolution: Who Lives? Who Dies? Who Pays?* (New York: Random House, 1986), p. 7.

53. Lewis Thomas, "Public Teaching Hospitals Face Life-Death Issues in Changing Times," *Modern Hospital* 109 (October 1967), p. 95.

54. Howard J. Brown, "Municipal Hospitals," *Bulletin of the New York Academy of Medicine* 43 (1967), p. 452.

55. Dr. Kerlikowske, quoted in "The Impact of Third-Party Insurance, Medicare, and Medicaid on City-County General Hospitals," *Modern Medical Topics,* October 1969, p. 3.

56. "Doctors at Philadelphia General Say Major Changes Needed to Save Hospital," *Modern Hospital* 109 (October 1967), p. 33.

57. "End of the Line for City Hospitals?" *Medical World News* 10 (May 9, 1969), pp. 34–39; "Crises Plague City, County Hospitals," *Hospitals* 42 (September 1, 1968), pp. 105–6.

58. Quentin B. Deming, I. Herbert Scheinberg, and Saul Moroff, "New York City's Municipal Hospitals Speak of Public Conscience," *New York Times,* February 17, 1987.

59. In 1967 a blue-ribbon committee, the Piel Commission, proposed abolition of the double standard among hospitals by fusing tax-supported and voluntary hospitals into a single, integrated system under a new nonprofit health-service corporation, the idea being to privatize the city-run institutions, but also to control other hospitals as well. This solution elicited little support, either from the voluntary hospitals (for whom city hospitals were a valuable support system) or from would-be reformers of municipal services (who saw no particular virtue in the private system). New York City Commission on the Delivery of Personal Health Services, *Health Services Delivery in New York City,* Piel Commission Final Report (New York, December 1967).

60. Barbara Ehrenreich, "New York City Tries a New Model," *Social Policy* 1 (January–February 1971), p. 26.

61. "Hospital Meeting Upset by Fighting," *New York Times,* June 12, 1971.

62. This was true even in California, where the Medicaid program, MediCal, promised major changes in California's county hospital system. California's county hospitals were, it is true, finally released from their limited role as welfare institutions; they became, in name at least, "community" hospitals, now legally open to the whole population. Individuals on public assistance or otherwise eligible for MediCal had the privilege of seeking service in voluntary and proprietary institutions. Nevertheless, a study of the implementation of MediCal in Los Angeles found that patients were driven more by custom, the convenience of hospital facilities, and the availability of transportation rather than by middle-class norms of "quality." Arnold I. Kisch and Foline E. Gartside, "Use of a County Outpatient Department by Medi-Cal Recipients," *Medical Care* 6 (November–December 1986), pp. 516–23.

63. True to a materialistic, "individualistic" legal philosophy for private institutions, the general rule prevailed, into the 1970s, that Americans possessed no right to be admitted to any hospital. Hospitals were not obliged to accept patients they did not desire—nor even to assign a reason for refusing to admit. Illinois was unusual, in the late 1960s, in imposing a legal duty on both public and private hospitals where surgical operations were performed, requiring them to give emergency medical treatment or first aid to any person who applied. Leonard S. Powers, "Hospital Emergency Service and the Open Door," *Michigan Law Review* 66 (1968), pp. 1462–63.

64. Jerome Mondesire and Donald Drake, "The PGH Battle Clamor Obscures Key Health-Care Issues," *Philadelphia Evening Bulletin,* March 1, 1976.

65. Joe Davidson, "Report Finds Hospital Closing Hasn't Backfired on Philadelphia," ibid., July 7, 1977.

66. Commission on Public-General Hospitals, *The Future of the Public-General Hospital: An Agenda for Transition* (Chicago: Hospital Research and Educational Trust, 1978).

67. For an excellent analysis, see Marilyn G. Rose, "Federal Regulation of Services to the Poor Under the Hill-Burton Act: Realities and Pitfalls," *Northwestern University Law Review* 70 (1975), pp. 168–201.

68.   See Institute of Medicine, *Health Care in a Context of Civil Rights: Report of a Study* (Washington, D.C.: National Academy Press, 1981).

69.   *Parker* v. *Port Huron Hospital,* 361 Mich. 1, p. 25, 105 NW 2nd 1, p. 13 (1960), quoted in *Parker* v. *Highland Park,* Mich. 273 NW 2nd, p. 413 (1978). Emphasis does not appear in the original case, but is added in the later case.

70.   *Parker* v. *Highland Park.*

71.   "84th Annual Report on Medical Education in the United States and Canada; 1983–84," *Journal of the American Medical Association* 252 (1984), p. 1536.

72.   The best statement is David E. Rogers and Robert J. Blendon, "The Academic Medical Center: A Stressed American Institution," *New England Journal of Medicine* 298 (1978), pp. 940–50.

73.   John Davidson, "Capital Area Health Consortium," in John D. Cochrane, *Hospital Consortia: Are They Just Another Layer of Bureaucracy or a Key to Survival?* (Sacramento: California Hospital Association, 1979), p. 44.

Chapter 12

1.   Alain C. Enthoven, *Health Plan: The Only Practical Solution to the Soaring Cost of Medical Care* (Reading, Mass.: Addison-Wesley Publishing Co., 1980), p. xv.

2.   See, e.g., William B. Schwartz and Paul J. Joskow, "Duplicated Hospital Facilities: How Much Can We Save by Consolidating Them?" *New England Journal of Medicine* 303 (1980), pp. 1449–57; Department of Health and Human Services, Health Resources Administration of 1980, *Report of the Graduate Medical Education National Advisory Committee to the Secretary;* Arnold S. Relman, "Determining How Much Medical Care We Need," *New England Journal of Medicine* 303 (1980), pp. 1292–93.

3.   U.S. General Accounting Office, "Information on Hospital Inspections, Reporting Requirements, and Life Safety Code Enforcement" and "Memorandum to the Honorable Herman E. Talmadge," July 2, 1980 (HRD-80-94) (B-199186).

4.   "Major Changes Made in Medicare Program," *Congressional Quarterly Almanac, 1983,* p. 391.

5.   Clinicians were asked to classify patient records into mutually exclusive groups; then these groups were further subdivided to reduce the variance in the patient's length of stay among the groups, in order to stratify services by differential demand, a proxy for costs. The goal was to measure the hospital's patient mix so that hospitals could be compared and rated by outside agencies—and eventually regulated according to their costs. An early version of the DRG system was first widely used in 1980. Early in 1982 the researchers issued revised categories, based on the latest version of the International Classification of Diseases and carved from twenty-three larger groups, each corresponding to a single organ system or a combination of an organ system and a disease etiology. Further divisions were based on whether the patient received a medical or a surgical procedure. It was these classifications that were assumed by the federal Medicare program the following year. R. B. Fetter et al., "Case-Mix Definition by Diagnosis-Related Groups," supplement to *Medical Care* 18 (February 1980); J. D. Thompson, R. B. Fetter, and C. D. Mross, "Case-Mix and Resource Use," *Inquiry* 12 (1975), 300–12; and see John D. Thompson, "Diagnosis-Related Groups," letter, *New England Journal of Medicine* 308 (1983), p. 1107. I rely here on Nancy L. Kelly, Diane E. Hamilton, and Ralph E. Berry, "A Brief Review of the Development of DRGs," in *Diagnosis-Related Groups (DRGs) and the Medicare Program: Implications for Medical Technology* (Washington, D.C.: Congress of the United States, Office of Technology Assessment, 1983), pp. 65–69.

6.   John K. Iglehart, "New Jersey's Experiment with DRG-based Hospital Reimbursement," *New England Journal of Medicine* 307 (1982), p. 1636. In the early 1980s, DRGs were the basis for several experiments in paying for hospital care. New Jersey was using the DRG system as an element in its reimbursement system. Maryland also had begun to regulate hospital rates, using DRGs as an element in this process, and Georgia used DRGs as part of its hospital grouping system in a 1981–82 Medicaid reimbursement experiment.

7.   An excellent review of this process in terms of the evolving federal role is Barry G. Rabe, "The Refederalization of American Health Care," *Medical Care Review* 44 (Spring 1987),

pp. 37–63; see also J. A. Morone and A. B. Dunham, "Slouching Towards National Health Insurance: The New Health Care Politics," *Yale Journal on Regulation* 2, no. 2, 263–91. A group of outside experts in health-care organization, financing, and research—the Prospective Payment Assessment Commission (ProPac)—sets the actual rates for each DRG.

8. Donald W. Simborg, "DRG Creep: A New Hospital-Acquired Disease," *New England Journal of Medicine* 304 (1981), p. 1602.

9. Ibid., p. 1604. Under the New Jersey system, for example, the average charge for the DRG for myocardial infarction was three times that for angina pectoris.

10. U.S. Congress, Senate, Special Committee on Aging, "Impact of Medicare's Prospective Payment System on the Quality of Care Received by Medicare Beneficiaries," Staff Report, September 28, 1985; and see James W. Moser, "Medicare Hospital Diagnosis-Related Groups and Quality of Patient Care," Center for Health Policy Research, American Medical Association, July 1986. And see Emily Friedman, "Those Wonderful People Who Brought You DRGs," *Hospitals* 58, no. 5 (1984), pp. 81–88.

11. "Is DRG Creep Spoiling the System?" *Washington Report on Medicine and Health: Perspectives,* September 3, 1984, pp. 1–3.

12. Reported in "DRGs and Quality of Care," *Washington Report on Medicine and Health: Perspectives,* November 25, 1985, p. 1.

13. Ibid., and see "Information Requirements for Evaluating the Impacts of Medicare Prospective Payment on Post-Hospital Long-Term Care Services: Preliminary Report" (GAO/PEMD-85-8) (Washington, D.C.: General Accounting Office).

14. John K. Iglehart, "Medicare Begins Prospective Payment of Hospitals," *New England Journal of Medicine* 308 (1983), pp. 1428–32. The other associations were the Association of American Medical Colleges, the Associated Hospital Systems, the National Council of Community Hospitals, and the Volunteer Trustees of Not-for-Profit Hospitals.

15. The new system for matching organ donors and recipients was to be run under a federal contract by the United Network for Organ Sharing, a nonprofit group in Richmond, Virginia. "New Law May Spur Organ Donations," *New York Times,* September 6, 1987.

16. Eli Ginzberg, "The Destabilization of Health Care," *New England Journal of Medicine* 315 (1986), p. 757.

17. *Surgery in the United States: A Summary Report of the Study on Surgical Services in the United States* (Chicago: American College of Surgeons and American Surgical Association, 1975). The report suggested, *inter alia,* regional reviews of surgical services, improved organization of surgical care, a decrease in the total number of persons carrying out surgical operations, and improved methods of distribution or referral for surgical patients.

18. Harold S. Luft, John P. Bunker, and Alain C. Enthoven, "Should Operations Be Regionalized? The Empirical Relation Between Surgical Volume and Mortality," *New England Journal of Medicine* 301 (1979), pp. 1364–69; see also Ann Barry Flood, W. Richard Scott, and Wayne Ewy, "Does Practice Make Perfect?" *Medical Care* 22 (1984), p. 98.

19. Dale G. Renlund et al., "Medicare-Designated Centers for Cardiac Transplantation," *New England Journal of Medicine* 316 (1987), 873–76; *Health Policy Week* 16 (August 17, 1987), pp. 3–4.

20. John E. Wennberg, Klim McPherson, and Philip Caper, "Will Payment Based on Diagnosis-Related Groups Control Hospital Costs?" *New England Journal of Medicine* 311 (1984), pp. 295–300.

21. Philip Caper, Robert Keller, and Paul Rohlf, "Tracking Physician Practice Patterns for Quality Care," *Business and Health* (September 1986), pp. 7–9.

22. See, e.g., Albert L. Siu et al., "Inappropriate Use of Hospitals in a Randomized Trial of Health Insurance Plans," *New England Journal of Medicine* 315 (1986), pp. 1259–66; and Ann Barry Flood et al., "Effectiveness in Professional Organizations: The Impact of Surgeons and Surgical Staff Organizations on the Quality of Care in Hospitals," *Health Services Research* 17 (Winter 1982), pp. 341–66; Robert G. Hughes, Sandra S. Hunt, and Harold S. Luft, "Effective Surgeon Volume and Hospital Volume on Quality of Care in Hospitals," *Medical Care* 25 (June 1987), pp. 489–503.

23. Susan D. Horn et al., "Interhospital Differences in Severity of Illness," *New England Journal of Medicine* 313 (1985), pp. 20–24.

24. A good review of the rise of the interest groups is John T. Tierney, "Organized Interests in Health Politics and Policy-making," *Medical Care Review* 44 (Spring 1987), pp. 89–118.

25. Reported in *Modern Healthcare,* March 26, 1986, p. 26; ibid., August 14, 1987, p. 66.

26. Pennsylvania Public Interest Coalition, *Public Interest News* 6 (Summer 1987), p. 3.

27. An AHA task force observed in 1982 that there might be specific problems with antitrust legislation (and thus a risk of prosecution) where there is explicit or implicit agreement among hospitals about prices or service allocation; where hospitals agree to consolidate services, based on a review of data disseminated among them (for example, that they would agree that one of two emergency rooms in the community should close and then move to implement that agreement); where hospitals and other coalition members, participants, and third-party payers cold-shoulder potential competition by, for example, agreeing not to reimburse new health-care facilities in an area; and where employers, with the active participation of competing hospitals, agree to refuse to deal with a particular hospital. *Report of the Adjunct Task Force on Anti-trust* (Chairman, Richard L. Epstein) (Chicago: American Hospital Association, 1982).

28. *Unfair Competition by Nonprofit Organizations with Small Business: An Issue for the 1980s* (Washington, D.C.: U. S. Small Business Administration, Office of the Chief Counsel for Advocacy, 1983); see also *U.S. Small Business Administration, Government Competition: A Threat to Small Business,* Report on the Advocacy Task Group on Government Competition with Small Business (Washington, D.C., 1980).

29. U.S. Department of Health and Human Services, Office of the Inspector General, *Financial Impact of the Prospective Payment System on Medicare Participating Hospitals—1984* (Washington, D.C., May 1986), reported in Daniel R. Waldo, Katharine R. Levit, and Helen Lazenby, "National Health Expenditures, 1985," *Health Care Financing Review,* Fall 1986, p. 7.

30. National Center for Health Statistics, *Advancedata* 127 (September 25, 1986), table 4.

31. *New York Times,* "Surgeons Try to Divide Twins," September 6, 1987; Anne Scitovsky, "Changes in the Costs of Treatment of Selected Illnesses, 1971–1981," *Medical Care* 23 (1985), pp. 1345–57.

32. The phrase is from Paul J. DiMaggio and Walter W. Powell, "The Iron Cage Re-Visited: Institutional Isomorphism and Collective Rationality in Organizational Fields," *American Sociological Review* 48 (1983), 147–60.

33. Steven D. Shortell, reported in *Modern Healthcare,* August 14, 1987, p. 40; and ibid., June 5, 1987, p. 44. *Modern Healthcare*'s survey of multihospital systems in 1987 found that 159 of the 164 centrally managed hospital systems operated freestanding facilities. In addition, 55 operated two or more nursing homes, 36 ran psychiatric hospitals, and 45 operated health maintenance organizations. Not-for-profit hospitals remain more diversified than their for-profit counterparts, at least with respect to those in systems. Currently 84% of not-for-profit hospitals operate ambulatory surgery centers compared with 77% of the for-profit hospitals. Thirty percent of the not-for-profits operate wellness programs, 25% skilled-nursing facilities, 21% kidney dialysis services, and 21% urgent care centers. In all of these areas, more of the not-for-profit hospitals have these formally diversified services than the for-profit hospitals. The only distinction was for outpatient CT scanners, where 55% of the for-profit hospitals and 40% of the not-for-profit hospitals reported services. On the early 1980s, see Emily Schulman Mendel, "Questions and Answers on Corporate Restructuring," *Trustee,* November 1981, p. 37.

34. "Business-Minded Health Care," *New York Times,* February 12, 1985.

35. "Hospital Systems Report 47.1% Drop in Profits Last Year," *Modern Healthcare,* June 5, 1987, p. 37.

36. Leah Rothstein, "Wishmann Design Targets Healthcare Design Growth," *Philadelphia Business Journal,* September 13, 1987, p. 18B. For another excellent example, see Emily Friedman, "The All Frills Yuppie Healthcare Boutique," *Transaction/Society* 28 (July–August 1986), pp. 42–48.

37. Paul Galloway, "Hospital Chic," *Chicago Tribune,* November 3, 1986.

38. Ibid.

39. Dan Ermann and Jon Gabel, "Investor-Owned, Multihospital Systems: A Synthesis of Research Findings," in Bradford H. Gray, ed., *For-Profit Enterprise in Health Care* (Washington, D.C., National Academy Press, 1986), pp. 475–76.

40. "Hospital Systems Report 47.1% Drop in Profits Last Year," *Modern Healthcare,* June 5, 1987, p. 37.

41. At Northwestern Memorial Hospital, Chicago, for example, a faculty group practice associated with Northwestern University established an independent corporation in 1981 and

the hospital responded by creating a for-profit management corporation to supply clinical and business support services to the practice. However, conflicts arose where the hospital acted as a service vendor to its medical staff and in 1986 the hospital's parent company sold the management firm to the practice. The hospital also began a for-profit interior design business. This too was sold. Following the integration of a freestanding radiology center with the hospital, the parent company's for-profit subsidiary found itself not operating any businesses. The hospital maintained two not-for-profit subsidiaries—one a real estate corporation and one a foundation to shelter the hospital's unrestricted funds. But its overall structure has now been resimplified, with the recognition, according to its president, that "our fundamental business is taking care of patients." Quoted by Judith Graham, "Diversified Hospitals Review Plans after Some Bumpy Rides," *Modern Health Care,* August 14, 1987, p. 32.

42. AMI has folded its insurance operations and other businesses including most of its ambulatory surgical centers. The company reportedly realized that through extending into the insurance business it was alienating physicians and failing to attract more patients. "AMI Ended Its Experiment with Diversification Last Year by Selling Several Operations," *Modern Healthcare,* August 14, 1987, p. 36.

43. See, e.g., Richard L. Johnson, "The Myth of Dominance by National Health Care Corporations," *Frontiers of Health Services Management* 3 (May 1987), pp. 3–22; Mark Schlesinger, "Investor-Dominated Health Care Is Not Inevitable," *Health Span* 3 (May 1986), pp. 13–17.

44. "For-profit Hospitals Loom Large on Health Care Scene," *Science* 23 (August 29, 1986), p. 928. And see Arnold S. Relman, "The New Medical Industrial Complex," *New England Journal of Medicine* 303 (1980), pp. 963–70.

45. Gray, ed., *For-Profit Enterprise in Health Care,* pp. 182–204.

46. Clark W. Bell, "Multihospital Systems," *Modern Healthcare,* June 5, 1987, p. 38.

47. Robert A. Go and Anne C. Bailey, "Selling the Not-for-Profit Hospital," *Hospital Capital Finance,* Fourth Quarter 1985, pp. 4–6.

48. See, for example, a series of articles in *Health Matrix* 3 (Spring 1985), including my own, "Voluntary and Governmental Activity," pp. 26–31.

49. Jerry Cromwell, "Impact of State Hospital Rate Setting on Capital Formation," *Health Care Financing* 8 (Spring 1987), p. 69.

50. Kari E. Super, "Building Activity Jumps 16 Percent in '86," *Modern Healthcare* (February 27, 1987), pp. 37–80.

51. Stephen Wood, "Survey Shows Changing Sources of Capital," *Hospital Capital Finance,* First Quarter 1986, p. 4.

52. Between 1975 and 1983, for example, corporate spending for health benefits rose an estimated 250%. Employers paid approximately $82 billion in 1983, up to $92.6 billion in 1984. Jennifer Conway and John Liebman, ed., *Employer Health Care Cost Containment* (Philadelphia: Leonard Davis Institute of Health Economics, University of Pennsylvania, 1986), p. 1. For an excellent review of the changes, see Jeff Goldsmith, "Death of a Paradigm: The Challenge of Competition," *Health Affairs* 3, no. 3 (1984), p. 8.

53. Ibid, p. 4.

54. Honeywell is a good example. In 1981 this large company's medical costs totaled nearly 40% of profits. As the chairman and chief executive officer remarked recently, until the 1980s most companies did not actually buy health-care services but just paid the bills: "Business was the payer and the health care industry was the payee. There was a respectful distance between us and, with it, a lack of understanding, sometimes even a lack of concern, on both sides." The company set up a task force in 1983 which concluded that Honeywell could better manage its expenditures by supporting health promotion, improving administrative procedures, cultivating cooperative provider relations and streamlining their benefit design. Thus self-insurance, oversight, and management of health expenditures, and working cooperatively with local health-care providers in coalitions were linked activities. Edson W. Spencer, "Honeywell's Perspective on Buying Health Care," *Trustee,* August 1987, p. 23.

55. Jonathan Betz Brown, "Employers Face High Stakes in Forging Capital Policy," *Business and Health,* June 1986, pp. 7–10.

56. HMOs are health maintenance organizations (prepaid group practices) which offer a relatively comprehensive menu of health-service entitlements from primary care to superspecialized hospitalization. HMOs boomed in the 1980s, both under not-for-profit and for-profit auspices. There are now approximately four hundred HMOs serving an estimated 20 million enrollees in the United States. PPOs are preferred provider organizations: organizations set

up to provide financial incentives to consumers to utilize a selected panel of doctors and hospitals, as well as other services. Providers are paid, in turn, usually on a negotiated fee-for-service basis, often with discounts for a certain volume of care. In short, a PPO is a mechanism designed to keep costs down by limiting choice and concentrating benefits. Competitive medical plans or CMPs are organizations similar to HMOs set up to provide services to Medicare beneficiaries under the provisions of legislation in 1982 (TEFRA). Under these provisions the federal government will pay eligible HMOs and CMPs 95% of what it would otherwise be paying for health care for the Medicare beneficiaries. In turn, the health plan may keep whatever profits it may make. For an excellent review of present arrangements, see *Introduction to Alternative Delivery Mechanisms: HMOs, PPOs and CMPs* (Washington, D.C.: National Health Lawyers' Association, 1986).

57. Richard D. Gifford, "Are Hospital Boards Turning 'Corporate'?" *Trustee* (August 1987), pp. 10–12.

58. David Mechanic, "The Transformation of Health Providers," *Health Affairs* 3 (Spring 1984), p. 64. And see Dundan Yaggy and Patricia Hodgson, eds., *Physicians and Hospitals: The Great Partnership at the Crossroads* (Durham, N.C.: Duke University Press, 1985).

59. I. Weinstein, "The Future of the MIO in a Price-Competitive, Price-Driven Market," *Topics in Health Care Financing* 11 (1984), pp. 84–92, quoted in Mark Schlesinger et al., "The Privatization of Health Care and Physicians' Perceptions of Access to Hospital Services," *Milbank Memorial Fund Quarterly* 65 (1987), p. 46.

60. Jacob Zatuchni, "Economic Incentives of Faculty Practice," letter, *Journal of the American Medical Association* 252 (1984), p. 899.

61. In 1984 the federal Court of Appeals found an exclusive arrangement for anesthesiology services in a New Orleans hospital to be a violation of the Federal Antitrust Laws, but this decision was overturned by the Supreme Court, whose members were persuaded that the arrangement in this particular situation was justified and did not unduly restrict competition in hospital and medical care in New Orleans. The hospital was one of approximately twenty hospitals in the New Orleans metropolitan area, thus patients had the choice of going to other hospitals if they wished. Moreover, the contract with this group of anesthesiologists assured the hospital of having all the services it needed, with anesthetics available at all times on a twenty-four-hour basis. Service was, in short, effective and the arrangement was found reasonable. William J. Curran, "Law-Medicine Notes," *New England Journal of Medicine* 311 (1984), pp. 243–44.

62. L. Stuart Ditzen, "Shunned by Hospitals, Some Doctors Go to Court," *Philadelphia Inquirer,* February 21, 1984.

63. James C. Dechene, "Physician Incentive Programs: Are They Legal?" *Health Span—The Report of Health, Business, and Law* 4 (January 1987), p. 9.

64. Jeff Goldsmith, "Death of a Paradigm," *Health Affairs* 3, no. 3 (1984), p. 14.

65. Good examples are: John D. Stoeckle, "Working on the Factory Floor: My God, They Want to Make us Employees!" *Annals of Internal Medicine* 107 (August 1987), pp. 250–51; S. A. Marcus, "Trade Unionism For Doctors: An Idea Whose Time Has Come," *New England Journal of Medicine* 311 (1984), pp. 1508–11; Alan L. Hillman et al., "Managing the Medical Industrial Complex," ibid. 315 (1986), pp. 511–13. The latter suggests that increasing the number of qualified physician executives is an "appropriate way to make the system more rational, before the stewardship of medicine is wrested from physicians altogether." Ibid, p. 511.

66. I have developed these ideas in "The Future of the Medical Profession," in Eli Ginzberg, ed., *From Physician Shortage to Patient Shortage* (Boulder, Colo.: Westview Press, 1986), pp. 75–93.

67. Robert Charles Clark, "Does the Non-Profit Form Fit the Hospital Industry?" *Harvard Law Review* 93 (May 1980), pp. 14, 17–89.

68. *Flagiello* v. *Pennsylvania Hospital,* 417 Pa. 486, pp. 493–94; 208, 913, pp. 196–97 (1965).

69. Italos Cappabianca, chairman of the Select Committee to Study Non-Profits, to James Redmond, Hospital Association of Pennsylvania, September 30, 1986, with attached document prepared by Ida Stabinski, in *Non-Profits: Potential Unfair Business Competition Analysis* (Harrisburg: Commonwealth of Pennsylvania, 1986).

70. Gregory Vigdor, *Hospital Tax Exempt Policy: Environmental Changes and Challenges* (Albuquerque: New Mexico Hospital Association, 1986).

71. *Utah County* v. *Intermountain Health Care Inc. and Tax Commissioner of the State of Utah,* no. 17699, Utah Supreme Court, June 26, 1985.

72. Sally Hanlon, "GAO Says Blue Cross/Blue Shield Would Not Be Tax Exempt," *Tax Notes,* July 14, 1986, pp. 98–99.

73. Reported in *Health Insurance News Digest,* March 15, 1986, p. 43.

74. Robert S. Bromberg, "The Charitable Hospital," *Catholic University Law Review* 20 (1970), pp. 237–58.

75. President's Commission for the Study of Ethical Problems in Medicine and Biomedical and Behavioral Research, *Securing Access to Health* (Washington, D.C.: Government Printing Office, 1983), vol. I, Report, pp. 2, 4.

76. Ibid., p. 5.

77. Nicole Luriel, "Termination of Medical Benefits: A Follow-up Study One Year Later," *New England Journal of Medicine* 314 (1986), pp. 1266–68.

78. Karen Davis and Diane Rowland, "Uninsured and Undeserved: Inequities in Health Care in the United States," *Milbank Memorial Fund Quarterly* 61 (1983), pp. 149–76.

79. John Yergan, et al., "Relationship Between Patient Race and the Intensity of Hospital Services," *Medical Care* 25 (July 1987), pp. 592–603.

80. The policy process is well documented by Randy Shilts, *And the Band Played On: Politics, People, and the AIDS Epidemic* (New York: St. Martin's Press, 1987).

81. Gilbert M. Gaul, "Health Coverage is Eluding Many," *Philadelphia Inquirer,* December 27, 1987.

82. Good examples are Stanley Jones, "What Distinguishes the Voluntary Hospital in an Increasingly Commercial Health Care Environment," paper prepared for the American Health Institute, Washington, D.C., April 14, 1986; B. C. Vladeck, "The Future of Voluntary Hospitals," *President's Letter* (United Hospital Fund), October 1986; J. David Seay and Bruce C. Vladeck, *Mission Matters: A Report on the Future of Voluntary Health Care Institutions* (New York: United Hospital Fund, 1987); J. David Seay and Bruce C. Vladeck, eds., *In Sickness and in Health: The Mission of Voluntary Health Care Institutions* (New York: McGraw-Hill, 1988).

Chapter 13

1. Kathleen Teltsch, "Volunteerism Finds New Adherents in New York," *New York Times,* March 13, 1988.

2. Leonard Krieger, "The Idea of a Welfare State in Europe and the United States," *Journal of the History of Ideas* 24 (1963), p. 556.

3. Maurice McGregor, "Hospital Costs: Can they be Cut?" *Milbank Memorial Fund Quarterly/Health and Society* 59 (1981), p. 93.

4. American Hospital Association, *Hospital Statistics, 1987 Edition* (Chicago: American Hospital Association, 1987), p. xxii.

5. The best statement of the value of (vague) language as a bridge for coalition-forming in the United States is Max Skidmore, *Medicare and the Rhetoric of Reconciliation* (University, Ala.: University of Alabama Press, 1970).

6. "U.S. Halts Funds to Develop Artificial Hearts for Humans," *New York Times,* May 13, 1988.

7. Daniel M. Fox, "The Consequences of Consensus: American Health Policy in the Twentieth Century," *Milbank Memorial Fund Quarterly/Health and Society* 64 (1986), pp. 76–99.

8. American Hospital Association, *Hospital Statistics, 1987 Edition,* p. x.

9. In thinking about the role of not-for-profit hospitals in the context of the "nonprofit sector" as a whole, I have benefited in particular from Harvey Brooks, Lance Liebman, and Corinne S. Schelling, eds., *Public-Private Partnership: New Opportunities for Meeting Social Needs* (Cambridge, Mass.: Ballinger Publishing Co., 1984), particularly the essays by Liebman, Robert C. Clark, and Thomas K. McCraw; and Walter W. Powell, ed., *The Nonprofit Sector: A Research Handbook* (New Haven, Conn.: Yale University Press, 1987), particularly the essays by Peter Dobkin Hall, James Douglas, John G. Simon, Lester M. Salamon, Paul DiMaggio, and (jointly) Theodore R. Marmor, Mark Schlesinger, and Richard W. Smithey.

10. This point has been made most forcefully by Robert M. Sigmond, in, for example, his *Remarks on Accepting the First C. Rufus Rorem Health Service Award,* pamphlet (Chicago: Blue Cross and Blue Shield Association, 1985).

11.   Regina E. Herzlinger, "Nonprofit Hospitals Seldom Profit the Needy," *Wall Street Journal,* March 23, 1987. And see Regina E. Herzlinger and William S. Krasker, "Who Profits from Nonprofits?" *Harvard Business Review* (January–February, 1987), pp. 93–106.

12.   Gregory D. Curfman, "Shorter Hospital Stay for Myocardial Infarction," *New England Journal of Medicine* 318 (1988), p. 1123.

13.   Joseph E. Hardison, "The House Officer's Changing World," *New England Journal of Medicine* 314 (1986), p. 1714.

14.   Sylvan Lee Weinberg, "The Patient with Heart Disease and the Cardiovascular Physician and Surgeon, 1958–1983," *Journal of the American College of Cardiology* 1 (1983), p. 11.

15.   John C. Bailar III and Elaine M. Smith, "Progress Against Cancer?" *New England Journal of Medicine* 314 (1986), p. 1226.

16.   Eugene Braunwald, "Effects of Coronary-Artery Bypass Grafting on Survival," *New England Journal of Medicine* 309 (1983), p. 1183.

17.   James W. Mold and Howard F. Stein, "The Cascade Effect in the Clinical Care of Patients," ibid. 314 (1986), pp. 512–14.

18.   Toby Citrin, "Trustees at the Focal Point," *New England Journal of Medicine* 313 (1985), pp. 1223–26. The best general analysis is John R. Griffith, *The Well-Managed Community Hospital* (Ann Arbor: Health Administration Press, 1987).

INDEX